Presidential Government

Presidential Government

Benjamin Ginsberg

Yale

UNIVERSITY PRESS

New Haven and London

Published with assistance from the Joan Patterson Kerr Fund.

Published with assistance from the Louis Stern Memorial Fund.

Yale University Press books may be purchased in quantity for educational,
business, or promotional use. For information, please e-mail
sales.press@yale.edu (U.S. office) or sales@yaleup.co.uk (U.K. office).

Set in Garamond type by Integrated Publishing Solutions,
Grand Rapids, Michigan.
Printed in the United States of America.

ISBN 978-0-300-21206-8 (paperback: alk. paper)

Library of Congress Control Number: 2015950946

A catalogue record for this book is available from the British Library.

This paper meets the requirements of ANSI/NISO Z39.48–1992
(Permanence of Paper).

10 9 8 7 6 5 4 3 2 1

For Sandy

Contents

Preface   ix

ONE. What Is an Executive, and Why Do We Need One?   1

TWO. The Constitutional Foundations of Presidential Power   18

THREE. A Brief History of the Presidency   59

FOUR. Presidential Elections   103

FIVE. The Executive Branch   160

SIX. The President, the Congress, and Domestic Policy   193

SEVEN. Presidential Policy Tools   231

EIGHT. The Executive and the Courts   280

NINE. Foreign Policy and National Security   323

TEN. Understanding the Presidency as an Institution:

  Advice for Citizens and Voters   391

Appendix: Gallery of Presidents   401

Notes   407

For Further Reading   449

Illustration Credits   455

Index   459

Preface

For most of the nineteenth century, the presidency was a weak institution. In unusual circumstances, a Jefferson, a Jackson, or a Lincoln might exercise extraordinary power, but most presidents held little influence over the congressional barons or provincial chieftains who actually steered the government. The president's job was to execute policy, rarely to make it. Policymaking was the responsibility of legislators, particularly the leaders of the House and Senate.

Today, the presidency has become the dominant force in national policy formation. Not all domestic policy springs from the White House, but none is made without the president's involvement. And when it comes to foreign policy and particularly security policy, there can be little doubt about presidential primacy. Congress retains the constitutional power to declare war, but that power has not been exercised in sixty-five years. During this period American military forces have been engaged in numerous conflicts all over the world at the behest of the president.

How did this transformation come about? To some, the study of the presidency is chiefly the study of personality and leadership in an attempt to distinguish between the attributes and conduct of strong and weak presidents—or great, near-great, and not-so-great presidents. Richard Neustadt, an influential presidential scholar, epitomized this focus on leadership styles and personality when he declared in 1960 that presidential power was the "power to persuade." In other words, the power of the presidency was derived from the charisma of the president.

Some scholars pushed this personalistic approach even further by engaging in psychoanalytic studies of presidents to determine which personality attributes seemed to be associated with presidential success. James David Barber's well-known book *The Presidential Character* is an exemplar of this school of thought.

The personal characteristics of presidents, however, while not unimportant, do not offer a satisfactory explanation for the utter transformation of the role of the executive in recent years. After all, while the power to persuade and other leadership abilities wax and wane with successive presidents, the power of the presidency has increased inexorably, perhaps growing more rapidly under the Roosevelts and Reagans and less so under the Fillmores and Carters of American politics, but growing nonetheless. The president is indeed a person, but the presidency is an office embedded in an institutional and constitutional structure and in a historical setting that limits some possibilities and encourages others. As Steven Skowronek has shown, leadership styles that are effective in one political era may be irrelevant or counterproductive in another. Even presidential character and style are institutionally conditioned. As we shall see, presidents today are generally more aggressive and ambitious than their predecessors because of an institutional change—a nominating process that tends to select for these characteristics. And as for the power to persuade, this formula was already beginning to be out of date in 1960 when it was introduced. The 1947 National Security Act had already vastly increased the president's institutional power to command. Presidents were already becoming more imperial and less dependent on the fine art of persuasion.

Accordingly, in this book I take what is generally called a historical-institutionalist approach. This perspective does not ignore leadership, but it nevertheless emphasizes history and institutions as the keys to understanding political phenomena. We will study presidential history to understand the ways in which past events and experiences shape current perspectives and frame the possibilities open to presidents. We will also pay a great deal of attention to institutional rules, particularly the Constitution, because these help set the parameters for decisionmaking and collective action.

Talented and ambitious presidents have pushed the boundaries of the office, adding new powers that were seldom surrendered by their successors. But what made this tactic possible was the inherent constitutional imbalance between the executive and Congress. As we will see, presidential power has grown less because of the leadership styles of particular presidents, and more because the Constitution puts Congress at an institutional disadvantage in its power struggles with the president. For example, under the Constitution, Congress legislates but it is the president who executes the law. In the course of executing the law, presidents have opportunities to enhance the power of the office. As we shall see, every time Congress legislates it empowers the executive to do something, thereby contributing, albeit inadvertently, to the onward march of executive power.

As this example suggests, understanding America's presidency requires us to do more than assess the relative merits of the presidents. It requires us to look carefully at the institution, including its constitutional place and history. Such an examination will be our starting point.

In the course of writing this book, I benefited from conversations with a number of colleagues, particularly Matthew Crenson, with whom I previously co-authored two books, and who helped shape my view of the presidency. It is customary to thank one's editor, but I can honestly say that this project would never even have been undertaken without the efforts of Sarah Miller of Yale University Press. Sarah appeared in my office one afternoon and, employing the fine art of persuasion, convinced me to write this book. Along with Ash Lago, Sarah has also provided excellent editorial guidance. My thanks also to my copyeditor, Julie Carlson; to Margaret Otzel, senior editor, who oversaw every aspect of production; to Poyee Oster and Melissa Flamson, who found the materials for our photo essays; to Liz Casey for her careful proofreading; and to Cynthia Crippen for preparing the index. My thanks also to the several readers engaged by the Press to review this manuscript while it was in preparation. As the readers will no doubt notice, I incorporated many of their suggestions and corrected the errors they had pointed out.

I have been a professor for more than forty years, the first twenty at Cornell and the remainder at Johns Hopkins. During these decades, I have lectured to thousands of students and spent a good deal of time chatting with more than a few undergraduate and graduate students at these schools and at the many others where I have been invited to speak. As I wrote this book, I tried to be mindful of the excellent questions and important concerns raised by students. It has been my experience that, assertions to the contrary notwithstanding, teaching and scholarship go hand in hand. Each contributes mightily to the other.

Benjamin Ginsberg
Summer 2015

ONE

What Is an Executive, and Why Do We Need One?

In This Chapter

The idea of a national executive seems self-evident today, but many of the Constitution's framers were suspicious of executive power. Only after trying to create a government that would work without a national executive did most framers agree, at the Constitutional Convention, that an executive was indeed essential for imparting badly needed "energy" to the goals and governance of the new republic. In this chapter I will identify the characteristics of an executive and explain the framers' concerns about executive power. I will also explore what they meant by the term "energy" and assess some of the special features of America's executive. Over the decades, Americans have come to believe that executive energy is so important that the untimely death or disability of America's chief executive has become a source of worry. Hence the chapter will conclude with a discussion of presidential succession.

What Is an Executive?

On any given day, the news media direct the attention of Americans to the activities, achievements, and shortcomings of our chief executive. We expect the chief executive to deal with recurrent crises in the Middle East, terrorist threats at home, the state of the nation's economy, health care, air quality, and a host of other matters. In times of crisis, in particular, we look to the president more than Congress or the courts for action, or at least reassurance.

A nation's *executive* is the individual or institution with the authority to administer and enforce the law. National executives have a variety of different titles: king, president, premier, sultan, and so forth—but this is their essential characteristic. The paramount executives of authoritarian regimes might also claim the right to say what the law is and to determine its application to individuals. In liberal democracies, however, these latter two powers are generally exercised by legislatures and courts, respectively. The citizens of several democracies, including the United States, retain the power to write some laws through popular referenda as well as to apply the law to individuals via service on juries. But even when citizens write or interpret the law, its implementation and enforcement are given over to the nation's executive.

In the United States the president is the chief executive and is empowered by the Constitution both to execute laws enacted or authorized by Congress (there are no national referenda in the United States), as well as to enforce the decisions of courts and juries. This American formula is known as a system of separated powers and was intended by the Constitution's framers to prevent a concentration of political authority in any one person or institution. The framers were heavily influenced by the theories of the French political philosopher Baron de Montesquieu, whose book *The Spirit of the Laws* "was taken as political gospel" at the Constitutional Convention.[1]

Montesquieu asserted that in order to guard against tyranny, political power must be dispersed among rival institutions. As every student of American government knows, Montesquieu recommended a tripartite division of power, locating the power to make, enforce, and interpret the law in three distinct institutions: a legislature to make the law, an executive to enforce it, and a judiciary to interpret the law and oversee its application to individuals. The framers understood this idea of separation of powers to mean that each of the three institutions should possess the capacity to check and balance the actions of the others. Hence the Constitution assigns each branch of government some power over the other branches. The president, for example, can veto acts of Congress. The Congress can block presidential appointments, treaties, and expenditures. Judges are subject to presidential appointment, with the advice and consent of the Senate but, at the same time, judges have the power to overrule presidential and congressional actions.

This system of checks and balances, as one scholar declared, means that the American system of government consists not so much of powers divided among institutions but of divided institutions sharing power.[2] The framers reinforced this institutional division by providing different mechanisms for selecting the holders of each national office—direct election for House members, selection by the state legislatures for senators, selection by members of an Electoral College chosen by the state legislatures for the president, and appointment for judges. The framers thought that this multifaceted selection system would give each institution a distinct constituency and different perspectives, and so encourage their tendency to check one another's actions. Today we sometimes blame this tendency for institutional "gridlock," but the framers thought that institutional division was necessary to preserve liberty.

In the centuries since America's founding, some of the sources of institutional division devised by the framers have eroded. Early in the nineteenth century, all the states adopted the principle of popular election of the presidential electors. The Seventeenth Amendment, ratified in 1913, provided for popular election of senators. And as we shall see, contrary to the idea of separated powers, America's executive, and particularly the agencies of the executive branch, have come to engage in a good deal of lawmaking and adjudication. Thus the president sometimes executes decisions made in the executive branch or by the White House itself. I shall return to this important point in Chapter 8.

Among democracies, America's executive is somewhat unusual, though not entirely unique. In most democracies, the executive is called a prime minister and is chosen by the national legislature, usually called a parliament, from among the leading members of that body. Usually, then, the leader of the parliament's largest party becomes prime minister. A prime minister has some political advantages and some disadvantages relative to America's president. On the one hand, prime ministers lead the parliamentary majority that selected them. If that majority is strong and stable, the prime minister can count on being able to bring about the enactment of laws without the legislative opposition that typically plagues America's presidents. If, on the other hand, the prime minister's parliamentary majority is weak, perhaps because it is based on an unstable coalition of political parties, an effort to enact important legislation can result in a legislative defeat. Such a defeat is defined as a parliamentary vote of "no confidence" in the prime minister and may lead to the dissolution of the parliament, new national elections, and, very likely, a new prime minister. By contrast an American president is independently elected and is not forced to leave office simply because Congress refused to approve some important presidential initiative. Thus while presidents may be more likely than prime ministers to suffer legislative losses, presidents are also better able to recover from defeats, lick their wounds, and live to fight another day.

To add just a bit more complexity to our picture, many nations boast presidents and prime ministers. Generally, the presidents associated with parliamentary systems are appointed by the parliaments and serve as symbolic heads of state. One major exception is France where, since 1962, the president has been independently elected and exercises significant power, especially in the military and foreign policy realms. France's prime minister is usually the dominant force in other policy areas. The relationship between the president and prime minister, however, can be complicated. France's prime minister is actually chosen by the president but can only be dismissed from office by the parliament. Hence a prime minister with strong parliamentary support can exercise a good deal of influence, but a prime minister lacking such support tends to become subordinate to the president.

Do We Need an Executive?

Most of us take for granted the idea that a nation needs an executive, but many Americans of the founding generation did not agree. Some thought the laws could be administered and enforced by the legislature itself, with the assistance of the courts and perhaps with some mechanism for the creation of a special executive during times of military emergency. This idea was inspired by the example of the Roman republic, whose day-to-day governance was in the hands of the senators and a number of magistrates with limited powers. In times of emergency, a dictator might be appointed by the senate to deal with the matter, but the dictator would lose his power when the senate had deemed the emergency to have ended. Famed Revolutionary War orator Patrick Henry recommended the Roman model. "Better a dictator in times of need," he said, than "this American presidency."[3]

Many equated executive power with the evils of monarchy. These evils included concentration of power, irresponsibility, arbitrary power, militarism, and licentiousness. This last idea seemed to stir the popular imagination. During the debates surrounding the ratification of the Constitution, Alexander Hamilton thought it necessary to point out that unlike some kings, the president would neither be surrounded by mistresses nor require his fellow citizens "to blush at the unveiled mysteries of a future seraglio."[4] In this matter, at least, Hamilton turned out not to be much of a prophet.

Even those not concerned with licentious conduct feared that an executive would be a threat to citizens' liberties. "If your chief be a man of ambition, and abilities, how easy it is for him to render himself absolute," thundered Patrick Henry at the Virginia State Convention, which had been called to consider ratification of the proposed Constitution.[5] Many who declared a general hostility to the idea of executive power argued that executives tended to find justification for almost anything they wanted to do and so would gradually expand their own powers vis-à-vis other public officials and bodies.[6] This concern, as we shall see, seems justified by the growth of presidential power over the past several decades.

The leading voices of the founding era, though, politicians like Alexander Hamilton and James Madison, were convinced that a government without a strong executive would be unable to promote and protect the nation's interests. They saw important virtues in executive power, including energy, national unity, and a capacity for prompt national action. As for national unity, Hamilton asserted that insofar as it provided the protection and services that citizens sought, executive power was the "great cement of society."[7] Even those who came to oppose the new Constitution agreed with this idea. One well-known anti-Federalist pamphleteer, writing under the pseudonym of "Federal Farmer," admitted that a vigorous executive could provide the unifying focus that even republics need.[8]

Even more important to advocates of executive power was the argument that an "energetic" executive was essential and that a weak executive would mean "feeble execution of the government."[9] To the framers of the Constitution, the term "energy" had great significance. By "energy" they meant the capacity to make decisions and take action in an expeditious and timely manner. Legislatures were understood to lack such energy because they were likely to engage in lengthy debates before agreeing on some way forward. Courts were seen as lacking energy because the rules of the legal process necessarily brought about delays in decisionmaking. Faced with important choices, legislatures and courts were inclined to dither and delay while an executive was more likely to act.

The energy of the executive, moreover, was seen as enhancing the energy of the entire government, providing the nation with a necessary instrument to deal with internal and external problems and foes. Among the internal problems that might be addressed by an energetic executive was the likely weakness of the new federal government vis-à-vis the already well-established state governments. In our own day, when the national government seems far more powerful than the state governments, it is difficult to remember that little more than two centuries ago the states had far more money, administrative capability, and citizen loyalty than did the federal government. Many of the states, however, were governed by legislatures and it was believed that an energetic federal executive might carry the day against the ponderous state assemblies. Indeed, many decades later, the energy of President Franklin D. Roosevelt in responding to America's economic crisis accelerated the onward march of federal power and concomitant decline in the relative autonomy of the states.

With regard to the energetic conduct of external affairs, consider a contemporary example. When Iraqi forces invaded Kuwait in August 1990, President George H. W. Bush mobilized a military force of more than 600,000 troops, along with warships and aircraft, to protect American access to Persian Gulf oil. While Bush acted quickly and decisively, Congress deliberated and debated. By the time Congress voted, by a narrow margin, to support a military campaign against Iraq, the president had already moved massive American air, naval, and ground forces into the region and was poised to strike with or without congressional approval. In some instances, of course, American presidents may be too energetic, rashly sending American troops into action when the nation's interests might better be served by avoiding war. Yet the point remains. Even if sometimes used unwisely, the energy of the executive empowers the entire government.[10]

During the founding period, many individuals saw this idea as having been incontrovertibly confirmed by the experience of the thirteen states under the Articles of Confederation. Absent an executive, the government seemed unable to protect America's interests abroad or safeguard its unity at home. For example, during the 1780s, Britain, other maritime powers, and even pirates harassed American maritime commerce. The so-called Barbary pirates were a particular menace. Privateers commissioned by the states of North Africa's Barbary Coast, including Tripoli, Algiers, Morocco, and Tunis, frequently attacked ships in the Mediterranean Sea, taking hostages who would be ransomed or sold into slavery. Before the Revolution, American shipping had been protected by Britain's Royal Navy, and during the Revolution, the French fleet had placed American vessels under its umbrella. After the American colonies won their independence, though, American merchant ships were on their own.[11] Lacking a navy or a national leader who could rally a response to the Barbary threat, America could only watch helplessly as ship after ship was captured and hundreds of sailors were carted off into what sometimes became a lifetime of slavery.

Events in the far-off Mediterranean, however, were eclipsed in importance by even more threatening developments at home. In the early 1780s, economically hard-pressed Massachusetts farmers began to organize protests in response to what they viewed as excessive taxation and property seizures for nonpayment of debts. Over the next several years, the protests spread and entire communities, including townsfolk, began to vehemently assert their grievances against the Massachusetts and national governments.[12] By 1786 the protests, now led by Daniel Shays, a former Revolutionary War soldier, had turned violent. Mobs seeking an end to land foreclosures forced the courts in several Massachusetts counties to shut down. To make matters worse, similar disturbances began to flare in other states. These events were much discussed by the Congress of the Confederation, as the national legislature was then called. The Congress, though, had no army or executive institutions to deal with the emergency. Eventually a group of wealthy Massachusetts merchants raised money to recruit a militia force and, in effect, hired a general to disperse the protestors, reopen the courts, and put down the rebellion.[13]

By contrast, after the adoption of the new Constitution, the chief executive was able to act quickly and decisively to bring an end to an uprising, in this case the so-called Whiskey Rebellion of 1791. Mobs of Pennsylvania farmers had prevented federal officials from collecting a new excise tax that was an important element of Treasury Secretary Hamilton's economic plan.[14] President Washington raised and personally led thirteen thousand troops to confront the protestors, who quickly dispersed without bloodshed.

Creating a Tame Prince

After the events of the 1780s, few delegates to the Constitutional Convention of 1789 were prepared to take issue with the need for a strong executive. James Wilson, a delegate from Pennsylvania, spoke for most when he declared at the convention, "An executive ought to possess the powers of secrecy, vigor and dispatch."[15] It may seem strange to our modern eyes to see "secrecy" cited as a major virtue of executive power, but secrecy was another concept that had taken on new importance for political leaders of the founding period due to their recent history. During the Revolutionary period, American political plans and military strategies had often became known to the British via the loose tongues of state legislators and even delegates to the Continental Congress, thus undermining the war effort.[16] As a result, it came to be generally agreed that legislatures could not keep secrets and that only an executive could make plans that would not reach the eyes and ears of the nation's foes. One wonders what the framers would make of the penchant for secrecy manifested by today's executive branch, which has deemed "classified" tens of billions of pages of documents—many of which, according to former solicitor general Erwin Griswold, seem to represent more of a threat to the reputations of political leaders than to the security of the nation.[17]

By the time of the Constitutional Convention, the necessity of executive power had come to be widely acknowledged. Yet Americans remained divided over the precise form that a national executive should take. Coupled with the generally shared agreement that an executive was needed was another consensus—that executive power was dangerous, posing a constant threat to liberty. Had not the Americans recently fought a bloody revolution to rid themselves of one executive? Should they now risk surrendering their hard-won freedom to another? Separation of powers would play an important role in restraining the ambitions of an executive, but how should the institutions of government be organized to provide the most reliable checks on improper uses of executive power?

At the Constitutional Convention—as well as in the discussions and debates held throughout the nation, and eventually in the state ratification conventions—a variety of schemes was proposed that, according to proponents, would secure the benefits of executive power without the attendant risks to popular liberties. As political theorist Harvey Mansfield put it so eloquently, almost all Americans acknowledged the need for what amounted to princely power in their government. The question was whether such a prince could be "tamed" to serve the people rather than tyrannize them.[18]

Many ideas were presented at the convention. Some delegates argued that the executive should consist of three individuals. Edmund Randolph of Virginia declared that a unitary executive was the "foetus of monarchy."[19] Randolph favored a three-person executive, an arrangement that he believed would allow different regions of the nation to be better represented and would reassure Americans that their new government was not headed by what amounted to a king.[20] Charles Pinckney of South Carolina asserted that the executive could consist of one person, but to check that executive's power, the individual should be elected by the legislature.[21] John Dickinson of Delaware said that the executive should be removable from office by the Congress at the request of a majority of the state legislatures.[22] Dickinson was certain that his plan would allow the state legislatures and the Congress to work together to restrain executive power. Roger Sherman of Connecticut called for the creation of an executive council with the duty to advise the executive and block actions by the executive if these were deemed to be unwise.[23] A handful of delegates favored popular election of the president, but most of the delegates were not friendly to direct popular democracy, which some declared to be the worst form of government, subject to incessant tumult and demagoguery.

Each of these proposals and many others were discussed at some length at the Constitutional Convention. Yet the basic principles to which most delegates adhered led, if not inexorably, at least gradually, to the eventual shape of the institution with which we are familiar. The importance they attached to energy and secrecy eventually led the framers to reject the notion of a three-person executive or executive council and to accept the principle of a unitary, or one-person, executive. The importance they attached to the principle of separation of powers led them to reject the idea of a president appointed by the Congress and to adopt the notion of an independently appointed president. The method of appointment chosen, the Electoral College system, which will be discussed in more detail in Chapter 4, was viewed as an ingenious arrangement that would maintain the president's independence from the Congress and the state legislatures while avoiding a direct popular election. The presidency was beginning to take shape.

The Broader Meaning of "President"

The president is an individual, but the term "presidency" or "administration" usually includes the president's cabinet, advisers, staff, the vice president, and the president's spouse. The term *cabinet* is a designation for the heads, called secretaries, of the fifteen government departments. Cabinet members are appointed by the president subject to senatorial confirmation. The president meets with the cabinet on a regular basis, but the cabinet as a group has no policymaking functions. Each cabinet secretary answers individually to the president for the conduct of his or her department, and the cabinet has little collective identity. The cabinet officers are generally chosen for their political standing with particular constituencies as well as for their subject-matter expertise. The secretaries of some departments, such as Treasury, State, and Defense, are expected to have considerable experience and expertise. But the secretaries of other departments, such as Agriculture and Commerce, are selected mainly for political reasons. Indeed, the commerce secretary is generally a former presidential crony or fundraiser.[24]

Since a 1993 executive order, cabinet secretaries who lead domestic agencies, along with a number of other high-ranking officials and presidential advisers, have come together in a Domestic Policy Council, which offers advice to the president on domestic policy issues much like the National Security Council does for national security concerns.[25] Thus far, however, the Domestic Policy Council has not been especially important. More important have been some thirty White House "czars" created by the Obama administration in order to coordinate policy in a variety of areas, including urban affairs, arms control, health reform, climate change, and manufacturing.[26]

For policy formulation and governance, presidents rely heavily on several other entities. Some presidents have assembled what is sometimes called an "inner cabinet," consisting of the National Security Council and senior White House staff officials. The National Security Council was established by the 1947 National Security Act, and consists of the president, the vice president, the secretaries of state and defense, and others designated by the president, usually including the director of the CIA and the president's national security adviser (formally the special assistant to the president for national security). Some presidents, including George W. Bush, have relied heavily on the Joint Chiefs of Staff for advice on military matters.

The inner cabinet usually also includes senior White House staff members such as the president's chief of staff and press secretary. The White House staff is a small group of close presidential advisers called "special assistants" to the president, and they often specialize in particular tasks or policy areas.[27] White House staffers include speech writers, legislative assistants, and communications office staffers.[28] The president's chief of staff typically has served the president as a campaign strategist and in some cases may be privy to the chief executive's innermost thoughts and secrets. The chief of staff generally controls access to the president and can become a powerful figure in Washington. For example, President Nixon's longtime chief of staff, H. R. Haldeman, along with his deputy, John Ehrlichman, were known in Washington as "the Berlin Wall" for their Germanic names and strict control of access to the Oval Office. Both Haldeman and Ehrlichman were convicted of perjury and obstruction of justice for their activities in the Watergate affair, discussed in Chapter 6.

Another important component of the presidency is the Executive Office of the President. The office was established by President Roosevelt via executive order in 1939 and includes several permanent agencies employing some two thousand individuals. The most important agency within the Executive Office of the President is the White House Office of Management and Budget, which was established in 1921 as the Bureau of the Budget and moved from the Treasury Department to its new home under President Roosevelt. The Office of Management and Budget prepares the president's budget, reviews the performance of executive agencies, and, through its Office of Information and Regulatory Affairs, prepares the president's rulemaking and regulatory agenda, which guides the activities of the executive agencies (more on this in Chapter 5). Other offices within the Executive Office of the President include the Council of Economic Advisers, which analyzes economic trends and recommends presidential actions in the economic realm; the Environmental Quality Council; and the National Security Council.

The administration also includes the vice president. Some presidents have ignored their vice presidents, having no further use for them after the election. This pattern seems to be the norm in presidential systems around the world.[29] In the United States, Harry Truman had barely met President Roosevelt before the 1944 presidential election and rarely saw him afterward. When Truman succeeded to the presidency after Roosevelt's death, he discovered that he had no idea what the administration had been doing; apparently, he was particularly surprised to learn of America's atomic bomb project. Dwight Eisenhower chose Richard Nixon as his running mate in 1952 but had little regard for Nixon and considered selecting a different running mate in 1956. John Kennedy added Lyndon Johnson to the 1960 Democratic ticket to win Texas's electoral votes but almost never consulted Johnson on policy matters.

In more recent years, presidential candidates have often chosen vice presidential running mates who would bring policy expertise to the administration, and then assigned them significant responsibilities. Thus Vice President Al Gore was charged with directing Clinton's plan to reorganize—or "reinvent"—the government. Vice President Dick Cheney directed the "war on terror," and was widely seen as the most powerful figure in the Bush administration. And Vice President Joe Biden has not had a formal policy portfolio in the Obama administration, but seems to be part of the president's circle of advisers.

Another often important actor in the administration is the First Spouse.[30] The president is the head of state as well as the chief executive, and the president's spouse has typically accompanied the president on foreign visits and ceremonial occasions. Some first spouses, though, have possessed considerable political and policy experience and have played important roles in the White House. During the 1992 campaign, Bill Clinton pointed to his wife's expertise as yet another reason to elect him to office. After the election, Hillary Rodham Clinton took a lead role in a number of policy areas. Later she was elected as a member of the U.S. Senate representing New York, and, after her own unsuccessful presidential candidacy, served as secretary of state in the Obama administration.

Presidential Succession

When Americans elect a president, they expect that individual to occupy the White House for four years. Yet eight presidents have died in office and one, Richard Nixon, was forced to resign.[31] The Constitution directs that in the event of a president's death, incapacity, resignation, or "inability to discharge the powers and duties" of the office, "the Same shall devolve" on the vice president. The precise meaning of the term "devolve" was vigorously debated in 1841 when President Harrison died and Vice President Tyler assumed the presidency. What actually "devolved," the office or merely the duties of the president? While Tyler declared himself to be president, many members of Congress said that Tyler was only the acting president and often addressed him as "Mr. Acting President." Tyler was highly offended by this usage and would return, unopened, letters addressed in this way. Behind his back, too, Tyler's detractors gave him a worse title: "His Accidency." But Tyler persevered, establishing a precedent. Subsequent vice presidents elevated to the presidency during an unfinished term were simply called president.[32]

The Twenty-Fifth Amendment, ratified in 1965, codifies this tradition by declaring that in the event of the death, resignation, or removal of the president, the vice president will become president. In addition, if the vice presidency becomes vacant, a new vice president will be nominated by the president, subject to approval by both houses of Congress. This provision became important in 1973 when Vice President Spiro Agnew was forced to resign in the face of a bribery investigation and President Nixon designated House Minority Leader Gerald Ford as vice president. Ford was confirmed by Congress and served as vice president for several months until President Nixon was forced to resign. At this point, Ford became president and nominated New York Governor Nelson Rockefeller to serve as his vice president. Rockefeller's confirmation hearings were somewhat contentious, but he ultimately assumed the office, giving the United States an unelected president and vice president.

The Twenty-Fifth Amendment also sets forward conditions for the permanent or temporary removal of presidents who have become incapacitated. Presidents may declare themselves to be unable to perform their duties or may be involuntarily declared incapacitated if the vice president and a majority of cabinet officers certify to Congress that the president is unable to serve. If the president's incapacity is temporary, the vice president serves as acting president. On three occasions, presidents have declared themselves to be temporarily incapacitated. Prior to colon surgery in 1985, President Reagan declared himself incapacitated and Vice President Bush was acting president for several hours. On two occasions, when he was undergoing minor medical procedures, President George W. Bush declared himself temporarily incapacitated and Vice President Cheney became acting president. No president has been involuntarily removed from office under the Twenty-Fifth Amendment. There was some discussion of using the procedure after President Reagan was shot in an attempted assassination in 1981, but Vice President George H. W. Bush refused to initiate the process. Prior to the adoption of the Twenty-Fifth Amendment, several presidents, including Woodrow Wilson, were incapacitated but no procedure existed for dealing with the problem.

Finally the 1947 Presidential Succession Act was created, then amended, to establish a precise, lengthy order of succession to the presidency (see Box 1). The act was adopted during the Cold War against the backdrop of a fear of nuclear attack. Today, the act is seen as important because of the danger of a catastrophic terrorist attack. To succeed to the presidency, an official must be eligible, that is, a natural-born citizen of the United States. Often one or another cabinet secretary is ineligible and so has no place in the line of succession. The line of succession is a ghostly presence in every presidency.

An issue of succession is also raised in the event of the death or incapacity of the president-elect before that individual is formally sworn into office. The Twentieth Amendment, ratified in 1933, provides that in the event of the death of

---

Box 1. Presidential Line of Succession

Vice President
Speaker of the House
President Pro Tempore of the Senate
Secretary of State
Secretary of the Treasury
Secretary of Defense
Attorney General
Secretary of the Interior
Secretary of Agriculture
Secretary of Commerce
Secretary of Labor
Secretary of Health and Human Services
Secretary of Housing and Urban Development
Secretary of Transportation
Secretary of Energy
Secretary of Education
Secretary of Veterans Affairs
Secretary of Homeland Security

---

the president-elect, the vice president–elect will become president. Should the vice president–elect also be unavailable, then Congress has the power to name an acting president, following the line of succession established by the 1947 Presidential Succession Act. This principle was nearly put into practice when, barely three weeks after the ratification of the Twentieth Amendment, a gunman, Giuseppe Zangara, sought to kill President-elect Franklin D. Roosevelt. The assassin's bullet missed Roosevelt and instead killed Chicago Mayor Anton Cermak. Had Roosevelt been killed, Vice President–elect John Nance Garner would presumably have been sworn in as president.

The Twentieth Amendment does not cover all possible contingencies associated with death or disability during the presidential selection process. If, for example, the apparent winner of the general election dies or is incapacitated before the Electoral College votes, or the apparent winner in the Electoral College is incapacitated before the electoral votes are officially counted by Congress, the results of the presidential election might be thrown into doubt and Congress forced to quickly adopt procedures to deal with the problem.

Thoughts on Executive Power

The framers of the Constitution thought that executive power was necessary for the proper promotion and protection of the nation's interests. Without the "energy" brought to a government by a strong executive, the framers feared that national unity and the government's capacity for action would be insufficient. At the same time, many of the nation's founders were concerned that a strong executive would pose a threat to citizens' liberties. Hence the strong executive was surrounded by checks and balances designed to impose restraints on executive power. Many saw the necessity for a strong executive but feared, nonetheless, that executive power would eventually overcome any restraints that could be devised to keep it in check. As we shall see, the events of the next two centuries can be understood as confirming both the hopes of advocates and the concerns of critics. In other words, the jury is still out on executive power.

America's First Spouses

The First Spouse can be an important figure in an American presidency. When Bill Clinton mounted his presidential bid in 1992, he underscored the contribution that he expected his wife, Hillary Rodham Clinton, to make to his presidency by declaring that by electing him Americans would receive "two for the price of one." During the nineteenth and early twentieth centuries, first spouses generally confined their public roles to hosting White House events, raising money for good causes, and greeting foreign leaders on ceremonial occasions. Some, including Abigail and Louisa Adams, were politically active and served as presidential advisers. In more recent times, several first spouses have played important roles in the governance of the nation, championing political causes and helping to formulate national policies.

Abigail Adams was the wife of John Adams, America's second president (elected in 1796) as well as the mother of John Quincy Adams, America's sixth president. Mrs. Adams is remembered today as a forthright spokesperson for racial equality and women's rights, helping to place both these matters on America's political agenda, particularly through her proposals to strengthen women's rights to own and inherit property.

Louisa Adams, wife of John Quincy Adams, was instrumental in Adams's 1824 election to the presidency. Mrs. Adams, an excellent writer, became the first prominent woman to

become involved in the sometimes venomous newspaper and magazine wars of the period, by writing articles for the pro-Adams press that defended herself and her husband.

Edith Wilson was the second wife of President Woodrow Wilson (elected in 1912), having married Wilson in 1915, a year after the death of the president's first wife. Unlike Abigail and Louisa Adams, Edith Wilson was no champion of gender or racial equality. Her diaries and memoirs are filled with prejudiced comments about African Americans, Jews, and other ethnic minorities, though she seems to have been proud that some of her own ancestors were Native Americans.

Eleanor Roosevelt, wife of President Franklin Delano Roosevelt (elected in 1932), was an active and significant political figure both during FDR's fourteen years in office and after his death. Through her political activities, Mrs. Roosevelt strengthened the administration's ties to black voters and to the labor movement while infuriating conservatives—especially conservative Southern Democrats, who viewed her as a socialist.

Betty Ford was the wife of President Gerald Ford, who assumed the presi-

dency when Richard Nixon was compelled to resign in 1974, in the wake of the Watergate scandal. After she underwent a mastectomy in 1974, Mrs. Ford campaigned for increased breast cancer awareness. Most notably, Mrs. Ford also revealed her own problems with alcoholism and championed the creation of programs for overcoming addiction and dependency.

Hillary Rodham Clinton, wife of President Bill Clinton (elected in 1992), has been among America's most important First Spouses. Like her husband, Clinton was a graduate of Yale Law School and was an influential attorney and public figure even before Bill Clinton's term in office. In 2001, Hillary Rodham Clinton became the only First Spouse in American history to be elected to office in her own right, winning a U.S. Senate seat to represent the State of New York. In 2008, she was an unsuccessful candidate for the Democratic presidential nomination. Subsequently, President Obama appointed Clinton to the position of secretary of state, in which office she served until 2013. In 2014, Clinton began the preliminary steps for a 2016 presidential bid. If she is successful, not only will she become America's first female president; she will also make Bill Clinton America's first male First Spouse.

Michelle Obama, wife of President Barack Obama (elected in 2008), played a role more like that of the first spouses of yesteryear than that of the modern First Spouse. She hosted White House events and served as a spokesperson, though not an activist, for a number of causes such as exercise and nutrition.

TWO

The Constitutional Foundations
of Presidential Power

In This Chapter

Presidents are individuals with varying abilities, interests, and inclinations. The presidency, however, is an institution whose shape and powers are defined by Article II of the Constitution. As we will see in this chapter, presidents claim four types of power under the Constitution. These are the *expressed* powers specifically granted by the Constitution; the powers not specifically listed but *implied* by the expressed powers; powers *delegated* to the president by the Congress; and powers that presidents claim to be *inherent* in the constitutional structure of the office. Some presidents are better able than others to exercise leadership and to wield the powers of the office. Yet over time, the presidency as an institution has grown in power. This growth, as we will see, has come about because of the institutional advantages that the Constitution gives to the presidency, namely unity, the power of execution, independence, and constancy. Taken together, these are the four principles of executive energy and the keys to understanding presidential power.

Article II

Article II of the Constitution established the presidency and provided the basis for presidential power.

ARTICLE II

SECTION. 1. The executive Power shall be vested in a President of the United States of America. He shall hold his Office during the Term of four Years, and, together with the Vice President, chosen for the same Term, be elected, as follows:

Each State shall appoint, in such Manner as the Legislature thereof may direct, a Number of Electors, equal to the whole Number of Senators and Representatives to which the State may be entitled in the Congress: but no Senator or Representative, or Person holding an Office of Trust or Profit under the United States, shall be appointed an Elector.

The Electors shall meet in their respective States, and vote by Ballot for two Persons, of whom one at least shall not be an Inhabitant of the same State with themselves. And they shall make a List of all the Persons voted for, and of the Number of Votes for each; which List they shall sign and certify, and transmit sealed to the Seat of the Government of the United States, directed to the President of the Senate. The President of the Senate shall, in the Presence of the Senate and House of Representatives, open all the Certificates, and the Votes shall then be counted. The Person having the greatest Number of Votes shall be the President, if such Number be a Majority of the whole Number of Electors appointed; and if there be more than one who have such Majority, and have an equal Number of Votes, then the House of Representatives shall immediately chuse by Ballot one of them for President; and if no Person have a Majority, then from the five highest on the List the said House shall in like Manner chuse the President. But in chusing the President, the Votes shall be taken by States, the Representation from each State having one Vote; A quorum for this Purpose shall consist of a Member or Members from two thirds of the States, and a Majority of all the States shall be necessary to a Choice. In every Case, after the Choice of the President, the Person having the greatest Number of Votes of the Electors shall be the Vice President. But if there should remain two or more who have equal Votes, the Senate shall chuse from them by Ballot the Vice President.

The Congress may determine the Time of chusing the Electors, and the Day on which they shall give their Votes; which Day shall be the same throughout the United States.

No Person except a natural born Citizen, or a Citizen of the United States, at the time of the Adoption of this Constitution, shall be eligible to the Office of President; neither shall any person be eligible to that Office who shall not have attained to the Age of thirty five Years, and been fourteen Years a Resident within the United States.

In Case of the Removal of the President from Office, or of his Death, Resignation, or Inability to discharge the Powers and Duties of the said Office, the Same shall devolve on the Vice President, and the Congress may by Law provide for the Case of Removal, Death, Resignation or Inability, both of the President and Vice President, declaring what Officer shall then act as President, and such Officer shall act accordingly, until the Disability be removed, or a President shall be elected.

The President shall, at stated Times, receive for his Services, a Compensation, which shall neither be increased nor diminished during the Period for which he shall have been elected, and he shall not receive within that Period any other Emolument from the United States, or any of them.

Before he enter on the Execution of his Office, he shall take the following Oath or Affirmation:—"I do solemnly swear (or affirm) that I will faithfully execute the Office of President of the United States, and will to the best of my Ability, preserve, protect and defend the Constitution of the United States."

SECTION. 2. The President shall be Commander in Chief of the Army and Navy of the United States, and of the Militia of the several States, when called into the actual Service of the United States; he may require the Opinion, in writing, of the principal Officer in each of the executive Departments, upon any Subject relating to the Duties of their respective Offices, and he shall have Power to grant Reprieves and Pardons for Offenses against the United States, except in Cases of Impeachment.

He shall have Power, by and with the Advice and Consent of the Senate, to make Treaties, provided two thirds of the Senators present concur; and he shall nominate, and by and with the Advice and Consent of the Senate, shall appoint Ambassadors, other public Ministers and Consuls, Judges of the supreme Court, and all other Officers of the United States, whose Appointments are not herein otherwise provided for, and which shall be established by Law: but the Congress may by Law vest the Appointment of such inferior Officers, as they think proper, in the President alone, in the Courts of Law, or in the Heads of Departments.

The President shall have Power to fill up all Vacancies that may happen during the Recess of the Senate, by granting Commissions which shall expire at the End of their next Session.

SECTION. 3. He shall from time to time give to the Congress Information of the State of the Union, and recommend to their Consideration such Measures as he shall judge necessary and expedient; he may, on extraordinary Occasions, convene both Houses, or either of them, and in Case of Disagreement between them, with Respect to the Time of Adjournment, he may adjourn them to such Time as he shall think proper; he shall receive Ambassadors and other public Ministers; he shall take Care that the Laws be faithfully executed, and shall Commission all the Officers of the United States.

SECTION. 4. The President, Vice President and all civil Officers of the United States, shall be removed from Office on Impeachment for, and Conviction of, Treason, Bribery, or other high Crimes and Misdemeanors.

The article begins by vesting the executive power, that is, the power to execute the laws, in the president of the United States. This language is known as the Constitution's "vesting clause." The president's executive power is underscored in Section 3 of Article II, the "take care clause," which confers on the president the duty to "take care that the laws be faithfully executed." The president's oath of office at the end of Section 1, moreover, obligates—and thus empowers—the chief executive to "preserve, protect and defend the Constitution of the United States." This language seems to require the president to take action, without specifying any limits to that action, if the constitutional government is threatened. President Abraham Lincoln cited his oath of office as justification for suspending the writ of habeas corpus in 1861. He declared that his oath would be broken if the government were to be overthrown. Suspension of the writ, he said, was necessary to prevent that calamity from taking place. By vesting the executive power in the president, Article II also implies that the president serves as America's head of state and is therefore entitled to special deference and respect. In Europe, the chief executives and heads of state were monarchs. While presidents are not monarchs, as the holders of executive power they might appear to be entitled to the kingly respect due a head of state.

Expressed Presidential Powers

The powers specifically mentioned in Article II are called the *expressed powers* of the office. These are mainly found in Section 2 and include the president's power as commander in chief of the Army and Navy of the United States, the president's power to grant reprieves and pardons, the president's power to negotiate treaties (subject to senatorial approval), the president's power to appoint and supervise all executive officers, and the president's power to appoint federal judges. Appointments must be confirmed by the Senate, though the president may make temporary "recess appointments" when the Senate is not in session. These constitutional powers may not be revoked by the Congress or the courts. Another expressed power of the president is contained in the "presentment clause" of Article I, Section 7 of the Constitution. After both houses of Congress have agreed on a piece of legislation, they must present it to the president, who is empowered to sign or veto the proposed law. Congress may override a presidential veto, but only by a vote of two-thirds of both houses.

On a number of occasions, presidents have also made use of what has come to be called the "pocket veto." The Constitution declares that the president has ten days to sign or veto a bill. If no action is taken, the bill becomes a law even without the president's signature. Bills that remain unsigned (in the president's pocket) after a session of Congress has ended, however, do not become law. Presidents favor the pocket veto because it cannot be overridden. Members of Congress, by contrast, have attempted to restrict the use of this presidential maneuver. They have appointed agents to receive bills and communications from the White House when the legislative body is not in session—agents whom presidents have sought to ignore.[1] The Supreme Court's June 2014 decision limiting presidential use of recess appointments, discussed later, may set a precedent for limits on the use of pocket vetoes. Maneuvers aside, as Table 1 indicates, a presidential veto is generally conclusive. Over the course of American history, only about 4 percent of all vetoes have been overridden.

Contemporary presidents have generally been more apt to use their veto power than were their nineteenth-century counterparts. In the early years of the republic, the veto was seen as an extraordinary measure, but as the power of the presidency increased, it became a more commonly used presidential instrument. We will return to this point in Chapter 3. President Obama has seldom used the veto power, but then again, as a result of the congressional stalemate during his administration, Congress has seldom presented the president with bills to sign.

Presidents often find themselves at odds with Congress over legislation and appointments, areas in which—under the principle of checks and balances—Congress

Table 1. Summary of Bills Vetoed, 1789–Present

President (years)	Coinciding Congresses	Vetoes			
		Regular	Pocket	Total	Overridden
Barack H. Obama (2009–present)	111–114	44	0		
George W. Bush (2001–2009)	107–110	12	0	12	4
William J. Clinton (1993–2001)	103–106	36	1	37	2
George H. W. Bush (1989–1993)[a]	101–102	29	15	44	1
Ronald Reagan (1981–1989)[b]	97–100	39	39	78	9
Jimmy Carter (1977–1981)	95–96	13	18	31	2
Gerald R. Ford (1974–1977)	93–94	48	18	66	12
Richard M. Nixon (1969–1974)	91–93	26	17	43	7
Lyndon B. Johnson (1963–1969)	88–90	16	14	30	0
John F. Kennedy (1961–1963)	87–88	12	9	21	0
Dwight D. Eisenhower (1953–1961)	83–86	73	108	181	2
Harry S. Truman (1945–1953)	79–82	180	70	250	12
Franklin D. Roosevelt (1933–1945)	73–79	372	263	635	9
Herbert Hoover (1929–1933)	71–72	21	16	37	3
Calvin Coolidge (1923–1929)	68–70	20	30	50	4
Warren G. Harding (1921–1923)	67	5	1	6	0
Woodrow Wilson (1913–1921)	63–66	33	11	44	6
William H. Taft (1909–1913)	61–62	30	9	39	1
Theodore Roosevelt (1901–1909)	57–60	42	40	82	1
William McKinley (1897–1901)	55–57	6	36	42	0
Grover Cleveland (1893–1897)	53–54	42	128	170	5
Benjamin Harrison (1889–1893)	51–52	19	25	44	1
Grover Cleveland (1885–1889)	49–50	304	110	414	2
Chester A. Arthur (1881–1885)	47–48	4	8	12	1
James A. Garfield (1881)	47	0	0	0	0
Rutherford B. Hayes (1877–1881)	45–46	12	1	13	1
Ulysses S. Grant (1869–1877)[c]	41–44	45	48	93	4
Andrew Johnson (1865–1869)	39–40	21	8	29	15
Abraham Lincoln (1861–1865)	37–39	2	5	7	0
James Buchanan (1857–1861)	35–36	4	3	7	0
Franklin Pierce (1853–1857)	33–34	9	0	9	5
Millard Fillmore (1850–1853)	31–32	0	0	0	0

continued

Table 1. *Continued*

President (years)	Coinciding Congresses	Vetoes			
		Regular	Pocket	Total	Overridden
Zachary Taylor (1849–1850)	31	0	0	0	0
James K. Polk (1845–1849)	29–30	2	1	3	0
John Tyler (1841–1845)	27–28	6	4	10	1
William H. Harrison (1841)	27	0	0	0	0
Martin Van Buren (1837–1841)	25, 26	0	1	1	0
Andrew Jackson (1829–1837)	21–24	5	7	12	0
John Q. Adams (1825–1829)	19–20	0	0	0	0
James Monroe (1817–1825)	15–18	1	0	1	0
James Madison (1809–1817)	11–14	5	2	7	0
Thomas Jefferson (1801–1809)	7–10	0	0	0	0
John Adams (1797–1801)	5–6	0	0	0	0
George Washington (1789–1797)	1–4	2	0	2	0
Total[d]		1,500	1,066	2,566	110

Source: U.S. Senate, available online at http://www.senate.gov/reference/Legislation/Vetoes/vetoCounts .htm (accessed July 24, 2015).

[a] Attempted intrasession pocket vetoes on H.R. 1 (101st Congress) and S. 333 (101st Congress) were disputed. Both bills were enacted into law so are not counted on this table.

[b] H.R. 4042 (98th Congress) is counted as a pocket veto.

[c] A pocket veto on H.R. 4476 (44th Congress) is not counted on this table because "it was not placed before the President for signature" (H.Doc. 493, 70th Congress, p. 24).

[d] The total number of vetoes tabulated is 2,565. This figure is one less than the numbered presidential vetoes because of the disputed pocket veto on H.R. 4476.

also exercises significant constitutional power. The relationship between presidential power and congressional power in these two domains will be among the major topics discussed in Chapter 6.

The War Power

Of the expressed presidential powers, none has been more important than the president's power as commander-in-chief of America's military forces. The framers assigned war powers to both Congress and the president. To Congress they gave the power to declare war and to raise and support military forces. To the president they gave the power to command those armies. Thus it was understood to be the province of the Congress to determine whether, when, and against whom to wage war, and the duty of the president to seek to bring the war to a successful conclusion.[2] The framers assigned the power to declare war to the Congress rather than the president because they thought representative assemblies that bore the costs of war were less inclined to engage in bloodshed than executives who might seek to reap the glory of military adventures. James Madison called war "the true nurse of executive aggrandizement" and declared it to be "an axiom that the executive is the department of power most distinguished by its propensity to war."[3]

Despite this concern, the framers knew that only the president could act quickly if the nation was actually attacked. Hence Article II gives Congress the power to "declare" war rather than, as was originally proposed, to "make" war. James Madison, along with Massachusetts delegate Elbridge Gerry, moved successfully to alter the proposed text, thereby "leaving to the executive the power to repel sudden attacks."[4] The framers thought this language was unambiguous. In an emergency, the president could defend the nation without waiting for congressional approval; otherwise only the Congress could send Americans to war. In practice, however, many questions remain unanswered. What is the scope of the president's power to "repel sudden attacks"? Might not a president argue that successfully repelling an attack required years of preparation and planning under the executive's command? Might not a president argue that an attack could best be repelled preemptively, that is, by striking first, perhaps after secret preparations that could not be revealed to Congress? The George W. Bush administration, for example, declared that the United States could not afford to wait to be attacked and so would, if necessary, disable terrorist groups and so-called rogue states before they could do harm to the United States.

Presidents, as we shall see, have asserted that their duties as commanders-in-chief give them an extra-constitutional "inherent" power to do whatever is needed to defend the nation, even to the extent of ignoring the objections of Congress and the courts. And indeed, over the decades, presidents have taken effective control over the power to initiate hostilities and in the process pushed Congress to the sidelines. Precisely how presidents gained primacy in this realm will be examined in Chapter 9. For now, let us simply observe that there is much truth to the framers' fear that presidents might be too ready to go to war. America's military leadership, moreover, has worked to enhance the president's role in America's economy and society as the constant preparation for war has reduced the difference between wartime and peacetime.

Presidential Pardons

Another of the president's expressed constitutional powers, the power to grant pardons, is often a source of controversy. A pardon is a presidential order, usually following an individual's petition and an investigation and recommendation from the

Table 2. Petitions for Presidential Pardons

Fiscal year	Petitions pending	Petitions received	Petitions granted	Petitions denied	Petitions closed without presidential action
2001 *(8.5 mos.)*	923	110	0	0	45
2002	988	152	0	519	53
2003	565	172	7	51	21
2004	659	235	12	108	42
2005	733	252	39	89	35
2006	822	254	39	255	53
2007	729	334	16	0	75
2008	972	555	44	513	107
2009 *(3.5 mos.)*	864	434	32	194	33
2009 *(8.5 mos.)*	1,040	232	0	0	132
2010	1,140	262	0	0	117
2011	1,285	331	17	872	84
2012 *(7 mos.)*	643	205	5	147	37
Totals:	11,363	3,528	211	2,748	834

Source: U.S. Justice Department data, available online at www.justice.gov/pardon/statistics.htm (accessed July 20, 2015).

Justice Department, that vacates a federal conviction and restores an individual to the state of innocence that existed before the conviction. In some cases, presidents may issue pardons before the fact, that is, they may pardon individuals for possible offenses related to some action even before actual charges are brought against them. The president may also commute a sentence without invalidating the original conviction. As Table 2 indicates, in recent years only about 5 percent of petitions for pardons have been granted.

In some instances, presidents pardon individuals whom they believe to have been wrongfully convicted, or when they believe that a pardon will help quell past social or political antagonisms. For example, Gerald Ford pardoned some fifty thousand Vietnam-era draft resisters, most of whom had never been brought to trial, asserting this would help to heal the political wounds produced by that conflict. And Jimmy Carter pardoned Patty Hearst, who had been kidnapped by a radical group and forced to participate in bank robberies.

Presidents will sometimes pardon politically prominent individuals, usually members of their own party, who have been convicted as a result of ethics probes.

Thus Gerald Ford pardoned Richard Nixon, setting off a heated national debate. George H. W. Bush pardoned a number of individuals involved in the Iran-Contra affair, including former defense secretary Caspar Weinberger and former national security adviser Robert McFarlane. George W. Bush issued a pardon to Vice President Cheney's chief of staff, Lewis "Scooter" Libby, who had been convicted of perjury. And Bill Clinton pardoned his own housing secretary, Henry Cisneros, who had been convicted of lying to the FBI.

Presidents will sometimes pardon friends and associates, leading to suspicion of favoritism. Bill Clinton, for instance, pardoned his half-brother, Roger, who had been convicted of cocaine possession, as well as his former Whitewater business partner Susan McDougal and fugitive financier Marc Rich, whose wife was a major Democratic Party contributor. Most pardons, however, appear to come about as a result of campaigns by a convicted individual's relatives, friends, and supporters to bring the case to a president's attention and provide the president with an opportunity to show that, like a medieval king, he or she could be merciful.[5]

Implied Presidential Powers

The list of expressed presidential powers is brief, but each expressed power has become the foundation for a second set of presidential powers, the *implied powers* of the office. An implied power is one that presidents need in order to exercise their expressed power. For example, the Constitution expressly gives the president the power to appoint "all other officers of the United States . . . which shall be established by law." Article II does not, however, expressly grant the president the power to remove such officials from office.

There is no reason to assume a priori that the power to appoint an official necessarily indicates the power to remove one. Recall that the president of France appoints the prime minister but only the national legislature can remove that official from office. From the earliest years of the republic, though, presidents claimed that the removal power was implied by the appointment power. This claim was generally accepted until 1867 when, during its struggles with President Andrew Johnson, Congress enacted the Tenure of Office Act (repealed in 1887), which required the president to obtain senatorial approval to remove those officials whose appointments had required Senate confirmation. Johnson's refusal to comply with this act led to his 1868 impeachment and trial. Johnson escaped his own removal from office by a one-vote margin. Fifty years later, the U.S. Supreme Court held in the case of *Myers v. United States* that the removal power was, indeed, implied by the appointment power.[6] The Court's decision also explicitly invalidated the long-defunct

Tenure of Office Act. In the much later case of *Bowsher v. Synar,* the Court made clear that the power to remove executive appointees belonged exclusively to the president, saying that Congress could not itself remove executive appointees, except by impeachment, even if it gave itself such a right in the statute establishing the office in question.[7]

The Constitution also authorizes presidents to recommend to Congress such measures as they may judge necessary and expedient. Consequently, presidents have endeavored to control the legislative agenda by recommending detailed annual budgets to the Congress. The White House expects these budgets to become the basis for the government's spending and revenue plans. Congress, of course, often has its own ideas about fiscal matters.

Presidents have also made much of the very first sentence of Article II, which declares, "The executive power shall be vested in a President of the United States of America." This grant of power, the subsequent admonition to presidents to see to it that the laws are faithfully executed, as well as the president's oath of office have all been cited by successive administrations as justifications for actions not expressly sanctioned by the Constitution. In recent years, the vesting clause has been said by presidents and their advisers to support what has come to be known as the "theory of the unitary executive."[8]

Unitary executive theory holds that all executive power inheres in the president except as explicitly limited by the Constitution.[9] According to this view, the president is a sovereign subject to some restraints such as Congress's control of revenues, its impeachment power, and its power to override presidential vetoes. Some proponents of unitary executive theory also aver that presidents have their own power to interpret the Constitution as it applies to the executive branch and need not necessarily defer to the judiciary. This claim was advanced by President George W. Bush when he signed a defense appropriation bill that included language on the treatment of terrorist suspects—the so-called anti-torture provision introduced by Senator John McCain—that the president had opposed. In his signing statement, Bush declared that he would construe the portion of the act relating to the treatment of detainees "in a manner consistent with the constitutional authority of the President to supervise the unitary executive branch and as Commander in Chief and consistent with the constitutional limitations on the judicial power."[10] The president was claiming, in other words, that particularly in the military realm, he possessed the authority to execute acts of Congress according to his own understanding of the law and the nation's interests. He also seemed to be claiming that the authority of the courts to interfere with his actions was limited. In 2014, President Obama acknowledged that a number of detainees had indeed been tortured by U.S.

authorities. In December 2014, a Senate investigation castigated the CIA for alleged abuses of detainees in secret prisons.

Unitary executive theory particularly holds that the president controls all policymaking by the executive branch, with Congress wielding only limited, if any, direct power over executive agencies. Only presidents, say unitary executive theorists, may exercise discretionary authority over the actions of these agencies. This idea has been the basis for such presidential programs as "regulatory review," discussed later, which has been used by every president since Ronald Reagan to guide rulemaking by the various federal agencies. Indeed sometimes presidents have used this process to write authoritative rules when they could not persuade Congress to enact the laws they were proposing.[11]

The president is a single, as opposed to a plural, chief executive, but under the principle of constitutional checks and balances, Congress has been given powers over the many important agencies of the executive branch through what has come to be called "congressional oversight" of the executive. Article I of the Constitution endows Congress with a number of powers, including the powers to appropriate funds, to raise and support armies and navies, to regulate interstate commerce, and to impeach officials of the executive branch. Article I also gives Congress the authority "to make all laws which shall be necessary and proper for carrying into execution the foregoing powers." Congressional oversight—which includes legislative hearings, investigations, studies, and reports—is arguably implied by this language. If Congress is to carry out its constitutional responsibilities, it must be able to obtain information regarding the activities of executive branch agencies and officials. Thus the stage is set for conflict between the implied powers of Congress and those of the president, a conflict we shall consider more fully in Chapter 6.

In this clash between the implied powers of Congress and the implied powers of the president, the advocates of presidential power claim the support of no less an authority than Alexander Hamilton, who pointed out that Article I, Section 1 of the Constitution limited congressional powers to those "herein granted," while no such limitation is attached to the executive powers of the president, which are, writes Hamilton, subject only to specific qualifications and limitations. If we agree with Hamilton, the idea of implied presidential power might thus carry more weight than the concept of implied congressional power.[12]

Even at the time of the founding, the question of what exactly might be implied by Article II raised some concerns in the nation at large. William Symmes, a member of the Massachusetts ratifying convention, expressed these misgivings when he said, "But was ever a commission so brief, so general, as this of our President? Can we exactly say how far a faithful execution of the laws may extend?

Or what may be called for or comprehended in a faithful execution? . . . Should a federal law happen to be as generally expressed as the President's authority; must he not interpret the Act. . . . And should the legislature direct the mode of executing the laws, or any particular law, is he obliged to comply, if he does not think it will amount to a faithful execution?"[13] Symmes showed remarkable perspicacity, apparently looking more than two centuries into the future and seeing President Bush's 2006 signing statement.

Delegated Presidential Powers

A third group of presidential powers is *delegated* by the Congress. When Congress settles on some course of action it will generally, by statute, delegate to the president or to the executive branch the authority to implement its decisions. This is an important way in which the law is executed. Often the president and the executive branch are allowed a good deal of discretion in deciding just how to implement a statute, and the more discretion the president is given, the greater is his or her authority to shape the law. In some instances, the delegation of power to the president is contingent, that is, granted by Congress but based on the president's finding that a particular state of affairs has come into existence. In other instances, Congress will simply and directly delegate to the president the power to implement a piece of legislation. In still other instances, Congress will delegate power to an administrative agency rather than the president, but the president, consistent with unitary executive theory, will usually claim to possess "directive" authority over the agency and will view Congress's action as delegating power to the White House.

After a statute is passed by the Congress and signed into law by the president, the various executive agencies charged with administering and enforcing the act will usually spend months and sometimes years writing rules and regulations to implement the new law and will continue to write rules for decades thereafter. Typically, a statute will assert a set of goals and establish some framework for achieving them but leave much to the discretion of the executive. In some instances, members of Congress are themselves uncertain of just what a law will do and depend on administrators to tell them. In the case of the 2010 Affordable Care Act, widely known as Obamacare, for example, several members admitted that they did not fully understand how the act would work and were depending on the Department of Health and Human Services (HHS), the executive agency with primary administrative responsibility for the act, to explain it to them.

Sometimes Congress is surprised by agency rules surrounding the enactment of a law. In 2012 the Internal Revenue Service (IRS) proposed rules to determine eligibility under the Affordable Care Act that would have excluded millions of working-class Americans whom members of Congress thought would be covered. Several congressional Democrats who had helped to secure the enactment of the legislation complained that the IRS interpretation would frustrate the intent of Congress.[14] The case of the Affordable Care Act is fairly typical. As administrative scholar Jerry L. Mashaw has observed, "Most public law is legislative in origin but administrative in content."[15] In Chapter 5, we will look more closely at agency rule-making and see how a bill actually becomes a law.

The roots of bureaucratic power in the United States are complex and date to the earliest decades of the republic.[16] Much of today's federal bureaucracy, however, can trace its origins to Franklin D. Roosevelt's New Deal. Under FDR's leadership, the federal government began to take responsibility for management of the economy, provision of social services, protection of the public's health, maintenance of employment opportunities, promotion of social equality, protection of the environment, and a host of other tasks. As the government's responsibilities and ambitions grew, Congress assigned more and more complex tasks to the agencies of the executive branch, which sometimes were only too happy to expand their own power and autonomy.[17] Executive agencies came to have responsibility for analyzing and acting on economic data; assessing the environmental impact of programs and projects; responding to fluctuations in the labor market; safeguarding the food supply; regulating the stock market; supervising telecommunications as well as air, sea, and land transport; and, in recent years, protecting the nation from terrorist plots.

When Congress writes legislation addressing these and a host of other complex issues, legislators cannot anticipate every question or problem that might arise under the law over the coming decades. Congress cannot establish detailed air quality standards, draw up rules for drug testing, or legislate the ballistic properties of artillery rounds for a new Army tank. Inevitably then, as the goals of Congress become more ambitious, more complex, and broader in scope, members of Congress must delegate considerable discretionary authority to the agencies charged with giving effect to the law. To be sure, if Congress delegates broad and discretionary authority to the executive, it risks seeing its goals subordinated to and subverted by those of the executive branch.[18] But if Congress attempts to limit executive discretion by enacting very precise rules and standards to govern the conduct of the president and the executive branch, it risks writing laws that do not conform to real-world conditions and that are too rigid to be adapted to changing circumstances.[19] As the Supreme Court explained in a 1989 case, "In our increasingly complex society, replete with ever changing and more technical problems, Congress simply cannot do its job absent an ability to delegate power under broad general directives."[20]

In some instances, Congress attempts to set standards and guidelines designed to govern administrative conduct. For example, the 1970 Clean Air Act specified the pollutants that the Environmental Protection Agency (EPA) would be charged with eliminating from the atmosphere, as well as a number of the procedures that the EPA was obligated to undertake.[21] But the act still left many other matters to EPA administrators, including enforcement procedures, who should bear the burden of cleaning the air, and even how clean the air should ultimately be.

Many other statutes give administrators virtually unfettered discretion to decide how to achieve goals that are only vaguely articulated by the Congress. For example, the statute establishing the Federal Trade Commission (FTC) outlaws "unfair methods of competition," though precisely what these methods might be is largely left to the agency to determine. Similarly, the statute creating the Occupational Safety and Health Administration (OSHA) calls on the agency "to protect health to the extent feasible," but what that extent might be is for the agency to determine. In its enabling act, the EPA was told to protect human health and the environment "to an adequate degree of safety."[22] As Congress continued to enact statutes setting out general objectives without specifying how the government was supposed to achieve them, the federal bureaucracy was left to fill in the ever-growing number of blanks.

In some instances, to be sure, Congress does write detailed standards into the law, only to see these rewritten by administrators. For example, in 2006, the Securities and Exchange Commission (SEC) announced that it was issuing new rules that would significantly change key provisions of the 2002 Sarbanes-Oxley Act, which had been passed in the wake of the Enron scandal to reform corporate governance and prevent fraud. As enacted by Congress, Sarbanes-Oxley contains very specific standards for accounting reform and investor protection. In response to industry lobbying, however, the SEC announced that it would issue new standards to ease corporate obligations under Section 404 of the act, which covers the financial statements issued by public corporations.[23] The agency determined that the law, as written by Congress, had forced corporations to engage in "overly conservative" practices.

In recent years, presidents have asserted a measure of direct control over rulemaking through a process called regulatory review. Presidents Clinton, Bush, and Obama, in particular, have declared that the White House has full authority to direct the rulemaking activities of executive agencies, both to block rules to which they object and to order the implementation of rules that will advance the administration's policy goals. Consistent with this idea, in June 2014 President Obama ordered the EPA to develop specific new rules in order to reduce carbon dioxide emissions from coal-powered generating plants. The Clean Air Act, enacted years earlier, had given the EPA authority to set various emission standards and now the president was asserting that this delegation of power authorized him to take the lead in setting such standards.

Inherent Presidential Powers

Presidents have also claimed a fourth source of constitutional power—an authority not specified in the Constitution but said to stem from "the rights, duties and obligations of the presidency." These are referred to as *inherent* powers and are most often asserted by presidents in times of war or national emergency. President Lincoln relied on a claim of inherent power to raise an army after the fall of Fort Sumter. Similarly, President Roosevelt (World War II), President Truman (Korean War), and both Presidents Bush (Persian Gulf and Middle East wars) claimed inherent powers to defend the nation. Since the Korean War, presidents have used their claim of inherent powers along with their constitutional power as commander-in-chief to bypass the constitutional provision giving Congress the power to declare war. Congress declared war after the Japanese attack on Pearl Harbor on December 7, 1941. Since that time, American forces have been sent to fight foreign wars on more than a hundred occasions but not once has Congress been asked for a declaration of war. In 1973, Congress passed the War Powers Resolution designed to restore its role in military policy, but presidents have regarded it as an improper limitation on the inherent powers of the presidency and so have studiously ignored its provisions.

The difference between inherent and implied powers is often subtle, and the two are frequently jointly claimed in support of presidential action. Implied powers can be traced to the powers expressed in the actual language of the Constitution.[24] Inherent powers, by contrast, derive from national sovereignty. Under international law and custom, sovereign states possess a number of inherent rights and powers. The most important of these are the right to engage in relations with other nations, the right of self-defense against attacks from other states, and the right to curb internal violence and unrest. Who actually has the right to give effect to the nation's various rights and powers? The executive power is vested by the Constitution in the president, who is acknowledged to have the power to "make" if not "declare" war, to negotiate treaties with other nations, and to see to it that the laws are faithfully executed. Thus it might be said to be constitutionally implied that it is the president who possesses the inherent power to defend the nation, to conduct its foreign relations, and to safeguard law and order.

Most presidents believe that they, and only they, are constitutionally authorized to manage the nation's relations with foreign states. If challenged, presidents and their aides will cite the words of John Marshall's 1800 speech to the House of Representatives, when the future chief justice of the Supreme Court called the president "the sole organ of the nation in its external relations, and its sole representative with foreign nations."[25] According to constitutional scholar Louis Fisher, Marshall meant that the president was the sole organ in implementing, not making, foreign policy.[26] Yet the Supreme Court took the more expansive view in its famous *Curtiss-Wright* decision, which cites Marshall in support of the idea that the president possesses broad inherent power in the making of foreign policy.[27]

A number of presidents have claimed that the presidency also has inherent powers in military affairs and in dealing with domestic emergencies—powers that were not necessarily spelled out in the Constitution nor sanctioned by law.[28] Justifying his 1803 decision to purchase Louisiana from France, President Thomas Jefferson wrote, "A strict observance of the written law is doubtless one of the high duties of a good citizen, but it is not the highest. The laws of necessity, of self-preservation, of saving our country when in danger, are of higher obligation. To lose our country to a scrupulous adherence to the written law, would be to lose the law itself, with life, liberty, property and those who are enjoying them with us, thus absurdly sacrificing the ends to the means."[29] In 1861, Abraham Lincoln suspended the writ of habeas corpus and declared martial law in a number of areas, called out the state militias, withdrew funds from the Treasury, and ordered a naval blockade of Southern ports, all without congressional authorization. In defending his suspension of habeas corpus, an action that clearly was without legal basis, Lincoln famously asked in a July 4, 1861, special session of Congress, "Are all the laws but one to go unexecuted, and the government itself go to pieces, lest that one be violated?" Congress retroactively validated all of Lincoln's actions. In the case of *Ex parte Merryman,* Chief Justice Roger Taney, sitting as a federal circuit court judge, ruled that only Congress, not the president, could suspend habeas corpus.[30] President Lincoln ignored the ruling and ordered the Army to maintain martial law, though he subsequently ordered the release of individuals being held by federal authorities.

During the Korean War, President Harry S. Truman relied on a claim of inherent powers to seize the nation's steel mills lest military production be interrupted by a threatened strike. Truman had deployed American military forces to Korea without a congressional declaration of war and in violation of a number of statutes, but he claimed that his action was an extension of the police power rather than a military action. In 1952, however, Truman asserted that his seizure of the steel mills was based on the inherent power of the executive and required no statutory basis. The president took the position that neither Congress nor the judiciary could contravene the president's inherent power to deal with an emergency.[31] The Supreme Court rejected Truman's seizure of the mills, but did not fully deny his claim that the president possessed inherent powers to deal with emergencies.

No president has acted so frequently on the basis of inherent powers as did President George W. Bush, who claimed that the inherent powers of the presidency gave him the authority to create military commissions, to designate U.S. citizens as enemy combatants, to engage in "extraordinary renditions" of captured suspects who were then moved to unknown facilities in unnamed countries for interrogation, and to authorize the National Security Agency (NSA) to monitor phone conversations between the United States and other nations.[32] When challenged, some but not all of these actions were overturned by the courts. We shall examine these decisions in some detail in Chapter 8. It is worth noting, however, that the decisions hardly put to rest the idea of inherent power. Indeed, Bush's successor, President Barack Obama, continued to rely on the concept of inherent power in ordering drone strikes against suspected terrorists and ordering American air strikes in Libya. Testifying before Congress in 2014, Attorney General Eric Holder defended the president's unilateral actions saying, "Given what the president's responsibility is in running the executive branch, I think there is an inherent power there for him to act in the way that he has."[33]

Congress has endeavored to place some limits on powers that presidents claim to be inherent. One example is the case of emergency powers. Presidents believe they have the inherent power to deal with emergencies. But Congress has, by statute, sought to circumscribe and guide the use of these powers. Under the 1976 National Emergencies Act, which was built on prior enactments, the president is authorized to declare a national emergency in the event of major threats to America's national security or economy.[34] An emergency declaration relating to foreign threats allows the president to embargo trade, seize foreign assets, and prohibit transactions with whatever foreign nations are involved. During a state of emergency, constitutional rights, including the right of habeas corpus, may be suspended. An emergency declaration, however, does not remain in force indefinitely; it continues for only one year unless renewed by the president. Several declarations have been renewed annually for quite some time: President Carter's 1976 declaration of an emergency during the Iranian hostage crisis has been renewed every year, as has been President Bush's 2001 emergency declaration following the 9/11 terror attacks. These declarations have provided a basis for various trade embargoes, asset freezes, and restrictions on money transfers ordered by successive presidents. Congress may, by a joint resolution of the two houses, terminate a state of emergency.

Another situation that presidents tend to view as involving their own inherent power, and that Congress has sought to regulate, is the nation's response to natural disasters. Under the 1988 Stafford Act, the governor of a state affected by a disastrous flood, hurricane, earthquake, or other calamitous event must ask the Federal Emergency Management Agency (FEMA) for a determination that the scope of the disaster is beyond the abilities of state and local authorities to handle. The president may then declare a disaster and make the state eligible for federal funds and relief. The purpose of the Stafford Act was to ensure that presidential disaster declarations were governed by statutory criteria. In recent years, however, critics have charged that presidential determinations and funding authorizations seemed nevertheless to be driven by political motivations.[35]

Checks and Balances

From the Constitution, presidents derive expressed, implied, and delegated powers. Claims of inherent powers are derived from the basic principles of national sovereignty coupled with the constitutional grant of executive power. The framers did indeed attempt to create a leader whose "energy" would power the entire government, but they were also concerned that executive power could be abused and might stifle citizens' liberties. To guard against this possibility, the framers contrived a number of checks on executive power. The president's term was to be limited to four years, though with the possibility of reappointment. The Congress was empowered to impeach and remove the president, to reject presidential appointments and refuse to ratify treaties, to refuse to enact laws requested by the president, to deny funding for the president's programs, and to override presidential vetoes of congressional enactments.

The framers viewed the threat of impeachment as an important check on executive power. The Constitution provides that a president may be impeached for "high crimes and misdemeanors." Such offenses are to be charged by the House and tried in the Senate, with the chief justice presiding and a two-thirds vote needed for conviction. At the Constitutional Convention, James Madison said it was "indispensable that some provision should be made for defending the Community against the incapacity, negligence or perfidy" of the chief executive.[36] Elbridge Gerry concurred on the necessity of impeachments, saying, "A good magistrate will not fear them. A bad one ought to be kept in fear of them."[37] During the course of American history, only two presidents, Andrew Johnson and Bill Clinton, have been impeached, though neither was convicted. Johnson's impeachment was triggered by his veto of the Tenure in Office Act, and Clinton's by charges of sexual improprieties. A third president, Richard Nixon, would almost certainly have been impeached for his misdeeds in the Watergate affair, but he chose to resign to avoid the impeachment process.

The requirement that the Senate concur in treaties and presidential appointments was seen by the framers as another important check on executive power. In *Federalist* 76, Alexander Hamilton wrote, "It will be readily comprehended that a man who had himself the sole disposition of offices would be governed much more by his private inclinations and interests, than when he was bound to submit the propriety of his choice to the discussion and determination of a different and independent body . . . The possibility of rejection would be a strong motive to care in proposing . . . He would be both ashamed and afraid to bring forward . . . [unsuitable] candidates."[38] Perhaps presidents have indeed been careful not to propose unsuitable nominees, because historically only about 2 percent of presidential nominees to top posts have been rejected by the Senate.[39]

In recent years severe partisan disagreements have led presidents often to resort to "recess appointments." These are authorized by Article II, Section 2, which states, "The President shall have Power to fill up all Vacancies that may happen during the Recess of the Senate, by granting Commissions which shall expire at the End of their next Session." Until recent years, recess appointments were made only between Senate sessions or when the Senate was adjourned for lengthy periods. In recent years, however, recess appointments have become more frequent and the Senate has resorted to an expedient similar to the one employed to prevent pocket vetoes: during periods of recess, one senator is assigned the task of calling the chamber to order for a few moments every day for a pro forma session so that the president cannot claim the Senate was closed for business. Presidents have viewed this procedure as nothing more than a subterfuge, since the Senate is incapable of actually conducting business during these periods.

In 2012, in a rare instance when the Senate was not even in pro forma session for three days of a ten-day recess, President Obama made three recess appointments to the National Labor Relations Board. All three appointees had been blocked by Republican senators using a variety of procedural maneuvers. In a unanimous June 2014 decision, however, the Supreme Court ruled that a ten-day recess was "presumptively too short" to permit a recess appointment. The Court did not indicate how long a recess would be necessary to permit recess appointments by the president.[40]

Under the Constitution, only the Congress has the power to enact legislation, levy taxes, or appropriate funds. Indeed so many were the constitutional checks on executive power that some delegates to the Constitutional Convention feared that the executive would be too weak and the potential energy of executive power lost.

Rufus King of Massachusetts said he was concerned that "an extreme caution in favor of liberty might enervate the government we were forming."[41]

King need not have worried. The constitutional character of the presidency ensured that checks and balances would not have an "enervating" effect on the executive branch. Far from it. Article II of the Constitution made the president too "energetic" for such an outcome to occur and virtually ensured that over time executive power would increase inexorably.

The Four Principles of Executive Energy

The powers granted to the president under Article II, whether expressed, implied, delegated, or inherent, are only part of the story of presidential power. Presidential power derives as much from the character and structure of the office as from the particular powers expressed or implied by Article II. Over time, successive presidents have been able to expand and augment the power of the office because the framers made the presidency an "energetic" institution, one with the capacity to make and implement decisions. The energy of the executive has allowed presidents to enhance their executive power sometimes even as their own programs and policy initiatives have been thwarted by congressional opposition.

Four great principles of executive energy are embodied in the Constitution, providing the president with advantages and possibilities that have allowed America's chief executives gradually to place the presidency at the forefront of American government. These principles of presidential energy are the unity principle, the principle of execution, the principle of independence, and the principle of constancy. Let us consider each in turn.

Unity

The unitary character of the presidency has provided presidents with a number of advantages in their dealings with other institutions of government, the Congress in particular. Unitary actors can, by definition, act unilaterally and are inherently more nimble than collective entities that must secure internal agreement before taking action. You may recall that this political agility was an important element of the framers' idea of presidential energy. They hoped that energetic executives would enhance the power of the federal government in a variety of contexts including vis-à-vis the states. The framers thought presidents would have the capacity to act while the state legislatures were still mired in debates. The same is true in the relationship between the president and Congress. In battles between the two institutions, as

Terry Moe observes, presidents often win by default because Congress cannot agree on a coherent strategy for opposing the chief executive.[42]

As unitary actors, moreover, presidents are not vulnerable to the collective action problems that almost inevitably afflict legislative bodies. To the president, self-interest and institutional power usually go hand in hand. For members of Congress, by contrast, the power and prerogatives of the institution are not unimportant but generally have little immediate effect on individual members and play, at best, a secondary role in members' calculations relative to constituency and electoral interests, as well as ideology and partisanship.

Presidents are almost always prepared to fight for their institutional prerogatives.[43] But when their collective interest in institutional power conflicts with members' individual electoral and constituency interests, as they often may, senators and representatives will generally put their individual and constituency interests first. Thus, for example, Jimmy Carter, who was often thought to be a weak president, was able to bring about the enactment of civil service reforms that strengthened the presidency and reduced congressional control over the bureaucracy. While legislators understood that this would be a result of the reforms, their attentions were focused mainly on provisions of the Carter proposal that affected important constituencies, including labor unions and veterans' organizations. Implications for the institutional balance of power, which were primary considerations for the president, were of no particular concern to individual senators and representatives.[44]

Similarly, in 2002, a number of Democrats supported presidential "fast track" trade promotion authority, which enhanced the power of the president to negotiate international agreements even though it would mean that Republican President George W. Bush could use his authority to negotiate trade deals according to his own conception of the national interest. Bush was able to obtain Democratic backing by agreeing that he would support expansion of several programs that were favored by important senators, including more assistance for unemployed factory workers.[45] For the president, the estimated cost of the new social programs, possibly $8.6 billion over ten years, was a small price to pay for an important expansion of executive power. And for the senators, institutional power was less important than constituency service.

Presidents are usually prepared to offer deals in exchange for important votes in Congress. To secure enactment of his health care proposals in 2009, President Obama engaged in a number of so-called horse trades: he offered members of Congress programs they deemed politically useful in exchange for their votes. The president's promises to Senators Mary Landrieu of Louisiana, Ben Nelson of Nebraska, and Blanche Lincoln of Arkansas came to be known in Washington respectively as the "Louisiana purchase," the "Cornhusker kickback," and the "streetcar named opportunism."

The fact that presidents are unitary actors, moreover, enhances their ability to behave as what might be called strategic innovators. When presidents or their staffers see an opportunity to enhance the power and prerogatives of the presidency, they are usually quick to take advantage of the possibilities. Collective bodies like the Congress generally lack institutional agility. When members of Congress wish to introduce a procedural or institutional change that might serve broad institutional interests, they must generally convince a majority of their colleagues to agree. Until the rules were changed in 2013, in fact, any proposed change in Senate procedures required the concurrence of sixty senators. Presidents, by contrast, are freer to follow the advice of the old television commercial that declared "Just do it." This agility tends to empower the president relative to the Congress.

Take, for example, the matter of signing statements. In 1986, Samuel Alito, a young deputy assistant attorney general in the Justice Department's Office of Legal Counsel, drafted a memo to his boss, Reagan administration Attorney General Edwin Meese, proposing the use of "interpretive signing statements."[46] Presidents almost always issue a signing statement when they sign a bill into law. Alito, a future Supreme Court justice, pointed out that a presidential signing statement was, however, "often little more than a press release." In his memo to the attorney general, Alito noted that, if carefully crafted, signing statements could become part of the legislative record, influencing judicial interpretations of the meaning of statutes for years to come. Attorney General Meese was impressed with Alito's idea and quickly grasped its further possibilities. If carefully crafted, the signing statement could become a form of presidential guidance to the executive agency charged with implementing the law and could, perhaps, be used to override congressional intent.

Meese began the practice of assigning Justice Department attorneys to write presidential signing statements and negotiated an agreement with the West Publishing Company to have signing statements included in its authoritative texts on federal law.[47] In place of the press-release signing statements of the past, President Reagan began to issue detailed statements carefully interpreting each section of important bills that reached his desk. In some cases, Reagan clearly reinterpreted Congress's acts or even sought to nullify them. In the case of a veterans' benefits bill, the president declared that several sections violated the integrity of the executive branch and would not be enforced.[48] And in a statement concerning a bill that prohibited construction on two Idaho waterways, Reagan declared that a portion of the bill was unconstitutional and would not be enforced by the executive branch.[49]

The Ninth Federal Circuit Court of Appeals found that the president lacked the authority to declare acts of Congress unconstitutional or to "excise or sever provisions of a bill with which he disagrees."[50] Successive presidents, however, have chosen to ignore this ruling and have continued to make use of signing statements to give their guidance to the executive branch and to rewrite legislative history. President George W. Bush, for example, used signing statements to alter at least five hundred legislative provisions.[51] Presidential persistence has paid off. Just as Samuel Alito predicted, the courts have begun to refer to signing statements when interpreting the meaning of statutes.[52]

Of course, Democrats were furious at the use of presidential signing statements by the Republicans. President Reagan, George H. W. Bush, and George W. Bush were all castigated by congressional Democrats for their usurpations of legislative power. Yet President Bill Clinton, a Democrat, found signing statements extremely useful in his battles with a Republican Congress. In one instance, taking a page from the Meese-Alito playbook, Clinton issued a statement when he signed a Defense Appropriation bill declaring that a provision requiring the military to discharge HIV-positive personnel was unconstitutional and would not be enforced by the executive branch.

Clinton's actions reveal that presidents are not only strategic innovators but also strategic accumulators of power and authority. Seldom, if ever, will any president surrender a power that has been claimed and used by a previous president. Congress, however, is sometimes prepared to surrender power for the sake of political expedience. In 2013, for example, the Senate, which then had a majority of Democratic members, surrendered some of its power to block presidential appointments to the executive agencies and the lower federal courts when it agreed that a sixty-vote supermajority would no longer be required to approve nominees— except, that is, for nominations to the Supreme Court, which are required by the Constitution to have a two-thirds majority for approval. The change was made for partisan reasons. Republicans had been blocking a number of President Obama's judicial nominees. The requirement of a sixty-vote majority, however, had enhanced the power of the Senate relative to the president by making it more difficult for the White House to secure approval for its nominees and by compelling the president to accede to the demands of senators in order to secure his goals.

Presidents are much more conscious of their institutional interests and will seldom surrender a power for any reason. During the 2008 campaign, for instance, candidate Obama denounced President Bush's use of signing statements as having no legal foundation. As president, however, Obama made use of signing statements to underscore presidential power and prerogatives. For example, Sections 1034 and 1035 of the 2014 Defense Authorization Act required the president to inform Congress at least thirty days prior to the release or transfer of any prisoner being held at the Guantanamo Bay military detention facility, which currently houses a number of accused terrorists and enemy combatants captured by American forces in Afghanistan. When he signed the act, President Obama included a statement that claimed in part, "Section 1035 does not, however, eliminate all of the unwarranted limitations on foreign transfers and, in certain circumstances, would violate constitutional separation of powers principles. The executive branch must have the flexibility, among other things, to act swiftly in conducting negotiations with foreign countries regarding the circumstances of detainee transfers."[53]

The president seemed to act on the principles of executive power articulated in this signing statement when in May 2014, he ordered the release of five Guantanamo detainees in exchange for an American soldier held captive by the Taliban. Congress was not consulted in advance, and the president barely bothered to respond to critics who questioned the legality of his actions. (See Chapter 7 for more on unilateral presidential action.)

Execution

The second principle of executive energy is that presidents derive power from their execution of the laws. Decisions made by the Congress are executed by the president, whereas presidents execute their own decisions. The result is an asymmetric relationship between presidential and congressional power. Whatever Congress does empowers the president; presidential actions, however, often weaken Congress. As we saw earlier, if members of Congress wish to accomplish any goal, they must delegate power to the executive. Sometimes Congress accompanies its delegation of power with explicit standards and guidelines; sometimes it does not. In either eventuality, over the long term, almost any program launched by the Congress empowers the president and more generally the executive branch, whose funding and authority must be increased to execute the law.

Take, for example, the 2010 Affordable Care Act. After much debate, Congress voted to enact this piece of legislation, which would cost billions of dollars and have an enormous impact on the nation's health care system. Congress certainly had no capacity to execute and administer the new law. Whatever the effects of Obamacare on the health care system, the statute entailed the granting of an enormous amount of power and funding to the executive branch. A brief summary of the law's provisions are instructive (Box 2). Each sentence, beginning with the words "the Secre-

Box 2. Excerpts from the Affordable Care Act
A Case Study in Congressional Empowerment of the Executive

(a) In General—Not later than 12 months after the date of enactment of the Patient Protection and Affordable Care Act, *the Secretary shall* develop standards for use by a group health plan and a health insurance issuer offering group or individual health insurance coverage, in compiling and providing to enrollees a summary of benefits and coverage explanation that accurately describes the benefits and coverage under the applicable plan or coverage . . .

The Secretary shall, by regulation, provide for the development of standards for the definitions of terms used in health insurance coverage, including the insurance-related terms described in paragraph (2) and the medical terms described in paragraph (3) . . .

IN GENERAL—Not later than 2 years after the date of enactment of the Patient Protection and Affordable Care Act, *the Secretary,* in consultation with experts in health care quality and stakeholders, *shall* develop reporting requirements for use by a group health plan, and a health insurance issuer offering group or individual health insurance coverage, with respect to plan or coverage benefits and health care provider reimbursement structures that—

(A) improve health outcomes through the implementation of activities such as quality reporting, effective case management, care coordination, chronic disease management, and medication and care compliance initiatives, including through the use of the medical homes model as defined for purposes of section 3602 of the Patient protection and Affordable Care Act, for treatment or services under the plan or coverage;

(B) implement activities to prevent hospital readmissions through a comprehensive program for hospital discharge that includes patient-centered education and counseling, comprehensive discharge planning, and post discharge reinforcement by an appropriate health care professional;

(C) implement activities to improve patient safety and reduce medical errors through the appropriate use of best clinical practices, evidence based medicine, and health information technology under the plan or coverage; and

(D) implement wellness and health promotion activities . . .

(c) Regulations—Not later than 2 years after the date of enactment of the Patient Protection and Affordable Care Act, *the Secretary shall* promulgate reg-

continued

Box 2 *Continued*

ulations that provide criteria for determining whether a reimbursement structure is described in subsection (a) . . .

In General—*The Secretary shall* award grants to States to enable such States (or the Exchanges operating in such States) to establish, expand, or provide support for—

(1) offices of health insurance consumer assistance; or

(2) health insurance ombudsman programs . . .

(1) IN GENERAL—*The Secretary,* in conjunction with States, *shall* establish a process for the annual review, beginning with the 2010 plan year and subject to subsection (b)(2)(A), of unreasonable increases in premiums for health insurance coverage . . .

(A) IN GENERAL—Beginning with plan years beginning in 2014, *the Secretary,* in conjunction with the States and consistent with the provisions of subsection (a)(2), *shall* monitor premium increases of health insurance coverage offered through an Exchange and outside of an Exchange . . .

(A) IN GENERAL—Out of all funds in the Treasury not otherwise appropriated, there are appropriated to the Secretary $250,000,000, to be available for expenditure for grants under paragraph (1) and subparagraph (B).

(B) FURTHER AVAILABILITY FOR INSURANCE REFORM AND CONSUMER PROTECTION—If the amounts appropriated under subparagraph (A) are not fully obligated under grants under paragraph (1) by the end of fiscal year 2014, any remaining funds shall remain available to the Secretary for grants to States for planning and implementing the insurance reforms and consumer protections under part A.

(C) ALLOCATION—*The Secretary shall* establish a formula for determining the amount of any grant to a State under this subsection. Under such formula—

(i) *the Secretary shall* consider the number of plans of health insurance coverage offered in each State and the population of the State; and

(ii) no State qualifying for a grant under paragraph (1) shall receive less than $1,000,000, or more than $5,000,000 for a grant year . . .

(a) In General—Not later than 90 days after the date of enactment of this Act, *the Secretary shall* establish a temporary high risk health insurance pool program to provide health insurance coverage for eligible individuals during the period beginning on the date on which such program is established and ending on January 1, 2014 . . .

continued

Box 2 *Continued*

The Secretary shall establish criteria for determining whether health insurance issuers and employment-based health plans have discouraged an individual from remaining enrolled in prior coverage based on that individual's health status . . .

There is appropriated to the Secretary, out of any moneys in the Treasury not otherwise appropriated, $5,000,000,000 to pay claims against (and the administrative costs of) the high risk pool under this section that are in excess of the amount of premiums collected from eligible individuals enrolled in the high risk pool. Such funds shall be available without fiscal year limitation . . .

The Secretary shall adopt a single set of operating rules for each transaction referred to under subsection (a)(1) with the goal of creating as much uniformity in the implementation of the electronic standards as possible. Such operating rules shall be consensus-based and reflect the necessary business rules affecting health plans and health care providers and the manner in which they operate pursuant to standards issued under Health Insurance Portability and Accountability Act of 1996 . . .

ELIGIBILITY FOR A HEALTH PLAN, HEALTH CLAIM STATUS, ELECTRONIC FUNDS TRANSFERS, HEALTH CARE PAYMENT AND REMITTANCE ADVICE—Not later than December 31, 2013, a health plan shall file a statement with the Secretary, in such form as *the Secretary may require,* certifying that the data and information systems for such plan are in compliance with any applicable standards (as described under paragraph (7) of section 1171) and associated operating rules (as described under paragraph (9) of such section) for electronic funds transfers, eligibility for a health plan, health claim status, and health care payment and remittance advice, respectively . . .

AUDITS OF HEALTH PLANS—*The Secretary shall* conduct periodic audits to ensure that health plans (including entities described under paragraph (3)) are in compliance with any standards and operating rules that are described under paragraph (1) or subsection (i)(5).

Source: Public Law 111–148 (124 Stat. 119), available online at http://www.gpo.gov/fdsys/pkg/PLAW-111publ148/html/PLAW-111publ148.htm (accessed July 20, 2015). Emphasis added.

tary shall," is a grant of power to the secretary of Health and Human Services, the agency mainly charged with administering the law. Utilizing these grants of executive power, HHS went on to develop thousands of pages of rules and regulations, all having the force of law.

The statute refers to "the Secretary," but the secretary works for the president of the United States. Many rules were drafted in consultation with the White House and while over the coming years HHS administrators will use their own judgment in developing new regulations, presidents will intervene in the process as they see fit. Thus in its attempt to promote health care, Congress inevitably added to executive and presidential power.

The Affordable Care Act is hardly unique. Every congressional statute—and there are thousands—empowers the executive to do something. Some statutes give the executive more discretion in its use of power, some less, but the end result is always to increase the power of the executive. A recent development, for example, has served as an executive power multiplier. This has been the advent of a new body of federal criminal law and enforcement power designed to ensure compliance with the thousands of statues enacted by the Congress. Recent estimates suggest that there now are nearly five thousand federal criminal laws, most enacted in the past several decades. It is worth remembering that the only federal crime defined by the U.S. Constitution is treason, though counterfeiting and piracy are also mentioned without being explicitly defined.

According to congressional testimony by former solicitor general Dick Thornburgh, moreover, in recent years federal agencies have created more than 300,000 new regulatory offenses, to promote compliance with the rules and regulations that they have enacted to execute the laws adopted by Congress.[54] For example, those who violate rules adopted by the Environmental Protection Agency (EPA) under the Clean Air Act or the Clean Water Act may be subject to arrest and prosecution under regulations adopted by the EPA. Those convicted of violating regulatory offenses may be fined or imprisoned. Further, to investigate rule-breaking and apprehend violators, every federal agency now employs armed agents. Thus in addition to the FBI and other law enforcement agencies, several thousand armed law enforcement officers are employed by such seemingly mundane agencies as the Fish and Wildlife Service, the Department of Education, and even the National Oceanographic and Atmospheric Administration. All this derives from the fact that the executive branch executes the law. The more laws that are enacted by Congress, the more that executive power is increased.

By contrast, when presidents undertake some action, they usually possess a broad menu of options regarding Congress. Once they have funding and authorization for some course of action, presidents and executive agencies may contrive to execute the laws in a way that marginalizes, circumvents, or simply ignores the Congress. For example, congressional Republicans have charged that the president ignored the provisions of his eponymous health care statute by unilaterally ordering delays in the implementation of various statutory requirements and by directing the Office of Personnel Management to ignore provisions of the act that required members of Congress and their staffs to obtain their own health insurance through the exchanges established by the law. In a similar vein, the Environmental Protection Agency was discovered to have ignored its statutory mandate under 2010 Clean Air Act amendments and expended its efforts to curb greenhouse gas emissions to sources specifically exempted by the statute.[55]

Even when they lack funding and authorization, presidents have increasingly made use of executive orders and a power called regulatory review, developed by Presidents Reagan and Clinton, to direct executive agencies to adopt rules and regulations—which have the force of law—without consulting the Congress. Thus, for example, in 2014 President Obama ordered the Environmental Protection Agency to develop new emission standards for coal-fired generating plants. If such standards are developed, they will be executed by the agency. The executive in this case will have unilaterally executed its own decisions and Congress will have been left on the sidelines. In June 2014, House Speaker John Boehner announced that a group of Republican members of Congress was preparing a lawsuit to block presidential powers of direct action. Given recent court precedents, as we shall see in Chapter 8, such a suit is unlikely to prevail. Presidential tactics of direct action will be discussed more fully in Chapter 7.

As to forcing Congress's hand, beginning with President Polk who sent forces to the U.S. border with Mexico, presidents have often made use of this ploy in the realm of military policy. If the president deploys American military forces, Congress cannot deny the troops food, fuel, and ammunition even if the White House did not secure congressional approval for its actions. Occasionally, Congress does cut off funds for ongoing military operations, as it did to bring the Vietnam War to a formal end, but lawmakers are hampered by the need to protect the lives of soldiers already in combat. Thus, for example, Congress voted in 1993 to prohibit further funding for American military operations in Somalia but attached a proviso that funds could be spent if the funds were needed for the protection of U.S. civilians or military personnel. Overt and covert operations by military and intelligence agencies have continued in Somalia to the present day. Thus, the executive power wielded by presidents means that the White House and Congress are in an asymmetric relationship. Congress can do little without empowering the executive. The president, however, can do much without the Congress.

Congress's most important power vis-à-vis the executive is its "power of the purse." Article I, Section 9 of the Constitution declares, "No money shall be drawn from the Treasury, but in consequence of Appropriations made by Law." When Congress writes legislation authorizing some program, it generally enacts an appropriation to pay the costs of the program for the next fiscal year. Except in the case of "entitlement programs" like Social Security whose appropriations are automatically tied to a statutory formula, Congress must agree to appropriate new funds for existing programs on an annual basis. Congress has the constitutional power to reduce or cut funding for every executive branch program except the entitlements, and even these could, at least hypothetically, be altered or even abolished. Republicans have always hoped to "privatize" Social Security. Article I, Section 8 further enhances Congress's power of the purse by assigning to Congress the power to levy taxes and borrow money. Without congressional approval, the executive could not pay its bills.

Article I, Sections 7 and 8 give Congress powerful weapons to use in struggles against the executive. These weapons, though, are often difficult to wield. Once created, federal programs can quickly develop political constituencies from among beneficiaries and service providers who will fight tooth and nail to protect their favorite programs from the budget axe. Take the case of "Super Twiggy," the cartoon squirrel. Super Twiggy was a character in web videos shown in Spain touting the health benefits of California-grown walnuts. The videos, which cost about $3 million to produce and air, were part of a $200 million per year Agriculture Department marketing effort to promote U.S. farm products overseas. When the program was threatened with cuts, walnut growers, farm groups, and farm-state representatives came to its defense and saved the little squirrel.

Nevertheless, under the terms of the 2011 Budget Control Act, Congress did impose mandatory across-the-board spending cuts for almost all nonentitlement programs. The cuts, referred to as "budget sequestration" and intended to slow the rate of increase in federal spending, went into effect in 2013 and are scheduled to continue until 2021. The 2011 Budget Act was itself reluctantly signed by President Obama in the face of a threat by House Republicans to refuse to raise the nation's debt limit (a constitutional power of Congress) and potentially cause a government default on some of its loans.

Thus, Article I, Sections 7 and 8 can give the Congress power to say no to the president. But if Congress decides that it wants to accomplish something rather than be perceived as merely obstructionist, it must resume empowering the executive.

Independence

The Constitution gave the president a considerable measure of independence from the Congress. The president is independently elected for a fixed term and, except under extraordinary circumstances, the president's tenure in office cannot be brought to an end by the Congress. Independence means that presidents can act without fear of being dismissed and hence have considerable freedom of action. This independence has allowed and encouraged presidents to carve out a number of unilateral powers —powers that can be exercised without congressional support. In recent years, for example, presidents have made growing use of executive orders and executive agreements to conduct the nation's domestic and foreign affairs without asking for congressional approval. An executive order bypasses Congress and the legislative process and is instead a direct presidential directive to the bureaucracy to undertake some action. Executive orders have a long history in the United States and have been the instruments for a number of important policies, including the purchase of Louisiana, the annexation of Texas, the emancipation of the slaves, the wartime internment of Japanese Americans, the desegregation of the military, the initiation of affirmative action, and the creation of a number of federal agencies including the Environmental Protection Agency, the Food and Drug Administration, and the Peace Corps.[56]

Historically, executive orders were most often used during times of war or national emergency. President Lincoln relied heavily on executive orders in the early months of the Civil War to mobilize troops, purchase warships, and obtain funds from the U.S. Treasury.[57] During World War II, President Roosevelt issued 286 executive orders establishing wartime agencies and authorizing the government to take control of factories and property for wartime needs.[58] In recent years, though, executive orders have become routine instruments of presidential governance rather than emergency wartime measures. President Clinton issued numerous orders relating to environmental programs, regulatory policy, affirmative action, and labor policy.[59] President George W. Bush issued more than three hundred executive orders, many relating to the "war on terror" but others pertaining to more mundane domestic policy matters such as his ban on the use of federal funds to support international family planning groups and his prohibition of the use of embryonic stem cells in federally funded research projects. President Obama has issued executive orders that have halted the deportation of undocumented immigrants who had come to the United States as children, prohibited federal agencies and contractors from discriminating against transgendered employees, and declared more than 700,000 square miles of the central Pacific Ocean off-limits to fishing. Charging that Congress was too slow to act on immigration reform, in 2014 Obama also issued executive orders blocking the deportation of several million undocumented immigrants.

Presidential use of executive orders is constrained by law. When presidents issue executive orders, in principle they do so pursuant to the powers granted to them by the Constitution or delegated to them by Congress. When presidents issue orders, they generally must state the constitutional or statutory basis for their actions. For example, when President Truman ordered the desegregation of the armed forces, he declared that the order was pursuant to his constitutional power as commander-in-chief. Similarly, when President Johnson ordered U.S. government contractors to initiate programs of affirmative action in hiring, he said the order was designed to implement the 1964 Civil Rights Act, which prohibited employment discrimination. Where the courts have found no constitutional or statutory basis for a presidential order, as in the case of President Truman's seizure of the steel mills in 1952, they have invalidated it. Such cases, however, are rare. Generally, the judiciary has accepted executive orders as the law of the land.

Executive orders are one form of presidential decree. Others include administrative orders, national security directives, presidential memoranda, presidential proclamations, and presidential findings.[60] Like executive orders, these other instruments establish policy and have the force of law; in fact, presidents often use them interchangeably. Generally, though, administrative orders apply to matters of administrative procedure and organization; directives seem most often associated with national or homeland security; memoranda are used to clarify or modify presidential positions and orders; and proclamations are usually hortative but are sometimes used to give emphasis to an especially important presidential decree, such as Lincoln's proclamation emancipating all slaves.

Congress is not entirely without power vis-à-vis executive decrees. Legislators can overturn presidential orders that were based on the president's legislative authority (as opposed to constitutional authority) via legislation declaring that the order "shall not have legal effect," or they can actually repeal the statute on which the order was based. In 1993, for example, Congress revoked an order by President George H. W. Bush to the Secretary of Health and Human Services to establish a human-fetal-tissue bank for research purposes. Congress directed that "the provisions of Executive Order 12806 shall not have any legal effect."[61] Efforts to overturn the orders of sitting presidents are, however, hindered by the fact that any such legislation can be vetoed by the president. Thus two-thirds of the members of both houses of Congress would have to agree to the move. One study indicates that only about 4 percent of all presidential orders have ever been rescinded by legislation.[62] Even these almost always were orders issued by presidents no longer in office. In one case, for example, a 2005 statute revoked a 1912 executive order.[63] Usually the best Congress can do is inhibit the implementation of an executive order by preventing funds from being spent to implement it. This, too, is relatively unusual.[64] Congress's failure to act, moreover, strengthens the legal validity of a presidential order. The Supreme Court has held that congressional inaction tends to validate an order by indicating congressional "acquiescence" in the president's decision.[65] This idea begs an important question. Many presidential orders take the form of secret national security directives and findings of which Congress is unaware. Can Congress be said to acquiesce in presidential decisions made without its knowledge?

Where the president has issued an order based on a claim of constitutional authority, as is almost always true of wartime orders, Congress cannot rescind the order via legislation. Claims of constitutional authority must be resolved by the courts, which, as we shall see in Chapter 8, tend to respect presidential claims. Whether based on constitutional or statutory power, the best instruments for the rescission of executive orders are the next president's orders. For instance, several of President Obama's executive orders revoked orders issued by President Bush, President Bush had issued orders revoking two of President Clinton's orders, and so forth. Nothing better illustrates the principle of executive independence than the fact that the only truly effective mechanisms for rescinding the orders of one president are the orders of another. At the beginning of 2015, congressional Republicans looked for ways to use their control of both houses of Congress to rescind President Obama's orders on immigration. The GOP's best hope, however, seemed to be to win control of the White House in 2016.

Constancy

The final principle of executive energy embodied in the Constitution is constancy. The Constitution gave the president control of agencies—the Army, the Navy, and the executive departments. Congress, by contrast, is an assembly of individuals. The difference is important. Bureaucratic agencies never sleep; they are constantly at work. Individuals eat, sleep, take vacations, and engage in a variety of personal activities. While individuals' minds are on other matters, bureaucracies move inexorably toward their goals. Henry Clay observed this phenomenon even in the early decades of the Republic. Observing events in 1841, Clay explained the executive's advantage over the Congress. "The executive branch of the government," he said, "was eternally in action; it was ever awake; it never slept; its action was continuous and unceasing, like the tides of some mighty river, which continued flowing and flowing on . . . till it swept away every impediment and broke down and removed every frail obstacle."[66] Perhaps a similar vision of executive power explains why Patrick Henry argued in favor of the Roman model, in which executives are appointed only as needed.

In the eighteenth and nineteenth centuries, Congress was in session only about half the year and presidents often made use of Congress's long absences to exercise power unilaterally. Jefferson's purchase of Louisiana, Andrew Jackson's order to remove government deposits from the Bank of the United States, Lincoln's suspension of the writ of habeas corpus, and many other executive decisions were conveniently made while legislators were absent from the capital.[67] Today Congress is in session most of the year, though, as noted earlier, presidents will try to take advantage of even the briefest congressional recess to veto legislation or make official appointments.

Even though Congress may spend more time in Washington, it cannot compete with the constancy of the executive. Agencies of the executive branch, particularly in the realms of national security, generally operate twenty-four hours a day, seven days per week. The executive is likely to become aware of developments and take action long before Congress is alerted. The executive, not Congress, makes decisions every hour of every day that affect the outcome of events. And the executive, not Congress, controls the daily flow of information that shapes public perceptions of events. When crises erupt in the Middle East, in Eastern Europe, in Asia, agencies of the executive branch are constantly on tap to act, while lawmakers must wait for the president to call, perhaps the next day or even a week later.

Thoughts on Article II: A Presidential Republic?

The institutions created by the Constitution are always given life by political developments in the nation. During much of the nineteenth and early twentieth centuries, Congress was usually the dominant branch of government, taking the lead in domestic and foreign policy. The War of 1812, for example, was very much a congressional war, planned, instigated, and lost by House Speaker Henry Clay and his "war hawk" allies. The power of Congress was, in part, a function of the emergence of a national party system. Strong parties brought about "party discipline" in the House and, to a lesser extent, the Senate—and this discipline allowed congressional leaders to speak for an entire house of Congress in their dealings with the president. The unitary House and unitary Senate could go toe to toe with the unitary executive. As we shall see, the coherence of America's political parties began to decay after 1900 following the Progressive reforms of America's party system. These reforms included civil service and the use of primary elections, all of which reduced the power of party leaders and gradually diminished the cohesion of the House and Senate. What followed was a gradual waning of congressional power relative to that of the executive.

What had been gradual became an accelerating shift in power after 1933. To implement his New Deal programs, and always claiming emergency needs during the Great Depression and World War II, President Franklin D. Roosevelt began adding offices, agencies, and personnel to the executive branch. Congress had been able to exercise reasonably effective oversight over the nation's relatively small pre–New Deal bureaucracy but found itself unable to do much more than occasionally intervene in the activities of the enormous post–New Deal executive. Political scientists Mathew McCubbins and Thomas Schwartz refer to this sporadic intervention, which usually occurs only after major problems have already arisen, as "fire alarm management."[68]

As Congress lost control over the executive, the executive began to supplant Congress. Through the rulemaking process, the agencies of the executive branch gradually became the nation's foremost legislators—and adjudicators—producing far more law than the Congress and far more adjudication than the courts.[69] We will return to the relationships among the president, Congress, the bureaucracy, and the courts throughout this book. For now, let us only observe that presidents have become more and more adept at using the agencies of the executive branch to circumvent Congress and the courts and so to overcome some of the constitutional restraints on their power. Many Americans applaud decisive presidential action to overcome "gridlock" on Capitol Hill. Yet we might do well to remember that the Constitution's framers were concerned to prevent concentration of power anywhere in the government, even at the cost of efficiency.

Presidential unilateralism (or "presidentialism")—through signing statements, executive orders, executive agreements, and regulatory review—has become an important force in American politics. Has the character of our government changed from a democratic republic to a presidential republic? And if so, should we as citizens be concerned? Some scholars assert that the presidency is a more democratic institution than the Congress because presidential elections boast far greater turnout than congressional races and because only the president can claim to speak for all the American people. But can one person actually represent all Americans in any meaningful way? Is presidential decisionmaking more consistent with democratic principles than congressional decisionmaking? These are questions that very American should ponder.

According to legend there is a spot in the Capitol, in today's statuary hall, where Congressman (and former president) John Quincy Adams once sat at his desk pretending to doze but eavesdropping on other members as wisps of their conversations echoed from the hall's parabolic ceiling. Today, as we consider the presidency, we can hear echoes of the debate at the Constitutional Convention between the advocates and opponents of a strong presidency. After so many decades, we might still wonder whose arguments were more compelling.

Presidential Eligibility

What Is a "Natural-Born Citizen"?

Article II of the Constitution states that in order to be eligible to serve as president, an individual must, among other things, be a natural-born citizen of the United States. This language seems simple but has provoked some controversy over the years. In 2008, some individuals declared that President Obama was not eligible for the presidency because his father had not been an American citizen. Others, dubbed "birthers," demanded proof that Obama had actually been born in Hawaii as he claimed. Generally speaking, "natural born" means a person born in the United States, regardless of the citizenship of his or her parents, or born abroad to parents who were U.S. citizens. An individual who is born a noncitizen but acquires citizenship through the

process of "naturalization" is not eligible. The Constitution's simple phrase has led to ambiguities and controversies and has never been interpreted by the U.S. Supreme Court. For example, if an individual was born abroad, must both parents have been American citizens to make that person eligible for the presidency? What if the parents of a foreign-born individual were naturalized rather than native-born citizens—is that person eligible? As a result of such ambiguities, questions have been raised about the eligibility of three presidents and several presidential aspirants in recent decades.

Chester A. Arthur. America's twenty-first president was born of parents who resided

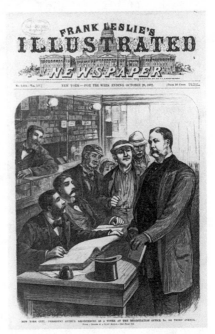

along the border between Vermont and Canada and, for a time, lived in Quebec. Arthur's political foes charged that he had actually been born in Canada. Moreover, while Arthur's mother had been born in the United States, his father had emigrated from Ireland and was not a U.S. citizen at the time of Arthur's birth.

Barry Goldwater. The 1964 Republican presidential nominee was born in Phoenix, Arizona. At the time of Goldwater's birth, however, Arizona had not yet been admitted to the Union as a state, though it was a U.S. territory. Some argued that Goldwater was ineligible for the presidency because, strictly speaking, he had not been born in the United States.

George Romney. In 1968, Romney was a leading contender for the Republican presidential nomination, though the nomination and the presidency were ultimately secured by Richard Nixon. Romney was born in Mexico, to which his Mormon grandfather had immigrated in 1886 when the United States outlawed polygamy. Some asserted that Romney's grandfather and parents had forfeited their U.S. citizenship. George Romney's son, Mitt, was definitely born in the United States.

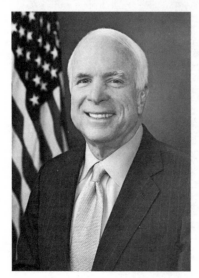

John McCain. The 2008 Republican presidential nominee was born in the Panama Canal Zone. His parents were both American citizens. Indeed, McCain's father was an officer on a U.S. submarine stationed in Panama and McCain's grandfather commanded the base. Since the Canal Zone was not legally regarded as U.S. territory, though, the citizenship status of those born there was ambiguous. Several authorities declared that McCain was actually a Panamanian citizen, and enough doubt was raised that in 2008 the Senate voted to approve a nonbinding resolution recognizing McCain as a natural-born citizen.

Barack Obama. President Obama was born in Hawaii. Obama's father was a British subject born in Kenya but this did not undermine Obama's eligibility. Claims that Obama had not actually been born in Hawaii were refuted by officials of that state.

STATE OF HAWAII	CERTIFICATE OF LIVE BIRTH	DEPARTMENT OF HEALTH
	FILE NUMBER 151	61 10641

1a. Child's First Name (Type or print) — BARACK 1b. Middle Name — HUSSEIN 1c. Last Name — OBAMA, II

2. Sex — Male 3. This Birth — Single 4. If Twin or Triplet, Was Child Born 1st 2nd 3rd 5a. Birth Date Month — August Day — 4 Year — 1961 5b. Hour — 7:24 P.M.

6a. Place of Birth: City, Town or Rural Location — Honolulu 6b. Island — Oahu

6c. Name of Hospital or Institution (If not in hospital or institution, give street address) — Kapiolani Maternity & Gynecological Hospital 6d. Is Place of Birth Inside City or Town Limits? If no, give judicial district — Yes

7a. Usual Residence of Mother: City, Town or Rural Location — Honolulu 7b. Island — Oahu 7c. County and State or Foreign Country — Honolulu, Hawaii

7d. Street Address — 6085 Kalanianaole Highway 7e. Is Residence Inside City or Town Limits? If no, give judicial district — Yes

7f. Mother's Mailing Address 7g. Is Residence on a Farm or Plantation? — No

8. Full Name of Father — BARACK HUSSEIN OBAMA 9. Race of Father — African

10. Age of Father — 25 11. Birthplace (Island, State or Foreign Country) — Kenya, East Africa 12a. Usual Occupation — Student 12b. Kind of Business or Industry — University

13. Full Maiden Name of Mother — STANLEY ANN DUNHAM 14. Race of Mother — Caucasian

15. Age of Mother — 18 16. Birthplace (Island, State or Foreign Country) — Wichita, Kansas 17a. Type of Occupation Outside Home During Pregnancy — None 17b. Date Last Worked

18a. Signature of Parent or Other Informant — (Stanley) Ann Dunham Obama Parent Other — 8-7-61

19a. Signature of Attendant — David A. Sinclair M.D. D.O. Midwife Other 19b. Date of Signature — 8-8-61

20. Date Accepted by Local Reg. — AUG -8 1961 21. Signature of Local Registrar — U.K. Lee 22. Date Accepted by Reg. General — AUG -8 1961

23. Evidence for Delayed Filing or Alteration

APR 25 2011

I CERTIFY THIS IS A TRUE COPY OR ABSTRACT OF THE RECORD ON FILE IN THE HAWAII STATE DEPARTMENT OF HEALTH

Alvin T. Onaka, Ph.D.
STATE REGISTRAR

Ted Cruz. The Republican senator from Texas has declared his candidacy for the presidency. Cruz was born in Canada. Cruz's mother was an American citizen but his father was a Cuban national. The senator's eligibility represents an interesting legal question.

THREE

A Brief History of the Presidency

In This Chapter

The history of America's presidency has been one in which the power and importance of the institution has gradually expanded. As political scientist Terry Moe has observed, "The political and historical reality is that presidents have largely defined their own constitutional role by pushing out the boundaries of their prerogatives."[1] Of course, presidential history includes both ups and downs, some coinciding with the rise and fall of national party systems and others linked to specific problems, issues, and personalities. We should train our analytic eyes, however, to see beneath the surface of day-to-day and even decade-to-decade political turbulence. We should focus, instead, on the pronounced secular trend of more than two and a quarter centuries of American history. Two hundred years ago, presidents were weak and often bullied by Congress. Today, presidents are powerful and often thumb their noses at Congress and the courts.

The Presidency Then and Now

In the early years of the Republic, Congress demonstrated its disdain for the chief executive by refusing to appropriate funds for even one secretary or assistant to help presidents carry out their day-to-day tasks. As a result, presidents often greeted visitors personally and were responsible for their own correspondence and recordkeeping. George Washington resorted to employing family members as informal private secretaries. During the Jackson administration, the president was able to secure a clerkship in the Land Office for his wife's nephew, Andrew Jackson Donelson, who then served informally as Old Hickory's private secretary. Donelson was succeeded in this post by Jackson's son, Andrew Jackson, Jr. President John Tyler also employed his son as a private secretary, while Presidents Polk and Buchanan made use of nephews in this capacity.[2]

It was not until 1857 that Congress finally appropriated money for a private secretary for the president. By 1871, Congress had grudgingly come to allow the president one secretary, one stenographer, and two clerks, as well as a steward and a messenger. Nevertheless, during his two terms in the late 1880s, President Grover Cleveland often found himself personally answering the telephone or White House doorbell, and he was the one who wrote checks to pay the bills for receptions and other White House expenses. According to administrative historian Leonard White, Congress believed that presidents did not play a sufficiently important role in the governmental process to merit a larger staff.[3] By refusing to provide the president with a larger staff, too, Congress hoped to make certain that presidents would have difficulty expanding their role. By 1900, White observed, it was obvious to Congress that presidents needed help if they were truly to function as chief executives, "but it was not certain that [Congress] intended a president to play such a role."[4]

Today, of course, the president directs a White House Staff of several hundred analysts, officials, and "special assistants," as well as some two thousand individuals working for the agencies of the Executive Office of the President. In addition, the president has considerable influence over the activities of nearly three million civilian employees of the executive branch and a great deal of influence over the actions of the Defense Department's nearly two million military and civilian employees.

Today's presidents are prepared to play a very important role in the governmental process. As we shall see, presidents dominate foreign and security policy and, while domestic policy in the United States today is not made entirely by the White House, it is never made entirely without its involvement. Events over the past two and a quarter centuries show that energetic presidents have indeed breathed life into the constitutional powers and principles established by the founders and discussed in Chapter 1.

Six Eras of American Presidential History

In terms of the shifting currents of American political history, the story of the American presidency can be divided into six eras: the Federalist and Jeffersonian era, the

Jacksonian era, the Civil War presidency, the Republican era, the era of the imperial presidency, and the era of the unilateral presidency.

The Federalist and Jeffersonian Era

The first era began with George Washington, who was virtually anointed by a grateful nation. Washington understood that his conduct in office would influence the way in which Americans viewed not only the presidency, but the new nation as well. He made a point of touring the country, making public appearances, and always comporting himself with great dignity so as to build respect for his office.[5] Virtually everything Washington did set a precedent.[6] Washington's proclamation of American neutrality in the 1793 war between Britain and France, followed by the signing of "Jay's Treaty" in 1794, which normalized trade relations with England, established the principle of presidential primacy in the realm of foreign relations. It was Washington, moreover, who insisted that the president be addressed as "Mr. President," a respectful and dignified form of address, but not one suggestive of the exaggerated courtesies favored by monarchies. Washington sent regular messages to Congress, and made a regular appearance and speech—the forerunner of today's State of the Union address. Washington took firm control over major government appointments, including, in 1795, making the first recess appointment. Washington also made it a practice to call meetings of the secretaries of the new government's departments, laying the foundations for the president's cabinet. Washington invented the principle of "executive privilege" when he refused to give the House documents that it requested regarding a diplomatic matter. Subsequent presidents expanded the idea that presidents were not obligated to give Congress records of their deliberations, and the Supreme Court ultimately recognized the doctrine in the 1974 case of *United States v. Nixon*—though, in the matter at hand, Nixon was ordered to give Congress the "Watergate tapes" that had recorded meetings in the Oval Office.[7] And by refusing to run for a third term, Washington created the two-term tradition, broken only by Franklin D. Roosevelt and codified in 1951 by the Constitution's Twenty-Second Amendment.

During Washington's administration, conflicts arose between Treasury Secretary Alexander Hamilton and Secretary of State Thomas Jefferson. Hamilton's supporters in Congress began to use the name "Federalists" to wrap themselves in the mantle of the Constitution's proponents, though some had actually been anti-Federalists during the ratification debates. These new Federalists generally spoke for New England commercial interests and supported a program of protective tariffs to encourage manufacturing, assumption of the states' Revolutionary War debts, the creation of a national bank, and the resumption of trade relations with England.

Jefferson's followers were known at first as the Jeffersonian Republicans, and later as the Democratic-Republicans. The Jeffersonian Republicans, who mainly represented Southern agricultural interests, are the forebears of the contemporary Democrats, making today's Democratic Party the oldest political party in the world. The Jeffersonian Republicans favored free trade, the promotion of agriculture over commercial interests, and friendship with France. Today's Democrats have complicated positions on free trade and agriculture but, so far as can be determined, continue to have good feelings toward France.

The Jeffersonians developed a partisan press, using newspapers, particularly the *National Gazette,* as well as handbills, to attack their political foes. They trained their sights in particular on Alexander Hamilton, whose illegitimate birth became grist for the mills of Jeffersonian publicists. The Federalists responded by passing the Alien and Sedition Acts, which outlawed criticism of the government. When these acts proved impossible to enforce, the Federalists established their own newspapers and launched vicious attacks against Thomas Jefferson.

The Jeffersonians proved to be more effective political organizers and campaigners than the Federalists and gradually expanded their political base from the South into the Middle Atlantic states. James Madison became the Democratic-Republicans' chief organizer and from his post as chair of the Orange County, Virginia, Democratic-Republican central committee, oversaw the new party's national political efforts.[8]

In 1800, Jefferson defeated Federalist president John Adams and led his party to power. The election revealed that the machinery of the Electoral College was seriously flawed. Under the Constitution, each elector was authorized to cast two votes, one for president and one for vice president. Each of the Democratic-Republican electors chosen by the Electoral College cast a vote for Jefferson and a vote for Aaron Burr, whom the Jeffersonians had intended to elect as vice president. Apparently the Democratic-Republicans had planned on one of their electors abstaining from casting a second vote, thus assuring Jefferson the majority, but this scheme somehow misfired. With a tie in the Electoral College, the House of Representatives would now choose between Jefferson and Burr. House Federalists saw an opportunity to strike a blow against their political enemy, Jefferson. Many voted to elect Burr to the presidency, producing thirty-five successive votes in which neither Jefferson nor Burr won a majority. Finally, on the thirty-sixth ballot, Jefferson was elected after several Federalists decided to abstain from voting to end the impasse.[9] This flaw in the Electoral College system was corrected by the Twelfth Amendment, which stipulated separate balloting for the president and vice president.[10]

Once in office, Jefferson sought to continue Washington's policy of neutrality in the wars between England and France. In 1807 the president ordered an embargo on all trade and shipping between America and both combatants. The 1807 Embargo Act, passed by Congress, was somewhat more damaging to England—which depended on trade—than to France, which did not. More important, however, was that the act was economically ruinous to the American economy and was widely evaded by merchants in the Northeast, who resorted to smuggling and subterfuge to maintain their trade routes.

Jefferson was more successful when it came to expanding America's territorial possessions. In 1803, without any specific authorization from Congress, Jefferson issued a decree—the forebear of today's executive orders—authorizing the expenditure of $15 million to purchase the Louisiana Territory from France, thus nearly doubling the size of the nation.[11] Congress later ratified the purchase despite many arguments that it was unlawful. The Louisiana Purchase was the first, but certainly not the last, case in American history when a president's capacity to act impelled Congress to follow in his wake. Jefferson's assertion of presidential power was somewhat more modest than is sometimes thought. Before Jefferson purchased Louisiana, Congress had authorized the use of force to seize both Florida and New Orleans. Jefferson ignored the authorization and mused that perhaps the Constitution should be amended to permit the acquisition of Louisiana.[12] Subsequently Jefferson authorized a number of exploratory expeditions, including the famous Lewis and Clark expedition, to map the new territory, thus setting the stage for America's westward expansion.

In addition, though Jefferson was a proponent of peaceful relations with other nations, continued threats along the frontier and on the high seas convinced him that America needed a professional army and navy. It was during Jefferson's presidency, then, that the organization of the Army was modernized and the U.S. military academy founded.

Jefferson's three Democratic-Republican successors, James Madison, James Monroe, and John Quincy Adams, were nominated by their party caucuses in Congress and elected to office by the Electoral College. Some states allowed electors to be chosen by popular vote, while in others the electors were appointed by the state legislatures. At the time, the nation's electorate was small, with most Americans disqualified from voting by property requirements or on account of their race or gender. After Jefferson's term, the presidency began to wane in importance.

Americans of this era felt little connection with the office of the presidency, and the center of national politics was the Congress, especially the House of Representatives. The War of 1812, for example, was planned, fought, and lost by the Congress, led by Speaker Henry Clay and the "war hawk" faction of Southerners and Westerners who hoped to conquer Canada. President Madison was barely consulted.[13] It should be mentioned, however, that Madison was bold enough to anger the Senate in 1812 when he became the first president to use the pocket veto.

The invasion of Canada failed and a British punitive expedition landed on America's coast and burned the nation's new capital, Washington, D.C. During the war, a group of politicians from the New England states met in Hartford, Connecticut, and nearly seceded from the Union to form their own New England Confederacy. The secession plan was ended by news of frontier general Andrew Jackson's victory over a British amphibious force attempting to seize New Orleans. The Battle of New Orleans was fought after the United States had formally sued for peace with England, but news of the end of the war had not yet reached far-off Louisiana.[14]

One unforeseen consequence of the War of 1812 was the collapse of the Federalist Party. Several important Federalist politicians had been associated with the Hartford Convention and in the wake of an upsurge of popular patriotism following Jackson's dramatic military victory, Federalism seemed to be linked with treason. The collapse of the Federalists left the Democratic-Republicans as America's only political party. Because of the elimination of partisan competition, some historians dubbed the period the "era of good feelings."

It might be more accurate to say that during this period, bad feelings took the form of factional struggle within one party. Various Democratic-Republican politicians, including Henry Clay, John Quincy Adams, John C. Calhoun, and William Crawford, jockeyed for position and sought their party's presidential nomination, which in the new one-party system was tantamount to election.

One important political outsider was also interested in the presidency. Andrew Jackson's fame made him an obvious presidential candidate. But the general was far more important in the nation at large than within the ruling party's tiny elite. Nominations were controlled by a small group of insiders—the members of the Democratic-Republican congressional caucus—and this group was jealous of the popular general.

Matters came to a head in the 1824 presidential election. During the two years prior to the election, Jackson's followers had adopted a strategy of discrediting the caucus by securing the endorsements of state legislatures. After the Tennessee legislature voted to nominate Jackson for the presidency, several states nominated Clay, two nominated John Quincy Adams, and South Carolina nominated its favorite son, John C. Calhoun.[15] One candidate, Treasury Secretary Crawford, hoped the party caucus would give him the nomination and declined to seek state legislative endorsements.

When the party caucus convened in 1824, most members of Congress believed that the days of nomination by party caucus had come to an end and few bothered to attend its meeting. A small group nominated Crawford but this had little significance and the main contenders—Crawford, Adams, Clay, and Jackson—essentially campaigned for the presidency as individuals. By 1824, some states had allowed the popular election of presidential electors while others clung to the original system in which the state legislatures chose the electors. Accordingly, the four candidates vied for both popular support and the support of the state legislatures. When the votes were counted, Jackson had won a plurality of the popular vote as well as a plurality, though not a majority, in the Electoral College. Absent an Electoral College majority, the House of Representatives was required to decide the outcome. In the House, Henry Clay threw his support to John Q. Adams, denying Jackson the presidency. Clay received Adams's promise to be named secretary of state. Jackson's supporters called this the "corrupt bargain" of 1824 and vowed to put "Old Hickory" into the White House in 1828.

Between 1824 and 1828, Jackson's allies, led by Senator Martin Van Buren of New York, constructed party organizations and worked to expand the suffrage. As we shall see again in Chapter 4, election rules are generally written to serve the interests of those in a position to write the rules. The Jacksonians knew that the general had overwhelming support among ordinary Americans. If property-ownership restrictions on voting could be removed, and if all the states could be induced to adopt direct popular election of the presidential electors, Jackson would surely win. Accordingly, these two reforms became major goals of the Jacksonian movement, which succeeded on both fronts between 1824 and 1828. Most property restrictions were removed and all but two states, Delaware and South Carolina, adopted a policy of popular election of electors. To deal with the fact that many of Jackson's supporters were poor and uneducated and had little experience with voting, the Jacksonians organized political clubs throughout the states to inform and mobilize the general's admirers and make sure that they voted. Before the 1832 election, the Jacksonians also constructed a nominating system that would take advantage of the general's popularity among rank-and-file local politicians, as opposed to elites in Washington. This was the party convention mode of nomination, and it began with the empowerment of local conventions to select delegates to state party conventions, which in turn would choose delegates to the national party convention. Local party activists would control the nomination, and the party caucus of Washington insiders was gone forever.

The Jacksonian Era

In the 1828 election, Jackson defeated his only rival, President John Q. Adams, by a solid margin, winning nearly 57 percent of the popular vote and close to 70 percent of the electoral vote. During the administrations of Madison, Monroe, and John Q.

Adams, the presidency had waned in importance. But Jackson moved to elevate the presidency within the American political structure. The democratization of the presidency had already increased the power of the office: unlike his predecessors, "Old Hickory" could call on the support of a national political following in his battles with his political foes. And as leader of what was now calling itself the Democratic Party, Jackson could usually count on the support of Democratic senators and representatives, who commanded majorities in both houses of Congress. To encourage Americans to view Jackson as the dominant force in American politics, Jackson's followers built a vigorous party press to promote his ideas and hired a group of painters to make certain that the president's image was everywhere, including on buttons, jugs, plates, and engravings—all of which were widely distributed among members of the American public.[16]

Many of Jackson's decisions as president, particularly in the realm of economic policy, were misguided and led the nation into serious economic distress. The Jacksonian Party mainly represented Southern and Western agricultural interests and local, as opposed to national, commercial and financial interests—today we might say "Main Street" as opposed to "Wall Street." Much of the struggle between the two centered on the Second Bank of the United States, a quasi-public entity that functioned as America's central bank. The Second Bank handled the federal government's financial transactions, maintained a stable currency, and protected the public credit. From the perspective of the Jacksonians, the Second Bank stifled local investment and land speculation and subjected local economic development in the South and West to the control of Northeastern bankers and financiers. Accordingly, Jackson vetoed a bill to renew the charter of the Second Bank, which was due to expire in 1836, and in 1833 organized the removal of government deposits from the bank. These deposits were sent, instead, to dozens of state and local banks, which used them as the basis for extending credit to marginal local business concerns and for issuing their own paper currency in the form of bank notes, which were nominally backed by their government deposits.

The inflationary results of this policy soon became apparent, leading Jackson in 1836 to issue an executive order requiring buyers of government lands to pay in gold or silver rather than the almost worthless notes promiscuously printed by the new legions of local banks. Jackson's "Specie Circular" led holders of state and local bank notes to attempt to redeem their notes for hard currency, but the issuing banks lacked sufficient currency reserves and were unable to honor their notes. The ensuing depreciation of the notes led to numerous bank failures and a severe economic depression, dubbed the Panic of 1837, as tens of thousands of individuals saw their nominal wealth transformed into worthless paper.[17]

Jackson also famously instituted the "spoils" or party patronage system for filling government offices. Patronage meant that party loyalty became the chief requirement for holding office in the various federal agencies. This practice was necessary because the Jacksonians were attempting to build a strong political party dependent not on a small number of wealthy patrons as had been true of the Federalists and Jeffersonians, but instead on the enthusiasm and energy of large numbers of impecunious activists. These individuals had to be rewarded for their efforts, and positions in the hundreds of federal land offices, customs houses, and post offices were the most obvious rewards available.[18] Often experienced federal employees were removed to make room for unqualified party activists. Jackson justified the practice by declaring, "The duties of all public officers are, or at least admit being made so plain and simple that men of intelligence may readily qualify themselves for their performance."[19]

Among Jackson's most important actions as president was his determination to oppose South Carolina's claim that states possessed the power to nullify the application of federal laws within their own territory. What came to be known as the Nullification Crisis began with opposition throughout the South to high tariffs on European manufactured goods. During this period of American history, the tariff was a central political issue, pitting the North, whose industries sought protective tariffs, against the South, which as an importer of manufactured goods and a low-cost producer of agricultural exports, favored free trade. In 1828, John C. Calhoun—who had been John Quincy Adams's vice president and subsequently became Jackson's vice president—anonymously drafted an "Exposition and Protest." In this document, Calhoun put forward South Carolina's claim that it had the right to prevent the federal government from undertaking any actions within the state's own territory that were deemed by the state legislature to run counter to the state's interests.

The issue remained hypothetical until 1832, when Jackson signed tariff legislation deemed injurious by South Carolinians. By this time, Jackson had broken with Calhoun and denied him the vice presidential nomination. The South Carolina legislature appointed Calhoun to the U.S. Senate, where he now openly advocated the doctrine of nullification. At Calhoun's urging, a state convention was called in South Carolina that declared the new tariff as well as prior tariffs to be null and void within South Carolina. President Jackson responded to the South Carolinians by securing the enactment of a "Force Bill," which authorized him to use troops to enforce the tariff.[20] Jackson declared himself to be ready to lead an army to South Carolina if it should become necessary, but a compromise ended the crisis. To appease the South Carolinians, Jackson signed a new tariff bill and rescinded the Force

Bill. South Carolina, for its part, rescinded its nullification ordinance but not before making a symbolic point by nullifying the about-to-be repealed Force Bill. Jackson had been willing to compromise, but had shown his determination to preserve the Union by military force if necessary.

One of the more unsavory aspects of Jackson's presidency was his support for a policy of Indian removal, which displaced tens of thousands of Southeastern Native Americans and forced them to relocate to arid lands west of the Mississippi. Jackson had earned his early fame as an "Indian fighter." Even before the Battle of New Orleans made him a national hero, Old Hickory had led the Tennessee, Georgia, and Alabama militia companies that defeated the Creek Indians in the 1814 Battle of Horseshoe Bend, fought in central Alabama. After the battle, Jackson forced the Creek Indians to sign a treaty ceding to the United States millions of acres of land, including lands that had belonged to Native Americans who had actually fought alongside Jackson's forces.[21] In an eerie foreshadowing of the 1941 forced relocation of Japanese Americans, the general deemed that security interests required the dispossession of even loyal Native Americans.

During Jackson's presidency, the land developers and speculators who were prominent in the Jacksonian Party pressed the president to make more Indian lands available for white settlement. Jackson complied, securing the enactment of the 1830 Indian Removal Act, which authorized the president to negotiate treaties that removed most Native American tribes from their Southeastern lands. In some instances, these relocations were forced and brutal.[22] More than one hundred million acres of land east of the Mississippi was wrested from Native Americans during Jackson's administration.[23]

One way in which Jackson permanently strengthened the presidency was his use of the veto power. Prior to Jackson's presidency, the veto had been seen as an extraordinary measure to be used only if the president believed that a congressional action would usurp the authority of the executive branch. The president was not viewed as having the authority to veto a bill simply because of a policy disagreement. Even George Washington had made use of only two vetoes, and Adams, Jefferson, and John Quincy Adams never vetoed a piece of legislation. Jackson, however, vetoed twelve bills and made it clear that he believed the president had the constitutional authority to veto bills that did not comport with his own view of the national interest. The most important example was, of course, Jackson's decision to veto reauthorization of the Second Bank. Even some of Old Hickory's supporters thought the president had overstepped his constitutional bounds in making this decision. In 1834, the Senate, now controlled by Jackson's political opponents, censured the president for refusing to turn over documents related to his bank veto, though the censure was expunged from the Senate's records in 1838 when Jackson's allies regained the majority. In subsequent decades, the veto would become a routine presidential instrument.

After Jackson left the White House, the power of the presidency waned. Jackson had believed in a strong presidency, so it was ironic that after he left office the political party that he and his followers had built, now calling itself the Democrats, weakened the presidency. The Democratic Party had been constructed as a congeries of state party organizations. Within each state, a clique of party notables reigned supreme, controlling political nominations, patronage positions, and—when the birth of the Whig Party reignited interparty competition—the armies of party workers charged with mobilizing voters. Each state's paramount party leaders often had themselves appointed to the U.S. Senate by the state legislatures they controlled.

After the departure of their supreme leader, Old Hickory, these state party notables saw no reason to defer to the wishes of meddlesome outsiders, such as presidents, when it came to managing the affairs of their own states. From their posts in the U.S. Senate, state party leaders became a log-rolling coalition for state power, confining the federal government to marginal activities and limiting its revenues to customs duties and the proceeds from public land sales. Each clique of state party leaders controlled its own state and united with other state party leaders in agreeing that the federal government should refrain from bothering them. The leaders of the Southern states were especially vehement members of this coalition for state power, seeing in the sovereignty of the states the best security against outside efforts to interfere with slavery.

This situation was not changed by the growing influence of the Whig Party, which won two of the seven presidential elections that followed Jackson's retirement. The Whigs consisted of a disparate coalition of politicians who held a variety of views on economic and social matters. They were united by only one political principle: opposition to Andrew Jackson. As a result, the Whigs eschewed discussion of issues, particularly the sectional differences that increasingly split the nation, and in presidential elections, they nominated famous military commanders like Generals William Henry Harrison and Zachary Taylor, who had no known political views.

Harrison, called "Old Tippecanoe" for his victory in an 1811 battle against Native Americans in Ohio, had sunk into political obscurity after briefly serving in Congress. He was not known to have taken any particular position on any of the issues of the day; his most recent public office had been clerk of the Court of Common Pleas in Hamilton County, Ohio, a position that did not require him to voice his opinion on slavery, the tariff, internal improvements, or any other potentially divisive question.[24] Similarly Taylor, a hero of the war with Mexico, had lived on military posts most of his adult life, had no interest in politics, and could not recall ever having voted. Both Harrison and Taylor died in office and were succeeded by their vice presidents, John Tyler and Millard Fillmore. Like the Democratic Party, the Whig Party was built as a congeries of state party organizations. Whig leaders joined their Democratic rivals in defending state power and constraining the power of the federal government.

Insofar as presidential power was concerned, one manifestation of party leaders' determination to protect the power of the individual states was the character of the presidential nominating process. The Jacksonians had introduced the idea of the party convention as a democratic political reform, albeit one designed to elect Jackson. Now the party convention became an institution designed to select presidential nominees who would not make trouble, lacked strong opinions on sectional issues, and would avoid interfering with the control that state party notables exercised within their own domains. Van Buren, Harrison, and Taylor were easy choices and posed no threat to established political interests.

In 1844 the Whigs broke their own rule and nominated Henry Clay, whose proposed "American system" of internal improvements was unpopular in the South and seen by other political notables as divisive. That same year, however, the Democrats began a practice that was to last for the next century and would, more often than not, produce mediocre nominees who might be electable but were unlikely to pose a challenge to party nabobs and potentates. Beginning with the 1844 Democratic convention, at each party's national nominating convention competing party factions, consisting of state delegations and coalitions of state delegations, would put forward the names of their own leaders as presidential candidates. Over the next several days or even weeks, competing party factions would fight one another to a standstill. At this point, serious negotiations would commence among these factions, leading to the choice of a nominee, sometimes a political unknown dubbed a "dark horse," who seemed weak and unlikely to pose a threat to the balance of power within the party or, if eventually elected, to the power of party leaders in the nation at large.

The first such dark horse candidate was James K. Polk, who was chosen by the Democrats after a nine-ballot deadlock. In 1852, the Democratic convention was deadlocked for a forty-eight-ballot battle between its Northern and Southern wings—only on the forty-ninth ballot did the Democrats turn to an obscure former senator, Franklin Pierce, who seemed to lack strong views on sectional issues. In 1856, the Democrats chose James Buchanan on the sixteenth ballot. Buchanan was helped by having been away from the country for several years as ambassador to Great Britain, so he lacked close ties to any faction. Buchanan also benefited from his diplomatic background, which had taught him to make flowery, platitudinous speeches with no content.

Nominees of this era were chosen because they were inoffensive and, once in the White House, most lived up to their lack of promise. The reputations of Martin Van Buren, William Henry Harrison, John Tyler, Zachary Taylor, Millard Fillmore, Franklin Pierce, and James Buchanan have, at least thus far, remained lackluster at best, despite the heroic efforts of the usual swarm of presidential hagiographers. Ironically, of the post-Jackson presidents, the one exception to the rule of inoffensiveness was the very first of the dark horses, James K. Polk.[25] In his previous positions, speaker of the U.S. House of Representatives and governor of Tennessee, Polk had shown little evidence of outstanding ability or ambition and was, for the most part, a Democratic "wheel horse" or loyal party lieutenant, first to Andrew Jackson and later to Martin Van Buren.

As president, however, Polk was "determined to use his party's power as aggressively as he could to realize great national achievements."[26] Today Polk is remembered chiefly for launching a war against Mexico that added more than a million square miles of territory to the United States, including the contemporary states of California, Arizona, New Mexico, Nevada, Utah, and Texas. Determined to secure American control of Texas, which was then a quasi-sovereign nation whose independence remained unrecognized by Mexico, and to seize California, Polk sent an army commanded by General Zachary Taylor to disputed territory along the border between the United States and Mexico. Taylor's forces then undertook a number of actions calculated to provoke the Mexicans, including crossing the Rio Grande to attack the Mexican city of Matamoros, which lies directly across the river from the contemporary American city of Brownsville, Texas. When Mexican forces responded, Polk asked Congress for a declaration of war on the grounds that Mexico had invaded the United States. Polk had used his power as commander-in-chief to force the issue and Congress's hand.[27]

Polk also reached an agreement with Great Britain, finally settling the Oregon boundary dispute that had soured relations between the two nations since a temporary joint administration of the territory had been agreed to in 1818. Under the terms of the new agreement, the northern boundary of the territory was set at the 49th parallel, where it remains today. Many Democrats had strongly favored setting the boundary line farther north, just above the 54th parallel and adjacent to the southern border of the then-Russian territory of Alaska. These Democrats had campaigned on the slogan "54–40 or fight," and saw Polk's acceptance of the

49th parallel as a betrayal. Polk nevertheless had secured American ownership of a huge territory encompassing the contemporary states of Washington, Oregon, and Idaho, along with portions of what would become Montana and Wyoming.

Polk also rectified one of Andrew Jackson's errors by ending the practice of depositing government funds in local and state banks. Polk introduced the independent treasury system, which, until its abolition in 1926, provided for the deposit of surplus government funds in the U.S. Treasury. The virtue of this system was that it reduced the likelihood of financial bubbles occasioned by rapid credit expansion—a situation that could result from profligate banking practices during periods of economic growth. Unfortunately, during periods of economic recession, the independent treasury system slowed the economy further by restricting the availability of credit. The system was eventually abandoned.

Polk also initiated a practice called central budgetary clearance that was later dropped but then revived and institutionalized during the 1920s. Prior to Polk, every government department had submitted its budget directly to Congress, which regarded direct review of agency budgets as essential to the exercise of its constitutional power of the purse. The problem, however, was that the budget of the United States became simply a sum of the individual departmental budgets with no overall mechanism for predicting annual outlays or linking expenditures to revenues. Polk's innovation was to require department heads to submit their budget requests to him rather than the Congress. The president then reviewed the requests and sent a consolidated budget to Capitol Hill. This new step was not only fiscally prudent, but also enhanced presidential power. When Polk's term ended, Congress put an end to the consolidated budget and resumed direct negotiations with department heads. Polk's innovation, however, was not forgotten and set the stage for the creation of the Bureau of the Budget about seventy-five years later.[28]

Abraham Lincoln and the Civil War Presidency

The political accession of Abraham Lincoln and the new Republican Party in 1861 touched off America's Civil War and changed the course of American history. For those who may not be familiar with this history, it may be worthwhile to review the steps that led to this cataclysmic event. Since the founding of the nation, the sectional struggle between North and South had threatened American unity. At the heart of the conflict was a sharp division of economic interest. The Southern states were among the world's low-cost producers of several important agricultural commodities, including cotton, rice, and tobacco, and Southern interests were thus vehement advocates of free trade. The Northern states, by contrast, had developed economies based on trade and manufacturing, and their interests advocated high tariffs to provide them with a captive national market. Consequently the tariff was the central issue of American politics in the early nineteenth century, leading, as we saw, to the Nullification Crisis of the 1830s.

Overlaying and exacerbating this economic controversy was the issue of slavery. Southern agriculture depended on a labor force that by 1860 consisted of more than three million black slaves descended from Africans who had been enslaved and transported to North America. The debate over slavery that roiled American politics from the founding to the Civil War was at once a matter of economics and morality. Southerners saw slavery as the lynchpin of their region's economic prosperity and political power. To some in the free states of the North, however, who called themselves *abolitionists,* slavery was a monstrous evil to be opposed without compromise. Abolitionist editor William Lloyd Garrison declared, "I am aware that many object to the severity of my language; but is there not cause for severity? I will be as harsh as truth, and as uncompromising as justice. On this subject I do not wish to think or speak or write with moderation."[29] Other Northerners viewed slavery mainly in terms of sectional power. Slavery empowered the South relative to the North and so restrictions on slavery would shift the sectional balance of power toward the North. This view represented a political and economic calculation rather than a moral stance and so, unlike the abolitionist view, could indeed be the subject of agreements and compromises.

At the Constitutional Convention of 1789, Northern and Southern delegates agreed that for purposes of representation in the House of Representatives, which was to be based on population, three-fifths of each state's slaves would be counted toward determining its quota of representatives. The delegates also agreed that slaves could continue to be imported, but only until 1808 when the practice would be banned, and they settled on a fugitive slave clause stipulating that slaves who escaped to the free states would be returned to their owners.

These compromises seemed to be a satisfactory basis for union, but the issue of slavery arose again in relation to the territories acquired for the United States by Jefferson's Louisiana Purchase. The question was whether slavery would or would not be permitted in these territories. If slavery was permitted, the power of the Southerners would be increased by the addition of an enormous new domain. But if slavery was prohibited, the new domain would likely be linked to the North, leaving the South to watch as Northern commercial and political power grew. Since expansion of slavery into the territories was at this time more a political than a moral concern, a compromise proved possible: the Missouri Compromise of 1820 banned slavery in the Louisiana Territory above 36 degrees, 30 minutes north—

except within Missouri, which would be admitted to the Union as a slave state—while, for political balance, Maine would be admitted as a free state. Practically speaking, the compromise seemed to give the advantage to the North. Missouri and the Arkansas territory would permit slavery, while, in addition to Maine, slavery would be prohibited in an enormous swath of territory that encompassed the future states of Kansas, Nebraska, Colorado, Wyoming, North Dakota, South Dakota, and Montana. The compromise was negotiated in the Congress, which was then the locus of national political power; President Monroe played only a minor role in the negotiations. Many in the South were not happy with the compromise, but most seemed to accept the idea that the addition of Missouri to the Southern domain was more important than the North's capture of the arid and barely populated Western territories.

The issue of slavery in the territories came to the fore again with the Mexican-American War. Many abolitionists had opposed the war, fearing that its result would be the acquisition of new lands for slaveholders. Texas's agricultural economy was already becoming dependent on slave labor and Texas laid claim to most of the New Mexico Territory. Recall that Henry David Thoreau wrote his famous essay justifying civil disobedience in direct response to what he and other Northern abolitionists viewed as a war to expand slavery. At the end of the war, Northerners and Southerners compromised again, with California admitted to the Union as a free state, Texas as a slave state, and voters in the New Mexico Territory, which included modern-day Arizona and a portion of Utah, allowed to decide later when they would petition to enter the Union as a state. Once again the main forum for negotiations was the Congress, with Senators Henry Clay and Stephen A. Douglas acting as the chief architects of the final series of bills that embodied the agreement. President Fillmore's main role in the matter was to sign the bills with which he was presented.

This Compromise of 1850 had been more difficult to achieve than previous compromises because the issue of slavery had become partially detached from its economic roots and had come to be seen as a compelling moral question. Over time, the abolitionists had convinced many in the North that slavery was evil. And in the course of responding to abolitionist arguments, Southerners had convinced themselves that many in the North wished only to steal their property, impoverish them, and deprive them of their freedom. What began as an economic dispute had become a moral issue. This meant that politicians seeking grounds for compromise were likely to be castigated by all parties as lacking moral fiber.

Matters came to a head in 1854 when Senator Douglas introduced a Kansas-Nebraska bill that would create the territories of Kansas and Nebraska, but contrary to the terms of the Missouri Compromise would permit the white residents of those territories to decide whether slavery would or would not be permitted within their borders. Douglas, who often served as a spokesman for railroad interests in the Senate, hoped to create territorial governments in Kansas and Nebraska as a necessary first step toward the construction of a transcontinental railroad through Nebraska. The railroad would open millions of acres of excellent agricultural land for cultivation, but by the terms of the Missouri Compromise, slaveholders would not have access to it. Accordingly, Southern senators had blocked both the railway project and the incorporation of the two new territories. Under the terms of the Kansas-Nebraska bill, Douglas offered a compromise—"popular sovereignty"—which he said meant that the settlers of the two territories could vote on whether to permit or prohibit slavery. Congress passed the bill, which was dutifully signed by President Pierce who had played little role in the negotiations. An unanticipated result of the act, though, was that pro- and anti-slavery forces flooded the two territories with settlers, paramilitary forces, and weapons to attempt to control the outcome of the vote. Sporadic fighting broke out in the territory and what reporters dubbed "bleeding Kansas" became a prelude to civil war.

One important response to these events was the formation of a new political party, which called itself the Republican Party of the United States and declared its opposition to the expansion of slavery in the territories. Formed in 1854, the party was a coalition of all the nation's opponents of slavery and the political power of the South. These included outright abolitionists who wanted slavery ended, "Free-Soilers" who opposed the expansion of slavery, commercial interests seeking higher tariffs, and a variety of others. Against the backdrop of political crisis, the new party's influence spread through the Northern states, where it began to supplant the Whigs as the main opposition party. Republican presidential nominee, frontier scout, and California senator John C. Frémont carried eleven states in the 1856 presidential race, finishing second to the Democrats and well ahead of the rapidly disintegrating Whigs.

Support in the North for the Republicans surged in the wake of the Supreme Court's 1857 *Dred Scott* decision, which invalidated both the Missouri Compromise and the Compromise of 1850 by declaring that the federal government had no constitutional power to regulate slavery in the territories.[30] The decision was cheered in the South but assailed in the North as a step in a Southern effort to compel even the free states to accept slavery. Within a year of the *Dred Scott* decision the Republicans had become the North's dominant party. Advancing under the slogan "Free soil, free labor, free men," Republicans won control of the House of Representatives in the 1858 national elections and prepared to do battle for the presidency in 1860.[31]

At its national party convention, held in Chicago, the Republicans nominated Abraham Lincoln for the presidency. Lincoln's political experience consisted of one term in Congress sixteen years earlier. But he had become nationally famous for his speeches during a series of debates during the 1858 Senate race, when he had sought to oust Senator Stephen A. Douglas from his Illinois seat. Since the Democrats carried the state legislature, Douglas was reappointed to the Senate in 1859, but Lincoln's eloquent and passionate assertion of opposition to slavery made him a hero to anti-slavery forces in the North. The debates were followed by other speeches, including a famous address at New York's Cooper Union where Lincoln asserted that slavery was morally wrong and that no compromise was possible between a principle that was morally right and one that was morally wrong. By nominating Lincoln, the Republicans were throwing down the gauntlet to the South. The economic issue with moral overtones had become a moral issue that could no longer be discussed peacefully.

The 1860 election gave Lincoln a popular plurality and an Electoral College majority. All his electoral votes came from the North; he failed to carry a single Southern state and only two counties in all the South went for Lincoln. Most Southerners believed that Lincoln intended to bring a rapid end to slavery, and they promised to support dissolution of the Union if Lincoln won the presidency. In preparation for this eventuality, constitutional conventions were called throughout the South. One month after the Electoral College results became official, South Carolina voted to secede from the Union. Six other states—Texas, Louisiana, Mississippi, Florida, Alabama, and Georgia—followed South Carolina out of the Union and banded together as the Confederate States of America. This new Confederacy chose Mississippi senator Jefferson Davis as its president. Despite these developments, many politicians in both the North and South continued to hope that some compromise might be reached and the crisis defused. Several of the Southern states, including Virginia, the South's most important state, had not seceded, and in the spring of 1861 their unionist politicians continued to search for some formula to avert the breakup of the United States. Perhaps such a formula might have been found, but events in Charleston's harbor soon made compromise impossible.

At the mouth of Charleston's harbor sits a tiny artificial island, Fort Sumter, which was constructed after the War of 1812 as part of America's system of coastal defenses. Sumter's artillery, along with guns positioned at Fort Moultrie, a point of land on Sullivan's Island across the harbor from Fort Sumter, guarded the approaches to Charleston. The Charleston forts and one Florida fort were the only federal installations in the seceded states that had not been quickly abandoned by federal authorities. On December 26, 1860, the federal commander in Charleston,

Major Robert Anderson, evacuated his troops from the indefensible Fort Moultrie to the more secure Fort Sumter and waited for orders from Washington. An attempt by the U.S. Navy to resupply Fort Sumter in January failed when South Carolina artillery opened fire on the supply ship *Star of the West* and drove it away.

The standoff at Fort Sumter continued through Lincoln's inauguration in March 1861. At this point, Confederate commissioners traveled to Washington to demand the surrender of the fort. They were officially rebuffed but received tacit assurances from Secretary of State Seward that the government would not attempt to reinforce the fort while discussions and deliberations continued. Both in Washington and in the temporary Confederate capital of Montgomery, Alabama, many influential politicians argued for a cautious approach. A number of Confederate officials thought secession could be accomplished without war, while a number of federal officials hoped a peaceful resolution to the Sumter question would help persuade Virginia to remain in the Union. By April, though, Sumter's supplies were running out and President Lincoln ordered a relief expedition to leave for Charleston. Confederate President Davis, in turn, ordered Southern artillery to open fire on the fort. Sumter's guns replied and for two days the citizens of Charleston cheered the artillery barrages from the waterfront.[32] Finally Major Anderson indicated that he was ready to surrender and a triumphal flotilla of soldiers and civilians headed for the little island. News of the fighting at Fort Sumter spread quickly via telegraph. President Lincoln asked the loyal states for 75,000 troops to suppress the rebellion. With Lincoln's call for troops, voices of moderation in Virginia, Arkansas, North Carolina, and Tennessee were drowned out: these states seceded and joined the Confederacy.

With the fall of Fort Sumter and the outbreak of the Civil War, President Lincoln issued a series of executive orders for which he had no clear legal basis. Without even calling Congress into session, Lincoln combined the state militias into a ninety-day national volunteer force, called for 40,000 new volunteers, enlarged the regular army and navy, diverted $2 million in unspent appropriations to military needs, instituted censorship of the U.S. mails, ordered a blockade of the Southern ports, suspended the writ of habeas corpus in the border states, and ordered the arrest by military police of individuals whom he deemed to be guilty of engaging in—or "contemplating"—treasonous actions.[33]

Lincoln was not indifferent to constitutional limitations on presidential power.[34] He asserted, though, that extraordinary measures were justified by what he called the presidential "war power," which he saw as constitutionally implied by the president's role as commander-in-chief, as well as the presidential oath of office and his duty to ensure that the nation's laws were faithfully executed.[35] Lincoln's assertion of presidential war powers did not stop in 1861. Over the course of the war, he instituted military conscription, emancipated the slaves by presidential proclamation, and instituted trial by courts martial throughout the nation for those accused of disloyal practices. As many as 30,000 persons were arrested for suspected disloyalty and some were held in prison as long as three years without formal charges being brought against them.[36] In 1863, a Democratic member of Congress from Ohio, Clement Vallandigham, was arrested after delivering a speech to the House denouncing the suspension of habeas corpus.[37] Vallandigham was tried by a military commission, sentenced to prison, and subsequently expelled to the Confederacy.

In almost every instance, Congress subsequently enacted legislation legitimating the president's actions. Thus after the president ordered the expansion of the Army and Navy, Congress enacted legislation to that effect. Similarly, after the president instituted military conscription, Congress voted a draft law. And after the president ordered the creation of military commissions to try individuals accused of treason against the United States, Congress enacted legislation governing the organization and conduct of such commissions. For its part, in the 1863 Prize Cases the Supreme Court upheld the president's power to order a blockade of the Southern ports.[38] In the 1866 case of *Ex parte Milligan,* the Court rejected the president's suspension of habeas corpus and indiscriminate use of military tribunals in areas of the nation that were not actually theaters of military operations, but it did recognize the president's power to declare martial law and to suspend civil liberties in areas actually subject to military threat.[39]

Lincoln not only expanded the power of the presidency; during the war he expanded the power of the national government more generally. The departure of virtually all the Southern Democrats from both the House and Senate meant that the coalition for state power that normally kept the federal government a small and toothless institution had, at least temporarily, disappeared. Some historians have asserted that Lincoln generally left nonmilitary concerns to Congress.[40] In wartime, however, the line between military and civilian matters is sometimes so thin as to be nonexistent. Lincoln used the absence of the Southern Democrats, along with claims of wartime emergency, to increase substantially the size and reach of the federal government, particularly in the realm of finance.

Before the war, Congress had sharply limited the federal government's resources to safeguard the primacy of the states. The war, however, created a justification for an enormous expansion of the federal government's financial base. Accordingly, Lincoln called Congress into special session in 1861 and pointed to the need for an escalation in revenues to support the war effort. One result was the 1861 Revenue Act, which established America's first federal income tax. Subsequently,

Lincoln and Treasury Secretary Salmon Chase persuaded Congress to authorize the issuance of $50 million in Treasury notes, redeemable in gold or silver specie, to meet military payrolls.

With financial needs increasing, Lincoln and Chase turned to Congress again, proposing an expedient suggested to Lincoln by an Illinois entrepreneur. The president asked Congress to empower the Treasury to authorize the issuance of $150 million in paper currency, not redeemable in specie, to meet military expenses. These notes were authorized by the 1862 Legal Tender Act, which created America's first national paper currency, declared to be "lawful money and a payment of all debts public and private."[41] The notes were nicknamed "greenbacks" because they were printed on both sides in green ink. During the course of the war, Congress authorized the issuance of nearly $450 million in paper currency by the Treasury and by the newly created national banks. The greenbacks gave the national government direct control over the money supply and a flexible capacity to fund its operations. As you might have guessed, the Civil War greenbacks were the direct forebears of the paper dollars in your wallet today.

Finally, needing still more money for the war, Lincoln and Chase turned to an Ohio banker, Jay Cooke, and asked him to place $500 million in government bonds in such a way that they could not be sold to domestic banks or foreign investors. Cooke developed a plan to market these securities to ordinary citizens who had never before purchased government bonds. He thought he could appeal to the patriotism of ordinary Americans, and he believed that widespread ownership of government bonds would give ordinary Americans a greater concern for their nation's welfare.[42] Cooke established a network of 2,500 sales agents throughout the North and used the press to promote the idea that purchasing government securities was both a patriotic duty and a wise investment. In every community, Republican Party organizations worked hand in hand with Cooke's sales agents, providing what historian Eric McKitrick calls the "continual affirmation of purpose" needed to sustain both popular support and the regime's finances through four long years of war.[43] Cooke's idea was used again during World War I and World War II, and indeed today's U.S. savings bonds are descendants of Cooke's bonds.

Thus not only did Lincoln enhance presidential power to fight the war; he also expanded the power of the national government. As the framers might have understood, presidential power energized the entire national government. Some of Lincoln's wartime measures ended with the Confederate surrender, but some, like the greenbacks, remained in place. And all became precedents for future chief executives.

Reconstruction: A Presidency in Decline

In the aftermath of the South's surrender and President Lincoln's assassination, the influence of the presidency was eclipsed by a resurgence of congressional power. This resurgence began with the impeachment of Lincoln's successor, President Andrew Johnson. The proximate cause of Johnson's impeachment was his veto of the Tenure in Office Act (see Chapter 2). The larger cause, however, was a clash between the president and Congress over postwar Reconstruction policy.

In the aftermath of the war, civil government was restored in the former Confederate states. New state constitutions were adopted and legislatures and governors were elected by the white citizenry. Blacks had been emancipated but possessed no civil rights such as the right to vote. To make sure that blacks would never vote or enjoy political, social, or economic equality with whites, most Southern states adopted "Black Codes," which restricted the legal and occupational rights of the newly emancipated slaves. These codes were often nullified by the federal military commanders who still oversaw the Southern states; nevertheless, publication of the codes caused howls of protest in the North. Republican newspapers throughout the North saw the Black Codes as nothing less than an effort by the defeated South to reimpose slavery. The Black Codes were declared to be an affront to those who had died fighting for freedom and another expression of the South's continuing hostility toward the Union. South Carolina's 1865 constitution, for example, was denounced by the Northern press as "a scandalous repudiation of democratic principles," and "a document enacted by men who have come red-handed from the battle field, and to whose garments the blood of our brothers and sons still clings."[44] Some influential Northerners averred that the South's loyalty and the safety of the freedmen could only be ensured if blacks were enfranchised.

Southern whites regarded the idea of black suffrage as an outrage. Northern Republicans, though, believed that black suffrage could ensure Republican electoral control of the entire region. In a number of Southern states, including Mississippi, Alabama, Louisiana, and South Carolina, blacks outnumbered whites by a considerable margin and, even where they were not a majority, blacks constituted a substantial minority of the population. The so-called Radical Republicans, led by Thaddeus Stevens of Pennsylvania in the House of Representatives and Charles Sumner of Massachusetts in the Senate, had long argued in favor of voting rights for blacks. But even those Northern Republicans who had no particular sympathy for blacks understood the electoral arithmetic. Enfranchised and politically organized, blacks could form a solid Republican base in the South, virtually guaranteeing that the Republican Party would control the nation for years to come. Thus even as President Johnson declared himself satisfied with events in the South and averred that it was time to fully restore civil authority in the former Confederacy, Congress responded to the Black Codes by refusing to seat the members elected in South Carolina and the other Southern states and by creating a joint Reconstruction committee to inquire into the question of whether the South was as yet entitled to congressional representation.

By the beginning of 1866, President Andrew Johnson and congressional Republicans were locked in an all-out struggle over Reconstruction. Johnson favored a conciliatory policy toward the defeated South and sought to restore the Southern states to the Union as soon as was practicable. Between January and November 1866, Johnson ignored congressional objections, reduced the number of federal troops stationed in the South—to only 2,700 in the entire state of South Carolina—and prepared for the complete elimination of the federal government's military presence in the former Confederacy. Congressional Republican leaders Stevens and Sumner, by contrast, were adamantly opposed to restoring the power of the South's prewar leadership and had already begun to develop their own plan for the region. Congress's plan would require a drastic reorganization of the governments of the Southern states as well as enfranchisement of the freedmen.

Early in 1866 Congress overrode Johnson's veto of the Civil Rights Act, which declared that all persons born in the United States had equal rights with regard to employment, property ownership, and judicial procedure. This act was Congress's direct response to the Black Codes, superseding and nullifying their provisions by federal law. In June 1866, Congress further strengthened this response by submitting to the states the Fourteenth Amendment to the Constitution. The Fourteenth Amendment prohibits the states from depriving citizens of rights to which they would be entitled by the federal Constitution, bars most former Confederate officials from holding public office without congressional approval, disallows any debts owed by the former Confederacy, declares that slaveholders will not be compensated for the loss of their slaves, and affirms that Congress has the power to enforce all these provisions whether the states like it or not. Reaction in the South was immediate and unanimous. To Southerners, the Fourteenth Amendment meant black suffrage, and every Southern legislature emphatically rejected the proposed constitutional change.

Events in the North, however, were quickly rendering their views moot. The congressional Reconstruction committee had filed its report in June 1866, and it was a damning indictment of the Southern states and Johnson's Reconstruction policies.

"In no instance in the Southern states was any regard paid to any other consideration than obtaining immediate admission to Congress under the barren form of any
election in which no precaution was taken to secure the regulatory of proceedings
or the ascent of the people," the report began. "Instead," the report continued, "all
feeling of conciliation on the part of the North has been treated with contempt."
"The burden rests," the report concluded, "upon the Southern people . . . to show
that they ought to resume their federal relations . . . They must prove that they have
established a republican form of government in harmony with the Constitution and
laws of the United States—that all hostile purposes have ceased, and that they have
given adequate guarantees against future treason."[45] The report went on to assert
that the Southern states lacked proper governments or constitutions, had forfeited
all political rights and privileges, and could be reestablished as governments only
through congressional action.

The Reconstruction report and its implications became a major focus of the
fall 1866 congressional campaign. President Johnson traveled about the country
speaking against the Radical Republicans and defending his own conciliatory policies toward the defeated Southern states. Republican congressional leaders, meanwhile, pointed to the joint committee report and to the Southern states' unanimous rejection of the Fourteenth Amendment as evidence of continued Southern
defiance of national authority. This was to be the first of many electoral campaigns
in which Republicans "waved the bloody shirt" of secession and war to retain the
allegiance of Northern voters. "Vote the way you shot," Republicans would remind
their supporters. The result of the 1866 election was an overwhelming victory for
congressional Republicans and a repudiation of the president. With enormous majorities in both houses, Congress's Radical Republican leadership could be confident
of overturning presidential vetoes and implementing whatever Reconstruction program it might choose.

Congressional Republicans lost no time in taking advantage of their new
numbers. In March 1867, Congress passed the First and Second Reconstruction
Acts, which declared that no legal government existed in any Southern state except
Tennessee. The remaining ten Southern states were divided into five military districts, each commanded by a general with the authority to remove local officials,
overturn state court proceedings, nullify state laws, and ignore state constitutions.
Under the terms of the acts, a state might be readmitted to the Union if and only
if it held a new constitutional convention whose delegates were chosen on the basis
of universal male suffrage. The convention, in turn, was required to write a new
constitution that, among other matters, provided for universal male suffrage in all
state elections. The new state legislature created under this constitution was re-

quired to ratify the Fourteenth Amendment. President Johnson argued that these congressional actions were unconstitutional, but the president's continuing efforts to thwart Congress's plans only led to his impeachment by the House and near-conviction in the Senate.

Though Johnson survived impeachment to complete his term in office, Congress had demonstrated that it, not the president, determined the policies of the U.S. government. President Grant, who was elected to succeed Johnson, was given to understand that Congress, and particularly the Senate, governed the nation and that the president should do as he was told. "The most eminent senators," wrote Massachusetts senator George Hoar, "would have received as a personal affront a private message from the White House expressing a desire that they should adopt any course in the discharge of their legislative duties that they did not approve. If they visited the White House it was to give, not receive advice."[46] President Grant understood his new place in the scheme of things and "yielded a quick deference to Republican leaders in the House and Senate, notably the latter."[47]

During the 1870s, the North grew tired of the turmoil and bloodshed associated with Reconstruction. Fueled by lurid press accounts of the depravity of the freedmen and the suffering of the white Southerners, Northern opinion turned solidly against continued efforts to impose a new order on the South. After 1876, Reconstruction was brought to a close and important elements of the prewar regime were rebuilt. Blacks were disenfranchised throughout the South and white Democratic rule was restored. As white Democrats regained their places in the House and Senate, the prewar coalition for state power reasserted itself—senators, in particular, were determined to rein in presidential power and reassert their own places as leaders of quasi-autonomous states. Much of the national administrative machinery built by Lincoln was abandoned, and the custom of nominating nonthreatening, "dark horse" presidential candidates was restored.

The Republican Era

Fifteen presidents governed America from Abraham Lincoln's election in 1860 to the inauguration of Franklin D. Roosevelt in 1932. Of these, thirteen were Republicans and only two, Grover Cleveland and Woodrow Wilson, were Democrats. Thus it seems appropriate to call this seventy-two-year period a Republican era. In terms of the role of the presidency, however, the era should be divided into three periods. The first is the Lincoln presidency, when America's chief executive exercised unprecedented wartime powers. During the second period, which includes the presidencies of Grant, Hayes, Garfield, Arthur, Harrison, Cleveland, and McKinley,

Congress regained its position as America's chief governmental institution. And in the third portion of the long Republican era, a portion that encompassed the presidencies of Theodore Roosevelt, Taft, Wilson, Harding, Coolidge, and Hoover, the importance of the presidency began to increase once again.

In the second of these periods, Grant, as we saw, deferred to Congress in almost all matters. And although President Hayes sought to restore a measure of presidential independence by ignoring the Senate when appointing the heads of the various government agencies, Congress had grown accustomed to being consulted on all appointments. Representatives exercised significant influence on all federal appointments within their districts, senators on appointments within their states and appointees from their states, and the Senate leadership on major executive appointments. When Hayes decided to nominate Cabinet officers without obtaining the prior approval of Senate leaders, the Senate initially refused to confirm the nominations; only after a major public campaign was Hayes able to secure confirmation of his appointees. One presidential historian declared that this battle marked the beginning of a decline in senatorial power.[48] Senate leaders, however, responded by implementing the practice of "senatorial courtesy," which required a president to obtain the assent of a nominee's home-state senators before the Senate would approve an appointment. In subsequent fights during the Hayes presidency and brief presidency of John Garfield, the White House sometimes succeeded in overcoming senatorial courtesy but was not able to overturn the principle.[49]

Despite occasional successes, presidents from Grant to McKinley were eclipsed by the Congress when it came to the formulation of national policy. The years from 1868 to the turn of the century included a good deal of struggle and strife in the nation. Conflicts arose over monetary policy, the role of organized labor, agricultural policy, immigration, political corruption, America's role in the world, and a host of other matters. For the most part, policies to deal with these issues were formulated by the leaders of Congress, rather than the president. Even America's 1898 war with Spain was declared by Congress despite President McKinley's misgivings.[50] Henry Adams summarized the relationship between the two branches during this period by writing, "So far as the president's initiative was concerned, the president and his cabinet might equally well have departed separately or together to distant lands. Their recommendations were uniformly disregarded."[51]

Even as Congress ignored the president's views, lawmakers made certain to impose their views on the administration of government. According to Leonard White, members of Congress "swarmed" in and out of government offices, investigating administrative practices, addressing constituents' complaints, and generally seeking to control administrative affairs. Congress also enacted numerous statutes dealing with the details of administrative procedures, ceding little discretionary authority to the executive.[52]

Progressivism

When President William McKinley was assassinated by an anarchist in 1901, he was succeeded by his abrasive, forceful, and energetic vice president, Theodore Roosevelt. The various state party leaders had long recognized Roosevelt as a threat to their own power and probably would never have given him the presidential nomination. Senate Republican leader Mark Hanna declared his opposition even to giving Roosevelt the vice presidential slot. Don't any of you realize, asked Hanna, "that there's only one life between that madman and the presidency?"[53]

Roosevelt was far more successful than his recent predecessors in influencing the legislative process and in using executive power to convince the public that the presidency was, indeed, a center of action and initiative. In 1903 Roosevelt was able to persuade Congress to enact the Elkins Act, which sought to strengthen railroad regulation; to approve the Expediting Act to speed antitrust cases against the steel, rail, oil, and meat-packing industries; and to bring about the creation of the Department of Commerce and Labor, which was to have important regulatory responsibilities. In 1906, Roosevelt pushed through the Hepburn Act, which gave the Interstate Commerce Commission rate-setting powers, as well as the Meat Inspection Act and the Pure Food and Drug Act, both of which were designed to deal with issues of food safety. This president did not yield "a quick deference" to Congress.

Roosevelt's ability to act forcefully in the legislative arena was not simply a matter of personality. The president was able to take advantage of a number of turn-of-the-century changes that created a potential for greater executive power. One such change was a communications revolution. Following the Civil War, the entire nation had been linked by telegraph lines that allowed news to travel electronically, rather than by horseback, from one part of the nation to another. Taking advantage of this new innovation were the "wire services"—news organizations that, for a fee, began to distribute national and international news to America's thousands of local newspapers. Calculating that the activities of the president were more likely to be of interest to a nationwide audience than the comings and goings of members of Congress, the wire services focused on the chief executive, providing same-day coverage of presidential actions and speeches to a national audience. It was this focus that gave Roosevelt a chance to become America's first media president. He used speeches to shape public opinion and bring public pressure to bear on members of Congress. Roosevelt said the presidency gave him a "bully pulpit," and he made "going public" an important weapon of presidential power.[54]

For Roosevelt's immediate successors, Taft and Wilson, speeches and press conferences became routine instruments. In his messages to Congress and public statements, President Taft regularly promoted a "laundry list" of objectives and legislative initiatives in an attempt to create an agenda for legislative action and to mobilize public and press opinion in support of his initiatives.[55] Taft lacked Roosevelt's skill as a speaker but the next president, Woodrow Wilson, combined oratorical ability with a determination to halt congressional encroachment into the powers of the executive. Wilson was determined to exert leadership in the legislative process. This he did, leading a successful effort to enact a number of major pieces of legislation, including the Federal Reserve Act, the Federal Trade Commission Act, the Clayton Anti-Trust Act, and a new income tax. Wilson also worked to overcome neutralist sentiment and lead America into war against Germany in 1917. Of course, at the end of the war, Wilson lost an epic battle with the Senate when he failed to obtain the two-thirds majority necessary to confirm the Treaty of Versailles and to establish the League of Nations. America instead agreed to make a separate peace with Germany and refused to join the league. Wilson suffered a stroke soon thereafter and was incapacitated for the remainder of his term.

In demonstrating new presidential leadership, Roosevelt, Taft, and Wilson benefited not only from their mastery of rhetoric, but also from a major political and institutional shift in the nation brought about by the Progressive movement.[56] Progressivism was a political movement that took hold at the turn of the century mainly among upper-middle-class, old-stock Americans who were deeply suspicious of the power of big business, opposed continued immigration, and were angered by the political corruption that seemed to be commonplace. Progressives believed that government could be a powerful instrument for the betterment of society and were willing to give their political backing to politicians who shared their views. Progressives also championed political reform. In particular, reformers attributed many of the ills of the political process to the political party "machines" that dominated politics in a number of states and major metropolitan areas. From the Progressive perspective the party machines fostered corruption and, perhaps even worse, contributed to the political power of the immigrant groups who were among the machines' chief clients.

Accordingly, Progressive reformers campaigned vigorously against machine politics and during the late nineteenth and early twentieth centuries were able to introduce reforms at both the state and national levels designed to weaken the power of the political parties and loosen their hold on the political process. Among the two most important of these Progressive reforms were civil service, which was introduced at the federal level by the 1883 Pendleton Act and then by numerous state and local acts, and the requirement of primary elections for the nomination of candidates for every office below the presidency. (Presidential primaries were introduced by some states in the early twentieth century, but did not become dominant until the 1970s.) These party reforms weakened political party organizations and, in turn, encouraged members of Congress to throw off party discipline in the House and Senate. The collapse of party discipline was emblemized by the 1910 "revolt" against House Speaker Joe Cannon, which stripped the leader of many of his powers and allowed members greater freedom in voting. This decline of party discipline, in turn, gave presidents more opportunity to exert leadership in the legislative realm. The House speaker and Senate leader no longer could count on the support of their members, and presidents were free to negotiate directly with members for their support. The unitary House and unitary Senate were able to go toe to toe with the unitary executive, but the president would soon become more than a match for two collections of individuals.

Progressive reform, along with oratorical strategies, helped Roosevelt, Wilson, and even Taft exert legislative leadership. The availability of possibilities is, of course, no guarantee that they will be used, and neither Warren Harding nor Calvin Coolidge seemed to have an agenda to promote. Harding did call Congress into session with a call for new programs, but thought his job was complete and that it was entirely up to Congress to decide what would be done.[57] In the 1920s some states had mandated primary elections for the selection of party convention delegates, but most had not and presidential nominations were still controlled by state party leaders. Republican Party bosses, meeting in their famous "smoke-filled rooms," had chosen in 1920 Harding, a tenth-ballot dark horse without much ambition; and party leaders gave Coolidge the 1924 nomination when his inoffensive completion of Harding's term, after Harding's death, convinced party bosses that Coolidge could be trusted to defer to them.

One very important presidential innovation, however, was introduced by Harding and cultivated by Coolidge: the Bureau of the Budget. A century earlier, President Polk had invented the idea of a consolidated presidential budget, but the idea soon fell into disuse in favor of the former practice of each agency submitting a separate budget estimate to Congress. In the aftermath of World War I, the federal budget had grown large enough that differences between federal taxing and spending had an impact on the economy, though that impact was difficult to predict. Economists had suggested giving the executive the responsibility for estimating future government revenues and linking these to a consolidated budget estimate. Although congressional leaders saw the creation of such an office as an infringement on Congress's power of the purse, economic realities could not be ignored: the 1921 Budget and Accounting Act created the Bureau of the Budget and placed it in the Treasury Department where it reported to the secretary and the president but could be overseen by Congress. Both Harding and Coolidge made a point of regularly consulting Charles Dawes, the first director of the bureau, and endeavoring to build presidential influence over its operations. Harding worked with the bureau to prepare an executive budget in 1922.[58] To keep an eye on the bureau, Congress created a new auditing arm, the General Accounting Office, which worked directly for the legislative branch. Decades later, the group was renamed the Government Accountability Office and its functions were expanded to include audits, evaluations, and investigations of government agencies.

The last president of the Republican era, Herbert Hoover, was bright, aggressive, and ambitious, and he owed his nomination as much to Republican primary voters as to party leaders. Hoover used executive orders, was not afraid to clash with Congress, and viewed the president as the nation's leader. Unfortunately, neither Hoover nor anyone else knew what to do when the global economy collapsed.

The New Deal and the Imperial President

Over the next thirty-six years, the Democrats were the nation's majority party in terms of voters' partisan identifications. Republicans held the White House during sixteen of those years. But no matter. The presidents of both parties presided over an expansion of presidential power that, for the most part, left the chief executive in control of the nation's government. Franklin D. Roosevelt broke the two-term tradition that had been established by George Washington and won election to four terms in office. FDR died before completing his last term but was succeeded by his vice president, Harry S. Truman, who won reelection in his own right in 1948.

With the support of overwhelming Democratic majorities in the Congress, FDR presided over an enormous expansion of the executive branch, enhancing the power of the nation's chief executive and the executive branch, and increasing the role of the federal government more generally. Since the administration of Andrew Jackson, ambitious presidents had seen themselves as legislative leaders, and FDR lost no time in proposing new legislation to the Congress. During his first one hundred days in office, sometimes called the "First New Deal," Roosevelt and his advisers introduced some fourteen new programs, each administered by a new government agency. These included creation of the Federal Deposit Insurance

Corporation, the Securities and Exchange Commission, the Agricultural Adjustment Administration, and the Civilian Conservation Corps. Between 1935 and 1938, sometimes called the "Second New Deal," Roosevelt presided over the passage of still more legislation, including the Social Security Act and the National Labor Relations Act. The administration of these and hundreds of other pieces of legislation required the creation of a score of new agencies and the recruitment of hundreds of thousands of additional federal workers.

The growth of the executive branch accelerated during World War II, when numerous new agencies were created to support the war effort in every area from the mobilization of troops, to the production of supplies and munitions, to maintaining civilian morale. New agencies also meant more federal employees. In 1930, the federal government had employed 966,000 workers, many of whom were scattered throughout the nation (postal workers were one example). By the end of the war, however, the national government employed more than three million civil servants, with many, if not most, of these workers employed in Washington.[59] Today, if one includes the contract employees who work side by side with federal employees in most government offices, the true number may be close to ten million.

Each time Congress enacted a new program, it also enhanced the power of the executive branch. The enormous expansion of government that took place during FDR's presidency, moreover, made it impossible for Congress to continue closely monitoring the activities of executive agencies as it had in the past. Congress resorted instead, as noted earlier, to "fire alarm" management, intervening only when called and leaving the day-to-day management of the executive branch to administrators and the president. To make certain that the fire alarm would be rung, Congress in 1946 enacted the Administrative Procedure Act, which required agencies to publish proposed new rules and regulations and provide an opportunity for affected interests to comment and come to Congress with complaints, thereby ringing the alarm. This procedure is called "notice-and-comment rulemaking," and it will be considered in more detail in Chapter 5.

President Roosevelt, for his part, made direct use of the enormously expanded executive branch by, insofar as possible, governing through executive order. An executive order, you may remember, is a presidential order to a federal agency to undertake some course of action, and the expanded executive branch made executive orders more important instruments. During his time in office, FDR issued 3,522 executive orders, almost surpassing the total that had been issued by the thirty presidents who preceded him (technically FDR was the thirty-second president, but Grover Cleveland is usually counted as the twenty-second and twenty-fourth president). Many of these orders had to do with military policy and others with domestic policy. One very important executive order, issued in 1937, created the Executive Office of the President and moved the Bureau of the Budget from the Treasury Department where it had been lodged since 1921 into the Executive Office. Creation of the Executive Office of the President gave FDR and his successors the staff and other resources with which to supervise the executive branch. In turn, presidents' control over the Bureau of the Budget, which was later renamed the White House Office of Management and Budget, gave them greater oversight and power over the nation's spending priorities and Congress's legislative agenda. Presidential budgets came to be packaged and sent to Congress as agenda-setting bundles of proposals. The terms New Deal, Fair Deal, New Frontier, Great Society, and so forth were labels for presidential budgets that were designed both to capture media and public attention and to guide the legislative process.

In terms of foreign policy, Roosevelt eschewed treaties in favor of the use of executive agreements, which often did not involve congressional approval. FDR often pointed to Wilson's failure to obtain Senate approval for the Treaty of Versailles, which the president claimed had paved the way to World War II, as a reason not to involve lawmakers in foreign relations unless absolutely necessary. Executive agreements continue to be favored by presidents who now seldom negotiate treaties that must be approved by the Senate. One of the cornerstones of postwar American international economic policy was the General Agreement on Tariffs and Trade (GATT). As the name implies, American participation was based on an executive agreement, not a treaty.

By the time Roosevelt died in 1944, the nation, the executive branch, and the presidency had been transformed. Americans—and even the Congress—now looked to the chief executive for leadership. Presidential power continued to grow during the administrations of Roosevelt's successors, Harry Truman and Dwight David Eisenhower. Against the backdrop of economic and international crises, Congress enacted the 1947 National Security Act, which created the Department of Defense, the Central Intelligence Agency, and the National Security Council, all designed as instruments of presidential power. Historian Arthur Schlesinger called the result the "imperial presidency," and presidents Eisenhower, Kennedy, Johnson, and Nixon made use of its power at home and abroad, though the imperial presidency would come under attack during the Johnson and Nixon administrations.

In 1960, John F. Kennedy was elected president. In his inaugural address, Kennedy announced a series of domestic initiative and budget priorities that he labeled the "New Frontier." These included expansion of domestic social programs, investment in science and space exploration, and a "peace corps" that would send young American volunteers to third-world nations to promote literacy and technology.

Kennedy did have some legislative successes and used executive orders to implement portions of his program, such as the Peace Corps, that encountered congressional opposition. The New Frontier, however, ended prematurely with Kennedy's November 1963 assassination.

Kennedy was succeeded by Vice President Lyndon Johnson, who seemed determined to make his mark on history, and in particular, to outshine Kennedy. During six years in office, Johnson led Congress in enacting a number of "Great Society" programs including Medicare and Medicaid, and in declaring a "War on Poverty" by establishing an Office of Economic Opportunity to inject federal funds into local anti-poverty programs. The Office of Economic Opportunity no longer exists, but other War on Poverty programs, such as Head Start, an educational enrichment program for poor children, continue its efforts.

Johnson, more than any president since Lincoln, promoted laws banning discrimination against black Americans. Particularly important was the 1965 Voting Rights Act, which promoted the registration of black voters throughout the South, sent federal officials to the Southern states to monitor election practices, and prohibited a number of jurisdictions that had been found to have been guilty of racial discrimination from changing any of their election laws without first obtaining the approval of the federal government. As a result of this legislation, millions of new black voters were registered throughout the South.

Unfortunately for his place in history, President Johnson's record was marred by the Vietnam War. During his six years in office, Johnson sent several hundred thousand American troops to Indochina, where they waged a bloody and inconclusive war against Vietnamese forces led by Ho Chi Minh, the president of what was then called North Vietnam. The war was extremely divisive within the United States and led to several years of violent demonstrations that unsettled a nation already shaken by nearly a decade of violent clashes between civil rights advocates and their foes. Stung by opposition within the Democratic Party, Johnson, who had won in a landslide in 1964, withdrew from the 1968 race.

Johnson's withdrawal and splits in the Democratic camp gave the 1968 presidential election to former Republican vice president Richard M. Nixon. The year 1968 would be the last one in which the party conventions actually selected the presidential candidates. In 1968, the liberal wing of the Democratic Party asserted that the presidential nomination had been stolen by party bosses and given to Vice President Hubert Humphrey. Prior to the 1972 presidential contest, the Democrats introduced major changes to their rules, requiring most convention delegations to be chosen in primary elections. The Republicans followed suit after 1972. Consequently, today's party conventioners ratify choices made by primary voters rather than make decisions of their own. One implication of this change is that the dark horse candidates of yesteryear, chosen because they were deemed unambitious and so unlikely to make trouble, have given way to ambitious and aggressive presidential candidates who have been willing to devote years to a singleminded quest for power.

Once elected, Nixon moved to end the Vietnam War by reaching an agreement with the North Vietnamese that entailed withdrawing American forces and effectively allowing President Ho to unite Vietnam under his rule. Nixon's term included a number of foreign policy successes, such as the establishment of relations with China. But he is chiefly remembered for the Watergate affair that drove him from office. Nixon had become involved in a major conflict with Congress over his efforts to reorganize federal agencies in a way that would increase presidential power and diminish congressional influence over their operations.[60] Angered by leaks from within the administration and convinced that the Democrats were planning "dirty tricks" to win the 1972 election, Nixon authorized the clandestine employment of a group of former intelligence agents, "the plumbers squad," to conduct covert operations against his political foes. The plumbers were caught breaking into Democratic headquarters at Washington's Watergate Hotel and in the subsequent investigation, Nixon's ties to these illegal efforts were revealed. The president resigned to avoid certain impeachment.

In the aftermath of Nixon's resignation, Congress enacted several pieces of legislation designed to curb presidential power. These included the War Powers Resolution, which was intended to restore a measure of congressional control over presidents' use of military forces; the Case Act, designed to compel presidents to disclose all executive agreements; the Ethics in Government Act, designed to facilitate congressional inquiries into executive conduct; and the Budget and Impoundment Control Act, which was intended to enhance Congress's power of the purse. Congress seemed to have the upper hand during the presidencies of Nixon's successors, Gerald Ford and Jimmy Carter. With Ronald Reagan's election in 1980, however, the onward march of presidential power resumed.

Presidential Unilateralism

President Reagan was determined to restore the presidential power that he and his advisers saw as having been dangerously "fettered" by the events of the preceding several years.[61] He embarked on a systematic effort to undermine the War Powers Resolution, ignored the Case Act, and sought to use the Budget Act for his own purposes. Moreover, Reagan continued to make use of executive orders and executive agreements while introducing new unilateral instruments of presidential governance such as regulatory review and signing statements. His successors, George H. W. Bush, Bill Clinton, George W. Bush, and Barack Obama, have followed in his footsteps, using and sharpening the weapons developed by Reagan. In the wake of the 9/11 terror attacks, for example, President George W. Bush claimed new emergency powers, including the power to order surveillance of U.S. citizens without judicial approval. And in 2014, declaring that he had waited too long for Congress to act, President Obama issued executive orders designed to begin the reorganization of America's immigration policy. Unilateralism has become a hallmark of the contemporary presidency.

Thoughts on Presidential History: The Onward March of Executive Power

In reviewing the six eras of presidential history, we see that presidents were affected by a variety of factors, including political issues, sectional conflicts, changes in the national party system, and so forth. During each of these eras, however, some presidents were able not only strategically to accumulate the powers claimed by their predecessors, but also to add their own innovations so as to transform the words of the Constitution into the foundations of today's presidency. Let us review some of the major powers introduced during each presidential era.

The Federalist and Jeffersonian Period

The president is head of state and a symbol of the United States (Washington).

The executive has primacy in the realm of foreign relations (Washington).

The heads of executive departments work for the president and may form his cabinet (Washington).

The president may use force to ensure that the laws are faithfully executed (Washington).

The president can make recess appointments (Washington).

The president has executive privilege (Washington).

There are inherent powers to the presidency (Jefferson).

A legislative sleight of hand called the pocket veto is introduced (Madison).

The Jacksonian Period

The president has the power to appoint and dismiss federal employees on the basis of political loyalty (Jackson).

The president is the leader of the political party (Jackson).

The veto can be used as a political weapon (Jackson).

The executive has control over money and credit (Jackson).

The president is commander-in-chief (Polk).

The president has budgetary powers (Polk).

Civil War Era

The presidential oath of office is a source of power (Lincoln).

The president has war powers (Lincoln).

The president has special powers in cases of national emergency (Lincoln).

The executive has the power to print paper money and create new forms of debt (Lincoln).

Republican Era

The president garners increased control over executive nominations (Hayes).

The bully pulpit becomes a part of presidential politics (Theodore Roosevelt).

The executive takes the lead with legislation (Theodore Roosevelt).

The Bureau of the Budget is created (Harding).

Imperial Presidency

The nation is governed through executive orders and executive agreements (Roosevelt).

The executive branch expands in size and influence (Roosevelt).

The Executive Office of the President is created (Roosevelt).

The Bureau of the Budget moves into the Executive Office of the President (Roosevelt).

The executive expands its legislative leadership (Roosevelt).

The Defense Department, CIA, and National Security Council are founded (Truman).

Unilateral Presidency

Presidential war powers are reasserted (Reagan).

The president begins to implement signing statements (Reagan).

Regulatory review becomes a tool of the executive (Reagan).

The vesting clause supposedly creates a unitary executive (G. W. Bush).

Emergency powers are used for expanded domestic surveillance (G. W. Bush).

Again, the powers of successive presidents have waxed and waned, but over 225 years, the power of the presidency has increased inexorably.

Presidential Greatness

Before we take leave of this part of our history, let us consider the frequently debated question of the relative merits of America's presidents. While the presidency is an article of the Constitution, the president is a person. Some presidents are generally acknowledged to have achieved great things in office, while others were dismal failures. While our first president, George Washington, did much to create the United States of America, our fifteenth president, James Buchanan, seemed unable to decide on any course of action as the Union dissolved into bloodshed. Buchanan believed that states had no right to secede but also believed that the federal government had no right to prevent them from doing so. Hence the president was paralyzed and unable to play any role whatsoever in the quickly unfolding events.

Every year, new presidential rankings are published, some based on surveys of historians who are asked to judge the relative merits of America's forty-four chief executives and some based on the opinions of ordinary Americans. Interestingly, members of the general public tend to give higher rankings to more recent presidents, while historians tend to find great merit in the presidents of yesteryear. Thus ordinary Americans give high marks to Presidents Reagan, Clinton, and Kennedy while professional historians generally agree that Washington, Lincoln, and Franklin D. Roosevelt were America's greatest presidents. Both groups have their biases and the rankings should be approached with caution.[62] Many Americans can recall the names of only the most recent presidents while historians and political biographers like to demonstrate their erudition by focusing on obscure facts about Warren Harding and Millard Fillmore.

Political biographers, in particular, tend to function as the cleanup crew of American political history by polishing the images of presidents of modest abilities. Biographers have a stake in touting the virtues of their subjects; otherwise why spend so much time writing a book? One biographer told me she had determined that her subject was a lout, but thought it would not serve her interests to emphasize that fact. Hence political biographers tend to depict the leaders of the past as giants. Presidents and other politicians who were known to be inept, foolish, duplicitous, or just plain scoundrels when they lived can, with a bit of scholarly touch-up, be presented as wise, albeit misunderstood, leaders. Thus in the hands of the cleanup crew, the somnolent Calvin Coolidge became a man who believed that a national leader should not try to "go ahead of the majestic army of human thought and aspiration, blazing new and strange paths."[63] Harry S. Truman, considered by his political colleagues in Kansas City to be a nice fellow but "too light" even for the Senate, where he served before becoming Roosevelt's vice-presidential running mate in 1944, was recast as a tribune of the people.[64] John F. Kennedy, a man with more style than substance, has become an individual every bit as courageous as those profiled in his ghostwritten work *Profiles in Courage*—for which the future president dishonestly accepted a Pulitzer Prize.[65] And Lyndon Johnson, a rather odd and troubled person who nearly wrecked the country with his Vietnam War policies, has been recast as a somewhat flawed but nevertheless great man.[66]

The images of these relatively recent politicians will almost certainly receive more polishing over the years to come. Have not the political hacks of the nineteenth century already joined the pantheon of the demigods? No doubt when political biographies are written two centuries or so from now, the somewhat stained reputations of some of our current leaders will enjoy a renaissance.

Perhaps we expect too much from our presidents and are too quick to be disappointed. Presidents who leave office without a strong record of achievement are considered failures even if no disasters occurred during their terms in the White House. The presidential rankings are instructive. Some presidents have risen and fallen in the rankings over time as historians have assessed and reassessed their administrations. But despite movement and quibbles, the same group is predictably at the top. Washington, Lincoln, and FDR are always ranked as America's best presidents, followed by our other energetic chief executives: Jackson, Jefferson, and Theodore Roosevelt. Historians seem to prefer those presidents who accomplished great things under adverse circumstances and to dismiss those like, say Warren Harding, Millard Fillmore, or Calvin Coolidge, who simply did little harm.

But what accounts for the fact that some presidents have done great things and others have not? Is it simply a matter of good fortune? Shakespeare wrote that some are born great, some achieve greatness, and some have greatness thrust upon them. If we apply the Shakespearean formula to presidents, we might observe that some are helped and others hindered by the power of the institution they inherit. Some presidents possess aggressive and outsized personalities and are determined to achieve greatness, while others are less ambitious. As we shall see, this outcome is not entirely random. Some modes of selection tend to produce more ambitious presidents than others. Finally, some presidents arrive at propitious moments in what political scientist Stephen Skowronek calls "political time," while others who perhaps are equally capable find themselves sailing against the currents of history. Over the course of American history, political time has been an important factor in determining presidential success and failure. As Skowronek indicates, some presidents have been elected as the champions and leaders of new political movements with mandates to transform America's political regime. Presidents who come to office in what Skowronek calls "reconstructive" elections—Jefferson, Jackson, Lincoln, Franklin Roosevelt, perhaps Ronald Reagan, and certainly George Washington as America's first president—have opportunities for dramatic political action. Greatness is thrust upon them. Their successors, however, have fewer opportunities, encounter more political resistance and, as an established political regime nears its end, may be hampered by being left with few allies and little public support, watching events they cannot control. Examples include John Quincy Adams, James Buchanan, Herbert Hoover, and Jimmy Carter.[67]

The opportunity presented, or not presented, by political time is not the whole story, however. The dynamism of the person and the power of the institution also matter. In recent years, the power of the presidency as an institution has increased markedly and the presidential selection system, as we shall see, has produced rather aggressive and ambitious presidents. Combine a powerful institution capable of exercising unilateral power with ambitious presidents determined to make their marks—to be America's "deciders" as George W. Bush once said—and we have leaders capable of standing outside political time and governing according to their own lights with less political support than presidents once required. More than their predecessors, today's presidents are, for better or worse, born great or at least capable of achieving greatness even if greatness is not thrust upon them. Presidential power alone can now sometimes stop the clock of political time.

The Growth of Presidential Power

P residential power has grown over the decades as presidents have undertaken strategic innovations and accumulated administrative and political
power in very calculated ways. To be sure, not every president has been
an innovator. While some have been quite energetic, others have been more
hesitant to use, much less expand, the powers of the presidency. Yet every era
of presidential history is associated with strategic innovations that have enhanced
the power of the White House.

Jefferson and the Louisiana Purchase. The constitutionality of President Jefferson's 1803 decree ordering the purchase of more than 500 million acres of land

Copyrighted 1904 by Ford P. Kaiser.   ALFRED RUSSELL

BORN TO COMMAND.

OF VETO MEMORY.

HAD I BEEN CONSULTED.

KING ANDREW THE FIRST.

from France was thought by many of Jefferson's contemporaries to be a violation of the Constitution, which gave no such power to the president. Jefferson in fact regarded himself as a strict constructionist, opposed to those who would claim powers not specifically granted by the Constitution. He did, however, strongly desire the acquisition of Louisiana and persuaded himself and some others that he was merely exercising the president's constitutional treaty power.

Jackson and the veto power. In the early decades of the republic, presidents seldom vetoed congressional legislation: it was thought that the presidential veto could only be used to defend the executive branch against legislative encroachments and not in cases where the president and Congress simply disagreed. In 1832, President Andrew Jackson ignored this idea when he vetoed the rechartering of the Bank of the United States, a piece of legislation with which he vehemently disagreed.

Lincoln and the war power. At the outbreak of the Civil War, President Lincoln issued a series of executive orders enlarging the army, instituting censorship of

the mail, and suspending the writ of habeas corpus in the border states. Lincoln justified his actions by what he called the presidential war power, which he claimed was implied by the president's role as commander-in-chief, his oath of office, and his duty to ensure that the nation's laws were faithfully executed.

FDR and the expansion of the executive branch. During his time in office, Franklin Delano Roosevelt was able, through legislation and executive orders, to bring about the creation of some one hundred new federal offices, which seemed to span the alphabet from the Agricultural Adjustment Administration (AAA) through the Works Progress Administration (WPA). These offices and agencies employed hundreds of thousands of workers and gave the federal government, the president in particular, enormous new administrative power and capabilities.

The imperial president. The 1947 National Security Act greatly strengthened the foundations of presidential power in the international realm. The act created

the Department of Defense, the CIA, and the National Security Council. These institutions enhanced presidential control over the use of military forces, presidential access to intelligence, and the president's ability to plan foreign and security policies.

The unilateral president. Today presidents often make use of executive orders, regulatory review, and signing statements to introduce (or ignore) policies unilaterally, sometimes circumventing the intent of Congress. In 2005, President Bush signed a defense appropriation bill that included a provision authored by Senator John McCain outlawing coercive forms of interrogation. In his signing statement, however, Bush indicated that the bill would be enforced in a manner consistent with the "constitutional authority of the president" and the president's duty to protect the American people from further terrorist attacks. In other words, the president indicated that he would or would not enforce the legislation as he saw fit.

FOUR

Presidential Elections

In This Chapter

Every four years, Americans elect a president. The process is long and complicated and has many stages. The first and longest stage is determining who among America's 325 million people might have a reasonable chance of mounting a successful presidential bid. As we shall see, some employ stepping stones, others rely on coattails, while still others are fortunate enough to start at the top in their quest for the White House. Members of this small group of individuals do battle in the primaries and in the general election, raising money, organizing national campaigns, engaging in televised debates, and struggling to master the intricacies of the Electoral College system. Eventually a winner is chosen, but for students of presidential elections how a winner is chosen is only the first question. The second question is what impact the process has on the character and identity of those elected.

The Independent Election

The president of the United States, unlike a prime minister, is independently elected in a process that takes place every four years, coincident with but not dependent on the results of the House and Senate races taking place at the same time. When elected, the president receives a four-year term of office. Under the provisions of the

Twenty-Second Amendment, ratified in 1951, no one may be elected to the presidency more than twice. A vice president who has succeeded to the presidency and served a portion of the previous president's term is also eligible to be reelected twice if that fractional term of service was less than two years. Those who serve more than two years, however, are only eligible for one additional term in office. Under these rules, Lyndon Johnson, for example, was eligible for reelection in 1968. After John F. Kennedy was assassinated in November 1963, Vice President Johnson succeeded to the presidency and served the remaining thirteen months of Kennedy's term. Johnson was then elected president in his own right in 1964 but dropped out of the 1968 presidential race after, as we shall see, an embarrassing showing in the New Hampshire primary.

The president's independent election is both a problem and a source of presidential power. It is a problem because the outcomes of congressional races often force presidents to work with their partisan and ideological opponents, and the result may be legislative gridlock. Independent election, though, can also be a source of presidential power because presidents are not dependent on the Congress for their selection or continuation in office and may use their powers to govern according to their own inclinations. In this chapter we shall examine how America's presidents are chosen, as well as the implications and significance of both the process and the choice.

Eligibility

Article II of the Constitution declares that the president must be a natural-born citizen at least thirty-five years of age. Generally the term "natural-born" is understood to mean anyone born either on U.S. soil, or on foreign soil to parents who are U.S. citizens. Individuals who are not citizens or are "naturalized" citizens—that is, who were granted citizenship after their birth—are not eligible to serve as president or vice president. This simple requirement occasionally leads to questions and controversies. Some Republicans challenged President Barack Obama's eligibility for office, noting that his father was a British subject rather than a U.S. citizen. Obama was born on American soil, however, a fact that rendered his father's citizenship irrelevant. Some Democrats, too, challenged the eligibility of 2008 Republican presidential nominee John McCain, pointing out that he had been born in Panama. But McCain's parents were both U.S. citizens. Indeed, McCain's father, a naval officer, commanded a submarine berthed at the U.S. naval base in Panama that was in turn commanded by McCain's grandfather. In 2008, the U.S. Senate adopted a nonbinding resolution recognizing McCain's eligibility to serve as president.

The eligibility of two Republican presidential candidates in 2016, Florida senator Marco Rubio and Louisiana governor Bobby Jindal, is sometimes questioned. Both were born to parents who were not U.S. citizens, but both are nevertheless clearly eligible to serve as president by virtue of having been born on U.S. soil. The most interesting current case is that of Texas Republican senator Ted Cruz, who is also running for president. Cruz was born in Canada to a U.S. citizen mother and Cuban national father. Had both of Cruz's parents been U.S. citizens, his eligibility would be clear, but given his foreign birth with only one U.S. citizen parent, Cruz's eligibility is a matter of some controversy.

Even if Cruz is disqualified from running, however, some 130 million Americans are technically eligible to serve as president. How do we choose one person from among these tens of millions?

Choosing a President

America holds its presidential elections every four years, but the selection of presidents is in fact a continuous process that only culminates (and in many ways, starts anew) on election day. In fact, politically ambitious Americans who might aspire to the presidency face a three-part selection process. The first part, which may take years, is achieving a sufficient level of political prominence to be considered by political notables and activists as a potential presidential nominee; the second part is securing the Democratic or Republican nomination; and the third part is actually mounting a national campaign and winning a presidential election. Each part of this process has its own rules and complexities, so let us consider each in turn.

Becoming Politically Prominent

One quaint bit of American mythology is the idea that any child can aspire to become president of the United States. In reality, only a tiny number of Americans can ever be serious contenders for the presidency or any other major political office.[1] Generally those who make themselves plausible candidates for high political office follow one of three paths, or in many instances, a combination. I call these paths stepping stones, starting at the top, and coattails.

A "Stepping Stones" Approach

The first path, as its name implies, entails following a series of political steps from lower, less important offices to higher, more important ones. A politician may begin as a local officeholder, move on to statewide office, and from there seek some significant national position. For example, America's eighth president, Martin Van Buren, began his political career in 1813 as a New York State senator, then served as New York's attorney general, then as a U.S. senator from New York, then as secretary of state, then as U.S. minister to England, then as Andrew Jackson's vice president, all before being elected to the presidency in 1836.

America's tenth president, John Tyler, also stepped on many stones but then slipped and fell. Tyler began in 1811 as a member of the Virginia House of Delegates, then was elected to the U.S. House of Representatives, then to the Virginia Senate. Next he became governor of Virginia, then was elected to the U.S. Senate, and in 1840, was elected vice president on the Harrison ticket. General Harrison was known as "Old Tippecanoe," and the 1840 Whig campaign slogan was "Tippecanoe and Tyler too." When the old general died soon after the inauguration, Tyler succeeded to the presidency (his new political nickname was "His Accidency"). So far, so good. Unfortunately, however, after Virginia seceded from the Union in 1861, Tyler stepped on one more stone, slipped, and permanently fell out of favor. He chose to run for a seat in the Confederate Congress and won, becoming the only U.S. president to serve as an official in the government of a hostile power.

In more recent years, Franklin D. Roosevelt was a president who rose to power through a series of stepping stones. FDR began his political career in 1910, shortly after graduating from law school, when he ran for the New York State Senate. In 1912, he was appointed assistant secretary of the Navy, and in 1920, Roosevelt became the party's vice presidential candidate behind presidential candidate James M. Cox. After recuperating from polio, Roosevelt was elected governor of New York in 1928 and became the Democratic standard bearer in 1932. During the twenty-two years between his initial state senate campaign and his eventual presidential race, Roosevelt held or campaigned for four offices and performed numerous political services, including working for Woodrow Wilson at the 1912 Democratic Convention and placing Al Smith's name into nomination in 1928 with what became known as his famous "Happy Warrior" speech.[2]

Politicians following the stepping stones strategy generally make use of whatever office they currently hold to enhance their public visibility and to expand their range of political contacts and allies. They regard any given office mainly as a platform from which to launch a campaign for higher office. For example, Barack Obama seemed to view his seat in the Illinois legislature mainly as a launching pad for a U.S. Senate campaign and his Senate seat primarily as a good place from which to mount a 2008 presidential campaign. Yet Obama's thin legislative record appeared not to discourage millions of Americans from viewing the attractive and well-spoken senator as an excellent presidential prospect.

The premier modern example of a successful stepping stones strategy is the career of the late John F. Kennedy. In 1955, then-congressman Gerald Ford asked his former House colleague, newly elected senator Jack Kennedy, how things were going in the Senate. Kennedy replied that he had "bigger plans."[3] In particular, Kennedy was campaigning for the 1956 Democratic vice presidential nomination, which he saw as a logical step from the Senate to his ultimate goal, the presidency. To further those plans, Kennedy ignored most of his legislative duties and used his Senate seat to enhance his national visibility. Many congressional leaders regarded Kennedy as an ineffectual lightweight. While other senators worked on legislation, Kennedy logged more than a hundred thousand miles in his plane, flying around the country to give speeches and polish his image.[4] Democratic House Speaker Sam Rayburn often referred to his former House colleague as "that little pissant Kennedy." Kennedy's speaking abilities and literary efforts, however, gradually increased his public stature.

Kennedy's 1955 book *Profiles in Courage,* which presented the stories of senators who had taken principled stands that ran counter to their political interests, was designed to transform the inexperienced senator into a recognized author, intellectual, statesman, and figure of national prominence. After the book's publication, Kennedy's father, Joseph P. Kennedy, was determined to secure a coveted Pulitzer Prize for his son. The elder Kennedy used his connections to convince the Pulitzer Prize committee to disregard its professional judges' recommendations and award John the Pulitzer Prize for biography. That the book was largely written by historian and Kennedy aide Theodore Sorensen became an issue when columnist Drew Pearson went on Mike Wallace's ABC television program to allege that *Profiles* was ghostwritten and that Kennedy's acceptance of the Pulitzer constituted a form of fraud.[5] In response to threats from Joseph Kennedy and his attorneys, ABC dropped the allegations.[6] Wallace, however, called the network's action a "craven" buckling to pressure from the Kennedys.[7]

Theodore Sorenson was a gifted writer and during the Kennedy presidency the book became a staple of high school civics classes. Students are seldom told that President John F. Kennedy was not the real author. Since Kennedy's literary triumph, many other ambitious politicians have also produced books, most often ghostwritten. For example, Hillary Rodham Clinton's 2014 book *Hard Choices,* published to promote her 2016 presidential aspirations, was reportedly written by a team consisting of Dan Schwerin, Ethan Gelber, and Ted Widmer.[8] Ben Carson, a 2016 GOP presidential hopeful, liked to boast that his well-known book *Gifted Hands* outsold Hillary Rodham Clinton's book—and that he had actually written it himself.

Roosevelt and Kennedy were both members of wealthy and prominent families and made frequent use of their money and connections to move from stepping stone to stepping stone. Not all successful candidates, though, have such fortunate backgrounds. Presidents Richard Nixon, Ronald Reagan, Bill Clinton, and Barack Obama, to cite recent examples, were impecunious but nevertheless managed to rise through the political ranks. The candidacies of all four of these men, and most individuals of similar backgrounds, were, however, supported by wealthy and powerful interests whose resources more than made up for the candidates' own lack of wealth and family connections. Richard Nixon's first congressional campaign was funded and launched by prominent California banker Herman Perry. Ronald Reagan's 1966 gubernatorial bid was promoted by a group of wealthy California business executives. Bill Clinton's initial political efforts, beginning with an unsuccessful 1974 House race followed by a successful 1976 campaign for the post of Arkansas attorney general, were backed by poultry billionaire Don Tyson.[9] Barack Obama's meteoric rise from community organizer to president was supported by Chicago billionaires Penny Pritzker and Alan Solow. Candidates may be propelled by personal ambition, but the path from stepping stone to stepping stone is smoothed by money and power. The more important the office, the greater the quantity of money and power needed to reach it.

Starting at the Top

Not every individual who aspires to high political office finds it necessary to negotiate a series of stepping stones to reach his or her objective. Some are able to jumpstart their political careers by capitalizing on the visibility, power, or prominence they achieved in some other endeavor. Such fortunate individuals can skip one or more of the usual steps and compete successfully for high political office without ever having held a lower office.[10]

One asset that often allows ambitious individuals to enter the political arena at a high level is fame. Since the founding of the Republic, for example, many famous generals have sought the presidency and six have actually won election. George Washington, Andrew Jackson, William Henry Harrison, Zachary Taylor, Ulysses S. Grant, and Dwight D. Eisenhower were the successful generals. Well-known generals who made unsuccessful bids for the White House include one-time NATO commander Wesley Clark and General Douglas MacArthur, who hoped that his command of American forces in the Pacific during World War II would induce a grateful public to reward him with the nation's highest office. Washington, Jackson, and Harrison, to be sure, had held other significant elective and appointive posts before their elevation to the presidency. Washington had been a member of the Continental Congress and served as chair of the Constitutional Convention. Jackson and Harrison had served in both the U.S. House of Representatives and the U.S. Senate, and both had been territorial governors.

The other three victorious generals, however, had no prior political experience whatsoever. Indeed, Taylor had never even been registered to vote and was not eligible to cast a ballot in support of his own election. Yet these generals' fame and popularity were powerful political assets, allowing them to ignore lesser political offices and set their sights directly on the White House. Taylor and Grant were convinced to seek the presidency by party leaders hoping to make use of the generals' popular standing. Eisenhower, for his part, needed no prodding. Though "Ike" always denied harboring political ambitions, his biographer, Stephen Ambrose, notes that from the end of World War II, Eisenhower's actions "could not have been better calculated to put him into the White House. His numerous public appearances, his association with the rich and powerful, and the content of his speeches all increased the demand that he become a candidate. No professional politician could have plotted as successful a campaign for the general as the one he directed himself."[11]

Martial prowess, of course, is not the only form of fame that has allowed politically inexperienced individuals to start at or near the top of the American political hierarchy. John Glenn's renown as an astronaut, for example, helped him win a seat in the U.S. Senate. In recent years, a number of well-known entertainers and professional athletes have sought to parlay their celebrity status into political careers. Ronald Reagan was a film actor and television host who had held no public office before running for governor of California. Similarly, California governor Arnold Schwarzenegger used the enormous fame he was able to garner as the star of blockbuster movies like *The Terminator* to launch his political career. (Since he had not been born in the United States, he could not entertain presidential ambitions.) Other entertainers who have successfully run for office in recent years include former California senator George Murphy; former Tennessee senator Fred Dalton Thompson, who briefly considered running for the presidency; and a former California representative, the late Sonny Bono.

The phenomenon of entertainers seeking political office is not limited to the United States. For instance, a well-known Indian actress, Jayalinthaa, used her fame to secure selection as governor of Tamil Nadu province. What may be a uniquely American phenomenon, though, is the number of professional athletes who run for office. To cite just a few recent examples, former pro football quarterback Jack

Kemp was elected to Congress and became the GOP's vice presidential candidate in 1996. NBA star Bill Bradley served as a senator from New Jersey and was a candidate for the Democratic presidential nomination. Hall of Fame pitcher Jim Bunning was elected to the U.S. Senate. University of Nebraska football coach Tom Osborne was elected to the U.S. House of Representatives, as were football stars Steve Largent and J. C. Watts. And former WWF professional wrestler Jesse Ventura, who was arguably both an athlete and an entertainer, was elected governor of Minnesota and was interested in the presidency.

Some candidates who start at the top are rich rather than famous. Wealth is always a useful political asset. Nearly half the members of the U.S. Senate and perhaps a third of the members of the U.S. House of Representatives are millionaires and hardly any of the others are poor. In recent years, the political importance of personal wealth has increased. To begin with, because of increased media expenditures, the cost of political campaigns has risen sharply over the past decade. For example, the average expenditure by a winning U.S. Senate candidate in 2012 was more than $10 million, while the average cost of winning a seat in the U.S. House of Representatives that same year was $1.6 million. Candidates able to at least partially finance their own campaigns are strongly preferred by party leaders and activists. Two notable recent examples of candidates with no political background who spent enormous amounts of money to win elections are John Corzine and Michael Bloomberg. Corzine, the multimillionaire former head of Goldman Sachs, one of the nation's most important investment banks, spent more than $60 million of his own money to win election to the U.S. Senate from New Jersey in 2000. Bloomberg, one of America's wealthiest men, spent more than $268 million of his personal fortune to win three New York mayoral contests. Wealthy entrepreneur Mitt Romney reportedly spent $45 million of his own money in his futile 2012 effort to wrest the White House from Barack Obama. And in 2015, entrepreneur Donald Trump indicated that he would make use of his personal fortune, estimated in the billions of dollars, to mount a 2016 presidential bid. Like fame, wealth is not a guarantee of victory. In the most expensive losing effort in modern political history, business entrepreneur Meg Whitman spent $140 million of her own money in an unsuccessful 2010 California gubernatorial campaign. Whitman won barely 40 percent of the vote.

A final sort of candidate who can sometimes start at the top is the leader of a new political movement or party. During the course of American political history, some new parties and political movements have been led by established politicians who failed to achieve their goals through conventional electoral processes. Abraham Lincoln, formerly a Whig, led the new Republican Party to victory in 1860. Former president Teddy Roosevelt formed his "Bull Moose" Party when it became clear that he would not be able to secure the Republican nomination in 1912. When he failed to win the Democratic nomination for president, in 1968 Alabama governor George Wallace formed the American Independent Party, which won more than 13 percent of the popular vote that year.

Other political movements have served as vehicles for political neophytes with a cause. For instance, James B. Weaver, Greenback Party candidate for president in 1880 and Populist standard bearer in 1892, was a champion of the eight-hour workday, the progressive income tax, and a host of other causes. Weaver had served briefly in the U.S. House of Representatives but could never have aspired to higher office through conventional party politics. A more recent example of an individual who used a political movement to start at the top is H. Ross Perot. In 1992, billionaire entrepreneur Perot, an individual who had held no prior political office, launched a presidential bid at the head of his own political movement, which he called "United We Stand America."

Perot spoke fervently on behalf of a number of causes, including a balanced federal budget, the introduction of electronic town hall meetings that would allow citizens a larger voice on policy matters, and defeat of the then-pending North American Free Trade Agreement (NAFTA), which Perot said would produce a "giant sucking sound" as American jobs rushed to Mexico. Perot spent $57 million of his own money on the campaign and won 18.9 percent of the national presidential vote. Perot's votes came mainly from individuals who might have supported the reelection of President George H. W. Bush, so the chief effect of Perot's candidacy was to smooth the way for Bill Clinton's election. Perot sought to revive his movement, renamed the Reform Party, for the 1996 presidential campaign, but his share of the vote dropped sharply. By 2000 the Reform Party had all but disappeared and Perot himself seemed to have lost interest in politics.

Riding a Sponsor's Coattails

Some individuals who reach high office do so by clinging firmly to the coattails of a powerful and successful sponsor. The sponsor may be a friend, political ally, or even a parent or spouse. Vice President Dick Cheney rose in politics by clinging tenaciously to the coattails of one of Washington's most powerful politician-bureaucrats, Defense Secretary Donald Rumsfeld.[12] Several U.S. presidents had been the political protégés of former presidents or other important politicians. James Monroe, for example, was handpicked by his predecessor, James Madison. Similarly, Martin Van Buren was Andrew Jackson's chief political lieutenant and was chosen by Old Hickory to succeed him in 1840. Lyndon Johnson had been the protégé of powerful House Speaker Sam Rayburn, who helped secure Johnson's spot on the Kennedy ticket in 1960. Most vice presidents have not been the protégés of the presidents with whom they served. Many, however, have hoped that their years of service in the president's shadow would pave the way for their own presidential nominations. And indeed, five of the past twelve presidents—Truman, Johnson, Nixon, Ford, and the first Bush—had previously been vice president. During the same period, two other former vice presidents—Walter Mondale and Al Gore—were defeated in presidential bids.

Family ties can also serve as powerful coattails. George W. Bush's political career was hardly hurt by his relationship to his father, George H. W. Bush, whose own career had been promoted by his father, Senator Prescott Bush. Former Florida governor Jeb Bush is a 2016 presidential hopeful, keeping the family tradition. The Kennedy family has been an important force in American politics for more than a half century. Ambassador Joseph P. Kennedy played an instrumental role in John Kennedy's rise to political prominence. John Kennedy, in turn, appointed his brother Robert to the post of U.S. attorney general, a position for which he had no obvious qualifications beyond his family ties. Robert was subsequently elected as a U.S. senator from New York and, had he not been murdered, might have won the presidency in 1968. Another of John Kennedy's brothers, Edward, served as a senator from Massachusetts, and a variety of Kennedy cousins have been elected to office on the strength of their family connection. Another example of the importance of familial coattails is the case of Hillary Rodham Clinton, wife of former president Bill Clinton. The former First Lady's prominence and contacts helped her win election to the U.S. Senate from New York, which she used as a stepping stone to a 2008 presidential bid. When she failed to secure the Democratic nomination, Clinton received the consolation prize of an appointment as Obama's secretary of state, which she has since used as a stepping stone for the 2016 presidential race.

Coattailers can turn out to possess considerable political talent of their own. Robert Kennedy, for instance, was a very astute politician whose rhetoric could sometimes inspire even the most cynical pundits. Other coattailers, though, seem lost when they are left to their own devices. One of the most inept campaigners in recent American history was Robert Kennedy's daughter Kathleen Kennedy Townsend, who suffered an abysmal loss to Republican Robert Ehrlich in the 2002 Maryland gubernatorial race, even though Maryland is a state where registered Republicans are about as rare as Eskimos. Like fame and fortune, coattails are not a guarantee of success.

Party Nominations: Many Are Culled, but Only Two Are Chosen

Of the some 130 million Americans nominally eligible to serve as president, only a handful achieve sufficient political prominence to become serious contenders for the Democratic and Republican presidential nominations. In principle, well-heeled and popular candidates might create their own political parties or run as an independent candidate. During every presidential race quite a number of new parties appear on the ballot in one or more states. In 2012 these included the Green Party, the Libertarian Party, the Constitution Party, the Socialist Party, and a host of others.

In practice, though, the third-party route is better suited to those wishing to make an ideological or personal statement than to those who hope to win an election. Take, for example, Donald Trump's threat to mount a third-party bid in 2016 if he failed to secure the GOP nomination. Trump's threat was intended to attract publicity and show his disdain for ordinary party politicians. An actual third-party bid seemed unlikely to place the flamboyant tycoon in the White House. Though Americans may sometimes sneer at their political parties, they rely on the Democratic or Republican label as a kind of certificate of authenticity for politicians, rightly or wrongly believing that the major party nominee has undergone peer review and vetting by his or her party colleagues. Many voters, moreover, are reluctant to throw away their vote by supporting a third-party candidate. The general belief that such candidates cannot win thus becomes a self-fulfilling prophecy. Finally, the Democratic and Republican labels give candidates guaranteed access to a place on the ballot. Even in national presidential contests, the ballot is regulated by the states, and state election laws often make it difficult for new parties to be listed on the ballot, usually by requiring the collection of thousands of petition signatures. In 2012, for example, most new parties were only listed on the ballots of a handful of states and several, such as the Modern Whig Party and the Boston Tea Party, were not able to achieve a spot on any ballot. It is worth remembering that only one American third party has ever captured the White House. In 1860, against the backdrop of the collapse of the Union, the new Republican Party secured the election of its nominee, Abraham Lincoln.

Prominent politicians with presidential ambitions thus almost invariably seek the Democratic or Republican presidential nomination. At one time, party leaders decided whom to nominate. Today, as we shall see, each state has created an array of primary elections and nominating caucuses that determine the votes of its delegates at the Democratic and Republican national conventions. The national conventions, which once were decisionmaking bodies, are now, insofar as candidate selection is concerned, mostly just pep rallies that ratify the results and trumpet the party's choice. The last time a party nominee was actually chosen by the convention was 1956, when the Democratic national convention selected Illinois governor Adlai Stevenson, a dark horse, on the third ballot.[13]

The party primaries and caucuses begin in January of each election year. But two, three, or even four years before these formal contests begin, well-known contenders seek to translate their political prominence into money and support. Political prominence means possessing sufficient visibility to attract the attention of the media, other politicians, and political activists; the support of volunteers; and, perhaps most critically, the interest of potential financial backers. A successful presidential candidacy requires spending hundreds of millions of dollars, including substantial amounts in the early stage of the race. Candidates who do not do well in the early primaries are likely to lose their donors and activists to the victors of those primaries.

As we shall see, some money for presidential campaigns is provided by small donors but most is contributed or directly spent by well-heeled backers. Generally, wealthy contributors do not wish to waste their money supporting politicians with no chance of success. Hence beginning about three years before the next national election, "prominent" politicians are invited to meet with potential backers. For the 2016 election, then, beginning in about 2013, prominent Republicans considering a race for the presidency began to meet with donors and to line up backers. Eventually, seventeen Republicans entered the race. These included current or former senators Ted Cruz, Jim Gilmore, Lindsey Graham, Rand Paul, Marco Rubio, and Rick Santorum, along with current or former governors Jeb Bush, Chris Christie, Mike Huckabee, Bobby Jindal, John Kasich, George Pataki, Rick Perry, and Scott Walker. The Republican field also included three individuals who had never held office but had achieved prominence in other areas. These were Johns Hopkins neurosurgeon Ben Carson, businesswoman Carly Fiorina, and real estate tycoon Donald Trump. Of the seventeen, Trump was the only one wealthy enough not to need financial backers. As the billionaire pointed out in the 2015 Republican debates, many of the other candidates usually depended on him for money.

On the Democratic side, Hillary Rodham Clinton, who had at various times been First Lady, a U.S. senator from New York, and secretary of state, overshadowed all other potential candidates. Most party activists and leading Democratic donors were eager to support a Clinton candidacy. Three other Democrats also announced their candidacies, though none were seen as serious rivals to Clinton. The most prominent of these was Vermont senator Bernie Sanders, a self-described democratic socialist. Sanders became the champion of the Democratic Party's liberal wing and could expect to garner support from these voters in Democratic primaries. Former Rhode Island governor (and former Republican) Lincoln Chafee, former Virginia senator Jim Webb, and former Maryland governor Martin O'Malley also declared their candidacies. In early 2014, O'Malley, a relative unknown, began visiting some of the early primary and caucus states to meet with local Democrats just in case a race became possible. O'Malley and some of the Republican hopefuls calculated that even a losing effort might increase their prominence sufficiently to be added to the ticket as a vice presidential nominee or to enhance their chances for the presidential nomination at some later date. Waiting in the wings on the Democratic side, Vice President Joe Biden considered announcing his candidacy for the presidency if Clinton's campaign faltered.

When a sitting president is planning to run for a second term—and so is truly starting at the top—other prominent politicians of the president's own party usually do not bother to mount their own bids. If events have made the president vulnerable, however, challengers may still emerge. In 1968, for example, Lyndon Johnson's disastrous Vietnam War policies led Senator Eugene McCarthy, and then Senator Robert Kennedy, to challenge Johnson for the Democratic nomination.

Organizing a Campaign

If candidates' informal visits, consultations, requests for pledges of support, and so on seem promising, the next steps are the formation of an "exploratory committee," which must be registered with the Federal Election Commission, and "staffing up," that is, retaining consultants, attorneys, media experts, and data analysts to organize primary campaigns and, for the two eventual nominees, general election campaigns.

In the nineteenth century, campaigns were planned and directed by party bosses, who employed the services of hundreds of thousands of patronage workers whose government jobs depended on their willingness to engage in political activity on the party's behalf. Contemporary political campaigns are led by political consultants who make use of activist volunteers, paid campaign workers, lawyers, and sophisticated communications technologies. Most consultants began their careers in advertising or marketing, though a small number actually have degrees in campaigning from such programs as George Washington University's Graduate School of Political Management. Consultants generally develop the campaign's overall strategy, frame issues, commission focus groups and opinion polls, recruit campaign workers, raise money, maintain relationships with the mass media, plan direct mail campaigns, and seek damaging information about the opposition: in short, they undertake all the activities needed for political success.

Some consultants have become political celebrities. Barack Obama's senior political adviser was Chicago media consultant David Axelrod. In the consulting world, Axelrod had worked for a number of African American politicians before signing on with Obama, and had become known for his ability to help black candidates overcome the suspicions of white voters. He is widely credited with developing the theme of "change" that helped carry Obama to the presidency in 2008. Since that election, he has become a very visible media commentator and has advised candidates in England and Italy. Another important Obama consultant, Jim Messina, is hardly known outside Washington political circles, but is famous among insiders: he crafted Obama's successful social media campaign and is credited with giving Obama a million Twitter followers. George Bush's chief strategist, Karl Rove, was a powerful figure in Washington for eight years and now heads a "super PAC" (for "political action committee," explained later) aimed at promoting the interests of Republican candidates and conservative causes.

Some consultants are associated with particular politicians. For example, political strategist Mark Penn has mainly worked for Bill and Hillary Clinton. Others have a larger group of clients. In 2008, for instance, David Axelrod found himself in the awkward position of having to decide which of his former clients to support. Axelrod had previously worked for presidential aspirants Barack Obama, Hillary Clinton, John Edwards, and Chris Dodd, as well as many other leading Democrats. Some consultants work only for Democrats and some only for Republicans, but a small number of firms boast partners from both parties and sell their services to the highest bidder. "This is not a political club, it's a business," said one well-known Washington political strategist.

Campaign Workers

With the disappearance of patronage employees, campaigns turned to volunteers and paid employees to work as staffers and fundraisers. Some candidates are better able to attract grassroots volunteers than others. Candidates supported by the religious right, organized labor, or senior citizens' groups like the AARP can rely on their allies to provide foot soldiers for the political trenches. Candidates who are not so fortunate often must rely on paid fundraisers and campaign workers. Prior to the 1980s, Democratic candidates were far better able than their Republican rivals to recruit volunteers. Organized labor provided the Democrats with workers, as did environmental and peace groups. During the 1980s, the balance of infantry power shifted. During the Reagan era the GOP forged an alliance with the

Christian right and mobilized regiments of Christian soldiers for political warfare. Democrats countered by increasing their efforts to recruit volunteers from feminist, gay rights, and student groups.

Lawyers

No contemporary campaign would be complete without the services of a phalanx of legal specialists. Fifty years ago, the courts seldom became involved in electoral processes and few attorneys knew much about election law. Today, election law is a major legal specialty and some large Washington law firms have created election law groups to deal with an ever-growing case load. Three types of electoral issues often become the foci of legal battles. One is the drawing of legislative district boundaries. Electoral engineering, or gerrymandering, is a longstanding electoral practice in which the party in power fortifies its position by drawing congressional and state legislative district boundaries that will reduce the number of districts its opponents might hope to win. This can be accomplished either by concentrating opposition voters into as few districts as possible or by scattering them across so many districts that they will not constitute a majority anywhere. Traditionally the courts would not review districting plans, calling them strictly political matters. Since the 1960s, though, the federal and state courts have heard many cases alleging that district borders were intentionally redrawn in order to discriminate against African American and other minority voters. And more recently, a number of cases have been generated by the GOP's very aggressive redistricting efforts in Texas, Pennsylvania, and other states. Traditionally states were redistricted once every ten years after the results of the new decennial census revealed changes in population patterns. But Republicans, led by former House majority leader Tom DeLay, have sought more frequent redistricting in states they controlled, so as to take fuller advantage of their power. Democrats, of course, have challenged these efforts, leading to protracted legal battles including a number of Supreme Court cases. In 2015, for example, the Supreme Court ruled against an effort by the Arizona state legislature to overturn a state voter referendum that created an independent commission to draw congressional district boundaries. Legislators had wanted to retain this power for themselves.

Gerrymandering can affect presidential outcomes because it is the state legislatures that control primary election rules and ballot laws. For example, Republican candidates are likely to benefit if a state legislature adopts strict voter registration laws and requires voters to show photo identification at the polling place. The

Democrats depend more on immigrant voters and others who may not possess the necessarily identification or understand the legal requirements for voting, so they generally benefit when a state legislature eases registration rules.

A second set of legal issues has been spawned by the campaign finance rules that Congress enacted in 1974, 1976, and 2002; by regulations developed by the Federal Election Commission; and by the Supreme Court's 2010 and 2014 campaign finance decisions. Finance laws govern many aspects of campaign fundraising and spending. They are often complex and confusing and even when they are reasonably clear, many politicians conceive campaign finance rules to be a challenge to be surmounted rather than a blueprint to be followed. In recent years, a number of prominent politicians or members of their staffs have been charged with campaign spending violations.

For example, in 2005, Hillary Clinton's Senate campaign treasurer paid a large fine for filing false reports with the Federal Election Commission. The reports hid the identity of one of Clinton's largest contributors, a convicted felon who was hiding in Brazil to escape a stock fraud indictment. In 2007, the Clinton campaign was forced to return $850,000 to about 260 donors whose funds had been solicited by Norman Hsu, who had engaged in illegal practices. In a similar vein, Republican House leader Tom DeLay was indicted in 2005 for campaign law violations in Texas. Following the indictment, DeLay was forced to relinquish his post as majority leader. Many election law violations involve efforts by individuals to circumvent contribution limits by persuading others to make contributions that they then reimburse. This was the basis for the 2014 guilty plea of prominent conservative pundit Dinesh D'Souza.[14] Other common election law violations involve commingling primary and general election campaign contributions. Candidates must keep the two separate, but campaign treasurers have been known to pay debts accrued by one account with surplus funds from the other. In April 2014, a Democratic primary rival charged former Democratic congressional candidate Marjorie Margolies, the mother of Chelsea Clinton's husband, with improperly commingling funds. The charge was denied by the Margolies campaign.[15]

A third set of campaign-related legal issues concerns the accuracy of vote counts. Since the 2000 Florida presidential election, which was decided in the courts after a statewide recount, every serious campaign has placed lawyers on retainer ready to challenge an unfavorable election outcome if the election was close, or to defend against such a challenge. Hundreds of attorneys were waiting in the wings, ready to attack or defend close outcomes in every state during the 2004, 2008, and 2012 national presidential elections as well as the off-year congressional races. Issues that can be raised to attack an election result include the eligibility of voters, the validity of ballots, the accuracy of counting procedures, the propriety of the instructions given to voters, and whether or not illegal incentives might have been offered to voters. For example, Republicans argued that the state's counting methods were flawed when they mounted a court challenge to the outcome of Washington's 2004 gubernatorial race. Eventually the count was upheld, but not before an expensive court battle. More recently, Starbucks ran afoul of election laws by offering to award a free cup of coffee to every patron who could show they had voted in the 2008 presidential race. Paying people to vote is unlawful, so the coffee chain was told that it could not lawfully keep its free-coffee promise.[16]

Several years ago, President Bush's attorney, Benjamin L. Ginsberg, called the 2000 Florida election struggle the "greatest peacetime mobilization of lawyers in American history." If so, the lawyers have never been fully demobilized.

The Primaries

Recruiting consultants, workers, and lawyers creates a *campaign*. The presidential campaign, say the Obama campaign or the Clinton campaign, is a political force organized to win a presidential election. The campaign's first objective is securing the nomination through a series of primary battles.

The Democratic and Republican nominations are formally awarded to the candidates who receive a majority of the delegate votes at the national party conventions. In 2016, Democratic rules called for 4,483 official delegates to attend the Democratic national convention, and the Republicans devised a formula resulting in the selection of 2,480 delegates. Delegate votes, in turn, are awarded to candidates mainly on the basis of their success in the state delegate-selection contests, which in 2016 were scheduled during a five-month period between February and June. Each party uses a somewhat different formula for determining how to apportion delegates among the states and the formulae are quite complex. In essence, however, both parties assign each state, U.S. territory, and the District of Columbia a number of delegates based on the jurisdiction's electoral votes and its support for the party during the several previous elections. Thus, large states receive more delegates, and large and loyal states even more delegates. The District of Columbia has three electoral votes, but the territories, such as Guam and the U.S. Virgin Islands, have none, so the party formula is adjusted to take those differences into account. States are also rewarded with extra delegates if they agree to schedule their primaries later in the season. This incentive is designed to discourage states from all scheduling primaries during the same few weeks.

In every state, territory, and the District of Columbia, the Democratic and

Republican parties hold nominating contests to apportion delegate support among the candidates for the nomination. Each jurisdiction's rules are different and, within each, the Democratic and Republican parties may employ different rules since the actual procedures are governed by a mix of state and party regulations (Box 3). The result is 112 distinct contests. And to make matters nearly impossible for students to follow, during any given year several states are certain to change their rules. There are, however, some general patterns and variations.

In the political world, rules generally reflect and are designed to reinforce the existing balance of power.[17] This principle certainly holds in the case of the rules governing presidential nominations. To begin with, in both political parties, proportional representation in primary elections reflects the fact that each party is a coalition of disparate groups and forces that insist on being included in the presidential selection process. The Democrats adopted proportional representation and caucuses prior to the 1972 elections as a result of a recommendation by the McGovern-Fraser Commission to make the party more open and inclusive to the civil rights, antiwar, and other so-called new politics groups of the period. Not coincidentally, the new rules helped lead to the presidential nomination of Senator George McGovern, the commission's chair. The Republican Party of the 1970s was relatively homogeneous and satisfied with winner-take-all rules, but during the 1980s the GOP added new groups such as white Southerners and Evangelicals to its coalition and changed its rules to accommodate its newfound diversity.

As to the nominating caucuses used in such states as Iowa and Nevada, these are something of a relic of the 1970s. The McGovern-Fraser Commission viewed local caucuses as an expression of direct democracy, allowing ordinary citizens to select the presidential nominees. Liberal Democrats thought the caucuses would be dominated by young, idealistic, and progressive Americans who would nominate presidential candidates who shared their views. Initially this prediction was correct, but as the idealists of the 1970s lost their political fervor, the caucuses lost their luster and survived only where some local interest found them useful. Thus in Nevada, for example, the organization of the caucuses enhances the political power of Las Vegas and its suburbs, while in Iowa the Democratic caucuses are dominated by organized labor and the Republican caucuses by Evangelicals. These forces favor keeping the caucuses. The events of the 1970s also played a role in the general preference for binding presidential primaries. Before 1972, many primary contests were nonbinding "beauty contests," with state party leaders controlling the actual delegate votes. The reformers of the 1970s outlawed these beauty contests and there has been little interest in restoring them.

The choice of open versus closed primaries is a matter of party strength. Party

Box 3. Delegate Selection Rules

1. *Primaries vs. caucuses.* Most convention delegates are chosen in primaries, though in some states, including Colorado, Iowa, and Nevada, delegates are chosen in Republican or Democratic caucuses. (The Democrats hold caucuses in a total of ten states; the Republicans, eleven.) The caucus is a meeting of registered party voters within each precinct or other designated area. Caucus rules vary, but in general, attendees group by candidate preference, hold an open discussion, and select from among themselves delegates to county conventions, where delegates are chosen to the state convention and, from there, to the national party convention. The caucus mode of nomination was popular in the 1970s but has gradually fallen out of favor since.

2. *Open versus closed primaries.* An open primary is one in which any registered voter may take part. Participation in a closed primary is restricted to individuals who have registered with that party. Some states hold semi-closed primaries in which registered independents may participate along with registered party members.

3. *Winner-take-all versus proportional representation.* The Democratic Party requires all states to elect delegates using some form of proportional representation, which will allocate delegates in proportion to each candidate's popular vote in the primaries or caucuses. The Republican Party allows states to use proportional representation or winner-take-all, in which the candidate receiving a plurality of the popular vote in the state's primary or convention receives all the state's national convention delegates. Despite the option, most state Republican parties have opted for proportional representation.

4. *Binding versus nonbinding primaries.* In most instances, the primaries determine how a state delegation's votes will be cast at the national party convention. Though the actual delegates may be appointed by the state party central committee, their votes are bound by the primary results. In a handful of states, including Iowa, the actual delegates are chosen via the primaries and caucuses, but they are not bound to support any particular candidate at the national convention. Most delegates have run as supporters of a particular candidate but are free to vote for another. This has occasionally become an issue in Iowa, where individuals supporting one candidate at the local caucus have reportedly switched to another at the county convention. In 2008, the Iowa Obama campaign charged the Clinton campaign with "poaching" delegates.[a]

continued

Box 3 *Continued*

> 5. *Superdelegates.* In addition to the elected delegates, each party has established a procedure to permit the appointment of a number of party notables as unpledged convention delegates. On the Democratic side several hundred elected officials and party notables are chosen by party officials, while on the Republican side each state's party chair and two national party committee members are entitled to attend the national convention as unpledged delegates. About 15 percent of the Democratic Convention delegates are unpledged superdelegates, while fewer than 5 percent of Republican delegates fall into that category.

[a] "Witness Account: Hillary Poaching Pledged Delegates (Updated)," *Daily Kos,* Mar. 10, 2008, available online at http://www.dailykos.com/story/2008/03/11/471945/-Witness-Account-Hillary-Poaching-Pledged-Delegates-Updated# (accessed July 20, 2015).

leaders are generally opposed to the involvement in party affairs of outsiders—that is, members of the other party and independents. Where parties are strong, this reluctance is likely to be reflected in the law. In states where parties are weak, by contrast, party leaders generally lack the political clout to insist on closed primaries.

Finally, there is the matter of the superdelegates. The leaders of both parties have been concerned that elected delegates could choose a presidential candidate who is too liberal (Democratic) or too conservative (Republican) to have much chance of winning the general election. This is a realistic threat, since voter turnout in primaries tends to be low and those who do vote tend to be more partisan and more ideologically committed than members of the general electorate. The task of the superdelegates is to nudge the convention to a more moderate position. Besides, the job of superdelegate gives party leaders a chance to attend their own party's convention.

For candidates and their campaigns, the primary rules and schedule are daunting. Candidates are faced with fifty separate contests in fifty states during a five-month period between February and June. In the larger states, candidates might rely mainly on media advertising and other campaign techniques often used for nationwide contests. In the smaller states, though, candidates are expected to make numerous personal appearances, getting to know the voters as though they were running for a local office. In 2008, Hillary Clinton visited Iowa on more than a dozen occasions prior to the caucuses, but many local politicians attributed her lackluster performance to her failure to visit the state as frequently as did political newcomer Barack Obama. Clinton became so frustrated after just a few visits to Iowa that she reportedly exclaimed, "I can't believe this! How many times am I going to have to meet these same people. This is so stupid. So unfair." Obama, by contrast, held 174 campaign events in Iowa and practically lived in the state between February 2007 and January 2008.[18]

In recent years, each party has sponsored televised debates among its own candidates beginning several months prior to the primaries. These debates, which are sometimes nationally televised, are occasionally rancorous. In the August 2015 Republican debate, New Jersey governor Chris Christie accused Kentucky senator Rand Paul of "blowing smoke" in Senate subcommittee hearings on intelligence and surveillance. Generally, however, candidates reserve their main attacks for the other party. These events should be seen as party showcases more than competitive debates. Each party is simply giving its main candidates a televised platform from which to speak to voters. The goal is to stimulate the interest of voters and to demonstrate to all the party's factions that their views are represented among the party's leaders. In 2012, for instance, some twenty Republican debates were held, featuring candidates who represented moderate conservatives (Mitt Romney and Newt Gingrich), the GOP's right wing (Michele Bachmann), Evangelicals (Rick Santorum), Libertarians (Ron Paul), Southerners (Rick Perry), and black conservatives (Herman Cain). The candidates seemed to get along well in these events, which were designed to demonstrate to Republican voters that all the GOP's factions needed to cooperate in order to win against the Democrats.

In 2016, so many candidates sought the Republican nomination that the organizers of the first debate, nationally televised on August 6, 2015, declared that only the top ten candidates, as determined by the polls, would be invited to the prime-time event. The remaining seven candidates participated in a forum held earlier in the day. The prime-time debate was generally dominated by Donald Trump, whose predictable bluster and swagger provided much of the evening's entertainment as well as most of the grist for the mills of the post-debate analysts. Some of the lesser-known candidates, including Senator Marco Rubio, Governor John Kasich, and Carly Fiorina, all of whom participated in the afternoon debate, impressed political analysts and benefited from the national exposure they received.

Though designed as party showcases, the candidate debates can affect electoral outcomes. In 2007–2008, then-senator Barack Obama's excellent television performance helped him overcome doubts among whites about the electability of a black president. In 2011, Governor Rick Perry raised questions about his own abilities during a Michigan debate when he was unable to recall the name of one of the three federal agencies that he claimed he would eliminate if elected. Mitt Romney mischievously tried to help Perry remember by suggesting several agencies as candidates for elimination, but Romney's help only added to Perry's discomfiture. And in 2015, many analysts thought Jeb Bush had hurt his presidential chances with a lackluster debate performance.

Currently, the nominating process is "front loaded." That is, most primaries are held in the first several weeks of the year, with eleven scheduled for the same Tuesday in March, sometimes known as Super Tuesday. Candidates who do well in the early primaries and caucuses—with Iowa and New Hampshire being the first—derive a considerable advantage, particularly if they run "better than expected." "Expected" is a media concept based on reporters' and pollsters' predictions of candidate strength. A candidate who does better than expected is often declared by the media to have "momentum" (George H. W. Bush called it Big Mo), and is better able to attract money and support for the next race. A candidate who does not fare as well as "expected" may have difficulty retaining supporters and funding.

Thus in 2004, John Kerry's first-place finish in the Iowa caucuses essentially ended the candidacies of Representative Dick Gephardt and Governor John Dean, who had both been expected to defeat Kerry. And in 2008, Barack Obama's candidacy was given an enormous boost by his success in the Iowa caucuses where he defeated the frontrunner and expected winner, Hillary Clinton.

Gaining momentum by doing better than expected raises the bar and may mean a stumble later if the subsequent performances do not match the new "expected" level. Thus in 2000 Senator John McCain, who had unexpectedly won the New Hampshire primary over Governor George W. Bush, lost his newfound momentum when he was defeated by Bush in the South Carolina primary.

This effort to manage expectations, of course, empowers pundits and reporters and increases popular attention to media coverage of campaigns. Moreover, this media management of expectations can affect the outcome of the primaries. In one famous instance, a primary candidate was routed by putative expectations even as he outpolled his actual opponent by a comfortable margin. This candidate was none other than President Lyndon Johnson who defeated his challenger, Senator Eugene McCarthy, in the 1968 New Hampshire Democratic primary by a 48–42 percent margin. Though McCarthy's was the only name on the actual ballot and Johnson's votes were write-ins produced by a last-minute campaign, the national media declared that Johnson had done much worse than expected against his little-known challenger. Apparently Johnson himself was convinced that he had been defeated, because the president soon thereafter declared that he would no longer be a candidate for reelection. Johnson had been driven from the race by a media creation: the "expected" performance of a candidate in an election.

No More Dark Horses

The current presidential primary process seems to give inordinate power to the primary voters and caucus attendees of two small and unrepresentative states. Candidates who do not perform well in Iowa and New Hampshire, or fail to at least meet expectations there, are not likely to win the nomination or even to continue the race. Many changes in the process have been discussed, including national party primaries and regional primaries, but for now, both parties seem content with the current arrangement. Serious pressure for change will eventually arise when some major political leader or important political force finds the existing system to be a stumbling block to its ambitions. For example, the Jacksonians denounced the party caucus and invented the convention system to promote their political fortunes, and antiwar and pro–civil rights forces denounced the convention system and demanded caucuses and primaries when it seemed that these would advance their interests. It serves little purpose to assess the abstract merits of various reform possibilities because we know that someday a major shift in the political climate will bring about the introduction of some new set of procedures.[19]

It is worth observing, however, that the current nomination procedures have ended the day of the dark horse, when the unknown was chosen by party leaders on the basis of inoffensiveness. Party leaders are not in a position to determine the outcome and only aggressive and ambitious politicians—not timorous dark horses—need bother to do battle for the nomination. We shall return to this point later in the chapter. For now, let us observe that among the handful of prominent politicians contesting the Democratic and Republican nominations, only two survive the primary contests. The others return to their senatorial, congressional, or gubernatorial posts; leave the political stage; or begin planning another presidential effort four or eight years hence.

The General Election

For two candidates and their campaigns, the effort now shifts to the general election. The first step in the general election campaign is the national party convention, where the Democratic and Republican candidates are formally awarded their parties' nominations and select vice presidential running mates. During the convention, too, competing party factions may battle over the party platform. The platform is seldom read by voters and is not intended mainly to stir public enthusiasm. Instead, the platform should be thought of as a contract among the party's various factions, one that sets forth their conditions for supporting the candidate in the general election. Platform battles are most likely to occur when new groups demand platform planks that are anathematic to established party leaders. During the 1950s and 1960s, for instance, liberal Democrats outraged Southern conservatives by demanding that the party platform denounce segregation. Currently, competing Republican factions are battling over the party platform's statements on social issues. Religious conservatives in the Republican camp say they cannot support the party unless the platform denounces same-sex marriage and abortion. But moderate conservatives, including gay Republicans, say they cannot support the party if the platform does include such planks.

As for the vice presidential nomination, by general agreement the presidential nominee is free to select a running mate. Often individuals are chosen to "balance the ticket." That is, the presidential campaign will select a running mate from a region, ethnic group, gender, ideological perspective, or combination of characteristics not represented by the presidential candidate, in hopes of broadening the candidate's electoral appeal or ability to govern. Thus, for example, in 2000 George W. Bush, an individual with little Washington experience (except as a president's son) chose Dick Cheney, an experienced longtime Washington insider, as his running mate. In 2008, John McCain, a politically moderate man, chose Sarah Palin, a politically conservative woman, as his running mate. And that same year, Barack Obama, a black, liberal, Protestant, Harvard Law School graduate, chose as his running mate Joe Biden, a white, moderate, Catholic who had attended neither Harvard nor Yale. Obama had also been criticized for lacking foreign policy experience, and Biden, chairman of the Senate Foreign Relations Committee, added foreign policy credibility to the ticket.

In many instances, the most important resources a running mate can bring to the ticket are the electoral votes of a key state.[20] John Kennedy chose Lyndon Johnson as his running mate in 1960 because Johnson promised to carry Texas, whose electoral votes Kennedy almost certainly needed to win the election. Also never far from consideration when candidates choose their running mates is the question of succession. Eight vice presidents have succeeded to the presidency because of the president's death and a ninth, Gerald Ford, succeeded when President Nixon was forced to resign. Campaigns will usually seek to choose running mates who will impress voters as capable of handling the duties of the presidency. In 2000, George W. Bush explained his decision to name Dick Cheney as his running mate, saying, "I didn't pick Dick Cheney because of Wyoming's three electoral votes . . . I picked him because he is without a doubt fully capable of being President of the United States."[21] In 2012, John McCain was widely criticized for selecting the inexperienced Sarah Palin as a running mate because many doubted that she was prepared to serve as president. Yet despite the media attention devoted to the announcement of vice presidential running mates, these individuals generally have only a marginal effect on the outcome of the race.[22]

The Electoral College

One of the enduring peculiarities of the American presidential election process is the Electoral College system. In the early history of popular voting, nations often made use of indirect elections. Voters would choose the members of some intermediate body that would, in turn, fill the relevant position. The last vestige of indirect elections in America is the Electoral College, the group of electors that formally selects the president and vice president of the United States.

Under the Constitution, each state is entitled to a number of electoral votes equal to its number of senators and representatives. In addition, the Twenty-Third Amendment, ratified in 1961, stipulated that the District of Columbia would be entitled to as many electors as the least populous state, currently Wyoming, which has three electors. Thus the Electoral College presently consists of 538 members. Of these, fifty-five are appointed by the most populous state, California, while the seven least populous states and the District of Columbia are each entitled to three electors (Table 3).

Article II of the Constitution stipulates that a majority of electoral votes is needed to elect the president and vice president. For its part, the Twelfth Amendment stipulates that the electors shall vote separately for the two offices. Thus 270 electoral votes are needed to win each office. Electoral votes are cast on the Monday after the second Wednesday in December, after the November presidential election. The electors never assemble as a body, but instead meet in their respective state capitals, cast votes, and submit the results to Washington, where the votes are formally counted in a joint session of Congress. The Speaker of the House declares the results. If no presidential candidate receives a majority, as happened in 1801 and 1825, the Twelfth Amendment declares that the House of Representatives will select the president from among the top three recipients of electoral votes. In such an eventuality, the House will vote by state with each state delegation casting one vote. If no vice presidential candidate receives a majority, as occurred in 1837, the choice is left to the U.S. Senate, which must choose from among the top two recipients of electoral votes, with each state casting one vote in that body. If the House of Rep-

Table 3. Electoral Vote Allocation by State, 2012–2020

State	Electors	State	Electors	State	Electors
Alabama	9	Kentucky	8	North Dakota	3
Alaska	3	Louisiana	8	Ohio	18
Arizona	11	Maine	4	Oklahoma	7
Arkansas	6	Maryland	10	Oregon	7
California	55	Massachusetts	11	Pennsylvania	20
Colorado	9	Michigan	16	Rhode Island	4
Connecticut	7	Minnesota	10	South Carolina	9
Delaware	3	Mississippi	6	South Dakota	3
District of Columbia	3	Missouri	10	Tennessee	11
Florida	29	Montana	3	Texas	38
Georgia	16	Nebraska	5	Utah	6
Hawaii	4	Nevada	6	Vermont	3
Idaho	4	New Hampshire	4	Virginia	13
Illinois	20	New Jersey	14	Washington	12
Indiana	11	New Mexico	5	West Virginia	5
Iowa	6	New York	29	Wisconsin	10
Kansas	6	North Carolina	15	Wyoming	3

Source: National Archives and Records Administration, available online at http://www.archives.gov/federal-register/electoral-college/allocation.html (accessed July 23, 2015).

resentatives is unable to choose a president in time for the official inauguration at noon on January 20, the Twentieth Amendment, ratified in 1933, specifies that the vice president–elect will serve as acting president until the House selects a president. If a vice president has not yet been chosen, the House speaker will serve as acting president until the House selects a president or the Senate chooses a vice president.

Originally, the electors were appointed by the state legislatures. By the end of the nineteenth century, however, all the states had mandated popular election of presidential electors. Within each state, party leaders appoint slates of electors, usually consisting of party officials and notables, equal to the state's number of electoral votes. The members of each slate pledge that, if elected, they will cast their votes for the party's presidential and vice presidential candidates. This process is usually invisible to voters. When, for example, a Republican voter in say, Texas, casts a presidential vote for the candidate named on the ballot, she or he is actually voting to select a slate of Republican electors pledged to support the GOP's presidential and vice presidential candidates. Under the winner-take-all rules used by forty-eight states and the District of Columbia, the slate of electors receiving a plurality of the statewide vote is elected and goes on to cast all its electoral votes for its own party's candidates. Complicating matters for students, Maine and Nebraska employ proportional representation in their allocation of electoral votes.

The framers of the Constitution viewed the Electoral College as an actual decisionmaking body that would reduce the uncertain impact of popular participation and increase the likelihood that only well-qualified individuals would be elected to the presidency. The electors, said Alexander Hamilton, would be individuals possessing "information and discernment."[23] Today the electors are not decisionmakers and the chief effect of the Electoral College is to shape the character and terrain of presidential races. Because of the Electoral College system, candidates must focus on winning a majority in the Electoral College rather than a national popular plurality. As a result, the presidential race is a series of fifty-one (counting the District of Columbia) separate contests for electoral votes. Moreover, since today the Northeast and West Coast states are reliably Democratic while many in the South and Southwest are dependably Republican, presidential elections are fought in a small number of "battleground" states that possess divided electorates and many electoral votes.

The battlegrounds usually include Pennsylvania, Ohio, Virginia, North Carolina, and Florida, with Minnesota, Wisconsin, and Iowa serving as lesser theaters of political warfare. Presidential campaigns pay scant attention to the remaining states, where candidates believe they are certain to win or highly likely to lose. This state of affairs means that some voters have more political clout than others. In particular, the Electoral College system reduces the political weight of America's urban and suburban centers of population, where candidates would concentrate if the presidential contest was a single nationwide election.

Three other problems are associated with the Electoral College system. First and most obvious is that it is mathematically possible for the candidate who secures the most popular votes to nevertheless lose the electoral vote. This has occurred on three occasions, most recently in 2000, when Al Gore won the popular election by some 500,000 votes but George W. Bush won in the Electoral College by four votes. Second is the problem of so-called faithless electors, that is, electors who fail to vote for the candidate whom they had pledged to support. In 1976, for example, the Republicans carried the state of Washington but one Republican elector refused to vote for Gerald Ford. Most states have enacted laws binding the electors, but these laws may be inconsistent with the Constitution's mandate. Finally, the emergence of a regionally based third party strong enough to carry several states would make it difficult for the Electoral College to produce majorities: consequently the House would effectively become the institution that chose presidents. This possibility was illustrated in 1968 when George Wallace's American Independent Party carried five Southern states with forty-six electoral votes. Just a handful of vote shifts in the other states would have sent the election into the House.

Since the Electoral College no longer serves its original purpose and the system adds a measure of uncertainty to presidential elections, why not abolish the Electoral College? Proposals to amend the Constitution and turn to direct national elections have frequently been introduced but seldom make much headway. The current system serves some significant political interests. Politicians from small states and battleground states believe that their influence would be reduced with the elimination of the Electoral College. Moreover, both of the two largest parties are reluctant to surrender their secure state bastions for the more uncertain and more costly environment of a nationwide election. Someday the Electoral College system will fail to produce a decision, lead to a political crisis, and be abolished. Until then, America will retain this quaint political relic.

Campaign Methods and Technologies

As we observed earlier, nineteenth-century presidential campaigns relied on the hundreds of thousands of workers, usually patronage employees, that each party could field like infantry armies on election day. These infantry armies still count in the primaries and in the general election. Many thousands of volunteers ring doorbells, hand out leaflets, and place signs in yards and posters on walls. In modern campaigns, however, a new array of weapons—perhaps we should label them "air and sea powers"—have joined, if not entirely supplanted, the infantry armies of the past.

Polling

Virtually all campaigns make extensive use of opinion polling. Campaigns collect data to assess the electorate's needs, hopes, and fears. Polls, conducted throughout the campaign, provide the basic information used to craft strategies, select issues, and check voter responses to candidate appeals. The theses, issues, and messages that candidates present are generally based on polls and small face-to-face sessions with voters called "focus groups." Pollsters have become important campaign consultants and often continue to work with presidents long after the election to help secure the enactment of legislation.

Broadcast Media

Extensive use of the broadcast media, television in particular, is the hallmark of the modern presidential campaign. Candidates endeavor to secure as much positive news and feature coverage as possible. This type of coverage is called *free media* because candidates do not pay for air time. Candidates can secure free media coverage by participating in newsworthy events. Sitting public officials, especially incumbent presidents, can call for new legislation, sponsor hearings, undertake inspection tours of fires and floods, and meet with foreign dignitaries to capture the attention of the television cameras. Challengers can announce new proposals or organize publicity stunts. In 2014, for example, Governor Rick Perry, who ran again for president in the 2016 race, picked a fight with President Obama over immigration and then held a well-publicized meeting with the president to discuss their differences. The contents of the meeting were not disclosed, but many photos were released for the evening news.

In addition to seeking free media coverage, primary and general election candidates, parties, and political advocacy groups collectively spend tens of millions of dollars to purchase television ads, most running for sixty, thirty, or even fifteen seconds. These so-called *spot ads* allow a candidate's message to be delivered to an audience before indifferent or hostile viewers can reach their dials to tune them out. In 2012, one fifteen-second anti-Romney ad showed an unhappy woman with a message claiming that Romney would outlaw abortion even in cases of rape and incest, while an anti-Obama ad declared that the president's health care program was a declaration of war against religion. Examples of extremely effective spot ads include George H. W. Bush's 1988 "Willie Horton" ad, which implied that Bush's opponent, Michael Dukakis, coddled criminals, and Lyndon Johnson's 1964 "daisy girl" ad, which suggested that Johnson's opponent, Barry Goldwater, would lead the United States into nuclear war. Ads generally do not present coherent arguments or evidence. They are designed to establish candidate name recognition, to create a favorable image of the candidate and a negative image of the opponent, to link the candidate with desirable groups in the community, and to signal the candidate's stand on salient issues. Generally negative ads that excoriate the opponent have a greater impact on voters than do positive ads that praise the candidate.[24] Voters profess to dislike negative ad campaigns, but they are more likely to remember negative images and be influenced by them, particularly when the targets of negative ads issue denials and defend themselves—and by doing so extend free coverage of the accusation.

The Internet

Since the 1990s, the Internet has become an increasingly important tool in political campaigns. In 2008 and 2012, both Democratic and Republican candidates developed an Internet strategy for fundraising, mobilizing support, and getting out the vote. The Obama campaign used the Internet to create events such as walkathons, community meet-ups, and fundraisers throughout the country. In 2012, both Obama and Romney developed social networking sites that allowed supporters to post information about themselves and chat with one another to build enthusiasm for their candidate. Through the Internet, messages transmitted by the campaign to its supporters are often retransmitted to ever-growing groups of Facebook friends, Twitter followers, and others in a process known as *crowdsourcing*. Crowdsourcing amplifies the power of political messages, bringing them to millions of individuals in a short period of time via friends and acquaintances, whose messages are considered more trustworthy than those that come directly from campaigns. Both political parties have also found that blogs are quite effective instruments for attacking the opposition. Often voters are unaware of the partisan leanings of particular blogs and are inclined to take at face value information that amounts to little more than partisan propaganda. Often, too, accounts presented by bloggers are picked up by the mainstream press and widely disseminated. Because of its growing importance, the two parties have been fighting vigorously for control of the "blogosphere."

In recent years, each party has also developed a database containing hundreds of pieces of information on every registered voter. The information is acquired from census reports; credit, banking, and store-purchase records; warranty cards; magazine subscription lists; memberships; travel records; answers to opinion-poll questions; and a myriad of other sources. Using this information and a number of sophisticated computer programs, consultants can infer a good deal about the attitudes, preferences, concerns, and likely political behavior of each voter. These inferences, in turn, allow campaigns to develop individualized advertising and fundraising messages that can be sent to voters via phone calls, mail, social media, and email—a practice called "microtargeting." This tactic not only reaches the right voters with the right messages, but also increases the efficiency of fundraising.

Mobilizing Core Constituencies

Each political party claims the allegiance of several core constituencies. For the Democrats, African Americans, Jews, and labor union members represent a solid bedrock of support whose levels of turnout are among the keys to victory and defeat. For the Republicans, rural small-town white voters, white Southerners, and Evangelical Protestants are solid constituencies. The electorate, however, is a dynamic rather than a constant force.

Over the past several decades, the American electorate has been undergoing a major transformation. As recently as the 1960s, the electorate was overwhelmingly white, while today Hispanic and African American voters account for nearly one-third of the voting-age population. Hispanics are the most rapidly growing group in America and are being courted by both parties. Soon a presidential ticket without a Hispanic presence will be at a decided disadvantage.

Campaign Themes and Tactics

In principle, democratic elections permit voters to make any choices they please. In practice, voters' choices are constrained by the options offered to them. The late V. O. Key once called electoral choices "echoes in an echo chamber."[25] The options offered to voters include not only the candidates themselves, but also the policy choices or other alternatives that these candidates have decided to present to the electorate. If the competing candidates mainly discuss foreign policy, voters would be hard-pressed to base their decisions on their own concerns about Social Security. And similarly, if candidates devote their energies to attacking one another's personal integrity, voters are likely to try to choose the more honest of the two.

Media accounts of battles over political issues seem to assume that these issues arise more or less spontaneously from popular needs and citizen demands. Yet the truth is that most political issues are developed by intellectuals, political consultants, academics, and staffers in Washington's partisan "think tanks," like the Brookings Institution, Heritage Foundation, American Enterprise Institute, Progressive Policy Institute, Cato Institute, and dozens of others. Indeed, "issues consulting" is a major Washington industry, with hundreds of experienced and would-be issue entrepreneurs peddling their ideas to public officials, political candidates, and interest groups. Sometimes these entrepreneurs create issues from whole cloth. That is, they offer a politician a potentially useful issue in which the public has exhibited no prior interest. For example, prior to the 1992 presidential election, consultants persuaded then senator and presidential hopeful Al Gore that he might enhance his standing among socially conservative Southern white voters by taking on the issue of sexually suggestive lyrics in rock music. This was not exactly an issue that had produced widespread popular concern. Indeed, the adults who might have been troubled by the problem could not understand the lyrics, while the teenagers who understood the lyrics probably liked them. Nevertheless, consultants convinced Gore that, once raised, the issue would attract popular notice and serve his political interests. Accordingly, Gore's wife, Tipper, made a series of speeches demanding that the music industry clean up its act and helped organize an effort to force the record industry to label albums containing offensive lyrics.

Rather than invent issues based on problems in which the public has exhibited no prior interest, issue entrepreneurs usually seek to identify potentially useful issues from among the many matters with which the public already has some concern. For example, issue specialists did not invent segregation or abortion. Instead, they found a vocabulary through which to frame and dramatize these matters, painting as moral evils needing to be rectified situations that some might have simply accepted as facts of life. An example is Martin Luther King's strategy of leading groups of peaceful marchers into Southern towns like Selma, Alabama, where they were sure to be attacked by the police.[26] By so doing, King demonstrated to millions of Northern whites watching on television that what they had previously ignored or downplayed as peculiar Southern "folkways" (to use President Eisenhower's characterization of the Jim Crow system) was a state of affairs fundamentally inconsistent with American values. King took a fact and created an issue.

Candidates can propose a seemingly infinite variety of choices to the electorate. In recent years, campaigns have focused on war and peace, public morality, candidates' personal integrity, social issues, the economy, and a host of other concerns. But while the possibilities may seem endless, there are essentially only four major themes that can be presented to the electorate individually or in some combination. These are *salutary* issues, *solidary* issues, *moral* issues, and *character* issues. Salutary issues are those focused on general social or economic benefits and solutions to national problems. Solidary issues involve questions of political, social, cultural, or ethnic identity and are designed to remind designated blocs of voters of their political loyalties and allegiances, or to signal to them that people like themselves have a stake in a particular political outcome. Moral issues address matters of personal and public rectitude. And issues concerning a candidate's character are designed to undermine the enthusiasm of the opposing side's normal supporters and to discourage them from coming to the polls by showing that their candidate lacks the moral stature required to be president. This is the chief purpose of "opposition research" or dirt digging: securing information that will discredit a candidate in the minds of all but his or her most ardent supporters.

Salutary Issues

The most important salutary issues are those relating to the nation's economy and to the nation's ability to stave off foreign attack and terrorism. Generally each political party will endeavor to blame the other for economic weakness and take credit for economic strength. Voters are inclined to blame the party in power for economic problems and credit it for a rosy economic outlook. The Consumer Confidence Index, a measure of Americans' level of optimism about the economy, has proven to be a reasonably reliable forecaster of presidential results, with a low score usually indicating that the party in power will be punished at the polls. The 2008 Democratic campaign focused on the economic fears of millions of voters and sought to blame the Republicans for having failed to anticipate or resolve the 2007 financial crisis and ensuing recession. Democrats also capitalized on the fact that American troops were still engaged in Iraq and Afghanistan with no particular goal or end in sight.

In 2012, with the nation's economy on the mend, the Obama campaign emphasized the president's legislative achievements—health care legislation, financial services regulation, economic stimulus legislation—as well as the withdrawal of most American forces from Iraq and Afghanistan. The Romney campaign seemed unable to develop a major issue of its own and focused on questioning the value of Obama's accomplishments.

In 2016, with the GOP on the attack against the incumbent Democrats, the major issues of the campaign included economic growth, foreign policy, and immigration. On the issue of growth, Republicans asserted that Democratic regulatory and trade policies cost Americans' jobs and hurt American business. Democrats replied that they stood for economic growth that would benefit all Americans, not just a wealthy few. On foreign policy Republicans charged that the Obama administration had risked the nation's security by signing an agreement with Iran that would only advance that nation's nuclear weapons program. Democrats defended the agreement as promoting stability in the Middle East and as the only alternative to war. On immigration, Republicans charged that the Obama administration had failed to deal with illegal immigration and border security and promised to do a better job of safeguarding the nation's borders.

Solidary Appeals

Voters' most important political identity is partisanship. In any given electoral contest, the voting choices of millions of Americans are barely affected by the issues and events of that particular campaign. These voters' choices are dictated, instead, by a long-term commitment to one or the other political party. While many partisans are sufficiently open-minded to switch their votes in response to campaign appeals, tens of millions of Americans identify so strongly with either the Democratic or Republican Party that they evaluate issues, candidates, and sometimes even potential marital partners through the lenses of their partisanship.[27] Through microtargeting, both presidential campaigns aim strong partisan appeals at their fellow partisans to remind them to come to the polls and support their party's candidate.

Partisanship is not unrelated to issues and identities. Typically, particular groups develop ties to one or another party on the basis of its stands on important issues or its efforts to cultivate the group's allegiance during some period of economic or political crisis.[28] In the 1930s, for example, Franklin D. Roosevelt and the Democrats used labor and social programs to win the support of unionized workers and members of urban ethnic groups whose prior partisan allegiances had been shaken by the Great Depression. Many African Americans and Jews, in particular, were drawn to the Democratic Party because it provided them with political opportunities that they had been previously denied. Once established though, partisan identification, like a brand preference in the marketplace, can become "sticky" and take on a life of its own. For many Americans, partisan loyalty is a lifelong commitment that they even seek to pass along to their children.

An individual's partisan identification can change. Most white Southerners were staunch Democrats until the 1960s. But the Democratic Party's support for the civil rights movement weakened its democratic allegiances and opened the way for the GOP to create Republican majorities in most states of the old Confederacy. Nevertheless, partisan ties can be quite resilient once established. Most Jewish citizens, for example, continue loyally to support the Democrats even though, as a generally wealthy group, Jews tend to benefit from Republican economic policies. One prominent Jewish GOP activist told me that the first time he voted for a Republican candidate he felt as though he had abandoned his religious faith and converted to Christianity.

Campaigns also appeal to voters on the basis of their social or political identities. Politicians typically make such appeals by emphasizing that they share or at least sympathize with some salient trait of the voters whose support they are seeking. Such traits include gender, ethnicity, race, religion, and various other physical or social characteristics that voters deem to be important. One well-known example of identity politics is the ethnically balanced ticket. In the nineteenth century, urban political machines typically enrolled voters from a variety of immigrant groups. To maintain voter loyalty, machine leaders always made certain that the party's slate of candidates included representatives from all the major groups. Even as recently as the 1960s, the Democratic Party's slate in New York City was led by candidates named Lefkowitz, Fino, and Gilhooley, which presumably reminded the city's numerous Jewish, Italian, and Irish voters that they had reason to support the Democrats.[29]

Occasionally a political party would identify a single candidate who represented multiple ethnic identities. One of the best-known examples is former New York Republican mayor Fiorello La Guardia, who served three terms between 1934 and 1945 and for whom one of New York's airports is named. La Guardia, whose first name meant "little flower," was the child of an Austrian-Jewish mother and an Italian-Catholic father, grew up in what is today Serbia, and was raised as a Protestant. La Guardia was fluent in Italian, German, Yiddish, and Serbo-Croatian, and campaigned in the language spoken by the voters he was addressing. He could also demonstrate equal piety in a Catholic church, a Protestant church, or a Jewish synagogue. La Guardia was such a successful practitioner of identity politics that to this very day New York's Italians and Jews argue over whether he was the city's first Italian mayor or its first Jewish mayor.

Since La Guardia's time, many new groups have become politically important while some of the older ethnic groups have waned in significance. In addition to Irish, Jewish, and Italian voters, politicians must endeavor to appeal to African Americans, women, Hispanics, Asian Americans, senior citizens, persons with disabilities, and a number of other communities. Today's political tickets frequently reflect this new diversity. In many parts of America, indeed, political commercials are as likely to be aired in Spanish as in English. Not even a modern-day La Guardia could personify all the diversity of contemporary American society.

In addition to balancing the ticket, contemporary politicians endeavor to balance their appeal by vigorously expressing their sympathy and admiration for groups to which they do not actually belong. Almost every New York politician, for example, is certain to make a political pilgrimage to Jerusalem, the Vatican, and Dublin, stopping en route at numerous senior citizen's centers, African Methodist Episcopal churches, and mosques. Many politicians have learned to speak a few words of Spanish or, like Florida's governor Jeb Bush, happily publicize their ties by marriage to America's rapidly growing Hispanic community. The Republican Party, as part of its attempt to broaden its ethnic base, has encouraged the political aspirations of senators Ted Cruz and Marco Rubio as well as Republican governor Bobby Jindal. And a variety of politicians have hoped to benefit from supporting affirmative action, women's rights, subsidized health care for seniors, and other programs aimed at cultivating the sympathy of one or another racial, social, or ethnic group.

Identity, though, is a slippery concept. Every individual has many identities and the potential for even more. A group's self-awareness seldom changes spontaneously. In most instances, group consciousness is created by political entrepreneurs who hope to derive some advantage from imbuing the members of a group with a sense of identity and common political purpose. For example, senior citizens have become an active and self-conscious force in contemporary American politics. Representatives of the senior lobby continually demand that the government provide enhanced pension and health care benefits for the elderly and, since seniors are more likely than other Americans to go to the polls, politicians vie with one another to express their concern and admiration for America's elderly citizens. The self-consciousness and political prominence of seniors did not arise spontaneously. Since time immemorial, aging simply had been a fact of every person's life, not a trait that distinguished some individuals from others. Seniors became a self-conscious group largely because of the activities of the American Association of Retired Persons (AARP) and other lobby groups during the 1960s. The development of group consciousness among older Americans has been electorally significant. In the past, as Americans aged, they either retained their preexisting partisan identifications or, as they became wealthier and more conservative in their thinking, tended to shift to the Republican camp. As self-conscious "seniors," however, older Americans have joined the Democratic coalition. Voters over the age of sixty-five historically tended to support the Republicans but have instead supported the Democrats in four of the last five presidential elections.

As the example of seniors suggests, the creation of new identities can be a powerful political weapon. By making individuals conscious of an alternative identity, politicians can change their political perceptions, partisan ties, and voting behavior. Since the 1980s, for example, the GOP's emphasis on religion and morality has helped to make Christian fundamentalists conscious of themselves as a defined group with distinct views and interests. Many of these individuals hold blue-collar jobs and, in their capacity as workers, certainly do not benefit from Republican economic and tax programs, which mainly serve upper-income groups. If these voters were primarily conscious of themselves as workers, they would probably be affiliated with the Democratic Party. Yet by persuading these blue-collar workers to identify themselves first and foremost as Christians, the GOP has been able to tie them to the Republican coalition. This feat of political magic, begun during the Reagan era, helped to elect both George H. W. Bush and George W. Bush.

Appeals Based on Moral Issues

Political campaigns employ moral appeals to energize their supporters and stigmatize their opponents. During the 1960s and 1970s, Democratic candidates attacked Republicans for failing to take stands on war and segregation. These moral appeals helped the Democratic Party to recruit hundreds of thousands if not millions of youthful new adherents. For the past three decades, Republicans have declared their opposition to abortion and their support for "family values" to distinguish themselves from the allegedly libertine Democrats. Moral issues have swelled the GOP's ranks with religious conservatives who came to identify with the Republicans and helped to elect four Republican presidents—Nixon, Reagan, and two Bushes. In 2004, the G. W. Bush reelection effort made special use of a particular moral issue, opposition to same-sex marriage, to mobilize religious conservatives in key states. The issues had arisen because of a series of legal and political efforts by gay-rights activists seeking to compel the states to recognize the right of same-sex couples to marry. Religious conservatives were incensed by what they viewed as an attempt to undermine the traditional family and to force the states to condone immoral conduct.

Republican campaigners saw an opportunity to convert this moral indignation into votes for the president. To this end, Republicans sponsored referenda on the issue of gay marriage to appear on the November 2004 ballots in a number of closely fought "battleground" states such as Ohio and Florida. The effect of the referenda was to energize religious conservatives and to bring them to the polls in large numbers to strike a blow against immorality. While at their polling places, they also voted for President Bush. These efforts were critical to the president's 2004 victory. Religious voters gave Bush the margin of victory in Florida, Ohio, and Missouri. On a national level, 22 percent of all voters cited moral values as the issue that meant the most to them. Of these individuals, 82 percent cast their votes for Bush.

In the past several years, Democrats have sought to turn the tables on the GOP by defining opposition to equal rights for gay, lesbian, and transgendered individuals to be a form of moral callousness. With each party using moral indignation to energize supporters, campaign events in some areas of the country have taken on the character of competing political demonstrations.

Appeals Based on Character Issues

Many Americans view good character as an essential attribute of political leaders. Character is a term that includes a number of traits, and most presidential candidates present themselves as honest, courageous, intelligent, and possessing good moral values. If they can, they will endeavor to suggest that their opponents manifest the opposite qualities.[30] Sometimes these charges and countercharges will degenerate into what politicians call a mudslinging contest. The most recent presidential mudslinging contest took place in 2004. That year, the Bush campaign made two principal contentions about the president's character. The first was that he was honest. "I say what I mean and I do what I say," was the president's frequent refrain. This claim was designed to distinguish Bush from politicians like Bill Clinton, whose personal integrity was considered suspect by many. Second, the president was presented as a strong and courageous leader who rallied the nation in the aftermath of 9/11 and took decisive action against the perpetrators of the attack and their supporters.

Democrats worked to challenge both these claims. The first was called into question when Democrats asserted that the president had not been fully candid about his Vietnam-era service in the Texas Air National Guard. Like the children of many prominent families, Bush had been able to secure a Guard appointment. Since the Guard was not assigned overseas duties in the Vietnam era, this appointment virtually guaranteed that Bush would be spared the rigors of combat in Indochina. Though this fact was a bit embarrassing for a president who now presented himself as a wartime leader, it was not politically fatal. The National Guard is a politically potent institution. Democrats could not afford to antagonize hundreds of thousands of people who had served in the National Guard by intimating that their service was somehow less than honorable, especially because the Guard did play an important combat role in the two Gulf wars.

Because of this consideration, Democrats focused instead on allegations that Bush had shirked many of his Guard duties while his commanding officers, concerned about offending his powerful father, looked the other way. These allegations had been circulating in the media for some time, but were given special prominence by a CBS news documentary narrated by longtime network anchor Dan Rather. The report averred that Bush had failed to report for Guard duties, had neglected to carry out assignments, and had generally treated his service in a cavalier manner. The potential for political damage to the president was enormous, but in the days following the program sources sympathetic to Bush revealed that CBS's main source of information was a longtime Bush adversary who could not prove any of his allegations. It appeared, moreover, that in its eagerness to present the story, CBS had failed to demand confirmation or evidence of the major charges being presented, in violation of the network's own rules. The resulting tumult led to the firing of a number of CBS executives and to Rather's precipitous "retirement." While the allegations against Bush were not factually disproved, they had been politically discredited and so were of little further value to the Democrats.

Democrats had a bit more success with their effort to undercut Bush's claim to be a strong and decisive wartime leader. The principal vehicle they developed for this purpose was the 9/11 Commission. In the spring of 2004, the 9/11 Commission examined events preceding the attack on the World Trade Center and the Pentagon, seeking to ascertain whether the president and other top officials had failed to respond appropriately to warning signs. Congressional Democrats hoped that a probe of the Bush administration's failure to anticipate the 9/11 attacks might embarrass the president in an election year and undermine public confidence in his ability to protect the nation's security—an area long seen as the president's chief political asset. Unfortunately for the Democrats, their party did not control either house of Congress and, therefore, lacked access to either the House or the Senate's formal investigative machinery. Nevertheless, the Democrats demanded an investigation and, through public pressure, ultimately forced congressional Republicans to agree to the creation of an ad hoc, bipartisan investigative panel to be appointed by the leaders of the two parties in Congress. There had been some expectation that the panel would consist of individuals with expertise in national security matters, and some panelists did indeed come from such backgrounds. But the Democrats placed on the panel several individuals whose expertise was prosecutorial rather than in the realm of national security. These included Richard Ben-Veniste, an attorney and Democratic activist who had helped to prosecute Nixon in the Watergate investigation and to defend Clinton in the Whitewater probe. The choice of prosecutors rather than national security experts underlines the role that congressional Democrats hoped the commission would play.

Recognizing the president's peril and seeking to limit possible political damage from the commission's findings, the GOP insisted that the investigation be completed and its report released by July 2004, some four months before the 2004 election. Because of the tight time limit, the commission was not as powerful an investigative instrument as a full-blown congressional inquiry might have been. Nevertheless, commission hearings in March and April of 2004 suggested that the Bush administration had not been sufficiently attentive to the terrorist threat prior to September 2001. This deeply embarrassed the president.

The hearings highlighted the testimony of a former national security aide Richard Clarke, who had just published a book criticizing Bush for his inattention to the threat of terrorism.[31] Committee Democrats led by Ben-Veniste praised Clarke while castigating the Bush administration's star witness, National Security Adviser Condoleezza Rice, whose testimony the commission had demanded despite presidential claims of executive privilege. Ben-Veniste interrupted Rice repeatedly while Democratic Commission member Jamie Gorelick, who had served as an assistant attorney general in the Clinton administration, delivered a lengthy statement critical of Rice's testimony.[32]

Indeed, long before publication of the official report, members of the commission made numerous public and media appearances to present their own views critical of the president. Ben-Veniste, Gorelick, and the others fully understood that the main purpose of the 9/11 probe was to undermine Bush's political standing—not to develop new intelligence and anti-terrorism policies. Democrats also mobilized a

group of widows of 9/11 victims—the so-called Jersey girls—to make television appearances during the hearings to express outrage at the presidential failures that had
allegedly been identified by the hearings. And as if to dramatize the commission's
findings, left-leaning movie maker Michael Moore produced a film entitled "Fahrenheit 9/11," which mocked President Bush and portrayed him as a clueless dope on
September 11, rather than as the forceful leader depicted by the White House.

Republicans launched a series of counterattacks. They demanded that Gorelick resign from the panel, charging that her own actions as assistant attorney general had hampered the FBI and now produced a conflict of interest with her service
as a commission member. And Republicans mobilized their own 9/11 survivors'
group to make television appearances in support of President Bush. Nevertheless,
through the 9/11 Commission and its ancillaries, Democrats did manage to call into
question the validity of President Bush's claims of strength and decisiveness.

While Democrats attacked the president's character, Republicans launched
their own efforts to impugn the character of Bush's opponent, Senator John Kerry.
The senator's two main claims were first that, unlike Bush, he had shown courage by
serving in Vietnam where he had commanded a patrol boat and had been decorated
for his heroism under enemy fire. Second, Kerry presented himself as possessing
greater intelligence than the president, whose alleged lack of intellectual ability had
been the subject of thousands of television comedy routines. In his public appearances, Kerry frequently sought to demonstrate his knowledge of history, economics,
and foreign languages. His linguistic abilities in particular distinguished him from
Bush, who often misspoke in English.

Republicans vigorously contested each of these claims. To dispute Kerry's
bravery in Vietnam, GOP operatives organized a group of conservative Vietnam
veterans who called themselves "Swift Boat Veterans for Truth." These so-called
Swifties traveled around the country asserting that Kerry had distorted and exaggerated his wartime record. Democrats countered, charging that the Swifties were
simply part of a GOP smear campaign. As evidence, Democrats pointed to the fact
that Bush attorney Benjamin L. Ginsberg was also the legal adviser to the Swifties.
Ginsberg was forced to resign from both positions. While Republicans were never
able to prove that Kerry had overstated his heroism in Vietnam, they did manage to
raise doubts and convert what had been widely viewed as a settled fact into a question.

To counter Kerry's claim that he was smarter than the president, Republicans
sought to redefine the issue a bit from intelligence to judgment. Bush and his aides
argued that Kerry had demonstrated poor judgment by frequently "waffling" on
major issues. In Republican campaign materials and even in the nationally televised
2004 presidential debates, Bush sought to give examples of instances, such as the

decision to invade Iraq, when Kerry seemed to shift from position to position. Democrats countered that Kerry changed his positions as events and circumstances changed and pointed out that the president's reluctance to change his mind might be seen as intellectual rigidity rather than moral steadfastness. Given the general view that President Bush was not the sharpest leader America had ever produced, Republicans were usually not too eager to engage in debates over the candidates' relative levels of intelligence. If, however, GOP operatives had managed to secure copies of Kerry's college records before the election, they might have welcomed a test of wits. Bush's academic record at Yale, to be sure, had been abysmal. But Yale grades disclosed after the election showed that Kerry's had been even worse.

While both campaigns saw issues as instruments for activating supporters, each saw questions of character mainly as means of dispiriting some who might vote for an opponent. Thus each 2004 campaign made a number of claims designed to persuade some of the other side's potential supporters that their candidate lacked sufficient moral fiber or intellectual stature to deserve their support. The Kerry campaign attacked Bush's stature as a wartime leader and intimated that the president was something of a dunce. The Bush campaign suggested that Kerry had not really been a war hero and lacked the firmness of judgment needed by a president. Attacks on character of this sort are not likely to convince a candidate's most committed supporters of his or her lack of virtue. Empirical studies suggest, however, that negative ads and other forms of character attack can discourage less certain and less committed individuals from going to the polls at all.[33] After all, who but the most rabid partisan would vote for a shirker, a dunce, or an inveterate flip-flopper?

Issues of character arose in the 2016 election as well. In mid-2014, in preparation for Hillary Clinton's presumed presidential candidacy, Republicans organized a congressional probe into events in Benghazi, Libya, where the American ambassador had been murdered in 2012. Since Hillary Clinton had been secretary of state at that time, Republicans hoped to show that she had been both to blame for errors and misjudgments leading up to the tragedy and unwilling to accept responsibility —and so lacked sufficient moral character to be president. Later Republicans raised questions about Clinton's use of a personal email account to conduct official business while she served as secretary of state. The obvious implication was that she had sought to hide her official actions, including matters relating to the Benghazi attack, from public scrutiny. Some suggested as well that these emails might contain references to foreign contributions to a charitable foundation established by the Clintons, which was itself receiving considerable scrutiny in the media. For Republicans, the emails became a useful reminder of the moral shortcomings that had plagued a previous Clinton's presidency.

The Debates

Many voters make judgments about candidates' characters during nationally televised presidential and vice presidential debates. Debates allow voters an opportunity to see how the candidates fare in direct, face-to-face exchanges where they are
not surrounded by staffers and consultants and must function with prepared scripts.
Voters believe that candidates' ability to think on their feet is a good test of presidential character. Candidate debates were common in the nineteenth century, but
the first modern debate occurred in 1960 when Richard Nixon faced John Kennedy.
Nixon was the much better known of the two and had been favored to win the election. In the debate, however, Kennedy seemed young and vigorous, and to many
Americans "looked presidential." Interestingly, television viewers were convinced
that Kennedy had won the debate, while those who only heard the candidates on
the radio thought Nixon had won.

Over the years, the debates have helped some politicians and hurt others.
Ronald Reagan used a debate with Walter Mondale to turn aside questions about
his advanced age by declaring that he would not criticize Mondale for his youth and
inexperience. Al Gore damaged his 2000 candidacy by appearing rude and super-
cilious in his debate with George Bush. Barack Obama's calm, professorial manner
convinced many white voters that they could, indeed, support a black candidate.
Vice presidential debates, too, have often had dramatic moments even though their
impact on the election might have been negligible. In the famous 1988 vice presidential debate, Republican candidate Senator Dan Quayle compared his own youth
and vigor to that of John Kennedy. His opponent, Democratic senator Lloyd Bentsen, cut Quayle short, saying, "Senator, I served with Jack Kennedy . . . Senator,
you're no Jack Kennedy." Bentsen's zinger permanently clouded Quayle's reputation
but the Bush-Quayle ticket nevertheless won the election.

Money and Presidential Elections

Some pundits are fond of declaring that money does not buy elections, but this
is not entirely true. Money may not buy love or happiness, nor does it guarantee
electoral victory, but success in these realms is difficult if not impossible without
substantial funding. Successful presidential candidates and their supporters spend
hundreds of millions of dollars. Some of these dollars are donated by individuals
who, under the law, may give up to $2,600 to each candidate as well as make con-
tributions to party committees and political action committees. Before 2014, individuals were subject to a limit of slightly more than $100,000 in total contributions

---

Box 4. Where the Money Comes From

Individuals—May contribute up to $2,600 per candidate, $5,000 per political
action committee (PAC), and an unlimited amount to 527s and 501(c)(4)s.
No limit on total contributions.

PACs—May contribute as much as $5,000 per candidate.

Bundlers—No overall limit, but individuals within bundles are subject to the
individual limit. Subject to record-keeping and disclosure requirements.

527 Committee—No limit on issue advocacy but may not coordinate with any
campaign. Subject to record-keeping and disclosure requirements.

527 Super PAC—No limit on express candidate advocacy, but may not coordinate with any campaign. Subject to record-keeping and disclosure requirements.

501(c)(4)—May spend up to half its revenue for campaign activity, including
express candidate advocacy, but may not coordinate with any campaign.
Not required to disclose donors.

Party Committees—May contribute up to $5,000 per candidate.

---

to all races per election cycle. This aggregate limit was, however, struck down by the
U.S. Supreme Court in the 2014 case of *McCutcheon v. Federal Election Commission*
as representing a limit on free speech.[34]

In the wake of the *McCutcheon* decision, coupled with the advent of the
Super PAC (see below), wealthy donors were free to spend as much as they wished
without fear of legal problems (Box 4). Some enthusiastically opened their wallets.
As of August 2015, four hundred families had made a total of nearly $200 million
in contributions both to politicians launching 2016 presidential bids and to the various forms of political action committees backing these politicians. These wealthy
donors were responsible for about half the money raised by candidates up to that
point in time.[35] Of course, these numbers do not take account of one of America's
wealthiest political donors, Donald Trump, who was spending his money on his
own campaign. Trump generally purchased campaign services from companies he
controlled. This practice kept Trump's net campaign costs low, since money was
moving from one Trump pocket to another.[36]

In addition to individual donations, candidates benefit from contributions from corporate and labor political action committees (PACs). A PAC is an entity established by a corporation or interest group to channel the contributions of its members into political campaigns. Under the terms of the 1971 Federal Election Campaign Act, PACs are permitted to make larger contributions to any given candidate than may be made by individuals. While individuals are limited to $2,600, PACs may give up to $5,000 per candidate. Some 4,500 PACs have been organized by corporations, trade associations, unions, and professional groups. In addition, many party leaders have established their own PACs, known as leadership PACs, to provide funding for their political allies. The impact of both individual and PAC contributions is often enhanced by a tactic known as "bundling." The bundler, usually a lobbyist or political activist, raises money from a variety of groups and individuals and presents it to the campaign in a single package or "bundle." The contributors hope to leverage the importance of their gifts, the campaign benefits financially, and the bundlers increase their own political clout. In 2012, for example, 769 bundlers brought more than $180 million to the Obama campaign.[37]

In 2016 hundreds of millions more will be spent in support of candidates by nominally independent nonprofit groups—the so-called 527s and 501(c)(4)s—that are not covered by federal campaign spending restrictions. These groups, named for the sections of the tax code under which they are organized, can raise and spend unlimited amounts on political advocacy so long as their efforts are not coordinated with those of any candidate's campaign. A 527 is a group established specifically for the purpose of political advocacy while a 501(c)(4) is a nonprofit group established for some other purpose that also engages in advocacy. A 501(c)(4) may not spend more than half its revenues for political purposes, but many political activists favor this mode of organization because, unlike a 527, a 501(c)(4) is not required to disclose where it gets its funds or exactly what it does with them. As a result, it has become a common practice for wealthy and corporate donors to route campaign contributions through 501(c)(4)s. The donor makes a contribution to the 501(c)(4), which keeps a cut and donates the remainder of the money to a designated "grassroots" campaign on behalf of the politician. In preparation for the 2016 race, several candidates aligned themselves with nonprofits essentially created to bolster their candidacies. While such alignments may seem inappropriate, neither the Federal Election Commission nor the IRS has challenged them.[38]

A third form of independent group, the independent expenditure-only committee, or "Super PAC," came about as a result of an interpretation by the Federal Election Committee of the Supreme Court's 2010 decision in the case of *Citizens United v. Federal Election Committee*. The committee ruled that the Supreme Court's decision permitted individuals and organizations to form committees that could raise and spend unlimited amounts of money to run political advertising so long as their efforts were not coordinated with those of the candidates.[39] Super PACs are organized under Section 527 of the tax code but unlike ordinary 527 groups, which do not expressly advocate on behalf of particular candidates, Super PACS do engage in express advocacy. In preparation for the 2016 race, backers of each of the major candidates established a Super PAC to promote the candidate's political fortunes. This might seem to constitute inappropriate coordination, but the Federal Election Commission has relaxed its standards to permit a good deal of cooperation between campaigns and supportive Super PACs. Indeed, many experts say that the rules barring coordination have virtually disappeared.[40]

In some instances, to be sure, candidates who spend lavishly come out on the short end. But even when this happens, they are usually defeated by opponents who spent almost as extravagantly. Though superior financial resources do not guarantee success, generally the candidate who raises and spends the most money wins. A study conducted by the Center for Responsive Politics found that 92 percent of the House races and 88 percent of the Senate races were won by the candidate who spent the most money.[41] The candidate without money, like Machiavelli's unarmed prophet, is usually doomed to failure.

That campaigns cost a great deal of money is hardly surprising. Marketing any product is expensive. One major cost is television advertising. Producing a thirty-second television commercial can cost $500,000 and airing it on network television can cost anywhere from $100,000 to $2 million each time it is presented. Local television time is much less expensive, but repeatedly airing ads even during off-peak hours on local TV can entail hundreds of thousands of dollars in expenditures. Another major cost to campaigns is staffing, particularly for attorneys. For example, in 1998, Senator Carol Moseley-Braun (D.-Ill.) raised nearly $5 million for her reelection effort. Of this, the senator spent more than $1.1 million—20 percent of her campaign war chest—on lawyers' and accountants' fees.[42]

Voters and Donors

In principle, there are two reasons to think that elections might allow citizens some measure of control over the government's conduct. These are, to put it simply, choice and accountability. Elections permit citizens an opportunity to choose representatives who share their own interests and preferences. They also give citizens a chance to hold officials accountable for their actions by threatening to depose those whose conduct in office is inconsistent with popular wishes. These ideas certainly seem plausible. The problem, though, is that these points of leverage in the relationship with politicians seem to accrue more to wealthy, organized, and interest-group-affiliated donors than to ordinary voters.

Most voters have relatively little information on which to base their choices. To a considerable extent, they rely on the candidates themselves to supply information about their campaigns and allow their preferences to be formed during the campaign by politicians' marketing efforts, which often include negative campaign ads. Organized groups, by contrast, are typically not very interested in candidates' campaign commercials. Corporate, labor, and ideological groups have well-defined interests and preferences and often employ staffers and lobbyists to identify the strategies through which these are most likely to be advanced.

In some cases, interest groups will simply provide financial help for politicians whom they believe to be likely to support their needs and goals. Typically, ideological groups support candidates who share their beliefs. For example, when he was a senator, former attorney general John Ashcroft, a longtime champion of the religious right, received hundreds of thousands of dollars in contributions from conservative religious groups who expected him to promote their agenda.[43] In a similar vein, liberal groups spend a good deal of their campaign money supporting the election of their ideological comrades and attempting to defeat conservatives. For example, during the 2004 contest, the Media Fund, a liberal 527, organized a $5 million advertising campaign attacking President Bush. "President Bush," the announcer intoned. "Remember the American dream? It's about hope, not fear. It's about more jobs at home, not tax breaks for shipping jobs overseas. It's about giving our children their chance, not our debt. It's about providing healthcare for people, not just profits. It's about fighting for the middle class, not special interests . . . It's time to take our country back from corporate greed and make America work for every American."

Corporate groups and PACs, for their part, tend to adopt a more pragmatic contribution strategy. Rather than limit their contributions to their existing allies, business groups continually seek to make new friends by giving money to candidates of all political stripes and sometimes to both candidates in the same race. When criticized during the August 2015 Republican debate for often donating money to Democrats as well as Republicans, Donald Trump replied indignantly that he was a "businessman." Often politicians approach interest groups and lobbyists to demand money and corporate interests will make contributions to keep friends and avoid making enemies.[44] Corporate donors even contribute to candidates who are fond of accusing them of seeking to subvert the political process. For example, in 2000 Senator John McCain loudly attacked special interest politics as he campaigned for the Republican presidential nomination. He asked voters to help him "break the

Washington iron triangle of big money, lobbyists and legislation that for too long has put special interests above the national interest."[45] But the very same special interests that McCain vilified were happy to contribute to his campaign and to raise money on his behalf. Firms were not about to allow a bit of populist rhetoric to stand in the way of maintaining a good relationship with the powerful chairman of the Senate Commerce Committee and, for his part, the senator was certainly not going to permit his own rhetoric to interfere with raising money. McCain's fundraising events were often organized by some of Washington's most powerful special interest lobbyists, who just happened to represent companies that had an enormous stake in legislation before McCain's committee, companies such as railroads, communications firms, wholesalers, and soft drink distributers.[46]

Corporate interests also endeavor to be strategic in their choice of lobbyists. Many of Washington's lobbyists also serve as campaign treasurers and major fundraisers for political candidates.[47] Individuals like Peter Hart, Tommy Boggs, Peter Knight, Ken Duberstein, and Vin Weber are influential, in part, because of their ability to raise money for politicians. Interest groups will often hire lobbyists whom they know to be key fundraisers for the politicians they hope to influence. In so doing, they are not making a campaign contribution that would have to be reported to the Federal Election Commission, but they are nevertheless seeking to make use of the fact that the lobbyist promoting their interests will be seen by the targeted politician as an important source of campaign money. For example, in 2003 a coalition of television networks seeking to loosen rules governing their ownership of local TV stations hired Gregg Hartley as their lobbyist. Hartley, formerly a top aide to the powerful House majority whip and now senator Roy Blunt, is one of Blunt's top fundraisers. Companies hiring Hartley to lobby for them are almost certain of receiving a positive reception from Blunt. Seventy-one members of Congress list lobbyists as treasurers of their reelection committees.[48] Seven members of the powerful House Appropriations Committee, five Republicans and two Democrats, have political action committees headed by lobbyists with business before the committee.[49]

In some instances, too, corporate groups form strategic alliances with ideological or not-for-profit groups. As indicated earlier, a corporate interest may find it useful to hide its campaign contributions by laundering them through a not-for-profit. For example, in the late 1990s a variety of gambling interests opposed a bill that would have prohibited Internet gambling. Members of Congress were reluctant to accept money directly from what might have seemed to be unsavory sources. At the direction of former Washington super lobbyist Jack Abramoff, the affected gambling interests made contributions to religious groups led by former Christian Coalition executive director Ralph Reed and Traditional Values Coalition founder Lou Sheldon, as well as tax reform groups headed by Grover Norquist. In turn, these groups lobbied against the Internet gambling ban, providing laundered campaign funds for prominent members of Congress.[50] This tactic, called money swapping, is fairly common. The Clinton administration allegedly engaged in extensive money swapping with such organizations as the International Brotherhood of Teamsters. In one case, a foreign national hoping to influence the administration was advised that a direct contribution would be illegal. Instead, Democratic fundraisers advised this individual to make a contribution to Teamster president Ron Carey's reelection campaign. The Teamsters, in turn, made a legal contribution to the Clinton campaign.[51]

Interest groups are not only in a better position than mere voters or even small donors to employ a strategic calculus in doling out their support; they also are far better able than voters to hold politicians accountable for their actions in office. As David Mayhew has observed, the average voter has only the "haziest awareness" of what a congressman or senator is actually doing in office.[52] Most voters pay no attention, and of those who do, many have little understanding of the complexities of the legislative process. Even attentive voters who read the newspapers and watch televised discussions would be hard-pressed to distinguish between a member of Congress who actually works hard to promote a particular cause and one who merely makes speeches or issues press releases.[53] Interest groups are in a much better position to make such judgments. Their lobbyists and staffers attend hearings, meet with legislators and members of their staffs, and prowl the corridors of Capitol Hill exchanging information with one another.

Of course, even interest groups can be duped. Native American gambling interests made millions of dollars in contributions and apparently got little for their money. Nevertheless, Washington's more savvy interest groups know precisely what legislators are doing and can react furiously if they feel betrayed. Take, for example, the AARP, which employs twenty-two full-time lobbyists, a thirty-two-scholar think tank, and more than two thousand volunteer organizers. AARP lobbyists monitor congressional activity on a daily basis and meet with members of Congress to present the organization's views and complaints. AARP organizers are prepared to touch off furious phone and letter campaigns in the districts of members whose attentiveness to senior issues is deemed lacking. In Washington, AARP is nicknamed "Darth Vader" and members of Congress know they will definitely see the dark side of the force if they take the organization's money and fail to follow through on their commitments.[54]

It is sometimes said that money and lobbying do not buy legislation; they merely buy "access" to lawmakers. This is a naive perspective. Unlike some star-struck voters, organized groups are not much interested in being photographed with famous politicians. Their goal is to secure the enactment of legislation that serves their interests. And from all indications, they accomplish this on a regular basis. To take just a few examples, over the past several years a coalition of sixty corporations, including Pfizer, Hewlett-Packard, and Altria, spent close to two million dollars in lobbying fees and campaign contributions to persuade Congress to lower the tax rate on earnings from their foreign operations. The result was legislation signed by the president in 2004 that has already saved the companies about $100 billion in taxes.[55] And after spending millions in campaign contributions and lobbying fees, corporations succeeded in bringing about the enactment of pension legislation in 2006 that allows them to sharply cut the amount they are required to contribute to the employees' pension funds. The savings to major corporations are expected to total as much as $160 billion over the next three years.[56] Similarly, the 2006 energy and Medicare bills contained billions of dollars in corporate benefits secured through millions of dollars in campaign contributions and lobbying expenditures.[57]

The same pattern can be found at the state and local levels. For example, in 2006, after handing out $1.4 million in campaign contributions to Virginia legislators, a coalition of builders, contractors, developers, and real estate agents persuaded the state legislature to kill the governor's proposal for limits on suburban development.[58] And a coalition of labor unions was able to halt Wal-Mart's expansion into Maryland by making substantial contributions to the campaigns of forty-eight members of the Maryland General Assembly during the month prior to the vote. Wal-Mart had hired a dozen lobbyists to promote its agenda through argument and persuasion. The unions, though, had a better understanding of Maryland politics. They skipped the arguments and paid cash for the votes they needed.[59] So much for buying only "access."

Can anything be done to address this problem? In 1971 and 2002, Congress enacted campaign finance legislation nominally designed to reduce the role of money in politics by limiting campaign spending and contributions, curtailing certain forms of campaign spending, and creating a voluntary form of public funding for presidential campaigns. Much of this legislation lies in shambles as a result of three Supreme Court decisions and a decision made by then-senator Obama. In 2008 Democratic candidate Obama decided not to accept public funding while his Republican rival, Senator McCain, agreed to accept such funding. By accepting public finding, McCain became legally ineligible to solicit private donations. In the ensuing campaign, Obama was able to outspend McCain by a wide margin. It seems unlikely that any future presidential candidate will make McCain's mistake.

As for court decisions, the Supreme Court's 1976 *Buckley v. Valeo* decision

struck down a provision of the 1971 Federal Elections Campaign Act that had limited candidate spending.[60] And, as we saw earlier, overall limits on campaign contributions were struck down by the Supreme Court's *McCutcheon* decision while the
high court's *Citizens United* decision ended most restrictions on campaign spending
by outside groups. The result is a campaign environment in which bundlers and
wealthy donors have a great deal of influence.

Consider, however, the implications of restricting campaign spending. The
2002 Bipartisan Campaign Reform Act (sometimes known as "McCain-Feingold")
contained a provision prohibiting interest groups and organizations from airing
ads advocating the victory or defeat of any federal candidate within thirty days of
a primary or caucus or sixty days of a general election. The nominal purpose of
this restriction was to prevent "attack ads" from being aired just before an election,
because the target would have little time to respond. But what might seem to most
Americans as an effort to ensure fair play was generally understood in Washington
as "incumbent relief legislation," that is, a law designed to make it more difficult to
unseat political incumbents. One of the central principles of campaign finance rules
is that those writing the rules are unlikely to overlook their own interests. Hence we
should be wary of proposed campaign finance reforms. If you and I are vying for
office and I write the rules, you might do well to begin planning your concession
speech. In this, as in so many areas of political life, there are no easy answers.

Thoughts on Presidential Elections: What Sorts of Presidents Do We Elect?

In the nineteenth and early twentieth centuries, when presidents were chosen by
party leaders, many were amiable, not especially ambitious individuals who were
happy to attend receptions and be treated with some deference. Today's presidents,
by contrast, generally spend years enhancing their prominence, running in the primaries, and perhaps suffering a defeat or two before securing the nation's highest
office. The days of the amiable, introverted Calvin Coolidge have given way to the
extroverted, aggressive, and ambitious Bill Clinton and, for that matter, Hillary
Clinton.

The political philosopher Thomas Hobbes once said, "A restless desire for
power is in all men . . . a perpetual and restless desire of power after power, that
ceaseth only in death."[61] To be sure, individuals vary in the extent to which they are
affected by Hobbes's "restless desire." Some seem content to lead quiet lives in which
they command nothing more challenging than their television tuners. Others, however, appear to strive perpetually for important offices and positions that place them

in charge of people, resources, and significant policy decisions. Every year, thousands of individuals compete for local, state, and national political office. Some seem driven to strive continually for higher and higher office, seemingly equating the desirability of the position with the power its occupant commands. Every year, local politicians seek opportunities to run for state office, state-level politicians eye national offices, and national politicians harbor presidential ambitions. A number of well-known American politicians invested years, even decades, seeking election to the presidency. Politicians like Al Gore and John Kerry (and in an earlier era, Henry Clay) devoted large fractions of their lives to unsuccessful presidential quests. Others, like Richard Nixon, Bill Clinton, and Barack Obama, struggled for years and finally succeeded. But what drives such individuals to commit themselves to a life of meetings, official dinners and deals, fundraising and negotiation, and media scrutiny? According to presidential scholar Richard Shenkman, these aspirants for high office are "frighteningly overambitious, willing to sacrifice their health, family, loyalty and values as they sought to overcome the obstacles to power."[62] Given the modern presidential selection system, which virtually requires aspirants to devote years to a single-minded quest for office, it seems reasonable to assume that at least many of the major contenders possess an extraordinary level of ambition, and perhaps ruthlessness.[63]

One longtime member of Congress told me that he had served through several presidencies and had become concerned that every recent occupant of the White House was, in his words, a "monster." We might do well to consider this representative's words when our presidents ask us to trust them.

A History of
Presidential Elections

Every four years, the national media and a gaggle of pundits assure Americans that the current election is of historic importance. To the extent that history consists of many small events, every election is historic. Some elections, though, are more important, either because they reflect the emergence of new political and social forces or because the elections themselves have played a unique role in American history. Let us consider several of these.

The election of 1828. America's first six presidents had been drawn from the narrow, political elite that governed the nation after the Revolution. Jackson, however, spoke for common Americans and the new social and political forces of the West. Jackson's candidacy had been opposed by almost the entire political establishment, so Old Hickory and his supporters worked to create a new nominating institution, the party convention, that would give control over the presidential nomination to politicians in the countryside rather than political leaders in the Capitol. The Jacksonians also worked to expand suffrage to give the general's tens of thousands of impecunious supporters the right to vote for him. And to make sure these inexperienced voters would come to the polls, the Jacksonians built party organizations throughout the nation. In 1828, these efforts swept Jackson into the White House and reshaped American politics.

The election of 1840. After the collapse of the Federalist Party following the War of 1812, the Jeffersonian Republicans, later known as the Democratic-Republicans or Democrats, was America's only political party. During the 1830s, however, a variety of dissident politicians established the Whig Party to compete for power. The Whigs were united by no principle besides the desire to win and so avoided discussion of issues. Whig candidates tended to be popular generals with

THE
HARD CIDER
CAMPAIGN
of
1840

VOTE FOR
TIPPECANOE
AND
TYLER
TOO!!!

DRAWINGS
by
JOHN WOLCOTT ADAMS

no known political views, and Whig campaigns were raucous affairs emphasizing slogans, singing, and drinking. In 1836, in what came to be known as the "hard cider" campaign, the Whigs elected General William Henry Harrison, known as "Old Tippecanoe" for his victory in a battle against Native American tribes. Harrison's running mate, John Tyler, was also an unknown commodity and was referred to as "Tyler too" in Whig campaigns.

The election of 1860. The issue of slavery divided the established Democratic and Whig parties and led to the formation of a new political party, the Republicans, which was determined to block the expansion of slavery into the territories. With

the election of Republican presidential candidate Abraham Lincoln, the Southern states seceded from the Union, convinced that Lincoln intended to outlaw slavery altogether. The defeat of the South preserved the Union, ended the institution of slavery, and confirmed the Republicans as America's dominant political party. During the seventy-two years between 1860 and 1932, the Republican Party won all but four presidential contests.

The election of 1896. During the 1880s, Southern and Western farmers organized against the growing economic and political power of railroads, bankers, and industrial corporations. Calling themselves the People's Party or Populists, these forces demanded a variety of political reforms such as the initiative referendum and recall, all of which were designed to democratize American politics. Populists won power in a number of states and in 1896 joined forces with the Democrats behind the presidential candidacy of William Jennings Bryan. The Bryan ticket was defeated by the Republicans under William McKinley. Populism faded as a political movement and Republican rule continued.

The election of 1912. In 1912, the Republican vote was split between supporters of President William Howard Taft and followers of former president Theodore Roosevelt. Roosevelt ran as an independent under the "Bull Moose" banner, emphasizing his strength and fearlessness. Division in the Republican camp paved the way for a rare victory by the Democrats, who had nominated Woodrow Wilson, a New

Jersey governor and former president of Princeton University. Wilson was reelected in 1916 under the banner "He kept us out of war." Soon afterward, Wilson brought about America's entry into World War I. This example should remind readers to exercise caution when evaluating campaign slogans.

The election of 1932. In the midst of the Great Depression, Americans were ready to abandon the Republicans and seek new leadership. Democrat Franklin D. Roosevelt won election in 1932 and reelection in 1936, 1940, and 1944, becoming the only U.S. president to serve more than two terms in office. Presidents are now limited to two terms by the Twenty-Second Amendment, ratified in 1951. During his time in office, FDR worked to strengthen the Democratic Party by adding new groups, forces, and institutions to the Democratic coalition. By the time of his death, the Democrats had become America's majority party.

The election of 2000. On election night, November 7, 2000, Democratic vice president Al Gore out-polled his Republican rival George W. Bush by more than 500,000 votes nationally. Bush, however, won a five-vote majority in the Electoral College to secure the presidency. This was the fourth instance in American history in which the popular vote winner lost in the Electoral College. This election was, how-

ever, unique in that the ultimate decision was made by the U.S. Supreme Court. An initial tally appeared to award the state to Bush by 537 votes, but the methods used to tally votes in several counties seemed open to question and the Florida Supreme Court ordered a partial recount. Three days later, on December 12, 2000, the recount was stopped by the U.S. Supreme Court in the case of *Bush v. Gore,* and Florida's electoral votes and the presidency were awarded to Bush.

The election of 2008. In 2008, America elected Barack Obama, its first African American president. Obama secured the Democratic nomination by besting Hillary Rodham Clinton in the primaries and defeating Republican senator John McCain in the general

election. Obama was reelected in 2012, defeating former Republican governor Mitt Romney. During his presidency Obama brought about the creation of a massive new national health care program, the Affordable Care Act, popularly known as Obama-care.

F I V E

The Executive Branch

In This Chapter

The president of the United States is the chief executive of America's national government. This is a job description as well as a title, since it was assumed from the first year of the Republic that presidents would need the support of a substantial bureaucracy to carry out their constitutional duties. The first Congress, meeting in 1789, created the Department of State, Department of Treasury, and Department of War (now Defense). In 1792, Congress established the Post Office Department (now the quasi-independent U.S. Postal Service), and in 1792 created the Department of the Navy (now part of Defense).

Today, the president oversees the activities of fifteen government departments as well as some seventy independent agencies and a host of boards, commissions, and quasi-public entities. Each of these departments and agencies consists, in turn, of a host of offices, bureaus, services, agencies, authorities, commissions, and other subdivisions—more than five hundred in the government departments alone. The oldest department is the Department of State, created in 1789; the newest is Homeland Security, which was created in the wake of the 9/11 terrorist attacks. Many of these bureaucratic entities possess the power to make rules that both have the force of law and directly affect citizens. Let us examine the agencies of the executive branch and their powers and responsibilities. Can the president

160

effectively manage these agencies? Is all this bureaucracy consistent with American democracy?

Agencies of the Executive Branch

All of America's cabinet departments and about half the other agencies were created by acts of Congress. The act establishing an agency is called its "organic statute." The remaining agencies were created by executive order, the orders of department secretaries, or through the reorganization of existing agencies.[1] Major agencies created by executive order include the Environmental Protection Agency (EPA), the Federal Emergency Management Agency (FEMA), and the Drug Enforcement Administration (DEA). Presidents have claimed the power to create agencies, and Congress has acquiesced by providing funding (Box 5).

Each of the fifteen government departments is led by a secretary who is also a member of the president's cabinet. Reporting to the secretary is a deputy secretary, while individual offices and activities are led by undersecretaries and assistant secretaries. The major independent agencies, such as the Social Security Administration, are usually headed by a senior official whose title might be commissioner, administrator, or director and who is, in turn, supported by deputies and assistant deputies. Government departments range in size from the tiny Department of Education, which employs only about 4,200 individuals, to the massive Department of Defense, which oversees some 700,000 civilian employees and 1.3 million military personnel. The Department of Defense is also responsible for maintaining the military readiness of 1.1 million reserve and National Guard troops. The independent agencies vary in size as well. The Social Security Administration employs about sixty thousand people while some of the smaller agencies are staffed by only a few dozen individuals.

Has the Government Gone Quasi?

In addition to these formal agencies of the federal government, America's federal bureaucracy includes a number of entities whose precise legal status is ambiguous. These are the so-called quasis. The quasis are hybrid organizations that exercise public power under congressional charters while remaining at least partially in private hands. These include such government-sponsored enterprises as the Corporation for Public Broadcasting, the Legal Services Corporation, and the National Passenger Railroad Corporation. One important form of quasi is the federally funded research and development center, a type of private entity organized at the

Box 5. Selected U.S. Government Departments and Agencies

Department of Agriculture

The U.S. Department of Agriculture (USDA) develops and executes policies related to farming, agriculture, and food. Its aims include meeting the needs of farmers and ranchers, promoting agricultural trade and production, assuring food safety, protecting natural resources, fostering rural communities, and ending hunger in America and abroad.

Department of Commerce

The Department of Commerce is the government agency tasked with improving living standards for all Americans by promoting economic development and technological innovation.

Department of Defense

The mission of the Department of Defense is to provide the military forces needed to deter war and to protect the security of the United States. It consists of the departments of the Army, Navy, and Air Force, as well as many agencies, offices, and commands, including the Joint Chiefs of Staff, the Pentagon Force Protection Agency, the National Security Agency, and the Defense Intelligence Agency.

Department of Education

The mission of the Department of Education is to promote student achievement and preparation for competition in a global economy by fostering educational excellence and ensuring equal access to educational opportunity.

Department of Energy

The mission of the Department of Energy is to advance the national, economic, and energy security of the United States.

Department of Health and Human Services

The Department of Health and Human Services is the U.S. government's principal agency for protecting the health of all Americans and providing essential

continued

Box 5 *Continued*

human services, especially for those who are least able to help themselves. Agencies of this department conduct health and social science research, work to prevent disease outbreaks, assure food and drug safety, and provide health insurance.

Department of Homeland Security

The missions of the Department of Homeland Security are to prevent and disrupt terrorist attacks; protect the American people, critical U.S. infrastructure, and key resources; and respond to and recover from incidents that do occur. The third largest cabinet department, it was established by the Homeland Security Act of 2002, largely in response to the terrorist attacks on September 11, 2001. The new department consolidated twenty-two executive branch agencies, including the U.S. Customs Service, the U.S. Coast Guard, the U.S. Secret Service, the Transportation Security Administration, and the Federal Emergency Management Agency.

Department of Housing and Urban Development

The Department of Housing and Urban Development is the federal agency responsible for national policies and programs that address America's housing needs, that improve and develop the nation's communities, and that enforce fair housing laws. The department plays a major role in supporting homeownership for lower- and moderate-income families through its mortgage insurance and rent subsidy programs.

Department of the Interior

The Department of the Interior is the nation's principal conservation agency. Its mission is to protect America's natural resources, offer recreation opportunities, conduct scientific research, conserve and protect fish and wildlife, and honor our responsibilities to American Indians, Alaskan Natives, and island communities.

Department of Justice

The mission of the Department of Justice is to enforce the law and defend the interests of the United States according to the law; to ensure public safety against threats foreign and domestic; to provide federal leadership in preventing and controlling crime; to seek just punishment for those guilty of unlawful behavior; and to ensure fair and impartial administration of justice for all Americans.

continued

Box 5 *Continued*

Department of Labor

The Department of Labor oversees federal programs for ensuring a strong American workforce. These programs address job training, safe working conditions, minimum hourly wage and overtime pay, employment discrimination, and unemployment insurance.

Department of State

The Department of State plays the lead role in developing and implementing the president's foreign policy. Major responsibilities include representing U.S. interests abroad, assisting foreign governments, providing training for foreign military services, countering international crime, and a wide assortment of services to U.S. citizens and foreign nationals seeking entrance to the United States.

Department of Transportation

The mission of the Department of Transportation is to ensure a fast, safe, efficient, accessible, and convenient transportation system that meets our vital national interests and enhances the quality of life of the American people.

Department of the Treasury

The Department of the Treasury is responsible for promoting economic prosperity and ensuring the soundness and security of the U.S. and international financial systems.

Department of Veterans Affairs

The Department of Veterans Affairs is responsible for administering benefit programs for veterans, their families, and their survivors. These benefits include pension, education, disability compensation, home loans, life insurance, vocational rehabilitation, survivor support, medical care, and burial benefits. Veterans Affairs became a cabinet-level department in 1989.

Note: The U.S. government also oversees seventy independent agencies and government corporations such as the Social Security Administration and the Veterans Administration.
Source: Data from WhiteHouse.Gov, available online at https://www.whitehouse.gov/1600/executive -branch (accessed August 12, 2015).

government's initiative to provide contract services to the government.[2] The oldest and best known of these is the Rand Corporation, which was created in 1948 to undertake research for the U.S. military.

Possibly America's most important quasis are the several government-sponsored enterprises that play key roles in the nation's financial services industry. The best known of these are the Federal National Mortgage Corporation, known as "Fannie Mae," and the Federal Home Loan Mortgage Corporation ("Freddie Mac"). The others are the Student Loan Marketing Association, which is often called "Sallie Mae"; the Farm Credit System; the Federal Home Loan Bank System; and the Federal Agricultural Credit Corporation ("Farmer Mac"). These enterprises are among the nation's largest banking institutions, collectively controlling assets of nearly $3 trillion. Risky lending activities by Fannie Mae and Freddie Mac may have contributed to the 2007–2008 financial crisis.

Also playing an important role in governance and national policymaking are a variety of nongovernmental organizations, some for-profit and some nonprofit, that offer advice, support, and contractual services to federal government agencies. The U.S. government relies on private firms to undertake such tasks as rating the credit-worthiness of securities, including government bonds, and accrediting colleges and universities. If a school is not accredited, its students are not eligible for federally guaranteed student loans.

The History of Federal Employees and Contractors

During much of the nineteenth century, federal employees were chosen on the basis of political loyalty and party "patronage." To secure a government job, an individual needed a political patron who might be a local party leader or even a member of Congress. After every election, presidents were besieged by politicians seeking offices for their supporters and individuals seeking offices for themselves. Competition for offices was fierce: President James A. Garfield was assassinated in 1881 by a disgruntled office seeker, Charles Guiteau. Patronage employees were expected to engage in campaigning and other political activities on behalf of their sponsors, and usually were expected to contribute a percentage of their salaries to their party's treasury.

The Pendleton Civil Service Act, signed into law in 1883, changed the system by requiring that federal government jobs be awarded on the basis of merit, usually determined by competitive examination. The act also made it illegal to fire or demote employees for political reasons. Over the ensuing years, civil service employees were afforded a variety of additional employment rights designed to protect them from arbitrary dismissal or demotion, making civil service employment among the most secure categories of employment in the nation. All but the very top tier of federal workers are covered by civil service protections. Civil service occupations today range from support jobs to positions as highly skilled scientists and physicians. Most blue-collar workers in the federal system are contract employees rather than civil servants.

Approximately 1,200 to 1,400 of the top leaders of government agencies, including those holding the rank of assistant secretary and above, as well as a number of other important officials, are appointed by the president with the approval of the Senate. These officials serve at the pleasure of the president and may be removed from office by the chief executive. Sprinkled through the bureaucracy are approximately 2,500 Schedule C appointees, who hold key positions and are recruited for their special expertise outside the civil service system. Schedule C appointees tend to be linked to particular presidential administrations.[3]

In addition to actual federal employees, the federal government relies heavily on private contractors to perform not only blue-collar tasks but virtually every other governmental function as well. As much as $400 billion in federal spending each year flows into the coffers of government contractors. The federal workforce is often described as a "blended" workforce with civil servants and contractors working side by side in most offices and performing overlapping tasks. Contractors generate reports, prepare meals, provide equipment, program computers, supervise projects, and, in the case of military contractors, provide security services for government agencies. Many of the rules and regulations promulgated by government agencies are drafted by contract employees. In 2007, when the General Service Administration sought to investigate allegations of fraud by federal contractors, the agency almost reflexively hired a contractor, CACI International, to manage the investigation.[4]

No firm numbers are available, but a number of federal agencies, including the Department of Energy and the Department of Education, employ the services of many more contractors than they have actual government workers.[5] Even agencies whose work is sensitive hand many tasks over to contractors. During the American occupation of Iraq, for example, the State Department allowed contract employees working for the BearingPoint Corporation to take part in discussions on war strategy. The State Department also contracted with a private security firm, Blackwater, to provide armed escorts for its personnel when they traveled through the country. Charges that Blackwater troops had, without provocation, killed a number of unarmed Iraqis forced the State Department to terminate the contract. Soon thereafter, however, it found another military contractor to provide security forces for its diplomats. Contract employees can be privy to the government's most closely guarded secrets. In 2013 Edward Snowden, an employee of the Booz Allen Hamilton Corporation, working under contract to the National Security Agency, leaked the details of the agency's electronic eavesdropping on American's phone calls and emails.

Depending on the mode of calculation, between 10 and 14 million individuals work for the federal government.[6] These include about 2.5 million civil servants, 1.4 million members of the armed forces, and six to seven million contract employees. Another three million individuals are generally engaged in government work for organizations that are not formally part of the government. Some of the employees in this blended workforce perform routine and mundane tasks, others undertake hazardous military missions, while tens of thousands of others hold positions that require them, do research, write reports, make recommendations, and help to shape and craft agency policies, including rules and regulations that have the force of law.

What Executive Agencies Do

Agencies in the executive branch undertake an enormous variety of tasks that can be thought of as falling into eight broad categories:

Foreign relations. The United States of America is one among roughly 196 independent countries in the world. (The number is approximate because not every country that claims independence is recognized as a sovereign state by every other country. The United States, for example, does not formally recognize several states including North Korea and Taiwan, though we have friendly relations with Taiwan, which we formally view as part of China. The Taiwanese government, of course, considers itself to be the legitimate government of China, though no other government agrees with this idea.) The Department of State handles America's normal diplomatic relations with other nations as well as with international bodies like the United Nations. The State Department manages and staffs several hundred American embassies and diplomatic missions around the world and monitors the activities of foreign diplomats assigned to the United States. U.S. embassies and diplomatic missions are staffed by career foreign-service officers who are trained in the arts of diplomacy as well as the culture and politics of the country in which they are stationed.

Other agencies also play important roles in managing America's foreign relations. The office of the U.S. Trade Representative, located within the Executive Office of the President, conducts America's trade negotiations with other nations; the Commerce Department promotes American exports; and the Treasury Department formulates international economic policy. Delicate negotiations and foreign policy planning are often conducted by the National Security Council staff on the president's behalf.

Revenue. All government activities require funding, so it is no accident that the Department of the Treasury was one of the first three agencies created by Congress. The Internal Revenue Service (IRS), an agency within the Treasury Department, every year collects more than $2.3 trillion in taxes from individuals and corporations. The IRS does not write America's tax laws; these are written by the Congress. The IRS does, however, write rules and regulations that implement the tax laws and so can have a major influence on the tax liabilities faced by individuals. We will return to the important topic of the relationship between laws and administrative rules later in this chapter. Several other agencies, including the Office of Customs and Border Protection within the Department of Homeland Security, also provide revenues for the federal government. Each year, customs duties on goods imported into the United States amount to several billion dollars.

A particularly important source of revenue is the Treasury Department, which markets U.S. government securities to the Federal Reserve, to financial institutions, and to foreign and domestic investors and which is responsible for making up the difference between government revenues and government expenditures. In 2014, the Treasury sold more than $700 billion in bonds to fund the government's operations. In 2010, when the government increased its deficit spending to bring the nation out of recession, the Treasury sold $1.6 trillion in bonds. Generally, Congress sets the legal limit on how much the Treasury can borrow. In principle, once the Treasury reaches the "debt ceiling," it is prohibited from marketing more securities and the president is left to decide which programs and services to cut if government expenditures exceed revenues. During the Obama administration, House Republicans declared that they would refuse to allow an increase in the debt ceiling unless the president agreed to various spending cuts. After a struggle, Congress agreed to suspend the debt ceiling until 2015, allowing the Treasury to borrow whatever it deemed necessary.

In recent years, among the largest purchasers of U.S. bonds has been the Chinese central bank, which holds nearly $2 trillion in U.S. debt. Some Americans fear that this debt makes the U.S. vulnerable to Chinese economic pressure, but the Chinese fear that any U.S. policy that lowers the value of the dollar would sharply reduce the value of their holdings. The interdependence of the world's two largest economies requires each to be cautious in its dealings with the other.

National security. The Department of War was the third executive department created by the first Congress in 1789 and the Department of the Navy was added a few years later. As a result of the 1947 National Defense Act, the Army, Navy (including the Marine Corps), and Air Force were all made parts of the Department of Defense or "DoD" (initially nicknamed the National Defense Establishment). Each of the three uniformed services has its own secretary, but these secretaries are not cabinet officers and are responsible mainly for military recruitment and logistics. For actual combat operations, there is only one secretary: the secretary of defense, a civilian cabinet official who reports directly to the president. Below the secretary of defense is the Joint Chiefs of Staff, an organization consisting of the commanders of each of the uniformed services and a uniformed Joint Staff, drawn from all four services and known in the military as "the purple" for the purple ribbons worn by its personnel. Reporting to the Joint Chiefs of Staff are the combatant commanders.

The Department of Defense has divided the world into six geographic regions. All American military forces within a particular region are under the command of a senior general or admiral who is in charge of any military action ordered by the president for that area. The combatant commander may draw personnel, weapons, and equipment deemed necessary for the particular combat mission from any of the services. Three additional combatant commands—Strategic Command, Transportation Command, and Special Operations Command—are charged with particular functions. The Navy Seals who killed Osama bin Laden at his compound in Pakistan in 2011, for example, came under the command of Admiral William McRaven, then head of the Special Operations Command.

The Department of Defense also houses a variety of intelligence agencies, including the Defense Intelligence Agency, the National Geospatial-Intelligence Agency, and the National Security Agency (NSA). The Defense Intelligence Agency is responsible for collecting and analyzing strategic and tactical intelligence relevant to American military operations. Since strategic intelligence might include political and economic matters, the agency does not limit its operations to purely military data and makes use of data collected electronically, known as signals intelligence, as well as data culled from open sources like foreign newspapers and material gathered by its agents throughout the world. Though its numbers are classified, the Defense Intelligence Agency is probably the nation's largest intelligence agency.

The National Geospatial-Intelligence Agency analyzes data collected by U.S. spy satellites. For example, its staff mapped Osama bin Laden's compound in preparation for the special operations strike that killed him. The NSA, for its part, intercepts electronic communications throughout the world and analyzes their content. In 2013, revelations by an NSA contractor of illicit NSA eavesdropping on American citizens caused a furor but probably did not halt the practices. This issue is discussed in detail in Chapter 9.

In addition to military intelligence agencies, the United States boasts several civilian agencies engaged in intelligence operations. The largest, the Central Intelligence Agency (CIA), is tasked with collecting and analyzing information throughout the world and using it to protect American security interests. The CIA employs both electronic methods of intelligence collection and traditional forms of espionage, known as human intelligence. The CIA also trains quasi-military units for "special operations" against foreign governments and terrorist groups. The agency's record in the special operations realm has been mixed. CIA agents allegedly toppled the Iranian government and the government of the Congo in the 1950s, organized an abortive attempt to overthrow the Castro government in the 1960s, and provided weapons and training for the mujahideen who forced the Soviet Union to retreat from Afghanistan in the 1980s. More recently, the CIA organized the local forces that helped the U.S. effort against the Taliban in Afghanistan. The CIA has also directed a campaign of drone attacks against suspected terrorists in Yemen, Pakistan, and elsewhere in the Middle East. In December 2014, the CIA was sharply criticized in a Senate report that accused the agency of unnecessary brutality in the methods it had used to interrogate suspected terrorists. No doubt the Senate's misgivings about the CIA were increased when senators learned that the agency had hacked into the computers used by Senate staffers conducting the investigation.

Domestic security and law enforcement. Until recent decades, domestic security was mainly left to state and local governments. Today, however, the federal government plays a major role in this realm. America's main law enforcement and domestic security agency is the Department of Justice, which is responsible for enforcing federal laws and prosecuting federal crimes. When an individual is charged with violating a federal criminal law, he or she is prosecuted in a federal court by an attorney assigned by the Criminal Division of the Department of Justice. One U.S. attorney, a presidential appointee, is assigned to each of the nation's ninety-four federal judicial districts to supervise the prosecution by assistant U.S. attorneys. In addition to prosecuting cases brought to them, U.S. attorneys conduct numerous investigations of misconduct and conspiracy to violate federal statutes. In recent years, Congress has enacted many new criminal laws related to everything from terrorism to bank robbery. These new laws have kept federal prosecutors busy and filled federal prisons with nearly a quarter of a million inmates.

One bureau within the Department of Justice is America's most important federal police force: the Federal Bureau of Investigation (FBI). Created by President Franklin D. Roosevelt on the foundation of an earlier agency, the FBI is the main agency tasked with investigating federal crimes and apprehending their perpetrators. Suspects arrested by the FBI are prosecuted, if that is warranted, by the appropriate U.S. attorney. The FBI is a law enforcement agency, not an intelligence agency. That is, the chief mission and orientation of the FBI is to investigate crimes that have taken place and find the guilty parties. An intelligence agency like the CIA, by contrast, analyzes information and seeks to anticipate dangerous developments before they actually occur. Since the 9/11 terror attacks, the FBI has worked to strengthen its intelligence capabilities, but its long-established culture has not changed much. The Department of Justice houses two other police forces: the Bureau of Alcohol, Tobacco, Firearms and Explosives (ATF), and the Drug Enforcement Administration (DEA).

In 2002, Congress created a new law enforcement agency, the Department of Homeland Security (DHS), to focus on border security and domestic terrorism. A number of existing agencies, including the Coast Guard, the Federal Emergency Management Agency, the Secret Service, Immigration and Customs Enforcement, the Transportation and Security Administration, U.S. Customs and Border Protection, and several others were moved into the new agency. The DHS has confronted many problems in its early years. To begin with, creation of the new agency was viewed by the FBI as a sharp and unwarranted rebuke for failing to prevent the 9/11 terror attacks. Every federal agency is anxious to guard what it sees as its own turf and the FBI, since the days of its legendary director J. Edgar Hoover, has been one of the most turf-conscious agencies in Washington. Accordingly, FBI staffers have shown reluctance to cooperate with the new agency.

Jurisdictional conflicts among various intelligence and security agencies are common and should not be viewed with alarm. Agency competition can give the president and the NSC multiple interpretations and perspectives, whereas interagency cooperation can produce a narrow viewpoint that ignores possibilities and restricts options. The congressional 9/11 Commission lost sight of this point when it recommended more coordination among agencies. In addition to possibly creating tunnel vision among U.S. intelligence resources, the formula suggested by the commission—creation of an intelligence czar and a new Department of Homeland Security—seems, instead, to have added new levels of competition to the world of intelligence.

The creation of DHS generated another set of problems. Moving agencies from their accustomed niches to new bureaucratic structures is almost guaranteed to produce cultural conflicts and clashes. Long-established bureaucratic agencies, like many of those that were moved to DHS, have usually evolved priorities and procedures that advance both the internal and external goals of their leadership cadres. That is, agency executives will identify a mission and set of practices that justify their own agency's budgetary claims and power vis-à-vis other institutions, while simultaneously reinforcing the established structure of power within the agency itself. Over time, this mission and associated practices can become so deeply ingrained in the minds of agency executives and staffers that adherence to them becomes a matter of habit and reflex. Students of bureaucracy refer to this set of established pattern of practices and beliefs about the organization's role and purpose as the agency's institutional "culture."[7]

Political scientist James Q. Wilson has observed, "Every organization has a culture . . . a persistent, patterned way of thinking about the central tasks of and human relationships within an organization. Culture is to an organization what personality is to an individual . . . it is passed from one generation to the next. It changes slowly, if at all."[8] Agency cultures are sometimes born with agencies' original missions, the personalities of their early leaders, and the character of their earliest supporters. Once established, agency cultures can be remarkably resistant to change as agencies recruit employees and executives thought to be sympathetic to the agency's values and, for good measure, subject them to a lengthy process of training and indoctrination.

Military indoctrination, including the curricula of the service academies and the training practices of the "boot camps" endured by new recruits, has become the stuff of folklore and the topic of many popular films. The new recruit, whether officer or enlisted person, is subjected to an intense period of indoctrination aimed, in large measure, at imbuing him or her with the culture and traditions of the service in question. Marine recruits are subjected to a week of "disorientation" designed to sever their ties to civilian life and then are taught the values of the Marine Corps. According to one authority, "To be in the Corps is to be in a state of mind that dictates one's relationship to the rest of the world."[9] While civilian bureaucracies do not run boot camps, most conduct orientation programs and some, most notably the U.S. Forest Service, approach the level and style of military methods in their efforts to ensure the loyalty of new personnel.[10]

Many agencies seem incredibly dedicated to missions defined long ago. The U.S. Fish and Wildlife Service, for example, was created in the nineteenth century to protect and conserve the nation's animal species and does so today, generally without regard for other economic and social interests. In recent years, for instance, the service has worked to return wolves and grizzly bears to the Northwest, even though these animals represent an economic and even physical threat to individuals engaged in ranching and recreational pursuits in the region.[11]

Often a cataclysmic event is required to alter an agency's long-established culture or sense of mission. All agencies, civilian as well as military, are almost certain to resist efforts to compel them to undertake activities that are foreign to their institutional cultures and thus seem to pose a threat to their institutional autonomy or internal balance of power. Seidman avers that attempts to compel agencies to engage in such activities are usually futile. "Alien transplants," he states, "seldom take root" and are continually "threatened with rejection."[12] The wholesale movement of agencies into DHS has produced contracting and procurement problems in the Coast Guard, discipline problems in the Secret Service, and performance issues in Immigration and Customs Enforcement. It remains to be seen whether DHS can evolve a new set of cultural understandings to placate unhappy officials and employees.

Promote the general welfare. A fifth set of federal agencies is responsible for promoting the general health and welfare of Americans. These agencies include the Department of Health and Human Services, the Department of Education, the Social Security Administration, a variety of agencies within other departments, as well as independent agencies such as the Environmental Protection Agency. The Department of Health and Human Services administers the Medicare and Medicaid programs and the new Affordable Care Act and oversees the National Institutes of Health (NIH), which is responsible for major medical research activities. Within the NIH, the Food and Drug Administration (FDA) is one of the agencies responsible for ensuring that pharmaceuticals are safe and effective and that various food products are safe. The EPA, for its part, administers environmental legislation and endeavors to reduce pollution from automobiles, power plants, and other sources.

The Social Security Administration is responsible for administering America's largest retirement program. Since its introduction in the 1930s, Social Security has collected premiums from working Americans and paid benefits to tens of millions of retirees. Social Security, like Medicare, is an entitlement program. Its benefits formulae are set by law and are not subject to annual congressional appropriation. Some Americans are concerned that Social Security benefits will exceed premiums sometime in the coming decades, leading to the system's bankruptcy and inability to honor its obligations to retirees. Actually, when the Roosevelt administration introduced Social Security the program was designed to have the appearance of an insurance plan to overcome political opposition to the idea of welfare. Consequently, Social Security can no more go bankrupt than can any other government program. If expenditures exceeded premiums, the government would be obliged to make up the difference from other tax revenues.

Fiscal and monetary policy. In the late nineteenth century, the federal government began to assume responsibility for managing the nation's economy. Its major tools of economic management are fiscal policy and monetary policy. Fiscal policy refers to taxing and spending and the relationship between the two. The Treasury Department is the agency chiefly responsible for advising Congress and the president on the implications of their tax and spending programs for the health of the economy. If the government spends much more than it collects in taxes, the result can be inflationary; if it taxes more than it spends, economic activity could be hampered. How to strike a balance is always problematic. Fiscal and monetary policies are also developed by the Congressional Budget Office, the White House Office of Management and Budget, and the president's Council of Economic Advisers.

Monetary policy refers to banks, credit, and currency. America's most important monetary policy agency is the Federal Reserve System, known as the Fed. Established by Congress in 1913, the Fed is generally responsible for adjusting the nation's money supply to meet the needs of banks and businesses while warding off both inflationary and deflationary pressures. One tool through which the Fed regulates the money supply is the "federal funds rate"—the rate that banks pay one another to borrow money. If the Fed raises the federal funds rate, banks and borrowers throughout the economy must pay higher rates for loans; lowering the federal funds rate has the opposite effect. The Fed is also tasked with regulating banks to ensure that they do not engage in risky lending practices that could threaten the financial system. In 2008, because of unwise lending practices, a number of major financial institutions were unable to meet their obligations, setting off a nationwide financial crisis and forcing the government to lend various banks and corporations $700 billion to avert a general economic collapse. Critics charged that the Fed, among other agencies, had been lax in its supervision. In 2010, Congress created the Financial Stability Oversight Council, chaired by the treasury secretary, to anticipate any future risks to the financial sector.

Regulatory agencies. Since the late nineteenth century, the federal government has undertaken to regulate citizens' conduct in almost every sphere of life. Most federal agencies make or administer regulations within their subject-matter jurisdictions. Some agencies have a primarily regulatory mission. These are the so-called independent regulatory commissions. These include the Federal Trade Commission (FTC), which was created to prevent monopolistic practices in the economy; the Federal Communications Commission (FCC), which regulates aspects of electronic communications; the Securities and Exchange Commission (SEC), which regulates the financial industry by applying various laws, including the 2010 Dodd-Frank Wall Street Reform and Consumer Protection Act, designed to curb abuses blamed for the 2008 financial crisis; and the Federal Election Commission (FEC), which regulates campaign practices.

Economic development agencies. A final set of agencies focuses on promoting the nation's economy. For example, the Department of Transportation oversees the nation's highway, rail, and air traffic systems. These systems are obviously the backbones of economic growth and development. A number of economic development agencies were also established to assist particular areas of the economy. The Department of Agriculture was created to serve the needs of farmers, the Small Business Administration to promote the health of small and medium-sized businesses, and so forth. These agencies typically work closely with the groups they serve and are often known as "clientele agencies."

Too Much Government?

For much of its history, America was known as a "stateless society." That is, the federal government was relatively small, most governmental activity was in the hands of states and localities, and Americans were governed more by the laws of the marketplace than by those of the Congress. The power of the federal government grew, mainly as a result of international threats and economic crises that required a collective response. The end of the crisis usually led to a reduction in the size of government, but never back to its pre-crisis level. Crisis has a ratcheting-up effect on government.[13] Moreover, government agencies, once established, tend to sink their tap roots into the political economy, providing services and benefits for some set of interests who will then mobilize to defend "their" agency.[14] This is especially true in the case of the clientele agencies whose benefits are concentrated but whose costs are diffused throughout the economy. For example, the Commerce Department is generally viewed in Washington as a do-nothing agency, but its friends in the business community are willing to protect it from attack. Individual programs, to be sure, are sometimes less durable.[15]

Thus Ronald Reagan and George H. W. Bush both proclaimed their dedication to cutting the size of government, but neither was able to eliminate even one agency or bureau in their combined twelve years in office. During the 2012 Republican presidential debates, all the prospective candidates proclaimed their desire to cut the size of the government. Yet although many Americans say they hate government, they appear to want its services. During the 1995 and 2013 "government shutdowns" prompted by struggles between Congress and the president over taxes and deficits, most Americans were concerned that government services would not be delivered (see Chapter 6). Few cheered the prospect of a disabled government.

The Importance of Rulemaking

As executive agencies carry out their assigned tasks, they engage in a host of activities from the most mundane to the most dangerous and controversial. Agencies conduct studies, publish reports, grant contracts, audit transactions, and identify violations of the law. Some agencies operate spy satellites, intercept communications, and send military forces to fight or disarm those who have been declared by the president to pose threats to the United States.

Among the most important tasks undertaken by executive agencies is rulemaking. Civics texts tell us that the law consists of statutes enacted by the Congress and signed by the president. This idea may have been correct in the early days of the American republic. Today, however, federal law is augmented by hundreds of thousands of rules and regulations possessing the force of law that are promulgated by a host of federal agencies—agencies staffed by officials whose names and job titles are unknown to the general public.

After a statute is passed by the Congress and signed into law by the president, the various federal agencies charged with administering and enforcing it will usually spend months and sometimes years writing rules and regulations to implement it, then continue to write rules for decades thereafter. Typically, a statute will assert a set of goals and establish some framework for achieving them, but much is still left to the discretion of administrators. In some instances, members of Congress are themselves uncertain of just what a law will do and depend on administrators to tell them.

In the case of the 2010 Affordable Care Act, widely known as Obamacare, as we saw earlier, several members admitted that they did not fully understand how the act would work and were depending on the Department of Health and Human Services, the agency with primary administrative responsibility for it, to explain it to them. Sometimes Congress is surprised by agency rules that seem inconsistent with congressional presumptions. Thus in 2012 the IRS proposed rules to determine eligibility under the Affordable Care Act that excluded millions of working-class Americans that Congress thought would be covered by the act. Several congressional Democrats who had helped to secure the enactment of the legislation complained that the IRS interpretation would frustrate the intent of Congress.[16] The case of the Affordable Care Act is fairly typical. As stated earlier, administrative scholar Jerry L. Mashaw notes that most public law is legislative in origin but administrative in content.[17]

When it deals with complex issues, Congress cannot realistically anticipate every problem that might arise and must give administrators discretion in implementing the law. The scope and complexity of governmental activities promotes congressional delegation of power to the bureaucracy in another way as well. When Congress addresses broad and complex issues, it typically has less difficulty reaching agreement on broad principles than on details. For example, every member of Congress might agree that enhancing air quality is a desirable goal. When it comes to deciding which approach to take to achieve this noble goal, however, many differences of opinion are certain to manifest themselves. Members from auto-producing states are likely to resist stiffer auto-emission standards and to insist that the real problem lies with coal-fired utilities. Members from districts that contain coal-fired utilities might argue that auto emissions are the problem. Members from districts that are economically dependent on heavy industry would demand exemptions for their constituents. Agreement on the principle of clean air would quickly dissipate as members struggled to achieve agreement on the all-important details. Delegation of power to an executive agency, by contrast, allows members to enact complex legislation without having to reach a detailed agreement. Congress can respond to pressure from constituents and the media to "do something" about a perceived problem while leaving the difficult details to administrators to hammer out.[18]

As a result of these and other factors, when Congress enacts major pieces of legislation, legislators inevitably delegate considerable authority to administrators to write rules and regulations designed to articulate and implement the legislative will. In some instances, Congress attempts to set standards and guidelines designed to govern administrative conduct. For example, the 1970 Clean Air Act specified the pollutants that the EPA would be charged with eliminating from the atmosphere as well as a number of the procedures that the EPA was obligated to undertake.[19] The act, however, left many other matters, including enforcement procedures, who should bear the burden of cleaning the air, and even how clean the air should ultimately be, to EPA administrators.

Many other statutes give administrators virtually unfettered discretion to decide how to achieve goals that are only vaguely articulated by the Congress. For example, the statute establishing the FTC outlaws, without expressly defining, "unfair methods of competition." Precisely what these methods might be is largely left to the agency to determine. Similarly, the statute creating the Occupational Health and Safety Administration (OSHA) calls on the agency "to protect health to the extent feasible." What that extent might be is for the agency to determine. And in its enabling act, the EPA is told to protect human health and the environment "to an adequate degree of safety."[20] As Congress continued to enact statutes setting out general objectives without specifying how the government was supposed to achieve them, the federal bureaucracy was left to fill in the ever-growing blanks.

To be sure, Congress sometimes does write detailed standards into the law only to see these rewritten by administrators. For example, in 2006 the SEC announced that it was issuing new rules that would significantly change key provisions of the 2002 Sarbanes-Oxley Act (also known as the Public Company Accounting Reform and Investor Protection Act). The act had been passed in the wake of the Enron scandal to reform corporate governance and prevent fraud. As enacted by Congress, Sarbanes-Oxley contains very specific standards. In response to industry lobbying, however, the SEC announced that it would issue new standards to ease corporate obligations under Section 404 of the act, which covers the financial statements issued by public corporations.[21] The agency determined that the law, as written by Congress, had forced corporations to engage in "overly conservative" practices.

Simply comparing the total volume of congressional output with the gross bureaucratic product provides a rough indication of where lawmaking now occurs in the federal government. The 106th Congress (1999–2000) was among the most active in recent years. It passed 580 pieces of legislation, two hundred more than the 105th Congress and nearly twice as many as the 104th. Some, like campaign-finance reform, seemed quite significant but many pieces of legislation were minor. During the same two years, executive agencies produced 157,173 pages of new rules and regulations in the official *Federal Register*.[22] For example, OSHA introduced new regulations affecting millions of workers and thousands of businesses, the EPA drafted new air quality standards, and the Securities and Exchange Commission and Commodities Futures Trading Commission announced significant revisions of futures trading rules that affected billions of dollars in transactions.

In principle, agency rules and regulations are designed merely to implement the will of Congress as expressed in statutes. In fact, agencies often draft regulations based on a broad statutory authority granted years or even decades earlier by congresses whose actual intent has become a matter of political interpretation.

Most of the laws enacted by Congress have little substance until federal agencies write the rules that give them effect. Take, for example, the Food Safety Modernization Act written by Congress and signed into law by President Obama in 2010. Four years later, the act still had little influence on American food safety because the FDA, charged with administering its provisions, had not yet finished writing the necessary rules and regulations that would give actual substance to the legislation conceived by the Congress.

Americans are often chided by the media and by academics for their lack of knowledge of current public issues and priorities. Many of the issues considered and policies promulgated by government agencies, however, are not only unknown to the public; they are also far below the radar of media and academic scrutiny. Each year, government agencies issue thousands of rules and regulations that have the force of law, along with orders, advisories, guidelines, and policy circulars that are fully enforceable by the courts. This mass of government edicts seldom receives much attention outside the small circle of stakeholders who are in continual and close consultation with rulemaking agencies.

Who outside a narrow segment of the investment community was aware of the debate surrounding a new rule adopted by the Commodity Futures Trading Commission in 2012 entitled "Business Conduct Standards for Swap Dealers and Major Swap Participants with Counterparties"? Similarly, who outside the trucking and agriculture industries was aware of the controversy over another 2012 rule adopted by the EPA entitled "Regulation of Fuels and Fuel Additives: 2013 Biomass-Based Diesel Renewable Fuel Volume"? As it happens, these two rules promise to have a large impact on the American economy. The new rule on business conduct, part of the lengthy and complex process of implementing the 2010 Dodd-Frank Act, imposes new standards for the "swaps" market, an over-the-counter market in which various financial instruments are traded by investors, usually as a means of hedging risks. The new rules, many of which were not specifically required by Dodd-Frank, establish anti-fraud, disclosure, and other standards for swaps dealers, and the estimated annual cost to investors of compliance with these rules is approximately $10 billion. The new EPA rule, for its part, sets standards for the use of biomass-based diesel fuel used mainly by trucks and by farmers. The cost to these groups of implementing the new standards is estimated to be $1 billion initially and perhaps $288 million per year thereafter.

According to one study, 131 rules and regulations defined as "major" (having a likely impact of $100 million or more), and adopted by federal agencies between 2009 and 2012, imposed $70 billion in new costs on the American public.[23] The various federal agencies writing these rules, however, assert that these costs were more than offset by the benefits derived by Americans from the rules in question.[24] Agencies are required by executive order to produce cost-benefit analyses of major new rules and, under the 2000 Right-to-Know Act, the Office of Management and Budget is required to submit an annual report to Congress summarizing the agencies' findings. Since many benefits are nonpecuniary—such as protection of homeland security—agencies are often creative in their accounting practices, monetizing presumptive benefits to justify actual costs. Or, as the office puts it politely, "Some rules produce benefits that cannot be adequately captured in monetary equivalents. In fulfilling their statutory mandates, agencies must sometimes act in the face of substantial uncertainty about the likely consequences."[25] Thus while these rules and regulations written by federal agencies usually do not capture the attention of the public or even the news media, they can have a substantial impact. They produce costs that are ultimately paid by the public in the form of higher prices and taxes, as well as benefits that may include safer products, cleaner air and water, a safer transportation system, and so forth.

Occasionally a proposed rule does come to the general public's attention. In

June 2014, at President Obama's behest, the EPA proposed new rules that would force coal-fired power plants to sharply reduce carbon-dioxide emissions. The standards threatened to increase the costs of energy produced from coal and led to howls of protest from coal producers and from politicians in states dependent on coal as an energy source. Typically, however, debates over the costs and benefits of proposed rules take place in obscure buildings in Washington and involve small groups of bureaucrats, interest-group "stakeholders," and congressional staffers, and do not come to the attention of the news media or the more general public.

The Elements of Federal Rulemaking

To begin with, some rules are written directly in response to, or at the behest of, Congress. In the most obvious case, when Congress enacts a piece of legislation, one or more executive agencies must write rules and regulations to flesh out and implement the statute. Complex pieces of legislation may result in hundreds of new rules. The 2010 Affordable Care Act (Obamacare) required years of rulemaking activity by the Department of Health and Human Services in order to implement the law.[26] Rules were also issued by the Department of the Treasury, the Department of Labor, the IRS, and a number of other agencies to implement portions of the legislation that fell into their bureaucratic domains.

Congress generally pays a great deal of attention to agency rulemaking when it comes to new legislation, sometimes giving agencies very precise directions and timetables, and occasionally reviewing agency efforts. Congress has also adopted the use of *deadlines* and *hammers,* embedding them in legislation as a way to compel agencies to expedite rulemaking. Political scientists Cornelius Kerwin and Scott Furlong point to the example of the Resource Conservation and Recovery Act of 1976, which contained a *hammer* mandating a total ban on land disposal of wastes, a disastrous outcome if the EPA failed to develop rules that articulated an alternative policy.[27] In this way, Congress sought to force timely agency action.

The White House is also likely to become involved in the shaping of rules for new programs, especially if these are part of the president's policy agenda. Since the Clinton administration, the Office of Information and Regulatory Affairs, an entity within the Office of Management and Budget, has been tasked by the White House with sending the agencies regulatory directives aimed at bringing about the development of rules and regulations that will promote the president's priorities.

More than 80 percent of the new rules promulgated in a typical year, however, involve existing rather than new programs.[28] Congress and the president certainly can become involved in this arena of rulemaking.[29] Major new rules are reviewed by the Office of Management and Budget and by the Government Accountability Office. The rulemaking agenda for existing programs, however, which includes statutes that have been in place for years or even decades, is largely based on the views and priorities of the agencies themselves.[30] Congress is only occasionally likely to become involved and then only if some important constituency interest makes a loud complaint.[31] Political scientists Mathew McCubbins and Thomas Schwartz have referred to this congressional practice as "fire alarm" oversight.[32]

Establishing Priorities

Agencies employ a variety of criteria to determine their rulemaking priorities for established programs. Large numbers of requests for interpretations and exemptions, for example, may serve as a cue to agency officials that some rule revision is needed.[33] According to political scientists William West and Connor Raso, agencies take into account such factors as economic and technological changes, shifts in the business environment, and experience acquired during the implementation of existing rules.[34] A number of agencies have priority-setting systems as well as teams tasked with the responsibility of reviewing the effectiveness of existing agency programs and recommending new courses of action.[35] In this way, agency priorities are, in considerable measure, the result of internal perspectives and decisions.

At the same time, the officials of most agencies are usually in regular contact with the groups and interests—the stakeholders—active in their own policy domains. These consultations play a significant role in shaping agency rulemaking agendas. West and Raso observe that agency officials and stakeholders, generally from the business community, are in frequent touch via informal communications, conferences, and meetings of trade associations. Also important is the so-called revolving door of personnel exchange between bureaucracies and (usually corporate) stakeholders.[36] When it comes to setting the agenda for new rules and regulations that affect existing laws, bureaucrats and stakeholders are "often impossible to separate."[37] To some extent, contacts between agencies and stakeholders are desirable if agencies are to fully understand the effects of the rules and regulations they promulgate. But the general picture that emerges from academic and press accounts is one in which rules and regulations are developed by an inside-the-Beltway crowd of agency executives and stakeholders who regularly exchange jobs with one another. This pattern is sometimes called "round up the usual suspects" rulemaking.

Once an agency has developed a proposed rule, or even during the process of development, it is required by Executive Order 12866, issued by President Clinton, to inform the Office of Information and Regulatory Affairs of significant new proposals. In some instances agencies are required by statute to inform the Council on Environmental Quality and the Small Business Administration as well, and rules made under some statutes mandate that agencies publish an "advance notice of proposed rulemaking" before the proposal is even fully formed. Agencies may also consult with Congress via the Government Accountability Office. Finally, the Office of Management and Budget has the authority to return proposed rules to the agency if they are deemed not to comport with the president's program or if the agency has not produced an adequate cost-benefit analysis of the impact of its proposal. In some limited instances, delineated by the 1990 Negotiated Rulemaking Act, agencies are then required to convene assemblies of representatives of affected interests to negotiate new rules.

After these reviews, the Administrative Procedure Act requires agencies to post proposed rules and regulations in the *Federal Register* for public comment. So-called notice-and-comment rulemaking is the hallmark of the system created in 1946 by this act. The notice posted in the *Federal Register* generally includes the language of the proposed rule and an invitation to any interested persons to post comments on the rule within some specified period of time. During this time frame, individuals and groups may send the agency their written comments on the proposed rule, and the agency is required to review and catalogue whatever comments it receives.

Public Disclosure

Despite the requirements of the Administrative Procedure Act, the Government Accountability Office has found that agencies often publish final rules without prior notice.[38] Agencies can do so if they are able to affirm that a proposed rule falls into one or another category that is exempt from the act's procedures. Some classes of rules administered by the EPA, the Department of Agriculture, the FAA, and several other agencies are exempt from the act because they apply to emergency situations. Rules dealing with military and foreign affairs are exempt. Interpretive rules are exempt in order to "allow agencies to explain ambiguous terms in legislative enactments without having to undertake cumbersome proceedings," while the general statements of policy are also exempt so as "to allow agencies to announce their tentative intentions for the future."[39] The reasons for these exemptions may be appropriate in principle, but in practice courts have found it difficult to distinguish between rules and policy statements, and agencies have been able to use policy statements to establish rules without notice and comment.[40]

One rather vague and large category of exemption is available if an agency finds and attaches to the final rule a statement that notice and comment were impractical, unnecessary, or contrary to the public interest. Such a "good cause" find-ing is unlikely to occur in the case of new and highly publicized programs. In cases where agencies are revising rules for long-established laws and believe that a rule is unlikely to attract much attention outside their established communities of stake-holders, however, they are as likely as not simply to publish the final rule without inviting comment. Since 9/11, agencies have increasingly invoked good cause as a reason not to seek notice and comment if their rule can somehow be justified by the threat of terrorism. For its part, the federal judiciary has been reluctant to question agency assertions.[41]

Agencies also make use of a variety of other subterfuges to avoid giving prior notice of rules. The Administrative Procedure Act requires that proposed "rules" be posted for comment, but it says nothing about other forms of agency orders such as policy circulars, technical corrections, advisories, and so forth. These forms of agency orders also have legal standing but are not subject to prior notice. The dif-ference between a rule and an order, as defined by the act, is essentially a question of an agency pronouncement's general applicability. A rule is a statement of general policy, while an order pertains to a particular instance.

This is another difference that may seem clear in theory but is often obscure in practice. Agencies frequently employ various sorts of orders, rather than rules, to assert general principles precisely because so doing allows them to avoid the Ad-ministrative Procedure Act. The U.S. Supreme Court has ruled that agencies have "informed discretion" in choosing whether to announce a new policy in the form of a rule or an order.[42] And while orders, unlike rules, do not have the full force and effect of law, the Supreme Court has ruled that orders must be given deference by courts in weighing the validity of agency actions because orders "constitute a body of experience and informed judgement to which courts and litigants may properly resort for guidance."[43]

When agencies do publish proposed rules and solicit comments, written sug-gestions and criticisms can have some impact.[44] Not surprisingly, the largest num-ber of responses comes from business and trade groups.[45] Changes resulting from such comments are, however, generally minor. William West, for example, found that informal communications between agencies and interest groups as rules were being developed were much more important than communications received by agencies during the comment period, which had an only marginal impact on what the final rules looked like.[46] Only in a very small number of statutes, such as the Fair Packaging and Labeling Act, has Congress required that agencies hold formal public hearings prior to the promulgation of a new rule. Formal rulemaking, as it is called, is cumbersome and rarely used.

In most cases, after the conclusion of the comment period, agencies are required to publish the final form of a new rule in the *Federal Register* for a period of thirty days to allow affected interests an opportunity to come into compliance with the revised law. Under the provisions of the 1996 Congressional Review Act, enacted as part of the Small Business Regulatory Enforcement Fairness Act, all new final rules must be submitted for review to both houses of Congress and to the Government Accountability Office. If the Office of Management and Budget has determined that the rule is "major" in terms of its potential economic impact, it cannot take effect for at least sixty days, nominally giving Congress time to disallow the rule if it wishes to do so. By 2011, the office had reviewed 1,029 major rules and just seventy-two joint resolutions of disapproval were introduced relating to forty-nine rules.[47] In only one case was a joint resolution of disapproval actually adopted and signed by the president. This involved an OSHA ergonomic rule enacted in the final month of the Clinton administration. The newly elected Republican Congress lost no time in disallowing the rule and President Bush was only too happy to sign the resolution.[48] Generally, agencies avoid the Congressional Review Act procedure by failing to file the required reports (see Chapter 6).

What might we conclude from this brief overview of federal rulemaking? Particularly when it comes to writing or revising rules for the implementation of established statutes, agencies have a good deal of discretion. Yet they certainly do not possess utter autonomy. Indeed there are numerous checks in the rulemaking process designed to ensure that agencies have a measure of accountability to Congress, the White House, and at least some constituency interests before a rule can be adopted and officially entered into the *Code of Federal Regulations.* As noted earlier, major rules are referred to the Office of Management and Budget so they can be assessed for their conformity with the president's objectives and for the accuracy of agencies' cost-benefit analyses. The impact of this review through the Office of Information and Regulatory Affairs has varied from administration to administration but has not been negligible.

Agencies must also demonstrate compliance with a variety of statutory obligations, generally involving the analysis and public dissemination of data relevant to their regulatory efforts. For example, the 1969 National Environmental Policy Act requires agencies to assess whether a proposed rule is likely to have a significant impact on the environment. If not, the agency must issue a "no significant impact" finding. If yes, the agency must prepare an environmental impact statement for the Office of Management and Budget describing the steps the agency will take to mitigate potential environmental damage.[49] Similarly, the Toxic Substances Control Act requires the EPA to conduct assessments of the threats posed by various toxic substances in the environment as compared to the technical possibility and financial cost of proposed reductions of these threats, and then explain how the risks justify the rules that are proposed. The 1980 Regulatory Flexibility Act requires agencies to consider the effects of proposed rules on small businesses, to assess potential alternatives that reduce the effects of such rules on small businesses, and to make their analyses public.[50] The 1992 Unfunded Mandates Reform Act requires agencies to show that they have assessed the impact of proposed rules on state, local, and tribal entities and to prepare a regulatory impact analysis for such rules. And the 2000 Data for Information Quality Act requires agencies to develop policies to ensure that the information they collect and utilize meets high standards in terms of quality and objectivity. The act allows private parties to petition agencies to correct what they believe to be errors in their information.[51] Several executive orders, too, require agencies to assess the impact of proposed rules on federalism.

These and the various other limits on agency actions discussed earlier are not insignificant, but they still leave agencies with considerable discretionary authority, for two reasons. First, agencies control much of their own regulatory agenda and set most of their own priorities. And second, many of the external checks on agency action apply to a small number of "major" regulations, leaving agencies more or less to their own devices on the minor rules that collectively can have a major impact. Indeed, small business groups have argued that there are so many of these seemingly minor rules in play that the result is a heavy regulatory burden. In response to such complaints, President Obama's 2011 Executive Order 13,963 ordered agencies to consider the cumulative impact of regulations, particularly insofar as small businesses were involved. It is not clear whether and how agencies have responded to this order. But it is perhaps telling that in 2012 the then-administrator of OIRA, Cass Sunstein, felt it necessary to issue a memorandum to the heads of executive departments and agencies reminding them of that order.[52]

Presidential Management of the Executive Branch

While Americans may debate governance as a philosophical problem, presidents tend to see it as a management problem. The president is the country's chief executive and so is responsible for overseeing the hundreds of agencies and millions of employees and contractors in the executive branch. Presidents are ultimately held responsible for problems and failures. President Truman kept a sign on his desk saying, "The buck stops here!"

As we saw, early presidents had virtually no staff and played little day-to-day role in the management of the government. Contemporary presidents, by contrast, have a large staff and play a very active role in management. Presidents possess three major management tools: appointments, executive oversight, and regulatory review. As to appointments, with senatorial approval, the president appoints 1,200 to 1,400 top officials of the various departments and agencies as well as several thousand additional high-ranking civil servants. Presidential appointees are chosen for their support for the president's goals and can be removed from their positions if the president believes that they are no longer useful. Usually senior officials are asked to resign to allow them to avoid the embarrassment of being fired. Thus, in 2014, Secretary of Veterans Affairs Eric Shinseki was asked to resign in the wake of widespread complaints about poor service at VA hospitals. Of course, an official who refuses to resign when asked to do so is likely to be discharged. For example, in 1993 President Clinton asked FBI Director William Sessions, a Reagan appointee, to tender his resignation. Sessions refused and Clinton fired him. There are variations to this scenario, however. One previous FBI director, J. Edgar Hoover, made certain that he could not be dismissed by collecting damaging information about the presidents and attorneys general to whom he reported. When Hoover was summoned by Attorney General Robert Kennedy and told that President Kennedy wanted him to resign, Hoover countered by explaining what information about the president would be released from his files if he were to be forced from office. Hoover kept his job.[53]

A second presidential instrument is executive oversight via the White House Office of Management and Budget, which encompasses four resource management offices, each led by an associate director, and each responsible for a particular set of government agencies. The resource management offices monitor the agencies' management and budgetary activities, including their compliance with the president's agenda. The Office of Management and Budget thus gives the president a mechanism to monitor government agencies and to direct their activities. Without that office, the president could not function as chief executive.

Finally, presidents can influence the bureaucratic rulemaking process. Their most important instrument for this purpose is regulatory review. The regulatory review process emerged from the 1979 Paperwork Reduction Act, which created the Office of Information and Regulatory Affairs within the White House Office of Management and Budget. Congress was responding to complaints from business owners about the time and money they were being forced to spend on the forms and records required by government regulations. The new office allowed the White House to monitor and limit the impositions of regulatory agencies on the businesses and industries that they regulated.[54] As we shall see in Chapter 7, every president since Ronald Reagan has used regulatory review to attempt to capture the agency rulemaking process and codify its policies without necessarily obtaining congressional assent.

Through appointments, the Office of Management and Budget, and regulatory review presidents exercise enormous power over the executive branch. Generally speaking, when presidents inform agency leaders of their goals and objectives, those leaders attempt to comply.[55] Thus, for example, in 2014 President Obama directed the EPA to "work expeditiously" to develop new standards governing pollutants produced by existing power plants. The agency's leaders had some doubts about the president's directives but nevertheless seemed ready to attempt to implement them. In this, as in most other cases, agency leaders have no particular incentive to fight with the president.

Alexis de Tocqueville once observed that the power of the Roman emperor was great but its reach was limited. The same could be said of presidents. Presidential power over the agencies is great but is exercised intermittently and limited to a small number of goals—the president's agenda. On a day-to-day basis, executive agencies have considerable latitude to manage their own affairs and to govern the United States according to their own lights. The executive branch governs with the authority of the president but not entirely at the president's behest.

Thoughts on Executive Power and Democracy

Americans expect their government to be effective and sensitive to the will of the people. These are high expectations. The president, America's chief executive, is an elected official. Effective government, however, requires the work of officials and contractors who are several steps removed from the electoral process. Much of the law is made not by America's elected legislature but by anonymous executive officials whose claim to legitimacy is expertise rather than democratic accountability. Is there a point beyond which effective government can no longer be democratic government? We shall return to these questions.

Executive Agencies and Their Missions

The executive branch consists of fifteen cabinet departments that, in turn, consist of some five hundred offices, bureaus, and agencies. In addition, the executive branch includes seventy independent agencies with their own subdivisions. The government employs about 2.7 million individuals as well as a much larger number of contract employees engaged in work for the government but not formally on the government payroll. Each year, executive agencies adopt some four thousand rules and regulations that have the force of law, in some respects making the executive branch, not the Congress, America's chief lawmaking body. Some have argued that the executive branch is too large and should be reduced in size. Once established, however, agencies develop constituencies for their services and are difficult to dislodge. Many agencies have a direct influence on the lives of millions of Americans.

Department of State. The State Department manages America's relations with other nations and with international organizations like the United Nations, and staffs American embassies and diplomatic missions around the world. At times, this can be a hazardous duty. In 2012, for instance, Islamic militants attacked the American diplomatic com-

pound in Benghazi, Libya, murdering U.S. Ambassador J. Christopher Stevens.

Internal Revenue Service. The Internal Revenue Service (IRS) is an agency within the Treasury Department charged with collecting the taxes that fund government operations. Each year, the IRS collects more than $2 trillion in taxes from individuals and corporations. The IRS also interprets the tax code written by Congress, acts on requests from charitable and religious groups for exemption from taxation, and investigates tax fraud.

Defense Department. The Department of Defense was created by the 1947 National Security Act, which united the several American military services under one umbrella. The department employs 700,000 civilians and about 1.3 million

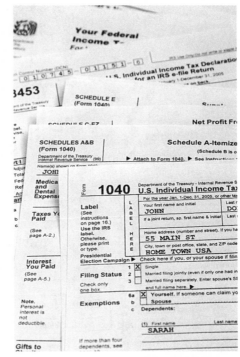

military personnel assigned to the Army, Navy, Air Force, and Marines. It has divided the world into six combatant commands under the authority of a commander who reports to the Joint Chiefs of Staff. The Joint Chiefs in turn report to the secretary of defense, who reports to the president. Within each combatant command, the

commander exercises control over troops from all the services and supervises their logistical support.

The Federal Bureau of Investigation. The federal government's primary law enforcement agency is the FBI, an agency within the Justice Department. The FBI has a broad mandate to investigate violations of federal criminal law, but sometimes engages in jurisdictional disputes with other federal police agencies. Competition among law enforcement agencies may produce inefficiencies, but can also provide Congress and the president with alternate perspectives on which to base their decisions. The FBI was led for nearly forty years by J. Edgar Hoover, its founding director. Hoover was feared in Washington because he was reputed to possess secret files on important politicians and officials.

The Transportation Security Administration. The TSA was created in the wake of the 2001 terror attacks in New York and Washington and was moved to the newly created Homeland Security Administration in 2003. TSA air marshals are assigned to many domestic and international flights and TSA screeners check every passenger and piece of luggage destined to board a flight within the United States. Most Amer-

icans complain about long lines at airports, but few would be willing to dispense with the screening process.

The Centers for Disease Control and Prevention. The CDC is America's main public health institute and its main responsibility is to control the spread of infectious diseases. During the 2014 Ebola outbreak, CDC scientists sought to help African nations deal with the disease and to prevent Ebola from reaching the United States. In 2011, the CDC's blog presented an article instructing the public on how to prepare for a zombie invasion. No such invasion was feared, but the CDC communication team thought the message would reach many who ignored public service announcements and teach them how to prepare for a disaster of any sort.

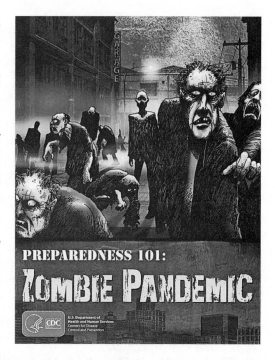

The Food and Drug Administration. The FDA is the primary agency responsible for ensuring the safety of the food consumed by Americans, and the pharmaceuticals and cosmetics used by Americans. FDA inspectors monitor every stage in food

production and FDA scientists test every pharmaceutical before it can be prescribed. Some critics charge that the FDA is too lax in its testing and inspection efforts while others say that the agency is too slow to approve potentially life-saving drugs.

Social Security. The Social Security Administration manages America's largest social program. During their working lives, Americans and their employers pay a mandatory Social Security tax that is automatically withheld from their paychecks. When they retire, Americans are then eligible to receive monthly pension checks whose size is based on the number of years they worked and their lifetime incomes. Millions of Americans depend on Social Security to pay their bills after they retire and are concerned when critics claim that the Social Security system will "go bankrupt" in the coming years. Such bankruptcy is impossible given the current legal obligations of this entitlement program. If the funds withheld from paychecks were not adequate to fund the system's obligations, Congress would be compelled to raise taxes to pay retirees.

SIX

The President, the Congress, and Domestic Policy

In This Chapter

Congress is the nation's legislature, responsible for formulating and making the law. The president's role, in principle, is to execute the laws enacted by Congress. Nowhere does the Constitution suggest that the president is expected to take a lead role in lawmaking. Yet many presidents have taken a broad view of their responsibilities and, since the 1930s and Franklin D. Roosevelt's "New Deal," every president has proposed packages of programs and policies to the Congress. Members of Congress can and do act as "policy entrepreneurs," promoting legislation dealing with domestic or foreign policy.[1] Such pieces of legislation as the Dodd-Frank financial services regulatory act, the McCain-Feingold campaign finance reform act, and the Kennedy-Kassebaum health insurance act were primarily congressional in origin and are known by their sponsors' names. Most major pieces of legislation, however, emanate from the White House.[2] Let us examine the patterns of conflict and cooperation between the president and Congress in the realm of domestic policy.

Presidential Initiative and Congressional Opposition

The most important sets of programs enacted by Congress in the past century, Franklin D. Roosevelt's "New Deal" and Lyndon Johnson's "Great Society," were developed by the two presidents and their advisers and were enacted, albeit with modifications, by Democratic congresses. The president has become the dominant figure in the realm of policy innovation for a number of reasons. First the president is a unitary actor while Congress consists of 535 individuals in two houses. It is difficult for Congress to act in a unified or coordinated manner and to agree on an agenda for action. Congress thus depends on the president to provide the agenda, and contemporary presidents are happy to oblige. The electoral process, as we observed in Chapter 4, generally produces ambitious presidents who hope to make a mark on history through their leadership and policy innovation.

Presidents, moreover, have developed an institutional capacity for policy innovation, through the White House staff, the executive office, and connections to America's universities and "think tanks" that provide every administration with plans and proposals. All presidents know they are graded on the new policies they develop and those who merely do no harm are not likely to join the pantheon of the greats.

President Obama has been no exception. The president can claim credit for quite a number of programs, though none as extensive in scope and reach as his signature health care initiative, the 2010 Affordable Care Act, known as Obamacare. Presidential initiatives also played a role in the enactment of a major economic stimulus package, a bailout of troubled banks and auto companies, the passage of a new pay-equity law, new tobacco regulation, policies that wound down the wars in Iraq and Afghanistan, and a variety of other programs.

As we shall see, when presented with presidential initiatives, members of Congress often have strong reason to oppose the chief executive. Members of the president's own party, to be sure, are usually supportive. The president's fellow partisans are more likely to share the president's views, to be responsive to similar interest groups and social forces, and to believe that the president's success or failure may affect their own electoral fortunes. Parallel reasons will usually lead members of the other party to oppose the president.[3] Hence presidents have their best chance of policy success when their own party controls Congress, and they work at a serious disadvantage when even one house of Congress is controlled by the opposition.

Political scientist Stephen Skowronek once characterized the president as a "blunderbuss," a muzzle-loading firearm with considerable power, if poor aim.[4] If the president is a blunderbuss, Congress is often "Dr. No," refusing to accede to presidential demands. Often the ability to say "no" is Congress's most important weapon, though in using its weapon it risks being called obstructionist by the White House and its allies. Nevertheless, unlike the president, members of Congress are seldom personally blamed or credited for their legislative accomplishments.[5] (Some, however, do seem to be especially adept at claiming credit.[6]) While voters may disparage the Congress collectively as a bunch of do-nothings, they generally like their own representative and, election after election, return that individual to office.[7] For many members, especially those not of the president's party, being a do-nothing, a Dr. No, is the only form of power available.

The Constitution: Separate Institutions, Shared Powers

Article I of the Constitution vests legislative power in the Congress, while Article II assigns executive power in the president. Yet under the principle of checks and balances, each is assigned an important role in the activities of the other. The Congress can refuse to pass legislation requested by the president or decline to provide funding for programs sought by the president. It can also reject presidential appointments or refuse to ratify treaties negotiated by the president. Congress can override presidential vetoes, impeach and remove the president from office, declare war, and order the president to take charge of the war effort. And though not specified in the Constitution, Congress has claimed the implied power to conduct investigations into the president's conduct and to oversee the activities of executive agencies.

Presidents, for their part, can veto acts of Congress, call Congress into special session, and adjourn Congress if the two houses cannot agree on a time of adjournment. The president is charged with executing the laws enacted by Congress and with commanding the nation's military forces in wars declared by Congress. The president must inform Congress "from time to time" on the state of the Union and recommend to Congress "such Measures as he shall judge necessary and expedient." The vice president serves as the presiding officer of the Senate and can cast a deciding vote in the case of ties in that body, though the most recent vice president to do so was Walter Mondale some forty years ago. Presidential scholar Richard Neustadt correctly observed that the constitutional separation between the presidency and the Congress is not a case of separation of powers, but is rather an example of separated institutions sharing powers.[8]

In principle, the president and Congress might cooperate, causing the constitutional system to operate smoothly in order to produce and implement legislation. The president might suggest necessary and expedient measures to Congress, which might then develop and enact legislation. The president might, without further ado, sign the legislation and go about the business of implementing and executing it. All this could happen and sometimes does, especially in the event of some national emergency such as the 9/11 terror attacks, when President Bush and congressional leaders worked swiftly to craft and implement a response.[9]

Even in more mundane areas, the president and the Congress sometimes act together in an expeditious manner. Take, for example, the 2009 Lilly Ledbetter Fair Pay Act. In keeping with the current fashion of naming laws for the person who nominally inspired them, this law is named after Ledbetter, a supervisor for Goodyear Tire and Rubber Company who discovered that she had been paid far less than her male counterparts. She filed a discrimination suit that went all the way to the U.S. Supreme Court but was ultimately dismissed in 2007 because Ledbetter had not filed suit within 180 days of her first paycheck, which was then the statutory requirement. A bill to change the law to allow suit to be brought within 180 days of any paycheck died in the Senate in 2007. The Ledbetter bill became an issue in the 2008 presidential campaign with Republican candidate John McCain expressing opposition to the bill and Democratic candidate Barack Obama saying he would make enactment of the Ledbetter bill a legislative priority. After the election, Democrats controlled not only the presidency but both houses of Congress as well. Obama had no difficulty prompting House Democrats to reintroduce the proposal, which was strongly supported by a host of labor, women's, and other groups in the Democratic constituency. The bill passed the House and Senate on party-line votes. President Obama then signed the bill, which went into effect on January 29, 2009. The president and Congress had cooperated, and within one month a new law had been enacted.

Yet this sort of cooperation is more the exception than the norm. Even when there is a success, the road to that success has usually been long and difficult. In the case of the Affordable Care Act, the White House was initially stymied by congressional opposition, with even some Democrats expressing skepticism. It found that the key to gaining approval was to craft the proposal so that it would serve the interests of major health insurance companies and the pharmaceutical industry. Health insurers hoped to sell millions of new policies to individuals who would be compelled to purchase insurance, and the pharmaceutical industry envisioned $35 billion in additional profits by selling drugs to these newly ensured consumers.[10] Yet despite the support of these powerful industries and their lobbyists, the bill passed the House and Senate on straight party votes with complex procedural maneuvers required to prevail in the Senate. After Democrats lost control of the House of Representatives in the 2010 national elections, most other elements of the president's agenda, especially immigration reform, were blocked by Republican leaders.

Embattled by Design

The relationship between the Congress and the president often can be more antagonistic than cooperative. To begin with, the electoral process guarantees that the president and many members of Congress will disagree, often strongly, on national priorities and directions. The president is independently elected in a set of fifty-one separate contests—fifty states plus the District of Columbia—taking place on the same day across the nation. Senators look for votes only in their states, with one-third of senators elected on the same day the president is chosen and two-thirds, following the constitutional principle of staggered terms, elected in previous years. House members are elected in districts, which are subdivisions of states. The framers of the Constitution believed that subjecting the principal officers of the government to separate elections, even at different times, would serve as a precaution against mass movements or unwise policies in response to some sudden shift in the public's mood. As Alexander Hamilton explained in *Federalist* 71, the complexity of the electoral system would prevent "an unqualified complaisance to every sudden breeze of passion; or to every transient impulse which the people may receive."[11]

Electoral complexity means that the president is likely to have different priorities than many members of Congress, subscribe to political beliefs that differ from those of many members of Congress, and often, since the president's electoral coattails are generally short, to have a different party affiliation than the majority in one or both houses of Congress. Presidents are far more likely to receive support from members of their own party than from members of the partisan opposition and are often frustrated when one or both houses of Congress are controlled by their partisan opponents. Divided government has become quite common in recent years in part because demographic changes have given the Democrats some advantage in presidential elections while the redrawing and gerrymandering of congressional district boundaries has given the GOP an advantage in House races.[12] Since 1995, Republicans have held majorities in the House during eight of ten elections while the Democrats, during the same period, won six of ten presidential contests. For only a brief, two-year period from 2009 to 2011 did one party—the Democrats—control the White House and both houses of Congress. Not coincidentally, it was during this period that President Obama was able to secure passage of his controversial health care legislation.

The difficulties caused by electoral complexity have been exacerbated in recent years because each party has sought to maximize "safe" congressional seats by drawing congressional district lines in such a way as to create heavily Democratic and heavily Republican districts.[13] As a result of this strategy to eliminate "swing" districts inhabited by voters with differing points of view, members of Congress no longer have much incentive to moderate their stands to appeal to a broad range of voters in their districts. To the contrary, Democratic members have become more liberal while Republican members have become more conservative.[14] Elected by an ideologically diverse national constituency, Republican presidents may have diffi-culty pleasing their more conservative copartisans in the House, while Democratic presidents are likely to be criticized by their more liberal Democratic House col-leagues. During the Obama years, for example, many House Democrats found the president insufficiently attentive to liberal causes while most House Republicans saw the president as a committed Leftist.[15]

The Role of Ambition

A second factor producing conflict between the president and Congress is presiden-tial ambition. As we saw in Chapters 1 and 2, during the early decades of the Repub-lic and even into the early twentieth century, presidential nominees were chosen by party leaders who preferred to see unassuming and deferential figures in the White House. Accordingly, most presidents were content to leave the work of governance to the Congress and harbored little desire to direct the affairs of the nation. Perhaps the extreme case was James Buchanan, elected in 1856, who defended his inactivity as the nation disintegrated by saying that he had "called the attention of Congress to the subject" of impending Southern secession and war, but believed that "it was the imperative duty of Congress," not the president, to determine what if any action needed to be taken.[16]

Complementing presidential diffidence was the much more aggressive con-duct shown by the leaders of the House and Senate during this era. Strong party discipline meant that the speaker of the House, in particular, led an institution of government more powerful than the presidency. House leaders and Senate leaders, as well, were anxious to defend their institutional prerogatives, to manage the affairs of the nation, and to keep meddlesome presidents in their place.

Around 1900, as a result of Progressive-era reforms, party discipline in Con-gress began to wane while new communications technologies allowed presidents to mobilize popular support on behalf of their own legislative objectives. These two changes provided an opportunity for presidents like Teddy Roosevelt, William Howard Taft, and Woodrow Wilson to present legislative programs to Congress, taking advantage of the constitutional admonition to present to Congress, from time to time, measures the president deems to be "necessary and expedient." In 1933, for instance, President Franklin D. Roosevelt called the Congress into special session to deal with the nation's economic crisis and presented it with proposed banking legislation that passed both houses within a few hours. Throughout his fourteen years in office, FDR seized the legislative initiative and presented Congress with dozens of major proposals that collectively became the "New Deal."

According to political scientist Andrew Rudalevige, Roosevelt's practice became institutionalized under Harry Truman.[17] President Truman and his advisers used the Bureau of the Budget, which an FDR executive order had moved into the Executive Office of the President, to develop legislative ideas. Staffers in the bureau solicited ideas from the executive agencies, from the White House staff, and from universities and research institutes like the Brookings Institution. These ideas were sifted, packaged, and sent to Congress in presidential messages that promoted a course of action based on the nation's legislative needs—as described by the president. FDR had generally bullied Congress and, by force of will and against the backdrop of national emergencies, had compelled legislators to accede to many of his demands. During the Truman administration, such presidential efforts to set the legislative agenda became institutionalized.

Roosevelt was an aggressive and extremely ambitious individual and so was Truman. But Roosevelt advisers like Dean Acheson and George C. Marshall, inherited by Truman, expected the new president to proceed in what they regarded as an appropriately presidential (Rooseveltian) manner and sought to create institutions that would compensate for FDR's absence. The presidents who followed Truman, though, were cut more in the FDR mold. Changes in the presidential nominating process, as we saw in Chapter 4, meant that the role of party leaders was all but eliminated and the selection process came to favor ambitious politicians willing to devote years to the singleminded pursuit of the nation's highest office. When elected, such individuals generally claimed to have a popular mandate and a plan, and were quick to present Congress with a presidential agenda. Some presidents, like Ronald Reagan, brought new ideas with them. Others shopped for ideas. John F. Kennedy and Lyndon Johnson, for example, made extensive use of the growing network of think tanks and university-based policy "wonks" to create task forces that would recommend innovative proposals. All post–New Deal presidents relied on the Bureau of the Budget, as well as the Council of Economic Advisers, the National Security Council staff, and other advisory groups within the Executive Office of the President, to propose new ideas and initiatives.

Since the 1921 Budget Act, presidents have been required to provide Congress with a consolidated annual budget that reconciles agency budget requests with expected revenues. Before FDR the annual budget was more an accounting exercise than an effort to set the nation's agenda. Roosevelt, Truman, and their successors, however, have used the annual budget message to introduce new packages of programs and initiatives. George W. Bush and Barack Obama essentially consolidated the budget message and State of the Union address in order to highlight presidential budget requests.

The public and even Congress have come to rely on the president to set a legislative agenda. A president who failed to present Congress with a package of new programs and initiatives would be widely castigated for lacking imagination and initiative. At the same time, however, the president's agenda is sure to create conflicts with those members of Congress who have partisan, ideological, or programmatic differences with the president. Thus presidential ambition is certain to produce clashes between the executive and the legislative branches.

Presidents are often gauged on their ability to steer legislation through the Congress, but unless the electorate has been kind enough to fill both houses with members of the president's party who share his or her agenda and beliefs, and the nation's enemies helpfully provide a crisis, this process can be quite problematic. Presidents vary in their personal ability to bargain with Congress. Lyndon Johnson was reportedly extremely adept at the arts of persuasion, intimidation, and greasing the wheels of government with special favors. Other presidents have been less adept and most have developed staff resources to smooth the way for their legislative requests. The Executive Office of the President includes a number of staff members whose chief task is legislative liaison—in other words, lobbying on behalf of the president's program. Like all good lobbyists, presidential staffers develop friends and contacts on Capitol Hill, provide information to congressional offices that supports the president's views, and seek to frame issues in a way that will increase presidential support in Congress.[18] Yet the bottom line is that presidents will generally receive the support of members of their own party and will generally not receive the support of members of the opposing party. At one time, presidents could change a few votes by offering special legislative favors and so forth to members of the other party, but today presidents must concentrate on making sure their own coalition remains intact. In recent, ideologically polarized congresses, party-line voting on major issues has become the norm and presidents have little room to pick up votes from the other side if their own party is in the minority.

Whose Law Is It Anyway?

A third source of conflict between the president and Congress derives from what might be called their principal-agent relationship. When Congress enacts a law, the executive is required to execute it. One might say that the president is serving as an agent for the Congress. Conflicts almost inevitably arise in any relationship of this sort. Whether the agent is a president or a plumbing contractor, the principal is likely to find instances in which the agent did not follow the precise terms of the contract or, perhaps, failed altogether to fulfill it.

Unlike most plumbing contractors, presidents are agents with their own agendas and their own ideas about the public interest. Presidents may decide to reject a congressional initiative, to nominally agree but not to do exactly what Congress mandated, or perhaps to accept Congress's mandate but take no action at all if they believe that Congress wants to take the nation in the wrong direction. As to outright rejection of a legislative initiative, the Constitution gives the president conditional veto power—conditional because Congress may override that veto. As we saw in Chapter 2, America's early presidents seldom vetoed laws, believing that the veto could only properly be used to protect the institution of the presidency from legislative encroachments. When Andrew Jackson vetoed a bank bill expressly because of a policy disagreement he was censured by the Senate, and when John Tyler vetoed a bank bill he was threatened with impeachment. More recently the veto became fairly common—FDR vetoed 635 bills—but during the Bush and Obama administrations, because of partisan gridlock, so few bills were passed that presidential veto pens grew rusty. In 2013, Congress passed only fifty-seven bills, the fewest in its history, and none were vetoed by the president. The media noted in 2014 that there was so little legislative activity that even the number of demonstrations and protests on Capitol Hill had dropped sharply. There seemed to be little point to demonstrating when so little legislative activity was taking place.[19]

The presidential veto is not as powerful a weapon as the veto power possessed by many state governors. Governors usually have "line-item vetoes," that is, they may veto portions of bills without having to veto the entire bill. The president possesses no such ability. Presidents must accept or reject bills in their entirety, which gives Congress a chance to include measures the president opposes along with measures the president would be hard-pressed to veto, such as defense appropriations bills. In 1996, Congress enacted legislation giving the president a line-item veto power, which President Clinton used a number of times. In 1998, however, the Supreme Court found that the line-item veto was not consistent with the Constitution's Presentment Clause because it improperly gave the president the power to amend legislation.[20] Recent presidents, as we shall see, have sought to use signing statements for just this purpose.

The veto is a presidential power expressed by the Constitution. The two other ways in which presidents and the executive branch more generally can thwart Congress are not. The first of these is through the execution of a law in a manner inconsistent with congressional intent. This practice is associated with the agencies of the executive branch as well as directly with the president. A recent case that caused a great deal of controversy involved a 2014 decision by the IRS to rewrite a portion of the Affordable Care Act. The act states that individuals who purchase health insurance through state exchanges are eligible for tax credits. These credits were intended to encourage individuals to purchase insurance through this mechanism and to encourage the states to establish such exchanges. By 2014, however, thirty-six states had declined to establish exchanges. In consultation with other agencies and the White House, the IRS decided to reinterpret the law to allow individuals who had not purchased their insurance in this manner to also receive tax credits. This seemingly minor change involved hundreds of millions of dollars in potential benefits and costs to businesses, individuals, and the national treasury. The problem, moreover, threatened the entire administrative structure of the Affordable Care Act. Opponents of the Act brought suit in federal court asserting the IRS had acted improperly. Eventually, though, the U.S. Supreme Court declared that the agency had not abused its discretion.[21]

When presidents themselves plan to execute the law in a manner inconsistent with statutory language, they often make their intent clear so that federal agencies will know what the chief executive expects of them. Signing statements are one vehicle that presidents have used for this purpose. For example, when President George H. W. Bush signed a bill that included a provision requiring contractors on a particular federal project to pursue affirmative action in their hiring practices, his signing statement directed the secretary of energy to ignore the requirement.[22] Similarly, when President George W. Bush signed legislation creating an inspector general to oversee U.S. operations in Iraq, he issued a signing statement asserting that this official should refrain from audits and investigations into matters involving intelligence and counterintelligence.[23] The legislation itself contained no such provision.

It hardly seems necessary to point out that when presidents plan to violate a prohibition or a criminal statute they usually seek to avoid public disclosure of that fact. Thus only through a determined congressional investigation was it learned that the Reagan White House had decided to violate a statutory prohibition known as the Boland Amendment, which forbade further government funding of the Nicara-guan Contras whom the president had strongly supported.

Another way in which presidents can use their executive powers to thwart Congress is by failing, or refusing, to execute the law. President Nixon, for example, several times refused to spend—that is, he "impounded"—funds appropriated by Congress. This practice was later severely restricted by the 1974 Budget and Impoundment Control Act. Presidential refusals to execute laws are not altogether uncommon, and they tend to be associated with presidential efforts to win favor with important constituency groups. President Clinton, for example, declared that a section of a defense appropriations bill requiring the discharge of military personnel found to be HIV-positive was unconstitutional and would not be enforced. President Obama, long before the Supreme Court acted to legitimate same-sex marriage, found reason not to enforce major portions of the Defense of Marriage Act, which had barred the government from recognizing such unions. The Obama administration also refused to enforce the Unlawful Internet Gambling Enforcement Act, which was aimed at blocking Internet gambling, and granted waivers to ten states freeing them from provisions of the No Child Left Behind Act. The statute, as enacted by Congress, makes no provision for such waivers. The administration also announced that it would refuse to deport undocumented immigrants who had come to the United States as children. Congress had considered and refused to enact legislation that would have adopted this policy. According to a White House official, "Often times Congress has blocked efforts and we look to pursue other appropriate means of achieving our policy goals . . . the president isn't going to be stonewalled by politics, he will pursue whatever means are available to do business on behalf of the American people."[24]

When the president refuses to enforce a statute or reinterprets a statute there is little Congress can do, at least in the short run. In 2014, Republican House Speaker John Boehner announced plans to sue the president in federal court for, among other matters, failing in his constitutional responsibility to see to it that the laws are faithfully executed. As we shall see in Chapter 8, however, the courts have generally been unwilling to intervene in disputes between Congress and the president, which in effect means that Congress has to fight its own battles.

How Congress Can Do Battle with the Executive

In fights with the executive, Congress is not without power. Actually, Congress has at least six major weapons at its disposal. These are its legislative powers, its quasi executive powers, the congressional power of the purse, legislative oversight, legislative investigations, and Congress's ultimate constitutional weapon, impeachment.

Legislative Powers

The simplest manner in which Congress can oppose the president is by enacting laws aimed at blocking presidential actions, or by refusing to enact laws favored by the president. On a routine basis, Congress declines to enact legislation sought by the president. In some instances the president has little recourse but to denounce congressional obstructionists. In other cases, the president may seek to circumvent Congress by using executive tools to achieve the desired effect. For example, Congress refused to enact the various environmental bills sought by President Clinton. The president, however, was able to implement much of his environmental agenda through executive orders and regulatory actions.[25] President Obama has similarly sought through executive action to implement various pieces of immigration legislation that Congress has declined to enact, including the DREAM Act, which would provide various rights and a route to citizenship for several hundred thousand undocumented immigrants. Many Republicans and some Democrats oppose the bill, and Obama has promised to continue using his executive powers to achieve his policy goals.

Two examples of lawmaking aimed at thwarting the president were mentioned earlier: the 1974 Budget and Impoundment Control Act and the 1982 Boland Amendment. The first of these was enacted in the wake of the Watergate battle between Congress and President Nixon (to be discussed more fully later). Since the administration of Thomas Jefferson, presidents had engaged in the practice of sequestering or impounding funds appropriated by Congress for programs they opposed. Jefferson, for example, refused to spend $50,000 appropriated by Congress for the construction of new gunboats to be used by the Navy to patrol the Mississippi River, saying that they were not needed.

Impoundment became a major issue during the Nixon administration. President Nixon made extensive use of impoundment both to block programs he opposed and to increase his leverage over executive agencies. In 1973–1974 alone, Nixon refused to disburse nearly $12 billion in funds that had been appropriated by the Congress. Following Nixon's resignation, Congress enacted legislation that provided detailed rules governing the president's impoundment authority. Subsequently, in the case of *Train v. City of New York,* the Supreme Court declared that the president had no authority to impound appropriated funds unless the appropriating legislation specifically granted such power.[26]

A second notable case of the use of legislation to curb presidential power grew out of a dispute between Congress and President Reagan over the administration's intervention into the Nicaraguan civil war. The administration supported several groups called the Contras, which sought to overthrow Nicaragua's Sandinista government, and it had ordered CIA special operations troops to engage in a number of acts of sabotage aimed at undermining the Nicaraguan government—all without informing congressional intelligence committees. Congressional Democrats strongly opposed American intervention in Nicaragua and were able to enact several pieces of legislation, known collectively as the Boland Amendment, that prohibited U.S. funding for the Contras. The legislation was attached as a rider to the Defense Appropriations Act, which the president would have found difficult to veto. Congress was thus able to use its legislative powers to block a presidential practice that it opposed.

What happened next, however, illustrates the difficulties that Congress can encounter in attempting to thwart a determined president through legislation. The administration decided that it would interpret the legislation very narrowly as applying only to funds appropriated for the operations of U.S. intelligence agencies, then employed the staff of the National Security Council, which is not an intelligence agency, to continue channeling money to the Contras. When Congress learned of this ploy and altered the Boland Amendment to clearly prohibit any and all funding of the Contras, the administration employed secret funds that it had acquired through a clandestine arms deal designed to help Iran in its war with Iraq—a maneuver that only came to light because of a report published in a Lebanese newspaper. This revelation, as we shall see, sparked congressional hearings that might have led to Reagan's impeachment. During the presidency of George H. W. Bush, Congress authorized a resumption of aid to the Contras, who were able to drive the Sandinistas from power electorally in 1990. In subsequent years, electoral politics mainly replaced civil war in Nicaragua.

Quasi Executive Powers

Reinforcing its legislative powers and consistent with Neustadt's notion of separated institutions sharing powers, the Constitution assigns Congress three powers that might be considered quasi executive. Congress can override executive vetoes, and the Senate must confirm presidential appointees and treaties, with treaties requiring a two-thirds majority. Each of these powers can bolster Congress's position vis-à-vis the executive.

The first of these quasi executive powers, the veto override, is often attempted but seldom successful (see Table 4).[27] A two-thirds majority of both houses is required to overturn the president's veto and, often enough, two-thirds of the members of both houses would fail to agree on the proposition that the marigold is a pretty flower. Generally speaking, presidential vetoes are most likely to be overridden when both houses of Congress are firmly controlled by the president's partisan and ideological foes. Not surprisingly, then, those presidents who saw their vetoes overridden most frequently were Andrew Johnson, Harry Truman, and Gerald Ford. Nine of Franklin Roosevelt's vetoes were also overridden but FDR was extravagant in his use of the veto power, turning back 372 bills. The most recent veto overrides came during the Clinton administration, when Congress overrode two of the president's vetoes. One of these overrides involved Clinton's use of the

Table 4. Vetoes Overridden, 1789–Present

President	Veto	Override	President	Veto	Override
Washington	2	–	B. Harrison	19	1
Adams	–	–	Cleveland (2nd term)	42	5
Jefferson	–	–	McKinley	6	–
Madison	5	–	T. Roosevelt	42	1
Monroe	1	–	Taft	30	1
J. Q. Adams	–	–	Wilson	33	6
Jackson	5	–	Harding	5	–
Van Buren	–	–	Coolidge	20	4
W. H. Harrison	–	–	Hoover	21	3
Tyler	6	1	F. D. Roosevelt	372	9
Polk	2	–	Truman	180	12
Taylor	–	–	Eisenhower	73	2
Fillmore	–	–	Kennedy	12	–
Pierce	9	5	L. B. Johnson	16	–
Buchanan	4	–	Nixon	26	7
Lincoln	2	–	Ford	48	12
A. Johnson	21	15	Carter	13	2
Grant	45	4	Reagan	39	9
Hayes	12	1	G. H. W. Bush	29	1
Garfield	–	–	Clinton	36	2
Arthur	4	1	G. W. Bush	0	0
Cleveland (1st term)	304	2	Obama	4	0
			Totals	1,488	106

Source: U.S. Senate, available online at http://www.senate.gov/reference/Legislation/Vetoes/vetoCounts .htm (accessed July 24, 2015).

line-item veto, which was later declared unconstitutional by the Supreme Court, to kill thirty-eight military construction projects. The second concerned a piece of legislation protecting accountants from class action suits, a bill that had been vigorously supported by the industry, which has considerable clout in Congress.

A second quasi executive congressional power is the Senate's power to deny appointments to individuals nominated by the president to executive positions or to the judiciary. Some 1,200 to 1,400 top federal officials and all federal judges require senatorial consent for their appointments and this is not always forthcoming. Over the course of American history, of some five hundred cabinet nominations, nine were rejected and twelve withdrawn in the face of Senate opposition.[28] Of 151

Supreme Court nominations, too, twelve were rejected and eleven withdrawn by the president.[29] The Senate's confirmation power is more important than these percentages might suggest, however. Knowing that they will face Senate confirmation, presidents will seldom nominate individuals who they think are unlikely to be confirmed.

In recent years, Supreme Court confirmations have produced epic battles between the Senate and the White House as Democrats and Republicans have struggled to maintain or secure control of the high court. In 1987 one Reagan nominee, Judge Robert Bork, was defeated in a 42 to 58 Senate vote, and a second, Judge Douglas Ginsburg, withdrew. Bork had been solicitor general during the Nixon administration and so had fired Watergate special prosecutor Archibald Cox at Nixon's order. During the confirmation hearings, Democratic senators read passages from Bork's scholarly writings and judicial opinions that seemed to portray him as an extremist. Using this tactic against nominees came to be known as "Borking." Ginsburg, for his part, withdrew from consideration in the face of allegations that he had smoked marijuana while a student.

George H. W. Bush encountered an unanticipated battle when he nominated Clarence Thomas to the Supreme Court. Bush calculated that Senate Democrats would be reluctant to attack an African American nominee, even though Thomas was politically quite conservative. Democrats, indeed, hesitated but launched a campaign against Thomas centering around allegations from one of his former subordinates at the Equal Employment Opportunity Commission that Thomas had engaged in inappropriate, sexually explicit banter with her. Thomas was confirmed after a nationally televised speech in which he accused his opponents of conducting a "legal lynching." Southern Democratic senators dependent on the votes of African American constituents quickly ascertained that these constituents agreed with Thomas, and so gave him their support.[30]

During the Clinton administration, two individuals whom the president had introduced as nominees were forced to withdraw even before their nominations were formally sent to the Senate. In what the media dubbed "Nannygate," corporate lawyer Zoe Baird and federal judge Kimba Wood both asked the president to drop them from consideration when Republicans pointed to evidence that they might have employed undocumented immigrants as nannies for their young children. This was a sufficiently widespread practice among wealthy Americans that Senate investigators had no doubt that they would find it if they looked.

Finally, during the presidency of George W. Bush, Supreme Court nominee Harriet Miers was forced to withdraw from consideration. Miers, then a White House counsel, had no judicial experience or experience in the constitutional areas dealt with by the Supreme Court. The Senate Judiciary Committee called her responses to questions inadequate, insufficient, and insulting, and made it clear to the president that she would not be confirmed.[31]

Presidential nominations, whether to the courts or federal agencies, are first considered by the appropriate subject-matter committee of the Senate. If the committee schedules hearings, nominees are expected to testify. Other witnesses purporting to have knowledge of the nominee's fitness may testify for and against the nominee. A vote is then taken to bring the nomination before the full Senate; the committee may or may not send a recommendation. When an appointment is presented to the Senate, there may be a debate, following which a majority of those senators present must agree to the motion "to advise and consent." Until 2013, filibusters requiring a three-fifths (formerly two-thirds) vote to override (a cloture vote) could prevent a nomination from being brought forward for a vote. During the first Truman administration, for example, Republican filibusters kept a number of nominations in committee while GOP senators waited hopefully for the 1948 elections to produce a Republican president.[32] In November 2013, to end Republican filibusters of Obama nominees, the Senate changed its rules to require only a simple majority for cloture. Democratic Senate majority leader Harry Reid said this rules change was justified because Republicans had blocked almost as many Obama nominees as the total blocked during previous presidencies since World War II. After the rules change, the stalled Obama nominees were confirmed by the full Senate.

Reid's claim had considerable validity. An unusual number of Obama nominees were being blocked in the Senate. Nevertheless, by changing Senate rules, Reid also diminished the power of the Senate vis-à-vis the White House, making it easier for presidents to secure confirmation of their nominees.

The Treaty Power

Article II, Section 2 of the Constitution provides that the president "shall have power by and with the advice and consent of the Senate, to make treaties provided two-thirds of the senators present concur." The two-thirds requirement was designed to curb presidential power and to ensure that relations between the United States and other nations had broad support, not just the support of a plurality. Formally, the Senate votes on a resolution of ratification. If the resolution passes, actual ratification takes place when the United States and the other nation exchange instruments of ratification.

Since 1789, the Senate has approved more than 1,500 treaties while rejecting only twenty-one. Another eight-five treaties were withdrawn because the Senate took no action on them.[33] Of course it is impossible to know how many potential agreements were never submitted by the president because Senate approval seemed unlikely. The most famous treaty rejected by the Senate was the Treaty of Versailles, which was rejected twice, in 1919 and 1920. The Treaty of Versailles was a multilateral agreement negotiated by President Wilson between the United States and a number of other nations that ended World War I and established the League of Nations. Senate isolationists opposed the league, however, so the administration was compelled to negotiate a number of separate treaties with the former belligerents in order to bring about a formal end to America's state of war with them. In 1999, the Senate also rejected a comprehensive nuclear test ban treaty negotiated by President Clinton.

Franklin Roosevelt regarded the treaty power as a constitutional error and often told his aides that the Senate's rejection of the Treaty of Versailles was one of the factors that had led to World War II. Roosevelt seldom brought treaties to the Senate but relied instead on executive agreements, to be discussed more fully in Chapter 7. Some executive agreements are brought to Congress as though they were ordinary legislation requiring a majority in both houses, but many others, especially those involving national security, are simply signed by the president without congressional approval. Executive agreements are enforceable by the courts but were traditionally seen as having less international authority and longevity than treaties since they could be abrogated by the next president. This distinction, however, seems no longer valid since the federal courts held in 1978 that the president could unilaterally abrogate even a treaty—in this case America's 1954 mutual defense treaty with Taiwan. Since presidents seem free to use executive agreements as they see fit, the importance of the Senate's constitutional treaty power has diminished sharply. Between 1947 and 2006, the United States has entered into more than seventeen thousand different agreements with other nations and international entities. Of these, only 6 percent were submitted to the Senate for approval.[34]

The Power of the Purse

As for spending powers, the framers of the Constitution conceived the "power of the purse" to be Congress's most fundamental prerogative. For more than a century this power was jealously guarded by powerful congressional leaders like Taft-era House speaker "Uncle" Joe Cannon, who saw congressional control of the budget as a fundamental safeguard against "Prussian-style" militarism and autocracy.[35] In the nineteenth century, Congress frequently itemized appropriations for executive branch agencies down to the last dollar, leaving no discretion in expenditures. An 1871 appropriation of $58,280 for one office was divided as follows: $3,000 for the first auditor, $2,000 for the chief clerk, and $720 for each of the other clerks.[36] Today when Congress appropriates funds for particular purposes, it generally allows administrators considerable discretion in their use, though it continues to take appropriations very seriously. The House and Senate have each established twelve matching appropriations subcommittees based on subject-matter jurisdictions. Each subcommittee holds hearings during which it considers the president's budget, congressional revenue, and expenditure targets, and hears testimony from agency officials and other parties before developing an appropriations bill that funds the agencies within its jurisdiction. The bill is subject to amendment by the entire chamber and eventually both houses must pass appropriations bills with precisely the same language.

When Congress is pleased with a program and its administrators, it can reward them by approving their budgets without subjecting them to much review or criticism. This gives administrators an incentive to seek good relations with their congressional appropriators. By contrast, if Congress is displeased with a federal program or agency, it can react by reducing or even eliminating the money appropriated for that function.[37] Congress may also attach riders to bills forbidding agencies from spending money for particular purposes.[38] In 2014 the House of Representatives voted to cut more than $1 billion from the IRS budget to punish the agency for allegedly targeting conservative political groups for special tax scrutiny. A variety of other cuts were also approved, including the elimination of funding for renovating the White House bowling alley. Absent a congressional appropriation, it appears that the president might be forced to find some other bowling venue.

Most federal programs operate on an annual budget. Notable exceptions are entitlement programs like Social Security and Medicare, whose spending and appropriation levels are set by legal formulae that are partially self-funded and remain in force unless changed by law, as well as agencies like the Federal Reserve that are fully self-funded. Under the Constitution, government spending must be approved via bills initiated in the House of Representatives, agreed to by the Senate, and signed by the president. If Congress and the president are unable to enact a budget, the 1884 Antideficiency Act requires that government activities begin shutting down so as to avoid violating the constitutional authority of Congress over spending. Usually, to avoid shutdowns, Congress and the president will agree on a continuing resolution to keep spending at or near existing levels. Indeed, the U.S. government operated on a series of continuing resolutions from 2009 until 2015 because Congress and the president were unable to reach an overall budget agreement. Congress may also appropriate funds for particular purposes even without an overall budget agreement.

Historically, congressional committees reviewed individual budgetary requests from every office and agency. These were made directly from the agencies to the Congress, and the federal budget consisted of the sum total of agreements between the agencies and congressional committees. The president was mainly out of the loop. The 1921 Budget Act, however, which created the Bureau of the Budget, ushered in a period of enhanced presidential influence over federal spending. Claiming powers not precisely specified by the act, President Harding introduced the principle of central legislative clearance.[39] Federal agencies were required to obtain bureau clearance for all requests and recommendations submitted to Congress. The agencies resisted but Harding's successor, Calvin Coolidge, mandated a central clearance procedure for all agency requests and recommendations with budgetary implications—a procedure that with modifications is still used today.

Since the New Deal, successive Congresses have yielded to steadily increasing presidential influence over the budget process. In 1939, Congress allowed Franklin D. Roosevelt to take a giant step toward presidential control of the nation's purse strings when it permitted him to bring the Bureau of the Budget into the newly created Executive Office of the President. Roosevelt and his successors have used the bureau (now called the White House Office of Management and Budget) to influence the nation's legislative and budgetary agenda by assembling a more or less coherent package of legislative proposals for the Congress to consider. Using the Office of Management and Budget as a presidential agenda setter rather than a mere clearinghouse for agency requests, successive presidents made their budgetary proposals the starting points for congressional action on taxing and spending, often relegating Congress to the subsidiary role of reacting to presidential initiatives rather than developing programs of its own.

In 1974 Congress responded to Richard Nixon's efforts to further enhance presidential control over spending when it enacted the Budget and Impoundment Control Act. The budget provisions of this piece of legislation centralized Congress's own budgetary process and established the Congressional Budget Office to rival the president's Office of Management and Budget.[40] Under the terms of the 1974 act, Congress undertook an independent budgetary process, leading to the creation of a unified congressional budget resolution on par with the president's budget. Many members of Congress hoped that the 1974 act would limit presidential power by restoring congressional control over the nation's taxing and spending agenda.

To some extent, the Budget Act was successful but the newly centralized budgetary process created a number of problems for lawmakers and, in many respects, served only to increase presidential influence. To begin with, it is enormously difficult for an inherently decentralized institution like the Congress to engage successfully in a single, centralized process.[41] The result is often stalemate and surrender to the White House. For example, in 1998, as a result of divisions between the parties, between the House and Senate, and among competing political factions, Congress was unable to agree on its own budget. This cleared the way for victory for President Clinton's spending priorities even though the GOP nominally controlled both houses of Congress and was engaged in an effort to impeach Clinton.[42]

A second problem created by the Budget and Impoundment Control Act is that a centralized process in Congress can, under some circumstances, serve the interests of the White House. Under the pre-1974 decentralized budget process, presidents sometimes found their appropriations and spending proposals subjected to piecemeal revision by numerous congressional committees and subcommittees. Presidents had difficulty intervening while their proposals were being nibbled into tatters by the sharp teeth of a host of congressional interests. The post-1974 centralized process, by contrast, created an opportunity for a president with a solid base of support in both houses of Congress to take control of the budget process in its entirety. This is essentially what happened in 1981 when President Reagan used Congress's budget resolution to cut taxes, increase defense spending, and curtail domestic social spending—a program that led to the enormous budget deficits of the 1980s and 1990s. Reagan almost certainly would not have been able to bring about his "revolution" if his budget had been subject to incremental attack.[43]

The deficit-reduction targets and spending caps negotiated by Congress and the president after the huge budget deficits of the Reagan era also played a role in reducing congressional influence and strengthening presidential oversight of the economy. Congress's power over the economy is based on its control of fiscal policy —the power to tax and spend. In the 1990 Budget Enforcement Act, however, Congress adopted pay-as-you-go, or "PAYGO," rules that require new spending or tax laws to be budget neutral. Any increase in spending had to be accompanied by an offsetting increase in taxes. The rule expired in 2002, but was reestablished in 2007 as a House rule and then, in modified form, enacted as a law in 2010. The PAYGO rules are highly politicized, and Congress can waive them in certain situations. For example, PAYGO was waived for the various stimulus packages designed to lift the United States out of recession in 2008–2009. Moreover, the Congressional Budget Office, which is responsible for "scoring"—the process of determining the budgetary impact of a new program—often employs "pay fors" to offset the projected cost of a program. A "pay for" is a projected future savings or revenue increase that may or may not ever take place. For example, the 2010 Affordable Care Act was scored as revenue neutral based on a number of possibly illusory "pay fors."

The PAYGO accounting rules may help to keep deficits in check, but they also tend to reduce the importance of Congress relative to the executive. The PAYGO accounting rules prohibit major changes in the relationship between taxes and spending and, by blunting fiscal policy, reduce congressional influence over economic affairs. The effect of this fiscal discipline is to increase the economic and political importance of monetary policy—control of interest rates and the supply of money and credit—which normally is the "fine tuning" of the economic policy process. Monetary policy is, of course, the province of the executive branch, particularly the Federal Reserve Board, and is heavily influenced, albeit not fully controlled, by the president. The elevated importance of monetary policy made the chairman of the Federal Reserve Board a major public figure while relegating the chairs of the key congressional tax and budget panels to positions of relative obscurity. Thus fiscal responsibility and congressional power do not necessarily go hand in hand. Ironically, the tax cuts and high levels of military spending of the Reagan and George W. Bush administrations exacerbated Congress's fiscal dilemma by leaving legislators without discretionary funds to spend. Over the past quarter century, the budgetary deck has been stacked sharply against Capitol Hill.

Finally, the centralized budgetary process has several times forced Congress to publicly confront rather than quietly subvert the president's budget. Such confrontations, some of which have led to partial shutdowns of the government, have occurred on a number of occasions, most notably in 1995–1996 when the government was shut down for twenty-one days, and 2013 when many government agencies were closed for eleven days. The results of these events suggest that it may be difficult, though not impossible, for Congress to gain the upper hand in direct budgetary confrontations with the White House.

The first major confrontation occurred after the 1994 elections gave Republicans control over both houses of Congress. Republican House Speaker Newt Gingrich was determined to bring about substantial cuts in spending on the domestic social programs championed by Democrats and led the House in proposing a budget that included cuts in environmental programs and public health and social programs, as well as an increase in Medicare premiums. As congressional Republicans had anticipated, President Clinton refused to accept GOP budget proposals. For several weeks, the federal government operated on a continuing resolution. A continuing resolution, which allows government agencies to operate on the basis of existing funding until a new budget is approved, must pass a vote in Congress and be signed by the president. One was in place through mid-November, but the president and Congress could not agree on its renewal, which meant that the federal government's spending authority lapsed in the closing weeks of 1995. Another continuing resolution was hastily approved, but when it expired, nonessential government agencies shut down for twenty-two days. During this period, nearly 800,000 government workers along with hundreds of thousands of individuals working for firms with government contracts were furloughed and government services curtailed. Government programs deemed essential, like national defense, remained unaffected by the shutdown.

Congressional Republicans had expected the shutdown to demonstrate the truth of their contention that America could get along without so many government agencies and services. But while many Americans might have agreed with the GOP in the abstract, each affected program had a constituency prepared to defend the agency that it saw as a source of benefits. As is so often the case, those who receive discrete benefits are far more ready to engage in political action than those who pay costs dispersed throughout the nation.

President Clinton, moreover, was able to make good use of the bully pulpit of the presidency to frame the battle as a case of intransigent members of Congress refusing to compromise and showing indifference to the hardships faced by furloughed federal employees and others. Every evening, television stories told of federal workers unable to make mortgage payments or buy Christmas gifts for their children as the holidays approached. Speaker Gingrich was widely caricatured as "the Gingrich who stole Christmas." Poll after poll showed a dramatic drop in support for the Republicans. In January 1996, the House Republicans surrendered and reached a budget agreement with President Clinton that achieved few of their goals.[44]

The House had slightly more luck using its power of the purse in a somewhat different form of confrontation with the president—a standoff over the nation's huge budget deficit created by wars in the Middle East and the various economic stimulus packages of the Bush and Obama administrations. Under the Constitution, only Congress can authorize the government to borrow money "on the credit of the United States." That means the Treasury cannot issue bonds without congressional authority—though if the government did not sell bonds, it could not meet its financial obligations and might default on its interest payments to bond holders. In the nineteenth century, each individual bond sale required congressional approval. Beginning in 1917, however, Congress established an overall ceiling on government borrowing. Since that time, the debt ceiling has been raised by statute hundreds of times to accommodate growing government borrowing needs.

Occasionally, in fights with the president, Congress has threatened to refuse to raise the debt ceiling unless the White House agreed to its terms. Such a battle erupted in 2011 when House Republicans declared that they would not allow an increase in the debt ceiling unless the president agreed to major cuts in federal spending. After tense negotiations, the president agreed to what became the 2011 Budget Control Act. The act provided for across-the-board federal spending cuts, called sequestration, on military and domestic programs in order to reduce the nation's budget deficit over a ten-year period if savings could not be realized any other way. At the same time, House Republicans agreed to seek further deficit reduction through tax increases embodied in the 2012 Taxpayer Relief Act. House Speaker Boehner, believing that confrontational tactics had been successful, was emboldened to seek a new public battle with the president—this time over the budget.

Congress was far less successful in this fight with President Obama, however. While battling the White House on the deficit, Republicans were also considering ways of reducing domestic social spending, particularly spending on Obamacare. By 2013, the Tea Party movement and other conservative activists were urging Republicans to shut down the government if that was necessary to block funding for the Affordable Care Act. In September, House Republicans, led by Speaker Boehner, said the House would not pass a continuing resolution to maintain government funding unless the Affordable Care Act was defunded. Neither the Democratic-controlled Senate nor President Obama would accept such a stipulation, so a government shutdown began on October 1, 2013. More than a million federal employees and contract workers were sent home. (As in the previous shutdown, services deemed essential, like the military, were not affected.)

Mindful of the public relations debacle they had suffered in 1995–1996, when they had been blamed for imposing hardships on citizens and federal workers, House Republicans passed a number of piecemeal appropriations bills providing funding for a variety of public services including the National Institutes of Health, the Food and Drug Administration, the National Park Service, and other agencies, and sought to blame the president for not signing them. But since the Senate would not pass any of these bills, they never made it to the president for a signature and Obama could simply ignore the ploy. After two weeks it became clear to House Republicans that Obama would not budge and that public opinion was turning against Congress, which was increasingly seen as petulant and intransigent. The House surrendered without wringing any concessions from the president. It seemed that, at least for the moment, government shutdowns were not a particularly useful congressional tactic in fights with the executive.

Nor, it seemed, were further threats on the debt ceiling. While threatening to shut down the government, House Republicans renewed their earlier threat to refuse to raise the debt ceiling, which was due to expire in February 2013. The president rejected any further concessions, calculating that Congress would not wish to be seen as responsible for what might be an economic disaster. Blustering until the last minute, the House finally capitulated and to add insult to injury accepted the No Budget, No Pay Act of 2013, which temporarily suspended the debt ceiling and barred any congressional pay raises until Congress had passed a budget. In the meantime, sequestration was imposing cuts in spending with Congress mainly being blamed for the pain felt by many affected interests.

This history of budgetary confrontations between Congress and the White House suggests that such battles may be difficult for Congress to win, for three main reasons. First, confrontations in which Congress seeks to bring the president to heel by closing the government are problematic because even though Americans favor the idea of less spending, each American favors spending on some programs. Thus a shutdown of the entire government is likely to upset everyone. Although in 2013 House Republicans sought to address this issue by reopening some but not all agencies, the president had refused to be taken in by this ploy.

Second, the president speaks with one voice, which offers a tactical advantage over Congress. During all the confrontations and crises we have considered, divisions between the House and Senate and within the House itself led to portrayals of members of Congress as a squabbling claque of politicians who were unable to agree among themselves, a position that undercut their opposition to the president. And third, in defending government agencies and the government's need to borrow money, the president generally seemed to be speaking for the national interest while his opponents in the House seemed to be threatening to push the country over what the media called the "fiscal cliff."

Legislative Oversight

A third arrow in Congress's quiver is legislative oversight. Oversight refers to congressional review and supervision of the activities of executive agencies. Through oversight, the Congress has an opportunity to determine whether the actions of the executive in administering programs are consistent with legislative intent, as well as to investigate the effectiveness and efficiency of government agencies. Charges of waste, illegal conduct, and abuse of citizens' rights are also topics for legislative inquiry.

As we observed in Chapter 2, the Constitution makes no mention of oversight but it seems implied by several of the enumerated powers of Congress, including the power to appropriate funds, to raise and support armies and navies, and even to impeach judges and members of the executive branch. Article I also gives Congress the power to make laws necessary and proper for carrying out its enumerated powers. It seems reasonable to assume that Congress is thereby empowered to hold hearings and conduct investigations into the conduct of executive branch agencies.

As noted in Chapter 2, Alexander Hamilton disagreed with this proposition, but no less an authority on government than the British philosopher John Stuart Mill saw oversight as among the chief duties of legislative assemblies.[45] In the 1927 case of *McGrain v. Daugherty,* the Supreme Court said that oversight was justified by Congress's legislative power and should concern matters "on which legislation could be had."[46] This principle does not impose much of a constraint on oversight since legislation "could be had" on just about any topic.

By statute, Congress has authorized House and Senate standing committees to oversee executive programs under their jurisdiction. And among the various provisions of the 1974 Budget Act was one authorizing congressional committees to conduct performance evaluations of executive agencies. By statute, too, agencies are required to furnish a variety of reports to Congress and each agency's inspector general is required to inform Congress of serious management and performance problems within his or her agency.

If Congress determines that an agency is not properly performing its tasks or is not acting in a manner consistent with its authority, legislators have a number of options. They may cut the agency's budget as exemplified by the House's decision to slash the IRS budget in 2014. They may restrict an agency's regulatory authority as occurred in the 1980s when Congress reduced the EPA's rulemaking discretion. They may also write new legislation to narrow the agency's jurisdiction or, in some instances, recommend that the Justice Department look into misconduct by agency executives.

Since the early days of the Republic, Congress has held hearings and conducted investigations to examine the activities of executive branch agencies. In 1792, the House of Representatives launched an investigation into the failure of a military expedition against a tribal confederation ordered by President Washington and led by General Arthur St. Clair. The House called for "such persons, papers and records as may be necessary to assist their inquiries," and justified its investigation by declaring that inquiries into the expenditure of all public money were the indispensable duty of the House.[47] President Washington was surprised by the congressional request for records and papers and was not certain that it was appropriate. After considering the matter carefully, though, Washington concluded that the House could appropriately institute such inquiries and was entitled to receive papers and records unless their disclosure "would injure the public."[48] This principle was repeated by Washington when he resisted congressional demands for papers relating to Jay's Treaty, which was negotiated with Great Britain in 1794.

As in many other instances, President Washington's decision set lasting precedents. He determined that Congress was entitled to conduct inquiries into the activities of the executive branch but that the president should exercise discretion in deciding what to disclose. This discretion came to be called "executive privilege," and was formally recognized by the Supreme Court in its Watergate tapes decision nearly two centuries later.[49] After investigating the causes of St. Clair's defeat, Congress concluded that much of the fault lay with the mismanagement of the Army's supply services. Accordingly, Congress enacted legislation transferring management of the supply services from the War Department to the Treasury Department. This was the first, but not the last, time that oversight of the executive branch led to an attempted legislative remedy.

In subsequent decades, Congress came to be recognized as the "grand inquest of the nation," and began to require regular reports from executive agencies on all their activities and expenditures.[50] In 1808, for example, Congress required detailed statements of all contracts made by the departments of the Treasury, War, Navy, and Post Office, and by collectors of customs. The next year Congress demanded full reports of all claims and expenses of the War and Navy departments, which were suspected of profligate spending.[51] In 1816, Congress created six standing committees on public expenditures, one respectively for the State, Treasury, War, Navy, and Post Office departments, and one on public buildings. These committees were established by House Speaker Henry Clay for the express purpose of overseeing the executive departments within their jurisdictions, and were responsible for "watching the conduct of business, criticizing laxness, and for the use of funds."[52]

Today, Congress exercises legislative oversight through a variety of tools and mechanisms.[53] Among the most important is the Government Accountability Office (GAO), originally called the General Accounting Office and established by the same 1921 Budget and Accounting Act that created the Bureau of the Budget. The GAO is headed by the comptroller general of the United States, who is appointed by the president, subject to senatorial confirmation, for a fifteen-year term. The GAO's original mission was to audit and report to Congress on executive agencies' use of appropriated funds. Over the years, however, GAO has gone beyond financial audits to undertake performance audits of executive departments and agencies on Congress's behalf. During the past year alone, GAO has reported widespread waste in government software spending, deficiencies in the operations of Veterans' Administration hospitals, faulty practices on the part of the Transportation Security Administration (TSA), problems with Federal Aviation Administration (FAA) pilot certification, and poor reporting practices by the Federal Reserve. In 2014, a GAO "secret shopper" found that the contractors employed to staff federal insurance exchanges made no effort to verify the identities of supposed clients and allowed individuals with false identifications and no documents to enroll for federally sponsored health insurance under the Affordable Care Act.[54]

In both the House and Senate, oversight is conducted by authorizing committees, appropriations committees, and various subcommittees, as well as the House Oversight and Government Reform Committee and the Senate Governmental Affairs Committee, which have broad oversight powers. To facilitate oversight, Congress has adopted several "whistleblower" statutes to encourage federal employees, who may have inside information on agency operations, to come forward if they are aware of abuses or misconduct. These whistleblowers are an important part of the oversight process. In 2014, for example, whistleblower testimony before the House Committee on Veterans' Affairs led to the resignation of the secretary of the U.S. Department of Veterans Affairs and other top officials, as well as legislation designed to reform practices in the department.

One oversight tool that has not been very effective is the Congressional Review Act procedure for disallowing new rules proposed by executive agencies. Under the provisions of the 1996 initiative, enacted as part of the Small Business Regulatory Enforcement Fairness Act, all new final rules must be submitted for review to both houses of Congress and to the GAO before they can be adopted. If the Office of Management and Budget has previously determined that the rule is "major" in terms of its potential economic impact, it cannot take effect for at least sixty days, nominally giving Congress time to disallow the rule if it wishes to do so. By 2011, the GAO had reviewed 1,029 major rules, and 72 joint resolutions of disapproval were introduced relating to 49 rules.[55] In only one case was a joint resolution of disapproval actually adopted and signed by the president. This involved an OSHA rule on ergonomics that had been enacted in the final month of the Clinton administration. The newly elected Republican Congress lost no time in disallowing the rule and President Bush was only too happy to sign the resolution.[56] Since 2012, federal agencies have avoided the Congressional Review Act procedure by the simple expedient of neglecting to report new rules to Congress.[57] Since Congress has no reliable capacity to monitor the thousands of rules promulgated by the agencies, it has no idea which, if any, it might like to disallow.

Many critics claim that despite nominally possessing various oversight tools, Congress is not especially adept at the routine supervision of federal agencies.[58] Reading the thousands of reports filed by the agencies and inquiring into their day-to-day activities, as was common in the nineteenth century, is seen today as a tedious activity that does not contribute to congressional career or electoral interests. Political scientists Mathew McCubbins and Thomas Schwartz call this routine form of oversight "police patrol" oversight and agree that members of Congress shun this activity; they assert that Congress is much better at what they call "fire alarm" oversight.[59] Fire alarm oversight takes place when a whistleblower, the media, a

GAO report, or other event brings a problem to Congress's attention. When the alarm rings, Congress may jump into action, schedule hearings, summon executive branch officials, and discuss possible legislation.[60]

For example, in 2013, when NSA contractor Edward Snowden revealed the existence of a massive NSA eavesdropping program that routinely intercepted U.S. citizens' electronic communications, a variety of congressional committees scheduled hearings to look into the matter, identify potentially illegal activity, and consider what, if any, legislative steps should be taken. The hearings, many of which were held behind closed doors, included testimony from top officials of the U.S. intelligence community who, not surprisingly, reassured Congress and the public that all of their actions were being monitored by the courts and were needed to protect America from terrorist threats. Several pieces of legislation to reform intelligence collection practices were introduced but none were enacted. The ringing of the fire alarm became somewhat muted but has not quite disappeared as new allegations of improper activities on the part of NSA and other agencies continue to surface.

More recently, the Senate Commerce Committee conducted hearings when cruise ship passengers complained that they had been mistreated and even criminally assaulted by employees of cruise lines while the ships were at sea and outside U.S. jurisdiction. Senator Jay Rockefeller, the committee chairman, said the passenger testimony pointed to the need for legislation to regulate the cruise industry and provide greater protection for Americans at sea.[61]

Legislative Hearings and Investigations

Another oversight tool is the congressional investigation, which may be launched by standing committees or specially created committees. In addition to the confirmation hearings discussed earlier, legislative hearings are of two types. In the most common variety, Congress conducts an investigation and hearings to see if some legislative remedy for the problems adduced might be needed. In recent years, Congress has held hearings and conducted investigations into a variety of matters, including the actions of the national intelligence community and the Internal Revenue Service, problems surrounding the launch of the Affordable Care Act, and a host of other matters. In 2014, members of the Senate Intelligence Committee, which had been looking into allegations of misconduct by the CIA and the possible need for legislative remedies, discovered evidence that the CIA had hacked into Senate computer systems to spy on the committee. CIA Director John Brennan first denied the allegations but then was forced to acknowledge their validity and apologize to committee members.

A second type of hearing, called an investigative hearing or ethics probe, has no direct legislative intent. The purpose of such a hearing is usually to look into allegations of misconduct on the part of one or more public officials, to undermine public support for the administration, and possibly to recommend the official's dismissal or even criminal charges.[62] Such hearings have a long history in the United States. In 1800, for example, a House committee held hearings to investigate charges that Mississippi territorial governor Winthrop Sargent had exceeded his authority, and two years later a second House committee investigated complaints that Sargent had caused one of his political opponents to be falsely arrested. As in Sargent's case, these hearings tend to be hostile.[63] In the 1990s, ethics probes led to the resignations of Agriculture Secretary Mike Espy and HUD Secretary Henry Cisneros.

Often, in conducting such hearings, Congress finds it difficult to compel executive branch officials, particularly members of the president's staff, to appear. In 2014, for example, the House Oversight and Government Reform Committee issued a subpoena to compel testimony from White House political adviser David Simas. The committee was looking into allegations that the White House Office of Political Strategy and Outreach, led by Simas, was illegally engaged in political fundraising. The president did not wish Simas to testify, and the White House Counsel sent committee chairman Darrell Issa (R.-Calif.) a letter stating that the subpoena posed a threat to executive branch interests as well as the president's ability to obtain candid advice and counsel. Issa pointed out that a similar claim, made by the Bush administration when then White House counsel Harriet Miers had been subpoenaed to testify before a congressional committee, had been rejected by a federal judge. The White House replied that it disagreed with the judge's opinion in the Miers case and would continue to resist the subpoena.[64] The stage appeared to be set for a long legal battle, though often in such cases Congress and the White House will negotiate an agreement allowing the subpoenaed official to testify but limiting the questions that can be asked.[65]

Watergate and Iran-Contra

The most notable set of investigative hearings in recent American history were the Watergate hearings into allegations of misconduct on the part of President Nixon, and the Iran-Contra probe into alleged violations of the law on the part of members of the Reagan administration. The first of these investigations arose from a struggle between President Nixon and Congress over Nixon's efforts to expand presidential power. Nixon had submitted a legislative reorganization plan to Congress that would have diminished legislators' ability to oversee the executive branch while enhancing presidential authority.[66] When Congress refused to take any of the actions recommended by the White House, Nixon began to implement his plan through executive orders.[67] As we saw earlier, Nixon also used the practice of impoundment to punish agencies that would not do his bidding, and he sought to limit congressional influence by withholding vital information such as the "secret bombing" of Cambodia from 1969 to 1973. Congressional Democrats rallied in opposition to these moves by Nixon. Among other strategies, they encouraged whistleblowers to come forward with damaging information about Nixon's activities and worked with pro-Democratic media such as the *New York Times, Washington Post,* and *CBS News* to underline the administration's shortcomings and publicize whistleblowers' claims.

To plug the "leaks" of information, the White House engaged a group of former intelligence agents and mercenaries, dubbed the "plumber's squad," to perform a number of covert operations. In 1971, for example, the plumbers broke into the office of Daniel Ellsberg's psychiatrist to see if they might find useful information. Ellsberg had leaked the classified "Pentagon Papers," which were then published by both the *Times* and *Post.* The administration also attacked its enemies in the media, threatening legislation to break up "media monopolies," which seemed to include mainly the *Times, Post,* and *CBS.*

The Watergate affair began against this backdrop. During the 1972 election campaign, Nixon had become convinced that the Democrats were planning "dirty tricks" to win the election. The plumbers were ordered to collect information on Democratic plans and broke into Democratic headquarters at the Watergate Hotel in Washington. They were interrupted by the Washington police and taken into custody, but released when they were able to obtain White House confirmation that their enterprise was somehow connected to national security.

Reporters for the *Post,* however, learned of the break-in and launched an inquiry. The reporters were covertly provided with information by a source they identified only as "Deep Throat," who turned out to be an assistant director of the FBI, an agency which may have had its own grievances against the president.[68] Gradually reports published in the *Post* and the *Times,* and publicized by the major television networks, linked the White House to the Watergate break-in and to other illicit activities. As revelations of misdeeds by the Nixon White House proliferated, the administration's opponents in Congress demanded a full-scale legislative investigation. In response, the Senate created a special committee, chaired by Senator Sam Ervin (D.-N.C.), to investigate White House misconduct in the 1972 presidential election. Investigators employed by the Ervin committee uncovered numerous questionable activities on the part of Nixon's aides, and these were revealed to the public during a series of nationally televised hearings.

Evidence of criminal activity unearthed by the Ervin committee led to congressional pressure for Attorney General Elliot Richardson to appoint a special prosecutor. In October 1973 that special prosecutor, Archibald Cox, issued a subpoena to the president demanding copies of conversations taped in the Oval Office. The president refused to comply and instead ordered the attorney general to dismiss Cox. Richardson refused and tendered his own resignation, as did Deputy Attorney General William Ruckelshaus. Cox was eventually dismissed by Solicitor General Robert Bork, who was now the senior Justice Department official. The media dubbed the resignations and firing the "Saturday Night Massacre."

A firestorm of protest erupted on Capitol Hill and public opinion turned sharply against the president. A new special prosecutor was appointed and the Supreme Court ordered Nixon to turn over the tapes. An attempt had obviously been made to erase portions of the recordings but sufficient evidence remained linking Nixon to the Watergate burglary and other illicit activities that the president was forced to resign to escape impeachment. Several presidential aides were indicted, convicted, and imprisoned.

One lesson learned from the Watergate affair is that even the president of the United States is not immune to determined congressional investigators, particularly if Congress is supported by the national news media and can obtain judicial acquiescence for its probes. To make certain that future presidents would remember this lesson, Congress in 1978 adopted the Ethics in Government Act to establish procedures for the appointment of special prosecutors (later called independent counsels).[69] One Reagan administration official later called such prosecutors "a loaded gun pointed at the executive branch."[70] The independent counsel provision of the 1978 act was allowed to lapse two decades later and an Office of Independent Council created within the Justice Department to conduct probes of misconduct in the executive branch. The combination of media revelations, congressional investigations, and subsequent prosecutions is a congressional weapon that Martin Shefter and I have called RIP, or revelation, investigation, and prosecution—a sometimes appropriate epitaph for executive officials in its line of fire.[71]

The Watergate affair also illustrates how difficult it is for even the most determined congressional effort to defeat the White House. Over months of struggle, only the fact that Congress was assisted by major segments of the media, the courts, top administration officials, and covertly, the FBI, allowed legislators to emerge victorious over the president. This point was underlined in the Iran-Contra investigation into whether the Reagan administration had made illegal arms transfers to the Nicaraguan "Contra" forces. The same RIP tactics employed against President Nixon were mobilized in the Iran-Contra affair, including a congressional investigation and the appointment of a special prosecutor. Reagan, however, was able to frustrate congressional investigators. The president made no objection to turning over to the special counsel records and papers, including his personal diaries. Having learned from Nixon's mistake, the White House had been careful not to document whatever misdeeds it might have committed. Several Reagan aides testified that the president knew nothing about any illegal activities. Indeed the televised testimony of one aide, Marine Colonel Oliver North, was so compelling that public opinion swung sharply in the president's favor, leading several members of Congress to declare newfound support for Reagan. Eventually three of the president's closest advisers were indicted for lying and obstruction, but all were either exonerated or received presidential pardons. A fourth individual with knowledge of the events surrounding the illegal arms deal, CIA Director William Casey, was hospitalized hours before his scheduled testimony and died soon thereafter.

Thus a full-scale congressional probe of White House activities known to be illegal failed largely because the president could not be shown to have been personally aware of the actions in question. Reagan was careful not to give investigators what the press called a "smoking gun," and so long as the president could be confident that no members of his innermost circle would turn against him, he was able to thumb his nose at his opponents on Capitol Hill. In a mundane criminal investigation, involving less exalted suspects, the president and all his aides would certainly have been found guilty of conspiracy and other charges. In a probe of the White House, however, the burden of proof on Congress is very high. A majority of legislators must be convinced, often including members of the president's own party. This in turn usually requires turning public opinion strongly against the chief executive, which is an almost impossible feat.

Impeachment

Congress's ultimate weapon against the executive is impeachment.[72] President Nixon would certainly have been impeached and very likely convicted if he had not resigned, and some members of Congress had hoped to present President Reagan with a similar choice in 1987. Impeachment is a two-step process. The Constitution gives the House of Representatives the power to impeach the president, vice president, and all other civil officers of the United States. To impeach means to charge an official with having committed "treason, bribery, or other high crimes and misdemeanors." An official who is impeached by a majority vote in the House then stands trial in the Senate with the chief justice of the Supreme Court presiding. During the trial, each and every article of impeachment forwarded by the House is considered and a separate vote is taken on each. A two-thirds vote is needed for conviction on each article. The defendant need only be convicted on one article to be removed from office. The question of what constitutes an impeachable offense is a political question. When he was House minority leader, future president Gerald Ford said, "An impeachable offense is whatever a majority of the House of Representatives consider it to be at a given moment in history."[73]

The impeachment process is seldom used and has historically been viewed as a power to be employed only in cases involving the most egregious forms of official misconduct. Since the nation's founding, resolutions calling for the impeachment of various officials have been introduced in the House many times. Quite a number of President Obama's foes claim that he has committed impeachable offenses, though Republican House leaders are leery of the idea of initiating an impeachment.[74] The House has actually initiated impeachment proceedings on only sixty-four occasions. Articles of impeachment have been voted nineteen times and seven individuals, all federal judges, have been convicted by the Senate. One judge, Alcee Hastings, was convicted and removed from the bench for taking bribes but was subsequently elected to Congress from Florida. The most recent judge to be convicted in the Senate was Thomas Porteous of the Eastern District of Louisiana, who was convicted of official corruption in 2010.

Twice, presidents of the United States have been impeached. The first, Andrew Johnson, was impeached in 1868. Johnson was charged with violating the new Tenure of Office Act, which prohibited the president from unilaterally dismissing officials whose appointments had required Senate confirmation, as well as a number of other crimes. The Senate fell one vote short of the two-thirds majority that would have convicted Johnson and removed him from office. In 1998, Bill Clinton was impeached by the House on charges of perjury and obstruction of justice relating to his sexual relationship with a White House intern.

Of course, just as his violation of the Tenure of Office Act was only the proximate cause of Johnson's impeachment, so the issue of sex in the Oval Office was hardly the full reason for Clinton's impeachment. In 1993 and 1994, Republicans had laid down a barrage of charges against Clinton and his wife, mainly related to their involvement in the failed Whitewater real estate development in Arkansas. While they were able to embarrass and harass the Clintons, Republicans were unable to disable the administration. In 1994, however, the GOP won control of both houses of Congress, thereby gaining control of the congressional authority to investigate and to secure appointment of independent counsels to investigate on its behalf. Some Republicans saw an opportunity to retaliate against the Democrats for the Watergate and Iran-Contra probes. Now headed by Republicans, congressional committees immediately launched wide-ranging investigations of Clinton's conduct during his years as governor of Arkansas.

At the same time, congressional Republicans launched several independent counsel probes to search for wrongdoing by Clinton and his associates. The most important of these prosecutors, Kenneth Starr, was able to extend the scope of his investigation to include sensational allegations that the president had an affair with a White House intern, Monica Lewinsky, and had later both perjured himself and suborned perjury on the part of the intern and others to prevent disclosure of his conduct. A month after Clinton was forced to appear before Starr's grand jury and acknowledge his affair with Lewinsky, the GOP-controlled House Judiciary Committee began impeachment proceedings. Clinton's impeachment was approved by the full House on a party-line vote. By another party-line vote, the Senate declined to convict. But Clinton's presidency had been damaged.

While the process spiraled to its conclusion, the Clinton administration was preoccupied with the president's defense. Clinton and his allies responded aggressively to every accusation and innuendo, leveling countercharges against his accusers and the special counsel's office, sometimes employing private detectives to collect damaging information about the president's adversaries.[75] Throughout the long struggle between Clinton and his adversaries, the president was vigorously defended by the Democratic Party. In January 1998, the Democratic National Committee (DNC) established a damage control center to coordinate strategies, disseminate information, respond to charges, and generally seek to protect the president from new revelations and accusations.[76]

Until Clinton's admissions of sexual misconduct compelled several prominent Democrats to distance themselves from him, not a single significant Democratic politician or interest group spoke against the president. Whatever their personal feelings, most Democrats believed that the destruction of the Clinton administration would bring a renewed Republican effort to undermine the domestic social institutions fashioned by the Democratic Party. Even the women's movement, which might have been expected to turn against a president who had admitted having a sexual relationship with a young female intern, decided that Clinton's support for abortion rights and federal funding for child care, as well as his record of appointing women to high office, outweighed his sexual indiscretions.

The lesson to be learned from the Clinton impeachment is that so long as a president is vigorously defended by his or her own political party and retains strong support in the nation, impeachment is rather unlikely to succeed. The process may disrupt an administration for a time but, barring cataclysmic revelations that completely strip a president of congressional and public support, when the smoke of political battle clears, the same president will still occupy the Oval Office.

Thoughts on the President and Congress: Power against Power

The Constitution's framers knew that the president and Congress would vie for power. They saw this competition as necessary to prevent a concentration of power that might threaten citizens' liberties. The government's "several constituent parts," said Madison, must be designed to check and balance one another. "Ambition must be made to counteract ambition."[77] What we sometimes call gridlock, the framers might have viewed as the proper operation of the federal machinery.

The framers thought that in the competition between the president and the Congress, it would be the Congress that would generally have the upper hand. After all, the Congress would be close to the people, directly elected from small constituencies, and in a republic would not popular support be the decisive factor? "In republican government," said Madison, "the legislative authority necessarily predominates."[78] On this matter, however, Madison proved to be a poor prophet. First, Madison did not anticipate a day when presidents themselves would be popularly elected, and so share Congress's electoral connection with the American people. Second, Madison did not foresee the advent of media and communications technologies that would focus on the White House and give the president more public visibility than any member of Congress. How could Madison have predicted that the president would have tens of millions of Twitter followers while most Americans would be unable to name their own congressional representatives?

Yet even if Madison cannot be faulted for failing to predict these characteristics of modern politics, he can be blamed for misunderstanding the essentially asymmetric relationship between legislative power and executive power. Congress may make the law, but it cannot execute the law it makes. It must instead turn to the president and grant funding and authority to the executive branch. This is Congress's great dilemma. To accomplish any goal other than maintaining stalemate and gridlock by saying no, it must enhance the power of the president. Congress may indeed use the powers discussed in this chapter to win some battles against the White House. Nevertheless, for more than two centuries, Congress has been losing the war against executive power. And in the meantime, as we shall see in Chapter 7, the executive has been developing new tools to circumvent even Congress's power to say no.

Congress Investigates the White House

The investigative hearing or ethics probe can be an important instrument of congressional power. The purpose of such a hearing is usually not to produce legislation but rather to look into allegations of misconduct on the part of one or more public officials, possibly leading to the official's dismissal or even a criminal indictment. Major ethics probes can throw the government into disarray. Ethics probes are a political weapon that Martin Shefter and I have called RIP—revelation, investigation, prosecution—and sometimes, rest in peace for the target.

Watergate. During the 1972 presidential campaign, a group of covert operatives employed by the White House broke into Democratic headquarters in the Watergate hotel and were apprehended by the Washington police. Although they were released at the bidding of the White House, *Washington Post* reporters learned of the break-in and conducted their own investigation, relying on information provided by a mysterious source they called "Deep Throat" who turned out to be a senior FBI executive. The investigation produced evidence of White House involvement in illicit activities and led to a congressional investigation and the appointment of a special prosecutor to look into allegations of criminality. After a flurry of resignations and firing, which the media dubbed the "Saturday Night Massacre," a firestorm of protest erupted on Capitol Hill and public opinion turned sharply against the president. When taped evidence surfaced of Nixon's involvement, he was forced to resign to escape impeachment. Several presidential aides were indicted, convicted, and imprisoned.

Iran-Contra. The congressional Iran-Contra investigation looked into allegations that President Ronald Reagan had ordered the illegal transfer of arms to Nicaraguan "Contra" forces supported by the White House. Reagan, however, was able to frustrate congressional investigators. He turned over records and papers, including his personal diaries, to the special counsel, but they included no incriminating evidence. Several Reagan aides testified that the president knew nothing about any illegal activities; the televised testimony of one aide, Marine Colonel Oliver North, was especially persuasive. Eventually, three of the president's closest advisers were

indicted for lying and obstruction but all were either exonerated or received presidential pardons. A fourth individual with knowledge of the events surrounding the illegal arms deal, CIA Director William Casey, was hospitalized hours before his scheduled testimony and died soon thereafter.

Whitewater. In 1993 and 1994, Republicans were actively embarrassing and harassing the Clintons, mostly with charges related to their involvement in the failed Whitewater real estate development in Arkansas. After the GOP won control of both houses of Congress in 1994, Republican congressional committees immediately launched wide-ranging investigations of Clinton's conduct during his years as governor of Arkansas and several independent counsel probes were initiated to search for wrongdoing by Clinton and his associates. The most important of these prosecutors, Kenneth Starr, extended the scope of his investigation to include sensational allegations that the president had had an affair with a White House intern, Monica Lewinsky. A month after Clinton was forced to appear before Starr's grand jury and acknowledge his affair with Lewinsky, the GOP-controlled House Judiciary Committee began impeachment proceedings. But although Clinton's impeachment was approved by the full House on a party-line vote, by another party-line vote, the Senate declined to convict.

SEVEN

Presidential Policy Tools

In This Chapter

In recent decades, America's presidential selection process has handed the reins of government to unusually driven or powerfully propelled individuals. Recent presidents, however, have all found at least some of their ambitions thwarted by the Madisonian system of separated powers—a series of hurdles and obstacles rendered all the more impassable by the divided government and intense partisan rancor that have characterized American political processes over the past half century. As we saw in Chapter 6, every recent administration has been frustrated by Congress's ability to thwart the president's legislative initiatives, to delay and obstruct major appointments, and to use its investigative powers to harry the administration and to disrupt its policy agenda. Let us see how presidents have learned to overcome and circumvent congressional opposition.

The Three Tools of Presidential Power

Presidents often seem like an embattled group. Richard Nixon was driven from office as the result of an investigation conducted by his congressional opponents. Jimmy Carter's "flagship" energy program was killed in the House of Representatives early in Carter's first term.[1] What was left of the "Reagan Revolution" was brought to a screeching halt during Ronald Reagan's second term by Congress's Iran-Contra probe. Congressional opponents forced President George H. W. Bush to accept a tax increase in 1990 despite Bush's famous "read my lips—no new taxes" pledge. President Bill Clinton's national health care plan, the centerpiece of his first administration, was defeated in Congress after a bitter partisan battle, as was another of the major proposals that Clinton offered during his first year in office: an economic stimulus package containing a number of social programs packaged as "investments" in America's supply of human capital. Clinton's second term, of course, was disrupted by scandal and a congressional impeachment process. President George W. Bush's efforts to enhance American energy independence by opening huge new portions of Alaska to oil exploration were scuttled by congressional Democrats. And President Obama's attempts to secure congressional enactment of legislation to reform America's immigration system were turned back by the House of Representatives.

Frequently, too, presidential appointments to cabinet agencies and the courts are sent packing by the administration's congressional opponents. During the Clinton years, for example, Senate Republicans used their majority on the Judiciary Committee to block so many of the president's judicial nominees that the federal courts experienced severe staffing problems. After George W. Bush's election in 2000, Senate Democrats took charge of the Judiciary Committee when the defection of Senator James Jeffords of Vermont cost the GOP control of the upper chamber. Now in control, Democrats refused even to hold hearings on President Bush's first eight nominations to the federal bench. More than eighty Obama nominees were delayed for several years in the Senate until Democrats were able to push through a rules change that permitted the upper chamber to vote on them.

These presidents, to be sure, also achieved major legislative victories. For example, in what proved to be an administrative change with far-reaching implications, President Nixon won congressional approval for renaming the Bureau of the Budget the Office of Management and Budget and expanding presidential control over its functions. President Carter secured the passage of major civil service reform legislation and was able to overcome intense opposition within the Senate to achieve ratification of the Panama Canal treaty. Ronald Reagan successfully championed the enactment of two major pieces of legislation that substantially altered the nation's tax structure while also persuading Congress to allow sharp increases in U.S. defense spending. George H. W. Bush moved Congress to authorize the use of force against Iraq in what came to be called the Persian Gulf War. Bill Clinton helped bring about congressional passage of the landmark North American Free Trade Agreement (NAFTA) and won a pitched battle against Republican House Speaker Newt Gingrich over the federal budget in 1995–1996. Gingrich had hoped to cut federal social spending, but after a protracted struggle during which several federal agencies were forced to close because the government's spending authority under the old budget had lapsed, Clinton strong-armed congressional Republicans into acceding to a budget that mainly reflected the president's spending priorities. Over the opposition of his own party's liberal wing in Congress, moreover, Clinton presided over the elimination of most welfare entitlement programs, thereby redeeming the president's 1992 campaign pledge to "end welfare as we know it." President George W. Bush secured congressional approval of a host of anti-terrorism measures, including massive reorganizations of government agencies, under the rubric of bolstering America's "homeland defense." And President Barack Obama was able to secure passage of his far-reaching health care program.

Certainly even the most embattled of recent presidents has been able to point to at least some legislative triumphs, but sooner or later all contemporary presidents have become frustrated by their constitutionally mandated partnership with the Congress and have searched for ways to overcome or circumvent their congressional foes. Presidents have sought to surmount and bypass Congress since the early days of the Republic—witness Jefferson's unilateral purchase of Louisiana—but as we shall see, these presidential efforts have become especially common in recent decades.

Generally there are three ways that presidents can expand their power vis-à-vis the Congress: party, popular mobilization, and administration. In the first instance, presidents may endeavor to construct or strengthen national partisan institutions with which to influence the legislative process and through which to implement their programs. Franklin D. Roosevelt's effort to purge his foes from the Democratic Party and to rebuild the party as a national institution responsible to the president is a case in point.[2] Alternatively, or in addition to the first tactic, presidents may use popular appeals to attempt to create a mass base of support that will allow them to overawe and subordinate their political foes. This tactic of popular mobilization has sometimes been called the strategy of "going public" or the "rhetorical" presidency.[3] And third, presidents may seek to bolster their control of established executive agencies or to create new administrative institutions and procedures that will reduce their dependence on Congress and give them more independence in governance and policymaking. Perhaps the most obvious example of this strategy is when presidents use executive orders in lieu of seeking to persuade Congress to enact legislation.

Party-based Organizations

Over the course of American political history, the first of these presidential strategies, the use of party, is most closely associated with the presidencies of Thomas Jefferson, Andrew Jackson, Abraham Lincoln, and Franklin D. Roosevelt. For Jefferson, the creation of a national party organization based on partisan clubs and sympathetic newspapers served as the chief means for defeating his Hamiltonian opponents in the Congress. Beginning in 1793, Jefferson and his supporters began creating Democratic societies to voice opposition to the Federalists, proffer friendship to France, and campaign for the election of Jefferson's political devotees. The clubs became the basis for a party organization that nominated candidates for office and mobilized voters to carry them to victory.[4] In addition, Jefferson gave journalist Philip Freneau a sinecure as a translator for the Department of State in exchange for Freneau's work in founding and operating a new newspaper, the *National Gazette,* to serve as the leading vehicle for Jeffersonian political propaganda.[5] As political scientist V. O. Key put it, Jefferson used his party organization to "line up the unwashed" in the countryside to secure the election of sympathizers who would support his legislative program.[6] These efforts have led some historians to view Thomas Jefferson as the virtual inventor of the political party. Historian Henry Jones Ford, for example, concluded that Jefferson's "great unconscious achievement" was "to open constitutional channels for political agitation."[7] By creating a political party, Jefferson was able to overwhelm his opponents at the polls, lead his own supporters to power, and dismantle much of the Hamiltonian legislative program of protectionism, public debt, and excise taxation.

Andrew Jackson, for his part, used patronage appointments—the so-called spoils system—to construct a party organization that would bolster his authority in Congress and the nation as a whole. The Jacksonians are credited (or blamed) for introducing the spoils system in order to reward their political friends and build a party machine at the expense of the public treasury. The charge is not unfounded. But patronage served other purposes too. After their 1828 victory, the Jacksonians faced not only their supporters' demand for government jobs, but also an executive branch staffed by holdovers from the Adams administration who might have sabotaged their efforts to set a new course for the federal government. The remedy was a "proscription" of public employees associated with the prior government, and their replacement by loyal Jackson partisans.[8]

Jackson brushed aside concerns about the competence of the new partisan administrators. Public administration, he said, required no special capabilities: "The duties of all public officers are, or at least admit of being made, so plain and simple that men of intelligence may readily qualify themselves for their performance; and I cannot but believe that more is lost by the long continuance of men in office than is generally to be gained by their experience."[9] Under Andrew Jackson, between 10 and 20 percent of the government's administrative personnel were removed to make room for supporters of the new regime. While the numbers were not as large as charged by Old Hickory's antagonists, the Jacksonians established the principle that the loyalty of public servants was to be ensured through the appointment of a new administration's partisan supporters. In 1840, when the Whig candidate, William Henry Harrison, captured the White House for the first time, the new cabinet met and resolved to replace Democratic appointees with loyal Whig supporters. Within a year, nearly 2,300 Democrats had been removed to make way for the new president's adherents. When the Democrats returned to office in 1844, they replaced thousands of Whig appointees with their own men.

Patronage helped to guarantee not only the loyalty of government functionaries, but also their ability to secure citizen compliance with government policy. In the United States, the power of the national government was weak and did not extend very far into the country, particularly after the Louisiana Purchase opened vast new lands to settlement. By the 1820s, frontier squatters were routinely ignoring federal land laws and imposing their own property settlements through armed violence and intimidation. Settlers who held their land under grants from the French or Spanish governments might have been less than fully loyal to Washington. In the South, doctrines of states rights and, eventually, of nullification, challenged the authority of a federal government that lacked the military force to impose its will on a recalcitrant population. Its civil servants, then, had to do more than administer: they had to win the loyalty of a people and shore up the legitimacy of the government that they served. A party politician who enjoyed popularity among his neighbors and commanded their votes (if not their deference) might also command their compliance with federal law and "win the good will and affections of the people for the government."[10] In this way, the construction of a party machine enabled Jackson to secure support for his initiatives both within the government and throughout the nation.

Abraham Lincoln, elected to office in 1860 as the nation's first Republican president, faced the extraordinary problem of Southern secession and civil war. In his effort to defeat the South and preserve the Union, Lincoln relied heavily on the support of the Republican Party in the Congress and in the states. Congressional Republicans supported measures for conscription, nationalization of the currency, railroad construction, tax increases, the use of slaves as soldiers, and variety of other measures needed to prosecute the war.[11] In all the loyal states, especially those controlled by Republican governors and legislatures, the Republican Party apparatus served as the president's strong administrative arm in a nation whose normal administrative machinery was inadequate to the daunting tasks at hand. For example, Republican governors played an important role in ensuring the success of the president's call for troops in 1862 and again from 1863 until the end of the war. The governors led aggressive recruiting campaigns in response to the president's calls for volunteers and cooperated in summoning the state militias for national service. After the adoption of military conscription with the enactment of the 1863 National Enrollment Act, Republican governors assisted federal authorities in enforcing what quickly became one of the most unpopular policies of the Civil War era.[12]

In a similar vein, Republican governors and legislatures supported Lincoln's controversial and often unilateral actions against dissent and suspected disloyalty. By a proclamation issued September 24, 1862, the president made "all persons discouraging volunteer enlistments, resisting militia drafts, or guilty of any disloyal practice . . . subject to martial law and liable to trial and punishment by Courts Martial or Military Commission."[13] While primary responsibility for enforcing this proclamation fell on the War Department, in the states that they controlled, Republican governors used their own powers to facilitate the identification and arrest of deserters, individuals suspected of circulating disloyal literature, and those who might actually organize against the Union. With the support of Republican governors and over the opposition of Democratic politicians, thousands of arrests were made during the war in an effort to suppress opposition to the president's policies.[14]

Finally, the Republican Party apparatus played an important role in the sale of the U.S. government securities that were critical to financing the nation's war effort. At the beginning of the war, the major European financiers who normally handled government securities had no confidence in the survival of the U.S. government. As a result, European financial markets were essentially closed to the federal treasury just when the government was facing enormous fiscal needs. In 1862, Treasury Secretary Chase invited Ohio Republican banker Jay Cooke to attempt to place some $500 million in government bonds that could not be sold to domestic banks or foreign investors. Cooke developed a plan to market these securities to ordinary citizens who had never before purchased government bonds. He thought he could appeal to the patriotism of rank-and-file Americans, and he believed that widespread ownership of government bonds would give large numbers of individuals a greater concern for their nation's welfare.[15] Accordingly, Cooke established a network of 2,500 sales agents throughout the North and used the press to promote the notion that purchasing government securities was both a patriotic duty and a wise investment. In every community, Republican Party organizations worked hand in hand with Cooke's sales agents, providing what McKitrick calls the "continual affirmation of purpose" needed to sustain popular support and the regime's finances through four long years of war.[16] By 1863, all the bonds had been sold and most were in the hands of private citizens rather than institutional investors. Thus in the realm of public finance, as in the other arenas discussed earlier, the Republican

Party served President Lincoln as both an administrative arm and a political prop, allowing him to muster support in the Congress and to implement his programs and policies in the nation. Ultimately the Republican Party played an enormous role in Lincoln's ability to defeat the Confederacy and preserve the Union.

Franklin D. Roosevelt was elected to the presidency in 1932, charged with saving the nation from the most severe economic crisis in its history. FDR soon launched the New Deal—an ambitious, if unwieldy, package of economic and social programs that would forever expand the federal government's role in American society. From the outset, faced with intense opposition from the business community and other conservative forces, Roosevelt "found it painfully obvious that control of his party was essential to execute any political program."[17] FDR counted on the Democratic Party for support in Congress and for political mobilization in the country at large. He depended heavily on the congressional Democratic leadership to muster support for his New Deal initiatives and worked closely with Democratic Party leaders on matters of patronage to bind together the fractious Democratic Party coalition.[18] Moreover, like Jefferson and Jackson, FDR saw the Democratic Party as an instrument of popular organization and mobilization that could be used to overwhelm his opponents at the polls. Accordingly, through a mix of material offerings and appeals for solidarity, Roosevelt worked to bring new forces into the Democratic coalition. These included organized labor, African Americans, members of urban ethnic groups, intellectuals, and professionals. Each of these groups that today are counted among the mainstays of the Democratic coalition had manifested divided loyalties before the New Deal era or, as in the case of African Americans, had been solidly Republican in political orientation.[19]

The New Dealers saw partisan mobilization as a strategy to add durability to their triumph over an opposition that had privileged access to the courts, the federal bureaucracy, most major corporations, universities, major law firms, and the national news media. Accordingly, the Roosevelt administration sought to establish or strengthen party organizations and to build ties to labor unions, which could bring blue-collar workers and their families to the polls. This effort brought substantial numbers of new voters into the electorate and helped to make the Democrats the nation's majority party for the next thirty-five years.[20]

As it responded to the nation's economic emergency, FDR's administration established a number of major domestic spending programs that would energize the Democratic Party's electoral machinery and attach millions of new voters to the New Deal coalition. In states and cities where established Democratic Party organizations were willing to give their allegiance to the new president, the administration used these organizations as conduits for the millions of dollars distributed to citizens under the aegis of such new federal initiatives as the Civil Works Administration, the Federal Emergency Relief Administration, the Works Progress Administration, the Civilian Conservation Corps, and the National Youth Administration. Over the course of the 1930s, nearly half of all American families would draw assistance from one or another of these programs, and by controlling its distribution Democratic machines in cities like Chicago and Pittsburgh were able to enroll millions of new voters. Most of the new adherents were drawn from the ranks of the unemployed and willingly gave their political support to the party organizations that had provided them with crucial jobs or emergency relief funds.

In states and localities where established Democratic organizations were controlled by the president's enemies, FDR channeled relief funds to insurgent Democratic factions and encouraged attempts to seize control of the party machinery.[21] In Michigan and Minnesota, for example, insurgents loyal to the president were able to take control of state party organizations and, with the help of federal relief funds, mobilize large numbers of new Democratic voters.[22] By strengthening his supporters in the Democratic camp and attacking his opponents, FDR sought to centralize his own control over the party machinery and to transform the Democratic Party from a congeries of semi-feudal local organizations into a national instrument capable of implementing the president's will.

Local party organizations were augmented by a variety of other political entities, especially labor unions affiliated with the newly created Congress of Industrial Organizations, or CIO. Roosevelt strongly supported the Wagner Act through which the government guaranteed labor's right to organize—a guarantee badly needed by the CIO's industrial unions, which had been locked in mortal combat with America's manufacturers. In response, the CIO gave all-out support to the Democratic Party. The CIO and its constituent unions contributed nearly $2 million to FDR's 1936 campaign for reelection. Where local Democratic Party organizations were weak or did not exist, the CIO in effect became the Democratic Party, organizing meetings and rallies, mounting registration drives, and delivering voters to the polls.[23] Conservative critics charged that FDR had become the captive of organized labor.[24] For the most part, though, it was labor that was FDR's political captive.[25]

By 1944, the CIO's Political Action Committee, which organized tens of thousands of union members to work on behalf of Democratic candidates, had become a central part of the national Democratic Party's campaign apparatus. Thanks to local party machines and labor unions, the Roosevelt administration was able to expand voter turnout in the North and to begin the process of permanently attaching millions of new voters to the Democratic Party. Presidential election turnout outside the South rose from fewer than 57 percent of eligible voters in 1928 to more than 73 percent by 1940. A large percentage of new voters were unemployed and had received some form of relief under the auspices of New Deal programs. The overwhelming majority of these voters supported the Democrats. According to the August 1936 Gallup poll, an astonishing 82 percent of Americans receiving some form of federal relief planned to vote for Roosevelt. Millions of the voters mobilized by the Roosevelt administration during this period became permanently attached to the Democratic Party coalition and provided the Democrats with a stable base of support that would contribute to Democratic control of American political institutions for a generation.

Finally, Roosevelt made intermittent efforts to transform the tens of thousands of individuals employed in New Deal agencies in every state and locality—as well as in Washington, D.C.—into a national patronage army that would centralize presidential control over the Democratic Party and allow the president to intervene directly in state and local electoral contests.[26] In Kentucky's 1938 Democratic senatorial primary, for example, the president employed Works Progress Administration employees, bolstered by federal work relief and farm funds, to ensure the renomination of his ally, Senate Majority Leader Alben Barkley, who was facing a strong challenge from Governor A. B. "Happy" Chandler.[27] Opponents feared that FDR was attempting to create a "new Tammany" on a nationwide scale to transform the Democratic Party into a national party machine, led by the president and funded and organized, at least indirectly, by the federal government.

Some presidents have been able to assume a position of national party leadership and to use this status to dominate the Congress and implement their political agendas. Yet during the course of American political history, party has generally been an unreliable instrument of presidential power. To begin with, federalism and the separation of powers have given America a decentralized electoral structure. Typically the national parties have been alliances of powerful local and state party organizations rather than the more hierarchically organized establishments that arose in unitary states with parliamentary systems such as Great Britain. Party power in America, for the most part, has resided at the partisan periphery rather than the core. Only on rare occasions have presidents or other national party leaders been able to subordinate the local party satraps and establish a modicum of national control over party affairs. Jefferson, Jackson, Lincoln, and FDR briefly centralized party power through a combination of personal prestige (Jefferson and Jackson, after all, were the founders of the parties they led), political skill—including the adroit use of patronage—and the force of extraordinary political circumstances, for instance the Civil War and Great Depression.

Under most circumstances, though, presidents have not been able to rely on party chieftains to do their bidding. Indeed, even the four presidents who exemplified strong party leadership often found themselves locked in bitter struggles with local leaders and important regional or ideological factions of their own party. Jefferson was opposed by John Randolph; Jackson engaged in a bitter feud with his vice president, John C. Calhoun; and Lincoln, on the eve of the 1864 presidential election, was faced with a virtual rebellion within the Republican Party led by radical Republican Senator Benjamin Wade and Representative Henry W. Davis. As for Roosevelt, FDR strengthened and expanded the Democratic coalition, but was not able to transform the Democratic Party into a reliable instrument of presidential power. FDR's efforts to expand New Deal welfare programs after his landslide victory in the 1936 presidential elections were strongly opposed by a group of powerful conservative Democrats, including Senators Josiah Bailey of North Carolina, Harry Byrd of Virginia, Edward Burke of Nebraska, Millard Tydings of Maryland, and Royal Copeland of New York, as well as House Rules Committee Chairman John J. O'Connor of New York.[28] To Roosevelt's chagrin, even his vice president, John Nance Garner of Texas, became identified with the group. These Democrats joined with Republicans in a conservative coalition that strongly opposed a number of significant New Deal initiatives, including the president's proposal to mandate minimum wages and maximum hours for working men and women.

Roosevelt responded in the so-called purge campaign of 1938. The president created an "elimination committee" headed by his trusted aide, Harry Hopkins, which was charged with the task of recruiting and supporting pro–New Deal candidates to oppose conservative Democrats in the 1938 primary elections. The purge had some success. It brought about O'Connor's defeat, which paved the way for passage of the administration's minimum wages and hours bill. Yet virtually all of the other incumbents targeted by FDR won renomination and reelection: that is, the president failed in his effort to intervene in local party affairs and drive his opponents from the Democratic Party. Indeed, the conservative coalition that formed during this era remained a major force in national politics for the next three decades. In 1939, the president's foes within the Democratic Party joined with Republicans to enact the Hatch Act, which barred federal employees from engaging in campaign work for candidates for national office—and so effectively blocked the creation of a national Democratic political machine under presidential supervision.

FDR's abortive purge campaign and its aftermath illustrate the difficulty that presidents have faced in attempting to use party as an instrument of power. Presidents, even exceptionally adroit and influential presidents, have never been able to seize local party machinery or reliably translate their own popularity into mastery of local and state electoral contests. Consequently, while party has been intermittently valuable to chief executives, it has not been a durable presidential tool. In recent years, of course, presidents have had less reason to even attempt to take control of political party organizations. A series of institutional changes have made party organizations less significant factors in American politics: for instance, the reforms of the Progressive era that reduced party control of nominations and severely curtailed patronage practices; the McGovern-Fraser reforms of the 1970s that reduced party influence over the presidential selection process; and most recently, the McCain-Finegold campaign finance reforms that delimit the role of the so-called soft money raised by the political parties.[29] Contemporary campaigns are more likely to rely on short-term volunteers, motivated by what may be evanescent political ardors, than permanent organizations of stalwart party workers. Moreover, since the 1950s new technologies, including television, polling, direct-mail fundraising, and computer-assisted campaigning, have partially supplanted the role of parties within the electoral process. The use of electronic campaign methods allows political candidates—especially at the national level—to run successfully for office without much organizational support.[30]

As a result of these developments, presidents have somewhat less reason to look to the parties as mechanisms for overcoming or circumventing congressional resistance or implementing their programs. Presidents, to be sure, are far more likely to find support among their fellow partisans in Congress than in the opposing camp. As we saw in Chapter 5, members of the president's own party have some stake in the president's success. This stake, however, does not make the party a reliable presidential tool. Presidents do not command their party's congressional delegations and may find themselves alone at critical moments. For example, in 2014, President Obama reached a "log-roll" agreement with Senate Republicans on a "package" of seven judicial nominees. Republicans promised to back the nominees the president wanted in exchange for confirmation of several Republican judges. One of the Republican judges, Michael Boggs, nominated to a post on the U.S. District Court for the Northern District of Georgia, was strongly opposed by Senate Democratic leaders, who said they would sink the entire package of nominees regardless of the president's views. In addition, members of Congress will almost always put their own electoral concerns ahead of the president's priorities. In 2011, for example, several congressional Democrats from more conservative districts who were facing reelection in 2012 voted against the president's $447 billion jobs bill, which went down to defeat.[31]

Hence, while hardly irrelevant, party leadership is not a fully reliable instrument of presidential power. Instead of, or in addition to, party, contemporary presidents are likely to use two other methods—popular mobilization and executive administration—to achieve their political goals.

"Taking It to the People"

Appealing to the people has become important to contemporary presidents and should be distinguished from the partisan endeavors discussed earlier. Popular mobilization may, of course, be part and parcel of a strategy of party building. The Jacksonians and the New Dealers, for example, both sought to mobilize new supporters for their party by appealing to disaffected members of the opposition and expanding the electorate to mobilize new voters. The difference, however, is that the contemporary presidential tactic of "going public" is more personal than partisan (as captured by the title of Theodore Lowi's critique of presidential manipulation of public opinion, *The Personal President*).[32] Jefferson and Jackson, the great party builders, rarely gave speeches and seldom made public appearances—though Jackson did once meet with a group of Native American tribal leaders.[33] Lincoln's train made stops to allow the president-elect to greet crowds en route to his inaugural, but Lincoln spoke only briefly at each stop, repeatedly stating that it would be inappropriate for him to offer public views on the pressing issues of the day.[34] Though all three of these presidents issued important public proclamations and, upon occasion, spoke eloquently, they mainly reached out to the people through the institutional mechanism of party organization rather than personally and directly.

Popular mobilization as a technique of presidential power has its historical roots in the presidencies of Theodore Roosevelt and Woodrow Wilson, and has become a weapon in the political arsenals of most presidents since the mid-twentieth century, especially for Franklin D. Roosevelt, John F. Kennedy, and Ronald Reagan. During the nineteenth century it was considered rather unseemly for presidents to engage in personal campaigning on their own behalf or in support of programs and policies. When Andrew Johnson broke this unwritten rule and made a series of impassioned public speeches asking the public to support his Reconstruction program, even some of Johnson's most ardent supporters were shocked at what was seen as his lack of decorum and dignity. For their part, the president's opponents cited his "inflammatory" speeches in one of the articles of impeachment drafted by the Congress pursuant to the first effort in American history to oust a sitting president.[35]

Over the next several decades, presidential communication with the public became more acceptable as direct popular election of presidential electors and the introduction of primary elections made the presidency a more democratic office. Moreover, during the same period, presidents found it increasingly possible to reach a mass audience because of improvements in mass communication. After the Civil War, the telegraph made rapid national communication possible and wire services began to carry national news, including news of political events and speeches, to every corner of the nation in a timely manner. The emergence of a powerful advertising industry also expanded mass communication by providing newspapers with an enormous new revenue base that allowed them to slash their prices and reach larger readerships. Moreover, in response to pressure from advertisers, who were anxious to avoid offending potential customers, newspapers toned down what had often been a rabidly partisan style and adopted the contemporary objective style for their news pages, relegating partisan ranting to their editorial pages. This change meant that a president's activities and speeches, disseminated through the telegraph by the wire services, would be reported, more or less objectively, by every newspaper in the country. These developments created new political possibilities that were quickly, albeit incompletely, seized upon by such presidents as Harrison, Cleveland, and McKinley, who used public speeches to bring their policy views before national audiences.[36] Direct presidential appeals for popular support, however, remained sporadically used devices until the presidencies of Theodore Roosevelt and Woodrow Wilson. Both these individuals made systematic use of speeches, the news media, and even professional public relations campaigns to reach the American people as they sought support for their programs and policies. Both presidents sought to link themselves directly to groups and forces in civil society that would rise to their defense vis-à-vis opponents in the Congress and, often, within their own political party.

According to political scientist Jeffrey Tulis, Theodore Roosevelt initiated this tactic in 1904 with a major presidential campaign to bring about the enactment of what eventually became the Hepburn Act—legislation aimed at preventing railroads from offering low rates to large shippers and authorizing the Interstate Commerce Commission to set maximum railroad rates.[37] Though this legislative effort won relatively quick passage in the House of Representatives, it was opposed in the Senate by influential members of the president's own party, including Majority Leader Nelson Aldrich. The measure was given little chance of passage. Rather than accept defeat, Roosevelt resolved to bring public pressure to bear on the Senate. He took off across the country, making a series of speeches designed to maximize press coverage of the issue—speeches that were reported on by the local newspapers in each city where he stopped and then carried by the wire services to every newspaper in the country. Roosevelt simultaneously cultivated the support of the so-called muckraking press, often leaking information damaging to the railroads and to his political opponents to friendly journalists—his so-called fair-haired boys—who, in turn, could be counted on to write newspaper and magazine articles support-ing the president's position. To help muckrakers make their case, the president made certain that government documents critical of the railroads were released—or leaked—at opportune moments. Roosevelt also maintained ties with friendly members of Congress, who were provided with material for their own speeches and letters. In these ways, Theodore Roosevelt pioneered the art of what has come to be understood as "reaching over the heads of Congress, directly to the American people." During the campaign on behalf of railroad regulation, Roosevelt and his allies encouraged Americans who supported the president's aims to demand that their political representatives stand with the president against the railroads. Though senators were not yet subject to popular election, they were susceptible to political pressure from the state legislatures and from party leaders in their home states, who in turn found themselves pushed to support the president. The result of this public campaign was near-unanimous Senate approval of a bill that included virtually all the features that Roosevelt had sought.

Woodrow Wilson was the second president to make systematic use of ap-peals to the public. Like Roosevelt, Wilson made use of speaking tours designed to generate press coverage and wide dissemination through the wire services. Wilson also introduced what has become an important presidential technique—the press conference. The president regularly invited correspondents for major newspapers to meet with him and ask questions about important policy issues. In some in-stances, Wilson planted questions with friendly reporters so that he could provide erudite—and prearranged—responses that would be carried by the national press. This practice was later adopted by other presidents, most notably John Kennedy.

Wilson was also the first president to make use of professional public relations to mobilize popular support. After his 1916 reelection, Wilson's efforts to align the United States with Britain and France and against Germany in the European war that had begun in 1914 were opposed by a number of important senators with isola-tionist inclinations, whom the president described as "a little group of willful men." To defeat these opponents, Wilson sought to bring popular pressure to bear upon the Senate, which since the ratification of the Seventeenth Amendment in 1913 had been made subject to direct popular election and so had become more responsive to popular pressure. The president asked New York journalist and publicist George Creel to develop a public relations campaign to convince Americans—many of whom had ties to Germany or, as in the case of the Irish, reason to oppose Great Britain—that they needed to support the British cause. These efforts became moot when German submarines caused American casualties and so brought the United States into the war. Nevertheless, Creel's usefulness did not come to an end. World

War I was an industrial war, requiring a total mobilization of popular support on the home front for military production as well as for the recruitment of enormous numbers of young men for military service. The war effort required the government to convince a skeptical civilian population to bear the costs and make the sacrifices needed to achieve success in industry and agriculture, as well as on the battlefield.

To this end, President Wilson asked Creel to head the Committee on Public Information, which organized a massive public relations and news management program aimed at promoting popular enthusiasm for the war effort. This program included the dissemination of favorable news; the publication of patriotic pamphlets, films, photos, cartoons, bulletins, and periodicals; and the organization of "war expositions" and speaker tours. Other related programs were aimed at maintaining the loyalty and productivity of the workforce. Much of the committee's staff was drawn from the major advertising agencies. According to Creel, the work of the committee "was distinctly in the nature of an advertising campaign . . . our object was to sell the war."[38]

Wilson's last great effort to mobilize popular sentiment was, of course, his campaign on behalf of Senate ratification of the Treaty of Versailles and of American membership in the League of Nations. As in the prewar years, the president found himself unable to overcome Senate opposition to his foreign policy. Refusing to consider a compromise that might have salvaged the essence of the agreement, he instead undertook a public campaign aimed, once again, at going over the heads of the senators, directly to the American people. The president said he needed to "purify the wells of public opinion."[39] He thus toured the nation, traveling eight thousand miles and delivering some forty speeches on behalf of his position. Wilson's strenuous efforts seem to have succeeded in increasing popular support for American participation in the League. Nevertheless, on a second vote, the Senate again refused to ratify the treaty. The stress of the campaign and what Wilson regarded as a personal and total repudiation by the Senate contributed directly to the president's 1919 stroke, which left him incapacitated for the remainder of his term in office.

Wilson's crushing failure by no means discouraged subsequent presidents from engaging in efforts to mobilize popular support. Indeed, only twelve years after Wilson left office, Americans elected another president who worked diligently to build a popular following that would support him in battles with Congress, the courts, and his foes in civil society. This president was, of course, Franklin D. Roosevelt. As noted earlier, FDR worked to make the Democratic Party an instrument of presidential power. But especially after the 1936 election and increasingly after the failure of his 1938 purge campaign, Roosevelt also sought to build a popular base of support independent from the institution of the Democratic Party. As political scientist Sidney Milkis observes, after 1938 FDR was "firmly persuaded of the need to form a direct link between the executive office and the public."[40]

Roosevelt developed a number of tactics aimed at forging such a link. Like his predecessors, he often embarked on speaking trips around the nation to promote his programs. On one such tour, he told a crowd that he felt like a modern-day Antaeus. "I regain strength just by meeting the American people," he said.[41] Often, the president announced new programs or policy directions in public speeches. Thus in October 1937 FDR told a huge throng in Chicago that the United States was threatened by events in Europe and Asia. Signaling a definitive turn away from American isolationism and neutrality, Roosevelt called for all civilized nations to join together to "quarantine" the perpetrators of "terror and international lawlessness."[42] The speech was carried throughout the nation by the wire services and broadcast live by the new radio networks, causing a sensation and serving notice to isolationist forces in the Congress that the president was prepared to do battle with them in the arena of public opinion.

In addition to this now-familiar presidential technique for reaching out to the public, FDR made limited but important use of the new electronic medium, the radio, to reach millions of Americans. In his famous "fireside chats," the president, or at least his voice, came into every living room in the country to discuss programs and policies as well as more generally to assure Americans that he was aware of their difficulties and working diligently toward solutions. Americans accustomed to "silent Cal" or the awkward Herbert Hoover found FDR's enthralling presence in their homes a heady experience and began to see the president as the center of government and an initiator of federal policies. So as not to wear out his welcome, Roosevelt gave relatively few fireside chats, but their influence on public opinion was substantial.

Roosevelt was also an innovator in the realm of what now might be called press relations. When he entered the White House, FDR had faced a mainly hostile press typically controlled by conservative members of the business establishment. As the president wrote, "All the fat-cat newspapers—85% of the whole—have been utterly opposed to everything the Administration is seeking."[43] Roosevelt hoped to be able to use the press to mold public opinion, but in order to do so he needed to circumvent the editors and publishers who were generally unsympathetic to his goals. To this end, the president worked to cultivate the reporters who covered the White House. Roosevelt made himself available for biweekly press conferences where he offered candid answers to reporters' questions and made certain always to make important policy announcements that would give the assembled reporters significant stories to file with their papers.[44] Roosevelt became the first president to designate a press secretary (Stephen Early), who was charged with organizing the press conferences and making certain that reporters observed the informal rules distinguishing presidential comments that were off the record from those that could be attributed directly to the president.

In his press conferences, FDR charmed and dazzled the reporters and converted most to administration partisans despite the conservative bias of their bosses, the newspaper owners. This meant that even though most major newspapers, in their editorial pages, continued to endorse Republican candidates and policy positions, their front-page news coverage emphasized the goals and accomplishments of the Roosevelt administration. Since most newspaper readers saw the front page but few read the editorial page, the overall impression they received from the press was one of an administration and, above all, a president, constantly working to promote the public good. As political scientist Samuel Kernell observes, "Roosevelt succeeded in splitting off Washington correspondents from the editorial stance of their papers." For twelve years, "Roosevelt lived with a hostile newspaper industry and a friendly press corps."[45]

Roosevelt also succeeded in making use of the motion picture industry to promote his policies. Early in his first term, FDR had been able to secure the support of Jack and Harry Warner, whose studio was a major producer of newsreels. As a result, the president and his programs frequently were featured on screens all across the nation, presenting tens of millions of moviegoers with an image of a president vigorously championing policies designed to help them. Later, as he sought to lead the nation into alliance with Great Britain against the threat posed by Nazi Germany, Roosevelt again turned to Hollywood to help him overcome isolationist and pro-German sentiment in the Congress and the nation. The film studios, often headed by Jewish Americans, were happy to cooperate. During the 1930s, when Roosevelt was engaged in bitter struggles with his isolationist foes, Hollywood produced a number of films, such as the 1938 classic *Confessions of a Nazi Spy*, that depicted the evils of the Nazi regime, presented Nazi Germany as a threat to the United States, and suggested that a pro-German fifth column was at work within the United States. Warner Brothers offered to make any short film addressing the need for military preparedness free of charge, while at the administration's request MGM produced such feature films as *Eyes of the Navy*, which emphasized the need for a strong national defense and an activist foreign policy. This propaganda campaign helped to build public support for American military preparedness, and assisted FDR in overcoming congressional opposition to his policy of gradually increasing support for Great Britain, long before the Japanese attack on Pearl Harbor silenced opponents of American involvement in the war. The White House showed its gratitude to Hollywood by ordering the Justice Department to settle an antitrust suit it had brought against the studios and by defending the filmmakers against charges of producing indecent materials.[46]

Not all of FDR's efforts to overcome congressional opposition by mobilizing popular support were successful. His 1937 campaign to "pack" the Supreme Court was a failure, as was his 1938 effort to expand relief spending. In 1939, Roosevelt launched a futile attack on the practice of senatorial courtesy by nominating to a federal district court vacancy a Virginian who was opposed by both of the state's senators and conducting a vigorous, but ultimately unsuccessful, public campaign on his behalf.[47] Despite these and other failures, however, Roosevelt demonstrated, especially in the realm of foreign policy, that an astute president could rally public support and use it to overcome his opponents in Washington. Indeed, every president since FDR has imitated and refined his methods for reaching the American people—though even with the introduction of television and other sophisticated electronic aides, no subsequent president has equaled FDR's communications skills.

President Dwight Eisenhower, for example, employed professional public relations firms to fashion his political messages, secured the assistance of Columbia University sociologist Robert Merton to analyze the public's view of his leadership qualities, and accepted coaching from television actor Robert Montgomery on the mechanics of delivering speeches.[48] Throughout his presidency, Eisenhower made extensive use of press conferences and the then new medium of television to present his views to the public. Beginning in 1955, Eisenhower allowed television crews to film his bimonthly press conferences for subsequent broadcast on the national television networks. Eisenhower's face became familiar to millions of Americans through the press conferences and through his televised addresses to the nation on matters of grave public concern, usually involving foreign policy crises. Political scientist Fred Greenstein observes that Eisenhower came to be seen by television viewers as a respectable and trustworthy person, "solid and full of common sense."[49]

In order to maintain an image of statesmanship, Eisenhower sought always to convey the impression that he was a man of principle, standing above the political fray. Occasionally Eisenhower might campaign for a specific piece of legislation such as his successful televised effort on behalf of the Landrum-Griffin labor relations act.[50] Generally, however, unlike Wilson or the Roosevelts, Ike eschewed direct public appeals on behalf of specific policies and usually avoided direct attacks against his political adversaries. Instead he focused on maintaining a high standing with the public, believing that so long as he maintained substantial levels of popular support, his friends in the Congress would be strengthened and his adversaries would be reluctant to oppose him. "One man," said Eisenhower, "can do a lot . . . if he happens to be ranking high in public estimation."[51] Thus during his bitter struggle against Joseph McCarthy, the president seldom mentioned the Wisconsin senator by name. Rather, Ike usually spoke obliquely of important American values and left it to the press to point out that McCarthy had violated these very same principles. Direct attacks on McCarthy were usually relegated to surrogates like Vice President Richard Nixon, who were less reluctant to dirty their hands.[52]

Eisenhower's successors were more willing than Ike to promote their programs and policies to the public. John Kennedy, for example, made use of live, televised press conferences, interviews with friendly reporters, and prime-time addresses to the nation to promote his policies. For example, in 1962, Kennedy spoke at thirty-three nationally televised rallies on behalf of his health care program.[53] Kennedy also employed carefully staged media events such as his famous July 1963 speech in Berlin, Germany, a city frequently under threat by the Soviet Union. Kennedy famously affirmed America's readiness to defend Berlin by declaring "Ich bin ein Berliner."[54] Kennedy presumably meant to say that he stood as one with the people of Berlin in the face of the Russian threat. The correct expression, though, would have been "Ich bin Berliner." Kennedy's phrase unfortunately declared to hundreds of thousand of assembled Germans that the American president saw himself as a locally popular form of puff pastry called "the Berliner."

Each of the past several presidents has sought to craft a public relations strategy that would emphasize his strengths and maximize his popular appeal. For Kennedy, handsome and quick-witted, the televised press conference was an excellent public relations vehicle. Johnson and Nixon lacked Kennedy's vaunted charisma, but both were effective television speakers, usually reading from a prepared text. For example, President Johnson's nationally televised address to a joint session of Congress following a brutal attack by local authorities against peaceful demonstrators in Selma, Alabama, in March 1965 is often credited with rallying popular opinion and overcoming congressional opposition to major voting-rights legislation.[55] Johnson also launched his "War on Poverty" with a series of televised appeals. After sending a special message to Congress outlining the need for new legislation, LBJ launched a publicity campaign in which the president and members of his family, trailed by television crews, made personal visits to impoverished families. Under intense media pressure, Congress passed the president's omnibus bill with a minimum of deliberation.[56]

Jimmy Carter and Bill Clinton occasionally addressed the nation and sometimes held press conferences, but both preferred other media formats. Both men made extensive use of televised town meetings—carefully staged events in which the president was asked questions by a friendly group of ordinary Americans. This format guaranteed that the president would not be asked the sorts of pointed questions preferred by reporters and gave the president an opportunity to appear to consult with rank-and-file citizens about his goals and policies. Like other presidents, Clinton also relied on friendly journalists to write favorable stories about his administration. Early in his career, Clinton had met and won the friendship of Sidney Blumenthal, a well-known writer for the *Washington Post* and *New Republic*. Throughout the Clinton years, Blumenthal wrote pieces lauding the president and assailing his foes.[57] Clinton eventually appointed Blumenthal a senior White House adviser.

Clinton also made the White House Communications Office an important institution within the Executive Office of the President.[58] In a practice continued by George W. Bush, the Communications Office became responsible not only for responding to reporters' queries, but also for developing and implementing a coordinated communications strategy that promoted the president's policy goals, developed responses to unflattering news stories, and made certain that a favorable image of the president would, insofar as possible, dominate the news. The Communications Office, in effect, institutionalized the functions undertaken on an ad hoc basis by media-savvy presidents like the Roosevelts and their staffers. George W. Bush's first communications director, Karen Hughes, sought to put the office "ahead of the news," frequently developing stories that would dominate the headlines, present the president in a favorable light, and deflect criticism. For example, after the administration responded to the September 11 terrorist attacks against the World Trade Center and Pentagon with a massive military campaign in Afghanistan, the Communications Office developed several stories that made it difficult for administration critics to gain much traction. One such story concerned the brutal treatment of women by Afghanistan's fundamentalist Taliban regime. Underlined in several speeches by First Lady Laura Bush, and communicated to the press in hundreds of news releases, the wave of publicity the Communications Office was able to generate concerning the Taliban government's harsh and demeaning posture toward women helped make it extremely difficult for the Bush administration's liberal critics to utter even a word of protest regarding America's efforts to oust the Taliban from power.

President Obama has preferred relatively short and less formal televised speeches from the White House or White House grounds. During these brief speeches he will typically explain some aspect of his administration's policy or past practices. In his August 1, 2014, speech, for instance, the president admitted that after 9/11, "We tortured some folks." Obama also likes photo opportunities where he is shown enjoying a beer or a hamburger with ordinary people in a family restaurant. These photo opportunities are known as "just plain folks" shots, and are designed to establish a relationship between the president and average American television viewers.

The recent president best known for his ability to build popular support through the media was, of course, Ronald Reagan—sometimes dubbed the "great communicator." According to journalist and Reagan biographer Lou Cannon, Reagan used his experience as an actor very effectively to reach out to the nation via the television screen. Reagan once said, "There have been many times in this office when I've wondered how you could do the job if you hadn't been an actor."[59] Reagan used televised broadcasts to the nation with great effectiveness to build public support for his programs and thereby to bring pressure to bear on the Congress. For example, on April 28, 1981, Reagan, whose budget proposals had been blocked in the Congress, made a nationally televised speech before a joint congressional session in which he touted his budget. The speech was a brilliant performance, a "smash" according to Newsweek, and seemed to produce a sharp increase in popular support for the president's proposals.[60] Taking note of constituency opinion, many congressional Democrats shifted their votes to support the president despite the efforts of House Speaker Thomas P. "Tip" O'Neill and others in the Democratic leadership to remind members that public opinion was fickle. After the president's speech, Democratic members of Congress received hundreds of calls from constituents urging them to support the president. One Democrat said of his colleagues, "They say they're voting for the president's budget because they're afraid."[61]

Though Reagan always seemed natural and relaxed on television, his actor's style required meticulous staffing just as any screen performance might need. "You need to have a very strong stage manager-producer-director," said Reagan's chief of staff Kenneth Duberstein. "You need to have very good technical men and sound men at all times."[62] The importance of stage management was especially evident when the president and his staff sought to create political spectacles. For example, midway through Reagan's first term, the president presided over the unveiling of the refurbished Statue of Liberty. The nationally televised ceremony included fireworks, tall sailing ships, and brass bands. At the climactic moment, the tarpaulin covering the torch was dropped to reveal the president, hand on heart, leading the national anthem. The identification of President Reagan with an important national icon was designed to create a powerful symbol of presidential authority, values, and patriotism that would capture the camera lens and be out of reach of congressional and media carping. The event required enormous preparation and stage management and allowed the president to communicate with the public at an almost visceral level that could not be touched by opponents' criticisms, because criticizing Reagan in this situation would have seemed tantamount to attacking the Statue of Liberty. During Reagan's first term in office, his actor's style, bolstered by solid staffing, helped the president to push major pieces of tax, budget, and defense legislation through a House of Representatives controlled by the Democrats.

Some presidents have been able to make effective use of a tactic of popular appeals to overcome congressional opposition. Popular support, though, has not been a firm and lasting foundation for presidential power.[63] As Tip O'Neill pointed out to his congressional caucus, popular support is notoriously fickle. President George W. Bush maintained a popular approval rating of over 70 percent for more than a year following the 9/11 terrorist attacks. This sustained popular response to the president's handling of a crisis, however, has been the rare exception to the general rule of a fickle public and unstable support for the president. Consider that after America's triumph in the 1990 Persian Gulf War, President George H. W. Bush scored a remarkable 90 percent approval rating in the polls. Just two years later, however, after the 1991 budget crisis, Bush's support plummeted and the president was defeated in his bid for reelection. And during Ronald Reagan's first two years in office, his approval score ranged from a high of 59 percent in 1981 to a low of 37 percent in early 1983.[64] As Reagan's standings in the polls fell, his ability to overawe Democratic opponents and retain the support of wavering Republicans diminished sharply.

Political scientist Theodore J. Lowi has argued that declines in popular approval during a president's term in office are nearly inevitable and follow a predictable pattern.[65] Presidents generate popular support by promising to undertake important programs that will contribute directly to the well-being of large numbers of Americans. Almost inevitably, presidential performance falls short of presidential promises and popular expectations, leading to a sharp decline in public support and a collapse of presidential influence. Lowi calls this phenomenon "the law of outcomes."[66] President Obama's public approval ratings have followed this same pattern, declining sharply during his second term. By mid-2014, many more Americans disapproved of the job the president was doing than approved of it.

Though they did not elevate this tendency to the status of a "law," the framers of the Constitution were aware of the ephemeral nature of popular political support. Indeed, the authors of the *Federalist Papers* argued that presidents and other public officials should be given fixed terms in office rather than the indefinite terms associated with parliamentary democracy, so that they would not be subjected to "an unqualified complaisance to every sudden breeze of passion; or to every transient impulse which the people may receive."[67] Unfortunately, when presidents depend heavily on popular support as an instrument of governance, they become vulnerable to "transient impulses" despite their fixed terms. As a foundation for presidential power, public opinion often turns out to be as unstable and treacherous as quicksand.

Reliance on public appeals makes presidents politically vulnerable in a second way as well. Appeals for popular support require presidents to make nearly constant use of the broadcast and news media to reach the public.[68] But this approach also makes presidents vulnerable to media attacks, which have been a feature of American politics since the Vietnam War. During the Vietnam War, the national print and broadcast media discovered a substantial middle- and upper-middle-class audience that was skeptical of administration policy and receptive to investigative coverage and adversarial journalism.[69] Consequently journalists became emboldened to present reports critical of the White House, and a constituency emerged that would rally to the defense of the media when the White House countered with its own attacks. This pattern has endured: newspapers and broadcasters have discovered that aggressive use of the techniques of investigation, publicity, and exposure have enhanced their autonomy and allowed them to carve out a prominent place for themselves in American government and politics.

Some media organizations, to be sure, are liberal in their political orientation and quicker to attack Republican presidents than their Democratic counterparts. The *Washington Post* and *New York Times,* for example, almost always endorse Democratic political candidates and have been sharply critical of the Nixon, Reagan, and Bush administrations. Other media outlets are conservative in their orientations and obviously present a different perspective to their readers and viewers. Such media as *FOX News,* the *Washington Times,* the *Weekly Standard,* and *American Spectator* are almost always more sympathetic to Republican causes and candidates and hostile to the Democrats. Once a story breaks, however, the print and broadcast media often seem to put partisanship and ideology aside in order to join in the attack and maintain their place and power. Thus some of the sensational charges against President Clinton received just as much play in the liberal *Washington Post* and *New York Times* as in the conservative *Washington Times.* Indeed, the *Washington Post* went so far as to savage its own former reporter, Sidney Blumenthal, in a series of articles, after Blumenthal wrote a favorable piece on Clinton during the height of the Whitewater affair.[70]

Providing the media with information is an enormous complex of ancillary institutions, including conservative and liberal "think tanks," various consulting firms specializing in developing damaging information on their clients' enemies (a tactic known as opposition research), and public relations firms. These enterprises, located mainly in Washington and New York, serve up an endless supply of press releases. Conservative institutions provide damaging information about liberal politicians, while liberal organizations provide damaging information about conservative politicians. The press hardly needs to engage in any investigative work of its own. It can choose the most tempting tidbits from the torrent of rumors, innuendos, accusations, and even the occasional fact conveniently delivered daily to newsrooms via fax.[71] In the summer of 2002, for example, the press gave extensive coverage to stories linking President George W. Bush and Vice President Dick Cheney to questionable practices by the corporations with which they had been associated before taking public office. The materials for the stories were generally provided by liberal public interest groups that were opposed to the administration's positions on economic and environmental issues.

Given the current penchant of the media for faultfinding and critical journalism, presidents who depend heavily on public relations as a source of political power are, in effect, making themselves vulnerable to a set of institutions with a stake in undercutting them. Every recent president has found himself the target of intense media attacks that in some instances seem designed merely to flex the muscles of the media. For example, in 1993 when Bill Clinton refused to submit to media demands that he hold more press conferences and fewer town meetings, the press and broadcast media ran a story they dubbed "Hairgate" purporting to show that the president was indifferent to the concerns of ordinary Americans. What was the evidence for this conclusion? Clinton had briefly delayed traffic at Los Angeles International Airport while a barber boarded *Air Force One* to give the president a haircut. While the facts were trivial, the story became the basis for a week of attacks on the president's character. Eventually, Clinton gave in to media demands for more press conferences and hired media consultant David Gergen to mend fences with the press. Long before the Monica Lewinsky affair completely sullied the president's image, Clinton concluded that the press was untrustworthy. No matter what he did, Clinton told a reporter, "You guys take it and you say . . . what else can I hit him about?"[72]

President George W. Bush and his staff, also distrustful of the news media, sought to carefully control the president's interactions with journalists. For example, Bush seldom held televised press conferences; he preferred instead to deliver speeches or to have staffers like press secretary Ari Fleischer engage in give and take with the reporters. As of March 2003, then, Bush had held only eight news conferences. At the same point in time in his first term in office, Bill Clinton, who had been criticized by the press for his failure to schedule press conferences, had held thirty while at a similar point in his presidency, George H. W. Bush had held fifty-eight televised press conferences. When asked about the paucity of press conferences held by the George W. Bush administration, White House Communications Director Dan Bartlett said, "If you have a message you're trying to deliver, a news conference can go in a different direction."[73]

Presidents who rely on popular support as an instrument of political power also often find themselves vulnerable to political opponents, especially opponents in Congress, who find ways of using publicity and the mass media to attack the president's ties to mass constituencies. When presidents first began to use their "bully pulpit" to reach over the heads of Congress directly to the American people, congressional opponents may have been dazzled and overawed, but in recent years, Congress has countered, often successfully, with its own publicity campaigns and sensational media revelations. The most important of these counterstrategies is the technique that Martin Shefter and I have called "RIP," or revelation, investigation, and prosecution (see Chapter 6).[74] As we saw, RIP was used with considerable effect against the Nixon, Reagan, and Clinton presidencies.

Nixon and Reagan's defenders charged that they had been the victims of left-wing conspiracies, while Clinton viewed himself as the victim of a vast right-wing conspiracy. In essence, they were all correct. There can be little doubt that all three presidents were guilty of most of the charges levied against them. Yet in each instance a president's foes were able to mount major media campaigns against the White House, leading to formal and well-publicized congressional investigations of presidential misconduct that drove Nixon from office and undermined the two other presidencies. In the opening years of the twentieth century, presidents learned how to mobilize popular support against their opponents in Congress. By the closing years of the same century, the tide had turned: members of Congress had learned how to use media revelations to attack and discredit presidents.

Presidents today have thus adopted what is essentially a defensive posture with regard to public opinion. Although they have certainly not abandoned "going public," they no longer do so as frequently as they once did—for example, there has been a decline in presidential appearances on prime-time television over the past four administrations.[75] Instead, presidents have directed their institutionalized public and media relations efforts more toward creating a generally favorable public image—following the example of Dwight Eisenhower—than toward promoting specific policies. Thus in 2002 President George W. Bush made several speeches to boost his proposed creation of a new Homeland Security department, while at the same time the White House Communications office was engaged in a nonstop, seven-day-a-week effort to promote news and feature stories aimed at bolstering the president's more general public image. Stories emphasized the president's empathy for retirees hurt by the downturn of stock prices; the president's anger over corporate abuses; the president's concern for the environment; the president's determination to prevent terrorism; the president's support for Israel; and so forth. These are all examples of image-polishing rather than going public on behalf of specific programs. Confronted with the limitations of a strategy of popular mobilization, presidents have shifted from an offensive strategy to a more defensive mode in this domain.[76] The limitations of going public as a route to presidential power have also led contemporary presidents to make use of a third technique—expansion of their administrative capabilities.

Flying Solo: The Administrative Strategy

Contemporary presidents have increased the administrative capabilities of their office in three ways. First, they have enhanced the reach and power of the Executive Office of the President. Second, they have sought to increase White House control over the federal bureaucracy. And third, they have expanded the role of executive orders and other instruments of direct presidential governance. Taken together, these three components of what might be called the White House "administrative strategy" have given presidents a way to achieve their programmatic and policy goals even when they are unable to secure congressional approval. Indeed, some recent presidents have been able to accomplish quite a bit without much in the way of congressional, partisan, or even public support.

Using the Executive Office of the President

Sustained presidential efforts to enhance the administrative power of the White House date back to the administration of Franklin D. Roosevelt. FDR, as we saw, made ample use of both partisan mobilization and direct popular appeals to bolster his political influence. But just as he turned to popular appeals in the wake of his failed purge of the Democratic Party, FDR began to turn to an administrative strategy when he saw the limitations and evanescent character of popularity as an instrument of power. In particular, during the struggles of the mid-1930s, including the battle over Roosevelt's failed "court-packing" plan, FDR's opponents showed that they too could make effective use of popular appeals and the news media. Accordingly the president realized that he could not pin all his political hopes on personal popularity. Following the 1936 presidential election, then, Roosevelt established the President's Committee on Administrative Management (also known as the Brownlow Committee) to consider reorganizing the executive branch of government so that the presidency could manage it more effectively.

In 1937, FDR proposed legislation based on the Brownlow report that was designed to expand the White House staff; strengthen the president's managerial and personnel powers, including the power to reorganize federal agencies; and eliminate the independent regulatory agencies. The president's opponents in Congress denounced this proposal as a blatant power grab by the White House and were able to defeat it. In 1939, however, a compromise proposal was enacted into law, giving FDR some of the powers he wanted. Most importantly, the 1939 act authorized the president to appoint six administrative assistants and gave him, for a period of two years, the authority to implement reorganizations of the executive branch, subject to congressional veto. Most of Roosevelt's foes saw these provisions as minor concessions to the president's ambitions. FDR, however, capitalized on them in September 1939 by issuing Executive Order 8248, which established the Executive Office of the President, a development that administrative scholar Luther Gulick has called an "epoch-making event in the history of American institutions."[77]

Under the terms of FDR's executive order, the administrative assistants allotted to the president by the 1939 Reorganization Act were defined as personal aides of the president charged with undertaking such duties as the president saw fit to entrust to them. Roosevelt quickly appointed a group of six assistants who became the basis of the White House staff, which today consists of nearly four hundred employees working directly for the president in the White House Office along with some 1,400 individuals staffing the several (currently eight) divisions of the Executive Office.[78] The creation and growth of the White House staff gave Roosevelt and his successors an enormously enhanced capacity to gather information, plan programs and strategies, communicate with constituencies, and supervise the activities of the executive branch. The staff multiplied the president's eyes, ears, and arms, becoming a critical instrument of presidential power.[79]

Executive Order 8248 established five divisions within the Executive Office. In addition to the White House Office itself, the most important was the Bureau of the Budget, today called the White House Office of Management and Budget. The Bureau of the Budget, as we saw in Chapter 3, had been established during the Harding administration as a mechanism for reviewing the budgetary requests of the various federal agencies and achieving economy in spending. President Harding had hoped that the bureau would become a presidential tool for controlling the U.S. budget. The Congress of that era, however, was unwilling to cede power to the White House. To prevent the president from gaining control over the bureau, Congress placed the new agency in the Treasury Department, the government agency it considered most responsive to congressional views. Over the next several years, successive presidents sought to use the bureau to enforce their own budgetary goals, but with limited success.

Franklin D. Roosevelt saw the Bureau of the Budget as a potential instrument of presidential control over federal spending and hence a mechanism through which the White House could greatly expand its power. Even before transferring the bureau into the Executive Office of the President, FDR had expanded its role, but once he had fully captured the agency he went even further, mandating that it would have the power of "central clearance." That is, all legislative proposals emanating from any federal agency, not only budgetary requests, had to be submitted to the bureau for analysis and approval before being sent on to Congress. Since the bureau now worked for the president, this procedure, which quickly became a matter of routine, greatly enhanced the president's control over the entire executive branch. Later, President Harry Truman added to the bureau's power by requiring that it draft all legislation emanating from the White House as well as all executive orders.[80] Thus, in one White House agency, the president had the means to exert major influence over both the flow of money as well as the shape and content of national legislation.

During the Truman administration, Congress added two more important divisions to the executive office: the Council of Economic Advisers in 1946 and the National Security Council in 1947. According to Milkis, some members of Congress saw these agencies as checks on the president's autonomy in military and fiscal matters.[81] Truman, however, quickly made these divisions part of the president's "team." Today, the chair of the Council of Economic Advisers is often a major architect of the administration's fiscal policy and provides the White House with substantial expertise in the realm of economic policy. In a similar vein, the head of the National Security Council, the president's national security adviser, is often a powerful voice in the international and military policy arenas. Some national security advisers, Henry Kissinger for example, have eclipsed the secretary of state in the making of American foreign policy. Like the Council of Economic Advisers, the National Security Council gives the president substantial expertise and decision-making power in a vital policy arena. Indeed, presidents have used these agencies to arrogate to themselves substantial power in these realms.

Making the Most of Regulatory Review

A second instrument that presidents have used to increase their power and reach is an agency within Office of Management and Budget called the Office of Information and Regulatory Affairs, which, as we saw in Chapter 5, supervises the process of regulatory review. Presidents have sought to use this process to seize control of rulemaking by the agencies of the executive branch. Whenever Congress enacts a statute, its actual implementation requires the promulgation of hundreds of rules by the agency charged with administering the law. For example, if Congress wishes to improve air quality, it must delegate to an agency—say the Environmental Protection Agency (EPA)—the power to establish numerous rules and regulations that will govern the actions of the government agencies, firms, and individuals whose conduct may have an impact on the atmosphere. The agency rulemaking process is itself governed by a number of statutory requirements concerning public notice (most importantly publication in the *Federal Register*), hearings, and appeals, but once completed and published in the massive *Code of Federal Regulations,* administrative rules have the effect of law and are enforced by the federal courts.

Some congressional statutes are quite detailed and leave agencies with relatively little discretion. Typically, however, Congress enacts a relatively broad statement of legislative intent and delegates to the appropriate administrative agency the power to fill in many important details.[82] One classic example is the 1914 Federal Trade Commission Act, which outlaws "unfair methods of competition" but fails to define such methods. This omission meant that the commission could develop its own standards of fairness.[83] In the words of administrative law scholar Kenneth Culp Davis, Congress typically says to an administrative agency, "Here is the problem: deal with it."[84]

The discretion that Congress delegates to administrative agencies has provided recent presidents with an important avenue for expanding their own power. Beginning with little fanfare during the Nixon administration, presidents—through regulatory review—gradually have endeavored to take control of the rulemaking process and to use it as a quasi-legislative mechanism through which they can engage in lawmaking without the interference of the legislature. After the EPA was established in 1970, business groups and their congressional representatives became alarmed at the enormous numbers and growing cost of new regulations issued by the agency to implement federal environmental laws. Nixon responded to these concerns by establishing a "quality of life" review process within the newly renamed Office of Management and Budget. Under this program, Nixon required the EPA to submit proposed new regulations for review a month prior to their publication in the *Federal Register*. The Office of Management and Budget, in turn, circulated the proposals to other agencies for comment, mainly to allow the measures' adversaries more time to mobilize an opposition. In 1974, President Ford issued an executive order formalizing this review process. Ford required that the Office of Management and Budget subject major proposed regulations to an "inflationary impact analysis" before their publication in the *Register*. Ford's successor, Jimmy Carter, issued a new executive order replacing this procedure with a requirement that the office analyze the cost of major proposed regulations, evaluate plausible alternatives, and approve the least cumbersome form of regulation.[85]

As Kenneth Mayer and Thomas Weko note, the Nixon, Ford, and Carter efforts fell short of full-blown presidential control over the rulemaking process. The various procedures these presidents established amounted to haphazard White House interference that lacked any clear pattern or enforcement power.[86] Though agencies might follow the presidentially mandated procedures, in the end they were not obligated to change their proposed regulations to comply with the president's policy goals. Because they lacked force, these initial White House efforts were largely ignored by Congress, which saw them merely as attempts by presidents to make symbolic gestures that would placate important constituency groups. This congressional view proved to be a mistake, since these early efforts by presidents to influence rulemaking created examples and precedents that opened the way for more determined efforts by Ronald Reagan and his successors in office, particularly Bill Clinton. Indeed, Congress unwittingly contributed to the expansion of presidential power in 1979 by enacting the Paperwork Reduction Act, which, among other things, provided for the creation of the Office of Information and Regulatory Affairs (OIRA). Congress was responding to complaints from businesses that government agencies were requiring them to complete and submit too many forms and records. Through this new office, the Office of Management and Budget was authorized to monitor and limit government agencies' paperwork collection requests.[87] This seemingly innocuous new agency was soon turned into an important new presidential tool.[88]

A month after taking office in 1981, President Ronald Reagan issued Executive Order 12291 establishing a process for centralized presidential oversight of agency rulemaking. The order required that regulatory agencies use cost-benefit analyses to justify proposed regulations. Significant new rules were not to be adopted unless the potential benefits to society outweighed the potential costs. To prove that they had complied with this mandate, agencies were required to prepare a formal regulatory impact analysis, which was to include an assessment of the costs and benefits of any proposed rule, as well as an evaluation of alternative regulations that might impose lower costs. The OIRA was responsible for evaluating these regulatory impact analyses. Agencies were prohibited from publishing major proposed rules without the office's clearance, and they were required to incorporate the office's recommended revisions into the rules that they eventually published. It could block the publication and implementation of any rule that it disapproved.

In effect, the Reagan administration used the statutory cover of the Paperwork Reduction Act to achieve a unilateral extension of White House power. The intention was not simply to reduce red tape for regulated business firms. Instead OIRA became an instrument through which the White House increased its control of the rulemaking process, so that it could block or amend rules at will. The Reagan administration quickly used the regulatory review process to curtail the impact of federal environmental and health and safety legislation. It blocked the promulgation of new rules by the EPA and the Occupational Safety and Health Administration (OSHA).[89]

During the eight years of the Reagan presidency, only a tiny number of proposals—an average of eighty-five per year—were returned to agencies for reconsideration or withdrawal.[90] Reagan's opponents in Congress denounced the president's intervention in the rulemaking process, but were able to wrest only minor concessions from the White House.[91] Administrators in the regulatory agencies raised few obstacles to the new regime in rulemaking. Under the Civil Service Reform Act of 1978, presidents had gained greater control over the assignment of senior bureaucrats to the top positions in federal agencies, and the Reaganites had taken full advantage of this opportunity to fill strategic positions with administrators sympathetic to the president's objectives.[92] The clarity of those objectives left little room for bureaucratic improvisation, especially since agency compliance was regularly monitored.[93] Given presidential control over budgets, staffing, and the general quality of agency life, most career bureaucrats found it more sensible to cooperate than to struggle with the White House.[94]

In 1985, President Reagan further expanded presidential control over rulemaking. By executive order, he required every regulatory agency to report annually to OIRA its objectives for the coming year. OIRA would then assess each agency's regulatory agenda for consistency with the president's program, and notify agencies of modifications needed to bring their plans into alignment with the views of the president. This new order went beyond Reagan's initial regulatory review program. Executive Order 12291 had authorized the White House to review rules after they were proposed; its sequel, Executive Order 12498, discussed later, enabled the White

House to intervene before rules were drafted.[95] Reagan's order forced agencies to take account of presidential goals and not just congressional intent when formulating the rules that carried legislation into effect.

President Bill Clinton extended presidential control of regulatory agencies by directing the OIRA to issue "regulatory prompts"—orders instructing agencies to adopt particular regulations. While Reagan had used regulatory review to prevent the imposition of rules to which he objected, Clinton took the further step of requiring agencies to formulate rules that he wanted.[96] Elena Kagan, a former official in the Clinton White House and now a Supreme Court justice, explains that Clinton felt hemmed in by congressional opposition during most of his presidential tenure. Determined to make his mark in domestic policy, Clinton used the bureaucratic rulemaking process to accomplish unilaterally what he was unable to achieve through Congress.[97]

In September 1993, Clinton issued Executive Order 12866 to replace Reagan's two orders regarding regulatory review. Clinton's new order preserved the essential components of Reagan's regulatory oversight system. He required agencies to submit major regulations to OIRA for review; he extended the use of cost-benefit analyses for the evaluation of proposed new rules; and he established an annual regulatory planning process similar to the one created by Reagan's Executive Order 12498.

Clinton, however, added two new elements to the regulatory review process established by Reagan. First, Clinton sought to extend regulatory review to the independent agencies such as the Social Security Administration.[98] President Clinton did not attempt to require the independent agencies to submit individual proposed rules for review. He did, however, require them to submit their annual regulatory agendas to OIRA for examination of their consistency with the president's priorities. Through this requirement, Clinton was seeking, at the very least, to begin to establish precedents that would lead to greater presidential control of the various independent agencies that Congress had placed outside the reach of presidential power.

Second, and more important in the immediate run, Clinton's order indicated that he believed the president had full authority to direct executive department heads in their rulemaking activities—not simply to block rules to which the president objected, but to order them to adopt such rules as the president thought might be appropriate. In the order itself, Clinton noted only that any conflicts between the Office of Management and Budget and an agency over proposed rules would be resolved by a presidential decision. It quickly became clear, though, that Clinton was seeking to assert that the rulemaking power delegated to agencies by the Congress was fully at the disposal of the president. Soon after issuing Executive Order

12866, the president began a regular practice of issuing formal orders to executive branch officials directing them to propose particular rules and regulations that the president thought were desirable.

During the course of his presidency, Clinton issued 107 directives to administrators ordering them to propose specific rules and regulations and, pursuant to the requirements of the Administrative Procedures Act, to publish them in the *Federal Register* for public commentary. In some instances, the language of the rule to be proposed was drafted by the White House staff, while in other cases, the president assigned a level of priority but then left it to the agency to draft the precise language of the proposal. Presidential rulemaking directives covered a wide variety of topics. For example, Clinton ordered the Food and Drug Administration (FDA) to develop rules designed to restrict the marketing of tobacco products to children. White House and FDA staffers then spent several months preparing nearly a thousand pages of new regulations affecting tobacco manufacturers and vendors.[99] On another occasion, President Clinton directed the secretary of labor to propose rules that would allow states to offer paid leave to new parents—mothers and fathers alike—through their unemployment insurance systems. In another instance, Clinton ordered the secretaries of the departments of Agriculture and the Interior to propose rules that would protect the nation's waters from pollution. Clinton also ordered the secretaries of Health and Human Services and the Treasury to propose a very specific set of standards governing the safety inspection of imported foods.[100] In two other cases, the president ordered the heads of all departments with health care responsibilities to adopt rules complying with a model "patients bill of rights" developed by a presidential advisory panel, and ordered the secretary of the treasury to develop rules that would ban the importation of assault pistols and improve the enforcement of gun-licensing requirements.

In principle, the agencies might have objected to these presidential directives and sought help from Congress. Clinton, however, was careful only to order agencies to adopt rules he believed they would support.[101] By telling agencies to do things they wanted to do, President Clinton avoided agency resistance and gave Congress no opportunity to object to his tactics, while establishing critically important precedents. In this way, Clinton was able to use the rulemaking process to circumvent his opponents in Congress. Indeed, President Clinton began issuing large numbers of administrative directives after the GOP took control of the House of Representatives in the 1994 elections and effectively paralyzed Clinton's legislative agenda. By controlling administrative rulemaking, Clinton was able to accomplish many of his goals in health care, parental leave, gun control, the environment, and many other areas without the need for legislative action.

Republicans denounced Clinton's actions as a usurpation of power.[102] Interestingly, however, after he took office President George W. Bush made no move to surrender the powers that Clinton had claimed. Quite the contrary. In September 2001, President Bush's OIRA administrator, John D. Graham, issued a memorandum asserting that the president's chief of staff expected the agencies to "implement vigorously" the principles and procedures outlined in former president Clinton's Executive Order 12866.[103] During the first seven months of Bush's presidency, OIRA returned twenty major rules to agencies for further analysis.[104] These included a rule drafted by the National Highway Traffic Safety Administration to implement legislation enacted by Congress in 2000 requiring the installation of tire-pressure monitoring devices on new cars. The auto industry objected to the cost of following the proposed rule and the OIRA responded by telling the National Highway Traffic Safety Administration to study alternative rules.

At the same time, Bush continued the Clinton-era practice of issuing presidential directives to agencies to spur them to issue new rules and regulations. These directives have been contained in "prompt letters" from OIRA to agency administrators. Five such letters were sent during Bush's first year.[105] One "prompt" encouraged OSHA to require companies to use automated external defibrillators to prevent heart-attack deaths. Another told Health and Human Services to require food labels to disclose the use of trans fats.[106] Since both agencies were eager to adopt the presidentially mandated regulations, it appears that Bush followed the Clinton example of ordering agencies to undertake actions they already favored in order to establish useful precedents for the use of presidential mandates. Serving notice that the administration planned to continue the practice of prompting agencies to adopt new rules, OIRA chief Graham said that the administration would welcome communication and advice both from groups and individuals who wanted existing rules abolished as well as from those who wished to see new rules proposed.

During the Bush years, OIRA became an increasingly powerful force in the rulemaking process. The extent of OIRA's influence became evident in 2003 when several members of Congress, concerned with the expansion of presidential influence over agency rulemaking, asked the General Accounting Office to prepare an assessment of OIRA's role. It examined eighty-five important rules adopted by federal agencies during the prior year. In twenty-five of these eighty-five cases, OIRA turned out to have had a significant influence on the substance and character of the rules adopted by federal agencies.[107] In several instances, representatives of interest groups affected by proposed rules had met directly with officials from the Office of Management and Budget and OIRA to press their cases, thereby circumventing the agencies and Congress. Apparently the lobbying community, ever sensitive to Washington's shifting political currents, sensed the new realities of institutional power.

Presidential involvement in agency rulemaking through regulatory review continued under Barack Obama. In 2014, Obama ordered the EPA to develop new standards limiting emissions from coal-fired generating plants. Under the leadership of Obama's OIRA director, Cass Sunstein, who stepped down in 2012, the White House reviewed several hundred proposed rules and sent more than thirty of its own proposals to the agencies for implementation. OIRA also embarked on a "look back" at existing regulations, seeking to eliminate outdated rules.[108] Agencies suggested some five hundred rules for elimination and OIRA secured congressional action on nearly one hundred. During that same year, it should be noted, federal agencies promulgated roughly 2,500 new rules and even this represented a decline from the 3,500 new rules issued in 2011.[109]

These numbers tell an important story. In any conflict with the bureaucracy over rules and regulations, the president will almost certainly prevail. Yet every year, agencies issue tens of thousands of rules and regulations that have the force of law. The president reviews a handful of these rules, proposes a few of his own, and secures the elimination of a few others. As we saw in Chapter 5, presidential power in this realm is similar to the power that de Tocqueville attributed to the Roman emperor. "The emperors possessed," he said, "an immense and unchecked power," but "it was confined to some few main objects and neglected the rest; it was violent, but its range was limited."[110] In a conflict, the president is almost sure to win. On a day-to-day basis, far below the president's radar, America is governed by its executive agencies.

It would nevertheless appear that the innovations introduced by presidents Reagan and Clinton have become accepted presidential practices. Through the process of regulatory review, successive presidents have acquired significant capacity to reshape legislation and, indeed, to achieve important policy goals without having to turn to an often hostile Congress for approval. Surprisingly they have achieved this success with relatively little fanfare or media scrutiny. Few Americans have heard of the OIRA, and the media give this small and obscure agency within the Office of Management and Budget little attention. Yet by working through OIRA, presidents have been able to substantially increase their power.

Governing by Decree

A third mechanism through which contemporary presidents have sought to enhance their power to govern unilaterally involves, as we saw in Chapter 2, the use of executive orders, presidential memoranda, and other forms of decrees, including executive agreements, national security directives, proclamations, reorganization plans, signing statements, and a host of others.[111] The administrative orders discussed earlier that presidents have used to implement the process of regulatory review are one form of executive order. But executive orders have a long history in the United States and have been the vehicles for a number of important U.S. government policies, including the purchase of Louisiana, the annexation of Texas, the emancipation of the slaves, the internment of the Japanese, desegregation of the military, initiation of affirmative action, and the creation of important federal agencies including the EPA, FDA, and Peace Corps.[112]

The most frequent presidential uses of executive orders are associated with wars and national emergencies (see Table 5). President Abraham Lincoln relied almost exclusively on executive orders during the initial months of the Civil War. He issued orders to activate federal troops, purchase warships, and expand the size of the military. He authorized payment of expenses for these initiatives via funds that were advanced from the treasury without congressional approval.[113] In the face of the emergency, Congress had no choice but to accept Lincoln's decisions and subsequently enacted legislation ratifying most of the president's actions. In a similar vein, between 1940 and 1945, President Franklin D. Roosevelt issued 286 executive orders related to military preparedness and the prosecution of World War II.[114] For example, FDR used executive orders to establish the National War Labor Board, the Office of War Mobilization, the Office of Price Administration, the Office of Civilian Defense, the Office of Censorship, the War Food Administration, the Office of War Mobilization, and a host of other agencies.[115] These agencies, created by executive order, played vital roles in managing the war effort, wartime production, labor relations, and the civilian economy. In addition, FDR issued executive orders to seize North American Aviation's plant in California, coal companies, a munitions plant, and other private businesses.[116] As in the Civil War case, Congress felt it had no choice but to follow the president's lead in view of the national emergency, and in 1943 Congress enacted the War Labor Disputes Act to authorize presidential seizure of factories, mines, and other facilities to ensure necessary military production. The volume of executive orders diminished after the end of World War II. During the Korean War, however, President Harry Truman also relied on a variety of presidential orders to place the economy on a wartime footing.

While the highest volume of executive orders occurs during times of war and national emergency, presidents also frequently make use of such actions in peacetime. In the realm of foreign policy, unilateral presidential actions in the form of executive agreements have virtually replaced treaties as the nation's chief foreign-policy

Table 5. Executive Orders, Washington–Obama

President	Number issued	Starting E.O. number
George Washington	8	n/a
John Adams	1	n/a
Thomas Jefferson	4	n/a
James Madison	1	n/a
James Monroe	1	n/a
John Quincy Adams	3	n/a
Andrew Jackson	12	n/a
Martin van Buren	10	n/a
William Henry Harrison	0	n/a
John Tyler	17	n/a
James K. Polk	18	n/a
Zachary Taylor	5	n/a
Millard Fillmore	12	n/a
Franklin Pierce	35	n/a
James Buchanan	16	n/a
Abraham Lincoln	48	
Andrew Johnson	79	
Ulysses S. Grant	217	
Rutherford B. Hayes	92	
James Garfield	6	
Chester Arthur	96	
Grover Cleveland (first term)	113	
Benjamin Harrison	143	
Grover Cleveland (second term)	140	
William McKinley	185	
Theodore Roosevelt	1,081	
William Howard Taft	724	
Woodrow Wilson	1,803	
Warren G. Harding	522	
Calvin Coolidge	1,203	
Herbert Hoover	968	5075
Franklin D. Roosevelt	3,522	6071
Harry S. Truman	907	9538
Dwight D. Eisenhower	484	10432
John F. Kennedy	214	10914
Lyndon B. Johnson	325	11128

continued

Table 5. *Continued*

President	Number issued	Starting E.O. number
Richard Nixon	346	11452
Gerald R. Ford	169	11798
Jimmy Carter	320	11967
Ronald Reagan	381	12287
George H.W. Bush	166	12668
Bill Clinton	364	12834
George W. Bush	291	13198
Barack Obama (as of 2015–07–23)	203	13510

Source: Data for 1999–2014 are from Gerhard Peters, *The American Presidency Project,* available online at http://www.presidency.ucsb.edu/data/orders.php (accessed July 23, 2015). Data for 2015 are from National Archives, Executive Orders Disposition Tables, available online at http://www.archives.gov/federal-register/executive-orders/obama.html (accessed July 23, 2015).

instruments.[117] Presidential decrees, however, are also often used for purely domestic purposes. For example, successive presidents developed federal antidiscrimination policies through executive orders. Roosevelt prohibited racial discrimination in defense industries and created the Fair Employment Practices Commission to work for the elimination of employment discrimination in the United States; Truman issued executive orders desegregating the armed services; Kennedy signed an order prohibiting banks from engaging in discriminatory mortgage-lending practices; Kennedy and Johnson issued executive orders prohibiting federal contractors from engaging in racially biased hiring practices; Johnson's Executive Order 11246 provided for minority hiring by government contractors, thereby establishing the basis for affirmative action programs; and Nixon ordered the so-called Philadelphia Plan, which required federal contractors to establish specific goals for hiring minority workers for federally funded jobs.[118]

Presidents may not use executive orders to issue whatever commands they please. The use of such decrees is bound by law. If a president issues an executive order, proclamation, directive, or the like, in principle he does so pursuant to the powers granted to him by the Constitution or delegated to him by Congress, usually through a statute. When presidents issue such orders, they generally state the constitutional or statutory basis for their actions. For example, when President Truman ordered the desegregation of the armed services, he did so pursuant to his constitutional powers as commander-in-chief. In a similar vein, when President Johnson issued Executive Order 11246 he asserted that the order was designed to implement the 1964 Civil Rights Act, which prohibited employment discrimination. Where an executive order has no statutory or constitutional basis, the courts have held it to be void. The most important case on this point is *Youngstown Sheet & Tube Co. v. Sawyer*, the so-called steel seizure case of 1952.[119] In this case, the Supreme Court ruled that President Truman's seizure of the nation's steel mills during the Korean War had no statutory or constitutional basis and hence was invalid.

Executive orders, moreover, may not supersede or contradict statutes. The president may not order what Congress has prohibited. For example, in 1995 President Clinton issued Executive Order 12954 prohibiting government agencies from contracting with firms that hired workers to replace striking employees. Legislation that would have accomplished this purpose had been blocked in the Senate during the previous year, and Clinton was dubious that such a bill could be enacted in the current session of Congress. The president's action was challenged in federal court and declared improper.[120] The District of Columbia Circuit Court held that Clinton's order had violated the National Labor Relations Act by interfering with the statutory right of private employers to replace strikers.

These and other court decisions, though, have established broad boundaries that leave considerable room for presidential action. Indeed, the courts have held that the statutory authority for executive orders need not be specifically granted but might instead be implied by the statute. For example, the Trading with the Enemy Act, designed to deal with wartime situations, was used by President Nixon as the basis for an executive order mandating wage and price controls.[121] The courts have also held that Congress might approve presidential action after the fact or, in effect, ratify presidential action through "acquiescence"—for example, by not objecting for long periods of time or by continuing to provide funding for programs established by executive orders.

In addition, federal judges have upheld presidential orders in what Supreme Court Justice Jackson, writing in the steel seizure case, called the "zone of twilight" where, despite the lack of statutory authorization for presidential action, Congress had not prohibited the action and Congress and the president might be seen as exercising concurrent authority.[122] The Supreme Court cited Jackson's opinion in upholding actions by Presidents Carter and Reagan prohibiting certain types of claims by American businesses against Iranian assets in the United States that had been frozen during the Iranian hostage crisis of 1979–1980.[123] Finally, the courts have indicated that some areas, most notably the realm of military policy, are presidential in character and have allowed presidents wide latitude to make policy by executive decree. Thus within the very broad limits established by the courts, presidential orders can and have been very important policy tools.

The total volume of executive orders and other presidential decrees issued in the past quarter century is not remarkable by historic standards. Franklin D. Roosevelt issued more directives than any subsequent chief executive. Except during wartime or in the realm of national security, however, presidents historically did not seek to implement a full-blown policy agenda through a program of unilateral executive action. Executive orders, though sometimes quite important, tended to be occasional supplements to the president's central policy focus—his legislative agenda. Recent presidents, however, have viewed executive orders—including, as we saw earlier, administrative directives—as mechanisms for circumventing Congress and achieving policy goals when they were unable to secure legislative cooperation. Presidents Reagan, George H. W. Bush, Clinton, George W. Bush, and Obama all developed strategies for unilaterally negating congressional actions as well as unilaterally implementing elements of their own policy agendas.

Employing Signing Statements

To negate congressional actions to which they objected, all five presidents made frequent and calculated use of presidential signing statements when signing bills into law.[124] As we learned in Chapter 2, the signing statement is an announcement made by the president at the time of signing a congressional enactment into law that usually includes innocuous remarks predicting the many benefits the new law will bring, but also sometimes declares the president's interpretation of the law. Indeed occasionally presidents have used signing statements to point to sections of the law that they deem improper or even unconstitutional, and to instruct executive branch agencies how to execute the law.[125] President Harry Truman, for example, accompanied his approval of the 1946 Hobbs Anti-Racketeering Act with a message offering his interpretation of ambiguous sections of the statute and indicating how the federal government would implement the new law.[126] Presidents have made signing statements throughout American history, though many were not recorded and did not become part of the official legislative record. Ronald Reagan's attorney general Edwin Meese, and his deputy, Samuel Alito, are generally credited with transforming the signing statement into a routine tool of presidential direct action.[127]

Reagan used detailed and artfully designed signing statements—prepared by the Department of Justice—to attempt to reinterpret congressional enactments. For example, when signing the Safe Drinking Water Amendments of 1986, President Reagan issued a statement that interpreted sections of the act to allow discretionary enforcement when the Congress seemed to call for mandatory enforcement.[128]

Reagan hoped the courts would accept his version of the statute when examining subsequent enforcement decisions. In other cases, as we saw in Chapter 2, Reagan used his signing statements to attempt to nullify portions of statutes. The same tactic of reinterpreting and nullifying congressional enactments was continued by Reagan's successor, George H. W. Bush. When he signed the 1991 Civil Rights Act, Bush asserted his concern that one of its provisions might be unfairly applied to businesses. By so doing, the president established his own reading to shape public understanding of the act's legislative history, provided guidance to administrators regarding the law's implementation, and attempted to influence future court interpretations.[129] On another occasion, Bush had unsuccessfully opposed a bill requiring the Department of Energy to employ affirmative action in contracting for the construction of the Superconducting Super Collider. When he signed the bill into law, Bush declared in a signing statement that there was no valid constitutional basis for an affirmative action program involving this project and directed the Energy secretary to ignore the requirement.[130] Bush had effectively nullified a law whose passage he had been unable to prevent.

For the most part, Presidents Reagan and Bush used signing statements to limit the scope of affirmative action programs, to block expansion of business regulation, to reduce the impact of environmental programs, and to thwart new labor laws. Bill Clinton followed the examples set by Reagan and Bush and made extensive use of signing statements both to reinterpret and nullify congressional enactments. But of course Clinton's agenda was far different from that of his two immediate predecessors. Faced with Republican-controlled congresses for six of his eight years in office, Clinton used his signing statements to attempt to block constriction of affirmative action programs, to limit efforts to weaken environmental standards, and to protect the rights of individuals with disabilities. For example, in 1996 Congress enacted a defense appropriations bill that included a provision requiring that any member of the military who was HIV-positive be discharged from service. President Clinton signed the appropriations bill, but asserted that this provision was unconstitutional.[131] He ordered the Justice Department not to defend the HIV ban in court if it was challenged—which, in effect, represented an announcement that the provision would not be enforced.

Thus, for Clinton as for his immediate predecessors, signing statements became an important weapon in the effort to block opponents' agendas. In recent years, as these presidents hoped, courts have given weight to presidential signing statements when interpreting the meaning of statutes.[132] More contemporary presidents have continued to use this tactic. As we saw in Chapter 2, President George W. Bush used more than five hundred signing statements to rewrite legislation pertaining to the war on terror, while President Obama has used a multitude of signing statements to push his foreign policy prerogatives.

Using Executive Orders

While Clinton followed Reagan's example in terms of using signing statements to blunt his opponents' agendas, he was an innovator in terms of crafting his own agenda through executive orders. We have already seen how Clinton used regulatory review to circumvent a hostile Congress. Even beyond this, according to legal scholar Todd Gaziano, President Clinton issued numerous orders designed to promote a coherent set of policy goals: environmental protection, strengthening of the federal government's regulatory power, shifting America's foreign policy from a unilateral to a multilateral focus, expansion of affirmative action programs, and helping organized labor in its struggles with employers.[133] In the area of environmental policy, for example, Clinton issued more than thirty executive orders relating to the environment and natural resources. For instance, in 1997 Clinton issued Executive Order 13061 establishing the American Heritage Rivers Initiative, which was designed to protect several major river systems from commercial and industrial development. The order also effectively overrode the land-use powers of state and local governments. During the same year, when the Senate failed to enact the Children's Environmental Protection Act, Clinton incorporated a number of its provisions into an executive order that he issued on Earth Day.[134]

Another Clinton order, Executive Order 12898, Environmental Justice for Minority Populations, required all federal agencies to show that they were taking account of environmental justice implications when they made decisions. Accompanying the order was a presidential memorandum that opened the way for minority groups to sue states and cities on environmental justice grounds.[135] During his final days in office, President Clinton issued orders closing off millions of acres of land in ten Western states to residential and commercial development by declaring them to be protected national monuments under the 1906 Antiquities Act. In the realm of labor relations, as noted earlier, President Clinton ordered the secretary of labor to develop rules prohibiting federal contractors from hiring replacement workers to fill in for strikers. This order, which was struck down by the U.S. District Court, actually represented an attempt to overturn a 1938 Supreme Court decision that had interpreted the National Labor Relations Act as specifically allowing employers to hire striker replacements.[136] The president also created labor-dominated government task forces to study workplace issues (Executive Order 12953) and mandated improved employment opportunities for Americans with disabilities (Executive Order 13164).

As in his use of regulatory review, President Clinton was able to craft a policy agenda through executive orders that he could not accomplish through legislation.[137] Faced with a hostile Congress, Clinton turned to unilateral instruments of executive power. He did not issue more executive orders than previous presidents: his innovation was instead to find a new use for an instrument that had been used only sporadically, and in the process to show that an activist president could develop and implement a significant policy agenda without legislation.

This lesson has surely not been lost on Clinton's successors. Indeed, just as he continued the practice of using regulatory review as a policy instrument, President George W. Bush did not hesitate to use executive orders—issuing more than forty during his first year in office alone. In his first months in office, Bush issued orders that prohibited the use of federal funds to support international family planning groups providing abortion-counseling services and that placed limits on the use of embryonic stem cells in federally funded research projects. Subsequently, Bush made very aggressive use of executive orders in response to the threat of terrorism —which the president declared to be his administration's most important policy agenda. In November 2001, for example, Bush issued a directive authorizing the creation of military tribunals to try noncitizens accused of involvement in acts of terrorism against the United States. The presidential directive also prohibited defendants from appealing their treatment in any federal or state court. In addition, the president issued orders that froze the assets of groups and individuals associated with terrorism, that provided expedited citizenship for foreign nationals serving in the U.S. military, and that instructed the CIA to use all means possible to oust President Saddam Hussein of Iraq, whom Bush accused of plotting terrorist actions.

While terrorism was certainly at the top of President Bush's agenda, he also issued a number of executive orders having to do with domestic policy. For example, to overcome congressional resistance to his efforts to increase domestic energy exploration and the rapid exploitation of domestic energy resources, in May 2001 Bush signed an executive order that closely followed a recommendation from the American Petroleum Institute, an oil industry trade association, to free energy companies from a number of federal regulations. Another executive order issued by President Bush, Executive Order 13303, effectively prohibited federal agencies from requiring union-only work crews on federally funded projects. Enforcement of the order was enjoined by the U.S. District Court, but the Court of Appeals held that

Bush had the authority to issue the order.[138] In still another executive order, 13212, President Bush created a task force charged with expediting the issuance of permits for energy-related projects.

Like his predecessors, Bush also turned to signing statements to undermine legislation that he was unable to block. For instance, in the course of signing campaign-finance-reform legislation in March 2002, Bush declared that the bill was "far from perfect" and implied that the provisions of the bill were "non severable," meaning that if the federal courts declared any portion of the bill unconstitutional, the entire bill would be rendered void.[139] The actual bill contains no such provision, but Bush was seeking to write his interpretation into the legislative history to increase the likelihood that if some future federal court is dissatisfied with any one portion of the law, it will strike down the entire measure.

In a similar vein, in July 2003 President Bush's solicitor general, Theodore Olson, asked the U.S. Supreme Court to reject a challenge mounted by conservative groups against a Clinton-era executive order that had restricted access to several national monuments and millions of acres of public land in the West. During the 2000 campaign, Bush had denounced Clinton's moves, which were very unpopular with voters in the Western states. Once in office, however, the president, like his predecessors, became vehemently opposed to any efforts to question the validity of executive orders. Indeed, the solicitor general questioned whether any legal basis even existed for the Court to review the executive orders in question.[140] During his eight years in office, Bush issued more than three hundred significant executive orders.

For his part, President Obama, as we saw, has issued a number of executive orders including orders at the end of 2014 that prevented the deportation of more than a million undocumented immigrants. Obama declared that he was compelled to overhaul the nation's immigration system through executive orders because Congress had failed to act on legislation desired by the White House.

Thoughts on Presidential Policy Tools

Throughout the course of American history, party leadership and popular appeals have both played important roles in presidential efforts to overcome political opposition. Both party and appeals to the people continue to be instruments of presidential power. Reagan's tax cuts and Clinton's budget victories were achieved with strong partisan support. George W. Bush, who lacked the oratorical skills of a Reagan or a Roosevelt, nevertheless made good use of sophisticated communications strategies to promote his agenda. Obama, too, relied on congressional Democrats to enact health care reform during his first term in office.

Yet in the modern era parties have waned in institutional strength, and the effects of popular appeals have often proven evanescent. These limitations have increasingly impelled presidents to try another strategy for achieving their policy goals: expanding the administrative capabilities of the office and their own capacity for unilateral action. To a certain degree, this strategy has been successful. In recent decades, the expansion of the Executive Office, the development of regulatory review, and the use of executive orders, signing statements, and the like have given presidents a substantial capacity to achieve significant policy results despite congressional opposition.

To be sure, the administrative strategy is not without pitfalls for the White House. In some instances over the years the federal courts have struck down unilateral actions by the president. As noted earlier, the Supreme Court invalidated Truman's seizure of the steel mills and a lower federal court nullified Clinton's order barring the hiring of replacements for striking workers. Similarly, Congress has the power to enact legislation overturning unilateral presidential actions. Both these hypothetical problems, however, seldom actually manifest themselves. For the most part the courts have shown considerable deference to the president. Only a small percentage of challenges to executive decrees have ever been upheld.[141]

Congress has been less passive in the face of this new strategy. Lawmakers frequently object vociferously to presidents' decrees and directives. For instance, President Clinton was often denounced on Capitol Hill for his uses of executive authority: Nebraska Republican senator Chuck Hagel accused him of "debasing the constitutional structure," while Oklahoma Republican congressman J. C. Watts suggested that Clinton thought he was "king of the world."[142] And occasionally Congress has gone beyond rhetoric to reverse presidential orders. For example, in 1999 Congress enacted legislation prohibiting the Department of Education from carrying out a presidential directive to administer national education tests.[143] And in 2014, the House of Representatives agreed to bring suit against President Obama for his use of unilateral powers. Though such a suit was never likely to succeed, it served notice to the White House that presidential unilateralism would be opposed.

In principle, perhaps, Congress could respond more vigorously than it has so far to unilateral policymaking by the president. Certainly a Congress willing to impeach a president should have the mettle to overturn his administrative directives. But the president has significant advantages in such struggles with Congress. In battles over presidential directives and orders Congress is on the defensive, reacting to presidential initiatives. The framers of the Constitution saw "energy," or the ability to take the initiative, as a key feature of executive power.[144] When the president takes action by issuing an order or an administrative directive, Congress must initiate the cumbersome and time-consuming lawmaking process, overcome internal divisions, and enact legislation that the president may ultimately veto. As Terry Moe has argued, moreover, in such battles Congress faces a significant collective action problem insofar as members are likely to be more sensitive to the substance of a president's actions and its effects on their constituents than to the more general implications of presidential power for the long-term vitality of their institution.[145] Congressional leaders might have reason to take a more institutionalist perspective, but in the contemporary Congress the titular leaders coax and cajole more than they command their nominal followers.

Thus Congress has yet to solve the problem of the administrative presidency. The contemporary American electoral system continues to produce extraordinarily ambitious and driven presidents who, year after year, expand their ability to circumvent the legislative process and to govern unilaterally. In the early months of 2002, fears of bioterrorism forced the evacuation of Capitol Hill offices and essentially put lawmakers out of business for several weeks. During this period, the president and his staff governed the country, issuing orders and decrees while members of Congress and their staffs checked their antibiotic supplies. This was an extraordinary situation and Congress moved to reassert its prerogatives once the safety of its offices and chambers had been reestablished. But it is difficult not to wonder if the brief image of a Capitol Hill empty and irrelevant, while the president was launching a war abroad and conducting the nation's domestic affairs, is not a portent of things to come.

Instruments of Presidential Government

There are three ways that presidents can expand their power vis-à-vis the Congress: party, popular mobilization, and administration. In the first instance, presidents may endeavor to construct or strengthen national partisan institutions with which to exert influence in the legislative process and through which to implement their programs. Franklin D. Roosevelt's effort to purge his foes from the Democratic Party and to rebuild it as a national institution responsible to the president is a case in point. Alternatively, or in addition to the first tactic, presidents may use popular appeals to attempt to create a mass base of support that will allow them to overawe and subordinate their political foes. This tactic has sometimes been called the strategy of "going public" or the "rhetorical" presidency. And third, presidents may seek to bolster their control of established executive agencies or to create new administrative institutions and procedures that will reduce their dependence on Congress and give them more independent governing and policymaking capabilities. Presidential use of executive orders to achieve their policy goals in lieu of seeking to persuade Congress to enact legislation is one example.

Party. America's first political party was built by Thomas Jefferson. Beginning in 1793, Jefferson and his supporters began the creation of Democratic societies to voice opposition to the Federalists, proffer friendship to France, and campaign for the election of Jefferson's political devotees. The clubs became the basis for a party organization that nominated candidates for office and mobilized voters to carry them to victory. Andrew Jackson took party building a step further. Jackson used patronage appointments—the so-called spoils system—to construct a party organization that would support the president and bolster his authority in Congress and the nation as a whole. The Jacksonians are credited (or blamed) for introducing the

spoils system in order to reward their political friends and build a party machine at the expense of the public treasury.

Going public. Theodore Roosevelt pioneered the art of what came to be understood as "reaching over the heads of Congress, directly to the American people." During the president's campaign on behalf of railroad regulation, Roosevelt

and his allies encouraged Americans who supported the president's aims to bring pressure to bear on their political representatives, and to demand that they stand with the president against the railroads. Though senators were not yet subject to popular election, they were susceptible to political pressure from the state legislatures and from party leaders in their home states, who in turn found themselves pushed to support the president. The result of this public campaign was near-unanimous Senate approval of a bill that included virtually all the features Roosevelt had sought. Today presidents can go public through electronic media. Here President Obama tweets his followers to mobilize their support.

Flying solo. Contemporary presidents have increased the administrative capabilities of their office in three ways. First, they have enhanced the reach and power of the Executive Office of the President. Second, they have sought to increase White House control over the federal bureaucracy. And third, they have expanded the role of executive orders and other instruments of direct presidential governance such as signing statements. Taken together, these three components of what might be called the White House "administrative strategy" have given presidents a capacity to achieve their programmatic and policy goals even when they are unable to secure congressional approval. Indeed, some recent presidents have been able to accomplish quite a bit without much in the way of congressional, partisan, or even public support. For example, charging that Congress was too slow to act on immigration reform, in 2014 President Obama issued executive orders blocking the deportation of several million undocumented immigrants.

EIGHT

The Executive and the Courts

In This Chapter

The American Constitution created a framework of checks and balances in which each of the three great branches of government exercises some measure of power over the other two, and in which the president seems to have considerable power vis-à-vis the courts. With the advice and consent of the Senate, the president appoints the justices of the Supreme Court and judges of the other federal courts. The judiciary, moreover, has only a limited power to enforce its own decisions: it depends on the president, and the executive branch more generally, for enforcement. This dependence makes the courts somewhat reluctant to enter into conflicts with the executive branch.

Constitutional Sources of Judicial Power

The federal courts can exercise power over the executive branch in three ways. First, in the course of exercising judicial review over acts of Congress, the federal courts may, in effect, rule on the constitutionality of the president's legislative program. In 2012, for example, the U.S. Supreme Court declared that President Obama's signature health care initiative met constitutional standards. Had the Court ruled against the law, the president's most important domestic initiative might have been blocked. In 2015, the Court upheld the law against another challenge that might have thwarted its effects.

Second, the federal courts are often asked to rule on the propriety of presidential actions. The power to review the president's actions was asserted by the Supreme Court early in American history. In the 1903 case of *Marbury v. Madison,* the Court declared that it had the power to review the actions of the executive branch but declined to exercise that power. The actual exercise of judicial power came in the 1804 case of *Little v. Barreme,* a case arising from military actions during America's undeclared naval war with France. In this case, the court invalidated an order issued by President Adams that it found inconsistent with the president's authority under an act of Congress.[1] Judicial authority to review presidential actions has seldom been questioned, though presidents have not always fully complied with judicial orders. In some instances, members of Congress have looked to the courts for support in their battles with the president. As recently as 2014, Republican House Speaker John Boehner announced that he planned to ask the federal courts to declare that President Obama had failed to live up to his responsibility to see to it that the laws were faithfully executed when he unilaterally delayed implementation of a section of the Affordable Care Act, or "Obamacare." The judiciary has generally found reason not to become involved in these struggles. In a number of cases dating from the 1970s, members of Congress filed suit in federal court to challenge a variety of presidential actions, including the use of military force without congressional authorization.[2] In the 1979 case of *Goldwater v. Carter,* however, the Supreme Court said, in effect, that it was up to Congress to fight its own battles with the president.[3] And in 1997, the Supreme Court essentially stopped such suits in a decision that distinctly narrowed the grounds on which members of Congress might claim standing to halt presidential actions even when the president had clearly nullified a legislative act and no other legislative remedy was available.[4] Legislators have nonetheless often filed amicus briefs in suits involving the exercise of presidential power and have cheered from the sidelines when the president has been challenged in federal court.[5]

Finally, the federal courts do frequently review the decisions and actions of executive agencies. The standards for such review are laid down by the 1946 Administrative Procedure Act, by various statutes, and by the precedents established over time by the courts themselves.

In this chapter, we will examine the appointment process, executive enforcement of judicial orders, judicial review of the president's legislative and nonlegislative actions, and judicial review of federal agency actions.

Judicial Appointments

Federal judges are appointed by the president, subject to confirmation by the Senate. Supreme Court justices and the judges of the federal appeals courts and district courts are appointed for life or "good behavior," which is to say they are subject to impeachment for misconduct. These courts are called Article III courts since their establishment is based on Article III of the Constitution. The president also appoints, subject to senatorial confirmation, the judges of what are known as Article I courts. These are the specialized courts, such as the U.S. Tax Court and the U.S. Court of Federal Claims, created by Congress. The judges of these courts receive ten-year appointments but are eligible for reappointment.

Judges are generally selected from among the more prominent or politically active members of the legal profession. Many federal judges previously served as state court judges or federal, state, or local prosecutors. Before the president makes a formal district or appeals court nomination, the senators from a candidate's own state must indicate that they do not oppose the nominee. This is an informal but seldom violated practice called *senatorial courtesy.* The practice of courtesy generally does not apply to Supreme Court appointments. Even before making a formal nomination to the Supreme Court, presidents will seek advice from their own party's senators as well as from the Justice Department and other members of the administration.

In general, presidents endeavor to appoint judges whose partisan and ideological views are similar to their own. Because judges receive lifetime appointments, presidents are very aware that their judicial appointees will continue to exert influence over national policy long after the president's own term has ended. As of 2014, thirty-nine judges appointed by President Nixon were still hearing cases, along with eight appointed by President Johnson and two appointed more than a half-century ago by President Kennedy. The late Supreme Court Justice William O. Douglas was appointed by Franklin D. Roosevelt and served for thirty-six years through the administrations of presidents Truman, Eisenhower, Kennedy, Johnson, Nixon, and Ford. To be sure that an appointee will be appropriate, the White House staff carefully evaluates him or her based on such factors as prior judicial opinions, writings and speeches, and background to determine ideological compatibility with the president's goals, as well as the likelihood that the candidate could be confirmed by the Senate.[6]

During two terms in office, presidents generally have an opportunity to appoint about a third of the 677 district court and 179 appellate court judges, as well as two or more of the nine Supreme Court justices. This allows every president to exercise significant influence over the character of the federal judiciary and means that two Democratic or two Republican presidents in a row can have a major impact on the ideological makeup of the courts. During his two terms in office, President George W. Bush appointed 261 district court judges, sixty-two appeals court judges, and two Supreme Court justices. Bush appointees were generally conservatives, offsetting the many liberal Clinton appointees. During his first six years in office, President Obama appointed 220 district court judges, fifty appeals court judges, and two Supreme Court justices. Obama's appointees were overwhelmingly liberals, but since his two Supreme Court designees, Sotomayor and Kagan, replaced Democratic appointees, their placement did not alter the ideological balance on the high court.

Once the president has formally nominated an individual, the nominee must be considered by the Senate Judiciary Committee and confirmed by a majority vote in the full Senate. In recent years, judicial appointments have sparked a great deal of partisan conflict. Senate Democrats have sought to prevent Republican presidents from appointing conservative judges, while Senate Republicans have worked to prevent Democratic presidents from appointing liberal judges. During the early years of the Obama administration, Republicans were able to slow the judicial appointment process through a variety of procedural maneuvers, including the filibustering of several nominees. In 2013, Senate Democrats pushed through a rules change to make it more difficult for the minority party to block nominations—though Republicans have vowed to make the Democrats regret the change the next time the GOP holds a majority in the Senate.

Political factors play an important role in the selection of district and appellate court judges and are decisive in the selection of Supreme Court justices. Because the high court has so much influence over American law, presidents seek to make absolutely certain to select justices who share their own political philosophies, though they make occasional mistakes. In recent history, two justices appointed by conservative presidents turned out to have liberal leanings. Chief Justice Earl Warren, appointed by Richard Nixon, ultimately became one of America's most liberal jurists, and David Souter, appointed by George H. W. Bush, usually voted with the Court's Democrats.

As of 2015, five of the nine Supreme Court justices had been appointed by Republican presidents. This conservative majority, consisting of Chief Justice Roberts and Justices Alito, Kennedy, Scalia, and Thomas, has generally cheered Republicans and outraged Democrats with a number of decisions, many on 5–4 votes, that have steered national policy in a more conservative direction than Democratic presidents and members of Congress would have liked. These decisions include lifting restrictions on campaign spending, invalidating state and local bans on firearms possession, upholding Michigan's ban on affirmative action in college admissions, and invalidating a key section of the 1965 Voting Rights Act that had prohibited nine southern states from changing their election laws without federal approval. Under the leadership of Justice Roberts's predecessor, Chief Justice William Rehnquist—a conservative jurist who had been appointed by President Reagan—the Court also effectively elected George W. Bush to the presidency when it decided in the 2000 case of *Bush v. Gore* that Florida's disputed electoral votes should be awarded to Bush.[7]

Thus, when they choose judges, especially Supreme Court justices, presidents can have an important and lasting influence on the courts and on American society. Not surprisingly, Supreme Court nominations have come to involve intense partisan struggle. Typically, after the president has named a nominee, interest groups opposed to the nomination mobilize opposition in the media, in the public, and in the Senate. During the late 1980s, for example, liberals were able to block the Supreme Court nominations of the prominent conservative judges Richard Bork and Douglas Ginsburg. In 1991, as we saw earlier, when President George H. W. Bush proposed appointing an African American conservative, Judge Clarence Thomas, to the Court, he calculated that liberal forces would be reluctant to attack a black nominee. Liberals nevertheless launched a campaign to discredit Thomas, charging him with making sexually inappropriate remarks to a woman whom he had supervised at the Equal Employment Opportunity Commission. After a rancorous debate, Thomas was nonetheless confirmed. During the Clinton administration, conservatives turned the tables and forced President Clinton to withdraw two nominees. Since then, battles have been less intense because the appointments that became available did not threaten the Court's ideological balance. Just to make a point, though, Republican senators spent several days questioning Obama nominees Sonia Sotomayor and Elena Kagan, without making serious efforts to derail the confirmations.

Presidential Enforcement of Judicial Decisions

Presidents not only appoint judges in their capacity as chief executives; they also bear a good deal of responsibility for the enforcement of court decisions. The president has a constitutional responsibility to see to it that the laws are faithfully executed, and this constitutional duty is generally understood to include enforcement of the decisions of the federal courts.

The judiciary depends on executive enforcement of its orders. While judges sitting on their benches in priestly robes seem to be imposing and powerful figures, they have only a limited capacity to implement or enforce the decisions they make. Generally judges must turn to executive agencies or even the president for help. Every day, local, state, and federal law-enforcement and correction agents—who are executive officials—enforce court judgments, custody orders, support orders, and sentences. Similarly, federal agencies enforce a host of court orders. For example, in the realm of anti-trust policy, the Federal Trade Commission routinely enforces federal court injunctions and cease-and-desist orders, as well as collects civil penalties from violators.

On rare occasions, the federal courts must turn to the president to enforce their orders. For example, a number of Southern governors adopted a posture of "massive resistance" in response to the Supreme Court's 1954 decision in the case of *Brown v. Board of Education*.[8] Federal judges, following the Supreme Court's ruling, ordered schools in their jurisdictions to end segregated instruction, but they were helpless to overcome the opposition of local authorities and mobs of protestors. This could only be accomplished by the executive branch. President Eisenhower sent military units to Little Rock, Arkansas, in 1957 to enforce the desegregation of Central High School and President Kennedy federalized the Alabama National Guard when Governor Wallace personally stood in the doorway to block the way for black students seeking to enroll in the previously all-white University of Alabama.

Dependence on the executive to enforce court decisions sometimes leaves the judiciary vulnerable to presidential refusals, some of which have been blunt and forceful. In 1831, President Jackson famously refused to enforce a Supreme Court order to the State of Georgia to free Samuel Worcester, a missionary arrested by Georgia authorities for violating a state law.[9] Jackson is reputed to have declared that Chief Justice John Marshall had made the decision so that Marshall could try to enforce it himself, but this account is probably apocryphal. In 1861, President Lincoln refused to obey an order from Chief Justice Taney to release John Merryman, who was being held in a military stockade.[10] Though presidential refusals to enforce a court order are rare—because presidents themselves are generally reluctant to be seen as having violated the law or subverted the judicial process—when they happen, there is little the judiciary can do.

Usually when presidents or other executive officials ignore or circumvent court orders, they do so in ways they deem unlikely to provoke a political outcry or a loss of public confidence in governmental institutions. For example, in 1969 the Nixon administration was faced with a series of federal court decisions demanding that school districts in Mississippi and elsewhere in the South be compelled to hasten the process of desegregation. During this same period, Nixon was pursuing his "southern strategy" of seeking to woo white southerners into the Republican political camp by suggesting that the pace of civil rights changes had been too rapid and needed to be slowed. The president was not about to offend his new political allies by vigorously implementing federal court desegregation orders. At the same time, Nixon did not wish to provoke a political crisis by directly defying the courts.

The administration settled on a strategy of obfuscation and subterfuge. Publicly, the administration expressed its intention to abide by court rulings and took some steps in this direction. But after enough had been done to shield the president from charges that he had failed in his lawful duties, the administration sharply reduced its efforts to promote desegregation. According to one biographer, Nixon was very cynical about the matter. "When [presidential chief of staff] Haldeman told him of the Court's decision, Nixon smiled and said, "Now let's see how they enforce it."[11]

For their part, federal agencies quite frequently circumvent or simply ignore federal court rulings, making use of various forms of subterfuge to avoid enforcing court orders with which they do not agree. Agencies are unlikely to thumb their noses at the Supreme Court but they frequently evade the orders of lower courts. One typical practice is reissuing or reinstating a practice nominally banned by the courts and claiming that the new practice is different from the previous one. In the recent case of *Hornbeck Offshore Services v. Jewell,* the Department of the Interior ignored a federal district court order that struck down an agency mandate and then reissued the former mandate as though it was a new action. The plaintiffs were put in the position of having to relitigate a case they had already won. The Supreme Court declined to hear the case.[12] Typically agencies will seek to identify minimal changes in their procedures that may give the appearance of compliance with judicial decisions and avert further intrusion into their affairs, while continuing the practices with which they are comfortable.[13]

Congressional hearings held in 2000 at the behest of the Judicial Conference of the United States found that agency noncompliance and nonenforcement of court decisions had become a serious problem for the federal courts. Legislation was introduced in the House to address the matter, and the "Federal Agency Noncompliance Act" was adopted by that chamber.[14] The act, which would have penalized executive agencies found to engage in a pattern of nonacquiescence, was opposed by the White House and died in the Senate.

Judicial Review of the President's Actions

While the federal judiciary is vulnerable to executive nonenforcement of its decisions, the president is vulnerable to judicial declarations that important elements of his or her legislative program or other actions are inconsistent with the Constitution. Since the nation's founding, to be sure, the Supreme Court has struck down more than 160 pieces of legislation in whole or in part. Thus in 2013, as we saw earlier, the Supreme Court invalidated key sections of the 1965 Voting Rights Act. That same year, the Court invalidated the Federal Defense of Marriage Act, which allowed states to refuse to recognize same-sex marriages sanctioned by other states. In some instances, invalidating statutes has had enormous political consequences. Perhaps the most important example is the Court's 1857 decision in *Dred Scott v. Sanford,* which invalidated the Missouri Compromise and pushed the nation toward Civil War.[15]

If we look at the Court's record in relation to the president, however, the picture that emerges is one of general judicial acquiescence to presidential authority. Since the nation's founding, the federal courts have invalidated all or portions of only a handful of executive orders. These include an order from President Clinton prohibiting the government from contracting with firms employing strikebreakers, President Truman's order seizing the nation's steel mills, and President Adams's order discussed earlier. Moreover, in only a small number of instances has the Court ever invalidated statutes that formed part of a sitting president's legislative program, and these came almost entirely within one political era. Briefly, during the 1930s, the Supreme Court stood against President Roosevelt, striking down portions of the Agricultural Adjustment Act, the National Industrial Recovery Act, and other New Deal programs. Roosevelt mounted a campaign against the Court that included a threat to increase the number of justices, and the Court retreated.

Two other examples of judicial confrontations with presidents are worth noting. In *Marbury v. Madison,* Chief Justice Marshall implicitly rebuked Jefferson but was careful not to give the president cause to ignore the Court's decision. Marshall wrote a decision simultaneously claiming the power of judicial review and finding reason not to intervene on Marbury's behalf, in order to avoid a direct confrontation with President Jefferson.[16] In *Ex parte Merryman,* Chief Justice Taney, sitting as a federal circuit court judge, incautiously ruled that President Lincoln lacked the power to suspend the writ of habeas corpus and ordered Confederate operative Merryman's release from military custody. Subsequently, Taney ordered the arrest of General Cadwalader, the commander of Fort McHenry where Merryman was being held. Lincoln ignored Taney's order and the marshal sent to arrest Cadwalader was turned away from Fort McHenry by the military. In that moment the actual, as opposed to theoretical, balance of power between the presidency and the judiciary was revealed.

The Supreme Court subsequently invalidated a number of Lincoln's legislative and executive initiatives but it did so long after the war had ended and the nation's political climate and occupancy of the White House had changed. In a similar vein, the Supreme Court struck down several pieces of Truman-era loyalty and security legislation such as the Subversive Activities Control Act of 1950. It did so, however, in 1965 when, again, the political climate had changed and the White House was in different hands.[17]

Perhaps the most dramatic instance since the New Deal when the Court directly confronted a sitting president was the Watergate tapes case, in which the Supreme Court ordered President Nixon to give congressional investigators the secret Oval Office tapes that had been subpoenaed by Congress.[18] In this instance the Court could count on the support of the Congress, as well as backing from leaders of both political parties and most of the national news media. Nixon, moreover, would have been certain of impeachment if he had refused the order. Even so, there was no guarantee that the president would obey and, as we shall see, in its opinion the Court was deferential to the idea of presidential power. In 1975, the Court ruled against Nixon's practice of impounding funds that Congress had appropriated when he did not approve of their use.[19] By this time, however, Nixon had already resigned and Congress had already placed restrictions on impoundment in the 1974 Budget Act. The Court's decision was anticlimactic, to say the least.

Against this backdrop of conflict avoidance, Chief Justice Roberts's 2012 decision to uphold the constitutionality of the 2010 Affordable Care Act, the central focus of President Obama's legislative agenda, seems consistent with the historic pattern. Many commentators expected the Court, with its conservative majority, to strike down major portions of the act on the grounds that the individual mandate (the requirement that individuals purchase health insurance) imposed by the legislation was inconsistent with congressional power under the Commerce Clause. In his opinion for the Court, though, Chief Justice Roberts asserted that the mandate was actually a tax, not an unwarranted expansion of congressional regulatory powers.[20] As a tax, the mandate fit well within the scope of congressional authority. Some critics pointed out that if the mandate was a tax it violated the constitutional requirement that tax bills originate in the House, since the Affordable Care Act had originated in the Senate. But whatever the constitutional niceties, the chief justice seemed determined to avoid a direct clash with the president and so found reason to uphold the act.

In a much less important case, to be sure, Justice Roberts was willing to rebuke the president. As we saw in Chapter 2, the Court ruled unanimously in 2014 that a ten-day recess had been "presumptively too short" to permit the president to make three recess appointments to the National Labor Relations Board. The president was annoyed, but the White House had merely been testing the limits of its power with no real expectation that its ploy would succeed.

Why the Courts Generally Support the Executive

The federal courts generally support the president and the executive branch not simply because they are afraid not to, but because they think they should. The support given the executive branch by the federal courts has often been noted by legal scholars and a number of explanations have been offered. The late constitutional historian Edward Corwin thought that the courts tended to defer to the president because presidential exercises of power often produced some change in the world that the judiciary felt powerless to negate.[21] Political scientists Terry Moe and William Howell have pointed to the fact that the courts depend on the goodwill of the executive branch for enforcement of their decisions.[22] Other scholars emphasize the reluctance of the courts to risk their prestige in disputes with popular presidents.[23]

All these explanations have some merit but there is another factor that has played an even more important role in linking the courts to the White House: judicial appointments. While much has been written about the appointment process, its political significance has often been misunderstood. Presidents obviously seek to appoint judges who will support them in the years to come, but, as has often been noted, this expectation is the equivalent of an unenforceable contract.[24] There is no guarantee that once ensconced in office jurists will support their patrons, much less their patrons' successors. And often enough, judges have surprised and disappointed the presidents who nominated them. We need look no further than the late Supreme Court chief justice Earl Warren or former justice David Souter for examples.

But the actual significance of the appointment process, especially as it pertains to presidential power, is somewhat more subtle. In their overall pattern, judicial appointments reflect the political milieu from which judges are drawn and to which they are tied. During the nineteenth century, federal judges were typically drawn from—and often had continuing ties to—the nation's electoral and representative systems. Not only were most judicial nominees active in party politics, but before their appointment to the bench, many district and circuit court judges, and even a number of Supreme Court justices, had also run for elective office and had served in the state legislators. Some had even served in the U.S. Congress. Chief Justice John Marshall, for example, served in both the Virginia House of Delegates and the U.S. House of Representatives. His successor, Roger Brooke Taney, had served in both houses of the Maryland legislature. Indeed, one comprehensive study has shown that among the two hundred district court judges appointed between 1829 and 1861, not only were most of the jurists themselves veterans of the electoral and legislative arenas, but more than 60 percent had fathers who had been active in electoral and legislative politics as well.[25]

The legislative experience once possessed by judges is now largely a thing of the past. Before the Civil War, more than 50 percent of all federal judges had previously served in a representative assembly, while today barely 4 percent have ever held elective office.[26] Contemporary federal judges are drawn mainly from the executive and judicial branches, and have little experience in the realm of legislative politics. This shift in the political backgrounds of federal judges reflects changes in the character of the American party system as well as the place of legislatures in the American institutional framework. In the nineteenth century, presidents looked to legislatures as a source of party notables whose appointment to the bench would strengthen their own political position. In the twentieth century, by contrast, political parties and legislatures have declined in importance and presidents are more likely to seek the favor of important interest and constituency groups like environmentalists and consumer activists (if they are Democrats), or anti-abortionists and pro-business forces (if they are Republicans). Unlike the old-time party leaders, these new political notables are often likely to be found in the executive and judicial branches, where such movements have sought and won privileged access in recent years. Many important political forces in recent years have been eschewing legislative combat in favor of bureaucratic politics and litigation, where they have been able to achieve satisfactory results without risking their fate to the vicissitudes of democratic politics.[27]

Does the institutional wellhead from which judges are drawn make a difference to their behavior on the bench? Conclusive proof is difficult to offer, but everyone who has lived and worked in Washington, D.C., sooner or later learns that most employees of the executive and judicial branches of the government are rather disdainful of the Congress and, if they notice them at all, dismissive of the state legislatures. Indeed from the perspective of many officials of the other two branches of government, the nation's elected representatives are mainly a collection of meddlers and bunglers who almost invariably place political considerations ahead of important national goals and priorities. It is revealing to read the unflattering assessment of Congress offered by the late Harold Seidman, one of the nation's greatest scholars of governmental organization and for twenty-five years a senior executive branch official in the Bureau of the Budget (now called the White House Office of Management and Budget). "Within the Congress," Seidman asserts, "words are sometimes equated with deeds . . . [and] concern . . . is focused principally on those elements [of public policy] that directly affect constituency interests or committee jurisdictions." He continues, "Legislative proposals are seldom debated from the viewpoint of their administrative feasibility [and] if things go wrong, failure can always be attributed [to others]."[28]

Seidman's views probably reflect the Washington consensus. It would be difficult to find any official with an executive or judicial background who has much respect for Congress, its processes, and—with a few exceptions—its members. Disparaging comments about legislative "interference" in the orderly processes of government are commonly heard in both formal and informal Washington settings. As the late senator Robert Byrd (D.-W.Va.) complained after White House officials referred to congressional rules and procedures as a set of "Lilliputian do's and don'ts," "Some of these people [executive branch officials] have complete disdain for Congress. They are contemptuous of Congress."[29]

Because nineteenth-century judges often had legislative backgrounds and were recruited from a political milieu in which legislatures were respected and powerful institutions, they had little difficulty deferring to legislative judgments. Contemporary judges, by contrast, seldom have served as members of representative bodies. They are, moreover, recruited from a political milieu in which legislatures are disdained by the political cognoscenti and during an era when executive power has, in fact, become more and more pronounced, while that of the Congress has gradually diminished. Contemporary judges are not even accustomed to viewing legislatures as institutions capable of taking sound and decisive actions. Perhaps the most significant exception to this rule was former Supreme Court justice Sandra Day O'Connor, who was the principal author of a number of decisions seeking to return power to the state legislatures. Perhaps it is no coincidence that Justice O'Connor was among the rare federal judges with state legislative experience, having served in the 1970s as a member and majority leader of the Arizona state legislature.

To a substantial extent, indeed, many federal judges have come to embrace a set of beliefs that were first fully articulated in the United States during the Progressive era. In the Progressive vision, only the judiciary and the executive branch are capable of dealing effectively with important national problems. Legislatures, by contrast, are inefficient, fit only to represent parochial, as opposed to broad, public interests, and are often corrupt. As one prominent federal appeals court judge observed, many contemporary federal judges, influenced by Progressive modes of thought, seek "rationality" in public policy and have an attitude of "hostility to a pluralist, party dominated, political process."[30] Such views are likely to find expression in distaste for legislatures and a preference for decisionmaking by courts and the executive—the nation's "rational" institutions. Recently, for example, a number of judges have objected vigorously to congressional efforts to control the policies of the U.S. Sentencing Commission, which was created by Congress in 1984 to ensure some measure of nationwide uniformity in sentencing for federal crimes. Though setting the appropriate penalties for violations of statutes would seem to lie within the purview of the nation's legislature, some federal judges seem to regard congressional efforts to establish sentencing rules as wholly misguided and illegitimate. The commission's rules were eventually modified and power over sentencing restored to the bench by a series of Supreme Court decisions.[31]

Four Areas Where the Federal Courts Have Empowered the Executive

Taken together, these considerations help to explain why, in recent decades, the federal courts have regularly intruded into a number of areas that once would clearly have been considered political—more specifically, congressional—domains. For example, in the 1962 case of *Baker v. Carr,* the U.S. Supreme Court held that legislative apportionment, a matter the Court had previously said was under the purview of Congress and the state legislatures, could, in fact, be determined by the federal courts.[32] Similarly, in the 1969 case of *Powell v. McCormack,* the Court heard on the merits former representative Adam Clayton Powell's claim that he had been improperly denied his seat in the Congress.[33] The House had voted to exclude Powell after it found that he had misappropriated congressional funds for personal use. Article I, Section 5 of the U.S. Constitution states explicitly that each house of Congress is empowered to judge the qualifications of its own members. The Supreme Court, nevertheless, held that it, rather than the Congress, should determine whether Powell was entitled to his seat.

Perhaps the most striking example of judicial intervention into the political arena in recent years was the Supreme Court's decision in the case of *Bush v. Gore,* one of several state and federal cases arising from the 2000 presidential election in the state of Florida. Here the Court, de facto if not de jure, awarded Florida's electoral votes to President George W. Bush in the disputed 2000 Florida presidential vote count.[34] On its face, the issue of whether Florida's electoral votes belonged to Bush or Gore seems to be precisely the sort of political question that the *Luther* court had assigned to Congress and the state legislature 170 years earlier. Though dismissed by the mainstream media—one national columnist referred to the state's legislative proceedings as "off-the-wall"—and the political establishment, the Florida legislature claimed to be prepared to resolve the issue as might have appeared to be its constitutional and legal right.[35] Alternatively, Congress might have settled the outcome. In a similar situation following the disputed 1876 presidential election, the U.S. Congress devised a procedure that ultimately awarded disputed electoral votes to Republican candidate Rutherford B. Hayes. In 2000, however, neither the Florida Supreme Court nor the U.S. Supreme Court saw any reason to even consider deferring to meddlesome, "off-the-wall" legislative bodies.

If the federal courts simply failed to bow to any other governmental institution, this might be taken as evidence for the judicial imperialism thesis once propounded by some conservative writers.[36] This imperialism, however, seems limited in scope, indeed mainly confined to wearing away the prerogatives of the Congress. When it comes to the actions of the executive branch, the federal courts have been far more tolerant in recent decades. Indeed, as judicial deference to Congress has waned, so has its solicitude for the presidency grown. Let us examine four areas—foreign policy, war and emergency powers, administrative authority, and legislative powers—in which the federal courts have acceded to and encouraged the expansion of presidential power.

Foreign Policy Decisionmaking

Foreign policy has come to be seen as a presidential preserve, but the Constitution assigns important foreign policy powers to the Congress. In fact, from the birth of the Republic through the early years of the twentieth century, the federal courts recognized Congress's role in shaping American policy toward other nations. For example, in the 1795 case of *Penhallow v. Doane,* the Supreme Court specifically held that the Constitution required the president and the Congress to share authority over the making of foreign policy.[37] Over the ensuing decades, the courts continued to emphasize congressional power. In the 1829 case of *Foster v. Neilson,* the Court indicated that Congress had the ultimate power to interpret the meaning of language in treaties between the United States and other nations.[38] In the 1850 case of *Fleming v. Page,* the Court held that only Congress, not the president, had the power to annex territory to the United States.[39] In the 1893 Chinese Exclusion Cases, the Court reaffirmed the dominance of Congress in the realm of international relations. Justice Gray, for the Court, said, "The power [in this instance, to exclude aliens] is vested in the political departments of the government, and is to be regulated by treaty or by Act of Congress."[40] In a similar vein, the 1901 Insular Cases conceded to Congress the power to determine the constitutional rights of the inhabitants of America's territories.[41]

This nineteenth-century deference to Congress in the realm of foreign relations gave way, in the twentieth century, to a distinct judicial presumption in favor of executive power in foreign affairs. The turning point was the 1936 case of *United States v. Curtiss-Wright Export Corporation*.[42] The company had been charged with conspiring to sell fifteen machine guns to Bolivia. This sale violated a May 1934 presidential proclamation issued pursuant to a congressional resolution that had authorized the president to prohibit arms sales to Paraguay and Bolivia, which were then engaged in a cross-border conflict. Attorneys for the company argued that the congressional resolution allowing the president discretion in the matter of arms sales was an unlawful delegation of legislative power to the executive branch. Indeed, as we shall see, in two earlier cases, *Schechter Brothers Poultry v. United States* and *Panama Refining Co. v. Ryan*, the Court had struck down acts of Congress on the grounds that they represented unconstitutionally broad delegations of legislative power to the executive branch.[43] Both decisions had prompted severe criticism from the White House and from congressional Democrats. Perhaps for that reason, the Court seemed anxious to distinguish the present case from the earlier decisions without seeming to retreat from its former position.

The Court might have accomplished this objective merely by asserting that the discretion allowed the executive branch under the 1936 act was more narrowly defined than the president's authority under the earlier acts. But the author of the Court's opinion, Justice George Sutherland, had long believed that America should pursue an active foreign policy guided by the president and the judiciary and free from the parochial concerns that, in his view, often dominated congressional policy-making. In essence, Sutherland thought politics should stop at the water's edge.[44] Thus, writing for the Court, Justice Sutherland made a sharp distinction between internal and external affairs. The congressional resolution delegating power to the executive, he wrote, might have been unlawful if it had "related solely to internal affairs." In the realm of foreign affairs, however, different standards and rules applied, permitting Congress to delegate powers to the president with only very general standards or even leaving "the exercise of power to his unrestricted judgement." Moreover, in the realm of foreign policy, the powers that Congress could appropriately exercise, and presumably delegate to the president, were not limited to the express and implied powers granted in the Constitution. This limitation was said to apply "only in respect of our internal affairs." Finally, in the realm of foreign affairs, said the Court, the president exercised "plenary and exclusive power," independent of any legislative authority, as "the sole organ of the federal government in the field of international relations."

Taken together, these three principles laid the legal groundwork for many of the claims of executive power made by presidents and sustained by the federal courts in subsequent years. The *Curtiss-Wright* decision implied that Congress, through action or inaction, could grant nearly any legislative authority to the president.[45] The president, moreover, possessing "plenary" powers, might in some instances act on his own authority without legislative authorization or even contrary to the express will of Congress. In particular, *Curtiss-Wright* helped to set the stage for presidential arrogation of one of Congress's most important foreign policy instruments—the treaty power—as well as the notion that presidential foreign policy actions not specifically prohibited by Congress had been tacitly approved through congressional acquiescence to the president's decisions.

With regard to the treaty power, Article II of the U.S. Constitution provides that proposed treaties between the United States and foreign states must be ratified by a two-thirds vote in the Senate before having the effect of law. On numerous occasions the Senate has exercised its Article II powers by refusing to ratify treaties negotiated and signed by the president. In recent years, the Senate has been especially unwilling to ratify human rights treaties and conventions that Senate Republicans have regarded as impositions on American sovereignty. These include the 1979 Convention to Eliminate All Forms of Discrimination against Women, the 1989 Convention on the Rights of the Child, the 1978 Convention on Human Rights, and the 2000 treaty creating a permanent International Criminal Court. After President Clinton signed the 2000 agreement, the late senator Jesse Helms, who then chaired the Senate Foreign Relations Committee, announced it would be "dead on arrival" in the U.S. Senate.[46]

In order to circumvent the Senate's Article II treaty powers, as we saw in Chapter 6, presidents have turned to the device of creating executive agreements with other nations. Largely at the president's discretion and based mainly on political considerations, these may be executive-congressional agreements, requiring a simple majority vote in each house of Congress for approval, or sole executive agreements, which are never submitted for congressional approval.[47] In the nineteenth and early twentieth centuries, executive agreements were most often trade pacts linked to prior congressional legislation.[48] For example, the Tariff Act of 1897 authorized the president to negotiate certain types of commercial agreements with other nations.[49] Though the resulting agreements were not submitted for ratification, their underlying purpose had been affirmed by the Congress and the president's discretionary authority had been limited.[50] There are, to be sure, examples from the nineteenth and early twentieth centuries of executive agreements undertaken by presidents on their own authority, sometimes at least nominally linked to the president's duties as commander-in-chief. For example, in 1900, without asking for authorization, President McKinley signed an agreement to cooperate with other nations to send troops to China to protect European legations during the Boxer Rebellion. Subsequently, in 1901, McKinley signed the Boxer Indemnity Protocol between China and other powers, again without seeking Senate approval. Yet despite these and other exceptions, the norm was that compacts between the United States and foreign nations were submitted to the Senate as required by the Constitution.

After taking office in 1933, President Franklin D. Roosevelt had no intention of allowing a small number of senators to block his foreign policy decisions and initiated what is the now standard practice of conducting foreign policy via executive agreement rather than Article II treaty. During his first year in office, Roosevelt signed what came to be known as the "Litvinov Assignment," which, among other things, provided for American recognition of the Soviet Union and assigned to the government of the United States all Soviet claims against American nationals. When the U.S. government ordered New York's Belmont Bank to turn over certain Russian assets, the bank refused to comply, asserting that the executive agreement on which the government's claim was based was not the equivalent of an Article II treaty and did not have the force of law. The case reached the Supreme Court in 1937 as *United States v. Belmont.*[51]

In its decision, the Court not only upheld the government's claim, but also affirmed the president's power to negotiate agreements without Senate approval—agreements that, for all intents and purposes, would have the legal effect of Article II treaties. Justice Sutherland, writing for the Court, reaffirmed his position in *Curtiss-Wright,* asserting that the president possessed the plenary authority to speak as the "sole organ" of the U.S. government in its foreign relations. As such, the president had the power to make binding international agreements that did not require Senate ratification. This decision was reaffirmed four years later in *United States v. Pink,* which also dealt with the disposition of Russian assets in the United States.[52]

Beginning with these decisions, the federal courts have nearly always accepted sole executive agreements and executive-congressional agreements as the equivalents of Article II treaties. A handful of cases, to be sure, have qualified executive agreements or limited their scope. In *Swearingen v. United States,* for example, an appeals court held that a sole executive agreement could not supersede the tax code.[53] Such cases, however, are the occasional exceptions. For the most part, the courts have held that, like treaties, executive agreements supersede previously enacted federal and state laws unless they are subsequently disallowed by the Congress. Thus, for example, in *Bercut-Vandervoort & Co. v. United States,* the Court of Customs and Patent Appeals ruled that a provision of the Internal Revenue Code must be interpreted in a manner consistent with the General Agreement on Tariffs and Trade, though the latter was a sole executive agreement.[54] And in *Coplin v. United States,* the Court of

Claims ruled that an executive agreement exempting some Americans working in the Panama Canal Zone from U.S. income taxes effectively repealed prior portions of the Internal Revenue Code with which it was inconsistent. (Interestingly, the court reached this conclusion even though attorneys for the government had argued that the president had exceeded his authority.)[55] Congress can, through the ordinary legislative process, seek to repeal or qualify an executive agreement. Where Congress fails to take action and specifically prohibit a presidential initiative, the Supreme Court has held that inaction constitutes a form of congressional acceptance or acquiescence.[56] In recent years, President Obama has signed a number of executive agreements including a "Strategic Partnership Agreement" with Afghanistan and several trade agreements. Members of Congress have grumbled, but grumbling has never been seen by the courts as a form of nonacquiescence.

At the same time that they have allowed presidents to substitute executive agreements for treaties when doing so suited the chief executive's purposes, the federal courts have also given the president broad latitude in interpreting existing treaties.[57] In one important case, moreover, the Supreme Court declined to intervene to block the president from unilaterally terminating an existing treaty.[58] When President Jimmy Carter decided to recognize the People's Republic of China, he also recognized China's claim to sovereignty over Taiwan and, accordingly, withdrew American recognition from the Taiwan government and terminated America's mutual defense treaty with the island's regime.[59] This precedent was then cited by the Bush administration in support of the president's decision in 2001 to unilaterally terminate the 1972 Anti-Ballistic Missile Treaty.[60]

If one common theme unites the numerous cases affirming the president's dominance in the realm of foreign policy, it is the theme of expertise. In case after case, the federal courts have been moved to declare that the president, and by implication, only the president, possesses adequate knowledge, information, and judgment to make foreign policy decisions. Legal historian Joel R. Paul calls this often-expressed judicial presumption "the discourse of executive expediency."[61] Thus in *Curtiss-Wright* Justice Sutherland refers to the special information the president may have and to the "unwisdom" of requiring too much congressional involvement in decisionmaking. In *Pink,* Justice Douglas writes that presidential primacy in the realm of external relations is necessary to promote "effectiveness in handling the delicate problems of foreign affairs." In *Dames & Moore v. Regan,* Chief Justice Rehnquist states his concern that Congress continue to allow the president the discretion he needs to conduct the nation's foreign policy and to meet the country's "challenges." The judges realize that the courts cannot conduct the nation's foreign policy and so, as they see it, they turn of necessity to the president. "The conduct of foreign relations is not open to judicial inquiry," and must be left to the president, Justice Sutherland said in *Belmont,* and Justice Douglas reiterated in *Pink.*

But what of the Congress? Reflecting the ideological legacy of Progressivism coupled, perhaps, with a sheer lack of firsthand legislative experience, contemporary courts do not seem to take seriously the notion that Congress should play a major role in conducting the nation's foreign affairs. What would the Congress contribute besides its parochial perspectives and "unwisdom" to delicate foreign policy matters? As we shall see, this judicial perspective is even more pronounced in considerations by contemporary federal courts of issues related to war and emergency powers.

Powers during War and Other National Emergencies

Contemporary presidents often behave as though they alone possess the authority to deploy military forces and lead the nation into war. Article I of the Constitution, however, seems to assign Congress the central role in this area. The framers gave Congress the power to declare war, to raise and support armies, to maintain a navy, to make rules for the conduct of the Army and Navy, to call out the militia, and to grant letters of marque and reprisal. Only Congress, moreover, can appropriate funds for the support of military forces. Article II, by contrast, appears to assign the president a lesser role. The president is to serve as commander-in-chief of the nation's military forces and to see to it that the nation's laws are faithfully executed. On the basis of the Constitution's text and from the debates at the Constitutional Convention, it appears that most of the framers intended Congress to decide whether, how, and when to go to war. The president's role as commander-in-chief would consist mainly of implementing congressional decisions by organizing actual military campaigns.[62] In addition, the president's duty to see to the faithful execution of the laws might include the task of responding to civil disorder or to foreign attack when Congress could not be convened in a timely manner.[63]

This was certainly the view expressed by James Madison at the Constitutional Convention's committee on drafting when he moved to give Congress the power to declare war while leaving to the executive only the power to "repel sudden attacks."[64] Thomas Jefferson saw Madison's handiwork as an important means of preventing the nation from becoming embroiled in conflicts. "We have already given in example," Jefferson wrote to James Madison, "one effectual check to the Dog of war by transferring the power of letting him loose from those who are to spend to those who are to pay."[65]

The early decisions of the federal courts supported this original conception of the distribution of war powers under the Constitution. In the 1800 case of *Bas v. Tingy*, the Supreme Court affirmed that only Congress had the power to commit the United States to war either by a formal declaration, which the justices called "perfect war," or to limited military engagements without a formal declaration of war (imperfect war) when "popular feeling might not have been ripe for a solemn declaration of war."[66] The following year, in *Talbot v. Seeman*, Chief Justice John Marshall, writing for the Court, said the Constitution gave Congress "the whole powers of war."[67] And, in *Little v. Barreme*, the Court held that the president could not go beyond Congress's explicit instructions when exercising his commander-in-chief powers.[68] The case arose from America's early eighteenth-century conflict with France. Congress had authorized the president to seize armed French vessels sailing to French ports. President Adams, however, had issued orders for the seizure of such ships sailing both to or from French ports. An American vessel, following this expanded order, had captured a French ship when it had emerged from a French port and the French owners had then sued to recover damages. The Court held that the captain of the American vessel was liable because the presidential orders under which he had acted had exceeded the president's authority and so were invalid. Later, in *Brown v. United States*, the Court invalidated an executive seizure of British property that took place after the initiation of hostilities but before the Congress had declared the War of 1812.[69]

Even in the early decades of the Republic, presidents sometimes deployed military forces without seeking congressional authorization. President Jefferson, for example, did not consult Congress before sending warships into the Mediterranean to prepare for action against the Barbary pirates. As legal scholar Jeremy Telman notes, however, the early presidents were well aware that the Constitution and the courts had reserved to Congress the power to authorize the use of force, and that Congress would act to defend its prerogatives. Accordingly, presidents were generally careful to avoid taking actions—even actions that defended Americans—that Congress would not support. In 1793, for example, George Washington refused a request from the governor of Georgia to send troops to protect settlers from Native Americans, on the ground that only Congress could authorize such action.[70] Similar examples are numerous. Indeed, as the U.S. State Department's foremost legal adviser Judge Abraham Sofaer writes, "At no point during the first forty years of activity under the Constitution, did a President . . . claim that presidents could exercise force independently of congressional control."[71] A similar point is made by David Currie, who indicates that the early presidents viewed only an actual attack on the United States as adequate justification for using armed force without congressional authorization.[72]

In some instances, presidents asked for congressional approval only after the fact. President Polk, for example, asked for a congressional declaration of war against Mexico after provoking an armed skirmish between American and Mexican forces. But even this post-hoc request indicates the president's recognition that he could not use force without congressional sanction. To underline the point, Congress voted to censure Polk for instigating the clash before it voted to declare war on Mexico.[73] Even Lincoln requested and received retroactive congressional approval of his decision to blockade Southern ports and suspend the writ of habeas corpus, actions he took during the early days of the Civil War while Congress was in recess.

Over the course of the Civil War, Lincoln issued numerous executive orders and military regulations without congressional sanction. He declared martial law far from combat zones, seized property, suppressed newspapers, expanded the Army, emancipated slaves, and censored the mails. When possible, the president tried to claim that his actions were justified not only by prospective congressional approval, but also by actual congressional legislation such as the 1795 and 1807 statutes authorizing the president to call out the militia and to use the military to suppress insurrection. When push came to shove, however, Lincoln justified his actions on his inherent powers as commander-in-chief and his presidential duty to see to it that the laws were faithfully executed. In part this was a constitutional claim based on an expansive reading of Article II as providing the president with powers beyond those delegated to him by the Congress. And in part this was a claim of extraconstitutional power similar to Locke's notion of the Crown's prerogative, which included "the power to act according to discretion for the public good, without the prescription of the law and sometimes even against it."[74]

In the two cases arising from Lincoln's actions during the Civil War, the Supreme Court did not accept this broadened conception of the presidential war power. The first denial came in 1863 in the so-called Prize Cases that challenged Lincoln's 1861 order to blockade Southern ports.[75] The Supreme Court upheld the validity of the president's order but did so primarily on the basis of the 1795 and 1807 congressional enactments mentioned earlier. The Court also cited the president's longstanding duty to repel attacks and invasions. In linking the president's actions to congressional authorizations and to well-established constitutional theory, the Court was affirming the traditional constitutional framework and refusing to give its imprimatur to the president's new claims. In effect, the Court refrained from challenging the then current reality of enhanced presidential power but refused to bolster that power's jurisprudential foundations.

In the second important case growing out of the Civil War, *Ex parte Milligan,* decided in 1866, the Court firmly rejected the president's claim to possess emergency powers outside the law or Constitution.[76] In 1861 Lincoln had, on his own authority, declared martial law and suspended the writ of habeas corpus even in states far removed from any theater of war. Milligan, a civilian and a citizen of Indiana, was an active "Copperhead," or supporter of the Confederate cause. In 1864, he was arrested at his home, tried by a military commission, and sentenced to be hanged for his seditious actions. At the time of Milligan's arrest, the civil courts in Indiana were functioning normally and could have heard the charges against him under an 1863 statute providing for the civil disposition of cases involving individuals arrested for disloyal activities.[77] Before Milligan's scheduled execution in 1865, the circuit court in Indianapolis issued a writ of habeas corpus and the case was brought before the Supreme Court. The Court held that the president had no authority to declare martial law in an area where the civil authorities and civil courts were operating without obstruction and where there existed no imminent threat of attack or invasion. Martial law could be declared only in the event of "compelling necessity." The Court, moreover, rejected any notion that in times of emergency the president possessed powers not prescribed by law or the Constitution. "The Constitution of the United Sates is a law for rulers and people, equally in war and in peace," wrote Justice Davis for the Court. "No doctrine, involving more pernicious consequences, was ever invented by the wit of man than that any of its provisions can be suspended during any of the great exigencies of government."[78] As has often been noted, the Court issued this judgment after the war had ended. During the war, the justices would likely have hesitated to protect a Confederate sympathizer and thwart the president and military authorities. Nevertheless, *Milligan* helped reassert the nineteenth-century principle of limited presidential authority. Indirectly, *Milligan* also cleared the way for the courts to reaffirm congressional power. While the late nineteenth-century Court was anxious to curb presidential war and emergency powers, it allowed Congress much more leeway. In the 1871 case of *Miller v. United States,* the Court carefully distinguished Congress's war powers from those of the president. While presidential war powers derived from congressional authorization, those of the Congress were limited only by the "law of nations."[79] In a number of post–Civil War cases, moreover, the Court invalidated presidential actions on the ground that the emergency had passed while upholding Congress's right to continue to exercise powers originally created to deal with the emergency.[80] According to legal historian Christopher N. May, at least until World War I it was generally agreed that war and emergency powers were primarily possessed by the Congress, not the president.[81]

At the end of the nineteenth century, however, the question of inherent presidential emergency powers had not been fully settled. Two turn-of-the-century domestic cases provided judicial sanction for the Lincolnesque notion that the president's duty to see to the faithful execution of the laws gave him inherent powers beyond those enacted by Congress or specified by the Constitution. In the first of these cases, *In re Neagle*, a U.S. marshal, David Neagle, assigned by the attorney general to protect Justice Stephen Field, shot and killed a disgruntled litigant who threatened the Justice as he was riding circuit in California.[82] When Neagle was arrested by state authorities and charged with murder, the federal government demanded his release, claiming that he was lawfully performing his duties as a marshal even though there was no specific statute authorizing the president to assign bodyguards to judges. The Court ruled that the president's duty to oversee the faithful execution of the laws gave him power that was not "limited to the enforcement of acts of Congress." The Court took this same position in the 1895 case of *In re Debs*.[83] Here the issue was whether to uphold a contempt citation against Debs and other union leaders for violating an injunction against a strike by rail workers. The executive had no statutory authority for seeking such an injunction, but the Court held that this action was nevertheless within the president's inherent powers.

World War I might have been expected to produce a profusion of cases involving presidential emergency powers. President Wilson, however, generally sought— and almost always received—clear statutory authorization for his actions during the war.[84] As a result, while a number of wartime and postwar cases dealt with the government's seizure of factories, mines, and railroads, as well as with wartime restrictions on freedom of speech, few if any disputes bore directly on the question of presidential power. For the most part, the courts were asked to review statutes enacted by the Congress, rather than unilateral actions undertaken by the president. The courts almost always upheld Congress's emergency and war powers during the war itself, and for several years thereafter, ignoring what normally might have been seen as unconstitutional exercises of governmental power and violations of civil liberties. These included convictions under the 1917 Espionage Act and the 1918 Sedition Law, which are often cited today as textbook violations of civil liberties. As Clinton Rossiter once observed, "The Court, too, likes to win wars."[85] Indeed, the Supreme Court rejected every challenge to emergency wartime legislation until long after the Armistice. In 1921 the Court invalidated portions of the Lever Act and in 1924 it struck down the District of Columbia emergency rent law.[86] At the same time, however, the Court did seek to affirm the principle—if not the immediate fact—that war powers are limited by the Constitution and subject to judicial review.[87]

Emergency and war powers issues arose again during World War II. Franklin D. Roosevelt issued numerous military and emergency orders during the war, generally claiming statutory authorization for his actions. Unlike Wilson, however, FDR was less than fastidious about the closeness of the relationship between his actions and their purported statutory basis. And indeed, in many instances the powers delegated by Congress to the executive were so broad as to provide the president with virtually unfettered discretion. For example, the Emergency Price Control Act of 1942 authorized the executive to set "fair and equitable" prices.[88] Like Lincoln a century earlier, Roosevelt saw his role as commander-in-chief and his duty to see to the faithful execution of the laws as conferring on his office constitutional and extraconstitutional powers—the Lockean prerogative—to defend the nation. Pursuant to this view, Roosevelt seized property, declared martial law, established military tribunals, and interned some seventy thousand American citizens of Japanese descent primarily on his own authority.

In May 1941, with Great Britain apparently on the verge of collapse, the president also issued a proclamation declaring a state of "unlimited national emergency," supplanting the "limited" emergency he had declared in 1939. As authority for these proclamations, the president vaguely cited some ninety-nine statutes, many forgotten for more than a century, as well as additional powers "not enumerated in the statutes," which could not be specifically defined but might require the president to take action.[89] A month after proclaiming the emergency, FDR ordered the seizure of a North American Aviation plant in Inglewood, California, that had been closed by a strike. This became the first of many such plant seizures retroactively ratified by the Congress in the 1943 War Labor Disputes Act, which authorized the president to seize mines or plants that produced materials required for the war effort. In a similar vein, Roosevelt, under his authority as "Commander-in-Chief in time of war," created a host of new executive agencies without consulting Congress.[90] And in 1942, the president told Congress that if it refused to repeal a particular provision of the Emergency Price Control Act, he would be left with "an inescapable responsibility" to prevent domestic economic factors from impeding the war effort. "In the event that the Congress should fail to act," said the president, "I shall accept the responsibility and I will act."[91] This view was echoed by President Obama in 2014 when he declared that Congress's failure to act on immigration policy would force him to act unilaterally.

During World War II, the Court, as it had during World War I, upheld the constitutionality of every statute enacted by the Congress for wartime purposes.[92] Because many of these statutes gave the executive branch broad discretionary authority, the Court's decisions, in effect, broadened the president's war and emergency powers. As Martin Shefter observes, during World War II the war powers of the nation became the war powers of the president, regardless of the "linguistic label."[93] Take, for example, the case of *Yakus v. United States,* which involved decisions of the Office of Price Administration under the Emergency Price Control Act of 1942.[94] A principal issue raised by the plaintiff, a wholesale butcher charged with selling beef for a higher price than allowed by the office, was whether the statute entailed an unconstitutional delegation of legislative power to the executive branch. The Supreme Court ruled that Congress clearly had the constitutional power to prescribe prices in a time of emergency. But because the executive's power under the statute was so broadly defined, the effect of the Court's decision was to allow the executive to prescribe prices during an emergency that had itself been declared by the executive.

In a number of other cases, the federal courts ruled more directly on the matter of presidential war and emergency powers, nearly always deciding in favor of the president's possession and exercise of such powers. One decision enhancing the president's emergency powers came in the 1942 case of *Ex parte Quirin,* which involved seven German agents apprehended by the FBI.[95] The men had been trained in sabotage and brought to the United States by submarine to attack American military facilities. President Roosevelt ordered the creation of a special military commission to try the accused saboteurs, but their attorneys argued that the president had no authority to issue such an order and that the men should be tried in the civil courts in the states where they had been captured. As we saw earlier, the 1866 *Milligan* court had held that the president could not convene military tribunals in places outside a theater of war where the civil courts were functioning normally. The Supreme Court in 1942, however, without explicitly overruling *Milligan,* distinguished the facts and circumstances of the two cases. The Court held that even where the civil courts were fully available and there existed no immediate threat of war or disorder, the president possessed the authority to create military commissions and to designate individuals as unlawful combatants subject to trial by such commissions. Sixty years later, the *Quirin* decision would be cited by the Bush administration in support of its decision to try terrorist suspects before military tribunals rather than the civil courts. In fact, President Bush intentionally modeled his executive order establishing such tribunals after Roosevelt's Executive Order 2561, which had authorized military trials for the German saboteurs.[96]

One additional World War II decision cited by the Bush administration was the Supreme Court's 1950 ruling in *Johnson v. Eisentrager.*[97] Eisentrager was a German spy in China. After Germany's surrender, he continued to work for the Japanese until his capture by the United States. Eisentrager was tried and convicted of various crimes by an American military commission in China and sentenced to life in prison. He was incarcerated in a U.S.-run facility in Bavaria, and his request for a writ of habeas corpus was rejected by the Supreme Court on the grounds that constitutional protections do not extend to enemy aliens held on foreign soil. The Bush administration relied on the *Eisentrager* precedent to bolster its claim that terrorist suspects held by American forces in Guantanamo, nominally part of Cuba, are beyond the reach of the civil courts.

Another group of important World War II cases involving the president's military powers stemmed from Roosevelt's February 1942 Executive Order 9066, which authorized the secretary of war and military commanders to establish "military areas" from which "any and all persons" might be excluded to prevent espionage and sabotage. Though the order was stated in general terms, its target was the Japanese American population of the West Coast states.[98] On the basis of this order, military authorities forcibly moved seventy thousand Japanese Americans to camps in Utah and elsewhere, where they were detained for the remainder of the war. Congress subsequently enacted legislation effectively ratifying the president's order. The most important of the cases generated by these events was *Korematsu v. United States,* which was decided in December 1944.[99] Korematsu, a U.S. citizen of Japanese ancestry, had violated a military exclusion order by refusing to leave his home in San Leandro, California, and been arrested. Korematsu attacked the validity of the exclusion order and the entire evacuation program as an unconstitutional exercise of presidential power. A sharply divided Supreme Court, however, held that the order was valid. In his opinion for the Court, Justice Black wrote, "The military authorities considered that the need for action was great, and time was short. We cannot . . . now say . . . these actions were unjustified." In essence, the Court held that it had no power to question the president's declaration of a military emergency or the actions he ordered pursuant to that declaration. More than any case since the Civil War, *Korematsu* affirmed the martial powers of the president and the deference shown by the courts in the face of a presidential declaration of military emergency.

Several other World War II cases upheld the president's use of emergency economic powers. One such case was *Employers Group of Motor Freight Carriers v. National War Labor Board,* decided by the Circuit Court of Appeals for the District of Columbia.[100] The National War Labor Board had been created by executive order in 1942 and authorized by the president to issue nominally nonbinding "advisory" orders that set wage rates in a variety of industries. Companies that failed to take the board's advice were inevitably denied government contracts, deprived of fuel and supplies, and in several instances, saw their plants and facilities seized by presidential orders under one of several statutes authorizing such action. The plaintiff, a trucking company, sought to appeal a board order "advising" it to grant a $2.75 per week wage increase to its employees, claiming that the board lacked any statutory standing, much less the authority to issue orders. The U.S. district and appeals courts, however, both ruled that the president possessed emergency power to establish executive agencies and declined to review the board's orders. In another major case, the courts affirmed the president's power to seize property on his own authority under his general war powers. This was the case of *Montgomery Ward & Co. v. United States*.[101] In December 1944, the president ordered the seizure of the plants and facilities of Montgomery Ward and Company after the firm's owner had refused to comply with the directives of the National War Labor Board. The government asserted that the seizure was justified under the Labor Disputes Act, but acknowledged that Montgomery Ward might not be a mine, manufacturing plant, or other facility described in the act. Even if it was not, said the government, the seizure was still justified under the president's "general war powers." These contentions were rejected by the U.S. District Court, but affirmed by the Circuit Court. The properties were returned to their owner before the Supreme Court could hear the case.

In sum, federal court decisions during World War II seemed to support strongly the notion that the president possessed emergency military and economic powers—powers that allowed him to declare martial law, seize property, set wages and prices, and generally act as a constitutional dictator during a time of emergency that the president himself had the power to declare.

The *Youngstown* Case

In 1952, however, the Supreme Court's decision in *Youngstown Sheet & Tube Co. v. Sawyer* placed some limits on these earlier holdings.[102] In 1950, after Chinese troops intervened in the Korean War, President Truman declared a state of emergency, reactivating various emergency statutes as well as laying the groundwork for emergency exercise of presidential authority. To halt a strike by steel workers in April 1952, Truman ordered the seizure of the nation's steel plants, asserting that an interruption of steel production would imperil the nation's defense. The steel companies opposed Truman's action and the case was soon considered by the Supreme Court.

The Court struck down Truman's actions, finding no constitutional or statutory basis for the president's seizure of the mills. Justice Hugo Black, author of the decision, noted that Congress had enacted legislation—in particular, the 1950 Defense Production Act—that the president might have used as a basis for seizing the mills. Black also noted that the president might have invoked the 1947 Taft-Hartley Act (which had been enacted over Truman's veto) to compel the steel workers to halt their strike. The president had instead relied on his powers as commander-in-chief and, on this basis, Black found no constitutional justification for the seizure of private property. The *Youngstown* decision appeared to place serious limits on the president's emergency powers and to indicate that the Court had serious doubts about the constitutionality of the numerous property seizures that had been ordered by presidents during previous wars.

In retrospect, though, the most important element of the Court's holding in *Youngstown* was not Black's decision for the Court; it was Justice Jackson's statement concurring with the ruling. Jackson asserted that presidential power varied with three sets of circumstances. The power of the president was, "at its maximum," he wrote, when the president acted "pursuant to an express or implied authorization of Congress." The president's power was "at its lowest ebb," when, as in the *Youngstown* case, he took action incompatible with the express or implied will of Congress. And when the president relied on his independent powers in the absence of a congressional grant or denial of authority, "there is a zone of twilight" where events and "imponderables" would determine the validity of presidential action. Jackson's three-part test became a standard by which the Court evaluated presidential actions in subsequent years, and on occasion it seemed to provide the basis for limiting presidential powers.[103] For example, in the 1971 case of *New York Times v. United States,* the Pentagon Papers case, three justices rested their rejection of the government's effort to enjoin publication of the Pentagon Papers on the ground that Congress had considered, but rejected, proposals to prohibit the disclosure of such information. Thus the president was acting contrary to the implied will of the Congress.[104] The next year, in *United States v. U.S. District Court,* the Court ruled that in the absence of congressional authorization and guidelines, the administration's domestic security surveillance program, which involved wiretaps and warrantless searches, violated the Fourth Amendment.[105]

For the most part, however, as Gordon Silverstein has observed, the Court has shrunk the definition of congressional action contrary to the will of Congress while expanding the meaning of congressional approval or acquiescence.[106] In other words, before the Court has been willing to rule that the president's actions were prohibited, it has usually demanded evidence that Congress has formally and explicitly forbidden the action in question. The Court has interpreted anything short of unambiguous formal prohibition as tacit approval. Thus, as we saw earlier in *Dames & Moore v. Regan,* where the Court claimed to explicitly rely on Jackson's *Youngstown* categories, the Court held that the absence of congressional disapproval of the president's actions could be constituted as approval. The Court came to a similar conclusion in the 1981 case of *Haig v. Agee,* where it held that the failure of Congress to give the president authority for his actions, "especially in the areas of foreign policy and national security," does not imply congressional disapproval of the president's actions.[107] Subsequently, in *Crockett v. Reagan,* a case in which several members of Congress claimed that the president was violating the War Powers Resolution by supplying military assistance to El Salvador, the district court found that before a court could intervene, Congress must take explicit action to apply the War Powers Resolution to the matter at hand.[108] Similar conclusions were reached by the court in 1987 in *Lowry v. Reagan* and in 1990 in *Dellums v. Bush.*[109] In 1999, several members of Congress brought suit against President Clinton, seeking to compel an end to the air war in Yugoslavia on the grounds that it had not been authorized by Congress and that the president's actions violated the War Powers Resolution. Here again, both the district and appellate courts held that in the absence of clearcut evidence of congressional disallowance of the president's actions, no action could be taken by the judiciary.[110]

The War on Terror

Thus, despite the *Youngstown* decision, the clear trend of case law since at least World War II, and most markedly since the Vietnam War, has been to support the president's use of emergency and war powers.[111] The scope of this discretion became especially evident in the response of the federal courts to President George W. Bush's "war on terrorism." Starting after September 11, 2001, the president issued numerous executive orders relating to the deployment of military and security forces and to the detention of captured terrorist suspects. While the president sought and received congressional support for many of his actions against terrorist groups, the White House did not concede that its policies related to the amount, character, and timing of the force to be used to combat terrorism were subject to congressional approval.[112]

In June 2004, the Supreme Court ruled in three cases involving the president's anti-terror initiatives and claims of executive power and in two of the three cases appeared to place some limits on presidential authority. Indeed, the justices had clearly been influenced by revelations that U.S. troops had abused prisoners in Iraq, and in these cases they sought to make a statement against the absolute denial of procedural rights to individuals in the custody of American military authorities. But while the Court's decisions were widely hailed as reining in the executive branch, they actually fell far short of stopping presidential power in its tracks.

The first case decided by the Court was *Hamdi v. Rumsfeld.* Yaser Esam Hamdi, apparently a Taliban soldier, was captured by American forces in Afghanistan and brought to the United States, where he was incarcerated at the Norfolk Naval Station. Hamdi was classified as an enemy combatant and denied civil rights, including the right to counsel, though he had been born in Louisiana and held American citizenship. A federal district court scheduled a hearing on Hamdi's habeas petition and ordered that he be given unmonitored access to counsel. This ruling, however, was reversed by the Fourth Circuit Court of Appeals. In its opinion, the court, quoting *Curtiss-Wright,* held that in the national security realm, the president wields "plenary and exclusive power." This power was even greater, said the court citing *Youngstown,* when the president acted with statutory authority from Congress. The court did not indicate which statute, in particular, might have authorized the president's actions, but went on to affirm the president's constitutional power, as supported in the Prize Cases, *Quirin,* and other rulings, to conduct military operations, to decide who is and who is not an enemy combatant, and to determine the rules governing the treatment of such individuals. In essence, said the court, the president had virtually unfettered discretion to deal with emergencies and it was inappropriate for the judiciary to saddle presidential decisions with what the court called the "panoply of encumbrances associated with civil litigation."[113]

In June 2004, the Supreme Court ruled that Hamdi was entitled to a lawyer and "a fair opportunity to rebut the government's factual assertions." The Supreme Court also affirmed, however, that the president possessed the authority to declare a U.S. citizen to be an enemy combatant and to order such an individual held in federal detention. Several of the justices intimated that once designated as an enemy combatant, a U.S. citizen might be tried before a military tribunal and the normal presumption of innocence suspended. One government legal adviser indicated that the impact of the Court's decision was minimal. "They are basically upholding the whole enemy combatant status and tweaking the evidence test," he said.[114]

A second case decided by the Court in June 2004 was *Rasul v. Bush.* In March 2003, the Circuit Court of Appeals for the District of Columbia had deferred to the White House with regard to the status of the 650 suspected terrorists and Taliban fighters held by the United States at the Guantanamo Bay naval base in Cuba. The government had never filed charges against any of the detainees and took the position that they could be held indefinitely "under the law of war" without legal process or access to counsel. In rejecting attorneys' motion for a writ of habeas corpus, the circuit court, citing the *Eisentragger* precedent, ruled that the detainees had no legal rights in the United States because, technically, they were being held on Cuban soil. The Supreme Court, though, reversed the lower court ruling, holding that Guantanamo Bay was territory under American jurisdiction, and so the prisoners were entitled to habeas corpus hearings. It was not clear how the decision would affect the thousands of foreigners detained by the United States in such places as Iraq and Afghanistan, and at least one justice, Antonin Scalia, vehemently rejected the idea that habeas corpus could be extended throughout the world.[115]

The third June 2004 case involved an American citizen, José Padilla, who was suspected by the government of conspiring with Islamic terrorists to explode a radiological "dirty bomb" in the United States. Padilla had been arrested at O'Hare Airport in Chicago and had subsequently been declared an enemy combatant by President Bush. As an enemy combatant, Padilla was subject to indefinite detention and possessed no legal rights. The Supreme Court declined on procedural grounds to rule on the Padilla case.[116]

Thus, in its June 2004 rulings, the Supreme Court did assert that presidential actions were subject to judicial scrutiny and place some constraints on the president's unfettered power. But at the same time, the Court affirmed the president's single most important claim—the unilateral power to declare individuals, including U.S. citizens, "enemy combatants" who could be detained by federal authorities under adverse legal circumstances. This hardly seems to threaten the foundations of the imperial presidency. Indeed, whatever the fate of Hamdi and the others classified as "enemy combatants," future presidents are likely to cite the Court's decisions as precedents for, rather than limits on, the exercise of executive power.

The President's Legislative Powers

The Constitution assigns the president significant legislative power in the form of the right to veto bills of which he disapproves. Over time, presidents have acquired additional legislative power. To begin with, presidents often recommend bundles of programs and policies such as Roosevelt's "New Deal" or Johnson's "War on Poverty" that shape Congress's legislative agenda. Second, under the terms of the 1921 Budget and Accounting Act, the president develops and submits to the Congress a unified executive budget.[117] Though Congress may revise the president's estimates, the executive budget usually becomes the template from which Congress works. Third, Congress is usually compelled to delegate considerable legislative power to the president to allow the executive branch to implement congressional programs. For example, if Congress wishes to improve air quality, it cannot possibly anticipate all the conditions and circumstances that may arise over the years with respect to its general goal. Inevitably, Congress must delegate to the executive substantial discretionary power to best bring about congressional aims in the face of unforeseen and changing circumstances. Thus over the years, almost any congressional program will result in thousands and thousands of pages of administrative regulations developed by executive agencies nominally seeking to implement the will of the Congress.

Such delegation is inescapable in the modern era, but it poses a number of problems for the Congress. If Congress delegates broad and discretionary authority to the executive, it risks seeing its goals subordinated to and subverted by those of the executive branch.[118] But if Congress attempts to limit executive discretion by enacting very precise rules and standards to govern the conduct of the president and the executive branch, it risks writing laws that do not conform to real-world conditions and that are too rigid to be adapted to changing circumstances.[119]

The issue of delegation of power has led to a number of court decisions over the past two centuries generally revolving around the question of the scope of the delegation. As a legal principle, the power delegated to Congress by the people through the Constitution cannot be redelegated by the Congress. This principle implies that directives from Congress to the executive should be narrowly defined and give the executive little or no discretionary power. A broad delegation of congressional authority to the executive branch could be construed as an impermissible redelegation of constitutional power. A second and related question sometimes brought before the courts is whether the rules and regulations adopted by administrators are consistent with Congress's express or implied intent. This question is closely related to the first because the broader the delegation to the executive, the more difficult it is to determine whether the actions of the executive comport with the intent of Congress.

With the exception of three cases from the New Deal era, the Court has consistently refused to enforce the nondelegation doctrine.[120] In the nineteenth century, for the most part, Congress itself enforced the principle of nondelegation by writing laws that contained fairly clear standards to guide executive implementation.[121] Congressional delegation tended to be either contingent or interstitial.[122] A contingent delegation meant that Congress had established a principle defining alternative courses of action. The executive was merely authorized to determine which of the contingencies defined by Congress applied to the circumstances at hand and to act accordingly. For example, the Tariff Act of 1890 authorized the president to suspend favorable tariff treatment for countries that imposed unreasonable duties on American products. In *Field v. Clark,* the Court held that this delegation was permissible because it limited the president's authority to ascertaining the facts of a situation. Congress had not delegated its lawmaking authority to the executive.[123] The Court also accepted what might be called interstitial rulemaking by the executive. This meant filling in the details of legislation where Congress had established the major principles. In the 1825 case of *Wayman v. Southard,* Chief Justice Marshall said Congress might lawfully "give power to those who are to act under such general provisions to fill up the details."[124] In 1928, the Court articulated a standard that, in effect, incorporated both these doctrines. In the case of *J. W. Hampton & Co. v. United States,* the Court developed the "intelligible principles" standard. A delegation of power was permissible "if Congress shall lay down by legislative act an intelligible principle to which [the executive] is directed to conform."[125]

As presidential power expanded during the New Deal era, one measure of increased congressional subordination to the executive was the enactment of laws that contained few, if any, principles limiting executive discretion. Congress enacted legislation, often at the president's behest, that gave the executive virtually unfettered authority to address a particular concern. For example, the Emergency Price Control Act of 1942 authorized the executive to set "fair and equitable" prices without offering any indication of what these terms might mean.[126] The Court's initial encounters with these new forms of delegation led to three major decisions in which the justices applied the "intelligible principles" standard to strike down delegations of power to the executive. In the 1935 *Panama* case, the Court held that Congress had failed to define the standards governing the authority it had granted the president to exclude oil from interstate commerce. In the *Schechter* case, also decided in 1935, the Court found that the Congress had failed to define the "fair competition" that the president was to promote under the National Industrial Recovery Act. In a third case, *Carter v. Carter Coal Co.,* decided in 1936, the Court concluded that delegating to the coal industry itself the authority to establish a code of regulations was impermissibly vague.[127]

These decisions were seen, with considerable justification, as a judicial assault on the New Deal and helped spark President Roosevelt's "court packing" plan. The Court retreated from its confrontation with the president and, perhaps as a result, no congressional delegation of power to the president has been struck down as impermissibly broad in the more than six decades since *Carter.* Instead, the Court has effectively rewritten the nondelegation doctrine in the form of the so-called *Chevron* standard. This standard emerged from the 1984 case of *Chevron v. Natural Resources Defense Council.*[128] An environmental group had challenged an Environmental Protection Agency (EPA) regulation as contrary to the intent of the statute that it was nominally written to implement. While a federal district court sided with the environmentalists against the agency, the lower court's decision was reversed by the Supreme Court. In its decision, the Supreme Court declared that so long as the executive developed rules and regulations "based upon a permissible construction" or "reasonable interpretation" of the statute, the judiciary would accept the views of the executive branch. This standard implies that considerable judicial deference should be given to the executive rather than to the Congress. Indeed the courts now look to the agencies to develop clear standards for statutory implementation rather than to the Congress to develop standards for the executive branch to follow.[129] In the 2001 case of *United States v. Mead Corp.*, the Court partially qualified the *Chevron* holding by ruling that agencies were entitled to *Chevron* deference only when they were making rules carrying the force of law, not when they were merely issuing opinion letters or undertaking other informal actions.[130] Despite this qualification, *Chevron* still applies to the most important category of administrative activity.

Two other cases concerning delegation of powers should be mentioned. These involve the legislative veto and the line-item veto. The legislative veto was a device often used by Congress to maintain some control over the executive's use of delegated powers. In the past, numerous statutes contained legislative veto provisions allowing one or both houses of Congress to reject actions by the president or executive agencies as inconsistent with congressional intent. But the *Chadha* case, noted earlier, struck down the one-house veto and raised serious questions about two-house veto provisions. Due to the Court's ruling in that case, which asserted that legislative veto provisions were separable from the statutes to which they were appended, restrictions on executive discretion were removed from more than two hundred statutes that had contained such provisions. As Silverstein observes, in its decisions the Court has effectively ruled that virtually any delegation of power to the executive branch is constitutional while devices designed to control delegation are unconstitutional.[131]

The major exception to this rule might appear to be the case of the line-item veto, invalidated by the Court in the case of *Clinton v. City of New York*.[132] Throughout the 1980s and 1990s, Republicans had argued that if the president had a line-item veto, it would allow him to delete fiscally irresponsible provisions of bills while preserving worthwhile legislation. The line-item veto became an important element in the GOP's "Contract with America," which served as the party's platform in the 1994 congressional elections. After Republicans won control of both houses of Congress that year, the party leadership felt compelled to enact a line-item veto even though the immediate effect of so doing so would be to hand additional power to Democratic president Bill Clinton. Many Republicans breathed a sigh of relief when the Court invalidated the measure. The actual impact of the line-item veto and the Court's decision was minor primarily because the United States of America does not employ a line-item budget. In most states, each budgetary outlay is, by law, a line item. In the federal budget, by contrast, Congress is free to lump together items as it sees fit and could prevent line-item vetoes by linking items the president opposed with those he strongly supported. Thus what appears to be the major exception to the rule of judicial support for increased presidential discretion is not that important of an exception. Over the past century, the federal courts have strengthened the legislative powers of the executive while showing scant concern for those of the legislature.

The President's Administrative Powers

A fourth realm in which the courts have helped to enhance the authority of the president is the area of executive power. Three issues, in particular, have been important. These are executive privilege, the power of appointment and removal, and executive orders. As for executive privilege, we noted at the beginning of the chapter that this concept had no firm standing in law until the Court's decision in *United States v. Nixon*. The actual term "executive privilege" was coined by President Eisenhower, who frequently refused to provide information to Congress when to do so, in his view, would violate the confidentiality of deliberations in the executive branch.[133] But long before Eisenhower introduced the phrase, presidents claimed the power to withhold materials from Congress and from the courts.[134] George Washington, for example, refused congressional requests for information about a disastrous campaign against the Indians and about the circumstances surrounding the negotiation of the Jay Treaty between the United States and Britain.

In the course of presiding over the criminal case against Aaron Burr, Chief Justice John Marshall gave some standing to such claims. Marshall indicated that in criminal cases the president could not be treated like an ordinary individual and might be compelled to produce evidence only if it was clearly shown by affidavit to be essential to the conduct of the case.[135] Because of the Watergate affair, the term "executive privilege" has developed a bad odor and subsequent presidents have sometimes used other phrases to deny congressional or judicial requests for information. For example, in refusing to allow the director of Homeland Security to testify before Congress in March 2002, President Bush asserted a claim of "executive prerogative."[136] In 2014, however, President Obama did use the term "executive privilege" in refusing to provide Congress with documents pertaining to an abortive "sting operation" by the Bureau of Alcohol, Tobacco, and Firearms that may have resulted in a Mexican drug gang acquiring firearms used in the murder of a U.S. Border Patrol agent and other crimes.

In *United States v. Nixon*, the Court, for the first time, explicitly recognized executive privilege as a valid presidential claim to be balanced against competing claims. The Court indicated that where important issues were at stake, especially foreign policy questions as well as military and state secrets, presidential claims of privilege should be given great deference by the courts. Finding no such issues in its present case, though, the Court ruled against Nixon. In a subsequent case, *Nixon v. Administrator of General Services,* the Court held that the former president's records were not privileged communications and could be transferred to the General Services Administration. Once again, though, the Court recognized the existence of executive privilege and said it could be used to protect the president's communications "in performance of [his] responsibilities . . . and made in the process of shaping policy and making decisions."[137] Thus, in both *Nixon* cases, precedents were established for claims of privilege, and in subsequent years the federal courts have upheld several such claims made by the president and other executive branch officials acting at the president's behest. For example, in *U.S. v. American Telephone & Telegraph,* in response to a presidential claim of privilege, the district court enjoined AT&T from providing a congressional subcommittee with the contents of a number of wiretaps conducted by the FBI.[138] Similarly, in *United States v. House of Representatives,* the district court refused to compel EPA administrator Anne Gorsuch to hand over to a House subcommittee what she claimed were privileged documents.[139]

In their more recent decisions, federal courts have continued to rule in favor of executive privilege in national security cases and others.[140] Both presidential deliberations and those of presidential advisers and their staffs have been held to be privileged.[141] The vice president has also claimed privilege, in *U.S. v. District Court for the District of Columbia.* In this case, a coalition of public interest groups, including Judicial Watch and the Sierra Club, sought to obtain the records of an energy task force led by Vice President Dick Cheney in 2001. The public interest groups brought the suit after a similar suit brought by the director of the General Accounting Office was dismissed for want of standing. The Cheney energy task force had been formed to make recommendations to the administration regarding federal energy policy. The public interest coalition charged that the task force gave inordinate influence to energy producers at the expense of consumer and environmental interests. A federal district court ordered Cheney to turn over his records. In a 7–2 opinion, however, the Supreme Court ruled that the vice president was entitled to the protection of executive privilege in order "to protect the executive branch from vexatious litigation that might distract it from the energetic performance of its constitutional duties."[142]

Another administrative realm in which the Court has generally shown deference to the president in recent decades is the area of appointment and removal. The president's appointment powers are defined in the Constitution and have produced little litigation. One important recent case, however, is *Buckley v. Valeo,* in which the Court ruled that Congress was not entitled to give itself the power to appoint members of the Federal Election Commission, an agency of the executive branch.[143] The removal power, by contrast, is not defined in the Constitution and has been a topic of some conflict between the president and Congress. In 1833, Congress censured President Jackson for removing the secretary of the treasury. In 1867, Congress enacted the Tenure of Office Act, which required Senate consent in order to remove cabinet officers over Andrew Johnson's veto. Johnson's subsequent attempt to remove Secretary of War Stanton played a major role in the president's impeachment. Congress enacted legislation in 1872 and 1876 requiring Senate consent for the removal of postmasters, but did repeal the Tenure of Office Act in 1887.[144]

The Supreme Court has made a number of decisions regarding the removal power that, for the most part, have supported the president. In the 1926 case of *Myers v. United States,* the Court struck down the 1876 law, ruling that the power to remove executive officials "is vested in the president alone."[145] In the 1935 case of *Humphrey's Executor v. United States,* however, the Court ruled against Franklin D. Roosevelt's efforts to remove a Federal Trade Commission (FTC) member before his term had expired. The Court noted that the FTC Act required the president to show cause for such actions and upheld Congress's right to impose such a requirement.[146] More recently, however, in the case of *Bowsher v. Synar,* the Court struck down a portion of the Gramm-Rudman-Hollings deficit reduction act, which had authorized the comptroller general, an official removable only by Congress, to review executive decisions.[147] And in *Mistretta v. United States,* the Court upheld the president's power under the Sentencing Reform Act to remove members of the U.S. Sentencing Commission, including federal judges.[148] In recent years, only in the politically charged cases involving special prosecutors have the courts significantly restricted presidential removal powers. In *Nader v. Bork,* the district court held that President Nixon's firing of Watergate special prosecutor Archibald Cox was illegal.[149] And in *Morrison v. Olson* the Supreme Court held that restrictions on the president's power to remove a special prosecutor did not invalidate the appointment.[150]

Finally, as for executive orders, it is sufficient to note that of the thousands of such orders that were issued from the birth of the republic through 1999, the overwhelming majority since 1933, one systematic study found that only fourteen were actually overturned by the courts. Of these fourteen, the federal judiciary struck down portions of twelve orders and overturned two others in their entirety.[151] One additional executive order was invalidated by a lower court in 2001.[152] Another 239 orders were modified or revoked by Congress between 1789 and 1999. One executive order overturned in its entirety was Truman's directive seizing the nation's steel mills, which was struck down in the *Youngstown* decision. A second was President

Clinton's order prohibiting the federal government from hiring permanent replacements for striking workers. This order, which contradicted both a Supreme Court ruling and specific federal legislation, was invalidated in the 1996 case of *Chamber of Commerce v. Reich.*[153] For the most part, the courts have been reluctant to examine executive orders, often ruling that the plaintiff lacked standing or that the dispute involved a political question. And when they have heard the case, they have almost always upheld the president's directive.[154]

Generally, the courts defer to the decisions of executive agencies and are satisfied if an agency's rulemaking process has complied with the provisions of the 1946 Administrative Procedure Act. This legislation requires agencies to give public notice of proposed rules (usually by publishing them in the *Federal Register*), to invite public comment, and to hold public hearings. The act does *not* require agencies to amend their proposals after receiving public comments.

An important recent decision that further enhanced administrative discretion came in the 2013 case of *City of Arlington v. FCC.*[155] The case concerned a provision of the Federal Communications Act that requires state and local governments to act on zoning applications for building wireless towers and antennas "within a reasonable period of time." The Federal Communications Commission (FCC) issued a ruling defining "reasonable period of time" as ninety days for modifications of existing facilities and 150 days for new ones. This may seem like a mundane ruling, but it has important implications. The plaintiff was arguing that the statute contained no provision authorizing the FCC to set rules defining "reasonable period of time." Hence, according to the plaintiff, the FCC was asserting a power that Congress never intended to grant. The Supreme Court's response, consistent with the *Chevron* doctrine, was that federal agencies should be seen as the best judges of their own power.

Thoughts about the Judiciary and Executive Power

Over the past century, the federal courts have bolstered the power of the executive branch and in particular, the presidency. To a considerable extent, the courts have reflected the changing realities of American political life. In the nineteenth century, Congress and the state legislatures were the dominant institutions of American government. Judges were typically recruited from the legislative arena and had reason to be confident that legislatures could govern. In the twentieth century, by contrast, the power of Congress waned, judges had little or no legislative experience, and increasingly, judges came to view the executive as the only branch of government capable of managing the nation's affairs. Congress may have looked to the courts for help in constraining presidential power, but the courts viewed Congress as incompetent at handling the nation's business and protecting its interests, especially in the realms of foreign policy and security affairs. Rather than delimiting the power of the president, then, they generally acted to expand the power of the presidency at the expense of the Congress.

It is notable that during six years of the Obama presidency, with a conservative majority on the Supreme Court, the president has suffered only one minor judicial setback—the recess appointments case. Meanwhile the chief justice in particular clearly labored over much more important cases to avoid giving offense to the president.

Perhaps the only realm in which the federal courts have served as a check on the White House is the area of the president's personal conduct. The Supreme Court has held, for example, that the president is not immune from civil suits relating to his person, as opposed to civil suits relating to official actions.[156] Yet even as the courts have recognized such limits on the conduct of the president, they have done much to remove those limits from the conduct of the presidency.

The President in Court

The federal courts can exert considerable power over the actions of the president. For example, in the course of undertaking judicial review of acts of Congress, the federal courts may, in effect, be ruling on the constitutionality of the president's legislative program. Moreover, the federal courts are often asked to rule on the propriety of presidential actions as well as the actions of executive agencies. The precise powers of the courts have been established through a series of judicial decisions that interpret and give meaning to the often ambiguous wording of the Constitution. In some instances the federal courts have clashed with the president. More often, though, the courts have found it expedient to defer to presidential authority.

Marbury v. Madison. In 1803, the Court was asked to rule on the constitutionality of an action by Secretary of State James Madison. Under the leadership of Chief Justice John Marshall, the Court declared not only that it had the power to review the actions of the executive branch, but also that the Judiciary Act of 1789 that had enabled Marbury to bring his claim to the Court was unconstitutional. In one fell swoop, Marshall claimed the power to review acts of Congress and of the president, all while prudently refraining from giving President Jefferson an opportunity to challenge his actions.

Frégate américaine, faisant sécher ses voiles.

Little v. Barreme. During America's undeclared naval war with France, an American frigate, the *USS Boston,* captured a Danish vessel sailing from a French port. The naval action was undertaken under orders from President Adams, though these orders seemed to contravene an act of Congress. In 1804 the Court held that the president could not lawfully order actions that contradicted congressional statutes.

United States v. Butler and the "court-packing" plan. In 1936, the Supreme Court struck down processing fees mandated by the 1933 Agricultural Adjustment Act. In response to this *Butler* decision and several other cases in which the Supreme Court had invalidated major pieces of New Deal legislation, President Roosevelt introduced a plan to increase the size of the Supreme Court, presumably to add enough liberal Democrats to the Court to ensure that New Deal programs would receive judicial approval. The court-packing plan provoked heated controversy but resulted in a judicial retreat that cheeky commentators called the "switch in time that saved nine."

Youngstown v. Sawyer. The Korean War strained resources at home. To avoid a steel strike that threatened military production during the conflict, President Truman ordered the mills seized and operated by federal authorities. In response to a complaint by the industry, the Court struck down Truman's order, ruling in 1952 that presidential actions must be based on constitutional or statutory authority. Though often treated as a landmark decision, the case has not particularly limited subsequent presidential actions.

United States v. Nixon. In 1974, President Richard Nixon refused to honor a congressional subpoena demanding that he turn over tapes that might show whether or not he had ordered illegal actions by his subordinates, claiming that the tapes fell under executive privilege. Congress asked the Supreme Court to order the president to turn over the tapes. In its ruling, the Court recognized the concept of executive privilege, but also determined that the special consideration did not apply in this

case. Nixon delivered a copy of the tapes that had been partially erased, though enough damaging information remained that he was forced to resign.

NFIB v. Sibelius. In 2012, the National Federation of Independent Business mounted a challenge to the constitutionality of the Affordable Care Act, or Obamacare. Commentators expected the Court's conservative majority to strike down the law as an unconstitutional expansion of the Commerce Clause. Chief Justice Roberts, however, sought to avoid a confrontation with the president and found reason to uphold the statute.

Here Americans learn how to sign up for a new health care plan using the Affordable Care Act's website.

NINE

Foreign Policy and National Security

In This Chapter

Management of America's relations with the outside world, in war as well as in times of peace, is at the heart of presidential power.[1] Presidential power in the realm of foreign relations is derived from Article II of the U.S. Constitution, which makes the president commander-in-chief of the nation's military forces and gives the chief executive the power to negotiate treaties, recognize foreign emissaries, and appoint ambassadors and consular officials. As is often the case, the precise meaning of these constitutional powers has been defined through practice and precedent. The Constitution also gives Congress important military and foreign policy powers, including the power to declare war, to raise armies, to regulate commerce with foreign nations and, in the case of the Senate, to ratify treaties and concur in the appointment of ambassadors. It is Congress, moreover, that must appropriate the funds to pay for presidential initiatives. To these various actors, the Constitution, as legal historian Edward Corwin has observed, proffered "an invitation to struggle" over who would control American foreign policy.[2]

How Presidents Came to Control Foreign Policy

As John Jay observed in *Federalist* 64, the president has a number of advantages in this struggle. The president is a unitary actor, with better access to information and a greater capacity for secrecy and action than the Congress.[3] Over the course of more than two centuries, moreover, successive American presidents, beginning with George Washington, have labored diligently to make their office the dominant force in American foreign and security policy and to subordinate Congress's role in this realm. From the perspective of 2016, it seems that they have succeeded.[4]

Already in 1793, President Washington initially accepted the French ambassador "Citizen" Genet, and several months later demanded his recall, both while deliberately refraining from consulting Congress.[5] During the same year, Washington issued a proclamation of American neutrality when war broke out between Great Britain and France, again, without congressional authorization.[6] In 1796, Washington refused to accede to congressional demands for documents relating to the negotiation of the Jay Treaty. Washington declared that in his judgment, the papers were "of a nature that did not permit disclosure at this time."[7] Indeed Washington was so determined to establish the primacy of the presidency in the realm of foreign policy that he objected vigorously to something as minor as a 1792 House resolution congratulating the French on their new constitution. Though the resolution was no more than a rhetorical gesture, Washington complained to his secretary of state, Thomas Jefferson, that Congress was seeking to "invade the executive."[8]

Washington's efforts to assert the primacy of the presidency in the foreign policy arena were strenuously defended by Alexander Hamilton. Writing under the pseudonym "Pacificus" in a series of 1793 articles in the *Gazette of the United States,* Hamilton argued that determining the direction of foreign policy was inherently the job of the executive.[9] He asserted, moreover, that the federal Constitution gave the president the power of initiative in foreign policy. The specific grants of power in the Constitution and their logical implications, he wrote, gave the executive the right to "determine the condition of the nation [and, if necessary,] to establish an antecedent state of things."[10] In other words, the president was free to undertake actions based on his judgment of the national interest and, if he deemed it appropriate, to confront the Congress and other governmental agencies with *faits accomplis.*[11]

The actions of subsequent presidents, from John Adams and Thomas Jefferson to George W. Bush and Barack Obama, have been consistent with Hamilton's vision of executive power. Thus America's second president, John Adams, dispatched a peace commission to France in 1799 despite the opposition of Congress and even the disapproval of most of his own cabinet members.[12] In a similar vein, America's third president, Thomas Jefferson, negotiated with France for the purchase of Louisiana and issued what today would be called an executive order consummating the bargain. Though Jefferson had previously condemned Hamilton's assertions of executive primacy in foreign affairs, as president he presented the Congress with a Hamiltonian *fait accompli* to which it gave its sullen acquiescence.[13]

Nearly two centuries later, in 1994, America's forty-second president, Bill Clinton, issued executive orders that provided Mexico with a $43 billion package of loans, including support from the International Monetary Fund and the International Bank of Settlements, to prevent the total collapse of the Mexican peso.[14] Congress had already rejected Clinton's request for a Mexican loan package. The president, however, believed that a Mexican economic crash would be disastrous for American economic interests and acted accordingly. In the wake of terrorist attacks in New York and Washington, America's forty-third president, George W. Bush, issued executive orders in 2001 that unleashed America's military might against the Taliban regime in Afghanistan and Saddam Hussein's regime in Iraq, created secret military tribunals for the prosecution of suspected foreign terrorists, established a program of international and domestic surveillance by the National Security Agency, and froze billions of dollars in foreign assets in the United States. Congress was barely consulted regarding any of these matters. The Obama administration, while withdrawing American forces from Iraq and Afghanistan, continued using special operations forces and unmanned aerial vehicles, popularly known as drones, to attack suspected terrorists, killing Al Qaeda leader Osama bin Laden, among others.

In 2015, President Obama signed an accord with Iran, promising to drop U.S. economic sanctions against the Iranians in return for Iran's promise not to build nuclear weapons. The president had previously agreed to submit any agreement to Congress for its approval, but the president subsequently stated that he would veto any congressional resolution of disapproval. Without waiting for Congress to act, Obama sent the agreement to the United Nations. On the basis of the proposed agreement, the U.N. authorized member states to immediately drop their economic sanctions against Iran, sharply reducing the effectiveness of any remaining American sanctions. The president, it seemed, had successfully circumvented Congress.

The U.S. Supreme Court has generally supported presidents' Hamiltonian view of their role in foreign policy. Justice Sutherland, citing John Marshall, declared in the landmark 1936 *Curtiss-Wright* case that the president was the "sole organ of the federal government in the field of international relations.[15] But while Congress nowadays usually defers to the president on foreign policy matters, it does not always give in to the chief executive. In 2015, for example, over President Obama's opposition, Congress invited Israeli prime minister Benjamin Netanyahu, a vehement foe of Obama's efforts to forge a nuclear arms treaty with Iran, to address a joint congressional session. Later, forty-seven Republican senators signed an open letter to the Iranian government designed to undercut Obama's negotiating stance.

Presidents and Their Advisers

Although during their terms U.S. presidents take the lead in foreign policymaking, before having the job most were domestic politicians whose chief interests and talents were in the realm of domestic policy. Among America's fourteen presidents during the past century, only four—Hoover, Eisenhower, Nixon, and George H. W. Bush—had extensive foreign policy experience before taking office; the others were forced to learn on the job.[16] During the 1992 presidential campaign, it was sometimes said that Bill Clinton's only international experience had been acquired at the International House of Pancakes. Clinton's immediate successors, George W. Bush and Barack Obama, similarly lacked foreign policy backgrounds.[17] All three presidents, like most of their predecessors, were nevertheless faced with momentous challenges to American security and to America's international interests. Bush, in particular, was compelled to develop a response to the September 11, 2001, terror attacks that destroyed the World Trade Center. By 2002, foreign policy had become the centerpiece of the Bush administration's agenda. In a June 1, 2002, speech at West Point, the president announced what came to be called the "Bush Doctrine" of unilateral action and preemptive war. Bush said that "our security will require all Americans . . . to be ready for preemptive action when necessary to defend our liberty and to defend our lives."[18] In his 2014 West Point speech, President Obama appeared to articulate a different policy when he said that the United States must reduce its reliance on military force and make more use of diplomacy.[19] But even though President Obama expressed reservations about unilateral preemption, during the Obama years America continued to launch many attacks against suspected terrorists before they were able to strike the United States.

As the dominant figure in the realm of American foreign and military policy, the president exercises substantial control over the nation's diplomatic and military institutions and so is in a position to decide with whom, when, and how the United States will interact in the international arena. Since World War II, for example, American military forces have fought in many parts of the world, including Korea, Indochina, the Middle East, Panama, and others. In every instance, the decision to commit troops to battle was made by the president, often without much consultation with the Congress. When President Obama ordered special operations soldiers to attack Osama bin Laden's compound in Pakistan, members of Congress learned of the operation and bin Laden's death from news broadcasts—just like other Americans. And it is the president and his emissaries who conduct negotiations with Russia, Iran, North Korea, and a host of other nations to deal with international problems and crises.

The president's foreign policy powers, particularly in the military realm, are far greater than the Constitution's framers had thought wise. The framers gave Congress the power to declare war, and made the president the nation's top military commander if and when Congress chose to go to war. Today, by contrast, presidents both command the troops and decide when to commit the nation to war.

The Foreign and National Security Policy Bureaucracy

Several government agencies play important roles in shaping and executing American foreign policy. These include the Treasury Department and the Commerce Department, as well as the departments of Defense and State, the Joint Chiefs of Staff, the Central Intelligence Agency (CIA), the National Security Council, the Department of Homeland Security, the Director of National Intelligence, the National Security Agency (NSA), and the Federal Bureau of Investigation (FBI). Because of the frequent intersections between foreign and domestic policy, other civilian agencies may become involved in foreign policy matters as well.

The National Security Council

The National Security Council, as described in Chapter 1, was created in 1947 as an entity within the Executive Office of the President to oversee the foreign policy establishment, to synthesize information coming from the bureaucracy, and to help the presidents develop their own foreign policy.[20] The council is a "subcabinet" made up of the president, the vice president, the secretaries of defense and state, plus other presidential appointees, including the heads of the CIA, Homeland Security, and the director of National Intelligence. Its heart is its staff, which consists of about two hundred subject-matter experts, often drawn from the academic world, who are capable of evaluating political, economic, and military events occurring worldwide. The head of the National Security Council's staff is the president's national security adviser.[21] Some national security advisers have been close presidential confidantes and have exercised considerable power because they had the president's ear and trust. For instance, Jimmy Carter seldom failed to consult Zbigniew Brzezinski on foreign policy and security matters, while both presidents Bush depended on the expertise of Brent Scowcroft.[22]

The State Department

Routine matters of international diplomacy come under the purview of the Department of State, which oversees more than three hundred U.S. embassies, consulates, and diplomatic missions around the world. Embassies are headed by ambassadors and consulates by consuls. Most embassy staff members are officers of the U.S. Foreign Service, the State Department's professional diplomatic corps. Some ambassadors, though, have no diplomatic expertise and are instead political appointees rewarded with an ambassadorial title for their campaign contributions to the president. Most of America's Western European embassies are nominally headed by political appointees but are actually run by their second in command, the deputy chief of mission, who is a foreign service professional.

The United States "recognizes" and maintains diplomatic relations with 186 countries. The United States does not recognize Iran or North Korea. Recognition means that the United States accepts the nation's government as lawful, will engage in routine trade and diplomatic exchanges with it, and will accept its citizens' passports for travel into America. To avoid angering India and China, respectively, the United States does not officially recognize Bhutan or Taiwan but is friendly with both and maintains diplomatic missions in both countries.

At the various embassies and other missions, State Department officials monitor American treaty and trade relations with the host country; they also provide assistance for American business interests and tourists and deal with foreign nationals attempting to emigrate to or visit the United States. Diplomatic officials are responsible for reporting on political and economic developments at their posts that might have implications for American policy. Some staff may officially or unofficially work for the CIA or other American intelligence services. Embassy staff are also tasked with developing good relations with prominent citizens of other nations in order to disseminate positive views of the United States and to secure information that might be useful to American interests. At the same time, the State Department monitors the conduct of the foreign nationals assigned to embassies and consulates in the United States. Though preventing outright foreign espionage is the responsibility of the FBI, the State Department is expected to keep an eye on the activities of foreign diplomats assigned by 176 nations to interact with the United States on American soil.

The State Department is headed by the secretary of state, a member of the president's cabinet and nominally America's most important foreign policy official after the president. The State Department was the first federal agency created by the first Congress in 1789, and the secretary's stature is underscored by the fact that he or she is fourth in line of succession to the presidency, behind the vice president, speaker of the House, and president pro tempore of the Senate. The secretary's actual importance varies with his or her relationship to the president. Some presidents completely ignore their secretaries. Franklin D. Roosevelt, for example, was barely aware that Cordell Hull existed, relegating him to an observer of the diplomatic scene. Other presidents rely heavily on their secretaries. The utterly inexperienced Harry Truman deferred to the very experienced Dean Acheson, who acted as the chief architect of U.S. foreign policy during the Truman years. In still other instances, presidents and secretaries work very well together and the secretary becomes the president's chief foreign policy adviser. Thus Richard Nixon and Henry Kissinger, George H. W. Bush and James David Baker, as well as George Bush and Condoleezza Rice, each worked closely together.

Some presidents use their secretaries as roving ambassadors more than advisers. John Kerry appeared to play this role in the Obama administration. But if the president is suspicious of the secretary's loyalty, the secretary is unlikely to play much of a part in making foreign policy. Thus George Bush did not take Colin Powell into his confidence, nor did Barack Obama rely much on the services of Hillary Clinton.

Major diplomatic initiatives are always undertaken at the behest of the president in consultation with the National Security Agency and, usually, the secretary of state. The president also attends a number of international conferences and is photographed in discussions with the heads of state of other important nations. Ceremonial visits to American allies and other important states are also made by the president, and foreign dignitaries are in turn hosted at the White House, in order to demonstrate America's friendship. These interactions are carefully orchestrated to ensure that no gaffes or breaches of protocol cause international hurt feelings.

Serious negotiations with other nations are usually handled by professional State Department diplomats deemed to have subject matter expertise as well as a good understanding of the priorities and sensibilities of their negotiating partners. The president is likely to become personally involved in only the highest-level talks. Usually talks begin at a lower level among professional diplomats; if progress is made, more important officials are summoned; and at the very end the president is called to meet with his counterpart to formally "seal the deal." Thus in the aftermath of the Russian annexation of Crimea, professional American and Russian diplomats were assigned to open talks, followed by meetings between U.S. Secretary of State John Kerry and Russian foreign minister Sergei Lavrov. When an agreement had been hammered out, President Obama and President Putin met, shook hands, and engaged in a brief round of credit claiming before each side accused the other of engaging in provocative acts. Relations deteriorated very sharply in 2014 when pro-Russian forces in Ukraine used a Russian-supplied missile to shoot down a Malaysian airliner that they apparently had mistaken for a Ukrainian transport plane.

Department of Defense

Since its creation in 1947 (when it was named the National Military Establishment), the Department of Defense has played a major role in the making of American foreign policy. The U.S. Department of Defense employs more than two million military and civilian personnel, and is a huge and complex bureaucratic entity whose organization charts fill many pages in the official *Department of Defense Organizations and Functions Guidebook.*[23] Reporting to the secretary of defense, known in Washington as the "SecDef," are twenty-seven assistant secretaries, undersecretaries, and directors, each of whom commands hundreds of staffers and is charged with such responsibilities as health affairs; budgets; and the acquisitions, testing, and evaluation of equipment and legal affairs. Working for these functionaries are tens of thousands of individuals in thirty-one agencies, including National Security, Geospatial Intelligence, Defense Intelligence, and Missile Defense. These and numerous other entities help to plan and sustain America's seemingly unending military efforts and allow America to put tens of thousands of combat troops into the field.

This set of agencies does not even include the three actual military services, each of which possesses its own civilian and military bureaucracies to administer and support its combat forces. A U.S. Army division, for example, will include, in addition to its combat troops, large numbers of military personnel, civilian employees, and civilian contractors whose functions include supply, maintenance, ordnance, ammunition support, quartermaster, transportation, finance, life support, signal infrastructure, public information, civil affairs, and administration. In the modern U.S. Army, approximately three noncombat personnel are devoted to the support of each combat soldier. This figure is sometimes known as the "tooth-to-tail ratio," or T3R, and some military analysts believe the Army's "tail" should be even longer to properly support its combat operations.[24] American combat forces are themselves exemplars of organizational complexity. A U.S. Army division, for instance, which typically deploys between ten and seventeen thousand troops, is usually composed of four brigades that are, in turn, divided into battalions that, in their turn, are composed of combat companies, each consisting of three platoons. Along with its combat companies (teeth) the division will include a host of logistical, administrative, and service units (tail) to provide the food, fuel, ammunition, and other supplies and services needed to support the division's activities.[25]

This entire military structure is, of course, supported by the vast industrial contracting system that developed during the Cold War and produces the aircraft, missiles, warships, tanks, electronics, transport systems, and other matériel and supplies on which the military depends. Though they are nominally civilian entities, such firms as Boeing, Lockheed Martin, Raytheon, Northrop Grumman, and General Dynamics are heavily dependent on military contracts and are functionally integrated into the military bureaucracies. Many of the executives of these firms, indeed, are retired military officers able to work closely with their still-serving counterparts. Military planning and research is undertaken by other private and quasi-private firms such as the RAND Corporation and the Institute for Defense Analysis. RAND and several of the others are technically "federally funded research and development centers"—that is, independent nonprofit corporations working for the federal government. RAND was originally created by the Douglas Aircraft Company to undertake research for the Air Force, and it continues to work primarily on Air Force projects.[26]

The Department of Defense implements American military policy by deploying troops anywhere in the world at the president's command. Increasingly, the department has assumed a leading nonmilitary, foreign policy role as well. To a significant extent, American foreign policy is driven by military and anti-terrorism concerns, and the agencies deemed capable of addressing these concerns are coming to play a larger and larger role in American foreign policy. In recent years, American ambassadors have complained that they have been relegated to secondary status as the White House has looked to military commanders for information, advice, and policy implementation. For every region of the world, the U.S. military has assigned a "combatant commander," always a senior general or admiral, to take charge of operations in that area. In many instances, these combatant commanders—who control troops, equipment, and intelligence capabilities—have become the real eyes, ears, and voices for American foreign policy in their designated regions. The combatant commanders report to the Joint Chiefs of Staff, who report to the secretary of defense, who in turn reports to the president.

Departments of Treasury and Commerce

The Treasury Department and Commerce Department coordinate America's international economic and monetary policies and work—along with the Office of the U.S. Trade Representative, housed in the Executive Office of the President—to implement America's international trade policies. The United States is the world's largest importer and exporter of goods and services. In 2013, the United States exported more than $1.5 trillion in goods and services while importing $2.2 trillion in goods and services. Roughly 11 million jobs in the United States are directly tied to international trade. Accordingly America has a vital interest in maintaining international trade and monetary practices that promote American prosperity. The United States works to discourage other nations from erecting tariff barriers to American goods and to maintain exchange rates between the dollar and other currencies that do not price American goods out of foreign markets, or flood the American market with foreign goods. The United States is also alert to efforts by other nations to drive American manufacturers out of business by underpricing exports, a practice known as "dumping," or stealing American technology through reverse engineering or outright piracy. Much of the current tension between the United States and China is a result of American charges that China engages in unfair trade practices—charges denied by China. The departments of Treasury, Commerce, and the U.S. Trade Representative are continually engaged in negotiations with America's trading partners, while overall policy is generally set by executive agreements negotiated between the White House and other nations.

Trade can become a weapon if the president declares that the United States will impose trade sanctions against another nation. Thus, for example, on the basis of Clinton and Bush executive orders as well as legislation enacted in 2010, the United States cut off all trade with Iran in an attempt to force that nation to halt its nuclear weapons program. The nuclear agreement between the U.S. and Iran negotiated in 2015 promised an end to the embargo in exchange for an Iranian promise to halt nuclear weapons development. The United States also maintains trade embargoes against North Korea. In 2014, the Obama administration imposed trade sanctions against Russia for its annexation of the Crimean Peninsula and to deter the Kremlin from further actions against Ukraine. A number of European nations resisted following America's lead because trade with Russia is important to their own economies, so the impact of the sanctions was not as severe as President Obama had hoped.

Of course, trade can be used as a carrot as well as a stick. By signing trade agreements with other nations, the United States promises to give them access to American markets. The North American Free Trade Agreement among the United States, Mexico, and Canada was, in part, an effort to strengthen Mexico's economy—and reduce Mexican immigration to the United States. The Commerce Department is the main agency monitoring compliance with the terms of NAFTA, and it frequently investigates charges of dumping made by American companies.

Intelligence Agencies

The CIA is America's chief civilian intelligence agency, collecting information throughout the world, preparing analyses, and launching covert operations if the president wishes to use force but is unwilling to acknowledge publicly America's involvement. CIA operators also pilot many of the drones used to attack and kill suspected terrorists. The CIA and Department of Defense were created by the same piece of legislation, but the secretary of defense and CIA director have generally viewed one another as rivals in the intelligence field. The secretary of defense controls substantial intelligence assets, including the Defense Intelligence Agency, that dwarf those of the CIA. In 2005, Congress created the position of director of national intelligence to coordinate intelligence activities and prepare the president's daily intelligence summary—a responsibility previously held by the CIA's director. This change came about because Congress believed that the intelligence community's failure to anticipate the 9/11 attacks was the result of a lack of coordination among the various agencies. Both the CIA and Department of Defense resented the creation of the director of national intelligence. They put aside their mutual suspicions to join forces against the interloper and have generally refused to share information with that person, who has no operational capabilities and so has been left in the dark on many intelligence matters. As was noted in Chapter 5, national intelligence agencies seem generally to regard one another as rivals, which they are for budgetary purposes. This phenomenon is not unique to the United States. In the former Soviet Union some in the military intelligence community would say that the Americans were the adversary but the KGB, the civilian intelligence agency, was the enemy.

Two other important executive agencies in the intelligence field are the FBI and the Department of Homeland Security. The FBI is generally responsible for the collection and analysis of intelligence data in the Western Hemisphere, since the CIA is barred by law from operating in the United States. The Department of Homeland Security was established after 9/11 through a merger of twenty-two existing agencies. One agency within DHS is Immigration and Customs Enforcement, which is charged with maintaining border security and enforcing America's immigration policies.

The National Security Agency

One additional intelligence agency worth discussing at length because of the enormous concern caused by its intelligence-gathering activities in recent years is the National Security Agency (NSA). Though housed within the Department of Defense, the NSA effectively reports directly to the president and provides the chief executive with the results of its worldwide electronic surveillance efforts. Surveillance of electronic communication has a long history in the United States, going back to a World War I government effort to read suspicious telegrams.[27] During the 1970s, however, Congress became concerned about a variety of secret White House surveillance efforts and in 1978 enacted the Foreign Intelligence Surveillance Act (FISA), which was designed to regulate electronic surveillance by government agencies.

The FISA stipulated that in order to undertake electronic surveillance of Americans, the government would be required to apply for a warrant from a special court created by the statute. This Foreign Intelligence Surveillance Court, known as the FISA Court, initially consisted of seven federal district-court judges who were appointed for seven-year terms by the chief justice of the U.S. Supreme Court. In 2001, it was expanded to eleven judges. A second court created by the act, the Court of Review, consisted of a three-judge panel empowered to hear appeals by the government of negative decisions by the FISA Court. In practice, the review court has been relatively quiescent since the government has had reason to appeal only a handful of the FISA Court's decisions. Both the FISA Court and Court of Review deliberate in secret and the content of their decisions is not made public.

According to the terms of FISA, the FISA Court would issue a warrant only if it found probable cause to believe that the target of the surveillance was acting in concert with a foreign power or agent. The 1978 act defined foreign power as a nation-state, but this was subsequently amended to include non-state actors such as terrorist groups. The act also allowed the president to authorize warrantless surveillance within the United States if the attorney general certified to the FISA Court that the target was a foreign intelligence agent, and if there was little chance that the privacy of any American citizen would be violated.

The effectiveness of the FISA process has been debated. On the one hand, between 1979 and 2012 only eleven of the nearly 34,000 requests for warrants made by government agencies, primarily the NSA and FBI, were turned down by the FISA Court.[28] This datum might suggest that the court was lax in its procedures. On the other hand, it may be that the FISA process forced the government to exercise at least some measure of caution in its surveillance activities, knowing that requests would need to withstand judicial scrutiny. Support for this latter view might be derived from the fact that following the 9/11 terror attacks, the Bush administration, determined to expand electronic data collection, decided to sidestep the FISA process and launch a large-scale program of warrantless wiretapping.

What would later be called the President's Surveillance Program, launched in 2001, involved warrantless monitoring of virtually all telephone calls and email messages between the United States and foreign countries. As in previous major surveillance efforts, the NSA, in collaboration with several other federal agencies, was able to secure secret cooperation from the major telecommunications companies for this purpose. The result was that millions of telephone and email conversations were monitored. In some instances, voice intercept operators actually listened to the calls. More often, the information was stored, subjected to keyword searches, and with the advent of the Defense Advanced Research Projects Agency (DARPA) total information awareness program in 2002, combined with other data such as credit card usage, social network posts, traffic camera photos, and even medical records so that NSA could search for suspicious patterns of activity.

Information not available electronically could be obtained by the FBI, which, via secret national security letters authorized by the 2001 Patriot Act, has compelled a variety of institutions ranging from universities to gambling casinos to turn over student or customer information without informing the subject. Congress ended DARPA funding for the total information awareness program in 2004, but by then the methodology had become well developed. In addition, tens of thousands of national security letters have been issued annually since 2001. These permit the collection of data that, particularly in conjunction with communications intercepts, allow federal authorities to learn an enormous amount about the activities of any individual or group.

In response to *New York Times* articles published in 2005 revealing the existence of the President's Surveillance Program, several members of Congress expressed outrage at what they saw as violations of FISA and vowed to fully investigate the matter. The Bush administration, however, was able to convince Congress that its actions had been necessary if not entirely legal means of thwarting terrorism. After some deliberation, Congress enacted the Protect America Act of 2007, which amended FISA to loosen restrictions on electronic surveillance and so, in effect, retroactively codified the legally questionable actions of previous years.[29] Thus under the amended act, the government was empowered to intercept communications that began or ended outside the United States without any supervision by the FISA Court. Moreover, telecommunications companies, whose cooperation had previously been voluntary, were directed to lend assistance to federal agencies engaged in electronic surveillance if ordered to do so by the government, and were immunized against any civil suits that might arise from providing such assistance.

The 2007 act contained a sunset provision requiring Congress to reconsider the surveillance issue in 2008. The resulting Amendments Act of 2008 was similar to the 2007 act, but did place restrictions on the power of NSA and other intelligence agencies to target Americans. At President Obama's behest, the act was renewed in 2012 for another five years. Between 2008 and 2013, the government insisted that it was not engaged in spying on Americans either at home or abroad. In March 2013, for example, Director of National Intelligence James Clapper, when testifying before the Senate, indignantly denied reports that the government was collecting data on millions of Americans. Similarly, NSA director General Keith Alexander denied charges by a former NSA official that the agency was secretly obtaining warrantless access to billions of records of Americans' phone calls and storing the information in its data centers.[30]

In June 2013, however, an NSA contractor named Edward Snowden leaked classified documents describing NSA's theretofore top-secret PRISM surveillance program, which had operated since 2007. Snowden's disclosures were published in the *Guardian* and *Washington Post* and revealed that through PRISM and several other programs, including BLARNEY, FAIRVIEW, LITHIUM, and the UPSTREAM surveillance of fiber optic cables, the NSA had been collecting data on its own as well as collaborating with virtually all major telecommunications companies to intercept, examine, and store the electronic communications of millions of Americans. These included emails, social network posts, Internet searches, and even local telephone calls. In essence, the NSA appeared to have the capacity to monitor all forms of electronic communication. The agency was storing monitored communications and was indeed in the process of constructing a huge new storage center in Utah in anticipation of a growing need for much greater storage capability.

While NSA's stated goal is to monitor communications between the United States and foreign countries, officials acknowledge that some purely domestic communications have been accidentally accessed but said they did not keep records of the number. Communications among Americans nominally cannot be viewed without a warrant from the FISA Court but, in practice, said one official who did not wish to be named, this rule is frequently violated. The NSA essentially is responsible for policing itself and according to one telecommunications executive formerly involved in the NSA program, whatever the nominal legal restrictions, "there's technically and physically nothing preventing a much broader surveillance."[31] A lawsuit that brought about the declassification in 2013 of a 2011 FISA Court opinion revealed that the NSA had been accessing as many as 56,000 "wholly domestic" communications each year without warrants. In the opinion, the then–chief judge of the FISA Court, Judge John D. Bates, clearly angry, wrote, "For the first time, the government has now advised the court that the volume and nature of the information it has been collecting [are] fundamentally different from what the court had been led to believe."[32]

Most of the data collected by the NSA apparently consisted of so-called metadata—that is, the times, senders, and recipients, but not the actual content of the communication. The NSA asserts that metadata are not covered by FISA. Consider, however, that through the successors to the Total Information Awareness program, the NSA and other federal agencies have the ability to use even these metadata in conjunction with other data sources to obtain a very good picture of the friends, activities, and proclivities of any American. Moreover, whether purposefully or accidentally, NSA has examined the actual contents of many tens of thousands of calls made by Americans within the United States without obtaining authorization from the FISA Court. According to some sources, NSA training manuals explain to data collectors and analysts how to record intercepts without providing "extraneous information" that might suggest that the actions were illegal if they happened ever to be audited.[33] As for the FISA Court, which is nominally charged with ensuring that the government does not violate laws governing surveillance activities, its chief judge, Reggie B. Walton, said in a written statement to the *Washington Post* that the court had no investigative powers and instead relied on the government itself to report any improper actions by its agents.[34]

In an August 2013 speech, President Obama addressed public concerns about the government's surveillance programs. The president pointed to the importance of interdicting terrorist attacks, declared himself to be confident that Americans' rights had not been abused, and said he hoped that ways could be found to make the public more "comfortable" with government surveillance activities. Unfortunately, given the history of government surveillance, there is little reason for Americans to feel a sense of comfort. Using methods that seem primitive today, J. Edgar Hoover's FBI collected information that made and broke political careers, disrupted dissident groups, and interfered with ordinary partisan politics. And much of what Hoover did was undertaken at the behest of the various presidents whom he served. From Franklin Roosevelt to Richard Nixon, and possibly since, presidents could not resist the chance to collect information to be used against their political foes as well as against dissident political forces.

Congress versus the President: An Unequal Battle

Our discussion of executive powers and institutions in the realm of foreign policy would be incomplete if we failed to consider the history and origins of these institutions and how their construction reflected and reinforced presidential power in the realm of foreign policy. In particular, the creation of the Defense Department, the various intelligence agencies, the National Security Council, and even the seemingly mundane office of the U.S. Trade Representative were the results of struggles for power in Washington that greatly bolstered presidential influence in the realms of defense, security, and foreign policy. Sometimes we tend to see great institutions of government as "givens" and fail to ask why they were established, by whom, for what purposes, and with what consequences. When we ask these questions, our attention becomes focused on the great institutional struggle between Congress and the executive that has been waged since our nation's founding.

Despite presidential efforts to monopolize foreign and security policy, from the time of the nation's founding the Congress has also sought to play a major role in both areas. Indeed, writing in response to letters by Hamilton ("Pacificus"), James Madison, using the pseudonym "Helvidius," argued that the president's powers in foreign affairs were instrumental only. That is, it was Congress's constitutional role to determine the substance and direction of American foreign policy while the task of the president was limited to implementing the will of the legislature.[35] The Constitution, as noted earlier, assigns the Congress specific powers in the realm of foreign affairs, including the power to declare war, the power to raise armies, and the power to regulate foreign commerce. On the basis of this constitutional authority, Congress has enacted numerous pieces of trade legislation; authorized the recruitment, training, and equipment of military forces; and, on at least one occasion—the War of 1812—declared war over the objections of the president. Not unlike presidents, Congress has occasionally sought to use its constitutionally mandated powers to claim additional powers as well. For example, when Congress declared war against Spain in 1897, it included recognition of the independence of Cuba in its resolution, even though President McKinley was opposed to recognizing the Cuban insurgent government.[36]

Through its general legislative powers, moreover, Congress can exercise broad influence over foreign policy. Congress may, for example, refuse to appropriate funds for presidential actions that it deems to be unwise or inappropriate. Thus in 1796 the House of Representatives was asked to appropriate funds to implement the Jay Treaty. Opponents of the treaty demanded that the House be given all papers and records pertaining to the negotiating process—a demand rejected by President Washington. The House narrowly approved funding but accompanied its acquiescence with a resolution affirming its right to refuse appropriations for the implementation of any treaty to which a majority of its members objected.[37] And on several occasions over the years, the House has indeed refused to appropriate funds needed to implement treaties negotiated by the president and ratified by the Senate.[38]

This power of the purse also extends to military action. Not only does Congress have the constitutional power to declare war, but also, under its general legislative powers, it must appropriate the funds needed to support military activities. In *Federalist* 69, Hamilton argues that Congress's power of the purse provides it with an ultimate check on the president's power as commander-in-chief.[39] This principle was illustrated during the Reagan administration when Congress enacted the so-called Boland Amendment. This piece of legislation prohibited the president from using any funds to provide military support for right-wing "Contra" guerilla forces in the civil war then raging in the nation of Nicaragua. The administration's response was to seek funds from Saudi Arabia, the Sultan of Brunei, and even from private individuals. This attempt to circumvent Congress's authority sparked the 1986 congressional Iran-Contra investigations, which led to criminal convictions for several high-ranking administration officials.

If foreign policy entailed only matters of trade, recognition, international accords, and other peacetime pursuits, the constitutional struggle between the president and Congress might have gone on indefinitely without any conclusive resolution. Unfortunately, however, throughout the nation's history, war and military affairs have been central foci of American foreign policy. Though the United States has fought only five formally declared wars, American armed forces have been involved in hundreds of military actions and "small wars" in every corner of the world.[40] America's first small war, the 1801 naval campaign against the Barbary States, involved a handful of ships and generated few casualties. Other so-called small wars have been quite large. American military action in Korea and Vietnam, for example, required the mobilization of hundreds of thousands of troops and resulted in tens of thousands of casualties.

Whether declared or undeclared, large or small, war has been the crucible of presidential power. During the nineteenth and early twentieth centuries, wartime expansion of presidential power tended to be temporary, generally limited to the duration of the war. In some respects, as we shall see, war mobilized the populace and empowered the Congress as much as it strengthened the presidency. Beginning with the Cold War, however, and perhaps even more markedly in recent years, preparation for war has helped presidents to substantially reshape the constitutional balance of power among the major institutions of government.

The Presidential Sword

In wartime, Congress has generally deferred to the president's leadership. Indeed, Congress has often granted presidents significant emergency powers and acceded to presidential claims of authority under the Constitution's commander-in-chief clause when urgent wartime conditions seemed to justify such approvals. Expansion of presidential power during wartime was particularly manifest during the Civil War and during World Wars I and II.

The Civil War

After the fall of Fort Sumter and the outbreak of the Civil War, President Lincoln, as we saw in Chapter 2, issued a series of executive orders for which he had no clear legal basis. In almost every instance, Congress subsequently enacted legislation legitimating the president's actions. Thus after the president ordered the expansion of the Army and Navy, Congress enacted legislation to that effect. Similarly, after the president instituted military conscription, Congress voted a draft law. And after the president ordered the creation of military commissions to try individuals accused of treason against the United States, Congress enacted legislation governing the organization and conduct of such commissions. For its part, in the 1863 Prize Cases the Supreme Court upheld the president's power to order a blockade of the Southern ports.[41] In the 1866 case of *Ex parte Milligan,* however, the Court rejected the president's suspension of habeas corpus and indiscriminate use of military tribunals in areas of the nation that were not actually theaters of military operations—even as it recognized the president's power to declare martial law and to suspend civil liberties in areas actually subject to military threat.[42]

World War I

Reflecting the state of emergency that existed after the initiation of hostilities in 1861, the Civil War pattern of presidential power enhancement was action by the president followed by congressional acquiescence. World War I, by contrast, was fought far from American soil and under circumstances that permitted reflective rather than reflexive congressional action. In some instances Wilson, like Lincoln, claimed powers under the "commander-in-chief" clause without waiting for Congress to act. For example, the president created a number of new executive agencies—including the Committee on Public Information, which was charged with disseminating government propaganda to the American public—without seeking specific congressional approval. For the most part, however, throughout the war, President Wilson sought legislative authority for his actions. And for the most part, Congress obliged by voting to grant the president extraordinary powers, not only over the organization of America's armed forces but also, on the theory that war required mobilization of economic as well as military might, over the nation's farms, mines, and factories as well. Thus over a period of less than two years, Congress enacted legislation that gave the president discretionary authority to mobilize and organize the nation's human resources and productive capabilities.

The 1916 and 1917 National Defense acts authorized the president in times of war to place obligatory orders with any firm for any product or material needed for the nation's defense. The 1917 Selective Service Act gave President Wilson the authority to raise an army through nationwide military conscription, while the Espionage Act made it unlawful to interfere with military recruitment. The Lever Food and Fuel Control Act authorized the president to regulate the manufacture, mining, and distribution of all articles he deemed necessary to the war effort: the power to requisition food and fuel; the power to take over and operate factories, mines, pipe lines, and storage facilities; and the power to set prices for food and fuel. The Trading with the Enemy Act gave the president additional emergency economic powers and empowered him to censor all communications with foreign countries. The Shipping Act gave the president authority to ration space for truck, rail, and ship cargo. Other statutes authorized the president to regulate foreign-language newspapers in the United States, and to take over and operate the nation's rail and water transport systems as well as its telephone and telegraph systems.[43] The Overman Act allowed Wilson to rearrange executive departments, their duties, and their jurisdictions without congressional approval. The president averred that such reorganization authority was needed in order to facilitate the national mobilization for war, but even the act's proponents acknowledged that it came close to giving the president dictatorial powers.[44]

Under the authority of these pieces of legislation, President Wilson created a number of sizeable new executive agencies such as the U.S. Food Administration and the U.S. Fuel Administration, both established to implement the Lever Act. The Fuel Administration proceeded to implement fuel rationing plans, including "heatless Mondays," while the Food Administration introduced price controls and distribution controls as well as rationing for major commodities such as beef.[45] Wilson used the Overman Act to reorganize agencies associated with wartime mobilization. His most important step was to separate an obscure agency called the War Industries Board from the National Defense Council. Wilson made the War Industries Board directly responsible to him and gave it enormous power to regulate the economy. Relying on a mix of threats and negotiation, the board set prices in such major industries as chemicals, textiles, metal, and construction and represented one of the most comprehensive intrusions of government into the marketplace ever attempted in the United States.[46]

Relying on the nominal authority given to him by Congress, Wilson also issued numerous executive orders aimed at both military and civilian functions. For example, he ordered the War Department to impose censorship on all telephone and telegraph lines, suspended civil service hiring rules for all government agencies, and discontinued the eight-hour work day for federal employees.[47] Among

Wilson's most important executive orders was his proclamation of December 26, 1917, that initiated a takeover of the nation's railroads, whose operations he deemed to have been hobbled by labor strife, car shortages, and traffic problems. The president created a U.S. Railroad Administration, headed by Treasury Secretary William McAdoo, which operated the rail lines until 1920, when they were returned to their former owners.

In a series of cases decided after the war, the U.S. Supreme Court upheld virtually all the president's actions as well as Congress's decisions to delegate enormous powers to the executive branch. In particular, the Court upheld the constitutionality of the government's takeover of the railroads, imposition of censorship, and enactment of military conscription laws. "In war," said Chief Justice White, the scope of governmental power becomes "highly malleable."[48] Even the limits on free speech brought about under the Espionage Act passed constitutional muster because, in the words of Justice Holmes, "When a nation is at war, many things that might be said in time of peace [are not] protected by any constitutional right."[49] Thus for the Court as for the Congress, the exigencies of war justified an enormous expansion of the powers for the chief executive.

World War II

World War II paved the way for an even more substantial expansion of presidential power than had occurred during the Civil War or World War I. As they had during World War I, members of Congress delegated substantial military and civil powers to the president. And what Congress did not give him by statute, President Roosevelt took by executive order. Even before the Japanese attack on Pearl Harbor brought America into the war, FDR sought to prepare the nation for armed conflict and endeavored to provide American support for Great Britain in its life-and-death struggle against Nazi Germany. As early as 1938, Roosevelt issued an executive order authorizing the Army to sell older weapons to private contractors who would then be free to sell them abroad. This was a thinly disguised ploy to sell weapons and munitions to Britain. Little more than a year later, after the fall of France, the administration made use of the same order to send more than a half million rifles and other arms and ammunition to the beleaguered British.[50]

Still later in 1940, the president violated the recently enacted Neutrality Act, as well as several other federal laws, by ordering the transfer to Britain of fifty U.S. Navy destroyers in exchange for the lease of sites for naval bases. Roosevelt was responding to an urgent plea from British prime minister Winston Churchill, who informed the president that nearly half of Britain's destroyer fleet had been lost, crippling the kingdom's capacity to protect its shipping from German U-boats. Roosevelt knew that Congress would not agree to the sale but decided he must proceed nevertheless. When the deal was announced, Attorney General Jackson argued that despite its apparent illegality, the exchange of destroyers for bases was validated by the president's constitutional authority as commander-in-chief, which gave him the power to "dispose" the armed forces of the United States. Jackson construed the term "dispose" as including "dispose of."[51] In March 1941, Congress enacted the Lend-Lease Act, which effectively ratified Roosevelt's policy of providing material aid to Great Britain.

In another executive order, issued in 1937, Roosevelt referred to an unnamed unit within the Executive Office of the President that would deal with unspecified emergencies. In 1940, the president issued a new executive order naming the unit the Office for Emergency Management. Roosevelt assigned the office major responsibilities for military preparedness and mobilization.[52] In the early years of the war, FDR used it as the institutional base for the creation of dozens of new wartime agencies such as the Office of Civilian Defense, the War Labor Board, the Office of Censorship, and the Office of Production Management.[53] These agencies, all created by executive orders, gave the president enormous direct power over the civilian economy and the life of the nation.

In May 1941, with war looming, Roosevelt declared a state of national emergency and issued a number of executive orders designed to promote military readiness. The next month, he issued an executive order seizing a North American Aviation plant in California where a labor dispute was threatening the production of fighter aircraft. Other plants threatened by strikes were subsequently commandeered.[54] Also acting on his own initiative, and without consulting Congress, Roosevelt sent American troops to garrison Greenland and Iceland in the spring of 1941 to thwart the threat of a German attack. During the same period, again without congressional authorization, the president ordered the U.S. Navy to protect American shipping in the North Atlantic and to "shoot-at-sight" any attackers.[55] This order effectively linked America to Britain's military efforts and brought the nation within a hair's breadth of war with Nazi Germany.

Throughout this prewar period, FDR faced enormous opposition from isolationist and pro-German forces in Congress, including even the congressman from his own home district, Representative Hamilton Fish of New York. Fish actually employed a number of anti-Semitic and pro-German staffers in his congressional office.[56] Despite such obstacles, the president was able to secure the enactment of several important pieces of legislation, in addition to the Lend-Lease Act mentioned earlier, that were designed to grant power to the White House so it could more effectively promote American security interests. The first was the September 1940

Selective Service Act, which authorized the president to reinstitute military conscription in the form of one year of compulsory military training and service for as many as 900,000 men. The draft law faced bitter opposition, especially in the West and Midwest where isolationist sentiment was strongest, but FDR launched an all-out and ultimately successful campaign to woo wavering legislators, promising that conscripts would only defend the shores of the United States and would never be sent outside the Western Hemisphere.[57]

The Selective Service Act also reinstated the provisions of the 1917 National Defense Act, which had authorized the president to require plants and factories to suspend other operations if he deemed their facilities necessary for the production of ships, munitions, or other war matériel. Subsequently, Congress authorized the president to establish production priorities for all factories, giving precedence not only to military hardware, but also to any goods he deemed necessary to the nation's defense.[58] In the summer of 1941, the first group of conscripts was nearing the end of its specified year of service. The president asked Congress to formally extend the period of service to two years. Despite the urgency of the times, the extension bill faced strong opposition. Finally, a six-month extension of service passed the House by a margin of only one vote.

A second important piece of prewar legislation was a 1940 act expanding the power of the Reconstruction Finance Corporation, which had been established earlier as a New Deal effort to spur business investment. In 1940, the Reconstruction Finance Corporation was given a new mandate to make government loans and investments aimed at ensuring the acquisition and production of materials and goods that the president said were needed for purposes of defense. It was also empowered to create government corporations or other entities for the purpose of producing strategic goods. During the war years, this corporation and its numerous subsidiaries engaged in a variety of economic activities, including rubber production, petroleum distribution, and insurance underwriting.[59]

The Japanese attack on Pearl Harbor ended debate over the wisdom of American involvement in the war. Pearl Harbor also brought an end to congressional resistance to conferring emergency powers upon the president. Within two weeks of the initiation of hostilities, Congress began to provide the president with an enormous array of economic as well as military powers designed to allow him to mobilize the nation for global war. In December 1941, Congress enacted the First War Powers Act, which, like the World War I Overman Act, gave the president the power to redistribute functions among executive agencies in any manner he saw fit. The act also gave the president the authority to regulate international financial transactions and censor private communications with any and all foreign countries.[60] Several months later, Congress enacted the Second War Powers Act, which allowed the president complete control over the distribution of scarce materials. This act also gave the Federal Reserve the authority to purchase government securities directly from the U.S. Treasury in order to finance the government deficits that would almost certainly be brought about by the war.

Another major piece of legislation, the Emergency Price Control Act, was enacted in January 1942, one month after the Pearl Harbor attack. The act established an Office of Price Administration with broad authority to control prices and rents. The purpose of the legislation was to prevent wartime inflation so as to make certain that the government could purchase needed goods at a low price. Inevitably, though, price controls produced shortages of many commodities, including gasoline, meat, and coffee. The Office of Price Administration then instituted a rationing system for such commodities that was retained throughout the war. In October 1942, Congress augmented the price control act by passing the Economic Stabilization Act, which expanded the president's control over wages and prices and paved the way toward a more comprehensive national economic policy.[61] The president received other emergency economic powers under the War Labor Disputes Act, which granted broad authority to seize companies threatened by strikes; the War Mobilization and Conversion Act; and a host of other pieces of legislation that left the White House in full control of the American economy.

As was true of the Civil War and World War I, the Supreme Court generally acquiesced in the expansion of presidential power during World War II. In *Yakus v. United States,* for example, the Court ruled that the Emergency Price Control Act was a proper delegation of power to the president.[62] In *Bowles v. Willingham,* the Court upheld the Office of Price Administration's control of apartment rents.[63] In *Korematsu v. United States,* the Court refused to invalidate Roosevelt's Executive Order 9006, ordering the internment of Japanese Americans.[64] In a similar vein, the Court ruled that under his powers as commander-in-chief, the president had the authority to establish a special military commission, outside the ambit of the civilian courts, to try eight Nazi agents, one of them an American citizen, who had entered the United States in 1942 for the avowed purpose of committing acts of sabotage.[65] In times of war, the Court was willing to allow the president broad leeway. Indeed, the war power did not automatically end with the war. In the 1948 case of *Woods v. Miller,* the Court ruled that a 1947 rent control statute was justified by the postwar housing shortage. "The war power," said Justice Douglas, "does not necessarily end with the cessation of hostilities."[66]

After the War: Reassertion of Congressional Power

James Madison had been determined to place the Constitutional war power in the collective hands of the Congress. Madison thought that executives, be they kings or presidents, had a tendency to become too fond of war. Congressional war powers, Madison thought, would leash what he and Jefferson liked to call the "dogs of war." Presidents and kings tended to see only the benefits of war, while members of Congress, who represented those who actually fought and died in wars, were inclined to be more cognizant of the costs.[67]

For more than a century, the Madisonian formula was effective. Congressional war powers, coupled with a lively popular politics, helped correct and curtail the expanded presidential war powers. Congress proved able to take back what it had given to the president during the period of national emergency. Sometimes kicking and screaming, the presidential genie was usually returned to its bottle soon after the guns were silenced. This process was made easier in part because many of the powers granted to the president were specifically military in character and lost their significance with the war's end. This was true of most of Lincoln's emergency powers, which, as the president said, "would be greatly diminished by the cessation of actual war."[68] After World War I, Congress moved to revoke the emergency military and economic powers that it had granted to President Wilson. Thus, by early 1920, the War Industries Board, Fuel Administration, War Trade Board, Grain Board, Shipping Board, Railroad Administration, and various other agencies that had been created to implement executive control over the economy had been disbanded. The War Finance Corporation survived in attenuated form for another five years before it, too, was liquidated.[69]

In a similar vein, after Japan's surrender ended World War II, most of the wartime agencies closed their doors by congressional, and in some cases even presidential, action. Within little more than a year, the entire structure of wartime wage, price, and production controls was dismantled. Some wartime programs, to be sure, survived. Because of growing concern about the Soviet Union, the system of military conscription instituted in 1940 was retained. Some employment and export programs survived. More generally, World War II promoted increased government intervention in the nation's economy, particularly through macroeconomic management.[70] Yet almost without exception, the instruments through which the president exercised his wartime powers during World War II, like those in past wars, were dismantled soon after the war's end.

In each of these instances, moreover, more than just the president's emergency powers were rescinded after the termination of hostilities. In the aftermath of the

Civil War and World War I, certainly, and to some extent after World War II as well, Congress laid political siege to the White House. As Arthur Schlesinger has observed, in each case the president's congressional opponents succeeded in dealing the chief executive a resounding political blow that underscored the Congress's determination to restore the temporarily swollen presidency to its prewar institutional banks.[71] Thus after the Civil War Congress impeached and very nearly convicted President Andrew Johnson when he sought to thwart congressional reconstruction plans for the defeated South. After World War I, after a gargantuan struggle with the White House, the Senate refused to ratify the Treaty of Versailles, dashing President Wilson's plans for the postwar world order. And in the aftermath of World War II, Congress savaged President Truman's domestic program; recommended passage of the Twenty-Second Amendment, which limited the president to two terms; and enacted over the president's veto a number of major pieces of legislation, including the 1947 Taft-Hartley Labor Act and the 1950 McCarran Internal Security Act. In addition, presidential control over foreign policy came under attack by proponents of the so-called Bricker Amendment, a group of initiatives that would have stipulated that no treaty or executive agreement could affect U.S. domestic law without action by Congress and, in some instances, the state legislatures. The amendment, which would have curtailed the executive's capacity to negotiate international agreements, ultimately failed but at one point appeared to have majority support in the Congress.[72]

More significantly, during this postwar period conservatives in both houses of Congress launched major attacks on the presidency in the form of investigations designed to demonstrate that the executive branch had been penetrated by Communist agents. Joseph McCarthy's Senate investigative committee as well as the House Committee on Un-American Activities charged that Communist spies had penetrated jobs at federal agencies ranging from sensitive positions in the State Department through mundane posts in the Commerce Department. The ultimate target of these investigations was the presidency itself. Some radical critics of the White House asserted that Roosevelt had "sold out" to the Communists during the Yalta Conference and that Truman had acquiesced in the appointment of "one-worlders" and Communist sympathizers to high government positions. McCarthy implied that these presidents had been part of an immense conspiracy to undermine the nation—"an infamy so black as to dwarf any previous such venture in the history of man."[73] These investigations placed the White House on the defensive, forcing it to devote energy and resources to answer a rapidly expanding array of charges. The investigations led, according to political scientist Wilfred Binkley, to a "gravitation of power into the hands of Congress, at the expense of the executive."[74]

For its part, the Supreme Court, which had championed presidential prerogatives during World War II, seemed to agree that it was time to deflate the powers of the executive. In April 1952, during the height of the Korean War, Truman feared that a threatened nationwide strike would close the steel industry and hamper the war effort. As would have been permissible under now-repealed World War I and World War II legislation, Truman ordered the secretary of commerce to seize and operate the mills.[75] In the case of *Youngstown Sheet & Tube v. Sawyer,* the Supreme Court held that the president lacked the power to issue such an order.[76] Nothing could be more sinister and alarming, said Justice Jackson for the Court, than an effort by the president "to enlarge his mastery over the internal affairs of the country" by his commitment of armed forces to a foreign war. Thus the Court now seemed prepared to side with Congress against the White House.

The patterns of postwar congressional assertiveness that we have observed in these three cases share a common underlying dimension. Generally speaking, though war initially expands the power of the presidency, it also has social and economic repercussions that can eventually embolden and empower the Congress. In particular, during much of American history, war has resulted in the mobilization of social and political forces that give Congress an opportunity to link itself to new groups and forces in American society and, with their backing, do battle with the White House.

The American government's historic reliance on ordinary citizens to fight in wars as well as finance war efforts has often sparked significant mass political mobilization both in support of and in opposition to presidential war policies. To begin with, the recruitment of troops—especially through conscription—as well as concomitant efforts to rally citizen support for military undertakings, often energizes popular political organization and activity both in support of and opposition to the war effort. For example, as Theda Skocpol has shown, the Civil War and both world wars prompted the formation of hundreds of patriotic, civic, and service organizations such as the Grange, the Women's Christian Temperance Union, and the Red Cross.[77]

At the same time, individuals and groups asked to bear the costs of war often felt emboldened to make new political demands and seek new political rights. In both America and Europe, war has been closely associated with expansion of the suffrage. Revolutionary War militiamen called to place their lives at the service of the nation thought themselves just as entitled to vote as their betters who risked only property. Indeed the Revolutionary militia was known as a breeding ground for radical democrats. In 1776, the Philadelphia Committee of Privates, an organization of Pennsylvania militiamen, advised voters to "Let no man represent you disposed to form any rank above that of Freeman."[78]

The sentiments of armed militiamen could not be ignored in the suffrage debates that followed the success of the revolutionary cause. Throughout the colonies, citizen soldiers pressed for and helped to win expanded voting rights. Organizations of state militiamen demanded an end to property restrictions on the suffrage on the ground that those asked to fight should not be barred from voting. In Maryland, groups of armed militiamen went to the polls in 1776 demanding to vote whether or not they could meet the state's existing property requirements for voters. In some instances those denied the right to vote threatened to stop fighting. The result in Maryland and other states was a general expansion of the suffrage during the Revolutionary period so as to accommodate the demands of those Americans being asked to fight. The War of 1812 also led to suffrage reforms in a number of states on the argument that "men who were good enough to fight were good enough to vote."[79] Women's suffrage in the United States, as in England and Canada, was partially brought about by World War I, on the basis of the notion that women were more likely to support the war effort if they possessed the right to vote.[80] Most recently, the Twenty-Sixth Amendment, which lowered the voting age to eighteen, was designed in part to bolster support among young men who were then being conscripted for service in the Vietnam War.

Mobilization for war particularly galvanized foes of the government's military efforts. Virtually every American war has engendered opposition from one or another quarter, and often opposition to war has been the basis for passionate rhetoric and intense bouts of organizational activity. Abolitionists, for example, castigated the 1846 Mexican War as a campaign to expand slavery and they organized a fierce, if ultimately ineffective, movement to oppose President Polk's policies. Though these opponents failed to block the war, their organizational efforts helped bring about the creation of the Free Soil Party, which later became a major component of the Republican coalition.[81]

In protracted conflicts, the hardships, casualties, and dislocations suffered by citizen soldiers and their families can inflame antiwar sentiments and drive the formation of political opposition to continued fighting. Resistance to military conscription often becomes a major focus of these efforts. The Civil War draft was bitterly resisted in many parts of the North and ignited major riots in New York and other cities in 1863.[82] The New York riot lasted four days before it was finally quelled by police and military authorities. So serious was the threat of continuing civil disorder that in the wake of the riot more than ten thousand soldiers were sent from the Army of the Potomac to garrison New York.[83] Opposition to the draft and growing popular weariness of the war very nearly led to Lincoln's defeat in the 1864 presidential election. Draft resistance was a major problem during World War I, when socialist organizers urged draft-age men to refuse induction and thousands of men were arrested for failing to register with their draft boards.[84] During the Vietnam War, liberal foes of American intervention in Indochina encouraged draft resistance and made conscription a major political issue.[85] Even World War II, a conflict that had overwhelming popular support, led to limited but vocal draft resistance.[86]

Finally, even after the cessation of hostilities, former critics of the war, including even some veterans, have often searched for political vehicles through which to express their alienation, while other Americans who served in the military have organized to trumpet their patriotism and to seek recognition for their sacrifices. Thus many individuals initially politicized by their opposition to the Vietnam War became active in the left-liberal "New Politics" movement of the 1970s.[87] New Politics supporters dominated the Democratic Party Convention in 1972 and secured the party's presidential nomination for liberal South Dakota senator George McGovern. In subsequent years, New Politics activists played important roles in the consumer, environmental, feminist, and other "postmaterial" political movements.[88] In a similar vein, many American war veterans joined organizations like the Grand Army of the Republic after the Civil War or the American Legion after the two world wars. These organizations became significant actors in American politics, pressing not only for such matters as the extensive system of veterans' pensions and benefits made available after the Civil War and World War I, as well as under the post–World War II G.I. Bill, but also for broader political goals. The Grand Army was a powerful force in Republican Party politics in the late nineteenth century while the American Legion became an important conservative pressure group during the twentieth.

These wartime and postwar mobilizations of new political forces, in turn, created new opportunities for political entrepreneurship on the part of sympathetic or even merely ambitious members of Congress. Occasionally during the war, but most often in the peacetime aftermath of military conflicts, groups within Congress have endeavored to reach out to the movements energized by the war. Members of Congress have espoused these groups' causes, advocated their views, and appealed to their solidary concerns and material interests—in the case of veterans, for example, by joining and associating themselves with veterans' groups and activities and by providing pensions, bonuses, and other benefits. In these ways, groups within Congress have been able to link themselves to energetic new political forces that, for their part, have a new stake in supporting congressional power vis-à-vis the executive branch. These alliances with new political forces often allowed postwar congresses to do what the nation's foreign foes could not do—take on and defeat the president.

Thus in the wake of the Mexican War, a number of northern congressional Democrats—including such New York "Barnburners" as David Wilmot, Preston King, and John A. Dix—turned against the national administration.[89] These members of Congress aligned themselves with the anti-slavery forces that had mobilized throughout the North in opposition to the attack on Mexico and subsequent American territorial expansion. This strengthened anti-slavery coalition became the basis for the Free Soil Party and, later, for the creation of the Republican Party. Anti-slavery forces in Congress harassed and weakened the Fillmore, Pierce, and Buchanan administrations. Though Pierce was able to secure the enactment of the 1854 Kansas-Nebraska Act, which repealed the Missouri Compromise in an attempt to appease both sides in the slavery controversy, the end result was to irrevocably divide the Democratic Party.

During the concluding years of the Buchanan administration, the new Republican Party controlled the House of Representatives. Republicans asserted that the power of the presidency should be curbed and established a special committee under the leadership of Representative John Covede of Pennsylvania to investigate the general topic of improper presidential efforts to influence congressional deliberations. The Covede committee charged President Buchanan with using bribes and other unsavory tactics to secure the enactment of legislation he favored, and recommended ways of reducing presidential influence in the legislative process.[90]

In a similar vein, in the aftermath of the Civil War, members of Congress opposed to President Andrew Johnson's Reconstruction policies relied heavily on the political support of the most important Union Army veteran's organization, the Grand Army of the Republic, which at its peak enrolled nearly a half million members, along with hundreds of thousands of their family members in its auxiliary organizations. The group supported the adoption of the Fourteenth Amendment, which the president opposed, and generally favored the radical Republicans' harsh policies toward the defeated South rather than the conciliatory program espoused by Johnson. Radical Republicans relied on grassroots support by the Grand Army of the Republic against Johnson's efforts to influence the outcome of the 1866 congressional elections. Subsequently, in 1867, Johnson attempted to oust Secretary of War Edwin M. Stanton, in defiance of the new Tenure of Office Act, which required congressional approval for the dismissal of cabinet officers. Many Republican radicals were convinced that Johnson's action was a prelude to some form of coup d'état and asked the Grand Army of the Republic to march a detachment of Union veterans to Washington to protect the Congress. House Speaker Colfax reported that explosives had been stolen in New York and were being brought to Washington to blow up the Capitol. The Grand Army prepared, unnecessarily as it turned out, to march on Washington at a moment's notice.[91] To emphasize the importance of the alliance between the president's congressional foes and the Grand Army, during the impeachment proceedings against President Johnson the group's national commander, Congressman John Logan of Illinois, served as one of the House impeachment managers.

A similar pattern of congressional alliances with emergent political forces manifested itself after the two world wars. After World War I, President Wilson's congressional opponents made common cause with German and Irish Americans and with postwar isolationists to block American participation in the League of Nations and thereby to destroy the Wilson presidency.[92] From the beginning, the Germans and Irish had opposed support for Great Britain in the European conflict but had been silenced by the administration's wartime suppression of dissent. But even many Americans who had supported the war were shocked by the carnage and disillusioned by the results. Now they opposed having "an American army policing the world and quelling riots in all peoples' back yards."[93] Interestingly, the treaty's most vehement foe, Senate Majority Leader Henry Cabot Lodge of Massachusetts, was himself a Rooseveltian internationalist who had supported America's entry into the war. Lodge, however, harbored a deep personal hatred for Wilson and was prepared to align himself with isolationists if to do so would thwart the president. Other Republicans had been angered by Wilson's wartime arrogation of power and were now eager to cut the president down to size and, especially, to derail any ambitions Wilson might have to seek a third term.[94] And after World War II, President Truman's congressional foes courted the support of patriotic veterans' groups like the American Legion and the Catholic War Veterans in their investigations of alleged Communist penetration of the executive branch. The American Legion, in particular, organized nationwide seminars on how to recognize and report subversive activities, publicized and enforced blacklists, supported anti-Communist members of Congress like Richard M. Nixon, and lent their political clout to the efforts of House Un-American Activities Committee and the McCarthy committee.[95]

During the late 1960s, groups in Congress aligned themselves with liberal forces that mobilized against the Vietnam War to undermine Lyndon Johnson's presidency in the late 1960s. This "New Politics" alliance remained active in American politics during the following decade and played an important role in the ouster of Richard Nixon. During Johnson's second administration, liberals—who had initially supported the war—turned against it largely because military needs began to divert substantial resources from Great Society social programs to which liberal Democrats were strongly committed. Liberals were joined by some civil rights leaders, like Martin Luther King, who viewed the war as a diversion of national energy and attention from the nation's effort to end segregation.[96] Supported by segments of the national news media, liberal forces began to criticize not only the administration's war policies, but also patterns and practices that had become commonplace in the years since World War II: lax Pentagon procurement practices, Pentagon public-relations activities, domestic spying by intelligence agencies, and the hiring of former military officers by defense contractors.[97]

Growing opposition to the war among liberals encouraged some members of Congress, notably Senator J. William Fulbright, chair of the Senate Foreign Relations Committee—along with such senators as George McGovern, Wayne Morse, and Ernest Gruening—to break with the president.[98] Fueling the growth of opposition to the war was the fact that increasing numbers of citizen soldiers, including conscripts, were being sent to fight in the jungles of Southeast Asia where they suffered substantial casualties.[99] Initially the system of deferments and exemptions surrounding military conscription ensured that most draftees were drawn from working-class and minority households—a segment of society not well represented in the political process or in possession of ready access to the media. In 1967, however, foes of the war charged that the draft was racist in character because its burden fell so heavily on minority communities.

Stung by these charges, President Johnson set in motion a set of changes in the draft law that limited student and other upper-middle-class deferments. As critics had hoped, the result was increased opposition to the war from more influential social strata who now saw their own children placed at risk. Between 1968 and 1970, tens of thousands of young men claimed conscientious objector status or presented dubious medical excuses, while tens of thousands more refused to register, or destroyed or returned their draft cards.[100] Others clogged the federal courts with challenges to draft orders. Antiwar sentiment among congressional liberals intensified in 1967 and 1968, and Senator Eugene McCarthy launched a bid to deny Johnson the 1968 Democratic nomination. Though he almost certainly would have been renominated despite liberal opposition, Johnson was politically wounded and chose to withdraw from the race. Antiwar Democrats went on to become an important element in the New Politics coalition that, in 1974, forced President Richard Nixon from office in the wake of the Watergate scandal.

After Nixon's resignation, congressional Democrats enacted a number of pieces of legislation designed to curb presidential power. These included the Budget and Impoundment Control Act to enhance congressional power in the budget process, the Ethics in Government Act to facilitate future prosecution of wrongdoing in the executive branch, and the Freedom of Information Act to open the files of executive agencies to congressional and media scrutiny. Congress also strengthened its own investigative arm, the General Accounting Office. Other legislation, such as the War Powers Resolution, specifically struck at presidential war and foreign policy powers.

Thus, in the wake of the Vietnam War as in a number of other instances, important groups within Congress were able to take advantage of war-induced political mobilization to do battle with the White House. On the one hand, military exigencies have frequently allowed chief executives to demand—and have compelled congresses to give—vast new powers to the president. On the other hand, the new political forces often brought into being by war have allowed groups in the Congress to forge political alliances that then enabled them to lay siege to the White House and retrieve some or all of the power that had been surrendered to the president—and perhaps then some. This democratic self-corrective served as a Madisonian vaccine against imperialist overreach.

An echo of this pattern helped bring an end to the wars in Iraq and Afghanistan, pressing Presidents Bush and Obama to end the fighting and bring American troops home sooner than they wanted. But during the fights over these and other American military actions during the past quarter century, it has become evident that Congress's ability to leash the dogs of war has declined considerably.

How to Separate Warmaking from Politics: A President's Guide

America's early wars were fought by citizen soldiers and financed in part by voluntary popular subscription. Not coincidentally, these wars also had an exhilarating effect on American political life, bringing about the mobilization of new political forces, the creation of new political rights and benefits, and significant congressional involvement. America's most recent military actions, by contrast, were fought by professional soldiers—in the case of the Afghan war, mainly special operations troops—utilizing sophisticated military technology and financed by the Federal Reserve System and contributions wrested from America's foreign allies. These conflicts did not stimulate much in the way of popular political mobilization, and for the most part Congress watched them from the sidelines. The transformation came about in part because of the Cold War and in part because of efforts by successive presidents, beginning most importantly with Harry Truman, to insulate presidential warmaking from popular politics. The end result has been to give presidents enormous freedom of action in the realm of foreign and security policy and, perhaps, to partially shield presidential power from the historic pattern of postwar retrogression.

Presidential Power and the Cold War

The Cold War had an enormous effect on presidential power. For more than forty years, the United States faced a dire military threat requiring the creation and permanent maintenance of powerful military forces ready to respond to an attack almost literally at a moment's notice. Indeed, the Cold War blurred the distinction between wartime and peacetime. Against the backdrop of the dangers facing the nation, successive Cold War and post–Cold War presidents were able to expand the power of the executive branch and affirm their own preeminence in security and foreign affairs. For the most part, in the face of what it perceived to be an existential threat from the Soviet Union, Congress acceded to presidential demands as it always had during wartime. Senator J. William Fulbright, who was later to become a major critic of presidential war power, said in 1961, "As Commander-in-Chief of the armed forces, the president has full responsibility, which cannot be shared, for military decisions in a world in which the difference between safety and cataclysm can be a matter of hours or even minutes."[101] Despite congressional deference, successive presidents did not place much trust in Congress or the democratic political process. Instead they sought to use the dangers facing the nation as a justification for building a set of institutions and procedures that would insulate from public scrutiny and congressional intervention presidential decisionmaking in the realms of security and foreign policy.

Unlike an actual war, moreover, the Cold War did not, in and of itself, produce the sort of political mobilization that has historically allowed Congress to confront the White House and restore the antebellum institutional balance. To be sure, major conflicts, especially the wars in Korea and Vietnam, were fought during the Cold War era. And, as we saw, particularly in the wake of the Vietnam War, Congress did move to curb presidential power. Unlike the ends of the Civil War or the world wars, however, which were followed by an interlude of peace, however brief, the conclusion of the Vietnam War merely meant a continuation of an underlying confrontation between superpowers. The continuing threat to American security allowed Presidents Ronald Reagan and George H. W. Bush to quickly throw off their congressional fetters and resume the onward march of presidential power.

In the immediate aftermath of World War II, the United States moved quickly to demobilize its military forces, and though it helped to bring about the creation of the United Nations, the Truman administration hoped to reduce its international commitments and concentrate on domestic concerns. President Truman had little foreign policy expertise or interest and expected to focus mainly on the domestic social and economic objectives embodied in his "Fair Deal" agenda. As late as October

1945, Truman had told the Joint Chiefs to expect sharp cuts in the military budget and steep reductions in the number of American troops stationed in Europe.[102] By 1946, however, crises in the Near East, the Balkans, and Europe had forced the president to devote his attention to international and security affairs. Truman's predecessor, Franklin D. Roosevelt, had dominated America's political landscape and governed the nation during a desperate worldwide military struggle. During the war, in historian Arthur Schlesinger's words, Roosevelt had "kept the military and diplomatic reins very much in his own hands."[103] The president was confident of his own judgment in these realms and had relied on a cadre of trusted aides like Harry Hopkins and later "Chip" Bohlen to conduct delicate negotiations.[104] FDR had generally bypassed Secretary of State Cordell Hull, whom he saw as useful merely for handling routine diplomatic business.[105]

In fact, while Roosevelt had gone through the motions of consulting Congress so long as he knew it would support him, he had frequently ignored Capitol Hill and regarded legislators, especially senators, "as a bunch of incompetent obstructionists" when it came to matters of national security.[106] Truman lacked the political standing that had allowed FDR to ride roughshod over the Congress, and he lacked FDR's confidence in his own capacity to make unilateral foreign policy decisions. Yet Truman believed strongly in the principle of executive control of foreign policy.[107] Accordingly, he and his advisers moved to create a set of institutions that would give an ordinary mortal like Harry S. Truman powers that once could only have been exercised by a giant like FDR.[108]

Two statutes, enacted within less than a year of one another, played an important role in institutionalizing the foreign policy and security powers of the presidency. The first, signed into law in August 1946, was the Foreign Service Reform Act, which merged the State Department and the Foreign Service into a single organization. This meant that experienced Foreign Service officers would routinely rotate back to Washington where they would be available for consultation and to help formulate policy. In 1947, Secretary of State George C. Marshall established the department's policy planning staff, which consisted mainly of Foreign Service officers on their Washington tours, to serve as an instrument through which the secretary and the president would be able to evaluate long-term foreign policy goals. From the perspective of Congress, the Foreign Service Act and the development of the policy planning staff would help to reduce the likelihood that future presidents would engage in FDR-style freewheeling diplomacy. But the actual result was to increase rather than curb presidential power. The policy planning staff gave the president a stronger institutional capacity to identify and evaluate foreign policy problems and consider alternative courses of action. The staff's first director, George

Kennan, became an important presidential adviser, as did his successor, Paul Nitze, and a number of subsequent directors.

An even more important piece of legislation, the National Security Act, was passed in July 1947. The National Security Act had three major parts. The first reorganized the military services by separating the Air Force from the Army and abolishing the historic division between the War Department and Navy Department. All three military branches were now placed within a single National Military Establishment (later renamed the Department of Defense), under the leadership of a civilian cabinet officer—the secretary of defense. Second, the act created the Central Intelligence Agency (CIA) to coordinate the government's activities in the realms of information gathering, espionage, and covert operations. Finally, the act established the National Security Council (NSC), which was chaired by the president and included the major cabinet secretaries, the chairman of the Joint Chiefs of Staff, the three service secretaries, and a number of other high-ranking officials. The NSC was to assist the president in coordinating national security planning and decisionmaking.

Members of Congress brought a mix of motives to the 1947 act. Some hoped to streamline national security decisionmaking to enable the nation to respond more effectively to crises. Others viewed the creation of the CIA and NSC as further means to prevent a return to Roosevelt-style presidential unilateralism. The CIA's predecessor, for example, the Office of Strategic Services, had been created by a Roosevelt executive order in 1942 and had operated as a semi-autonomous instrument of the White House.[109] From Truman's perspective, however, the National Security Act promised to create important mechanisms for presidential control over American foreign and security policy. Though he was not fully satisfied with all its provisions, Truman made passage of the act a major presidential priority.[110]

Presidential Control of the Military

Indeed, subsequent events were to affirm Truman's view: the 1947 National Security Act created the basis for what later critics would call the "imperial presidency." To begin with, the 1947 act represented a further step in the professionalization of the military services and their subjection to presidential control. As noted earlier, America's military effort had historically depended on state militias, which often answered as much to governors, senators, and members of Congress as to the president. During the Civil War, for example, many politicians secured gubernatorial commissions in state militia units and through them, as well as through the state governors, Congress frequently sought to interfere with Lincoln's military plans.

Presidential control of the military was enhanced at the beginning of the Spanish American War when Congress passed the 1898 Volunteer Act. Under its terms, the general officers and their staffs of all state militia units, now renamed the National Guard, were to be appointed by the president rather than the state governors. The 1903 Dick Act further increased presidential control of the nation's military forces by authorizing the president to dissolve state guard units into the regular Army in times of emergency, while the 1916 National Defense Act gave the president the authority to appoint all commissioned and noncommissioned National Guard officers in time of war. The 1916 act also began the creation of the national military reserves, which eventually supplanted the state units as the force employed to fill out the military's ranks in time of emergency.[111]

While these pieces of legislation gradually gave the president and the military brass in Washington fuller control over what originally had been primarily state forces, the longstanding division of the military into two cabinet departments— War (Army) and Navy—also undermined presidential control. Historically each of the services, as well as branches within the services, most notably the Marine Corps and the Army Air Corps, had their own ties to supporters in the Congress and used these to circumvent their nominal superiors. For example, during World War I the Marines mobilized their allies in Congress to induce the president to accept their participation in the American expeditionary force over the objections of the secretary of war, the secretary of the Navy, and General Pershing, the force's commander.[112] In a similar vein, between the wars some lawmakers became enchanted with the idea of military aviation and supported General Billy Mitchell's quixotic crusade against the War and Navy departments. Over the objections of the president and the secretary of war, Congress enacted the 1926 Air Corps Act, which made the Air Corps a virtually autonomous entity within the Army.[113] Even more important, the War Department and the Navy Department presented Congress with separate budgets and competing visions of the nation's military needs and priorities. The annual struggle for funding between the two service branches, complete with competing testimony by the nation's foremost military authorities, opened the way for increased congressional intervention into military decisionmaking.

The 1947 National Security Act created a single defense secretary responsible for all defense planning and the overall military budget. As amended in 1949, the act diminished the status of the individual service secretaries, who were no longer to be members of the president's cabinet or the National Security Council. Instead these secretaries were to focus on manpower and procurement issues and to report to the secretary of defense and his assistant secretaries. To further centralize military planning, the 1949 amendments created the position of chair of the Joint Chiefs of Staff to denote the officer who was to serve as the principal military adviser to the defense secretary and the president. By creating a more unified military chain of command and a single defense budget, the National Security Act diminished Congress's ability to intervene in military planning and decisionmaking and increased the president's control over the armed services and national security policy. In 1948, under the auspices of the first defense secretary, James Forrestal, the chiefs of the three military services met at Key West and negotiated a set of agreements on missions and weapons that were expected to mute interservice squabbles and the congressional intervention that inevitably ensued.

Truman also brought about the creation of an enormous standing army. Historically, the United States had built large armies in wartime and quickly disbanded them at the war's end. Opposition to maintaining standing armies in peacetime predated even the birth of the Republic. To meet the needs of the Korean War, however, Truman was forced to halt the force reductions that had been under way since the end of World War II. Moreover, by 1951, Truman and his advisers were concerned with more than America's immediate military requirements. The president had concluded that American security required the construction of a permanent military force capable of deterring military attack from the Soviet Union and its allies anywhere on the globe. This had been the conclusion reached in a planning document known as NSC-68, drafted primarily by Paul Nitze and the State Department's policy planning staff and presented to the National Security Council in April 1950. This document, which became a cornerstone of American security policy, asserted that the principal goal of Soviet policy was the subversion or destruction of the United States. Preventing the Soviet leadership from achieving this goal would require a long-term commitment on the part of the United States. "Containment" of its adversary would necessitate the development of enormous military forces—forces so powerful that the Soviets would be deterred from committing acts of aggression against the United States and its allies by the knowledge that the United States could retaliate with overwhelming force. In short, the authors of the document advised that the United States commit itself, for the first time in its history, to maintaining powerful military forces in peacetime.

Truman did not act on the recommendation of NSC-68 until the next year, when he called for expanded military spending and American rearmament to meet long-term challenges.[114] By 1952 the United States had tripled its military spending, expanded its nuclear weapons programs, begun the deployment of a fleet of heavy bombers capable of attacking the Soviet Union, doubled the size of the Army and Marine Corps, and increased rather than diminished the size of its naval forces. To make certain that sufficient manpower would be available to meet military needs,

Congress enacted the Universal Military Training and Service Act of 1951 and the Armed Forces Reserve Act of 1952. The first of these pieces of legislation expanded the military draft, which had already been reinstated under the 1948 Selective Service Act. In principle, all eighteen-year-old men would now be required to undertake military training. To mute political opposition, however, the law allowed the Selective Service System to provide for educational and occupational deferments. In practice, these deferments, like the Civil War commutation fee that had allowed men to pay three hundred dollars in lieu of conscription, permitted individuals wealthy enough to remain in school or puissant enough to secure occupational deferments from local draft boards to avoid service. Labor leaders like Walter Reuther and African American leaders like A. Philip Randolph objected to the elitist character of the draft.[115] The system of deferments and exemptions, however, helped to forestall objections from the nation's more influential strata. As Selective Service System Director Lewis Hershey warned, if any effort was made to eliminate the deferments, "All hell will break loose."[116] Those who did serve in the military, whether as conscripts or volunteers, were required under the Reserve Act to remain in the ready reserves, available for call-up in the event of emergency. By 1953, nearly 4 million Americans were a part of the active military, backed by sizeable National Guard and reserve forces.[117]

To make certain that the nation's military forces had adequate matériel and equipment, Congress enacted the 1950 Defense Production Act, which gave the president the authority to purchase strategic materials and order industries to give priority to military needs. Three years earlier, the 1947 National Security Act had provided for the creation of a National Security Resources Board to help the president coordinate military and industrial planning in wartime.[118] Rather than attempt to command industry to meet military needs, however, the president opted to expand and institutionalize the World War II contracting system. At the beginning of World War II, Secretary of War Henry Stimson had advised Roosevelt to "hire" industrialists by providing them with lucrative military contracts. "If you are going to try to go to war, or to prepare for war, in a capitalist country, you have got to let business make money out of the process or business won't work," Stimson said.[119]

During the Truman era, this hiring of industrialists became a permanent feature of the American industrial and political landscape. Hundreds of firms received contracts for military equipment ranging from meals, uniforms, and vehicles to missiles, aircraft, and naval vessels. Where existing enterprises did not meet the government's needs, the government sponsored the creation of new ones. One of the most important is the RAND Corporation. Originally sponsored by the U.S. Air Force, and formally known as a federally funded research and development center,

RAND and a number of other corporations were established with the support of the military to engage in weapons research and operational planning.[120]

Most major contracts, moreover, required subcontracting, so that thousands of firms throughout the nation profited from defense work.[121] For some, like the Lockheed, Northrup, and Grumman aviation companies, military undertakings became the principal focus of their business. These contractors made themselves virtual arms of the military, usually working closely, if not exclusively, with one particular service branch that then made sure that its contractors always received a share of military business. The contractors and subcontractors, in turn, offered the military a powerful base of support, in dozens of congressional districts, for maintaining high levels of spending on weapons and procurement programs.[122] The concentration of these firms in the South led some observers to rename the region below the old Mason-Dixon Line the "Gunbelt."[123] The intense political support of thousands of firms and their unionized workers, in what President Eisenhower called the "military-industrial complex," helped successive administrations ensure that the president would always have at his disposal an enormous and powerful military machine.

Some contractors, their executive ranks filled with retired admirals, generals, captains, and colonels who now sold weapons to their former services, have come to resemble officers' clubs. Indeed, Military Professional Resources, Inc. (MPRI), a division of high-technology defense contractor L3 Communications, boasts that it employs "more generals per square foot than the Pentagon."[124] MPRI administers much of the Army's ROTC program and has played a major role in support of American policy in Croatia and Bosnia. Other firms operate military bases, provide security for foreign leaders allied with the United States, conduct surveillance and covert operations, and even field sizeable bodies of combat troops.[125]

Thousands of heavily armed private contractors were employed by American public and corporate entities in Iraq in 2003–2004 to provide security and other services for U.S. operations. These contractors were involved in intense fighting alongside regular U.S. troops in the spring of 2004 and incurred significant casualties.[126] Indeed, the existence of these private soldiers was brought to the attention of the American public in March 2004 when four employees of Blackwater, U.S.A., a North Carolina security firm, were ambushed and killed in the Iraqi town of Felujah and their bodies mutilated and dragged through the streets. The four men, former Army Special Operations personnel, were serving as security officers for American firms working in Iraq.[127] Later that year, eight Blackwater commandos, assisted by the firm's helicopters, repelled an attack by Shiite militiamen against U.S. headquarters in the town of Najaf. At the peak of the fighting, the various U.S. security firms working in Iraq formed an operational alliance to share intelligence and resources.[128]

The ability of private firms to deploy heavily armed professional soldiers has given presidents access to military capabilities outside the scope of public or congressional scrutiny. Indeed, several recent presidents have employed private military contractors to engage in activities that Congress has expressly forbidden U.S. military forces to undertake. For example, when authorizing assistance to Columbia to prosecute the "War on Drugs" in the 1990s, Congress placed strict limits on the use of American military forces to support the Columbian military. U.S. forces were prohibited from engaging in counterinsurgency efforts and from providing assistance to Columbian military units with poor human rights records. The Clinton administration, however, believed that drug gangs and anti-government insurgents were often difficult to distinguish and found it hard to identify Columbian military units with unblemished human rights records. Accordingly, the administration employed private military contractors to circumvent what it saw as burdensome congressional restrictions.

The use of private contractors allowed the administration to claim it was following the letter of the law and, at the same time, to provide "deniability" and political cover if military plans went awry.[129] Thus, MPRI was given a contract to develop the Columbian government's overall military plan and another contractor, Northrup Services, was engaged to provide technical specialists for such tasks as staffing radar sites. Two additional firms, Virginia Electronics and DynCorp, provided what amounted to fully equipped combat troops. Virginia Electronics employed former U.S. Navy Seals to operate gunboats along the supply lines used by Columbian rebel groups, while DynCorp provided training and support for the Columbian air force. According to many reports, DynCorp pilots actually flew combat missions against Columbian rebel groups.[130] Private military contractors also were employed by the Clinton administration in Bosnia, Angola, Equatorial Guinea, and Liberia to circumvent congressional restrictions on the use of American military forces.[131] In these and many other instances, military contractors have provided presidents with the means to pursue their own policy goals without having to defer to congressional views and priorities.

Private soldiers, to be sure, can pose certain risks for presidents who rely on them. For centuries, mercenary troops have earned a reputation for a lack of discipline and a lack of commitment to the interests of the states that employ them. In recent years, as might have been expected given this history, American presidents occasionally have been embarrassed by the actions of their contractors. For example, in May 2004, President Bush was forced to make a televised apology for the mistreatment of Iraqi prisoners held at the Abu Ghraib detention facility near Baghdad. Among those implicated in the scandal were employees of two private military contractors, CACI International based in Arlington, Virginia, and Titan Corp. of San Diego. The two firms had provided interrogators and translators to U.S. military intelligence agencies.[132] In a similar vein, during the Clinton administration, several employees of DynCorp working in Bosnia had to be sent home in the wake of allegations of statutory rape, corruption, and abetting prostitution.[133] When presidents seek to escape congressional scrutiny by contracting out for military services, they may discover that the contract contains fine print they had not expected.

Intelligence and Planning

In addition to centralizing military decisionmaking, the 1947 National Security Act increased the White House's capacities for foreign policy and security planning, intelligence gathering and evaluation, and covert intelligence operations. The first of these results stemmed from the creation of the National Security Council. The council itself was never more than a loose-knit presidential advisory body and seldom had any independent influence. Beginning during the Kennedy presidency, however, the NSC staff became an important presidential instrument. Truman and Eisenhower relied on the State Department's policy planning staff and the Joint Chiefs of Staff for policy analysis and advice. These groups, however, did not work directly for the president and had other institutional loyalties. Kennedy expanded the NSC staff and designated McGeorge Bundy, an Ivy Leaguer and former intelligence officer, to serve as his special assistant for national security affairs and head of the NSC staff. During subsequent presidencies, the NSC staff, eventually consisting of nearly two hundred professional employees organized in regional and functional offices, along with the national security assistant, became important forces in the shaping of foreign and security policy, often eclipsing the State Department and its leadership. For example, when he served as Richard Nixon's national security assistant, Henry Kissinger effectively excluded the secretary of state, William Rogers, from most foreign policy decisionmaking. Similarly, during the Carter administration, the president allowed his national security assistant Zbigniew Brzezinski to marginalize Secretary of State Cyrus Vance. Both Rogers and Vance eventually resigned.[134]

The construction of a national security bureaucracy within the executive office of the president made possible the enormous postwar expansion of presidential unilateralism in the realm of security and foreign policy. Beginning with Truman, presidents would conduct foreign and security policy through executive agreements and executive orders and seldom negotiate formal treaties requiring Senate ratification. Presidents before Truman—even Franklin D. Roosevelt—had generally submitted important accords between the United States and foreign powers to the Senate for ratification, and had sometimes seen their goals stymied by senatorial opposition. Not only did the Constitution require senatorial confirmation of treaties but, before Truman, presidents had lacked the administrative resources to systematically conduct an independent foreign policy. It was not by accident that most of the agreements—particularly the secret agreements—negotiated by FDR concerned military matters where the president could rely on the administrative capacities of the War and Navy departments.[135]

The State Department's policy planning staff, especially the National Security Council staff, created the institutional foundations and capabilities that enabled Truman and his successors to conduct and administer the nation's foreign and security policies directly from the Oval Office. For example, American participation in the International Trade Organization, one of the cornerstones of U.S. postwar trade policy, was based on a sole executive agreement, the GATT Provisional Protocol, that was signed by President Truman after Congress failed to approve the organization's charter.[136] Truman signed some 1,300 executive agreements and Eisenhower another 1,800, in some cases requesting congressional approval and in other instances ignoring the Congress. Executive agreements take two forms: congressional-executive agreements, and sole executive agreements. In the former case, the president submits the agreement to both houses of Congress as he would any other piece of legislation, with a majority vote in both houses required for passage. This is generally a lower hurdle than the two-thirds vote required for Senate ratification of a treaty. A sole executive agreement, by contrast, is not sent to the Congress at all. Either way, all executive agreements and treaties have the power of law, though a sole executive agreement cannot contravene an existing statute.[137] Since the Truman and Eisenhower presidencies, few treaties have been submitted to the Senate as stipulated by Article II of the Constitution.[138] Indeed, two of the most important recent international agreements entered into by the United States, the North American Free Trade Agreement and the World Trade Organization agreement, were confirmed by congressional executive agreement, not by treaty.[139]

It is also important to note that in recent years, through a combination of executive orders and institutional changes, presidents have been able to sharply reduce congressional authority in the realm of trade policy. The 1934 Reciprocal Trade Agreements Act gave the president expanded authority to negotiate trade agreements with other countries and reduced Congress's ability to interfere with or reject such presidential agreements. In 1974, similar authority was granted to the president to negotiate the reduction of nontariff barriers under so-called fast track procedures, which limit congressional power to overturn presidential decisions.[140] The 1974 act also expanded the role of the U.S. Trade Representative, an office originally authorized by Congress in 1962 and established by President Kennedy via executive order in 1963. This office has enhanced the institutional ability of the White House to set the nation's overall trade policy agenda, often relegating Congress to the task of vetoing specific measures within a larger plan—a reversal of the constitutionally mandated relationship between the two branches.

In a similar vein, the policy planning staff and National Security Council opened the way for policymaking by executive order in the areas of security and foreign policy. Executive orders issued to implement presidents' security policy goals have been variously called national security presidential directives and national security decision directives, but are most commonly known as national security directives, or NSDs. These, like other executive orders, are commands from the president to an executive agency.[141] Most NSDs are classified and presidents have consistently refused even to inform Congress of their existence, much less their content. Generally, NSDs are drafted by the National Security Council staff at the president's behest. Some NSDs have involved mundane matters, but others have established America's most significant foreign policies and security postures. As mentioned earlier, NSC-68, developed by the State Department's policy planning staff prior to the creation of an NSC staff, set forward the basic principles of containment on which American Cold War policy came to be based. A series of Kennedy NSDs established the basic principles of American policy toward a number of world trouble spots.[142] Ronald Reagan's NSD-12 launched the president's massive military buildup and force modernization program, while his NSD-172 began the development of anti-missile programs. Thus the creation of new administrative capabilities gave presidents the tools through which to dominate foreign and security policy and to dispense with Congress and its "incompetent obstructionists."

Presidential power was further augmented in the 1947 act by the creation of the CIA, which became a centrally important presidential foreign policy tool. The CIA gave the president the capacity to intervene in the affairs of other nations without informing Congress or the public. At the president's behest, the CIA undertook numerous covert operations and clandestine interventions in foreign countries during the Cold War and afterward. The agency's covert operations branch was established by a top secret presidential order, NSC-10/2, issued in June 1948. These operations were to include propaganda, economic warfare, sabotage, subversion, and assistance to underground movements. The U.S. government was to be able to "plausibly disclaim responsibility" for all covert operations.[143] Carrying out successive secret presidential orders, usually framed as NSDs, the CIA overthrew the Iranian government in 1953 and installed the shah, who ruled Iran for the next quarter century. During the 1950s, the CIA also overthrew governments in Guatemala, Egypt, and Laos that were deemed to be unfriendly to the United States.[144] The CIA helped organize, and for a number of years subsidized, anti-Communist politicians and political parties in Western Europe. In some instances, of course, CIA operations resulted in embarrassing failures such as the abortive "Bay of Pigs" invasion of Cuba in 1961. Nevertheless, covert CIA operations have been used by presidents to advance American interests in virtually every corner of the globe, from Afghanistan to Zaire.

From its inception, the CIA was a presidential instrument with the Congress exercising little or no supervision over its activities. Indeed, until the 1970s the agency lacked procedures for even responding to congressional concerns about its activities; such procedures were deemed not necessary. To the extent that Congress was even informed about CIA operations, such information usually came after the fact.[145] In the wake of the Vietnam War and Watergate investigations, both houses of Congress established intelligence oversight committees with subpoena powers and budgetary authority over intelligence agencies. Nevertheless, Congress continues to accept the general notion that intelligence is an executive function, and congressional intervention in the operations of the CIA and other intelligence agencies has been superficial at best.[146]

For the most part, the nation's new intelligence capabilities were directed outside its own borders. Truman hoped to avoid infringements on the civil liberties of Americans and opposed Director J. Edgar Hoover's efforts to expand the domestic intelligence activities of the FBI.[147] By executive order, however, Truman created a Loyalty Review Board, which brought together a number of World War II programs designed to screen prospective government employees and to investigate charges of treasonable or disloyal conduct. Individual agencies were authorized to develop their own loyalty programs.[148] Truman also issued a number of executive orders establishing a classification system for government secrets that ultimately led to the classification of millions of pages of documents and allowed the president and the various federal agencies to stamp as "secret" almost any information they chose not to reveal to the public and the Congress.[149]

Revenue

The construction and expansion of America's new standing Army and other national security institutions would require the nation to bear, on a permanent basis, levels of military spending previously seen only during wartime emergencies. Stated in constant dollars, President Truman's 1952 defense budget of more than $46 billion represented a twenty-fold increase over America's defense spending in 1940 and approached World War II spending levels—outlays that the nation was expected to sustain into the indefinite future. To accomplish this Herculean task, Truman could rely on the tremendous extractive capabilities of the federal tax system developed by the Roosevelt administration during World War II, a watershed period in U.S. government finance. First, the Revenue Act of 1942 substantially broadened the nation's tax base, increasing the number of households subject to the income tax from 13 million to 28 million. By 1944, tax rates began at 3 percent on incomes between $500 and $2,000, rose to 20 percent for incomes above $2,000, and climbed steeply to reach a nominal rate of 91 percent on incomes over $200,000.[150]

The second important innovation associated with the war was the enactment of the Current Tax Payment Act of 1943. Before 1943, federal income taxes were to be paid quarterly in the year after the income was received. This system depended heavily on the honesty, goodwill, and foresight of individual taxpayers. Under the terms of the 1943 act, however, employers were required to withhold 20 percent of wages and salaries and to remit these to the government as the income was earned. The 1943 Current Tax Payment Act partially freed the government from its historic dependence on the support and integrity of the individual taxpayer. It made the collection of income taxes automatic and involuntary from the perspective of the taxpayer and, together with higher rates, increased federal income tax revenues from slightly more than $1 billion in 1940 to more than $45 billion by 1945. At the end of World War II, there was considerable political pressure to cut taxes and Congress did enact a tax cut over the president's veto in 1948.[151] The outbreak of the Korean War, however, produced a series of temporary tax increases that in many instances became permanent, leading to $65 billion in revenues in 1955 and beginning the march toward today's $2 trillion in federal income tax receipts.

To make this tax burden more palatable to millions of ordinary Americans, the government relied on the principle of progressivity. Enshrined in American tax law since the Revenue Act of 1862, progressivity was a concession to the popular sense of justice. According to tax historian Sidney Ratner, progressivity accompanied the extension of new and relative high rates of taxation to citizens with small incomes.[152] In principle, at least, the relative handful of wealthy Americans had to be taxed at even higher rates in order to convince tens of millions of their less prosperous fellow citizens that the tax system was fair and that they should comply with its demands. At the same time, however, to prevent those very same wealthy and powerful Americans from mobilizing to block the imposition of high tax rates, Congress filled the income tax with numerous "loopholes" that were mainly designed to reduce the tax burdens of upper-income wage earners, investors, and business owners.[153] As in the case of "universal" military conscription, those with sufficient influence to make trouble were bought off.

In addition to taxes, the White House sought to generate financial support for an expanded military effort from two other sources. One was the sale of arms and military equipment to friendly and neutral nations. Allowing American military contractors to sell arms to other countries helped to increase production runs and hence reduce the unit costs to the American military of expensive weapons; it also brought the armies of foreign countries into the American military orbit.[154] At the same time, arms sales would help maintain the vitality of the American arms industry—the so-called defense industrial base—and its contribution to the nation's security.[155] Today, some $20 billion worth of American military hardware is sold abroad every year.[156]

A second and more important source of financial support for America's military effort was "burden sharing." America expected its allies to share the costs of defense either by contributing financially or by contributing troops and equipment in times of need. Burden sharing was certainly not a novel idea. As long ago as 430 B.C.E., Periclean Athens supported its fleet by creating the Delian League and requiring the islands of Chios, Lesbos, and Samos to make financial contributions for the maintenance of Athenian military and naval forces.[157] But at the end of World War II, America's chief allies were financially exhausted. To ensure that the Western European democracies would possess the means to resist Communism and to bolster America's own security, the United States thus launched major programs to promote European economic recovery, including the 1948 Marshall Plan.[158] The success of these efforts, in turn, made the Europeans worthwhile alliance partners. The British, in particular, were expected to contribute significantly to the American defense burden and were, in return, given privileged access to U.S. decisionmaking.[159]

In the 1950s the United States built a number of military alliances, most notably the North Atlantic Treaty Organization (NATO), which required participants to shoulder a portion of America's military costs. During that decade NATO added some twenty divisions of British, German, and other European troops, along with thousands of aircraft and tanks, to the six American divisions defending Western Europe.[160] Other American military agreements ultimately involved more than fifty nations in Europe and the Pacific region.[161] Military burden sharing continues to the present day. In the 1950s, America sought troops and material assistance from its allies. Today the United States is more likely to demand that its allies contribute financially.

In addition to defraying America's military expenses, treaties and defense pacts served presidential interests in another way: presidents could use the cover of one of America's thousands of treaty obligations to undertake actions, especially in the military realm, that faced significant opposition in the Congress. International commitments became a presidential trump card to be used against the Congress even as more and more of these commitments were based on executive agreements made by the president without congressional consultation. Early in the Vietnam War, for example, Secretary of State Dean Rusk explained to the Senate Foreign Relations Committee that American assistance to Vietnam was required under the terms of bilateral assistance agreements. It turned out that all of these agreements, which the administration now cited as American obligations, had been entered into by the White House without the knowledge of Congress. Upon further inquiry, the Foreign Relations Committee uncovered hundreds of American international obligations negotiated by presidents without congressional sanction.[162]

Winning authorization from the U.N. Security Council has been a particularly important presidential ploy. President Truman sought and received Security Council approval to intervene against North Korea before even consulting with congressional leaders, and then cited the United Nations resolution rather than congressional approval as the basis for going to war.[163] In a similar vein, President George H. W. Bush used U.N. Security Council Resolution 678, authorizing the use of force against Iraq, to pressure a reluctant Congress to approve the deployment of American forces in the Persian Gulf in preparation for the 1990 Gulf War.[164] Indeed, on numerous occasions presidents have ordered American forces to join U.N. "peacekeeping" missions without seeking any endorsement from Congress.[165]

One method of financing military operations that has been emphatically rejected by recent presidents is the mass marketing of government bonds. During the Civil War, World War I, and World War II, millions of ordinary citizens purchased billions of dollars in small-denomination government securities. These bonds, often called liberty bonds or victory bonds, gave ordinary Americans an important role in financing the nation's war efforts.[166] From the government's perspective, selling securities in small denominations to millions of purchasers not only is inefficient, but also has the unwanted effect of linking funding for military efforts to popular support. If citizens opposed the president's military policies, they might refuse to purchase bonds. Contemporary presidents have sought to remove political constraints from their ability to deploy military forces and so have sought to create funding mechanisms that were as insulated as possible from the vagaries of domestic politics. These considerations help to explain President Bush's strong opposition to legislation introduced by Senator Mitch McConnell of Kentucky after the September 2001 terrorist attacks. McConnell's bill called for the development of a Treasury Department war bond program to help finance the war on terrorism that had been declared by President Bush. The bill was enacted despite the president's objections, but the administration essentially ignored the legislation. The Treasury Department renamed an existing series of U.S. savings bonds "patriot bonds," but made no particular effort to bring these securities to the attention of those Americans who were seeking ways to contribute to the war effort.[167]

Thus, in the early years of the Cold War, President Truman built a huge, permanent military establishment and solidified the principle of centralized presidential control over the military. The president also laid the foundations for funding this military machine and began to assemble a political constituency that would support high levels of military spending. While levels of military spending would fluctuate with international events and political currents over the next several decades, the maintenance of a huge standing army, once unthinkable, had now become a matter of course. Truman, moreover, established a national security staff within the executive office and began to construct an intelligence service capable of covert operations around the globe. These resources, in turn, helped Truman and future presidents circumvent Congress and engage in unilateral management of the nation's foreign and security policies. Possession of institutional capacity does not guarantee its use, but it certainly makes its use possible, and the White House emerged from the Truman era with what Schlesinger and others have called "imperial" capabilities.

Lessons from the Korean War to the War on Terrorism

The imperial presidency overcame challenges from Congress and from members of its own military, notably General MacArthur, to fight for, and if anything, strengthen, its power during the Korean War. In June 1950, when North Korean forces invaded South Korea, President Truman and his advisers believed that if they failed to respond forcefully, they would encourage Soviet aggression throughout Europe and Asia. Uncertain about Congress's mood, the president decided that rather than turn directly to Capitol Hill, he would first secure a U.N. Security Council resolution authorizing military intervention. He then met with a bipartisan group of congressional leaders, informed them of the U.N. resolution, and received their support. Congressional leaders expected Truman to ask for a formal resolution approving the use of force, if not for a full-blown declaration of war. Truman, however, influenced by the views of Secretary of State Dean Acheson, decided he would not ask for a congressional vote. Instead he accepted Acheson's view that his constitutional powers as commander-in-chief, coupled with America's obligation to enforce the U.N. resolution, were adequate grounds for ordering American forces into combat. By deploying massive forces without asking congressional approval, even though he had been assured that approval was forthcoming, Truman sought to assert the principle that the president, not Congress, could decide whether and when to go to war. Members of Congress complained, but given the growing sense of national emergency, they acquiesced by voting to appropriate the necessary funds and to extend the draft.[168] A fundamental principle had been established. In the future, even when presidents sought congressional assent to the use of force, there was a tendency to view this as a courtesy rather than a constitutional requirement. Indeed, as we saw earlier, President George H. W. Bush's defense secretary, Dick Cheney, told the president he shouldn't even bother seeking congressional support for the use of military force in the Persian Gulf in 1991.[169]

Over the next two years, the Korean War became unpopular as the fighting dragged on inconclusively. The new powers of the presidency, however, proved equal to the tasks of fighting a war and resisting efforts by the Congress and others to interfere with presidential prerogatives. Two factors worked in Truman's favor: the economy and the draft. To begin with, Truman chose to finance the war chiefly through increases in federal income tax rates. Though higher taxes are never popular, the early 1950s were a period of economic growth in the United States and higher taxes were more than offset by rising incomes. The nation could afford both guns and butter.[170] Korean War tax increases, moreover, were not as substantial as they might have been, because two other sources of revenue were helping to support the costs of the war. First, a number of American allies contributed troops and matériel. These included Great Britain, Australia, Turkey, and above all, South Korea. Moreover, under the newly established Bretton Woods financial system, the U.S. dollar was the world's reserve currency. During this period, billions of dollars were held by foreign banks and the seigniorage to the U.S. Treasury was enormous.[171] At the same time, as we saw earlier, conscription in the Korean War era was driven by a system of deferments and exemptions that permitted members of influential social strata to escape military service if they so chose. These economic and social factors helped to mute domestic opposition to the war. The end result on the battlefield was a stalemate. At home, however, the White House won a resounding victory as the exigencies of war made it all the more difficult for Congress to carp about the president's expansion of military power and covert capabilities.

The next two presidents made ample use of the capabilities forged by Truman. Eisenhower further centralized presidential control over the military establishment and continued the Truman-era loyalty program. In 1955 and 1956, President Eisenhower in effect demanded a blank check from Congress for possible military action in the Taiwan Straits and the Middle East and, in 1958, sent fourteen thousand marines into Lebanon without asking Congress for authorization. Indeed Eisenhower issued numerous national security directives and made ample use of the CIA's covert capabilities. And in 1954, he made his own contribution to the enhancement of presidential power when he made a virtually absolute claim of executive privilege in refusing to turn over records to the Congress.[172] John F. Kennedy, for his part, seemed cut from the same mold. He expanded the executive's capacity for covert operations by creating the Special Forces, an elite military corps reporting more fully to the president than to the regular Army command, and he then sent those Special Forces and other American military elements to assist the South Vietnamese without consulting Congress. By the Kennedy era, these sorts of actions on the part of the president were more or less taken for granted by Congress, by the public, and by most scholars.[173]

The expansion of presidential power in the realm of foreign and security policy, however, seemed for a time to be halted and even reversed by the clash between Congress and President Lyndon Johnson over the Vietnam War and, later, the Watergate struggle between Congress and President Richard Nixon. Unlike the war in Korea, the Vietnam War sparked enormous opposition in the American public and in the Congress. While this opposition had a number of sources, one aspect of the problem was economic. By the late 1960s, America no longer was as dominant in the world economy as it had been during the previous decade. It would not be so easy for a president to ask the United States to produce both guns and butter. America's allies had no interest in helping to defray the costs of the war. And to make matters worse, a powerful domestic constituency, the liberal wing of the president's own political party, was deeply committed to a set of enormously expensive social programs that President Johnson had himself defined as the nation's top priority. Diversion of funds from the president's Great Society programs to pay for the war generated enormous opposition. Later, changes in draft rules made politically potent constituencies more vulnerable to conscription and intensified their opposition to the war. The result was to drive Johnson from office and to compel his successor, Richard Nixon, to withdraw American forces under circumstances that made the victory of Communist forces, led by Ho Chi Minh, all but inevitable.

The end of the Vietnam War represented not only a military defeat for the United States, but also a setback for the presidency. In the aftermath of the war and, in particular, after the disintegration and eventual collapse of the Nixon administration, Congress seized the opportunity to enact a number of pieces of legislation designed to curb presidential power in the foreign policy and security domains. These included the 1972 War Powers Resolution to limit presidential control over the deployment of American military forces, the 1973 Case-Zablocki Act, requiring that Congress be informed of all executive agreements, the 1974 Hughes-Ryan Amendments to regulate foreign military assistance, the 1976 National Emergen-

cies Act to regulate the exercise of presidential emergency power, the Foreign Intelligence Surveillance Act of 1978 and the Intelligence Oversight Act of 1980 to
provide for congressional oversight of intelligence operations, and the 1976 Arms
Export Control Act to limit presidential use of proxy forces. Congress also created
intelligence oversight committees to monitor the president's use of the nation's intelligence agencies. It appeared that the classic pattern of presidential politics had
reasserted itself. Political mobilization induced by war had strengthened the Congress and weakened the presidency.

The post-Vietnam retrogression of presidential power, however, proved to be
short-lived. Johnson's successors took a number of steps to ensure that within two
decades after the last American troops were evacuated from Saigon, presidential
power in war and foreign relations had been more than restored. The first of these
steps involved the recruitment and internal structure of the military and its relationship to American society. For two centuries, America had relied on citizen soldiers to fill the ranks of its armed forces and had spurned the idea of a professional
army as being inconsistent with democratic values. In the wake of the Vietnam
War, however, presidents and military planners realized that dependence on citizen
soldiers could impose serious constraints on the use of military forces. The risks
facing citizen soldiers provided opponents of the use of military force with a potent
issue to use against the government. The casualties and hardships borne by citizen
soldiers, moreover, reverberated through the society and might, as the Vietnam case
illustrated, fuel antiwar movements and resistance to military conscription. University of Chicago economist Milton Friedman, who served as a member of the Gates
Commission created by President Nixon to examine the elimination of military
conscription, argued that three-fourths of the opposition to the Vietnam War was
generated by the draft.[174] Citizen soldiers might be appropriate for a national war in
which America was attacked and domestic opposition was driven to the margins.
Anti–Vietnam War protests, however, convinced President Richard Nixon and his
successors that an army composed of professional soldiers would give them greater
flexibility to use military power when they deemed it necessary.[175]

Accordingly, Nixon ended the draft in 1973 and began to convert the military
into an all-volunteer force of professional soldiers. The presumption was that sending military professionals into battle would be less likely to incite popular and political resistance than would deploying reluctant conscripts. This supposition seems
to have been borne out. Indeed, in 2002, some opponents of President George W.
Bush's buildup of American forces for an attack against Iraq argued for a renewal
of conscription precisely because they believed that the president would be constrained from going to war if the military consisted of draftees.[176]

Members of this new professional force, especially those recruited for its elite combat units, receive extensive training and indoctrination designed to separate them from civilian society, and to imbue them with a warrior ethic that emphasizes loyalty to the group and organization.[177] This training is designed to immunize the military against possible contagion from antiwar and defeatist sentiments that may spring up in civilian America, and it appears to have produced a military, especially an officer corps, that views itself as a distinct caste.[178]

To a significant extent, the current military lives as a state within a state, subject to its own rules, norms, and governance.[179] Many members are recruited from families with a strong military tradition and from areas of the country, primarily the South and West, where conservative politics and support for the military are widespread.[180] This is a military better prepared for the idea that war is a normal state of affairs and whose members are less likely to complain to the media and members of Congress about the hardships and dangers they may endure in their nation's service. The creation of this all-volunteer force has sharply reduced the constraints on the use of military power and has rendered it more difficult to mobilize opposition to the continuing use of military force once a campaign is launched. Thus, for example, while the national news media and opposition politicians sought to make an issue of the American casualties suffered during the occupation of Iraq in 2003, the public's response was muted. Military families were generally prepared—albeit not pleased—to accept the risks to which their loved ones were exposed. They had been "trained to be stoical" in the words of defense analyst Eliot Cohen.[181] Meanwhile most Americans, secure in the knowledge that their children would not be called on to serve in the armed forces, were more concerned with other political issues.[182]

To be sure, the active-duty, all-volunteer force is backed by approximately one million reservists and National Guard troops who train on a regular basis but are called into service only when needed. Reservists make up a large percentage of troops trained in a number of support specialties—such as water supply, medical specialties, and chemical warfare—that are usually needed only in actual combat situations.[183] Tens of thousands of reservists were mobilized during the 1990 Persian Gulf War, then for the various military operations conducted during the Clinton years, and again in 2002–2003 in preparation for a second war with Iraq. Though the reservists are volunteers and many are veterans of the regular military, calling them up for service can disrupt the civilian economy and society and sometimes cause hardship and resentment among the reservists, their families, and their employers. During the Vietnam War, both Lyndon Johnson and Richard Nixon refrained from calling up the reserves, believing that such an order would intensify political opposition to the war. Because of these problems, in 2003 Defense Secretary Donald Rumsfeld ordered military planners to find ways to diminish or even eliminate the armed force's reliance on reserve troops. Such a shift will entail some expansion of the ranks of active-duty military as well as training regular forces to take over the specialties currently dominated by reservists.[184] Though both steps will add to defense costs, lessening the government's dependence on the last of its citizen soldiers would create a military force even more readily available for use whenever and wherever it was deemed to be needed. Consistent with Rumsfeld's wishes, the 2004 defense budget already called for the conversion to active-duty status of thousands of civil affairs, psychological operations, and special operations jobs that had been the domain of reserve forces.[185]

In the aftermath of Vietnam, the military was not only professionalized; it was also further centralized. The Goldwater-Nichols Department of Defense Reorganization Act of 1986 significantly increased the power of the chairman of the Joint Chiefs of Staff, the defense secretary, and the president to determine military missions and set procurement policies.[186] This change not only promised to improve military effectiveness, but also further reduced opportunities for the individual services to air their squabbles publicly and so open the way for congressional intervention. This had been a continuing, albeit muted, problem since the struggles of the Truman era and had broken out anew during the Vietnam War when the Army publicly accused the Air Force of failing to provide adequate close air support for its ground combat troops.[187]

While a more professional and centralized military might diminish the political constraints on presidential warmaking, it could not fully eliminate them. Many Americans might be willing to accept the idea of sending professional soldiers into harm's way, especially if their own children were not subject to conscription. But even professional soldiers are Americans with hometowns, parents, relatives, and friends, and the Vietnam conflict had demonstrated that American casualties could become a political liability—and ultimately, a constraint on the use of military force. This problem was one of the factors that led successive administrations to search for means of waging warfare that would minimize American casualties. After the carnage of the Civil War, American military doctrine had already begun to emphasize technology and maximum firepower, in order to keep casualties low and maintain public support.[188] In the years after the Vietnam War, the military services invested tens of billions of dollars in the development of cruise missiles, drone aircraft, precision-guided munitions, and a multitude of other advanced weapons systems capable of disabling or destroying America's opponents while reducing the risks to which American troops were exposed.[189]

Thus, in the 1990 Persian Gulf War and even more so in the 2001–2002 Afghan campaign, precision-guided weapons inflicted enormous damage on enemy forces while reducing the risks to U.S. troops. In the 2003 Iraq war, pilotless aircraft, precision-guided munitions, battlefield computers, and new command-and-control technology helped bring about a rapid victory over substantial Iraqi forces with what once might have been seen as impossibly low casualties.[190] Military analysts have pointed to these developments—sometimes called a revolution in military affairs—as indicative of a technological revolution in the conduct of war. Like past transformations in military tactics, however, this one has been caused as much by political pressures as by technological or exclusively military factors.[191] To the extent that U.S. casualties can be limited to smart bombs and pilotless aircraft, popular opposition to the use of military force is less likely to become a political problem. After one Predator drone aircraft was downed in 2002, an Air Force officer involved in the program said, "It was on page six of the *Washington Post*. If that had been a [manned] F-16, it would have been page one."[192] Along the same lines, in March 2004 the U.S. Army announced the cancellation of its $39 billion Comanche helicopter program. The Comanche required two crewmen and many of its planned missions could now be undertaken by pilotless drones that would not present the risk of casualties. "The Comanche is no longer consistent with the changed operational environment," said acting Army secretary Les Brownlee.[193]

Presidents and the military learned two other lessons from the Vietnam War, concerning media and money. Most military officers and defense officials were convinced that negative media coverage had played an important role in the waning of popular support for America's intervention in Southeast Asia. Stories of atrocities and casualties and a steady diet of media accounts questioning or contradicting official views of the war undoubtedly played a role in turning public opinion against the war during the mid-1960s.[194] After the war, then, all of the military services devised procedures and tactics to prevent negative media coverage of future conflicts. One of these tactics was to restrict media access to theaters of combat. In the Persian Gulf, Grenada, Panama, Afghanistan, and the other regions where American forces were sent into battle, reporters were restricted to pool coverage and were strictly prohibited from making unescorted visits to war zones. In general, the press was able to show only what the military wanted the public to see. At the same time, the defense brass made a major effort to cultivate good relations with reporters and media personalities and assigned only the most articulate military and media-savvy civilian defense officials—Generals Colin Powell and Norman Schwartzkopf in 1990, and Defense Secretary Donald Rumsfeld in 2001—to brief the media and answer questions.

In preparation for an attack on Iraq in 2003, reporters were sent to military "boot camps" where they were prepared for the rigors of combat and given a chance to absorb military perspectives. Some reporters were attached to particular combat units in the hope that they would file favorable stories about the soldiers with whom they lived and worked on a daily basis. One journalist observed that the purpose of this practice was to induce reporters "to bond, to feel part of a unit and to get the military good press."[195] This program of "embedding" reporters with military units was extremely successful. Many journalists clearly identified with their units and typically used the pronoun "we" when describing military actions undertaken by those units. Such press criticism as was heard during the war generally came from reporters far from the front or from military analysts in New York and Washington. These critics, however, could not compete with the enthusiastic "embeds" who provided dramatic real-time combat photos and coverage via satellite. Experienced and capable White House communications staffers, like Deputy Communications Director James Wilkinson, were simultaneously assigned to serve temporarily as information managers for senior military officers.[196] This move was intended to prevent generals who might lack communications skills from making statements that were inconsistent with White House views or that might be deemed politically incorrect.

The combination of restriction and astute public relations had a generally positive effect on the tenor of media coverage of U.S. military action. The networks themselves, to be sure, engaged in a good deal of self-censorship. Stung by Republican charges that they lacked patriotism, the major news networks generally made a point of treating Americans to favorable coverage of America's war effort. CNN went so far as to assign a more upbeat anchor team for its domestic broadcasts than for its international service. International audiences heard critical coverage from a team consisting of Jim Clancy, Michael Holmes, and Becky Anderson, who consistently questioned the claims of American officials. American viewers, by contrast, saw the team of Paula Zahn, Aaron Brown, and Wolf Blitzer, who seemed to find considerably more to praise than to question in their review of America's military effort.[197]

While the White House had been eager to encourage press coverage of the battles for control of Iraq, it took a very different approach during the subsequent occupation of the country. Media access to most of Iraq was severely limited and coverage of military actions restricted. The administration also imposed an almost total ban on coverage of wounded soldiers as they returned to the United States. Stories about individual casualties appeared in the press, but no coverage was permitted of the almost nightly flights from Iraq that brought the dead and wounded troops back to America.[198]

As for money, the U.S. government learned two lessons during the Vietnam War. One lesson was that attempting to buy both guns and butter with funds extracted from its own taxpayers could be politically harmful. The second was that

Congress might employ its power of the purse to interfere with military operations. During the course of American history, Congress has seldom refused to provide funding for military action when asked to do so by the president. In 1973, however, Congress voted to cut off funding for combat operations in Cambodia, a move that hastened the end of the Vietnam War.[199] Two years later, moreover, Congress voted to block the use of any funds for U.S. military intervention in Angola.[200] In order to make themselves less dependent on taxpayers and Congress, post-Vietnam presidents redoubled their efforts to induce American allies and others to share the military burden.

This tactic first became apparent during the Reagan administration when the White House solicited funds from the Sultan of Brunei to pay for military aid to the Nicaraguan Contras. Apparently, the funds were placed in the wrong Swiss bank account and never actually reached the Contras.[201] Despite this fiasco, the ploy of turning to foreigners to fund America's military efforts has been increasing in importance. In the 1990 Persian Gulf War, for example, the Bush administration made much of the fact that the United States had organized a coalition of nations to liberate Kuwait. But with the exception of Great Britain, which contributed valuable combat forces, America's coalition partners provided only token military units. Instead, members of the coalition were expected to contribute financially to the American military effort. Thus Saudi Arabia, Kuwait, the United Arab Emirates, Germany, Japan, and France—nations threatened by Iraq or dependent on Middle Eastern oil—collectively paid the United States some $54 billion as their contribution to the war effort. This sum was actually slightly more than the final cost of the war.[202] The president had wanted the payments to be tendered as "gifts" directly to the Defense Department, which could then spend the money as the administration saw fit. Congress, however, insisted that the funds be paid to the treasury, where any subsequent disbursements would require a congressional appropriation.[203] The importance of fiscal considerations in the Persian Gulf War is one reason that the United States was anxious to keep in its coalition nations like Saudi Arabia and the United Arab Emirates that had money but virtually no military prowess, but kept out of its coalition militarily potent but impecunious nations like Israel. The United States had enough firepower; it needed cash.

Lessons from Vietnam to Afghanistan and Beyond

Having learned the lessons of Vietnam, albeit not the lessons that antiwar protestors of the 1960s had hoped, successive presidents, most notably Ronald Reagan and George H. W. Bush, worked to break the legal fetters through which Congress had sought to constrain presidential warmaking. Some of these fetters proved illusory.

For example, the 1980 Intelligence Oversight Act lacked sanctions or penalties and seemed to assume that the president would cooperate with Congress.[204] No subsequent president, however, showed any intention of cooperating and, indeed, beginning with President Reagan, the White House interpreted the act as authorizing the executive to conduct covert operations.[205]

Other fetters were removed by the courts. For example, Congress had drafted the 1976 National Emergencies Act to narrow the president's emergency powers and had attached a legislative veto provision to ensure its ability to control presidential actions under the act. The legislative veto is a procedure allowing Congress to overturn a president's specific use of a power that has been granted by Congress. The U.S. Supreme Court, however, in the 1981 case of *Dames & Moore v. Regan,* stemming from President Carter's handling of the Iranian hostage crisis, construed the president's emergency powers broadly.[206] And in the 1983 case of *Immigration and Naturalization Service v. Chadha,* the Court invalidated legislative veto provisions.[207] The result was to leave the president with broader emergency powers and less congressional control than Congress had hoped. Though Congress can still end a presidentially declared emergency by a congressional joint resolution, such a resolution is subject to presidential veto.[208]

A third presidential fetter was broken by aggressive presidential action beginning in the early Reagan years. The 1973 War Powers Resolution provided that presidents could not use military forces for more than ninety days without securing congressional authorization. Many in Congress saw this time limit as a restraint on presidential action, though, as has often been observed, it gave the president more discretion than had been provided by the framers of the Constitution. President Gerald Ford had carefully followed the letter of the law when organizing a military effort to rescue American sailors held by North Korea. But this was the first and last time that the War Powers Act was fully observed.[209] The demise of the act began during the Reagan administration. President Reagan and his advisers were determined to eliminate this restriction, however negligible, on presidential war power.[210] Accordingly, between 1982 and 1986 Reagan presented Congress with a set of military *faits accomplis* that undermined the War Powers Act and, in effect, asserted a doctrine of sole presidential authority in the security realm. In August 1982, Reagan sent U.S. forces to Lebanon, claiming a constitutional authority to do so.[211] After terrorist attacks killed a number of Marines, Congress pressed Reagan to withdraw American forces, and to underscore its displeasure, activated the sixty-day War Powers clock. But after the administration accused lawmakers of undermining America's military efforts, Congress extended the president's authority to deploy troops to Lebanon for another eighteen months.

The president essentially ignored Congress, but withdrew American forces in February after further casualties and no prospect for success. Then in October 1983, while American forces were still in Lebanon, President Reagan ordered an invasion of the Caribbean island of Grenada after a coup had led to the installation of a pro-Cuban government on the island. Once again, the president claimed that his position as commander-in-chief gave him the power to initiate military action on a unilateral basis. Congress threatened to invoke the War Powers Act, but Reagan withdrew American troops before the Senate acted. The invasion of Grenada was quick, virtually without casualties, and quite popular, especially after the president claimed to have rescued a group of American medical students attending classes on the island. Also generating considerable popular approval was the 1986 bombing of Libya in response to a terrorist attack in Berlin that the administration had blamed on Libyan agents. Again Reagan acted without consulting Congress and claimed that his authority had come directly from the Constitution.

President Reagan was thus able to use American military forces on three separate occasions while denying that he was required to seek congressional authorization for his actions. Congress threatened and grumbled but in each instance was outmaneuvered by the president. In 1987, too, several of the president's aides were prosecuted for violations of federal law when it was revealed that the administration had transferred arms to Nicaraguan "Contra" guerillas then fighting against the Sandinista regime in that nation, despite specific congressional prohibitions. Nevertheless Reagan's successor, George H. W. Bush, resumed using American military forces on his authority as commander-in-chief. In December 1989, Bush ordered an invasion of Panama designed to oust Panamanian strongman General Manuel Noriega. Bush claimed that American citizens living in the Canal Zone were in danger and charged that Noriega had become involved in drug trafficking. Since drugs are shipped to the United States from many nations, often with the connivance of high-ranking officials, this seemed a rather flimsy pretext. Congress nevertheless made no official response to the invasion. A nonbinding House resolution expressed its approval of the president's actions, but urged Bush not to use drug smuggling as a reason to invade Mexico or the remainder of Latin America.[212]

In 1990–1991, the Bush administration sent a huge American military force into the Persian Gulf in response to Iraq's invasion and occupation of Kuwait, actions that posed a substantial threat to American economic and political interests. Consistent with the tactics devised by Harry Truman, the administration quickly secured a U.N. Security Council resolution authorizing member states to use "all necessary means," that is, military force, to compel Iraq to restore Kuwaiti independence. The president's spokespersons, then-defense-secretary Richard Cheney in particular, asserted that the U.N. resolution was a sufficient legal basis for American military action against Iraq. Given the U.N. resolution, said Cheney, no congressional authorization was required.[213] After House Democrats expressed strong opposition to unilateral action by the president, Bush asked Congress for legislation supporting the U.N. resolution. Both houses of Congress voted to authorize military action against Iraq—the Senate by the narrowest of margins—but the president made it clear that he did not feel bound by any congressional declaration and was prepared to go to war with or without Congress's assent. Indeed, the president later pointed out that he had specifically avoided asking Capitol Hill for "authorization" since such a request might improperly imply that Congress "had the final say in . . . an executive decision."[214]

President Clinton continued the Truman and Bush practice of securing authorization to use military force from a compliant international body and then presenting Congress with a *fait accompli:* in 1994, he planned an invasion of Haiti under the cover of a U.N. Security Council resolution. The president hoped to oust the military dictatorship that had seized power in a coup and to reinstall President Jean-Bertrand Aristide. Congress expressed strong opposition to Clinton's plans but he pressed forward nonetheless, claiming that he did not need congressional approval. The invasion was called off when the Haitian junta stepped down, but Clinton sent ten thousand American troops to occupy the island and help Aristide secure power. Congress was not consulted about the matter. In a similar vein, between 1994 and 1998, claiming to act under U.N. and NATO auspices, the administration undertook a variety of military actions in the former Yugoslavia, including an intensive bombing campaign directed against Serbian forces and installations, without formal congressional authorization. The air campaign lasted some seventy-nine days, involved more than thirty thousand American troops and more than eight hundred aircraft, and was conducted exclusively on the president's own authority.[215] The War Powers Resolution seemed to have entered the same legal limbo as state laws prohibiting lascivious carriage.

By the end of the Clinton administration, it was no longer clear what war powers, if any, remained in the hands of the Congress. Ronald Reagan, George H. W. Bush, and Bill Clinton had all ordered American forces into combat on their own authority; outmaneuvered, bullied, or ignored the Congress; and repeatedly asserted the principle that the president controlled security policy and especially the use of military force. Early in the administration of President George W. Bush, Islamic terrorists destroyed the World Trade Center and damaged the Pentagon. The president responded by organizing a major military campaign designed to eliminate terrorist bases in Afghanistan and to depose the Taliban regime that had sheltered the terrorists. Congress, for its part, quickly passed a joint resolution authorizing the president to use all necessary and appropriate means to prevent future acts of terrorism. This resolution continues to be cited by presidents as the legal basis for their various military actions. For example, the Obama administration has launched hundreds of drone attacks against suspected terrorists without ever consulting Congress about the propriety of the missions. If pressed, the administration will point to the 2001 resolution as the legal basis for its power.

The 2001 congressional resolution was little more than a blank check, barely mentioned by the press and ignored by the public. Both were, by now, fully aware that whatever its rhetoric, Congress had very little real control over the use of American military might. Subsequently, President Bush issued a variety of executive orders establishing military tribunals to try suspected terrorists, freezing the assets of those suspected of assisting terrorists, and expanding the authority of the CIA and other intelligence agencies. America's allies were also asked to contribute material and financial support for the endeavor.

Congress was not completely quiescent. Within a month of the terrorist attacks, the White House had drafted and Congress had quickly enacted the USA Patriot Act, which expanded the power of government agencies to engage in domestic surveillance activities, including electronic surveillance, and restricted judicial review of such efforts. The act also gave the attorney general greater authority to detain and deport aliens suspected of having terrorist affiliations.[216] The following year, Congress created the Department of Homeland Security, which combined offices from twenty-two federal agencies into one huge new cabinet department that would be responsible for protecting the nation from further acts of terrorism. The new agency, with a tentative budget of $40 billion, was to include the Coast Guard, Transportation Safety Administration, Federal Emergency Management Administration, Immigration and Naturalization Service, and offices from the departments of Agriculture, Energy, Transportation, Justice, Health and Human Services, Commerce, and the General Services Administration. The actual reorganization plan was drafted by the White House, but Congress weighed in to make certain that the new agency's workers would enjoy civil service and union protections.

It should also be mentioned that in October 2002, Congress voted to authorize the president to attack Iraq, which the administration had accused of supporting terrorism and constructing weapons of mass destruction. As had become customary, the congressional resolution gave the president complete discretion and the president, while welcoming congressional support, asserted that he had full power to use force with or without Congress's blessing. Only the late Senator Byrd, who took congressional power seriously, even bothered to object to the now obvious political if not constitutional truth of Bush's claim. In a reversal of the usual pattern, however, the president used his congressional resolution to pressure the U.N. Security Council to approve the use of force. Without such a resolution, an attack on Iraq would appear politically less legitimate and, more important, some of the nations expected to bankroll the war might well refuse, fearing their own domestic political repercussions.

The Security Council, though, stopped short of the authorization sought by President Bush, agreeing only to return U.N. weapons inspectors who had been ousted from Iraq some years earlier. Members of the council, especially France and Russia, argued that Iraq should be given an opportunity to disarm before being attacked. So while the inspectors shuffled rather aimlessly around the suburbs of Baghdad, the president mobilized land, sea, and air forces in preparation for a military assault. And once again, American diplomats worked to build a coalition. The president called it a "coalition of the willing," and said different nations would play various roles in it, according to their abilities. Presumably, this meant that the British were expected to provide military support while Kuwait and Qatar, among others, were expected to provide bases for American forces. Several other nations, including Japan and Germany, nominally opposed to the war, signaled their willingness to help finance the postwar reconstruction of Iraq in exchange for access to Iraqi oil. For their part, American officials indicated that even without financial contributions from America's allies, the war would not impose a burden on the American economy. In the immediate aftermath of the war, the administration was frustrated by unexpected costs encountered in the occupation of Iraq and by the hugely expensive task of rebuilding the nation's shattered economy and infrastructure. In a conference organized under U.N. auspices in October 2003, the United States succeeded in extracting pledges of some $13 billion in aid from a number of European and Asian countries. Arab nations, including Saudi Arabia, Kuwait, Qatar, and the United Arab Emirates, were expected to contribute billions more.[217]

After his election in 2008, President Obama brought an end to the wars in Iraq and Afghanistan but not to the president's power to wage war. The administration authorized scores of special operations and drone strikes against suspected terrorists. Some of these strikes have involved the execution of U.S. citizens suspected of terrorist activities. In 2011, for example, a drone strike in Yemen killed Anwar al-Awlaki, a U.S. citizen and imam of a Virginia mosque suspected of being a senior Al Qaeda recruiter. The administration had allegedly placed al-Awlaki's name on a CIA "target list" and obtained a Justice Department memorandum authorizing the killing. Several months later, another drone strike killed al-Awlaki's sixteen-year-old son, also a U.S. citizen born in Denver. The CIA and military have also been authorized to launch what are sometimes called "signature strikes." These are drone attacks against groups or individuals whose identities are unknown but whose activities seem suspicious to the drone operator. These strikes inevitably cause civilian casualties since it is often impossible to distinguish terrorist actions from innocent civilian activities. A group of persons loading fertilizer onto a pickup truck may be terrorists building bombs or farmers planting crops. Like its predecessors, the Obama administration has resisted congressional efforts to look into its uses of presidential war powers.

Thoughts on the President's Role in Foreign and Security Policy: Where Do Presidential War Powers End?

Franklin D. Roosevelt is often credited with the creation of the modern presidency. Indeed, during the Great Depression and World War II, FDR greatly expanded the executive branch and increased the powers of the Oval Office. In the realms of foreign and security policy, however, it was Harry S. Truman who laid the foundations for presidential supremacy. Roosevelt had been a wartime president who made use of his personal dynamism and political skill to fashion a series of ad hoc arrangements to control the national security arena. Truman, however, built the institutions and invented the procedures that allowed a rather inexperienced legislator from Missouri—and his successors of varying abilities, backgrounds, and political persuasions—to manage the foreign and security policies of what became a great imperial power. Through the mix of military and civil institutions developed during the Truman era, the United States contained the Soviet Union and, ultimately, prevailed in the Cold War. Through these same institutions, though, the presidency came to dominate the realm of national security while the Congress was gradually pushed into the background.

Part of the problem was the Cold War itself. Historically, as we saw, presidential power had waxed in wartime and waned afterward as Congress, in alliance with the forces inevitably mobilized by the effects of war, moved to reassert its role. The Cold War erased the distinction between war and peace. The emergency, and presidential demands for emergency powers, were both constant and, unfortunately, with the conclusion of the Cold War, new emergencies have arisen. The growth of presidential power, though, was not inevitable. Presidential power expanded not only due to the Cold War, but also because successive presidents devised institutions that bolstered their power at the expense of Congress. And when Congress managed to rein in presidential power after the Vietnam War, presidents did not respond by passively submitting to legislative authority. Instead, they licked their wounds, learned from past mistakes, and introduced institutional innovations intended to restore and enhance the authority of the Oval Office in the realm of security affairs. Among the most important of these has been the end of the nation's dependence on citizen soldiers and the construction of a military force and military tactics designed to reduce political constraints on the presidential use of military power. Wars fought by professional soldiers and drones are not likely to generate large-scale opposition to presidential war policies. As much as military success, that is the purpose of professional soldiers and drones.

Increased presidential control of security policy has had implications for presidential power in domestic affairs as well. Since the Civil War, presidents have demanded and received the power to regulate civilian production in wartime. Since the early years of the Cold War, moreover, military contracts have been a major factor shaping domestic industrial production and priorities. But presidential national security powers have intruded into other domestic areas as well.

Since the initiation of President Bush's War on Terror, the Patriot Act and the Homeland Security department have brought the president's national security powers home, much as the loyalty and security classification systems of the Cold War era once did.[218] As we saw, the Patriot Act, coupled with executive orders, has given the NSA the power to eavesdrop on every American and has enhanced the authority of the Justice Department to launch investigations, to obtain warrants for wiretaps, and to seize tainted assets. These powers have already been employed in a number of cases having no relationship whatsoever to terrorism.[219] And since the threat of terror is not likely to end in the foreseeable future, these policies are likely to become deeply ingrained in American political life. Moreover, as the distinction between foreign policy and domestic policy diminishes, the president's growing foreign policy powers are certain to take on ever greater domestic importance.

The President Goes to War

Since the Washington administration, presidents have claimed to possess powers not specified in the Constitution but said to stem from "the rights, duties and obligations of the presidency." These are referred to as inherent powers and are most often asserted by presidents in times of war or national emergency. President Lincoln relied on a claim of inherent power to raise an army after the fall of Fort Sumter. Similarly, Presidents Roosevelt (World War II), Truman (Korean War), and both Presidents Bush (Persian Gulf and Middle East Wars) claimed inherent powers to defend the nation. Since the Korean War, presidents have used their claim of inherent powers along with their constitutional power as commander-in-chief to bypass the constitutional provision giving Congress the power to declare war. Congress declared war after the Japanese attack on Pearl Harbor on December 7, 1941. Since that time, American forces have been sent to fight foreign wars on more than one hundred occasions but not once was Congress asked for a declaration of war. In 1973, Congress passed the War Powers Resolution designed to restore its role in military policy. Presidents, however, have regarded the resolution as an improper limitation on the inherent powers of the presidency and have studiously ignored its provisions.

War of 1812. The "War Hawk" faction in Congress, led by Speaker Henry Clay, hoped to seize Canada in a short war against Britain. President Madison was dubious about the matter but was ignored. The war was a disaster and sparked a secessionist movement in New England, as well as retribution by the British, who in 1814 burned the White House and other government buildings in Washington, D.C. Andrew Jackson's famous victory at New Orleans came after the war had ended.

Mexican-American War. In 1846, President Polk used the pretext of a supposed Mexican attack on the United States to launch an invasion of Mexico. Congress fa-

CAPTURE AND BURNING OF WASHINGTON BY THE BRITISH, IN 1814.

vored the war but resented Polk's unilateralism, and agreed to a formal declaration of war only after lambasting Polk. The war resulted in the American annexation of a huge swath of Mexican territory in the current American Southwest.

Civil War. When South Carolina militia forces attacked Fort Sumter, President

BOMBARDMENT OF VERA CRUZ, MARCH 1847
ATTACK OF THE GUN BOATS UPON THE CITY, & CASTLE OF SAN JUAN DE ULLOA.
COMMANDED BY JOSIAH TATNALL ESQ U.S.N.

Lincoln undertook a variety of military responses without waiting for congressional acquiescence. Congress subsequently ratified Lincoln's actions.

World War I. Woodrow Wilson campaigned for reelection in 1916 on the slogan, "He kept us out of war." Once reelected, however, Wilson worked to bring about America's entry into the war. Wilson believed that it was America's duty to create a more orderly and peaceful world—to "make the world safe for democracy." The German policy of unrestricted submarine attacks on ships bound for England helped persuade Americans that Wilson was correct.

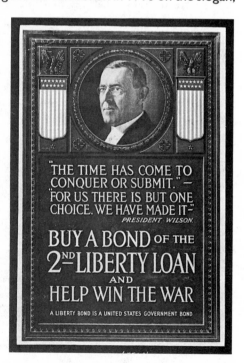

World War II. Many Americans believed that the nation's sacrifices in World War I had been a mistake and, thereafter, supported a posture of isolationism. President Roosevelt, however, viewed the expanding power of Nazi Germany and Imperial Japan as a mortal threat to the United States and worked to prepare the

nation for war. All debate ended when Japanese carrier forces attacked the American Pacific fleet at Pearl Harbor on December 7, 1941. The Japanese surrendered after four years of bloody conflict.

Korean War. North Korean forces, supported by China, invaded South Korea in 1950. President Truman ordered American troops into combat to save the beleaguered South Koreans. Truman did not ask Congress for a declaration of war; he chose instead to act on his own authority under the general auspices of a U.N. mandate. The Korean War thus became the first of several undeclared wars.

Indochina War. In the 1960s, Presidents Kennedy and Johnson deployed American forces to Vietnam and other nations of Southeast Asia in opposition to North Vietnamese and various other indigenous forces. Eventually several hundred thousand American troops were embroiled in bloody and inconclusive fighting. The war sparked a peace movement in the United States and eventually, in 1973, produced congressional legislation compelling the withdrawal of American forces and the eventual evacuation of remaining American personnel from Saigon.

TEN

Understanding the Presidency
as an Institution
Advice for Citizens and Voters

Now that we have reviewed the constitutional status, history, and institutional features of America's presidency, I would like to offer, for further reflection and discussion, three concluding thoughts about what the framers liked to call our executive magistracy.

1. The president is a person and possesses neither divine nor satanic power. This point would appear to be obvious, but many Americans seem either enraptured or overcome by hatred when thinking about the president. Some say they "believe" in the president, as in the lyrics of the 2008 Obama campaign song "We Believe in Barack Obama" by a popular group, the Hush Sound.[1]

Veneration of rulers is hardly a new phenomenon. The rulers of ancient Egypt, ancient China, and ancient Japan, to name a few, were regarded as divine figures and medieval European kings claimed to rule by divine right. America's founders, however, hoped to discourage this sort of primitive thinking. Article I, Section 9 prohibits the federal government from granting titles of nobility, and Article I, Section 10 applies the same prohibition to the states. America's rulers were to be plain citizens temporarily appointed to serve their country, not titled demigods. George Washington underscored this point when he insisted that he be addressed simply as Mr. President.

Some presidents and their advisers, as we saw in Chapter 7, have encouraged the development of personality cults, and presidential biographers have, for their own reasons, worked to elevate ordinary mortals into godlike figures. The first of these hagiographers was Mason Weems, who invented many of the myths that came to surround George Washington—the cherry tree, the silver dollar, and so on—to boost the flagging sales of his biography of the first president. Others have followed in Weems's footsteps. A sampling of the titles tells the story—*Presidential Courage: Brave Leaders and How They Changed America, Polk: The Man Who Transformed the Presidency and America, Franklin Roosevelt: Soldier of Freedom, American Lion: Andrew Jackson in the White House.* My apologies to the authors; some of these books make excellent reading. Unfortunately, though, their overall effect is to encourage presidential veneration by elevating ordinary individuals into saints.

On the other side of veneration is hatred. Some will project onto this seemingly larger-than-life presidential figure their own ugly vitriol and fears. President Obama has complained that many Americans seem to hate him and he is right to be concerned. President of the United States is the most dangerous job in America. Four of America's forty-three presidents, 9.3 percent of the occupants of the White House, have been assassinated. The next most dangerous occupation in America is lumberjack, with an on-the-job fatality rate of only .09 percent. In addition to the four presidents killed, one chief executive (Reagan) was shot but recovered, while serious but unsuccessful attempts were made on the lives of twelve other presidents, most by their fellow citizens.

These data underline the point that citizens of a republic should neither venerate nor loathe their elected officials. Those who venerate the president are foolish; those who loathe the president should search for explanations within themselves.

2. Presidents are politicians who have spent their lives competing for office and power. As a result most are ambitious, cynical, and ruthless, and do not view the world from the same perspective as ordinary Americans. In some cases, say that of Richard Nixon, their character flaws become obvious. Others are better able to hide their political traits. Americans of the 1950s liked a man they saw as genial "Uncle Ike" but even Richard Nixon, who saw the real Eisenhower, was actually afraid of the general, who he said was the coldest, most ruthless individual he had ever met.[2]

For presidents, just as for other politicians, words and principles are weapons, evaluated for their utility rather than their truth value. Programs and policies are tools of political power, advanced if they promote the president's interests, opposed if they do not. Friends and allies are embraced so long as they are useful, and sometimes jettisoned if they become liabilities.

"I have previously stated and I repeat now that the United States plans no military intervention in Cuba." said President John F. Kennedy in 1961 as he planned military action in Cuba. "As president, it is my duty to the American people to report that renewed hostile actions against United States ships on the high seas in the Gulf of Tonkin have today required me to order the military forces of the United States to take action in reply," said President Lyndon Johnson in 1964 as he fabricated an incident to justify expansion of American involvement in Vietnam. "We did not, I repeat, did not—trade weapons or anything else [to Iran] for hostages, nor will we," said President Ronald Reagan in November 1986, four months before admitting that U.S. arms had been traded to Iran in exchange for Americans being held hostage there. "Simply stated, there is no doubt that Saddam Hussein now has weapons of mass destruction," said Vice President Dick Cheney in 2002. When it turned out that these weapons did not exist, Assistant Defense Secretary Paul Wolfowitz explained, "For bureaucratic reasons, we settled on one issue, weapons of mass destruction[, as justification for invading Iraq,] because it was the one reason everyone could agree on."[3] "First of all, if you've got health insurance, you like your doctor, you like your plan—you can keep your doctor, you can keep your plan. Nobody is talking about taking that away from you," said President Obama as he prepared to launch a program that would compel many Americans to change their physicians and health plans. As was true of all the others, Obama's positions on various issues, such as same-sex marriage, "evolved" to suit changing political circumstances, and over the course of his two terms, he jettisoned several longtime friends whose embrace proved inexpedient.

Most Americans seem unprepared for the realities of politics and are dismayed when they are deceived—again. Part of the problem is that American civic education seems designed to encourage political naiveté. What are citizens currently taught about government and politics? The main lessons currently taught to elementary and secondary school students in the citizenship-education programs mandated by every American state consist of three broad principles: government is necessary and America's government is particularly beneficent; it is important to follow rules and pay taxes; and appropriate political activity by citizens consists mainly of voting. These civics lessons are certainly not ill-intentioned. Yet they do not seem calculated to encourage lively or robust forms of citizenship, nor to give rise to a very sophisticated understanding of politics.

What should be taught in place of or in addition to these rather ingenuous lessons? Not surprisingly, both Plato and Aristotle had some useful thoughts on this topic. The Athenians thought that every person was born an ιδιώτης (idiot) but, through proper education, some might become citizens capable of effective participation in public life. Plato, later echoed by Aristotle, thought a citizen must know both how to rule and how to be ruled. Of course, in the fifth and sixth centuries B.C.E., many Athenian citizens might literally have taken turns ruling and being ruled. But the real point is that rulers who understand what it is like to be an ordinary member of the public will treat their subjects justly and with respect. At the same time, ordinary individuals who understand the perspectives and purposes of rulers will not only be willing to accept just rule, but also be less vulnerable to mistreatment and manipulation. If Americans are not to be ἰδιῶται (idiots), they need to understand how authority is exercised on them—the tricks of the ruler's trade—so that they can be prepared to consider the effects of this authority and to distinguish truth from lies. Being taught how to rule might prepare Americans to understand their presidents and avoid being flummoxed by them.

3. *Do not succumb to the fallacy of "presidentialism."* Whether they like a particular president or not, many Americans seem convinced that Congress is stupid and inefficient—the "broken branch" according to one recent book—and that only the president has the ability to properly govern the nation. This is a fallacy for three reasons.[4]

Emergency Power

The first element of presidentialist thinking is that executive power is needed to deal with emergencies and to ensure the nation's security.[5] While no one could argue with this position in the abstract, particularly in an age of global terrorism, the problem is that presidents can sometimes be too anxious to act forcefully in response to what they perceive as security threats. The framers of the Constitution gave Congress, not the president, the power to make war precisely because they feared that presidents might be altogether too willing to commit the nation to armed conflicts.[6]

But if the president is too anxious to go to war, is Congress too reluctant to respond to emergencies? The short answer is no. It would be difficult to identify an instance during the past half century in which the nation's security was compromised because Congress refused to act. In contrast, there have been a number of cases, including perhaps the recent Iraq war, in which the president was, as Madison feared, too quick to take vigorous action. When the nation has faced actual emergencies, Congress has seldom refused to grant appropriate powers to the president.

Contemporary executive power, moreover, is not held in reserve for national emergencies but is instead employed by presidents on a routine basis, often to implement mundane elements of their agenda that lack sufficient support in Congress to be enacted into law. Thus President Clinton used the power of regulatory review to launch an environmental program that had been blocked in the Congress. Similarly, President Bush used an executive order to place limits on stem cell research, a decision that pleased religious conservatives but could never have mustered majorities in the House and Senate. President Obama has issued executive orders to implement portions of an immigration bill that failed to pass the Congress. Right or wrong, these decisions hardly involved national emergencies. In all three instances, the president was simply asserting his policy preferences and using his executive powers to override or ignore those of his opponents.

The Public Interest

A second presidentialist argument is that the president champions the national interest as opposed to the particularistic interests defended by members of Congress. This position was frequently articulated by nineteenth-century Progressives, who asserted that only a powerful presidency could stand outside the realm of partisan conflict, exercise stewardship over the economy as a whole, and advance the national interest.[7] Today similar arguments are voiced by critics of Congress who accuse the legislative branch of an inherent incapacity to surmount special interest politics.[8] A similar perspective informs the writings of administrative theorists who support the notion of the unitary executive. For example, Steven Calabresi has written elsewhere, "The President who is alone vested with all of the executive power and is elected by all of the people, can be lobbied to rein in special interests . . . He can be urged to prevent special interest groups or ideologues from diverting public policy into immoderate or non-public-interested directions."[9]

This notion of the president above party seems reminiscent of the premodern yearning for a wise and beneficent king who would brush aside the selfish claims of manipulative courtiers and rule on behalf of the best interests of all his subjects. Perhaps such kings existed from time to time, but historically the behavior of kings should not inspire much confidence in the notion that powerful executives are a good antidote to factional selfishness and rent-seeking special interests. Presidents, to be sure, are unitary actors. As such they may find it more difficult than members of Congress to escape responsibility for their conduct or, through inaction, to become free riders on the efforts of others. To this extent, the presidentialist argument might have some merit. Empirically, however, presidents do not appear much less likely than senators and representatives to set aside personal concerns in favor of some abstract public good. Presidents often enough seem to promote programs designed mainly to reward important political backers and contributors even when these initiatives clearly do not serve the larger public interest. What public interest was served by President Clinton's decision to pardon fugitive financier Marc Rich?

Why did President Bush block stem cell research even though such work is important to maintaining America's technological edge? In both instances, personal or political calculations appear to have outweighed presidential concern for the public interest. Even the Progressives, who invented the idea of presidentialism, had a particular axe to grind. They did not actually think presidents could be above politics. Progressives thought, rather, that presidents would be more oriented to the needs of major national corporations than to those of local and regional firms.[10]

Presidentialism and Democracy

Beyond assertions of the need for a strong presidency and the allegedly superior commitment of the president to the national interest, a third presidentialist argument is frequently made: that the presidency is a more democratic institution than the Congress.[11] This argument has a certain surface plausibility. As the only official who is elected by the entire nation, the president can indeed claim to be the only person to represent all Americans. And though only half of all eligible voters participate in presidential elections, the percentage for congressional races is sharply lower. Issues of gerrymandering, committee structure, seniority, and incumbency also taint Congress's democratic credentials. Nevertheless the notion that the presidency is a more democratic institution than the Congress is ultimately misleading and mischievous. The notion is misleading, first, because the Congress inevitably represents a greater variety and range of interests and perspectives than the president. The notion that the presidency is a more democratic institution than the Congress is wrong for another, more important, reason as well. Both presidents and members of Congress are products of electoral democracy. But while modern presidents are elected through a democratic, even if imperfect, process, only the Congress governs in anything approaching a democratic and pluralistic manner. The congressional process, to be sure, seldom conforms to the ideals of democratic theory. Indeed, its defects are much discussed and well known. Yet at its core, the congressional policymaking process revolves around open hearings, public debate, and vigorous contention among a host of disparate groups. Though a small number of congressional hearings are closed, usually because executive branch witnesses claim national security concerns, the great majority of committee and subcommittee hearings are open to the public and the press. In short, despite its many imperfections, the U.S. Congress is a democratic decisionmaking body.

In addition, whatever Congress's shortcomings as a democratic policymaking body, its credentials shine by comparison to those of the White House. Presidential decisionmaking generally takes place in private and is often shrouded in secrecy.

The agencies of the executive branch are required by law to engage in an extensive process of open consultation with interested parties when they make decisions. Presidents, however, have no such obligation. Recent presidents have vehemently asserted that the secrecy of the processes leading up to their decisions is shielded by executive privilege, which means that these deliberations are often removed from the public domain. Even the decisions themselves are sometimes not revealed to the public or even to the Congress. Many so-called national security directives issued by presidents in recent years have been used to initiate secret missions by intelligence and defense agencies.[12] The recent case of NSA eavesdropping revelations is an example. For many years, too, presidents signed secret executive agreements with other governments obligating the United States to various forms of action without congressional knowledge, much less approval. In 1972, Congress enacted the Case-Zablocki Act, which requires the president to annually provide it with a list of all international agreements entered into during the previous year. Presidents have never fully complied with the terms of this act, claiming that it does not cover national security directives and other sensitive matters.[13]

America's founders thought a strong executive was necessary to give the government "energy." They would not, however, have recommended glorifying the presidency or viewing presidential government as the solution to the nation's problems. The framers of the Constitution had just overthrown one king and were very much aware of the value of checks and balances. In their desire for effective leadership, Americans today, like the founders, should not lose sight of the importance of democratic governance.

The President as a Lightning Rod

Some Americans seem inclined to excessively venerate or loathe our chief executives. Presidents are neither demigods nor demons, yet every American president has become the target of malicious campaigns designed to persuade their fellow citizens that America is governed by monstrous, malicious, or supremely incompetent chief executives.

Lyndon Johnson. Opponents of the Vietnam War often chanted, "Hey, hey, LBJ. How many boys did you kill today?" This poster depicts Johnson as King Kong atop the

nation, destroying its institutions and sending young Americans to war like lambs to the slaughter.

Richard Nixon. Nixon, here drawn as a pig, was often depicted as a loathsome figure, unfit for office.

Ronald Reagan. Reagan was politically conservative and often decried

THE FASCIST GUN

IN THE WEST

as a Fascist by his political enemies. During his days as an actor, Reagan had starred in several westerns. Juxtaposition of these two elements produced this poster.

Bill Clinton. In the wake of Clinton's involvement with a young intern, the president

was impeached, though not convicted. This bumper sticker, with a line drawn through the president's image, was commonly displayed during this period.

George W. Bush. Though a graduate of Yale and scion of a distinguished American family, Bush was often portrayed as uncouth and unlettered—the village idiot.

Barack Obama. Many conservatives viewed Obama as too liberal and too weak to lead America. Some caricatures of the president exhibited distinct elements of racism.

Appendix
Gallery of Presidents

1. George Washington, 1789–1797

2. John Adams, 1797–1801

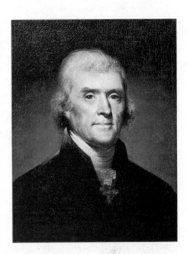

3. Thomas Jefferson, 1801–1809

4. James Madison, 1809–1817

5. James Monroe, 1817–1825

6. John Quincy Adams, 1825–1829

401

7. Andrew Jackson, 1829–1837

8. Martin Van Buren, 1837–1841

9. William Henry Harrison, 1841

10. John Tyler, 1841–1845

11. James Knox Polk, 1845–1849

12. Zachary Taylor, 1849–1850

13. Millard Fillmore, 1850–1853

14. Franklin Pierce, 1853–1857

15. James Buchanan, 1857–1861

16. Abraham Lincoln, 1861–1865

17. Andrew Johnson, 1865–1869

18. Ulysses S. Grant, 1869–1877

19. Rutherford Birchard Hayes, 1877–1881

20. James Abram Garfield, 1881

21. Chester Alan Arthur, 1881–1885

22. Grover Cleveland, 1885–1889

23. Benjamin Harrison, 1889–1893

24. Grover Cleveland, 1893–1897

25. William McKinley, 1897–1901   26. Theodore Roosevelt, 1901–1909   27. William Howard Taft, 1909–1913

28. Woodrow Wilson, 1913–1921   29. Warren Gamaliel Harding, 1921–1923   30. Calvin Coolidge, 1923–1929

31. Herbert Clark Hoover, 1929–1933   32. Franklin Delano Roosevelt, 1933–1945   33. Harry S. Truman, 1945–1953

34. Dwight David Eisenhower,
1953–1961

35. John Fitzgerald Kennedy,
1961–1963

36. Lyndon Baines Johnson,
1963–1969

37. Richard Milhous Nixon,
1969–1974

38. Gerald Rudolph Ford, 1974–1977

39. James Earl Carter, Jr., 1977–1981

40. Ronald Wilson Reagan,
1981–1989

41. George Herbert Walker Bush,
1989–1993

42. William Jefferson Clinton,
1993–2001

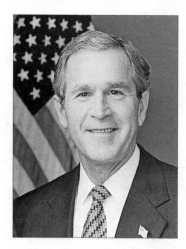

43. George Walker Bush, 2001–2009

44. Barack Hussein Obama, 2009–2017

Notes

CHAPTER ONE
What Is an Executive?

1. Max Farrand, *The Framing of the Constitution of the United States* (New Haven: Yale University Press, 1962), 49.

2. Richard Neustadt, *Presidential Power* (New York: Wiley, 1960), 33.

3. Quoted in Herbert Storing, *What the Anti-Federalists Were For: The Political Thought of the Opponents of the Constitution* (Chicago: University of Chicago Press, 1981), 49–50.

4. Alexander Hamilton, James Madison, and John Jay, *The Federalist Papers,* ed. Edward Mead Earle (New York: Random House, Modern Library, n.d.), no. 70, 454.

5. Quoted in Herbert Storing, ed., *The Anti-Federalist* (Chicago: University of Chicago Press, 1981), 311.

6. Storing, *What the Anti-Federalists Were For,* 49.

7. Hamilton, Madison, and Jay, *Federalist Papers,* no. 17, 105.

8. Storing, *What the Anti-Federalists Were For,* 49.

9. Hamilton, Madison, and Jay, *Federalist Papers,* no. 70, 455.

10. Ray Raphael, *Mr. President: How and Why the Founders Created a Chief Executive* (New York: Knopf, 2012).

11. Frank Lambert, *The Barbary Wars: American Independence in the Atlantic World* (New York: Hill and Wang, 2005).

12. Leonard L. Richards, *Shay's Rebellion: The American Revolution's Final Battle* (Philadelphia: University of Pennsylvania Press, 2003).

13. Ibid.

14. William Hogeland, *The Whiskey Rebellion: George Washington, Alexander Hamilton and the Frontier Rebels Who Challenged America's Newfound Sovereignty* (New York: Simon & Schuster, 2010).

15. Quoted in Max Farrand, ed., *Records of the Federal Convention of 1787* (New Haven: Yale University Press, 1937), vol. 1, 70.

16. John Nagy, *Spies in the Continental Capital: Espionage across Pennsylvania during the American Revolution* (Yardley, PA: Westholme, 2011).

17. Benjamin Ginsberg, *The Worth of War* (New York: Prometheus Books, 2014), 198.

18. Harvey Mansfield, Jr., *Taming the Prince: The Ambivalence of Modern Executive Power* (New York: Free Press, 1989).

19. Quoted in Farrand, *Records*, vol. 1, 66.

20. Ibid., 88.

21. Ibid., 91.

22. Ibid., 85.

23. Ibid., 97.

24. A. M. Bertelli and C. R. Grose, "The Lengthened Shadow of Another Institution? Ideal Point Estimates for the Executive Branch and Congress," *American Journal of Political Science* 55 (2011): 767–781.

25. Michael Nelson and Russell Riley, eds. *Governing at Home: The White House and Domestic Policymaking* (Lawrence: University Press of Kansas, 2011).

26. Mark Rozell and Mitchell Sollenberger, "Obama's Executive Branch Czars: The Constitutional Controversy and a Legislative Solution," *Congress and the Presidency* 39, no. 1 (2012): 74–99.

27. Bradley Patterson, *To Serve the President: Continuity and Innovation in the White House Staff* (Washington, DC: Brookings, 2008).

28. Michael Nelson and Russell Riley, eds., *The President and Words: Speeches and Speech Writing in the Modern White House* (Lawrence: University Press of Kansas, 2011).

29. Jody C. Baumgartner and Rhonda Evans Case, "Constitutional Design of the Executive: Vice Presidencies in Comparative Perspective," *Congress and the Presidency* 36, no. 2 (2009): 148–163.

30. MaryAnne Borrelli, *The Politics of the President's Wife* (College Station: Texas A&M University Press, 2011).

31. Philip Abbot, *Accidental Presidents: Death, Assassination, Resignation, and Democratic Succession* (New York: Palgrave Macmillan, 2008).

32. Michael J. Gerhardt, *The Forgotten Presidents: Their Untold Constitutional Legacy* (New York: Oxford University Press, 2013).

CHAPTER TWO

Constitutional Foundations of Presidential Power

1. Louis Fisher, "The Pocket Veto: Its Current Status," *CRS Report for Congress,* Mar. 30, 2001, available online at http://www.senate.gov/reference/resources/pdf/RL30909.pdf (accessed

July 18, 2015). See also Robert J. Spitzer, "The Historical Presidency: Growing Executive Power; The Strange Case of the 'Protective Return' Pocket Veto," *Presidential Studies Quarterly*, 42, no. 3 (Sept. 2012): 637–655.

2. James Madison, "Helvidius Letter I," in *The Letters of Pacificus and Helvidius* (Delmar, NY: Scholars' Facsimiles and Reprints, 1976), 27–30.

3. James Madison, "Helvidius Letter IV," in *The Letters of Pacificus and Helvidius* (Delmar, NY: Scholars' Facsimiles and Reprints, 1976), 90.

4. Max Farrand, ed., *Records of the Federal Convention of 1787* (New Haven: Yale University Press, 1966), vol. 2, 318.

5. Jeffrey Crouch, *The Presidential Pardon Power* (Lawrence: University of Kansas Press, 2009). Also Jeffrey Crouch, "The Toussie Pardon, 'Unpardon,' and the Abdication of Responsibility in Clemency Cases," *Congress and the Presidency*, vol. 38, no. 1 (2011): 77–100.

6. 272 U.S. 52 (1926). In the later case of *Humphrey's Executor v. United States*, 281 U.S. 602 (1935), the Court ruled that the executives of independent commissions could be removed only for cause.

7. 478 U.S. 714 (1986).

8. John Yoo, *The Powers of War and Peace* (Chicago: University of Chicago Press, 2003). See also Dana Nelson, "The Unitary Executive Question: What Do McCain and Obama Think of the Concept?" *Los Angeles Times*, Oct. 11, 2008, available online at http://www.latimes.com/opinion/la-oe-nelson11-2008oct11-story.html (accessed July 18, 2015).

9. See Eric Posner and Adrian Vermeule, *The Executive Unbound: After the Madisonian Republic* (Chicago: University of Chicago Press, 2011).

10. "Unchecked Abuse," *Washington Post*, Jan. 11, 2006, available online at http://www.washingtonpost.com/wp-dyn/content/article/2006/01/10/AR2006011001536.html (accessed July 18, 2015).

11. Elena Kagan, "Presidential Administration," *Harvard Law Review* 114 (June 2001): 2262.

12. Alexander Hamilton, "Pacificus Letter I," in *The Letters of Pacificus and Helvidius* (Delmar, NY: Scholars' Facsimiles and Reprints, 1976), 11.

13. Quoted in Storing, *What the Anti-Federalists Were For*, 49.

14. Robert Pear, "Ambiguity in Health Law Could Make Family Coverage Too Costly for Many," *New York Times*, Aug. 12, 2012, 10.

15. Jerry L. Mashaw, *Greed, Chaos, and Governance: Using Public Choice to Improve Public Law* (New Haven: Yale University Press, 1997), 106.

16. Kimberly Johnson, *Governing the American State* (Princeton: Princeton University Press, 2006); also Elizabeth Sanders, *Roots of Reform: Farmers, Workers and the American State* (Chicago: University of Chicago Press, 1999) and Theda Skocpol, *Protecting Soldiers and Mothers: The Political Origins of Social Policy in the United States* (Cambridge, MA: Harvard University Press, 1995).

17. Daniel Carpenter, *The Forging of Bureaucratic Autonomy* (Princeton: Princeton University Press, 2001).

18. See Theodore J. Lowi, *The End of Liberalism,* 2nd ed. (New York: Norton, 1979); also David Schoenbrod, *Power without Responsibility: How Congress Abuses the People through Delegation* (New Haven: Yale University Press, 1993).

19. Kenneth Culp Davis, *Discretionary Justice* (Baton Rouge: Louisiana State University Press, 1969), 15–21.

20. *Mistretta v. United States,* 488 U.S. 361, 372 (1989).

21. Schoenbrod, *Power without Responsibility,* 61.

22. William F. Fox, *Understanding Administrative Law,* 4th ed. (New York: Lexis Publishing, 2000), 36–37.

23. Kara Scannell and Deborah Soloman, "Business Wins Its Battle to Ease a Costly Sarbanes-Oxley Rule," *Wall Street Journal,* Nov. 10, 2006, 1.

24. Louis Fisher, "The Unitary Executive and Inherent Executive Power," *Journal of Constitutional Law* 12, no. 1 (Feb. 2010): 586.

25. *Annals of Congress* 10 (1800): 613.

26. Louis Fisher, "Presidential Inherent Power: The 'Sole Organ' Doctrine," *Presidential Studies Quarterly* 37, no. 1 (Mar. 2007): 139.

27. *United States v. Curtiss-Wright Corp.,* 299 U.S. 304 (1936).

28. Clement Fatovic, *Outside the Law: Emergency and Executive Power* (Baltimore: Johns Hopkins University Press, 2009).

29. Quoted in Paul Brest et al., *Processes of Constitutional Decisionmaking: Cases and Materials,* 6th ed. (New York: Aspen, 2006), 65–67.

30. 17 F. Cas. 144 (C.C.D. Md. 1861), no. 9487.

31. Louis Fisher, "Invoking Inherent Powers: A Primer," *Presidential Studies Quarterly* 37, no. 1 (Mar. 2007): 1–22.

32. Ibid.

33. John Gramlich, "Holder Sees Constitutional Basis for Obama's Executive Actions," *Roll Call,* Jan. 30, 2014, available online at http://www.rollcall.com/news/holder_sees_constitutional_basis_for_obamas_executive_actions-230528-1.html?pg'1 (accessed July 18, 2015).

34. Harold C. Relyea, "National Emergency Powers," *Congressional Research Service,* 2007, available online at http://fas.org/sgp/crs/natsec/98-505.pdf (accessed July 18, 2015).

35. Andrew Reeves, "Political Disaster: Unilateral Powers, Electoral Incentives, and Presidential Disaster Declarations," *Journal of Politics* 73, no. 4 (Oct. 2011): 1142–1151.

36. Farrand, *Records of the Federal Convention of 1787,* vol. 2, 65.

37. Ibid., 66.

38. Alexander Hamilton, James Madison, and John Jay, *The Federalist Papers,* ed. Edward Mead Earle (New York: Random House, Modern Library, n.d.), no. 76, 494–495.

39. Peter Grier, "Hagel, Brennan and History: How Often Does Senate Reject Cabinet Nominees?" *Christian Science Monitor,* Jan. 7, 2013, available online at http://www.csmonitor.com/USA/DC-Decoder/Decoder-Buzz/2013/0107/Hagel-Brennan-and-history-How-often-does-Senate-reject-cabinet-nominees (accessed July 18, 2015).

40. Josh Gerstein, "Supreme Court Strikes Down Obama Recess Appointments," *Politico,* June 26, 2014, available online at http://www.politico.com/story/2014/06/supreme-court-recess -appointments-108347.html (accessed July 18, 2015).

41. Farrand, *Records of the Federal Convention of 1787,* vol. 2, 66.

42. Terry M. Moe, "The President and Bureaucracy," in Michael Nelson, ed., *The Presidency and the Political System,* 4th ed. (Washington, DC: CQ Press, 1995), 429.

43. William Howell and David Brent, *Thinking about the Presidency: The Primacy of Power* (Princeton: Princeton University Press, 2013).

44. Moe, "President and Bureaucracy," 438–439.

45. "Fast Track May Be Just a Horse Trade Away," *Bloomberg BusinessWeek Magazine,* Apr. 21, 2002, available online at http://www.businessweek.com/stories/2002-04-21/fast-track-may -be-just-a-horse-trade-away (accessed July 18, 2015).

46. Christopher Lee, "Alito Once Made Case for Presidential Power," *Washington Post,* Jan. 2, 2006, available online at http://www.washingtonpost.com/wp-dyn/content/article/2006/ 01/01/AR2006010100788.html (accessed July 18, 2015).

47. Philip J. Cooper, *By Order of the President: The Use and Abuse of Presidential Direct Action* (Lawrence: University Press of Kansas, 2002), 201.

48. Ronald Reagan, "Statement on Signing a Veterans' Benefit Bill," Nov. 18, 1988, *Public Papers of the President,* 1988–1989 (Washington, DC: U.S. Government Printing Office, 1990), book 2, 1558.

49. Ronald Reagan, "Statement on Signing the Bill Prohibiting the Licensing or Construction of Facilities on the Salmon and Snake Rivers in Idaho," Nov. 17, 1988, *Public Papers of the President, 1988–1989* (Washington, DC: U.S. Government Printing Office, 1990), book 2, 1525.

50. *Lear, Siegler v. Lehman,* 842 F. 2nd 1102 (1988).

51. Andrew Sullivan, "We Don't Need a New King George: How Can the President Interpret the Law as if It Didn't Apply to Him?" *Time,* Jan. 24, 2006, 27–28.

52. Cooper, *By Order of the President,* 217.

53. Quoted in Lauren Carroll, "After Ignoring Provision about Notifying Congress of Guantanamo Detainee Transfers, This Moves to Promise Broken," *Tampa Bay Times,* June 4, 2014, available online at http://www.politifact.com/truth-o-meter/promises/obameter/promise/ 516/no-signing-statements-nullify-instruction-congress (accessed July 18, 2015).

54. Marc A. Levin, "So-Called Crimes Are Here, There, Everywhere," *Criminal Justice* 28, no. 1 (Spring 2013): 4–10.

55. *United Air Regulatory Group v. E.P.A.* 573 U.S. (2014).

56. Terry M. Moe and William G. Howell, "The Presidential Power of Unilateral Action," *Journal of Law, Economics, and Organization* 15, no. 1 (Jan. 1999): 133–134.

57. Todd F. Gaziano, "The Uses and Abuses of Executive Orders and Other Presidential Directives," *Texas Review of Law and Politics* 5 (Spring 2001): 267–315.

58. Kenneth R. Mayer, *With the Stroke of a Pen: Executive Orders and Presidential Power* (Princeton: Princeton University Press, 2001), 71–73.

59. Todd Gaziano, "The New Massive Resistance," *Policy Review* (May–June 1998): 283.

60. Harold C. Relyea, "Presidential Directives: Background and Overview," *Congressional Research Service,* Nov. 26, 2008, available online at http://fas.org/sgp/crs/misc/98-611.pdf (accessed July 15, 2015).

61. Quoted in Vivian S. Chu and Ted Garvey, "Executive Orders: Issuance, Modification, and Revocation," *Congressional Research Service,* Apr. 16, 2014, available online at http://fas.org/sgp/crs/misc/RS20846.pdf (accessed July 18, 2015).

62. Adam L. Warber, *Executive Orders and the Modern Presidency* (Boulder, CO: Lynne Rienner, 2006), 118–120.

63. Chu and Garvey, "Executive Orders."

64. Ibid., 10.

65. *Dames & Moore v. Regan* 453 U.S. 654 (1981).

66. Henry Clay, *The Works of Henry Clay: Comprising His Life, Correspondence, and Speeches* (Ann Arbor: University of Michigan Library, 1904), vol. 6, 309.

67. Scott C. James, "The Evolution of the Presidency: Between the Promise and the Fear," in Joel D. Aberbach and Mark A. Peterson, eds., *The Executive Branch* (New York: Oxford University Press, 2005), 10.

68. Mathew D. McCubbins and Thomas Schwartz, "Congressional Oversight Overlooked: Police Patrols versus Fire Alarms," *American Journal of Political Science* 28 (1984): 165–179.

69. Philip Hamburger, *Is Administrative Law Unlawful?* (Chicago: University of Chicago Press, 2014).

CHAPTER THREE

A Brief History of the Presidency

1. Terry Moe, "The Presidency and the Bureaucracy: The Presidential Advantage," in Michael Nelson, ed., *The Presidency and the Political System,* 7th ed. (Washington, DC: CQ Press, 1995), 430.

2. Leonard D. White, *The Jacksonians: A Study in Administrative History, 1829–1861* (New York: Free Press, 1954), 82–83.

3. Leonard D. White, *The Republican Era: A Study in Administrative History, 1869–1901* (New York: Free Press, 1958), 101.

4. Ibid., 103.

5. Jeffrey Tulis, *The Rhetorical Presidency* (Princeton: Princeton University Press, 1987), 69.

6. Fred Greenstein, *Inventing the Job of President: Leadership Style from George Washington to Andrew Jackson* (Princeton: Princeton University Press, 2009).

7. 418 U.S. 663 (1974).

8. Ralph Ketcham, *James Madison: A Biography* (Charlottesville: University Press of Virginia, 1990), 329.

9. Noble Cunningham, Jr., "The Election of 1800," in Arthur Schlesinger, Jr., ed., *History of American Presidential Elections* (New York: Chelsea House, 1972), vol. 1, 101–134.

10. James Roger Sharp, *The Deadlocked Election of 1800: Jefferson, Burr, and the Union in Balance* (Lawrence: University Press of Kansas, 2010).

11. Jeremy Bailey, *Thomas Jefferson and Executive Power* (New York: Cambridge University Press, 2007).

12. Joseph Ellis, *American Sphinx: The Character of Thomas Jefferson* (New York: Vintage Books, 1998), 245.

13. Robert Remini, *Henry Clay: Statesman for the Union* (New York: W.W. Norton, 1991), 88–89.

14. Donald Hickey, *The War of 1812: A Forgotten Conflict,* rev. ed. (Champaign: University of Illinois Press, 2012).

15. James F. Hopkins, "Election of 1824," in Arthur Schlesinger, Jr., ed., *History of American Presidential Elections* (New York: Chelsea House, 1972), vol. 1, 361–364.

16. Matthew Crenson and Benjamin Ginsberg, *Presidential Power: Unchecked and Unbalanced* (New York: W.W. Norton, 2007), 76–77.

17. Alasdair Roberts, *The Panic of 1837* (Ithaca, NY: Cornell University Press, 2013).

18. Martin Shefter, *Political Parties and the State* (Princeton: Princeton University Press, 1993), 61–98.

19. James D. Richardson, ed., *Messages and Papers of the Presidents* (Washington, DC: U.S. Government Printing Office, 1899), vol. 2, 449.

20. William Ellis, *The Union at Risk: Jacksonian Democracy, States' Rights, and the Nullification Crisis* (New York: Oxford University Press, 1989).

21. Tom Kanon, *Tennesseans at War: 1812–1815: Andrew Jackson, the Creek War, and the Battle of New Orleans* (Tuscaloosa: University of Alabama Press, 2014).

22. Anthony Wallace, *The Long, Bitter Trail: Andrew Jackson and the Indians* (New York: Hill & Wang, 1993).

23. Robert Remini, *Andrew Jackson and His Indian Wars* (New York: Penguin, 2002).

24. Richard McCormick, *The Presidential Game: The Origins of American Politics* (New York: Oxford University Press, 1984), 169.

25. Walter R. Borneman, *Polk: The Man Who Transformed the Presidency and America* (New York: Random House, 2009).

26. F. I. Greenstein, "The Policy-Driven Leadership of James K. Polk: Making the Most of a Weak Presidency," *Presidential Studies Quarterly* 40 (2010): 725–733. See also Stephen Skowronek, *The Politics Presidents Make: Leadership from John Adams to Bill Clinton* (Cambridge, MA: Belknap Press of Harvard University Press, 1997), 157.

27. Amy S. Greenberg. *A Wicked War: Polk, Clay, Lincoln, and the 1846 U.S. Invasion of Mexico* (New York: Knopf, 2012).

28. Michael Riccards, *The Ferocious Engine of Democracy: A History of the American Presidency* (Lanham, MD: Madison Books, 1995), vol. 1, 162–163.

29. Quoted in William E. Cain, ed., *William Lloyd Garrison and the Fight against Slavery: Selections from the Liberator* (New York: Macmillan, 1994).

30. 60 U.S. 393 (1857).

31. Eric Foner, *Free Soil, Free Labor, Free Men: Ideology of the Republican Party before the Civil War* (New York: Oxford University Press, 1995).

32. Mary Boykin Chestnut, *A Diary from Dixie* (New York: Random House, 1997), 38.

33. James G. Randall, *Constitutional Problems under Lincoln* (New York: Appleton, 1926), ch. 1.

34. Daniel Farber, *Lincoln's Constitution* (Chicago: University of Chicago Press, 2003).

35. Edward S. Corwin, *The President: Office and Powers,* 4th rev. ed. (New York: NYU Press, 1957), p. 229.

36. Geoffrey Perret, *Lincoln's War* (New York: Random House, 2004).

37. Ibid.

38. Prize Cases, 67 U.S. 635 (2 *Black*) (1863).

39. *Ex parte Milligan,* 71 U.S. 2 (4 Wall.) (1866).

40. David Donald, *Lincoln Reconsidered: Essays on the Civil War Era* (New York: Vintage, 2001), 191–192.

41. Margaret Myers, *A Financial History of the United States* (New York: Columbia University Press, 1970), 155.

42. Ellis Paxson Oberholtzer, *Jay Cooke: Financier of the Civil War* (Philadelphia: Jacobs, 1907).

43. Eric L. McKitrick, "Party Politics and the Union and Confederate War Efforts," in *The American Party Systems: Stages of Political Development,* ed. William N. Chambers and Walter Dean Burnham, 2nd ed. (New York: Oxford University Press, 1975), 147.

44. Quoted in Francis B. Simkins and Robert H. Woody, *South Carolina during Reconstruction* (Chapel Hill: University of North Carolina Press, 1932), 53.

45. Quoted in John S. Reynolds, *Reconstruction in South Carolina* (Columbia, SC: The State Co., 1905), 49.

46. George F. Hoar, *Autobiography of Seventy Years* (New York: Scribner's, 1903), vol. 2, 46.

47. Quoted in Leonard D. White, *The Republican Era: A Study in Administrative History, 1869–1901* (New York: The Free Press, 1958), 23.

48. Wilfred E. Binkley, *President and Congress* (New York: Knopf, 1947), 155.

49. White, *Republican Era,* 33–34.

50. Lewis L. Gould, *The Spanish-American War and President McKinley* (Lawrence: University Press of Kansas, 1982).

51. Quoted in White, *Republican Era,* 41.

52. Ibid., 68.

53. Quoted in Arthur W. Dunn, *From Harrison to Harding* (New York: Putnam, 1922), 334–335.

54. Jeffrey K. Tulis, *The Rhetorical Presidency* (Princeton: Princeton University Press, 1987), ch. 4.

55. Ibid., 118.

56. Peri Arnold, *Remaking the Presidency: Roosevelt, Taft, and Wilson* (Lawrence: University Press of Kansas, 2011).

57. Eugene Trani and David L. Wilson, *The Presidency of Warren G. Harding* (Lawrence: University Press of Kansas, 1977), 56–59.

58. Peri Arnold, *Making the Managerial Presidency* (Lawrence: University Press of Kansas, 1998), 54.

59. U.S. Census, "Statistical Abstract," 1945, table 176, available online at http://www2 .census.gov/prod2/statcomp/documents/1944-04.pdf (accessed July 18, 2015).

60. Richard Nathan, *The Plot That Failed: Nixon and the Administrative Presidency* (New York: Wiley, 1975).

61. Gordon Crovitz and Jeremy Rabkin, *The Fettered Presidency: Legal Constraints on the Executive Branch* (Washington, DC: American Enterprise Institute, 1989).

62. Robert W. Merry, *Where They Stand: The American Presidents in the Eyes of Voters and Historians* (New York: Simon and Schuster, 2012).

63. Robert Sobel, *Coolidge: An American Enigma* (Washington, DC: Regnery, 1998), 5.

64. David McCullough, *Truman* (New York: Simon & Schuster, 1992), 204.

65. Arthur M. Schlesinger, Jr., *A Thousand Days: John F. Kennedy in the White House* (New York: Houghton-Mifflin, 1965).

66. Robert Dallek, *Flawed Giant: Lyndon Johnson and His Times* (New York: Oxford University Press, 1999).

67. Stephen Skowronek, *The Politics Presidents Make: Leadership from John Adams to Bill Clinton* (Cambridge, MA: Belknap Press of Harvard University Press, 1997).

CHAPTER FOUR
Presidential Elections

1. Jennifer Lawless, *Becoming a Candidate: Political Ambition and the Decision to Run for Office* (New York: Cambridge University Press, 2011).

2. Barbara G. Salmore and Stephen A. Salmore, *Candidates, Parties, and Campaigns,* 2nd ed. (Washington, DC: CQ Press, 1989), 2–3.

3. Christopher Matthews, *Kennedy and Nixon: The Rivalry That Shaped Postwar America* (New York: Simon and Schuster, 1996), 105.

4. Ibid., 117.

5. Ibid., 115.

6. Ibid.

7. Quoted in ibid., 116.

8. Paul Farhi, "Who Wrote That Political Memoir? No, Who Actually Wrote It?" *Washington Post,* June 9, 2014.

9. David Maraniss, *First in His Class* (New York: Simon and Schuster, 1995), 331–332.

10. David T. Canon, *Actors, Athletes, and Astronauts: Political Amateurs in the U.S. Congress* (Chicago: University of Chicago Press, 1990).

11. Stephen E. Ambrose, *Eisenhower: Soldier and President* (New York: Simon and Schuster, 1990), 245–246.

12. Joan Didion, "Cheney: The Fatal Touch," *New York Review of Books* 80, no. 15 (Oct. 5, 2006): 51–56.

13. J. Bello and R. Y. Shapiro, "On to the Convention!" *Political Science Quarterly* 123 (2008): 149.

14. Joseph Ax, "Anti-Obama Author D'Souza Pleads Guilty to Campaign Finance Violation," *Reuters,* May 20, 2014, available online at http://www.reuters.com/article/2014/05/20/us-usa-politics-dsouza-idUSBREA4JoH520140520 (accessed July 18, 2015).

15. Samantha Lachman, "Daylin Leach Accuses Marjorie Margolies of Violating Campaign Finance Law," *Huffington Post,* Apr. 24, 2014, available online at http://www.huffingtonpost.com/2014/04/24/daylin-leach-marjorie-margolies_n_5205398.html (accessed July 18, 2015).

16. "Starbucks Free Java Violates Election Law, State Says," *Bloomberg News,* Nov. 3, 2008.

17. Elaine C. Kamarck, *Primary Politics: How Presidential Candidates Have Shaped the Modern Nominating System* (Washington, DC: Brookings, 2009).

18. Mark Halperin and John Heilmann, *Game Change: Obama and the Clintons, McCain and Palin, and the Race of a Lifetime* (New York: HarperCollins, 2010). See also David Redlawsk, Caroline J. Tolbert, and Todd Donovan, *Why Iowa? How Caucuses and Sequential Elections Improve the Presidential Nominating Process* (Chicago: University of Chicago Press, 2010).

19. C. J. Tolbert, A. Keller, and T. Donovan, "A Modified National Primary: State Losers and Support for Changing the Presidential Nominating Process," *Political Science Quarterly* 125 (2010): 393–424; also C. Panagopoulos, "Are Caucuses Bad for Democracy?" *Political Science Quarterly* 125 (2010): 425–442.

20. Jody Baumgartner, "Vice Presidential Selection in the Convention Era: Experience or Electoral Advantage?" *Congress and the Presidency* 39, no. 3 (2012): 297–315.

21. "George W. Bush Selects Dick Cheney as Running Mate," *Green Papers*, July 25, 2000, available online at http://www.thegreenpapers.com/News/20000725-0.html (accessed July 18, 2015).

22. B. Grofman and R. Kline, "Evaluating the Impact of Vice Presidential Selection on Voter Choice," *Presidential Studies Quarterly* 40 (2010): 303–309.

23. Alexander Hamilton, James Madison, and John Jay, *The Federalist Papers,* ed. Edward Mead Earle (New York: Random House, Modern Library, n.d.), no. 68, 442.

24. John Geer, *In Defense of Negativity: Attack Ads in Presidential Campaigns* (Chicago: University of Chicago Press, 2006).

25. V. O. Key, Jr., *The Responsible Electorate* (Cambridge, MA: Harvard University Press, 1966).

26. David Garrow, *Protest at Selma* (New Haven: Yale University Press, 1980).

27. The classic study is Angus Campbell et al., *The American Voter* (New York: Wiley, 1964).

28. Walter Dean Burnham, *Critical Elections and the Mainsprings of American Electoral Politics* (New York: Norton, 1970).

29. Paul Greenberg, "The Invisible Ethnic Group," JewishWorldReview.com, Oct. 29, 2004, available online at http://www.jewishworldreview.com/cols/greenberg102904.asp (accessed August 12, 2015).

30. Emmett H. Buell, Jr., and Lee Sigelman, *Attack Politics: Negativity in Presidential Campaigns since 1960* (Lawrence: University Press of Kansas, 2008).

31. Richard Clarke, *Against All Enemies: Inside America's War on Terrorism* (New York: Free Press, 2004).

32. Jim Rutenberg, "9/11 Panel Comments Freely," *New York Times,* Apr. 15, 2004, 1.

33. Steven Ansolabehere and Shanto Iyengar, *Going Negative: How Attack Ads Shrink and Polarize the Electorate* (New York: Free Press, 1995).

34. 572 U.S. _____ (2014).

35. Nicholas Confessore, Sarah Cohen, and Karen Yourish, "A Wealthy Few Lead in Giving to Campaigns," *New York Times,* Aug. 2, 2015, p. 1.

36. Rebecca Ballhaus, "By Funding Self, Trump Gains Edge," *Wall Street Journal,* July 25, 2015, p. A4).

37. "Barack Obama's Bundlers," OpenSecrets.org, available online at https://www.open secrets.org/pres12/bundlers.php (accessed July 18, 2015).

38. Susan Schmidt and James Grimaldi, "Nonprofit Groups Funneled Money for Abramoff," *Washington Post,* June 25, 2006, 1; also Matea Gold, "Secret Donors Are Poised to Take Prominence in 2016 Campaigns," *Washington Post,* July 15, 2015, p. A4.

39. 558 U.S. 50 (2010).

40. Matea Gold, "Super PACs' Role Grows Even Larger: Line Blurs between Campaigns and Groups," *Washington Post,* July 7, 2016, p. A4.

41. "Barack Obama's Bundlers."

42. Ibid.

43. David Johnston and Neil A. Lewis, "How the Religious Right Pushed for Ashcroft's Nomination," *San Francisco Chronicle,* Jan. 7, 2001, 1.

44. Richard Dunham and Eamon Javers, "Shakedown on K Street," *BusinessWeek,* Feb. 20, 2006, 34–36.

45. Jeffrey H. Birnbaum, *The Money Men* (New York: Crown, 2000), 75.

46. Ibid.

47. Eliza Carney, "Cleaning House," *National Journal,* Jan. 28, 2006, 36.

48. Brody Mullins, "Growing Role for Lobbyists: Raising Funds for Lawmakers," *Wall Street Journal,* Jan. 27, 2006, 1.

49. Jonathan Weisman and Charles H. Babcock, "K Street's New Ways Spawn More Pork," *Washington Post,* Jan. 27, 2006, 1.

50. Frank Clemente and Craig Holman, "Fallout from Abramoff: Congress for Sale? Religious Right for Sale?" Institute for Public Accuracy, Jan. 4, 2006, available online at http://

www.accuracy.org/release/1196-fallout-from-abramoff-congress-for-sale-religious-right-for-sale (accessed August 12, 2015).

51. Darrell West, *Checkbook Democracy* (Boston: Northeastern University Press, 2000), 117.

52. David Mayhew, *Congress: The Electoral Connection* (New Haven: Yale University Press, 1974), 40.

53. Ibid., 116–119.

54. Birnbaum, *Money Men,* 164.

55. Jeffrey Birnbaum, "Clients' Rewards Keep K Street Lobbyists Thriving," *Washington Post,* Feb. 14, 2006, A1.

56. Mary Williams Walsh, "Major Changes Raise Concerns on Pension Bill," *New York Times,* Mar. 10, 2006, 1.

57. See Jonathan Weisman, "Closed-Door Deal Makes $22 Billion Difference," *Washington Post,* Jan. 24, 2006, 1.

58. Michael D. Shear, "Va. Growth Bolstered by Well-Funded Voting Bloc," *Washington Post,* Jan. 30, 2006, B1.

59. John Wagner and Ann E. Marimow, "Largess Preceded Vote on Wal-Mart," *Washington Post,* Feb. 10, 2006, B1.

60. 424 U.S. 1 (1976).

61. Thomas Hobbes, *Leviathan* (New York: Collier, 1962), 80.

62. Richard Shenkman, *Presidential Ambition* (New York: Harper, 1999).

63. Matthew A. Crenson and Benjamin Ginsberg, *Presidential Power: Unchecked and Unbalanced* (New York: W.W. Norton, 2007).

CHAPTER FIVE
The Executive Branch

1. William G. Howell and David E. Lewis, "Agencies by Presidential Design," *Journal of Politics* 64, no. 4 (Nov. 2002): 1095–1114.

2. Harold Seidman, *Politics, Position, and Power* (New York: Oxford University Press, 1998), 208.

3. David Lewis, *The Politics of Presidential Appointments: Political Control and Bureaucratic Performance* (Princeton: Princeton University Press, 2008).

4. Scott Shane and Ron Nixon, "U.S. Contractors Becoming a Fourth Branch of Government," available online at http://www.nytimes.com/2007/02/04/world/americas/04iht-web.0204contract.4460796.html (accessed July 18, 2015).

5. For estimates of the "true" size of America's government, see Paul C. Light, *The True Size of Government* (Washington, DC: Brookings, 1999).

6. Ibid.

7. Seidman, *Politics, Position, and Power.*

8. James Q. Wilson, *Bureaucracy: What Government Agencies Do and Why They Do It* (New York: Basic Books, 1989), 91.

9. Thomas E. Ricks, *Making the Corps* (New York: Touchstone, 1997), 138.

10. Herbert Kaufman, *The Forest Ranger: A Study in Administrative Behavior* (Baltimore: Johns Hopkins University Press, 1960).

11. See Anita Huslin, "Grizzly Proposition Aims to Return Bears to Idaho," *Washington Post,* July 3, 2000, A3.

12. Seidman, *Politics, Position, and Power,* 118.

13. Robert Higgs, *Crisis and Leviathan: Critical Episodes in the Growth of American Government* (New York: Oxford University Press, 1987).

14. Daniel Carpenter, *The Forging of Bureaucratic Autonomy* (Princeton: Princeton University Press, 2001).

15. C. R. Berry, B. C. Burden, and W. G. Howell, "After Enactment: The Lives and Deaths of Federal Programs," *American Journal of Political Science* 54 (2010): 1–17.

16. Robert Pear, "Ambiguity in Health Law Could Make Family Coverage Too Costly for Many," *New York Times,* Aug. 12, 2012, 10.

17. Jerry L. Mashaw, *Greed, Chaos, and Governance: Using Public Choice to Improve Public Law* (New Haven: Yale University Press, 1997), 106.

18. Schoenbrod, *Power without Responsibility,* ch. 2.

19. Ibid., p. 61.

20. William F. Fox, *Understanding Administrative Law,* 4th ed. (New York: Lexis Publishing, 2000), 36–37.

21. Kara Scannell and Deborah Soloman, "Business Wins Its Battle to Ease a Costly Sarbanes-Oxley Rule," *Wall Street Journal,* Nov. 10, 2006, 1.

22. Harold W. Stanley and Richard G. Niemi, *Vital Statistics on American Politics* (Washington, DC: Congressional Quarterly Press, 2001), 262.

23. James L. Gattuso and Diane Katz, "Red Tape Rising: Regulation in Obama's First Term," *Heritage Foundation Backgrounder #2793,* May 1, 2013, available online at http://www.heritage.org/research/reports/2013/05/red-tape-rising-regulation-in-obamas-first-term (accessed July 18, 2015).

24. White House Office of Management and Budget, "2013 Draft Report to Congress on the Benefits and Costs of Federal Regulations and Agency Compliance with the Uniform Mandates Reform Act," available online at http://www.whitehouse.gov/sites/default/files/omb/inforeg/2013_cb/draft_2013_cost_benefit_report.pdf (accessed July 18, 2015).

25. Ibid., 4.

26. Center for Healthcare Research and Transformation, "ACA 2013 Implementation Timeline," available online at http://www.chrt.org/publication/aca-2013-implementation-timeline (accessed August 12, 2015).

27. Cornelius M. Kerwin and Scott R. Furlong, *Rulemaking: How Government Agencies Write Law and Make Policy* (Washington, DC: CQ Press, 2011), 226.

28. William F. West and Connor Raso, "Who Shapes the Rulemaking Agenda? Implications for Bureaucratic Responsiveness and Bureaucratic Control," *Journal of Public Administration Research and Theory* 23 (Oct. 2012): 495–519.

29. Christopher Foreman, for example, was able to identify efforts by the committees overseeing the Food and Drug Administration to induce the agency to develop new rules. Christopher Foreman, *Signals from the Hill: Congressional Oversight and the Challenge of Social Regulation* (New Haven: Yale University Press, 1988).

30. West and Raso, "Who Shapes the Rulemaking Agenda?," 504.

31. Joel Aberbach, *Keeping a Watchful Eye: The Politics of Congressional Oversight* (Washington, DC: Brookings, 1990).

32. Mathew McCubbins and Thomas Schwartz, "Congressional Oversight Overlooked: Police Patrols versus Fire Alarms," *American Journal of Political Science* 28 (1987): 165–179.

33. Sidney A. Shapiro, "Agency Priority Setting and the Review of Existing Agency Rules," *Administrative Law Review* 48, no. 3 (Summer 1996): 370–374.

34. West and Raso, "Who Shapes the Rulemaking Agenda?," 506–507.

35. Kerwin and Furlong, *Rulemaking,* 132.

36. William F. Fox, Jr., *Understanding Administrative Law,* 4th ed. (New York: Matthew Bender, 2000), 192.

37. West and Raso, "Who Shapes the Rulemaking Agenda?," 508.

38. Kerwin and Furlong, *Rulemaking,* 190.

39. Jeffrey S. Lubbers, *A Guide to Federal Agency Rulemaking,* 5th ed. (Chicago: American Bar Association, 2012), 63.

40. Ibid., 64.

41. Ibid., 95.

42. *SEC v. Chenery Corp.,* 332 U.S. 194 (1947).

43. *Skidmore v. Swift,* 323 U.S. 134 (1944). See also Fox, *Understanding Administrative Law,* 202.

44. Susan Webb Yackee, "Sweet-Talking the Fourth Branch: The Influence of Interest Group Comments on Federal Agency Rulemaking," *Journal of Public Administration Research and Theory* 16 (2005):103–124.

45. Marissa Golden, "Interest Groups in the Rule-Making Process: Who Participates? Whose Voices Get Heard?" *Journal of Public Administration Research and Theory* 8 (Apr. 1998): 252–253; also Jason Webb Yackee and Susan Webb Yackee, "A Bias toward Business?: Assessing Interest Group Influence on the Bureaucracy," *Journal of Politics* 68, no. 1 (2006): 128–139.

46. William West, "Formal Procedures, Informal Processes, Accountability, and Responsiveness in Bureaucratic Rulemaking: An Institutional Policy Analysis," *Public Administration Review* 64 (Jan.–Feb. 2004).

47. Morton Rosenberg, "The Congressional Review Act after Fifteen Years: Background and Considerations for Reform," paper given at the Administrative Conference of the United States, Sept. 16, 2011, available online at http://www.acus.gov/sites/default/files/documents/COJR-Draft-CRA-Report-9-16-11.pdf (accessed July 18, 2015).

48. Kerwin and Furlong, *Rulemaking*, 231.

49. Ibid., 60.

50. Small Business Administration Office of Advocacy, "A Guide for Government Agencies: How to Comply with the Regulatory Flexibility Act," June 2010; available online at https://www.sba.gov/advocacy/guide-government-agencies-how-comply-regulatory-flexibility-act (accessed July 18, 2015).

51. Kerwin and Furlong, *Rulemaking*, 60.

52. Executive Office of the President, Office of Management and Budget, "Memorandum for the Heads of Executive Departments and Agencies," available online at http://www.whitehouse.gov/sites/default/files/omb/assets/inforeg/cumulative-effects-guidance.pdf (accessed July 18, 2015).

53. Curt Gentry, *J. Edgar Hoover: The Man and the Secrets* (New York: Norton, 1991).

54. James F. Blumstein, "Regulatory Review by the Executive Office of the President: An Overview and Policy Analysis of Current Issues," *Duke Law Journal* 51 (Dec. 2001): 856.

55. Marissa Martino Golden, *What Motivates Bureaucrats* (New York: Columbia University Press, 2000).

CHAPTER SIX

The President, Congress, and Domestic Policy

1. Ralph Carter and James Scott, "Taking the Lead: Congressional Foreign Policy Entrepreneurs in U.S. Foreign Policy," *Politics and Policy* 32, no. 1 (Mar. 2004): 34–71.

2. Matthew N. Beckmann, *Pushing the Agenda: Presidential Leadership in U.S. Lawmaking, 1953–2004* (New York: Cambridge University Press, 2010); also Jeffrey E. Cohen, *The President's Legislative Policy Agenda, 1789–2002* (New York: Cambridge University Press, 2012); George C. Edwards III, *The Strategic President: Persuasion and Opportunity in Presidential Leadership* (Princeton: Princeton University Press, 2009); Paul Light, *The President's Agenda*, 3rd ed. (Baltimore: Johns Hopkins University Press, 1999).

3. Gary C. Jacobson, "Partisan Polarization in Presidential Support: The Electoral Connection," *Congress and the Presidency* 30, no. 1 (2003): 1–36; also Gary C. Jacobson, "The President's Effect on Partisan Attitudes," *Presidential Studies Quarterly* 42, no. 4 (Dec. 2012): 683–718: Matthew Lebo and Andrew J. O'Geen, "The President's Role in the Partisan Congressional Arena," *Journal of Politics* 73, no. 3 (July 2011): 718–734; Frances E. Lee, "Dividers, Not Uniters: Presidential Leadership and Senate Partisanship," *Journal of Politics* 70, no. 4 (Oct. 2008): 914–928.

4. Stephen Skowronek, *The Politics Presidents Make* (Cambridge, MA: Belknap Press of Harvard University Press, 1997).

5. David Mayhew, *Congress: The Electoral Connection* (New Haven: Yale University Press, 1974).

6. Justin Grimmer, Solomon Messing, and Sean J. Westwood, "How Words and Money Cultivate a Personal Vote: The Effect of Legislator Credit Claiming on Constituent Credit Allocation," *American Political Science Review* 106, no. 4 (Nov. 2012): 703–719.

7. Stephen Frantzich, "Congress, the Houses of Ill Repute: Editorial Cartoonists Take on the House and Senate," *Congress and the Presidency* 40, no. 2 (2012): 152–164.

8. Richard Neustadt, *Presidential Power* (New York: Signet, 1964).

9. W. G. Howell and J. C. Rogowski, "War, the Presidency, and Legislative Voting Behavior," *American Journal of Political Science* 57 (2013): 150–166.

10. Bruce Japsen, "Obamacare Will Bring Drug Industry $35 Billion in Profits," *Forbes,* May 25, 2013, available online at http://www.forbes.com/sites/brucejapsen/2013/05/25/obamacare -will-bring-drug-industry-35-billion-in-profits (accessed July 18, 2015).

11. Alexander Hamilton, James Madison, and John Jay, *The Federalist Papers,* ed. Edward Mead Earle (New York: Random House, Modern Library, n.d.), no. 71, 464.

12. G. C. Jacobson, "Partisan Polarization in American Politics: A Background Paper," *Presidential Studies Quarterly* 43 (2013): 688–708.

13. Gary Cox and Jonathan Katz, *Elbridge Gerry's Salamander: The Electoral Consequences of the Reapportionment Revolution* (New York: Cambridge University Press, 2002).

14. N. McCarty, K. T. Poole, and H. Rosenthal, "Does Gerrymandering Cause Polarization?," *American Journal of Political Science* 53 (2009): 666–680; also Jamie Carson et al., "Redistricting and Party Polarization in the U.S. House of Representatives," *American Politics Research* 35, no. 6 (2007): 878–904; Morris Fiorina, with Samuel J. Abrams and Jeremy C. Pope, *Culture War? The Myth of a Polarized America* (New York: Longman, 2004).

15. T. Skocpol and L. R. Jacobs, "Accomplished and Embattled: Understanding Obama's Presidency," *Political Science Quarterly* 127 (2012): 1–24.

16. Andrew Rudalevige, "The Executive Branch and the Legislative Process," in Joel Aberbach and Mark Peterson, eds., *The Executive Branch* (New York: Oxford University Press, 2005), 421.

17. Ibid., 423.

18. Russell L. Riley, *Bridging the Constitutional Divide: Inside the White House Office of Legislative Affairs* (College Station: Texas A&M University Press, 2010); also Matthew N. Beckmann, "The President's Playbook: White House Strategies for Lobbying Congress," *Journal of Politics* 70, no. 2 (Apr. 2008): 407–419.

19. Ben Terris, "A Congress Too Pathetic to Picket: Political Gridlock Has Turned a Onetime Magnet for Protest into a Virtual Ghost Town," *Washington Post,* July 23, 2014, C1.

20. *Clinton v. City of New York,* 524 U.S. 417 (1998).

21. *King v. Burwell,* 576 U.S. ___ (2015).

22. Phillip J. Cooper, *By Order of the President* (Lawrence: University Press of Kansas, 2002), 206.

23. Elizabeth Bumiller, "For President, Final Say on a Bill Sometimes Comes after the Signing," *New York Times,* Jan. 16, 2006, A11.

24. Steve Friess, "Obama's Policy Strategy: Ignore Laws," *Politico,* June 16, 2012.

25. Elena Kagan, "Presidential Administration," *Harvard Law Review* 114, no. 2245 (June 2001).

26. 420 U.S. 35 (1975).

27. David Bridge, "Presidential Power Denied: A New Model of Veto Overrides Using Political Time," *Congress and the Presidency* 41, no. 2 (2014): 149–166.

28. "Nominations," U.S. Senate website, available online at http://www.senate.gov/artand history/history/common/briefing/Nominations.htm (accessed July 18, 2015).

29. "Supreme Court Nominations, Present–1789," U.S. Senate website, available online at http://www.senate.gov/pagelayout/reference/nominations/Nominations.htm#official (accessed July 18, 2015).

30. Jonathan Kastellec, Jeffrey Lax, and Justin Phillips, "Public Opinion and Senate Confirmation of Supreme Court Nominees," *Journal of Politics* 72, no. 3 (July 2010): 767–784.

31. Jan C. Greenburg, *Supreme Conflict* (New York: Penguin, 2007), 281.

32. "Nominations" (with detail), U.S. Senate website, available online at http://www.senate .gov/artandhistory/history/common/briefing/Nominations.htm#10 (accessed July 18, 2015).

33. "Treaties," U.S. Senate website, available online at http://www.senate.gov/artandhistory/ history/common/briefing/Treaties.htm (accessed July 18, 2015).

34. Glen Krutz and Jeffrey Peake, *Treaty Politics and the Rise of Executive Agreements* (Ann Arbor: University of Michigan Press, 2009).

35. Kenneth Mayer and Thomas Weko, "The Institutionalization of Power," in Robert Y. Shapiro et al., eds., *Presidential Power* (New York: Columbia University Press, 2000), 195.

36. Leonard D. White, *The Republican Era: A Study in Administrative History, 1869–1901* (New York: The Free Press, 1958), 55.

37. Louis Fisher, "Presidential Budgetary Duties," *Presidential Studies Quarterly* 42, no. 4 (Dec. 2012): 754–790.

38. Jason A. MacDonald, "Limitation Riders and Congressional Influence over Bureaucratic Policy Decisions," *American Political Science Review* 104 (2010): 766–782.

39. Charles Dawes, *The First Year of the Budget of the United States* (New York: Harper, 1923).

40. Philip G. Joyce, *The Congressional Budget Office: Honest Numbers, Power and Policymaking* (Washington, DC: Georgetown University Press, 2011).

41. John B. Gilmour, *Reconcilable Differences? Congress, the Budget Process and the Deficit* (Berkeley: University of California Press, 1990), 229.

42. Allen Schick, *The Federal Budget: Politics, Policy, Process* (Washington, DC: Brookings, 2000), 94–95.

43. Louis Fisher, *Congressional Abdication on War and Spending* (College Station: Texas A&M Press, 2000), 128.

44. David Rogers, "Spending Pact Marks Major Retreat by GOP Leaders," *Wall Street Journal,* Sept. 30, 1996, A20.

45. John Stuart Mill, *Considerations on Representative Government* (London: Parker, Son and Bourne, 1861), 104.

46. 273 U.S. 135 (1927).

47. Leonard D. White, *The Federalists: A Study in Administrative History, 1789–1801* (New York: Free Press, 1948), 80.

48. Ibid., 81.

49. *U.S. v. Nixon,* 418 U.S. 683 (1974).

50. Leonard D. White, *The Jeffersonians: A Study in Administrative History, 1801–1829* (New York: Free Press, 1951), 94.

51. Ibid., 96.

52. Ibid., 102.

53. Joel D. Aberbach, "What's Happened to the Watchful Eye?" *Congress and the Presidency* 29, no. 1 (2002): 3–23.

54. Maggie Fox, "GAO Sting Finds It Easy to Fake It, Get Obamacare Premiums," *NBC News,* July 23, 2014, available online at http://www.nbcnews.com/health/health-news/gao-sting -finds-it-easy-fake-it-get-obamacare-premiums-n162456 (accessed August 12, 2015).

55. Morton Rosenberg, "The Congressional Review Act after 15 Years: Background and Considerations for Reform," paper given at Administrative Conference of the United States, Sept. 16, 2011, available online at http://www.acus.gov/sites/default/files/documents/COJR -Draft-CRA-Report-9-16-11.pdf (accessed July 18, 2015).

56. Kerwin and Furlong, *Rulemaking,* 231.

57. Juliet Eilperin, "Technically, Hundreds of Administration Rules are Invalid," *Washington Post,* July 31, 2014, A19.

58. Morris S. Ogul, *Congress Oversees the Bureaucracy: Studies in Legislative Supervision* (Pittsburgh: University of Pittsburgh Press, 1976).

59. Mathew McCubbins and Thomas Schwartz, "Congressional Oversight Overlooked: Police Patrols versus Fire Alarms," *American Journal of Political Science* 28, no. 1 (Feb. 1984): 165–179.

60. Steven Balla and Christopher Deering, "Police Patrols and Fire Alarms: An Empirical Examination of the Legislative Preference for Oversight," *Congress and the Presidency* 40, no. 1 (2013): 27–40.

61. "Cruise Passengers Recount Horror Stories to Senate," *Salon,* July 23, 2014, available on-line at http://www.salon.com/2014/07/24/cruise_passengers_recount_horror_stories_to_senate (accessed August 13, 2015).

62. Douglas Kriner and Eric Schickler, "Investigating the President: Committee Probes and Presidential Approval, 1953–2006," *Journal of Politics* 76, no. 2 (Apr. 2014): 521–534.

63. White, *Jeffersonians,* 99.

64. Josh Hicks, "Rep. Issa Ends Hearing after White House Defies Subpoena," *Washington Post,* July 17, 2014, A15.

65. David A. Yaloff, *Prosecution among Friends: Presidents, Attorneys General, and Executive Branch Wrongdoing* (College Station: Texas A&M University Press, 2012).

66. Mordecai Lee, *Nixon's Super-Secretaries: The Last Grand Presidential Reorganization Effort* (College Station: Texas A&M University Press, 2010).

67. Richard Nathan, *The Plot That Failed: Nixon and the Administrative Presidency* (New York: Wiley, 1975).

68. Curt Gentry, *J. Edgar Hoover: The Man and the Secrets* (New York: Norton, 1991).

69. Kiki Caruson, "Public Watchdogs or Imperial Pitbulls: An Evaluation of Special Prosecutor Investigations of Executive Branch Misconduct," *Congress and the Presidency* 36, no. 1 (2009): 80–114.

70. Quoted in John Harwood and Edward Felsenthall, "Independent Counsels Range Far Afield," *Wall Street Journal*, Jan. 29, 1998, 1.

71. Benjamin Ginsberg and Martin Shefter, *Politics by Other Means* (New York: Basic Books, 1990).

72. Michael Gerhardt, *The Federal Impeachment Process*, 2nd ed. (Chicago: University of Chicago Press, 2000).

73. "Remarks in the U.S. House of Representatives in an Effort to Impeach Supreme Court Justice William O. Douglas," Apr. 15, 1970, recorded in the *Congressional Record*, 91st. Cong., 2nd sess., 1970, vol. 116, 11913.

74. Nia-Malika Henderson and Wesley Lowery, "Talk of Impeaching Obama Could Help, Not Hurt Democrats," *Washington Post*, July 24, 2014, A4.

75. Peter Baker and Susan Schmidt, "Starr Searches for Sources of Staff Criticism: Private Investigator Says Clinton Team Hired Him," *Washington Post*, Feb. 24, 1998, 1.

76. John F. Harris, "Office of Damage Control," *Washington Post*, Jan. 31, 1998, 1.

77. Hamilton, Madison, and Jay, *Federalist Papers*, no. 51.

78. Ibid.

CHAPTER SEVEN
Presidential Policy Tools

1. Fred I. Greenstein, *The Presidential Difference* (Princeton: Princeton University Press, 2000), 135.

2. Sidney M. Milkis, *The President and the Parties* (New York: Oxford University Press, 1993), chs. 3 and 4.

3. Samuel Kernell, *Going Public: New Strategies of Presidential Leadership*, 3rd ed. (Washington, DC: Congressional Quarterly Press, 1997); also Jeffrey K. Tulis, *The Rhetorical Presidency* (Princeton: Princeton University Press, 1987).

4. V. O. Key, *Politics, Parties, and Pressure Groups*, 5th ed. (New York: Crowell, 1964), 202–203.

5. Joseph Charles, *The Origins of the American Party System* (New York: Harper, 1961), 84.

6. V. O. Key, *Politics, Parties, and Pressure Groups*, 4th ed. (New York: Crowell, 1958), 221–223.

7. Henry Jones Ford, *The Rise and Growth of American Politics* (New York: Macmillan, 1898), ch. 7.

8. Martin Shefter, *Political Parties and the State* (Princeton: Princeton University Press, 1994), ch. 3.

9. James D. Richardson, comp., *Messages and Papers of the Presidents*, vol. 2 (Washington, DC: U.S. Government Printing Office, 1896–1899), 448.

10. Quoted in Matthew A. Crenson, *The Federal Machine: Beginnings of Bureaucracy in Jacksonian America* (Baltimore: Johns Hopkins University Press, 1975), 175.

11. Richard Franklin Bensel, *Yankee Leviathan: The Origins of Central State Authority in America, 1859–1877* (New York: Cambridge University Press, 1990), 226–227.

12. Eric L. McKitrick, "Party Politics and the Union and Confederate War Efforts," in William N. Chambers and Walter Dean Burnham, eds., *The American Party Systems,* 2nd ed. (New York: Oxford University Press, 1975), 117–151.

13. Ibid., 137.

14. Ibid.

15. Ellis Paxson Oberholtzer, *Jay Cooke: Financier of the Civil War* (Philadelphia: Jacobs, 1907).

16. McKitrick, "Party Politics," 147.

17. Paul Van Riper, *History of the United States Civil Service* (Evanston, IL: Row, Peterson, 1958), 320.

18. Milkis, *President and the Parties,* 55.

19. See Samuel Lubell, *The Future of American Politics* (Garden City, NY: Doubleday, 1956).

20. Kristi Andersen, *The Creation of a Democratic Majority, 1928–1936* (Chicago: University of Chicago Press, 1982).

21. Martin Shefter, *Political Parties and the State* (Princeton: Princeton University Press, 1994), 83–84.

22. James Sundquist, *Dynamics of the Party System* (Washington, DC: Brookings, 1975).

23. J. David Greenstone, *Labor in American Politics,* 2nd ed. (Chicago: University of Chicago Press, 1977).

24. Steven Fraser, *Labor Will Rule: Sidney Hillman and the Rise of American Labor* (New York: The Free Press, 1991), ch. 17.

25. Grant McConnell, *Private Power and American Democracy* (New York: Knopf, 1966), 308.

26. Milkis, *President and the Parties,* 92–93.

27. Ibid., 93.

28. Ibid., 80.

29. On the effects of Progressive-era reforms, see Walter Dean Burnham, "Theory and Voting Research," *American Political Science Review* 68 (Sept. 1974): 1002–1023; also Walter Dean Burnham, "The Changing Shape of the American Political Universe," *American Political Science Review* 59 (Jan. 1965): 7–28. On the McGovern-Fraser reforms see Austin Ranney, *Curing the Mischiefs of Faction* (Berkeley: University of California Press, 1975).

30. Benjamin Ginsberg, "Money and Power: The New Political Economy of American Elections," in Thomas Ferguson and Joel Rogers, *The Political Economy: Readings in the Politics and Economics of American Public Policy* (New York: M. E. Sharpe, 1984).

31. Rosalind S. Helderman, "Why Some Democrats Oppose Obama's Jobs Bill," *Washington Post*, Oct. 12, 2011, available online at http://www.washingtonpost.com/politics/why-some -democrats-oppose-obamas-jobs-bill/2011/10/12/gIQAILfBgL_story.html (accessed July 19, 2015).

32. Theodore J. Lowi, *The Personal President: Power Invested, Promise Unfulfilled* (Ithaca, NY: Cornell University Press, 1985).

33. Jeffrey K. Tulis, *The Rhetorical Presidency* (Princeton: Princeton University Press, 1987), 73.

34. Ibid., 79.

35. Ibid., 91.

36. Ibid., 86.

37. Ibid., ch. 4.

38. George Creel, *How We Advertised America* (New York: Harper and Brothers, 1920).

39. George Brown Tindall, *America: A Narrative History* (New York: W.W. Norton, 1992), 1013.

40. Milkis, *President and the Parties*, 97.

41. James MacGregor Burns, *Roosevelt: The Lion and the Fox* (New York: Harcourt, Brace, 1956), 317.

42. Ibid., 318.

43. Ibid., 317.

44. Samuel Kernell, *Going Public: New Strategies of Presidential Leadership*, 3rd ed. (Washington, DC: Congressional Quarterly Press, 1997), 79.

45. Ibid., 81.

46. Clayton R. Koppes and Gregory D. Black, *Hollywood Goes to War: How Profits and Propaganda Shaped World War II Movies* (Berkeley: University of California Press, 1987), chs. 1–3.

47. Burns, *Roosevelt*, 370.

48. Fred I. Greenstein, *The Hidden-Hand Presidency: Eisenhower as Leader* (New York: Basic Books, 1982), 96.

49. Ibid., 19.

50. Elmer Cornwell, *Presidential Leadership of Public Opinion* (Bloomington: Indiana University Press, 1981), 117–135.

51. Quoted in Greenstein, *Hidden-Hand Presidency*, 99.

52. Stephen Ambrose, *Eisenhower: Soldier and President* (New York: Touchstone, 1990), ch. 14.

53. Arthur M. Schlesinger, Jr., *A Thousand Days: John F. Kennedy in the White House* (New York: Houghton-Mifflin, 1965), 662.

54. Ibid., 809.

55. David Garrow, *Protest at Selma: Martin Luther King and the Voting Rights Act of 1965* (New Haven: Yale University Press, 1978).

56. Tulis, *Rhetorical Presidency,* 168–172.

57. Sidney Blumenthal, *The Clinton Wars* (New York: Farrar, Straus and Giroux, 2003).

58. Martha J. Kumar, *Managing the President's Message: The White House Communications Operation* (Baltimore: Johns Hopkins University Press, 2007).

59. Lou Cannon, *President Reagan: The Role of a Lifetime* (New York: Public Affairs Press, 1991), 32.

60. David Alpern, "The Second Hundred Days," *Newsweek,* May 11, 1981, 23.

61. Tulis, *Rhetorical Presidency,* 147.

62. Cannon, *President Reagan,* 35.

63. Brandon Rottinghaus, *The Provisional Pulpit: Modern Presidential Leadership of Public Opinion* (College Station: Texas A&M University Press, 2010).

64. Tulis, *Rhetorical Presidency,* 161.

65. Lowi, *Personal President.*

66. Ibid., 11.

67. Alexander Hamilton, James Madison, and John Jay, *The Federalist Papers,* ed. Edward Mead Earle (New York: Random House, Modern Library, n.d.), no. 71, 464.

68. Matthew Eshbaugh-Soha and Jeffey S. Peake, *Breaking through the Noise: Presidential Leadership, Public Opinion, and the News Media* (Stanford, CA: Stanford University Press, 2011).

69. Benjamin Ginsberg and Martin Shefter, *Politics by Other Means: Politicians, Prosecutors and the Press from Watergate to Whitewater,* rev. ed. (New York: W. W. Norton, 1999), 35–39.

70. Joseph Lelyveld, "In Clinton's Court," *New York Review,* May 29, 2003, 11–15.

71. Jill Abramson, "Washington's Culture of Scandal Is Turning Inquiry into an Industry," *New York Times,* Apr. 26, 1998, 1.

72. Quoted in Robert Shogan, *The Double-Edged Sword: How Character Makes and Ruins Presidents from Washington to Clinton* (Boulder, CO: Westview, 1999), 224.

73. Mike Allen, "Bush's Distaste for News Conferences Keeps Them Rare," *Washington Post,* Mar. 7, 2003, A20.

74. Ginsberg and Shefter, *Politics by Other Means,* 39–46.

75. Kernell, *Going Public,* 114.

76. Lori Cox Han, *A Presidency Upstaged: The Public Leadership of George H. W. Bush* (College Station: Texas A &M University Press, 2011).

77. Cited in Clinton Rossiter, *The American Presidency,* 2nd ed. (New York: Harcourt, Brace and World, 1960), 129.

78. Harold W. Stanley and Richard G. Niemi, *Vital Statistics on American Politics, 2001–2002* (Washington, DC: Congressional Quarterly Press, 2001), 250–251.

79. Milkis, *President and the Parties,* 128.

80. Ibid., 160.

81. Ibid.

82. The classic critique of this process is Theodore J. Lowi, *The End of Liberalism* (New York: Norton, 1969).

83. Ibid., 97.

84. Kenneth Culp Davis, *Administrative Law Treatise* (St. Paul: West Publishing, 1958), 9.

85. Mayer and Weko, "Institutionalization of Power," 199.

86. Ibid.

87. James F. Blumstein, "Regulatory Review by the Executive Office of the President: An Overview and Policy Analysis of Current Issues," *Duke Law Journal* 51 (Dec. 2001): 856.

88. A. Acs and C. M. Cameron, "Does White House Regulatory Review Produce a Chilling Effect and 'OIRA Avoidance' in the Agencies?," *Presidential Studies Quarterly* 43 (2013): 443–467.

89. Terry M. Moe, "The President and Bureaucracy," in Michael Nelson, ed., *The Presidency and the Political System,* 4th ed. (Washington, DC: CQ Press, 1995), 432.

90. Elena Kagan, "Presidential Administration," *Harvard Law Review* 114 (June 2001): 2262.

91. Moe, "President and the Bureaucracy," 430–431.

92. Joel D. Aberbach and Bert A. Rockman, *In the Web of Politics: Three Decades of the U.S. Federal Executive* (Washington, DC: Brookings, 2000), 169.

93. Marissa Martino Golden, *What Motivates Bureaucrats? Politics and Administration during the Reagan Years* (New York: Columbia University Press, 2000).

94. Ibid., ch. 1.

95. Blumstein, "Regulatory Review," 859.

96. Richard H. Pildes and Cass Sunstein, "Reinventing the Regulatory State," *University of Chicago Law Review* 1 (1995): 62.

97. Kagan, "Presidential Administration," 2247.

98. Ibid., 2247.

99. Ibid., 2265.

100. Ibid., 2271.

101. Blumstein, "Regulatory Review," 860.

102. For example, Douglas W. Kmiec, "Expanding Executive Power," in Roger Pilon, ed., *The Rule of Law in the Wake of Clinton* (Washington, DC: Cato Institute Press, 2000), 47–68.

103. Blumstein, "Regulatory Review," 854.

104. Stephen Power and Jacob M. Schlesinger, "Bush's Rules Czar Brings Long Knife to New Regulations," *Wall Street Journal,* June 12, 2002, 1.

105. Ellen Nakashima, "Chief Plans Overhaul of Regulatory Process," *Washington Post,* Mar. 20, 2002, A31.

106. Robert Percival, "Presidential Management of the Administrative State," *Duke Law Journal* 51 (Dec. 2001): 1015.

107. John D. McKinnon and Stephen Power, "How U.S. Rules Are Made Is Still a Murky Process," *Wall Street Journal,* Oct. 22, 2003, A6.

108. John M. Broder, "Powerful Shaper of U.S. Rules Quits, Leaving Critics in Wake," *New York Times,* Aug. 4, 2012, 1.

109. Maeve Carey, "Counting Regulations: An Overview of Rulemaking, Types of Federal

Regulations, and Pages in the Federal Register," *Congressional Research Service,* May 1, 2013, available online at http://www.fas.org/sgp/crs/misc/R43056.pdf (accessed July 20, 2015).

110. Alexis de Tocqueville, *Democracy in America,* ed. Phillips Bradley (New York: Vintage, 1945), vol. 2, book 4, ch. 6, 335.

111. A complete inventory is provided in Harold C. Relyea, "Presidential Directives: Background and Review," The Library of Congress, Congressional Research Service, report 98–611, Nov. 9, 2001.

112. Terry M. Moe and William G. Howell, "The Presidential Power of Unilateral Action," *Journal of Law, Economics, and Organization* 15, no. 1 (Jan. 1999): 133–134.

113. Todd F. Gaziano, "The Use and Abuse of Executive Orders and Other Presidential Directives," *Texas Review of Law and Politics* 5 (Spring 2001): 274.

114. Kenneth R. Mayer, *With the Stroke of a Pen: Executive Orders and Presidential Power* (Princeton: Princeton University Press, 2001), 71.

115. Ibid., 72–73.

116. Louis Fisher, *Constitutional Conflicts between Congress and the President,* 4th ed. (Lawrence: University Press of Kansas, 1998), 110.

117. Moe and Howell, "Presidential Power," 164.

118. Mayer, *With the Stroke of a Pen,* ch. 6.

119. 346 U.S. 579 (1952).

120. *Chamber of Commerce v. Reich,* 74 F.3rd 1322 (D.C. Cir. 1996).

121. Phillip J. Cooper, *By Order of the President: The Use and Abuse of Executive Direct Action* (Lawrence: University Press of Kansas, 2002), 22.

122. Ibid., 24.

123. *Dames & Moore v. Regan,* 453 U.S. 654 (1981).

124. Mark Killenback, "A Matter of Mere Approval: The Role of the President in the Creation of Legislative History," *University of Arkansas Law Review* 48 (1995): 239.

125. Cooper, *By Order of the President,* 201.

126. Edward S. Corwin, *The President: Office and Powers,* 4th rev. ed. (New York: NYU Press, 1957), 283.

127. Cooper, *By Order of the President,* 201.

128. Ibid., 216.

129. Cooper, *By Order of the President,* 207.

130. Ibid., 206.

131. Ibid., 217.

132. Kristy Carroll, "Whose Statute Is It Anyway? Why and How Courts Should Use Presidential Signing Statements When Interpreting Federal Statutes," *Catholic University Law Review* 16 (1997): 475.

133. Gaziano, "Use and Abuse of Executive Orders," 283.

134. Tara L. Branum, "President or King? The Use and Abuse of Executive Orders in Modern-Day America," *Journal of Legislation* 28, no. 1 (2002): 1–59.

135. Cooper, *By Order of the President,* 108–109.

136. *National Labor Relations Board v. McKay Radio and Telephone Co.,* 304 US 333 (1938).

137. Jeffrey Fine and Adam Warber, "Circumventing Adversity: Executive Orders and Divided Government," *Presidential Studies Quarterly* 42, no. 2 (June 2012): 256–274.

138. *Building Construction Trades Department v. Allbaugh,* 295 F. 3rd. 28 (2002).

139. George Will, "Reforming Free Speech," *Washington Post,* Mar. 31, 2002, B7.

140. Frank J. Murray, "Justice Fights to Keep Clinton Monument Edicts Intact," *Washington Times,* July 28, 2003, A3.

141. Moe and Howell, "Presidential Power," 174; Cooper, *By Order of the President,* 77.

142. Kagan, "Presidential Administration," 2270.

143. Ibid., 2351.

144. Alexander Hamilton, James Madison, and John Jay, *The Federalist Papers,* ed. Clinton Rossiter (New York: Signet, 1961), no. 70, 423–430.

145. Moe, "Presidency and the Bureaucracy," 416–420.

CHAPTER EIGHT
The Executive and the Courts

1. 2 *Cranch* 170 (1804).

2. The first was *Mitchell v. Laird,* 488 F. 2nd 611 (1973), in which thirteen members of Congress asked the court to order the president to bring an end to the Vietnam War on the grounds that it had not been properly authorized by the Congress.

3. 444 U.S. 996 (1979).

4. *Raines v. Byrd,* 521 U.S. 811 (1997). See also *Campbell v. Clinton,* 52 F.Supp. 2d 34 (D.D.C. 1994). For an interesting discussion of efforts by legislators to use the courts to bring about changes in presidential policies, see Anthony Clark Arend and Catherine Lotrionte, "Congress Goes to Court: The Past, Present and Future of Legislator Standing," *Harvard Journal of Law and Public Policy* 25 (Fall 2001): 209.

5. For an example of a congressional *amicus* brief see Roy E. Brownell, "The Unnecessary Demise of the Line-Item Veto Act," *American University Law Review* 47 (June 1998): 1273.

6. *Exploring Constitutional Conflicts,* available online at http://law2.umkc.edu/faculty/projects/ftrials/conlaw/senateconfirm.html (accessed July 19, 2015).

7. 531 U.S. 98 (2000).

8. 347 U.S. 483 (1954).

9. *Worcester v. Georgia,* 31 U.S. 515 (1832).

10. *Ex parte Merryman,* 17 F. Cas. 144 (1861).

11. Quoted in William Howell, *Power without Persuasion: The Politics of Direct Presidential Action* (Princeton: Princeton University Press, 2003), 142.

12. The entire brief, 13–15 (2013), is available for review online at the Washington Legal Foun-

dation website, http://www.wlf.org/upload/litigation/briefs/WLFHornbeckvJewellBrief.pdf (accessed August 13, 2015).

13. Bradley Canon, "Studying Bureaucratic Implementation of Judicial Policies in the United States: Conceptual and Methodological Approaches," in Marc Hertogh and Simon Halliday, eds., *Judicial Review and Bureaucratic Impact* (Cambridge, UK: Cambridge University Press, 2004), ch. 3.

14. H.R. 1924, available online at http://www.gpo.gov/fdsys/pkg/CRPT-106hrpt976/html/CRPT-106hrpt976.htm (accessed July 19, 2015).

15. 60 U.S. 393 (1857).

16. 5 U.S. 137 (1803).

17. *Albertson v. Subversive Activities Control Board,* 382 U.S. 70 (1965).

18. *United States v. Nixon,* 418 U.S. 683 (1974).

19. *Train v. City of New York,* 420 U.S. 35 (1975).

20. *National Federation of Independent Business v. Sibelius,* 132 S.Ct. 2566 (2012).

21. Edward Corwin, *The President: Office and Powers,* 4th rev. ed. (New York: NYU Press, 1957), 16.

22. Terry M. Moe and William G. Howell, "The Presidential Power of Unilateral Action," *Journal of Law, Economics, and Organization* 15, no. 1 (1999): 151–152.

23. Thomas E. Cronin and Michael A. Genovese, *The Paradoxes of the American Presidency* (New York: Oxford University Press, 1998), 271.

24. Moe and Howell, "Presidential Power," 150.

25. Kermit L. Hall, *The Politics of Justice: Lower Federal Judicial Selection and the Second Party System, 1829–1861* (Lincoln: University of Nebraska Press, 1979), 152–156.

26. Matthew Crenson and Benjamin Ginsberg, *Presidential Power: Unchecked and Unbalanced* (New York: W.W. Norton, 2007), 313.

27. Matthew A. Crenson and Benjamin Ginsberg, *Downsizing Democracy: How America Sidelined Its Citizens and Privatized Its Public* (Baltimore: Johns Hopkins University Press, 2002), 14–19.

28. Harold Seidman, *Politics, Position and Power: The Dynamics of Federal Organization,* 5th ed. (New York: Oxford University Press, 1998), 52.

29. David Baumann, "Budget Debates Leave White House with Foes in Both Parties," *GovExec.com,* Feb. 15, 2002, 1.

30. Ralph K. Winter, "The Activist Judicial Mind," in Mark W. Cannon and David M. O'Brien, *Views from the Bench* (Chatham, NJ: Chatham House, 1985), 291.

31. John S. Martin, Jr., "Let Judges Do Their Jobs," *New York Times,* June 24, 2003, A31.

32. 369 U.S. 186 (1962).

33. 395 U.S. 486 (1969).

34. 531 U.S. 98 (2000). For the background and details of the case see E. J. Dionne and William Kristol, eds., *Bush v. Gore: The Court Cases and the Commentary* (Washington, DC: Brookings, 2001). For a defense of the Court's actions, see Richard Posner, *Breaking the Dead-*

lock: The 2000 Election, the Constitution and the Courts (Princeton: Princeton University Press, 2001).

35. Benjamin Ginsberg and Martin Shefter, *Politics by Other Means* (New York: W. W. Norton, 2002), ch. 6. The quoted comment regarding the Florida legislature is from Thomas Oliphant, "Gov. Bush's Cynical End-Around in the Florida Legislature," *Boston Globe,* Dec. 3, 2000, D8.

36. For a critique of the notion of judicial imperialism, see Mark Kozloski and Anthony Lewis, *The Myth of the Imperial Judiciary* (New York: NYU Press, 2003).

37. 3 Dall. 54 (1795).

38. 2 Pet. 253 (1829).

39. 50 U.S. 602 (1850).

40. *Fong Yue Ting v. United States* 149 U.S. 698 (1893).

41. 182 U.S. 1 (1901).

42. 299 U.S. 304 (1936).

43. *Schechter Bros. v. United States,* 295 U.S. 495 (1935); *Panama Refining Co. v. Ryan,* 293 U.S. 388 (1935).

44. Gordon Silverstein, "Judicial Enhancement of Executive Power," in Paul Peterson, ed., *The President, the Congress and the Making of Foreign Policy* (Norman: University of Oklahoma Press, 1994), 28–29.

45. Randall W. Bland, *The Black Robe and the Bald Eagle: The Supreme Court and the Foreign Policy of the United States, 1789–1953* (San Francisco: Austin & Winfield, 1996), 172.

46. Sarah H. Cleveland, "Crosby and the 'One Voice' Myth in U.S. Foreign Relations," *Villanova Law Review* 46 (2001): 975.

47. John C. Yoo, "Laws as Treaties?: The Constitutionality of Congressional-Executive Agreements," *Michigan Law Review* 99 (Feb. 2001): 757.

48. Corwin, *President,* 212–213.

49. Bland, *Black Robe,* 177.

50. See *Field v. Clark,* 143 U.S. 649 (1892).

51. 299 U.S. 304 (1936).

52. 301 U.S. 324 (1937).

53. 565 F.Supp. 1019 (D. Colo. 1983).

54. 151 F.Supp. 942 (1957).

55. 6 Cl. Ct. 115 (1984). The decision was later reversed on appeal by the U.S. Court of Appeals for the Federal Circuit primarily because both the U.S. and Panamanian governments asserted that the executive agreement had not been intended to relieve Canal Zone workers of their federal tax obligations. See 761 F. 2nd 688 (1985).

56. *Dames & Moore v. Regan* 453 U.S. 654 (1981).

57. Relevant cases include *Rust v. Sullivan,* 500 U.S. 173 (1991) and *U.S. v. Alvarez-Machain,* 504 U.S. 655 (1992).

58. *Goldwater v. Carter,* 444 U.S. 996 (1979).

59. Victoria M. Kraft, *The U.S. Constitution and Foreign Policy: Terminating the Taiwan Treaty* (New York: Greenwood, 1991), ch. 3.

60. Joshua O'Donnell, "The Anti-Ballistic Missile Treaty Debate: Time for Some Clarification of the President's Authority to Terminate a Treaty," *Vanderbilt Journal of Transnational Law* 35 (Nov. 2002): 1601.

61. Joel R. Paul, "The Geopolitical Constitution," *California Law Review* 86 (July 1998): 671–672.

62. Ronald J. Sievert, "*Campbell v. Clinton* and the Continuing Effort to Reassert Congress' Predominant Constitutional Authority to Commence, or Prevent, War," *Dickinson Law Review* 105 (Winter 2001): 157.

63. D. A. Jeremy Telman, "A Truism That Isn't True? The Tenth Amendment and Executive War Power," *Catholic University Law Review* 51 (Fall 2001): 135.

64. Max Farrand, ed., *Records of the Federal Convention of 1787* (New Haven: Yale University Press, 1937), vol. 2, 318.

65. Julian C. Boyd, ed., *The Papers of Thomas Jefferson* (Princeton: Princeton University Press, 1950), vol. 15, 397.

66. 4 U.S. 37 (1800).

67. 5 U.S. 1 (1801).

68. 6 U.S. 170 (1804).

69. 12 U.S. 110 (1814).

70. Telman, "A Truism That Isn't True?," 144.

71. Abraham D. Sofaer, "The Power over War," *University of Miami Law Review* 50 (Oct. 1995): 33.

72. David Currie, "Rumors of War: Presidential and Congressional War Powers, 1809–1829," *University of Chicago Law Review* 67 (Winter 2000): 1.

73. Telman, "A Truism That Isn't True?," 145.

74. John Locke, *Treatise of Civil Government and a Letter Concerning Toleration* (New York: Appleton-Century Crofts, 1937), 109.

75. 67 U.S. 635 (1863).

76. 71 U.S. 2 (1866).

77. Martin S. Sheffer, *The Judicial Development of Presidential War Powers* (Westport, CT: Praeger, 1999), 25.

78. *Ex parte Milligan*, 71 U.S. (4 Wall.) 2 (1866).

79. 78 U.S. 268 (1871).

80. For example, *Stewart v. Kahn* 78 U.S. 493 (1871).

81. Christopher N. May, *In the Name of War: Judicial Review and the War Powers since 1918* (Cambridge, MA: Harvard University Press, 1989), 19.

82. 135 U.S. 546 (1890).

83. 158 U.S. 564 (1895).

84. Wilson did undertake a number of measures on his own authority as commander-

in-chief, such as the creation of the Committee on Public Information, the War Industries Board, and the War Labor Board, but for the most part he relied on statutory authority for his actions. Corwin, *President,* 237.

85. Clinton Rossiter, *The Supreme Court and the Commander in Chief* (Ithaca, NY: Cornell University Press, 1951), 91.

86. May, *In the Name of War,* 258.

87. For example, see *Hamilton v. Kentucky Distilleries,* 251 U.S. 146 (1919).

88. Corwin, *President,* 241.

89. Arthur Schlesinger, *The Imperial Presidency* (Boston: Houghton-Mifflin, 1973), 111.

90. Corwin, *President,* 243.

91. Quoted in ibid., 250.

92. May, *In the Name of War,* 258.

93. Sheffer, *Judicial Development of Presidential War Powers,* 53.

94. 321 U.S. 414 (1944).

95. 317 U.S. 1 (1942).

96. Lisa M. Ivey, "Ready, Aim, Fire? The President's Executive Order Authorizing Detention, Treatment and Trial of Certain Non-Citizens in the War against Terrorism Is a Powerful Weapon, But Should It Be Upheld?" *Cumberland Law Review* 33 (2002–2003): 107.

97. 339 U.S. 763 (1950).

98. Rossiter, *Supreme Court,* 43.

99. 323 U.S. 214 (1944).

100. 143 F.2nd 145 (D.C. Cir. 1944).

101. 150 F. 2nd 369 (1945).

102. 343 U.S. 579 (1952).

103. Patricia Bellia, "Executive Power in Youngstown's Shadows," *Constitutional Commentary* 19 (Spring 2002): 87.

104. 403 U.S. 713 (1971).

105. 407 U.S. 297 (1972).

106. Gordon Silverstein, *Imbalance of Powers: Constitutional Interpretation and the Making of American Foreign Policy* (New York: Oxford University Press, 1997), 176.

107. 453 U.S. 280 (1981).

108. 558 F.Supp. 893 (1982).

109. *Lowry v. Reagan,* 676 F.Supp. 333 (1987); *Dellums v. Bush,* 752 F.Supp. 1141 (1990).

110. 340 U.S. App. D.C. 149 (2000).

111. Harold H. Koh, *The National Security Constitution* (New Haven: Yale University Press, 1990), 137.

112. Robert J. Delahunty and John C. Yoo, "The President's Constitutional Authority to Conduct Military Operations against Terrorist Organizations and the Nations That Harbor or Support Them," *Harvard Journal of Law and Public Policy* 25 (Spring 2002): 487.

113. 542 U.S. 507 (2004).

114. Charles Lane, "Justices Back Detainee Access to U.S. Courts," *Washington Post,* June 29, 2004, 1.

115. 542 U.S. 466 (2004).

116. Ibid.

117. Several agencies, however, are not subject to presidential budgetary review. See Louis Fisher, *Constitutional Conflicts between Congress and the President,* 4th ed. (Lawrence: University Press of Kansas, 1997), 201.

118. See Theodore J. Lowi, *The End of Liberalism,* 2nd ed. (New York: Norton, 1979). Also David Schoenbrod, *Power without Responsibility: How Congress Abuses the People through Delegation* (New Haven: Yale University Press, 1993).

119. Kenneth Culp Davis, *Discretionary Justice* (Baton Rouge: Louisiana State University Press, 1969), 15–21.

120. David M. O'Brien, *Constitutional Law and Politics,* vol. 1, 4th ed. (New York: Norton, 2000), 368.

121. Lowi, *End of Liberalism,* 94–97.

122. Jeffrey A. Wertkin, "Reintroducing Compromise to the Nondelegation Doctrine," *Georgetown Law Journal* 98 (Apr. 2002), 1012–1013, 1055.

123. 143 U.S. 649 (1892).

124. 23 U.S. 1 (1825).

125. 276 U.S. 394 (1928).

126. 56 Stat. 23 (Jan. 30, 1942).

127. 298 U.S. 238 (1936).

128. 467 U.S. 837 (1984).

129. See *Whitman v. American Trucking Associations,* 531 U.S. 457 (2001) and *AT&T Corp. v. Iowa Utilities Board,* 525 U.S. 366 (1999).

130. 533 U.S. 218 (2001).

131. Silverstein, *Imbalance,* 187.

132. 524 U.S. 417 (1998).

133. Archibald Cox, "Executive Privilege," *University of Pennsylvania Law Review* 122 (1974): 1383.

134. Raoul Berger, *Executive Privilege* (Cambridge, MA: Harvard University Press, 1974).

135. *United States v. Burr,* 25 F.Cas. 187 (1807).

136. Jeffrey Carlin, "Walker v. Cheney: Politics, Posturing and Executive Privilege," *Southern California Law Review* 76 (Nov. 2002): 235, 245.

137. 433 U.S. 425 (1977).

138. The appeals court, however, developed a procedure that gave the subcommittee limited access to documents under court supervision. 551 F.2nd 384 (D.C. Cir. 1976).

139. 556 F. Supp. 150 (D.D.C. 1983). As in the *AT&T* case, the court developed a procedure providing limited access to the contested documents.

140. See, for example, *Bareford v. General Dynamics Corp.,* 973 F.2nd 1138 (5th Cir. 1992).

141. See, *In re Sealed Case,* 121 F.3rd 729 (D.C. Cir. 1997).

142. 124 S.Ct. 1391 (2004).

143. 424 U.S. 1 (1976).

144. Robert V. Percival, "Presidential Management of the Administrative State: The Not-so-Unitary Executive," *Duke Law Journal* 51 (Dec. 2001): 963, 972.

145. 272 U.S. 52 (1926).

146. 295 U.S. 602 (1935).

147. 478 U.S. 714 (1986).

148. 48 U.S. 361 (1989).

149. 366 F. Supp. 104 (D.D.C., 1973).

150. 487 U.S. 654 (1988).

151. William J. Olson and Alan Woll, "How Presidents Have Come to Run the Country by Usurping Legislative Power" (Washington, DC: Cato Institute, 1999).

152. *Building and Construction Trades Department v. Allbaugh,* 172 F. Supp. 2nd 138 (D.D.C., 2001).

153. 74 F. 3rd 1322 (D.C. Cir. 1996).

154. Tara L. Branum, "President or King? The Use and Abuse of Executive Orders in Modern-Day America," *Journal of Legislation* 28 (2002): 1, 18.

155. 133 S.Ct. 1863 (2013).

156. *Clinton v. Jones,* 520 U.S. 681 (1997).

CHAPTER NINE
Foreign Policy and National Security

1. Brandice Canes-Wrone, William G. Howell, and David E. Lewis, "Toward a Broader Understanding of Presidential Power: A Reevaluation of the Two Presidencies Thesis," *Journal of Politics* 70, no. 1 (Jan. 2008): 1–18.

2. Edward S. Corwin, *The President: Office and Powers,* 4th rev. ed. (New York: NYU Press, 1957), 171.

3. Alexander Hamilton, James Madison, and John Jay, *The Federalist Papers,* ed. Clinton Rossiter (New York: Mentor, 1961), no. 64, 390–396.

4. Joseph S. Nye, Jr., *Presidential Leadership and the Creation of the American Era* (Princeton: Princeton University Press, 2013).

5. James W. Davis, *The American Presidency* (Westport, CT: Praeger, 1995), 246.

6. Corwin, *The President,* 178–179.

7. Quoted in ibid., 182.

8. Quoted in Leonard White, *The Federalists* (New York: Free Press, 1948), 55.

9. Alexander Hamilton and James Madison, *Letters of Pacificus and Helvidius* (New York: Scholars Facsimiles & Reprint, 1999).

10. Ibid.

11. Corwin, *The President,* 181.

12. Sidney M. Milkis and Michael Nelson, *The American Presidency: Origins and Development* (Washington, DC: Congressional Quarterly Press, 1999), 91.

13. Leonard White, *The Jeffersonians* (New York: Free Press, 1951), 32.

14. Davis, *American Presidency,* 242.

15. *United States v. Curtiss-Wright Export Corporation,* 209 U.S. 304 (1936).

16. Kurt M. Campbell and James B. Steinberg, *Difficult Transitions: Foreign Policy Troubles at the Outset of Presidential Power* (Washington, DC: Brookings Institution Press, 2008).

17. Elizabeth N. Saunders, *Leaders at War: How Presidents Shape Military Interventions* (Ithaca, NY: Cornell University Press, 2011).

18. "Text of Bush's Speech at West Point," *New York Times,* June 1, 2002, available online at http://www.nytimes.com/2002/06/01/international/02PTEX-WEB.html (accessed August 13, 2015).

19. White House Office of the Press Secretary, "Remarks by the President at the United States Military Academy Commencement Ceremony," May 28, 2014, available online at https://www.whitehouse.gov/the-press-office/2014/05/28/remarks-president-united-states -military-academy-commencement-ceremony (accessed August 13, 2015).

20. D. Miller, "The Contemporary Presidency: Organizing the National Security Council: I Like Ike's," *Presidential Studies Quarterly* 43 (2013): 592–606.

21. Ivo H. Daalder and I. M. Destler, *In the Shadow of the Oval Office: Profiles of the National Security Advisers and the Presidents They Served* (New York: Simon and Schuster, 2009).

22. John Burke, *Honest Broker? The National Security Adviser and Presidential Decision Making* (College Station: Texas A&M University Press, 2009).

23. *Department of Defense Organizations and Functions Guidebook,* excerpt available online at http://marshallcenterciss.contentdm.oclc.org/cdm/ref/collection/p16378coll5/id/503 (accessed August 12, 2015).

24. John J. McGrath, *The Other End of the Spear: The Tooth-to-Tail Ratio (T3R) in Modern Military Operations* (Fort Leavenworth, KS: Combat Studies Institute Press, 2007), available online at http://www.cgsc.edu/carl/download/csipubs/mcgrath_op23.pdf (accessed July 20, 2015).

25. D. Robert Worley, *Shaping U.S. Military Forces* (Westport, CT: Praeger, 2006), ch. 3.

26. Harold Seidman, *Politics, Position and Power,* 5th ed. (New York: Oxford University Press, 1998), 209.

27. Benjamin Ginsberg, *The Worth of War* (New York: Prometheus Books, 2014), ch. 5.

28. "Foreign Intelligence Surveillance Act Court Orders, 1979–2012," Electronic Privacy Information Center, available online at https://epic.org/privacy/wiretap/stats/fisa_stats.html (accessed July 20, 2015).

29. James Bamford, "They Know Much More Than You Think," *New York Review of Books,* Aug. 15, 2013, 4.

30. Ibid., 4.

31. Siobhan Gorman and Jennifer Valentino DeVries, "HSA Reaches Deep into U.S. to Spy on Net: Fresh Details Show Programs Cover 75 Percent of Nation's Traffic, Can Snare Emails," *Wall Street Journal,* Aug. 21, 2013, A8.

32. Quoted in Ellen Nakashima, "NSA Collected Thousands of Domestic E-mails," *Washington Post,* Aug. 22, 2013, 1.

33. Barton Gellman, "Audit: NSA Repeatedly Broke Privacy Rules," *Washington Post,* Aug. 16, 2013, 1.

34. Carol D. Leonnig, "Surveillance Judge Says Court Relies on Government to Report Its Own Actions," *Washington Post,* Aug. 16, 2013, 1.

35. Hamilton and Madison, *Letters of Pacificus and Helvidius.*

36. Corwin, *The President,* 189.

37. White, *The Federalists,* 64.

38. Louis Fisher, *The Politics of Shared Power,* 4th ed. (College Station: Texas A&M Press, 1998), 186.

39. Hamilton, Madison, and Jay, *Federalist Papers,* no. 64, 418.

40. See Max Boot, *The Savage Wars of Peace: Small Wars and the Rise of American Power* (New York: Basic Books, 2002).

41. Prize Cases, 67 U.S. 635 (2 *Black*) (1863).

42. *Ex parte Milligan,* 71 U.S. 2 (4 Wall.) (1866).

43. Corwin, *The President,* 235.

44. Robert Higgs, *Crisis and Leviathan* (New York: Oxford University Press, 1987), 139.

45. Paul Koistinen, *Mobilizing for Modern War: The Political Economy of American Warfare* (Lawrence: University Press of Kansas, 1997), chs. 10 and 11.

46. Higgs, *Crisis and Leviathan,* 141.

47. Philip J. Cooper, *By Order of the President* (Lawrence: University Press of Kansas, 2002), 72.

48. *United States v. Cohen,* 255 U.S. 81 (1921).

49. *Shenck v. United States,* 249 U.S. 47 (1919).

50. Corwin, *The President,* 238.

51. Ibid., 238.

52. Kenneth R. Mayer, *With the Stroke of a Pen* (Princeton: Princeton University Press, 2001), 111.

53. Corwin, *The President,* 243.

54. Davis, *American Presidency,* 224.

55. Arthur M. Schlesinger, Jr., *The Imperial Presidency* (Boston: Houghton-Mifflin, 1973), 110–111.

56. Benjamin Ginsberg, *The Fatal Embrace: Jews and the State* (Chicago: University of Chicago Press, 1993), 118.

57. J. Garry Clifford and Samuel R. Spencer, Jr., *The First Peacetime Draft* (Lawrence: University Press of Kansas, 1986).

58. Corwin, *The President,* 240.

59. Higgs, *Crisis and Leviathan,* 204.

60. Ibid., 205.

61. Ibid., 210.

62. 321 U.S. 414 (1944).

63. 321 U.S. 503 (1944).

64. 323 U.S. 214 (1944).

65. *Ex parte Quirin,* 317 U.S. 1 (July special term, 1942).

66. 333 U.S. 138 (1948).

67. Hamilton and Madison, *Letters of Pacificus and Helvidius.*

68. Schlesinger, *Imperial Presidency,* 66.

69. Higgs, *Crisis and Leviathan,* 154.

70. Bartholomew H. Sparrow, *From the Outside In: World War II and the American State* (Princeton: Princeton University Press, 1996).

71. Schlesinger, *Imperial Presidency,* 127.

72. Ibid., 151.

73. David Oshinsky, *A Conspiracy So Immense* (New York: Free Press, 1985).

74. Wilfred Binkley, "The Decline of the Executive," *New Republic,* May 18, 1953.

75. Maeva Marcus, *Truman and the Steel Seizure Case: The Limits of Presidential Power* (New York: Columbia University Press, 1977).

76. 343 U.S. 579 (1952).

77. Theda Skocpol et al., "Patriotic Partnerships: Why Great Wars Nourished American Civic Voluntarism," in Ira Katznelson and Martin Shefter, ed., *Shaped by War and Trade: International Influences on American Political Development* (Princeton: Princeton University Press, 2002), 143–180.

78. Michael D. Pearlman, *Warmaking and American Democracy* (Lawrence: University Press of Kansas, 1999), 57.

79. Chilton Williamson, *American Suffrage from Property to Democracy, 1760–1860* (Princeton: Princeton University Press, 1960), ch. 6.

80. Benjamin Ginsberg, *The Consequences of Consent* (New York: Random House, 1982), ch. 1.

81. Eric Foner, *Free Soil, Free Labor, Free Men: The Ideology of the Republican Party before the Civil War* (New York: Oxford University Press, 1970).

82. Iver Bernstein, *The New York City Draft Riots* (New York: Oxford University Press, 1997).

83. Jack F. Leach, *Conscription in the United States* (Rutland, VT: Charles E. Tuttle, 1952), 296.

84. David M. Kennedy, *Over Here: The First World War and American Society* (New York: Oxford University Press, 1986), 144–167.

85. Stephen Kohn, *Jailed for Peace* (Westport, CT: Greenwood Press, 1986).

86. Kennedy, *Over Here,* 144–167.

87. Martin Shefter, *Political Parties and the State* (Princeton: Princeton University Press, 1994), 88–91.

88. For a discussion of "postmaterial" politics, see Jeffrey M. Berry, *The New Liberalism* (Washington, DC: Brookings, 1999).

89. Herbert D. A. Donovan, *The Barnburners* (New York: NYU Press, 1925).

90. George L. Mayer, *The Republican Party, 1854–1966* (New York: Oxford University Press, 1967), 71.

91. Ibid., 161.

92. Howard Jones, *Crucible of Power* (Wilmington, DE: SR Books, 2001), 103–105.

93. Senator Hiram Johnson, quoted in Mayer, *Republican Party,* 354.

94. Ibid., 353.

95. Ellen Schrecker, *Many Are the Crimes* (Boston: Little, Brown, 1998).

96. Herbert Shapiro, "The Vietnam War and the American Civil Rights Movement," in Walter Hixson, ed., *The Vietnam Antiwar Movement* (New York: Garland, 2000), 71–95.

97. Benjamin Ginsberg and Martin Shefter, *Politics by Other Means,* 3rd ed. (New York: Norton, 2002), 91.

98. Robert D. Johnson, "The Origins of Dissent: Senate Liberals and Vietnam," in Walter Hixson, ed., *The Vietnam Antiwar Movement* (New York: Garland, 2000), 151–275.

99. Scott Gartner, Gary Segura, and Michael Wilkening, "Local Losses and Individual Attitudes toward the Vietnam War," in Walter Hixson, ed., *The Vietnam Antiwar Movement* (New York: Garland, 2000), 193–218.

100. Bartholomew Sparrow, "Limited Wars and the Attenuation of the State," in Ira Katznelson and Martin Shefter, ed., *Shaped by War and Trade: International Influences on American Political Development* (Princeton: Princeton University Press, 2002), 277–278.

101. Schlesinger, *Imperial Presidency,* 166.

102. Michael J. Hogan, *Cross of Iron: Harry S. Truman and the Origins of the National Security State, 1945–1954* (New York: Cambridge University Press, 1998), 72–73.

103. Schlesinger, *Imperial Presidency,* 118.

104. Robert Sherwood, *Roosevelt and Hopkins* (New York: Universal Library, 1950), 636–640.

105. Matthew J. Dickinson, *Bitter Harvest: FDR, Presidential Power and the Growth of the Presidential Branch* (Cambridge, UK: Cambridge University Press, 1996), 178–181.

106. Charles E. Bohlen, *Witness to History* (New York: Norton, 1973), 210.

107. Milkis and Nelson, *American Presidency,* 280.

108. Robert D. Schulzinger, *U.S. Diplomacy since 1900* (New York: Oxford University Press, 1998), 212.

109. Rhodri Jeffreys-Jones, *The CIA and American Democracy,* 2nd ed. (New Haven: Yale University Press, 1998), ch. 1.

110. Alonzo Hamby, *A Man of the People: A Life of Harry S. Truman* (New York: Oxford University Press, 1995), 309–311.

111. Allan R. Millett and Peter Maslowski, *For the Common Defense: A Military History of the United States* (New York: Free Press, 1984), ch. 10.

112. Allan R. Millett, *Semper Fidelis: The History of the United States Marine Corps* (New York: Free Press, 1991), 292–296.

113. Millett and Maslowski, *For the Common Defense,* 366.

114. Ibid., 515.

115. Hogan, *Cross of Iron,* 151.

116. Quoted in George Q. Flynn, *The Draft* (Lawrence: University Press of Kansas, 1993), 141.

117. Millett and Maslowski, *For the Common Defense,* 517.

118. Aaron L. Friedberg, "American Antistatism and the Founding of the Cold War State," in Ira Katznelson and Martin Shefter, ed., *Shaped by War and Trade: International Influences on American Political Development* (Princeton: Princeton University Press, 2002), 254.

119. Paul Koistinen, *The Hammer and the Sword: Labor, the Military, and Industrial Production, 1920–1945* (New York: Arno Press, 1979), 580.

120. Harold Seidman, *Politics, Position, and Power,* 5th ed. (New York: Oxford University Press, 1998), 208–211.

121. Ken Silverstein, *Private Warriors* (London: Verso, 2000), ch. 5.

122. General Wesley K. Clark, "Iraq: What Went Wrong," *New York Review of Books* Sept. 22, 2003, 52–54.

123. Ann Markusen et al., *The Rise of the Gunbelt: The Military Remapping of Industrial America* (New York: Oxford University Press, 1991), ch. 10.

124. Quoted in Anthony Bianco and Stephanie Anderson Forest, "Outsourcing War," *Business Week,* Sept. 15, 2003, 72.

125. W. Singer, *Corporate Warriors: The Rise of the Privatized Military Industry* (Ithaca, NY: Cornell University Press, 2003); also Chalmers Johnson, *The Sorrows of Empire* (New York: Henry Holt, 2004), ch. 5.

126. Dana Priest, "Private Guards Repel Attack on U.S. Headquarters," *New York Times,* Apr. 6, 2004, 1.

127. James Dao, "Private Guards Take Big Risks, for Right Price," *New York Times,* Apr. 2, 2004, 1.

128. Dana Priest and Mary Pat Flaherty, "Under Fire, Security Firms Form an Alliance," *Washington Post,* Apr. 8, 2004, 1.

129. Singer, *Corporate Warriors,* 207.

130. Ibid., 208.

131. Ibid., 210–211.

132. Ellen McCarthy, "CACI Wants to Review Report on Alleged Abuse," *Washington Post,* May 4, 2004, A18.

133. Greg Jaffe, David S. Cloud, and Gary Fields, "Iraq Contractors Pose Problem," *Wall Street Journal,* May 4, 2004, A4.

134. John Burke, *The Institutional Presidency,* 2nd ed. (Baltimore: Johns Hopkins University Press, 2000), 37–40.

135. Joel R. Paul, "The Geopolitical Constitution: Executive Expediency and Executive Agreements," *University of California Law Review* 86 (July 1998): 713–714.

136. Ibid., 720–721.

137. Ibid., sec. 3; also Fisher, *Politics of Shared Power,* 190–191.

138. Harold W. Stanley and Richard Niemi, *Vital Statistics on American Politics, 2001–2002* (Washington, DC: Congressional Quarterly Press, 2001), 334.

139. John C. Yoo, "Laws as Treaties?: The Constitutionality of Congressional-Executive Agreements," *University of Michigan Law Review* 99 (Feb. 2001): 757.

140. Judith Goldstein, "International Forces and Domestic Politics: Trade Policy and Institution Building in the United States," in Ira Katznelson and Martin Shefter, ed., *Shaped by War and Trade: International Influences on American Political Development* (Princeton: Princeton University Press, 2002), 214–221.

141. Cooper, *By Order of the President,* 144.

142. Ibid., 158.

143. Jeffreys-Jones, *CIA and American Democracy,* 55–56.

144. Schlesinger, *Imperial Presidency,* 167.

145. Keith Whittington and Daniel Carpenter, "Executive Power in American Institutional Development," *Perspectives on Politics* 1, no. 3 (Sept. 2003): 495–513.

146. Ibid., 505–506.

147. Robert J. Donovan, *Conflict and Crisis: The Presidency of Harry S. Truman, 1945–1948* (New York: W.W. Norton, 1977), 296–297.

148. Athan Theoharis, ed., *The Truman Presidency: The Origins of the Imperial Presidency and the National Security State* (Stanfordville, NY: E.M. Coleman, 1979), 257–261.

149. Schlesinger, *Imperial Presidency,* ch. 10.

150. Margaret Myers, *A Financial History of the United States* (New York: Columbia University Press, 1970), ch. 15.

151. Friedberg, "American Antistatism," 250.

152. Sidney Ratner, *American Taxation: Its History as a Social Force in Democracy* (New York: W.W. Norton, 1942), 72.

153. Joseph A. Pechman, *Federal Tax Policy,* 5th ed. (Washington, DC: Brookings, 1987), 355–363; also B. Guy Peters, *The Politics of Taxation* (Cambridge, MA: Blackwell, 1991), 1–15.

154. Todd Sandler and Keith Hartley, *The Economics of Defense* (Cambridge, UK: Cambridge University Press, 1995), ch. 10. Also Michael T. Klare, *American Arms Supermarket* (Austin: University of Texas Press, 1984), 34.

155. David Gold, "The Changing Economics of the Arms Trade," in Ann Markusen and Sean Costigan, eds., *Arming the Future* (New York: Council on Foreign Relations Press, 1999), 249–268.

156. Leslie Wayne, "Polish Pride, American Profits," *New York Times,* Jan. 12, 2003, sec. 3, p. 1.

157. Larry Neal, *War Finance* (Brookfield, VT: Edward Elgar Publishing, 1994), vol. 1, p. 3.

158. Dean Acheson, *Present at the Creation* (New York: W.W. Norton, 1987), ch. 26.

159. Malcolm Chalmers, *Sharing Security: The Political Economy of Burdensharing* (London: Macmillan, 2000), 33.

160. Millett and Maslowski, *For the Common Defense,* 519.

161. Schlesinger, *Imperial Presidency,* 165.

162. Ibid., 200–207.

163. Ibid., 132–133.

164. Edward C. Luck, *Mixed Messages: American Politics and International Organization, 1919–1999* (Washington, DC: Brookings, 1999), 61–62.

165. Ibid., ch. 7.

166. Lawrence R. Samuel, *Pledging Allegiance* (Washington, DC: Smithsonian Institution Press, 1997).

167. John J. Miller, "Get Your War Bonds: Why Doesn't the Administration Shout It?" *The National Review,* Dec. 22, 2003, 25–26.

168. Schlesinger, *Imperial Presidency,* 132–135.

169. Bob Woodward, "Cheney Upholds Power of the Presidency," *Washington Post,* Jan. 20, 2005, A7.

170. Jonathan Hughes and Louis Cain, *American Economic History,* 5th ed. (Reading, MA: Addison-Wesley, 1998), 529.

171. Neal, *War Finance,* 17.

172. Schlesinger, *Imperial Presidency,* 156–158.

173. Louis Fisher, *Congressional Abdication on War and Spending* (College Station: Texas A&M Press, 2000), 49–52.

174. Flynn, *The Draft,* 265.

175. Douglas Bandow, "Fixing What Ain't Broke: The Renewed Call for Conscription," *Policy Analysis* 351 (Aug. 31, 1999): 2.

176. Charles B. Rangel, "Bring Back the Draft," *New York Times,* Dec. 31, 2002, A21.

177. Thomas E. Ricks, *Making the Corps* (New York: Simon & Schuster, 1997), ch. 5.

178. Ole R. Holsti, "Of Chasms and Convergences: Attitudes and Beliefs of Civilians and Military Elites at the Start of a New Millennium," in Peter D. Feaver and Richard H. Kohn, *Soldiers and Civilians* (Cambridge, MA: MIT Press, 2001), 15–100.

179. Jonathan Turley, "The Military Pocket Republic," *Northwestern University Law Review* 97 (Fall 2002): 1–126.

180. David M. Halbfinger and Steven A. Holmes, "Military Mirrors a Working-Class America," *New York Times,* Mar. 30, 2003, 1; also David Shiflett, "An Army That Drawls: Johnny Reb Goes to Iraq and Everywhere Else," *National Review,* May 5, 2003, 29–30.

181. Quoted in Vernon Loeb, "In Iraq, Pace of U.S. Casualties Has Accelerated," *Washington Post,* Dec. 28, 2003, 1.

182. Lawrence F. Kaplan, "Willpower: Why the Public Can Stomach Casualties in Iraq," *New Republic,* Sept. 8, 2003, 19–22.

183. In the aftermath of the Vietnam War, some generals supported placing critical spe-

cialties in the reserves to prevent presidents from asking the army to fight without popular support. See Greg Jaffe, "Today, Military Kids Often Say Goodbye to Dad—and Mom," *Wall Street Journal,* Mar. 11, 2003, 1.

184. Thom Shanker, "U.S. Considers Limits on Role of the Reserves," *New York Times,* Jan. 26, 2003, 1.

185. Vernon Loeb, "Rumsfeld Turns Eye to Future of Army," *Washington Post,* June 8, 2003, A12.

186. James R. Locher III, *Victory on the Potomac: The Goldwater-Nichols Act Unifies the Pentagon* (College Station: Texas A&M Press, 2002).

187. Franklin C. Spinney, "Notes on Close Air Support," in Donald Vandergriff, ed., *Spirit, Blood and Treasure: The American Cost of Battle in the 21st Century* (Novato, CA: Presidio Press, 2001), 199–213.

188. Geoffrey Perret, *A Country Made by War* (New York: Random House, 1989), 305–308.

189. George and Meredith Friedman, *The Future of War* (New York: St. Martin's, 1996), ch. 10.

190. Matthew Brzezinski, "The Unmanned Army," *New York Times Magazine,* Apr. 20, 2003, 38–80.

191. MacGregor Knox and Williamson Murray, *The Dynamics of Military Revolution, 1300–2050* (New York: Cambridge University Press, 2001), 188–192.

192. Quoted in Christopher Palmeri, "A Predator That Preys on Hawks?" *Business Week,* Feb. 17, 2003, 78.

193. Renae Merle, "Army Scraps $39 Billion Helicopter," *Washington Post,* Feb. 24, 2004, 1.

194. David Halberstam, "Televising the Vietnam War," in Doris A. Graber, ed., *Media Power in Politics* (Washington, DC: Congressional Quarterly Press, 1984), 290–295.

195. Jennifer Harper, "Journalists Prepare to See War from the Battlefield," *Washington Times,* Mar. 4, 2003, A5.

196. Tim Reid, "Texan Sent to Be Voice of War," *The Times* (London), Nov. 14, 2002, 19.

197. Michael Massing, "The Unseen War," *New York Review,* May 29, 2003, 16–19.

198. Loeb, "In Iraq."

199. John Lehman, *Making War: The 200-Year-Old Battle between the President and the Congress over How America Goes to War* (New York: Scribner's, 1992), 263.

200. Ibid., 265.

201. Louis Fisher, "The Spending Power," in David Gray Adler and Larry N. George, *The Constitution and the Conduct of American Foreign Policy* (Lawrence: University Press of Kansas, 1996), 234.

202. Neal, *War Finance,* 18.

203. Fisher, *Congressional Abdication,* 76.

204. Gordon Silverstein, *Imbalance of Powers: Constitutional Interpretation and the Making of American Foreign Policy* (New York: Oxford University Press, 1997), 145.

205. Lori F. Damrosch, "Covert Operations," in Louis Henkin, Michael J. Glennon, and William D. Rogers, eds., *Foreign Affairs and the U.S. Constitution* (Ardsley-on-Hudson, NY: Transnational, 1990), 87–97.

206. 453 U.S. 654 (1981).

207. 462 U.S. 919 (1983).

208. Christopher N. May, *In the Name of War: Judicial Review and the War Powers since 1918* (Cambridge, MA: Harvard University Press, 1989), 256.

209. Thomas M. Franck, "Rethinking War Powers: By Law or by 'Thaumaturgic Invocation'?," in Louis Henkin, Michael J. Glennon, and William D. Rogers, eds., *Foreign Affairs and the U.S. Constitution* (Ardsley-on-Hudson, NY: Transnational, 1990), 59.

210. Caspar W. Weinberger, "Dangerous Constraints on the President's War Powers," in L. Gordon Crovitz and Jeremy Rabkin, eds., *The Fettered Presidency: Legal Constraints on the Executive Branch* (Washington, DC: American Enterprise Institute, 1989), 95–116.

211. Fisher, *Congressional Abdication*, 68.

212. Ibid., 75–76.

213. Ibid., 77.

214. George Bush and Brent Scowcroft, *A World Transformed* (New York: Knopf, 1998), 441.

215. Robert J. Delahunty and John C. Yoo, "The President's Constitutional Authority to Conduct Military Operations against Terrorist Organizations and the Nations That Harbor Them," *Harvard Journal of Law and Public Policy* 25 (Spring 2002): 487.

216. For an analysis of the act, see Michael T. McCarthy, "USA Patriot Act," *Harvard Journal on Legislation* 39 (Summer 2002): 435.

217. Steven R. Weinman, "U.S. Is Confident Conference Will Produce Enough Donations to Rebuild Iraq," *New York Times,* Oct. 23, 2003, A4.

218. See, for example, Ronald Dworkin, "Terror and the Attack on Civil Liberties," *New York Review of Books,* Nov. 6, 2003, 37–41.

219. Eric Lichtblau, "U.S. Uses Terror Law to Pursue Crimes from Drugs to Swindling," *New York Times,* Sept. 28, 2003, 1.

CHAPTER TEN
Understanding the Presidency

1. You can see the group Hush Sound performing its song "We Believe in Barack Obama" online at https://www.youtube.com/watch?v=oScp-IikAW4 (accessed August 13, 2015).

2. Chris Matthews, *Kennedy and Nixon: The Rivalry That Shaped Postwar America,* repr. ed. (New York: Free Press, 2011).

3. Quoted in Alexander Cockburn and Jeffrey St. Clair, eds., "Weapons of Mass Destruction: Who Said What When," in *Counterpunch,* May 29, 2003, 1.

4. Thomas Mann and Norman Ornstein, *The Broken Branch* (New York: Oxford University Press, 2008).

5. A contemporary statement of this position is Harvey C. Mansfield, Jr., *Taming the Prince: The Ambivalence of Modern Executive Power* (New York: Free Press, 1989), ch. 1.

6. Alexander Hamilton and James Madison, *The Letters of Pacificus and Helvidius,* ed. Richard Loss (Delmar, NY: Scholars Facsimiles and Reprints, 1976), 91–92.

7. Martin Shefter, *Political Parties and the State* (Princeton: Princeton University Press, 1994), 78–79.

8. C. Boyden Gray, "Special Interests, Regulation, and the Separation of Powers," in L. Gordon Crovitz and Jeremy Rabkin, eds., *The Fettered Presidency: Legal Constraints on the Executive Branch* (Washington, DC: American Enterprise Institute Press, 1989), 211–223.

9. Steven Calabresi, "The Virtues of Presidential Government," *Constitutional Commentary* 18 (Spring 2001): 51, 72.

10. Shefter, *Political Parties,* 79.

11. Grant McConnell, *The Modern Presidency* (New York: St. Martin's, 1976).

12. Christopher Simpson, *National Security Directives of the Reagan and Bush Administrations* (Boulder, CO: Westview Press, 1995).

13. Philip J. Cooper, *By Order of the President* (Lawrence: University Press of Kansas, 2002), 145.

For Further Reading

CHAPTER ONE

Barilleaux, Ryan J., and Christopher S. Kelley, eds. *The Unitary Executive and the Modern Presidency.* College Station: Texas A&M University Press, 2010.

Borelli, Mary Anne. *The Politics of the President's Wife.* College Station: Texas A&M University Press, 2011.

Fatovic, Clement. *Outside the Law: Emergency and Executive Power.* Baltimore: Johns Hopkins University Press, 2009.

Kleinerman, Benjamin. *The Discretionary President: The Promise and Peril of Executive Power.* Lawrence: University Press of Kansas, 2009.

Miller, Aaron D. *The End of Greatness: Why America Can't Have (and Doesn't Want) Another Great President.* New York: Palgrave MacMillan, 2014.

Neustadt, Richard. *Presidential Power.* New York: Wiley, 1960.

Patterson, Bradley. *To Serve the President: Continuity and Innovation in the White House Staff.* Washington, DC: Brookings, 2010.

Skowronek, Stephen. *Presidential Leadership in Political Time,* 2nd ed. Lawrence: University of Kansas Press, 2011.

Sollenberger, Mitchell A., and Mark Rozell. *The President's Czars.* Lawrence: University Press of Kansas, 2012.

Tatalovich, Raymond, and Steven Schier. *The Presidency and Political Science.* Armonk, NY: M.E. Sharpe, 2014.

Warshaw, Shirley Anne. *The Co-Presidency of Bush and Cheney.* Stanford, CA: Stanford University Press, 2009.

Witcover, Jules. *The American Vice Presidency: From Irrelevance to Power.* Washington, DC: Smithsonian Press, 2014.

CHAPTER TWO

Corwin, Edward S. *The President: Office and Powers,* 4th rev. ed. New York: NYU Press, 1957.

Crouch, Jeffrey. *The Presidential Pardon Power.* Lawrence: University of Kansas Press, 2009.

Farrand, Max, ed. *Records of the Constitutional Convention of 1787.* New Haven: Yale University Press, 1966.

Fisher, Louis. "The Unitary Executive and Inherent Executive Power." *Journal of Constitutional Law* 12, no. 1 (Feb. 2010): 586.

Gerhardt, Michael J. *The Forgotten Presidents: Their Untold Constitutional Legacy.* New York: Oxford University Press, 2013.

Hamburger, Philip. *Is Administrative Law Unlawful?* Chicago: University of Chicago Press, 2014.

Hamilton, Alexander, and James Madison. *The Letters of Pacificus and Helvidius.* Delmar, NY: Scholars Facsimiles and Reprints, 1976.

Hamilton, Alexander, James Madison, and John Jay. *The Federalist Papers.* Ed. Clinton Rossiter. New York: New American Library, 1961.

Howell, William, and David Brent. *Thinking about the Presidency: The Primacy of Power.* Princeton: Princeton University Press, 2013.

Posner, Eric, and Adrian Vermeule. *The Executive Unbound: After the Madisonian Republic.* Chicago: University of Chicago Press, 2011.

CHAPTER THREE

Arnold, Peri. *Remaking the Presidency: Roosevelt, Taft and Wilson.* Lawrence: University Press of Kansas, 2011.

Bailey, Jeremy. *Thomas Jefferson and Executive Power.* New York: Cambridge University Press, 2011.

Beirne, Logan. *Blood of Tyrants: George Washington and the Forging of the Presidency.* New York: Encounter Books, 2014.

Brands, H. W. *Traitor to His Class: The Privileged Life and Radical Presidency of Franklin Delano Roosevelt.* New York: Anchor, 2009.

Ellis, Richard J. *The Development of the American Presidency.* New York: Routledge, 2012.

Ferling, John. *Jefferson and Hamilton: The Rivalry That Forged a Nation.* New York: Bloomsbury Press, 2013.

Greenberg, Amy S. *A Wicked War: Polk, Clay, Lincoln and the 1846 U.S. Invasion of Mexico.* New York: Knopf, 2012.

Greenstein, Fred. *Inventing the Job of President: Leadership Style from George Washington to Andrew Jackson.* Princeton: Princeton University Press, 2009.

Milkis, Sidney M., and Michael Nelson. *The American Presidency: Origins and Development.* Washington, DC: CQ Press, 2008.

Pasley, Jeffrey. *The First Presidential Contest: 1796 and the Founding of American Democracy.* Lawrence: University Press of Kansas, 2013.

White, Leonard D. *The Federalists: A Study in Administrative History.* 4 vols. New York: Free Press, 1950–1958.

CHAPTER FOUR

Erikson, Robert, and Christopher Wlezien. *The Timeline of Presidential Elections: How Campaigns Do and Do Not Matter.* Chicago: University of Chicago Press, 2012.

Geer, John. *In Defense of Negativity: Attack Ads in Presidential Campaigns.* Chicago: University of Chicago Press, 2006.

Halperin, Mark, and John Heilman. *Game Change: Obama and the Clintons, McCain and Palin, and the Race of a Lifetime.* New York: HarperCollins, 2010.

Kamarck, Elaine C. *Primary Politics: How Presidential Candidates Have Shaped the Modern Nominating System.* Washington, DC: Brookings, 2009.

Lawless, Jennifer. *Becoming a Candidate: Political Ambition and the Decision to Run for Office.* New York: Cambridge University Press, 2011.

Shaw, John T. *JFK in the Senate: Pathway to the Presidency.* New York: Palgrave Macmillan, 2013.

Sides, John, and Lynn Vavreck. *The Gamble: Choice and Chance in the 2012 Presidential Election.* Princeton: Princeton University Press, 2014.

CHAPTER FIVE

Aberbach, Joel D., and Mark A. Peterson, eds. *The Executive Branch.* New York: Oxford University Press, 2005.

Bachner, Jennifer, and Benjamin Ginsberg. *What the Government Thinks of the People.* New Haven: Yale University Press, 2015.

Carpenter, Daniel. *The Forging of Bureaucratic Autonomy.* Princeton: Princeton University Press, 2001.

Gailmard, Sean, and John W. Patty. *Learning while Governing: Expertise and Accountability in the Executive Branch.* Chicago: University of Chicago Press, 2013.

Golden, Marissa Martino. *What Motivates Bureaucrats.* New York: Columbia University Press, 2000.

Johnson, Kimberly. *Governing the American State.* Princeton: Princeton University Press, 2006.

Lewis, David E. *The Politics of Presidential Appointments: Political Control and Bureaucratic Performance.* Princeton: Princeton University Press, 2008.

Lubbers, Jeffrey S. *A Guide to Federal Agency Rulemaking.* 5th ed. Chicago: American Bar
    Association, 2012.

CHAPTER SIX

Beckman, Matthew N. *Pushing the Agenda: Presidential Leadership in U.S. Lawmaking.* New
    York: Cambridge University Press, 2010.
Cohen, Jeffrey E. *The President's Legislative Policy Agenda.* New York: Cambridge University
    Press, 2012.
Edwards, George C., III. *Overreach: Leadership in the Obama Presidency.* Princeton: Princeton
    University Press, 2012.
Fisher, Louis. *Constitutional Conflicts between President and Congress.* 6th ed. Lawrence: Univer-
    sity Press of Kansas, 2014.
Genovese, Michael A., and Todd L. Bell. *The Presidency and Domestic Policy.* Boulder, CO:
    Paradigm, 2014.
Joyce, Philip G. *The Congressional Budget Office: Honest Numbers, Power and Policy Making.*
    Washington, DC: Georgetown University Press, 2011.
Riley, Russell L. *Bridging the Constitutional Divide: Inside the White House Office of Legislative
    Affairs.* College Station: Texas A&M University Press, 2010.
Rudalevige, Andrew. "The Executive Branch and the Legislative Process." In Joel Aberbach and
    Mark Peterson, eds., *The Executive Branch.* New York: Oxford University Press, 2005.
Yaloff, David. *Prosecution among Friends: Presidents, Attorneys General and Executive Branch
    Wrongdoing.* College Station: Texas A&M University Press, 2012.

CHAPTER SEVEN

Cooper, Philip. *By Order of the President: The Use and Abuse of Executive Direct Action.* Law-
    rence: University Press of Kansas, 2002.
Doherty, Brendan. *The Rise of the President's Permanent Campaign.* Lawrence: University Press
    of Kansas, 2012.
Edwards, George C. *On Deaf Ears: The Limits of the Bully Pulpit.* New Haven: Yale University
    Press, 2003.
Eshbaugh-Soha, Matthew, and Jeffrey S. Peake. *Breaking through the Noise: Presidential Leader-
    ship, Public Opinion, and the News Media.* Stanford, CA: Stanford University Press, 2011.
Han, Lori Cox. *A Presidency Upstaged: The Public Leadership of George H.W. Bush.* College
    Station: Texas A&M University Press, 2011.
Howell, William G. *Power without Persuasion: The Politics of Direct Political Action.* Princeton:
    Princeton University Press, 2003.

Kernell, Samuel. *Going Public: New Strategies of Presidential Leadership.* 4th ed. Washington, DC: CQ Press, 2007.

Mayer, Kenneth R. *With the Stroke of a Pen: Executive Orders and Presidential Power.* Princeton: Princeton University Press, 2001.

Milkis, Sidney M. *The President and the Parties.* New York: Oxford University Press, 1993.

Tulis, Jeffrey K. *The Rhetorical Presidency.* Princeton: Princeton University Press, 1987.

CHAPTER EIGHT

Bellia, Patricia. "Executive Power in Youngstown's Shadows." *Constitutional Commentary* 19 (Spring 2002): 87.

Bessette, Joseph M., and Jeffrey K. Tulis. *The Constitutional Presidency.* Baltimore: Johns Hopkins University Press, 2009.

Canon, Bradley. "Studying Bureaucratic Implementation of Judicial Policies in the United States." In Marc Hertogh and Simon Halliday, *Judicial Review and Bureaucratic Impact.* Cambridge, UK: Cambridge University Press, 2004.

Goldsmith, Jack. *The Terror Presidency: Law and Judgment inside the Bush Administration.* New York: W.W. Norton, 2009.

Kozloski, Mark, and Anthony Lewis. *The Myth of the Imperial Judiciary.* New York: NYU Press, 2003.

Posner, Richard. *Breaking the Deadlock: The 2000 Election, the Constitution, and the Courts.* Princeton: Princeton University Press, 2001.

Silverstein, Gordon. "Judicial Enhancement of Executive Power," in Paul Peterson, ed. *The President, the Congress, and the Making of Foreign Policy.* Norman: University of Oklahoma Press, 1994.

Simon, James F. *FDR and Chief Justice Hughes: The President, the Supreme Court, and the Epic Battle over the New Deal.* New York: Simon & Schuster, 2012.

CHAPTER NINE

Burke, John P. *Honest Broker? The National Security Advisor and Presidential Decision Making.* College Station: Texas A&M Press, 2009.

Campbell, Kurt M., and James B. Steinberg. *Difficult Transitions: Foreign Policy Troubles at the Outset of Presidential Power.* Washington, DC: Brookings, 2008.

Fisher, Louis. *Presidential War Power.* Lawrence: University Press of Kansas, 2013.

Gardner, Lloyd C. *The Killing Machine: The American Presidency in the Age of Drone Warfare.* New York: New Press, 2013.

Hendrickson, Ryan. *Obama at War.* Lexington: University Press of Kentucky, 2015.

Howell, William, and Jon Pevehouse. *When Dangers Gather: Congressional Checks on Presidential War Powers.* Princeton: Princeton University Press, 2007.

Klaidman, Daniel. *Kill or Capture: The War on Terror and the Soul of the Obama Presidency.* New York: Houghton Mifflin, 2012.

Nye, Joseph S., Jr. *Presidential Leadership and the Creation of the American Era.* Princeton: Princeton University Press, 2013.

Polsky, Andrew. *Elusive Victories: The American Presidency at War.* New York: Oxford University Press, 2012.

Saunders, Elizabeth N. *Leaders at War: How Presidents Shape Military Interventions.* Ithaca, NY: Cornell University Press, 2011.

Yoo, John. *The Powers of War and Peace: The Constitution and Foreign Affairs after 9/11.* Chicago: University of Chicago Press, 2005.

CHAPTER TEN

Healy, Gene. *The Cult of the Presidency: America's Dangerous Devotion to Executive Power.* Washington DC: Cato Institute, 2008.

Wood, Dan. *The Myth of Presidential Representation.* New York: Cambridge University Press, 2009.

Illustration Credits

Page

15		Library of Congress, Prints & Photographs Division, LC-DIG-hec-13515
16	top left	Library of Congress, Prints & Photographs Division, LC-USZ62-14438
16	top right	Library of Congress, Prints & Photographs Division, LC-USZ62-17634
16	bottom	Library of Congress, Prints & Photographs Division, LC-USZ62-108091
17	top	Image courtesy of Betty Ford Center
17	middle	Image courtesy of U.S. Department of State
17	bottom	Library of Congress, Prints & Photographs Division, LC-DIG-ppbd-00357
55		Library of Congress, Prints & Photographs Division, LC-USZ62-60395
56	top	Library of Congress, Prints & Photographs Division, LC-DIG-ppmsca-19601
56	middle	Library of Congress, Prints & Photographs Division, LC-DIG-ds-02746
56	bottom	Senator McCain Official Photo
57		© Hawaii Department of Health/ZUMAPRESS/Newscom
58		© ZUMA Press, Inc / Alamy
99		Library of Congress, Prints & Photographs Division, LC-USZ62-2089
100	top	Library of Congress, Prints & Photographs Division, LC-USZC4-12983
100	bottom	Library of Congress, Prints & Photographs Division, LC-DIG-ds-05202. President Obama chairing the National Security Council
101	top	© World History Archive / Alamy
101	bottom	© White House Photo / Alamy
102		© Matthew Cavanaugh/EPA/Newscom
155	top	Library of Congress, Prints & Photographs Division, LC-USZ62-1805
155	bottom	Library of Congress, Prints & Photographs Division, LC-USZ62-58633
156		© akg-images/Newscom. Lincoln inauguration
157	top	Library of Congress, Prints & Photographs Division, LC-USZ62-54836. William Jennings Bryan
157	bottom	Library of Congress, Prints & Photographs Division, LC-DIG-acd-2a05497
158	top	Franklin D. Roosevelt Presidential Library and Museum, National Archives
158	bottom	© St Petersburg Times/ZUMAPRESS/Newscom. Florida vote recount in 2000
159		© Everett Collection/Shutterstock.com
188		© epa european pressphoto agency b.v. / Alamy

Page

189	top	© jpbcpa/iStockphoto
189	bottom	© TsuneoMP/Shutterstock.com
190	top	Library of Congress, Prints & Photographs Division, LC-DIG-ppmscc-03262
190	bottom	© EdStock/iStockphoto
191	top	Courtesy of Centers for Disease Control
191	bottom	© Food Collection / Alamy
192		© zimmytws/iStockphoto
228		Library of Congress, Prints & Photographs Division, LC-DIG-highsm-15095. Watergate Hotel
229		© Arthur Grace/ZUMAPRESS/Newscom
230		© Chuck Kennedy/KRT/Newscom
278	top	Library of Congress, Prints & Photographs Division, LC-DIG-ds-05242
278	bottom	© zodebala/iStockphoto
279		© Mike Theiler/UPI/Newscom
319		Courtesy of Virginia Memory. John Marshall
320	top	U.S. Naval Historical Center Photograph
320	bottom	© Fotosearch /Getty Images
321		Library of Congress, Prints & Photographs Division, LC-USZ62-72424
322	top	© Everett Collection/Newscom
322	bottom	© Jim West / Alamy
387	top	Library of Congress, Prints & Photographs Division, LC-USZ62-117176
387	bottom	Library of Congress, Prints & Photographs Division, LC-USZ62-13
388	top	Library of Congress, Prints & Photographs Division, LC-USZC4-528
388	bottom	Library of Congress, Prints & Photographs Division, LC-USZ62-107229
389	top	© akg-images/Newscom
389	bottom	© John Frost Newspapers / Alamy
390		© Hugh Van ES UPI Photo Service/Newscom
398	left	King Kong's Song Black Light, Wet Petal Press, Offset, 1967–1968, Los Angeles, CA. Courtesy of Center For the Study of Political Graphics (CSPG)
398	right	Nixon with Pig Face Wimps Collective Offset, 1970, New York, NY. Courtesy of Center For the Study of Political Graphics (CSPG)
399	top	The Fascist Gun in the West. Vic Dinnerstein, Offset, 1980, Los Angeles, CA. Courtesy of Center For the Study of Political Graphics (CSPG)
399	bottom	© Scott Mc Kiernan/ZUMA Press/Newscom
400	top	© Ashley Cooper / Alamy
400	bottom	© Dennis Tarnay, Jr. / Alamy

Appendix: Gallery of Presidents

A.1. The White House Historical Association

A.2. Library of Congress, Prints & Photographs Division, LC-USZ62-13002

A.3. The White House Historical Association

A.4. The White House Historical Association

A.5. Library of Congress, Prints & Photographs Division, LC-USZ62-117118

A.6. Library of Congress, Prints & Photographs Division, LC-USZ62-117119

A.7. National Gallery of Art

A.8. Library of Congress, Prints & Photographs Division, LC-USZ62-13008

A.9. Library of Congress, Prints & Photographs Division, LC-USZ62-7985

A.10. Library of Congress, Prints & Photographs Division, LC-USZ62-13010

A.11. Library of Congress, Prints & Photographs Division, LC-USZ62-13011

A.12. The White House Historical Association

A.13. The White House Historical Association

A.14. Library of Congress, Prints & Photographs Division, LC-USZ62-13014

A.15. Library of Congress, Prints & Photographs Division, LC-USZ62-96357

A.16. Library of Congress, Prints & Photographs Division, LC-DIG-highsm-03733

A.17. Library of Congress, Prints & Photographs Division, LC-USZ62-13017

A.18. Library of Congress, Prints & Photographs Division, LC-USZ62-91985

A.19. Library of Congress, Prints & Photographs Division, LC-DIG-pga-01375

A.20. Library of Congress, Prints & Photographs Division, LC-DIG-cwpbh-03740

A.21. The White House Historical Association

A.22. Library of Congress, Prints & Photographs Division, LC-USZ62-46194

A.23. Library of Congress, Prints & Photographs Division, LC-USZ61-480

A.24. Library of Congress, Prints & Photographs Division, LC-USZ62-46194

A.25. Library of Congress, Prints & Photographs Division, LC-USZ62-103844

A.26. Library of Congress, Prints & Photographs Division, LC-DIG-ppmsca-35700

A.27. Library of Congress, Prints & Photographs Division, LC-USZ62-105141

A.28. Library of Congress, Prints & Photographs Division, LC-USZ62-107577

A.29. Library of Congress, Prints & Photographs Division, LC-H25- 38567-C

A.30. Library of Congress, Prints & Photographs Division, LC-USZ62-103191

A.31. Library of Congress, Prints & Photographs Division, LC-DIG-hec-18540

A.32. Library of Congress, Prints & Photographs Division, LC-USZ62-117121

A.33. Library of Congress, Prints & Photographs Division, LC-USZ62-117122

A.34. Courtesy of US Army

A.35. Library of Congress, Prints & Photographs Division, LC-DIG-ds-02311

A.36. Library of Congress, Prints & Photographs Division, LC-USZ62-13036

A.37. Courtesy Richard Nixon Presidential Library & Museum

A.38. Courtesy Gerald R. Ford Library & Museum

A.39. Courtesy Jimmy Carter Presidential Library & Museum

A.40. Courtesy Ronald Reagan Presidential Library & Museum

A.41. The White House Historical Association

A.42. Library of Congress, Prints & Photographs Division, LC-USZ62-107700

A.43. Library of Congress, Prints & Photographs Division, LC-DIG-ppbd-00371

A.44. Library of Congress, Prints & Photographs Division, LC-DIG-ppbd-00358

Index

Note: Page numbers in *italic* type indicate illustrations. Page numbers followed by *b* indicate boxes. Page numbers followed by *t* indicate tables.

AARP (American Association of Retired Persons), 138, 150
abolitionists, 73, 74, 75, 349
abortion, 134, 138, 273
Abramoff, Jack, 149–150
Abu Ghraib prisoner abuse (Iraq), 308, 362–363
Acheson, Dean, 199, 329, 370
Adams, Abigail, 15, *15*
Adams, Henry, 84
Adams, John, 62, 68, 281, 299, 320, 324, *401*; First Spouse, 15, *15*
Adams, John Quincy, 53–54, 63, 64, 65–66, 68, 97, 234, *401*; First Spouse, 15–16, *16*
Adams, Louisa, 15–16, *16*
administrative directives, 50, 263, 264. *See also* executive orders
Administrative Procedure Act (1946), 89, 263, 317; exemptions, 182–183
advertising, 115, 122, 132, 147, 148, 243; "attack" ads, 152; negative ads, 131, 143
affirmative action, 49, 50, 137, 202, 271; executive orders and, 49, 266, 268–269; federal contractor minority hiring, 268; Supreme Court rulings, 284
Affordable Care Act (2010), 30–31, 42–46, 47, 135, 159, 194, 196, *322*; challenges to, 202, 215, 218, 220, 281, 322; congressional passage of, 39–40, 197, 275; constitutionality rulings, 280–281, 288; excerpts from, 43–45*b*;

funding battles, 215; implementation of, 173, 176; IRS reinterpretation of, 201–202; Obama's promises about, 393; as revenue neutral, 212
Afghanistan war, 42, 135, 297, 354, 375–376, 384; CIA activity, 170; enemy combatant, 308–309, 310; as 9/11 response, 250, 325, 381–382; Obama's wind-down policy, 194
African Americans: campaign appeals to, 137; desegregation and, 49, 50, 266, 268, 285; draft inequality and, 353, 360; first U.S. president (*see* Obama, Barack); political affiliation of 132, 133, 136, 237; as political candidates, 116, 144; Southern discrimination, 80–81, 83, 134; Supreme Court nominee hearing, 207, 284. *See also* affirmative action; civil rights movement; desegregation
African slave trade ban (1808), 73
Agnew, Spiro, 12
Agricultural Adjustment Act (1933), 287, 320
Agricultural Adjustment Agency, 89, 101
agriculture, 48, 62, 66, 84; government programs, 165; slave labor economy, 73, 74; Western expansion and, 75
Agriculture Department, 48, 175, 182, 221, 263, 382; functions of, 162*b*; secretary of, 9
Air Corps Act (1936), 358
Air Force, 189, 331, 357, 375
Air Force Department, 162*b*

airline security, 190–191, *190*
air pollution. *See* emission standards
Alabama National Guard, 285
Alaskan oil pipeline, 232
Aldrich, Nelson, 243
Alexander, Keith, 336
Alien and Sedition Acts (1798), 62
Alito, Samuel, 41, 49, 270, 283
Altria, 151
ambassadors. *See* diplomacy
Ambrose, Stephen, 109
American Association of Retired Persons, 138, 150
American Enterprise Institute, 133
American Heritage Rivers Initiative, 272
American Independent Party, 111
American Legion, 350, 352
American Petroleum Institute, 273
American Spectator, 253
American system, 70
Anderson, Robert, 77
Angola, 362
Anti-Ballistic Missile Treaty (1972), 297
Antideficiency Act (1884), 210
antimissile program, 365
Antiquities Act (1906), 272
antitrust, 85, 86, 285
antiwar movements, 91, 125, 349–350, 352, 353, 373
appellate courts, 41, 282, 283, 309–310
appointments, 2, 9, 20–21, 22, 61, 186, 187, 314–316; congressional consultation on, 84; congressional obstruction of, 231, 232; to judiciary, 280, 282–286, 289; Senate advice and consent for, 20–21, 22, 36, 37, 42, 208–209, 280. *See also* recess appointments; removal power
appropriations, 28, 29, 36, 37, 48, 51, 60, 72, 88, 92, 202; as fundamental congressional prerogative, 2, 43, 209–216
Arisride, Jean-Bertrand, 381
Aristotle, 393–394
armed forces. *See* military forces; *specific branches*
Armed Forces Reserve Act (1951), 350
Arms Export Control Act (1976), 373
arms sales, 368
Army, 63, 189, 298, 330, 340, 357, 358, 359

Army Air Corps, 358
Army Department, 51, 162*b*, 358
Arthur, Chester A., 55–56, *55*, 83, *403*
Article I, 29, 48, 198, 216, 292, 391; on limit to congressional powers, 29; presentment clause, 22; war powers, 298
Article I courts, definition of, 282
Article II, 18–38, 52–58, 104, 195, 295, 296, 298, 300, 323, 364; delegated presidential powers, 30–33, 36, 201, 208, 310–314; elector majority, 127; recess appointments authorization, 37; text of, 18–21
Article III courts, definition of, 282
Articles of Confederation, 6–7
Ashcroft, John, 148
Asian Americans, 137
assassinations, 85, 91, 104, 112, 165, 392; attempts, 12, 13, 392
athletes, political careers of, 109–110
atomic bomb project, 10
attack ads, 152
attorney general, 382
Australia, 371
automobile industry bailout, 194
Awlaki, Anwar al-, 382
Axelrod, David, 116

Bachmann, Michele, 123
Bailey, Josiah, 240
Baird, Zoe, 207
Baker, James, 329
Baker v. Carr (1962), 292
balance of power. *See* checks and balances
banking system, 72, 79, 268, 371; Dodd-Frank reform act, 174, 179, 193; federal quasi agencies and, 165; federal regulation of, 174, 193; fiscal crisis (2008) and, 174, 194; Great Depression and, 198
Bank of the United States, 61, 66. *See also* Second Bank of the United States
Banning, Jim, 110
Barbary pirates, 6, 299, 339
Barkley, Alban, 239
Barnburners, 351
Bartlett, Dan, 255
Bas v. Tingy (1800), 299
Bates, John D., 336
"battleground" states, 129, 130, 139

Bay of Pigs invasion (1961), 366
BearingPoint Corporation, 166
Belmont Bank, 296
Benghazi attack (2012), 143, 188–189, *188*
Bentsen, Lloyd, 144
Ben-Veniste, Richard, 141
Bercut-Vandervoort & Co. v. United States
    (1957), 296
Bhutan, 328
Biden, Joe, 11, 115, 126
Binkley, Wilfred, 347
bioterrorism, 276
Bipartisan Campaign Reform Act or BCRA
    (2002), 152, 193, 241
"birthers," 55, 57, 104
Black, Hugo, 306–307
Black Codes, 80
Blackwater U.S.A., 166, 361
"bleeding Kansas," 75
Blitzer, Wolf, 377
Bloomberg, Michael, 110
blue-collar workers, 138, 166, 237
Blumenthal, Sidney, 250, 253
Blunt, Roy, 149
Boehner, John, 47, 203, 215, 281
Boggs, Michael, 241
Boggs, Tommy, 149
Bohlen, Charles E. ("Chip"), 356
Boland Amendment (1982), 202, 204–205, 339
bond market. *See* government bonds
Bono, Sonny, 109
Booz, Allen Hamilton Corporation, 167
Bork, Robert, 207, 223, 284, 316
Bosnia, 362, 363
Boston, USS (frigate), *320*
Boston Tea Party (political faction), 113
Bowles v. Willingham (1944), 345
Bowsher v. Synar (1986), 28, 316
Boxer Rebellion, 295–296
Bradley, Bill, 110
Brennan, John, 220
Bretton Woods system, 371
bribery, 12, 21, 224
Bricker Amendment, 347
Britain. *See* Great Britain
broadcast media. *See* radio; television
Brookings Institution, 133, 199
Brown, Aaron, 377

Brownlee, Les, 376
Brownlow Committee, 257
Brown v. Board of Education (1954), 285
Brown v. United States (1920), 299
Brunei, Sultan of, 378
Bryan, William Jennings, 156
Brzezinski, Zbigniew, 327, 363
Buchanan, James, 60, 70–71, 95, 97, 198, 351, *402*
Buckley v. Valen (1976), 151–152, 315–316
budget, U.S., 28, 88, 210–215, 252, 258; com-
    ponents of, 188–192; congressional power
    and, 48, 72, 353; continuing resolution
    and, 213–214; deficit spending and, 168,
    175, 212, 214–215; deficit reduction act, 316;
    entitlement programs, 48, 173, 192, 210, 233;
    impoundment and, 202, 204, 222; line-item
    veto and, 313–314; presidential power and,
    90, 94, 199, 211–212, 232–233, 251, 274, 310;
    sequestration and, 48, 204, 215, 216. *See also*
    Bureau of the Budget; defense budget
Budget Act (1921), 199, 211
Budget Act (1974), 217, 288
Budget and Accounting Act (1921), 88, 218, 310
Budget and Impoundment Control Act (1974),
    92, 202, 204, 353; problems created by,
    211–212
Budget Control Act (2011), 48, 215
Budget Enforcement Act (1990), 212
Bull Moose Party, 111, 156, *157*
bully pulpit, 86, 94, 214, 255
bundlers (campaign finance), 145*b*, 146
Bundy, McGeorge, 365
burden sharing, 368
bureaucracy. *See* federal bureaucracy
Bureau of Alcohol, Tobacco, Firearms, and
    Explosives (ATF), 171, 314
Bureau of the Budget, 10, 72, 87–88, 94, 290;
    creation of, 211, 218, 257; move into Exec-
    utive Office, 90, 95, 199, 211, 232, 257–258.
    See also White House Office of Manage-
    ment and Budget
Burke, Edward, 240
Burr, Aaron, 62, 314
Bush, George H. W., 6, 12, 50, 111, 124, 131, 138,
    139, 144, 175, 326, *405*; decline in popular
    support for, 252; foreign policy advisers,
    327, 329; Iran-Contra affair pardons, 27;
    judicial appointments, 207, 283, 284;

Persian Gulf War authorization, 33, 232, 252, 369, 371, 378, 380–381; political family of, 112, 140; presidential reelection loss, 252; presidential unilateralism and, 93, 270; signing statement, 202, 271; tax increase by, 232; televised news conferences of, 255; as vice president, 112

Bush, George W., 9, 12, 27, 39, 98, *102*, 184, 199, 201, 219, 221, 326, *406*; budget deficits and, 214; character issues and, 140–143; communication strategies, 250, 274–275; congressional relations, 232, 233; domestic surveillance program, 93, 95, 325, 334–335; emergency powers, 93, 95; executive orders, 49, 51, 270, 273, 304, 325, 332, 395, 396; executive privilege and, 314; foreign policy advisers, 327, 329; inherent power claim, 33, 35 (*see also* Afghan war; Iraq war); judicial appointments, 283; judicial rejected appointments 207–208, 232; malicious characterization of, 400, *400*; media relations, 253, 254–256; military commissions and, 35, 273, 304, 305, 309, 325, 382; political family of, 112; political strategist, 116; preemptive war doctrine, 326; presidential campaigns, 124, 138, 139–143, 144, 148; presidential election (2000) disputed votes, 158, 284, 292–293; presidential electoral vs. popular votes for, 118, 119, 129, 157–158, 284; presidential unilateralism and, 93, 95, 270, 325; regulatory review, 32, 264–265, 273; signing statements, 28, 30, 41, 202, 271–272, 274; treaty power and, 297; vice president of, 11, 12, 126, 315; war on terror policies, 11, 28–29, 35, 49, 93, 95, 102, 140–142, 195, 233, 250, 252, 256, 273, 304, 308–310, 325, 326, 334–335, 369, 381–382, 385; World War II precedents and, 304–305

Bush, Jeb, 112, 116, 124, 137
Bush, Laura, 250
Bush, Prescott, 112
Bush v. Gore (2000), 158, 284, 292–293
business regulation, 271
Byrd, Harry, 240
Byrd, Robert, 291, 382–383

cabinet, 9–10, 160, 161; appointments to, 84, 232; department components, 9, 188–189;

dismissal of members, 351; impeachment of members, 21; presidential line of succession and, 13*b*; Senate confirmation of appointment, 206; Washington's foundation for, 61, 93. *See also specific departments*
CACI International, 166, 363
Cadwalader, John, 287
Calhoun, John C., 64, 65, 67, 240
Cambodia, 378; "secret bombing" of, 222
campaign spending, 114, 132, 144–153; reform, 118, 151–152, 174, 193, 241, 274, 283; Supreme Court lifted restrictions on, 146–147, 152, 283
Canada, 64, 332, 349
Cannon, Lou, 251
Cannon, Joseph ("Uncle Joe"), 87, 209–210
Capitol building, 53–54, 64
Caplin v. United States (1983), 296–297
Carey, Ron, 150
Carson, Ben, 116; *Gifted Hands,* 107–108
Carter, Jimmy, 26, 35, 92, 97, 231, 232, 269, 297, *405*; civil service reform; 39; foreign policy adviser, 327, 363; Iranian hostage crisis and, 379; regulatory review, 260; televised town meetings, 249–250
Carter v. Carter Coal Company (1936), 312
Case Act (1988), 92
Casey, William, 224, 230
Case-Zablocki Act (1973), 372, 397
Catholic War Veterans, 352
Cato Institute, 133
caucuses. *See* nominating caucus
CBS News, 140, 222
celebrity politicians, 116
censorship, 77, 100–101, 341, 342, 343, 345
Center for Responsible Politics, 146
Centers for Disease Control and Prevention (CDC), 191, *191*
Central Intelligence Agency (CIA), 9, 204, 273, 328; covert activities, 365–366, 371–372; creation of, 90, 95, 102, 357, 365; drone strikes and, 170, 383–384; foreign policy and, 327; functions of, 170, 171, 332–333, 365–366; Iran-Contra affair and, 224, 230; secret prisons of, 29; Senate hearings on, 170, 220; terror-related expanded authority of, 382
Cernak, Anton, 13
Chadha case (1983), 313, 379

Chafee, Lincoln, 115
Chamber of Commerce v. Reich (1996), 317
Chandler, A. B. ("Happy"), 239
character issues, 139–143, 392
Charleston (S.C.), 76–77
Chase, Salmon, 79, 236
checks and balances, 2–3, 8, 14, 29, 36–38, 397; congressional-presidential conflicts and, 22, 24, 39, 227, 338–339; judiciary and, 280–322
Cheney, Dick, 27, 111, 126–127, 254; justification for war and, 371, 380–381, 393; vice presidential executive privilege claim, 315; vice presidential power of, 11, 12
Chevron v. Natural Resources Defense Council (1984), 312–313, 317
chief of staff, 9, 10
China, 295–296, 297, 304, 328; Nixon visit to, 92; U.S. debt holding by, 168
Chinese Exclusion Cases (1893), 293
Christian Coalition, 149–150
Christian Right. *See* religious right
Christie, Chris, 123
Churchill, Winston, 342–343
CIA. *See* Central Intelligence Agency
CIO (Congress of Industrial Organizations), 238
Cisneros, Henry, 27, 221
Citizens United v. Federal Election Commission (2010), 146–147, 152
City of Arlington v. FCC (2013), 317
civic education, 393–394
civil disobedience, 74
Civilian Conservation Corps, 89, 238
civil liberties, 4, 8, 14; intelligence collecting and, 366; wartime suspension of, 78, 302, 340
civil rights: antidiscrimination measures and, 49, 50, 266, 268–269, 273, 285, 295, 353; executive orders and, 49; judicial decisions on, 284, 285, 286; school desegregation, 285–286; Southern denial to blacks, 80, 83; voting rights and, 91, 249, 284, 287
Civil Rights Act (1964), 50, 269
Civil Rights Act (1991), 271
civil rights movement, 91, 125, 134, 136, 249, 352–353
civil service, 39, 52–53, 87, 165–166, 232, 261; World War I rules suspension, 341. *See also* federal bureaucracy

Civil Service Act (1883). *See* Pendleton Civil Service Act
Civil Service Reform Act (1978), 261
Civil War, 62, 72–80, 357, 369, 387–388, *388*; blockade of South, 34, 77, 300, 340; civic and service organizations, 348; Confederate surrender, 79, 156, 237; conscription commutation fee, 360; draft riots, 349; economic and moral roots of, 72–75; executive orders, 49, 77–78, 266; factors leading to, 72–83, 287; Fort Sumter fall (1861), 33, 76–77, 340, 386, 387, *388*; major presidential powers introduced, 94; military commissions, 78, 236, 340; opening actions of, 76–77; postwar congressional power, 347; postwar political alliances, 351–352; president's inherent powers and, 33, 34, 77–78, 94, 100–101, *101*, 235–236, 300, 339, 340; Republican Party and, 72, 79, 235–237, 239; Supreme Court rulings, 287–288, 300–301, 340; veterans organization, 350, 351–352. *See also* Reconstruction era
Civil Works Administration, 238
Clapper, James, 335–336
Clark, Wesley, 108
Clarke, Richard, 141
classified information, 7, 365, 366
Clay, Henry, 51–52, 63–64, 65, 70, 74, 218, 386
Clayton Anti-Trust Act (1914), 86
Clean Air Act (1970), 32, 33, 46, 177; amendments (2010), 47
Clean Water Act (1972), 46
Cleveland, Grover, 60, 83, 89, 243, *403*
clientele agencies, 175
Clinton, Bill, 141, 150, 153, 184, 186, 219, *230*, 295, 308, 326, *405*; budget confrontation, 213–214, 274; character issue and, 139–140, 254, 399–400; congressional opposition to, 232–233, 273; execution of laws and, 202–203, 204; executive orders, 49, 51, 181, 262–263, 264, 269, 270, 272–273, 274, 275, 317, 325, 332; First Spouse, 11, 15, 17, *17*, 112 (*see also* Clinton, Hillary Rodham); foreign policy, 325, 332; impeachment of (1998), 36, 211, 225–226, 230, 232, *399*, 400; judicial appointments, 283, 284; line-item veto use, 201, 206, 313–314; media relations, 249–250, 253, 254, 255; military force authorization,

381; pardon power use, 27, 395; perjury charges against, 225, 226; personality of, 152; political consultant, 116; popular approval of, 96; presidential unilateralism, 93, 270; private military contractors and, 361, 362, 363; regulatory review, 32, 47, 260, 262–264, 265, 272, 273, 394; Senate rejections and, 207, 209; sexual misconduct of, 225, 226, 230, 232, 254, 399–400; signing statements, 41, 271; spending priorities, 212; stepping stones to presidency, 108; striking worker replacement issue, 269, 272, 275, 287, 317; televised town meetings, 249–250, 254; veto overrides and, 205–206; vice president of, 11; Whitewater probe, 141, 225–226, 230, 253, 255

Clinton, Chelsea, 118

Clinton, Hillary Rodham: Benghazi investigation and, 143; email issue and, 143; as First Spouse, 17, *17*; *Hard Choices*, 107, 108; personality of, 152; political background of, 11, 15, 17, 112, 118; political consultant for, 116; presidential candidacies of, 114, 121, 122–123, 124, 143, 158; as secretary of state, 329; Whitewater probe and, 225, 230

Clinton, Roger, 27

Clinton Foundation, 143

Clinton v. City of New York (1998), 313

closed primary, 120, 122; vs. open, 121*b*

CNN cable network, 377

coal power emissions, 47, 180, 265

Coast Guard, 163, 171, 173, 382

Code of Federal Regulations, 184, 259

coercive interrogation. *See* torture

Cohen, Eliot, 374

Cold War, 12, 249, 330, 339, 354, 385; arms race and, 360–361; containment policy, 359, 365, 384; presidential powers and, 355–357, 365, 370, 384, 385

Colfax, Schuyler, 351

Colombia, U.S. private military contractors in, 362

Comanche helicopter, 376

commander-in-chief, 20, 22, 24, 25, 29, 33, 47, 50, 71, 94, 195, 308, 327, 345; as executive order rationale, 268; presidential extraordinary wartime measures as, 77, 101, 303, 340, 343, 370, 386; presidential foreign

policy power as, 323, 338. *See also* inherent presidential powers

commerce. *See* trade policy

Commerce Clause, 288, 322

Commerce Department, 85, 175, 382; foreign policy and, 327, 331–332; functions of, 162*b*; secretary of, 9

Committee on Public Information, 245, 340

Commodities Futures Trading Commission, 178, 179

communications technology, 85, 198, 243, 246, 275. *See also* electronic communications; media; surveillance; *specific types*

Communist threat, 347; loyalty program, 288, 347, 352, 366, 371, 385. *See also* Cold War

Compromise of 1850, 74–75

Confederate States of America, 106, 287; founding of, 76, 77; postwar treatment of, 80; surrender of, 79, 156, 237

Confessions of a Nazi Spy (film), 247

Congress: activity diminishment (2013), 201; antislavery forces, 351; apportionment ruling, 292–294, 314–315; appropriation power, 28, 29, 36, 37, 48, 51, 60, 72, 88, 92, 202, 209–216, 323, 338–339; controversial national issues (1868–1900), 84; courts created by (Article I courts), 282; criminal laws, 170; debt ceiling and, 48, 168, 214–216; delegation of powers, 30–33, 36, 310–314; democracy and, 396; divided government and, 231; Electoral College and, 19, 127; emergency powers of, 35–36, 301, 302; entitlement programs and, 173; federal bureaucracy and, 161, 176–177; "fire alarm" oversight and, 181; first (1789), 160; foreign policy role of (*see under* foreign policy); General Accounting Office, 88; hearings and investigations, 29, 123, 216–224, 228–232, 255, 286, 339, 347, 354, 396; historical power of, 59–60, 63–64; impeachment power of, 224–226; intelligence oversight committees, 366; judicial power and, 280, 292–293; legislative oversight, 216–220; lobbyists and, 137, 146, 149–151; military funding cutoff by, 47; negative views of, 290–291, 394; 9/11 resolution (2001) of, 171, 382–383; nineteenth and early twentieth-century dominance of, 52, 301; nondelegation doctrine and, 311; "notice-

Congress (*continued*)
and-comment rulemaking" and, 89–90, 182; oversight tools of, 216–224; partisanship and, 37, 41, 197, 198, 200, 201, 231, 232, 241, 256, 274, 279, 283; party discipline and, 198, 200; pay raises for, 216; postwar assertiveness patterns of, 80–83, 346–387; power of the purse of (*see subhead* appropriations power *above*); powers reserved to, 29, 36, 37–38, 47–48, 195–198, 203–227; presidential power and (*see* congressional-presidential relations); president's state of the union address to, 21, 61, 195, 199; qualifications of members, 292; quasi executive powers of, 205–208; Reconstruction report of, 81–82; removal power of, 28, 36, 316; RIP (revelation, investigation, and prosecution) technique and, 223–224, 228, 255; special interests and, 395; state party organizations vs., 69; twentieth-century waning of powers of, 52–54; unitary executive theory and, 28, 29; veto override by, 22, 36, 195, 201, 205–206, *206t*, 347; Vietnam withdrawal legislation, 390; War of 1812 and, 52, 63, 64, 386; war power of (*see under* war powers).
  See also House of Representatives; Senate
Congressional Budget Office, 174, 211, 212
congressional-presidential relations, 193–227; Article I on, 29; Article II on, 20–21; budget confrontations, 213–216; checks and balances, 22, 24, 36–38, 39, 227, 338–339; conflict factors, 47–48, 196–203, 231–232; constitutional nature of, 195–198; curbs on presidential power, 92, 204–205, 372–373; delegation of powers, 30–33, 38, 310–314; government shutdowns, 175, 213–214, 215, 216, 232–233; gridlock conditions, 53, 104, 201; hearings, 217–218, 255, 286, 396; investigative hearings, 29, 220–224, 228–230, 354; legislative oversight and, 216–220; president's power vs., 84, 195, 325–326, 384–385; president's relative empowerment and, 38–48, 50, 61, 84–85; supremacy over presidency, 84–85; taxation and spending, 175. *See also* veto power
Congressional Review Act (1996), 184, 219
Congress of Industrial Organizations (CIO), 238

Congress of the Confederation, 6–7
conscription, 78, 236, 340, 341, 342, 344, 346, 348; Civil War riots (1863), 349; inequalities of, 360, 367, 371; post–Vietnam end to, 373; post–World War II expansion of, 360; Vietnam era resistance to, 26, 350, 353, 372, 373
Constitution: judicial power and, 280–286; Presentment Clause, 201; presidential oath to protect, 21; presidential succession and, 11; ratification debates, 4; separation of powers, 2; slavery issues and, 73; war powers and, 298–299. *See also* Article I; Article II; checks and balances; separation of powers; *specific amendments*
Constitutional Convention (1789), 5–9, 109, 397; Article II implied powers, 29–30; Electoral College intent, 129; executive energy concept, 38, 276; executive power debate, 1, 4, 14, 37–38, 54; fear of monarchy, 4, 397; fixed terms of office and, 252–253; foreign policy debate, 323, 338; political philosophies and, 2, 217, 300, 303; presidential impeachment provision, 36; prohibition of titles of nobility, 391; slave state representation and, 73; war powers and, 25, 298, 327, 394
Constitution Party, 113
consultants, 133–134
Consumer Confidence Index, 135
consumer movement, 350
containment policy, 359, 365, 384
Continental Congress, 109
contractors. *See* private contractors
Contract with America, 313
Contras (Nicaragua), 202, 204–205, 223–224, 229, 339, 378, 379
Convention on Human Rights (1978), 295
Convention on the Rights of the Child (1989), 295
Convention to Eliminate All Forms of Discrimination against Women (1979), 295
Cooke, Jay, 79, 236
Coolidge, Calvin, 84, 87, 88, 96, 97, 152, 211, *404*
Copeland, Royal, 240
Corporation for Public Broadcasting, 161
corporations, 32, 146, 254; bureaucratic revolving door with, 181; presidential campaign donors, 148–149

corruption, 84, 86

Corwin, Edward, 289, 323

Corzine, Jon, 110

Council of Economic Advisers, 10, 173, 199, 258

Council on Environmental Quality, 182

counterfeiting, 46

Court of Customs and Patents Appeals, 296

Court of Federal Claims, 282

Court of Review, 334

courts. *See* judiciary

courts martial, 78, 236

Covede, John, 351

covert operations, 361, 365–366, 371–372, 379

Cox, Archibald, 207, 223, 316

Cox, James M., 106

Crawford, William, 64–65

Creek Indians, 68

Creel, George, 244–245

criminal law, 46, 170

Crockett v. Reagan (1983), 308

crowdsourcing, 132

cruise missiles, 375

cruise ship hearings, 220

Cruz, Ted, 105, 116, 137; natural-born citizen status, 58, *58*

Cuba, 366, 393

currency, 174, 371; exchange rates, 332; paper, 66, 79, 94

Current Tax Payment Act (1943), 367

Currie, David, 299

Curtiss-Wright ruling (1936). See *United States v. Curtiss-Wright Export Company*

Customs and Border Control, 163, 171, 333

customs collection, 218

Dames & Moore v. Regan (1981), 297–298, 307, 379

"dark horse" candidates, 70–71, 83, 87, 92, 116, 125

Data for Information Quality Act (2000), 185

Davis, David, 301

Davis, Henry W., 240

Davis, Jefferson, 76, 77

Davis, Kenneth Culp, 259

Dawes, Charles, 88

Dean, John (Iowa governor), 124

Debs, Eugene, 302

debt, U.S., 61, 234

debt ceiling, 48, 168, 214–216

declaration of war: as congressional power, 24–25, 33, 84, 298, 327, 338, 386, 387; undeclared wars and, 34–35, 339, 379–380, 386

"Deep Throat" (Watergate investigation source), 222, 229

Defense Advanced Research Project Agency (DARPA), 335

Defense Appropriations Act (1982), 204–205

Defense Authorization Act (2014), 42

defense budget, 212, 213, 215, 232, 338–339, 359, 360, 366–367, 367

defense contracts, 331, 360–361

Defense Department, 60, 161, 189–190, *189*, 337, 378; agencies under, 330, 333; creation of, 90, 95, 102, 169, 189, 330, 357; foreign policy and, 327, 330–331; functions of, *162b*, 189; intelligence agencies and, 169–170, 333; private contractors and, 330–331, 353; reorganization of, 375; secretary of, 8, 359; War Department as predecessor, 160

Defense Intelligence Agency, *162b*, 169, 330, 333

Defense of Marriage Act (1996), 203, 287

defense pacts, 368–369

Defense Production Act (1950), 306, 360

deficit spending, 168, 175, 212, 214–215; Gramm-Rudman-Hollings reduction act, 316

DeLay, Tom, 117, 118

Dellums v. Bush (1990), 308

democracy: direct, 8, 120; executive power and, 3, 187; presidentialism and, 396–397

Democratic National Committee (DNC), 226

Democratic Party, 83, 88–92, 156–157; campaign issues, 135; conservative coalition, 240; convention system, 70, 114, 154, 350; core constituency, 132–133, 136, 138, 237; division over slavery, 155, 351; electorate expansion and, 237–239; Jacksonian era and, 64–72, 125, 239, 277–278; Jeffersonian forerunners of, 62, 277; judicial nominees and, 283, 284; as majority party (1933–1952), 157, 237; media endorsement and, 253; national convention, 125–126; New Politics (1970s) and, 350; partisan identification, 88–90, 136; as presidential mobilization tool, 234–235, 237–239, 240, 245; primary elections, 91–92, 119–125, *121b*; volunteer workers, 116, 117;

Democratic Party (*continued*)
    Watergate headquarters break-in, 92, 222, *228*, 229
Democratic-Republican Party, 62–65, 154, 234, 277
departments and agencies. *See* federal bureaucracy
desegregation, 49, 50, 285; armed forces, 49, 50, 266, 268, 330; school, 285–286
DHS. *See* Homeland Security Department
Dick Act (1903), 358
Dickinson, John, 8
diplomacy, 188–189, 296, 323, 324, 331; appointments, 20; Foreign Service and, 328, 356; Foreign Service-State Department merger, 356
direct democracy, 8, 120
direct election, 3, 65, 242, 244
direct mail, 241
disabled people, 137, 271, 273
district courts, 282, 283
District of Columbia: British burning of, 64, 386, *387*; emergency rent laws, 302; presidential electors, 119, 127, 129
district redrawing. *See* gerrymandering
Dix, John A., 351
Dodd, Chris, 116
Dodd-Frank Wall Street Reform and Consumer Protection Act (2010), 174, 179, 193
domestic policy, 49, 193–227
Domestic Policy Council, 9
domestic surveillance. *See* surveillance
Donelson, Andrew Jackson, 60
Douglas, Stephen A., 74–75, 76
Douglas, William O., 282, 297, 298, 345
Douglas Aircraft Company, 331
draft. *See* conscription
DREAM Act (proposed), 204
Dred Scott v. Sandford (1857), 75, 287
drones, 375, 376; military use of, 35, 170, 325, 333, 334, 382, 383–384
Drug Enforcement Administration (DEA), 161, 171
drug trafficking, 314, 362
D'Souza, Dinesh, 118
Duberstein, Kenneth, 149, 251
Dukakis, Michael, 131
DynCorp, 362, 363

Early, Stephen, 247
ebola outbreak (2014), 191
economic depression. *See* Great Depression
Economic Stabilization Act (1942), 345
economy: basis of congressional control over, 212; Civil War and, 73, 76; emergency war powers and, 305–306; federal agencies and, 173–175; government intervention into, 346; North-South division, 72–73; presidential Council of Economic Advisers, 10, 173, 199, 258; as salutary campaign issue, 134, 135; stimulus packages, 194, 212, 214, 232; wartime regulation of, 341, 343, 344, 345; worldwide collapse (1929) of, 88. *See also* monetary policy
Education Department, 46, 161, 166, 173, 275; functions of, 162*b*
Edwards, John, 116
Egypt, 365–366
Ehrlich, Robert, 112
Ehrlichman, John, 10
eighteen-year-old vote, 349
Eisenhower, Dwight D., 285, 326, 392, *405*; executive agreements, 364; executive power expansion, 371–372; "executive privilege" initiation as term, 314; imperial presidency, 90; military career of, 108, 109; on military-industrial complex, 361; national security advisers, 363; national security and, 371–372; Nixon as vice president of, 10, 249; popular mobilization and, 248–249, 255
Eisentrager (German agent), 304–305, 309
elderly people, 137–138
elections: direct vs. indirect, 3, 8, 85, 120, 127–130; district redrawing and, 117–118, 196–197, 396. *See also* presidential election campaigns
Electoral College, 8–9, 13–14, 17–30, 63, 126, 127–130; "battleground" states, 129, 130, 139; constitutional revisions for, 62, 127; contested elections and, 62, 65, 127–128, 158, 292–293; critics of, 130; date of vote casting, 127; elector selection, 63, 65, 119–120, 128–129, 242; loss of popular vote winner to, 157, 284; problems of, 129–130; purpose of, 197; Twelfth Amendment correction of, 62, 127; vote allocation by state, 127, 128*b*; winner-take-all rule, 129

electronic communications, 35, 167, 169, 174, 220, 334–335, 336; popular mobilization with, 243, 244, 246, 248, 279; presidential campaigns and, 241; secret surveillance of, 35, 167, 220, 307, 315, 325, 333–337, 382

Elkins Act (1903), 85

Ellsberg, Daniel, 222

El Salvador, 308

email monitoring, 335, 336

emancipation proclamation (1863), 49, 50, 78

Embargo Act (1807), 63

embryonic research. *See* stem cell research

emergency powers, 4, 301–308; cessation of war and, 346; congressional, 35–36, 301, 302; executive orders and, 49, 266; judicial decisions and, 293; presidential, 33–34, 301–303, 339, 340–341, 379, 384–390; presidentialist thinking and, 394–395; presidential limits on, 306–308; F. D. Roosevelt declaration of, 53, 302–303, 343; as surveillance basis, 93, 95, 373

Emergency Price Control Act (1942), 303, 304, 312, 345

emission standards, 47, 177, 178, 180, 187, 265

Employers Group of Motor Freight Carriers v. National War Labor Board (1944), 305–306

employment discrimination, 50, 196, 268, 269

enemy combatants, 42, 308–310, 325; U.S. citizens as, 35, 309, 310, 382

energy (executive). *See* executive energy, principles of

Energy Department, 27, 166, 382; functions of, 162b

energy policy, 232, 273–274, 315

enfranchisement. *See* suffrage

Enron scandal, 32

entitlement programs, 48, 173, 192, 233; set legal funding formula for, 210. *See also* Medicare and Medicaid; Social Security

environmental programs, 394–395; *Chevron* standard and, 312–313; emission standards, 47, 177, 178, 180, 187, 265; executive orders and, 49, 263, 265, 272; impact statements and, 184–185; New Politics and, 350; "quality of life" review and, 259–260, 261; signing statements and, 271; standards and guidelines, 177

Environmental Protection Agency (EPA), 32–33, 46, 47, 173, 178, 180, 182, 312–313;

coal emissions and, 47, 180, 265; congressional curbs on, 217; creation of, 49, 161, 266; impact statements and, 184–185; presidential directive, 187; regulatory review and, 259–260, 261

Environmental Quality Council, 10

Equal Employment Opportunity Commission (EEOC), 207, 284

Equatorial Guinea, 162

Ervin, Sam, 222–223

Espionage Act (1917), 302, 341, 342

Espy, Mike, 221

Ethics in Government Act (1978), 92, 223, 353

ethics probes. *See* investigative hearings

ethnic identities, 133, 136–137, 237

Evangelicals. *See* religious right

exchange rates, 332

excise tax, 234

executive, 1–8, 14, 36–38; definition/essential characteristics of, 1–4; expansion of, 95, 101, 300; forms of, 8; rationale for, 4–7; unitary theory of, 8, 28–29, 30, 38–42. *See also* president

executive agreements, 49, 53, 92, 94; as Article II treaty equivalent, 90, 209, 295, 296, 297, 363; compelled disclosure of, 93; foreign and national security policy and, 90, 363, 369, 397; two forms of, 364

executive branch, 160–192. *See also* federal bureaucracy; president

executive budget. *See* budget, U.S.

executive energy, principles of, 5–6, 8, 14, 38–52, 276; constancy and, 51–52; execution of laws and, 42–48; independence and, 49–51; unity and, 38–42

Executive Office of the President, 10, 60, 167, 199, 211, 256–258, 279, 327; advisory groups, 199; creation of, 90, 95, 257; expansion of, 275; five divisions within, 257–258; legislative liaison, 200; national security bureaucracy, 363–366; wartime emergencies and, 343; White House Communications Office, 250, 255, 256

executive offices, 3, 22, 27, 101

executive orders, 8, 47, 49–51, 53, 88, 92, 93, 94, 185, 256, 261–270, 272–274, 275, 279, 314, 325, 332, 366, 385, 395; agencies created, 161; agency rulemaking, 181–182, 261–263,

executive orders (*continued*)
264; to circumvent Congress, 204, 222; congressional constraints on, 50, 51, 316; constitutional/statutory basis for, 268–269; definition of, 89; executive agency creation, 161; foreign and national security policy, 363, 364, 365; historical use of, 49, 63, 77–78, 89–90, 100–101, 300; judicial invalidation of, 287, 316–317; per president, 267–268*t*; revoking previous orders, 51; F. D. Roosevelt extensive use of, 89–90, 257–258, 342, 343; unilateral president and, 102; World War I, 341–342

executive oversight, 186–187

executive power. *See* presidential powers

executive privilege, 93, 217–218; secrecy and, 397; Supreme Court rulings, 61, 218, 223, 314–315, 321–322

Ex parte Merryman (1861), 34, 287

Ex parte Milligan (1866), 78, 300–301, 304, 340

Ex parte Quirin (1942), 304, 309

Expediting Act (1903), 85

expressed presidential powers, 22–27, 36

Eyes of the Navy (film), 247

Fahrenheit 9/11 (film), 143

Fair Deal, 90, 355–356

Fair Employment Practices Commission, 268

Fair Packaging and Labeling Act (1967), 183

family planning funding, 49, 273

family values, 138

Fannie Mae, 165

Farm Credit System, 165

Farmer Mac, 165

farmers. *See* agriculture

FBI. *See* Federal Bureau of Investigation

FDA. *See* Food and Drug Administration

Federal Agricultural Credit Corporation (Farmer Mac), 165

federal budget. *See* budget, U.S.

federal bureaucracy, 160–192; administrative regulations, 311; antidiscrimination policies, 49; budget shutdowns (1995–1996, 2013), 175, 213–214, 215, 216, 232–233; Civil War expansion of, 78, 79; Communist infiltration charges, 347, 352; components of, 162–164*b*, 188–192; congressional appropriations for, 209–215; congressional hearings and oversight of, 29, 72, 216–220; constant

action by, 51–52; critics of size of, 175, 188, 214; electronic surveillance by, 333–334, 382; executive agencies, 167–175; expanded powers of, 31–33; foreign policy and, 327–337; Freedom of Information Act and, 353; institutional culture of, 172–173; judicial districts and, 170; judicial rulings and, 280–281, 286, 317; New Deal expansion of, 31, 88–89, 101, 238, 239; oldest (*see* State Department); personnel (*see* federal employees); political patronage and, 67; post–New Deal, 53; presidential management of, 185–187, 256, 279; presidential unilateral powers and, 47, 51–52, 93; private contractors and, 166–167, 268, 272, 273–274; public disclosure exemptions, 182–183; quasi entities, 161, 165; regulatory review and, 32–33, 259–265; research and development center, 161, 165; revolving door with corporate stakeholders, 181; F. D. Roosevelt reorganization plan, 257–258; rulemaking process, 175–187, 217, 259–262, 317; Schedule C appointees, 166; World War I new agencies, 340, 341; World War II new agencies, 343, 346. *See also specific departments and agencies by key word*

Federal Bureau of Investigation (FBI), 46, 186, 190, 315, 337; creation of, 170; functions of, 170–171, 190, 333; Watergate affair and, 222, 223, 229

Federal Communications Act (1934), 37

Federal Communications Commission (FCC), 174, 317

federal courts. *See* judiciary

Federal Deposit Insurance Corporation, 88–89

Federal Election Campaign Act (1971), 146, 151, 152

Federal Election Commission (FEC), 118, 147, 174, 316

Federal Election Committee, 146–147

Federal Emergency Management Agency (FEMA), 36, 161, 163, 171, 382

Federal Emergency Relief Association, 238

federal employees, 39, 165–166, 186, 188, 232, 261; ban on political campaigning by, 240; government shutdowns and, 214, 215; patronage and, 234; private contractors, 166–167, 169, 188; whistleblower protection statues, 219. *See also* civil service federal funds rate, 174

Federal Home Loan Bank System, 165

Federal Home Loan Mortgage Corporation (Freddie Mac), 165

Federalist and Jeffersonian era, 60, 61–65, 233–234; major presidential powers introduced, 93

Federalist Party, 61, 62, 64, 154, 234, 277, 386

Federal National Mortgage Corporation (Fannie Mae), 165

Federal Register, 182, 184, 259, 260, 263, 317

Federal Reserve Act (1913), 86

Federal Reserve System, 213, 218, 345, 354; creation of, 174; funding of, 210

federal spending. *See* budget, U.S.; defense budget

federal-state relations. *See* state-federal relations

Federal Trade Commission (FTC), 32, 174, 285, 316

Federal Trade Commission Act (1914), 86, 177, 259

fetal tissue research. *See* stem cell research

Field, Stephen, 302

Field v. Clark (1892), 311

filibuster, 208

Fillmore, Millard, 70, 71, 74, 96, 97, 351, *402*

financial bubbles, 72

financial crisis (2007–2008), 135, 165, 168, 174, 194; stimulus packages, 212, 214

financial services. *See* banking system

Financial Stability Oversight Council, 174

Fiorina, Carly, 116

First and Second Reconstruction Acts (1867), 82

First Spouses, 9, 11, 15–17, *15, 16, 17*

First War Powers Act (1941), 344

FISA. *See* Foreign Intelligence Service Act

FISA Court, 334, 335, 336, 337

fiscal cliff, 216

fiscal policy, 173–174, 258; congressional control over, 212. *See also* budget, U.S.; monetary policy; taxes

Fish, Hamilton, 343

Fish and Wildlife Service, 46, 172

Fisher, Louis, 34

501(c)(3), status, 145*b*, 146

527 committee, 145*b*, 147

527 Super Pac committee, 145*b*, 146

Fleischer, Ari, 254

Fleming v. Page (1850), 293

Florida, 139; presidential election 1876 vote dispute, 293; presidential election 2000 vote recount, 118, 119, 158, *158,* 284, 292–293; as presidential election battleground state, 129; secession of, 76

focus groups, 130

Food Administration (World War II), 341

Food and Drug Administration (FDA), 49, 173, 178, *191,* 215, 263; creation of, 266; functions of, 191–192

Food Safety Modernization Act (2010), 178

Force Bill (1833), 67–68

Ford, Betty, 16–17, *17*

Ford, Gerald R., 12, 92, 107, 260, 379, *405;* First Spouse of, 16–17, *17;* on impeachable offenses, 225; pardon of Nixon, 27; pardon of Vietnam draft resisters, 26; presidential campaign (1976), 129; regulatory review and, 260; succession to presidency, 126; veto overridef, 205; as vice president, 112

Ford, Henry Jones, 234

foreign assets, 296, 325; seizure of, 35, 269, 385

foreign commerce. *See* trade

foreign emissaries. *See* diplomacy

Foreign Intelligence Surveillance Act (FISA, 1978), 334, 373; amendments (2007, 2008), 335

foreign policy, 323–390; congressional role in, 20, 84, 245, 293–294, 298, 323, 325–326, 338–339, 346–354; covert and clandestine operations (*see* Central Intelligence Agency); diplomatic recognition and (*see* diplomacy); executive agencies and, 167–168, 363; executive agreements and, 90, 363, 369, 397; expertise and, 297–298; judicial decisions and, 293–298; National Security Council and, 258; neutrality and, 61, 62, 324, 342; presidential advisers and, 326–327, 356; presidential inherent powers and, 33–34, 52; presidential national emergency declaration and, 35; presidential power statutes and, 356–357; presidential primacy and, 34, 93, 101–102, 248, 294–298, 323–326, 337–339; presidential unilateralism and, 266, 268, 297, 324–325, 363, 370, 379–380; signing statements and, 272; State Department

foreign policy (*continued*)
and, 164, 188–189, 328–330. *See also* national
security; trade policy; treaty power; war
powers
Foreign Service, 328, 356
Foreign Service Reform Act (1946), 356
foreign trade. *See* trade policy
Forest Service, 172
Forrestal, James, 359
Fort McHenry, 287
Fort Moultrie, 76–77
Fort Sumter, fall of (1861), 33, 76–77, 340, 386,
387, *388*
Foster v. Neilson (1829), 293
founders. *See* Constitutional Convention
Fourteenth Amendment (1866), 83, 351; provi-
sions of, 81, 82
Fourth Amendment, 307
Fox News, 253
France, 61, 63, 383; executive system, 4, 27;
Quasi War with, 281, 299, 320, 324. *See also*
Louisiana Purchase
Freddie Mac, 165
Freedom of Information Act (1966), 353
Free Soil Party, 75, 349, 351
free speech, 145, 302, 342. *See also* censorship
free trade, 62, 67, 72
Frémont, John C., 75
Freneau, Philip, 234
Friedman, Milton, 373
Fuel Administration, 341, 346
Fuel Control Act (1917), 341
fugitive slave clause, 73
Fulbright, J. William, 353, 355
Fundamentalists. *See* religious right
Furlong, Scott, 180

GAO. *See* Government Accountability Office
Garfield, James A., 83, 84, *403*; assassination
of, 165
Garner, John Nance, 13, 240
Garrison, William Lloyd, 73
Gates Commission, 373
GATT. *See* General Agreement on Tariffs and
Trade
gay rights, 117, 139, 203, 287
Gaziano, Todd, 272
Gelber, Ethan, 107

General Accountability Office (formerly Gen-
eral Accounting Office), 88, 218, 219, 264,
335, 354
General Agreement on Tariffs and Trade
(GATT), 90, 296; Provisional Protocol, 364
General Service Administration, 166, 382
general welfare, federal agencies promoting, 173
Geospatial Intelligence Agency, 330
Gephardt, Dick, 124
Gergen, David, 254
German Americans, 352
Germany, 244, 247, 304; World War II and,
342, 345, 388
Gerry, Elbridge, 25, 36
gerrymandering, 117–118, 197, 396
G.I. Bill, 350
Gilmore, Jim, 116
Gingrich, Newt, 123, 213, 214, 232–233
Ginsberg, Benjamin L., 119, 142
Ginsburg, Douglas, 207, 284
Glenn, John, 198
Goldwater, Barry, 56, *56*
Goldwater-Nichols Department of Defense
Reorganization Act (1986), 375
Goldwater v. Carter (1979), 281
Gore, Al: presidential ambition, 153; presiden-
tial campaign, 112, 133–134, 144; presidential
popular vote, 129, 157–158; presidential loss,
284, 292; as vice president, 11, 112
Gore, Tipper, 134
Gorelick, Jamie, 141, 142
Gorsuch, Anne, 315
Government Accountability Office (GAO,
formerly General Accounting Office), 88,
180, 182, 184, 218, 219
government bonds, *33*, 168, 345, 369–370, *388*;
private citizen ownership of, 79, 236–237
government departments and agencies. *See*
federal bureaucracy
government shutdowns (1995–1996, 2013), 175,
213–214, 215–216, 232–233
governors. *See* state governors
Graham, John D., 264
Graham, Lindsey, 116
Grain Board, 346
Gramm-Rudman-Hollings Act (1985), 316
Grand Army of the Republic, 350, 351–352
Grange, 348

Grant, Ulysses S., 83, 84, 108, 109, *403*

Gray, Horace, 293

Great Britain, 6, 71, 371, 378, 383; French wars, 61, 63; Jay Treaty with, 61, 217, 314, 324, 338; parliamentary system, 239; U.S. alliance, 368; women's suffrage, 349; World War I, 352; World War II, 244, 247, 342–343. *See also* War of 1812

Great Depression (1930s), 136, 157, 198, 237–239, 384

Great Society, 90, 91, 193–194, 352, 372

Greenback Party, 111

greenbacks (paper currency), 79

greenhouse gas emissions, 47

Green Party, 113

Greenstein, Fred, 248

Grenada invasion (1983), 380

Griswold, Erwin, 7

Gruening, Ernest, 353

Guantanamo Bay prisoners, 42, 305, 309–310

Guardian (newspaper), 336

Guatemala, 365–366

Guiteau, Charles, 165

Gulf of Tonkin, 393

Gulf wars. *See* Iraq war; Persian Gulf War

Gulick, Luther, 257

gun control, 263, 283

habeas corpus, writ of: enemy combatants and, 309, 310; Lincoln suspension of, 21, 34, 52, 77, 78, 101, 287, 300, 301, 340; national emergency suspension of, 35

Hagel, Chuck, 275

Haig v. Agee (1981), 307–308

Haiti, Clinton planned invasion (1991) of, 381

Haldeman, H. R., 10, 286

Hamdi, Yaser Esam, 308–309

Hamdi v. Rumsfeld (2004), 308–309

Hamilton, Alexander, 4, 5, 7; argument for electors, 129; Federalists and, 61, 62, 234; foreign policy and, 324–325, 338–339; policies of, 234; presidential checks and, 37; presidential vs. congressional powers and, 29, 217, 338

Hanna, Mark, 85

Harding, Warren G., 84, 87, 88, 94, 96, 97, 211, 257, *404*

Harrison, Benjamin, 83, 243, *403*

Harrison, William Henry, 69–70, 71, 108, 109, 156, *402*; death in office of, 11, 106; political parties and, 235

Hart, Peter, 149

Hartford Convention, 64

Hartley, Gregg, 149

Hastings, Alcee, 225

Hatch Act (1939), 240

Hayes, Rutherford B., 83, 84, 94, 293, *403*

heads of state, 21, 93

Head Start program, 91

Health and Human Services Department (HHS), 50, 263, 382; Affordable Care Act and, 30, 46, 176; functions of, 162–163*b*, 173; presidential "prompt letter" to, 264

health and safety legislation, 261

health care, 232, 249, 263. *See also* Affordable Care Act; Medicare and Medicaid

Health Insurance Accountability and Portability Act (1996), 193

hearings and investigations, 123, 216–224, 228–232, 255, 286, 339, 396; investigative hearings, 26–29, 220–224, 228–230, 231–232, 255, 354; legislative oversight, 216–220; loyalty hearings, 347, 352

Hearst, Patty, 26

Helms, Jesse, 295

Henry, Patrick, 4, 52

Hepburn Act (1906), 85, 243

Heritage Foundation, 133

Hershey, Lewis, 360

Hewlett-Packard, 151

high crimes and misdemeanors, 21, 36, 224

Hispanics, 133, 137

history of presidency. *See* presidential history

HIV-positive military personnel, 41, 271

Hoar, George, 83

Hobbes, Thomas, 152

Hobbs Anti-Racketeering Act (1946), 270

Ho Chi Minh, 91, 92, 372

Holder, Eric, 35

Hollywood, 247–248

Holmes, Oliver Wendell, Jr., 342

Homeland Security Act (2002), 163

Homeland Security Department (DHS), 160, 171–172, 314, 327, 385; agencies combined under, 382; G. W. Bush speeches promoting, 256; creation of, 382; customs and

Homeland Security Department (DHS)
(*continued*)
　border protection, 168, 333; functions of,
　163*b*, 171, 333, 382. *See also* Transportation
　Security Administration
Hoover, Herbert, 84, 88, 97, 326, *404*
Hoover, J. Edgar, 171, 186, 190, *190*, 337, 366
Hopkins, Harry, 356
Hornbeck Offshore Services v. Jewell (2013), 286
Horseshoe Bend, Battle of (1814), 68
Horton, Willie, 131
House of Representatives: appropriations
　subcommittees, 210; budget-cut meas-
　ures, 48; campaign spending and, 147;
　celebrity members, 10; debt ceiling and,
　168, 214–215; district redrawing, 117–118,
　197–198, 396; early importance of, 63; first
　Republican control of (1858), 75; impeach-
　ment initiation by, 36, 224, 225, 226, 230;
　initiatives against Obama, 47, 203, 215, 281;
　party discipline and, 198; presidents with
　prior service in, 109; presidential contested
　election decision by, 62, 65, 127–128, 130,
　292–293; presidential line of succession and,
　13*b*, 62, 65; Radical Republicans in, 80–81;
　revolt against Speaker Cannon (1910), 87;
　"war hawk" faction, 52, 63–64
House Oversight and Government Reform
　Committee, 217, 219, 221
House Rules Committee, 240
House Un-American Activities Committee,
　347, 352
House Veterans Affairs Committee, 219
Housing and Urban Development Department
　(HUD), functions of, 163b, 221
Howell, William, 289
Hsu, Norman, 118
Huckabee, Mike, 116
Hughes, Karen, 250
Hughes-Ryan Amendments (1974), 372–373
Hull, Cordell, 356
human rights treaties, 295
Humphrey, Hubert, 91
Humphrey's Executor v. United States (1935), 316
Hussein, Saddam, 273, 325, 382

Idaho, 72
identity politics, 135, 136–138

immigrants: political parties and, 86, 116, 118,
　136; undocumented, 203, 204, 207, 274,
　307, 382
immigration: border security enforcement,
　333; Obama reform efforts, 49–50, 51, 93,
　131, 135, 196, 204, 232, 274, 279, 303, 395; as
　political issue, 131, 135, 196, 232
Immigration and Customs Enforcement, 171,
　173, 303, 333
Immigration and Naturalization Service, 382
Immigration and Naturalization Service v.
　Chadha (1983), 313, 379
impeachment, 20, 21, 28, 36–37, 92, 201, 205,
　216; of Clinton (1938), 36, 211, 225–226, 230,
　232, *399*, *400*; definition of, 224; of federal
　judges, 216, 282; of A. Johnson (1868), 27,
　36, 80, 83, 225, 242, 316, 347, 352; Nixon's
　probability of, 36–37, 92, 223, 224, 229;
　offenses for, 21, 36, 224, 225; process of, 36,
　224–226
imperial presidency, 61, 90, 357, 370; major
　presidential powers introduced, 94–95
implied presidential powers, 27–30, 32–33,
　101–102; constitutional derivation of, 33, 36;
　definition of, 27; inherent powers vs., 33–34
impoundment of funds, 202, 204, 211, 222, 288
income tax. *See* Internal Revenue Service; taxes
independent counsel, 223, 225, 226, 230
independent regulatory commission, 174
independent treasury system, 72
India, 328
Indian Removal Act (1830), 68
indirect election, 3, 127–130
Indochinese war. *See* Vietnam War
industrial unions, 238
inflation, 66, 345
inherent presidential powers, 25, 33–36, 52, 93,
　394–395; emergency powers and, 33–34,
　301–302, 339, 385, 386–390; implied powers
　vs., 33–34; war powers and, 77–78, 100–101,
　300, 385, 386–390
In re Debs (1895), 302
In re Neagle (1890), 302
Institute for Defense Analysis, 331
institutional culture, 172–173
Insular Cases (1903), 293
insurrections, 6–7, 300
intellectuals, 237

intelligence operations, 4, 123, 169–170, 171, 220, 331, 332–333, 337, 363–366, 370, 382; congressional oversight of, 366, 373; national security directives and, 397; signing statement, and, 202. *See also* Central Intelligence Agency; National Security Agency; surveillance

Intelligence Oversight Act (1980), 373, 379

intelligible principles standard, 312

interest groups, 144–152, 163, 194

interest rates, 213

Interior Department, 263, 286; functions of, 163b

internal improvements, 30–31, 70, 168

Internal Revenue Code, 296, 297

Internal Revenue Service (IRS), 220; Affordable Care Act administration and, 30–31, 176, 201–202; functions of, 168, 189; House punitive budget cut (2014) for, 210, 217

international agreements, 372, 397

International Bank of Settlements, 325

International Criminal Court, 295

international law, 33

International Monetary Fund, 315

international relations. *See* foreign policy

International Trade Organization, 364

Internet, 150, 203; presidential campaigns and, 132, 241; surveillance of searches, 335, 336

interpretive signing statements. *See* signing statements

interrogation methods, 28–29, 170, 202

interstate commerce, 29

Interstate Commerce Commission, 85, 243

investigative hearings (ethics probes), 26–29, 220–224, 228–230, 231–232, 354; presidential pardons and, 26–27; RIP (revelation, investigation, and prosecution), 223–224, 228, 255

Iowa: caucus, 120, 121b, 122, 124, 125; presidential electors, 129

Iran: CIA intervention (1953) in, 365; U.S. non-recognition of, 328; U.S. nuclear agreement (2015) with, 135, 325–326, 332

Iran-Contra affair, 232, 378, 380, 393; as Boland Amendment violation, 202, 204–205; congressional hearings, 221, 223–224, 225, 229, 255, 339; details of, 229–230; presidential pardons and, 27, 224

Iranian hostage crisis (1979–1980), 35, 269, 379

Iraq war (1990–1991). *See* Persian Gulf War

Iraq war (2003–2011), 6, 373; abuse of Iraqi prisoners, 308, 362–363; American allies ("coalition of the willing") and, 383; congressional authorization vote, 382–383; financial costs of, 383; justifications for, 33, 325, 382–383, 393, 394; National Guard and, 140, 374; Obama policy, 194, 325, 355; occupation policy, 202, 374, 377, 383; popular movement to, 354; as presidential election issue, 135; private contractors and, 166, 361–363; reporters embedded with troops, 376–377

Irish Americans, 136, 137, 244, 352

isolationists, 209, 244, 245, 246, 247, 343, 352, 388, 344.46

Israel, 325–326

Issa, Darrell, 221

Italian Americans, 136, 137

Jackson, Andrew, 60, 64–69, 71, 72, 88, *100*, *402*; historical view of, 97; Indian removal and, 68; inherent presidential power and, 52; judiciary and, 285; military career of, 64, 68, 108, 109, 386; Nullification Crisis and, 67–68; party organization and, 234–235, 239, 240, 242, 277–278; popular mobilization and, 242; presidential election and, 125, 154; Senate censure of (1834), 68–69, 201, 316; spoils system and, 67, 94, 234–235, 239; veto use by, 52, 66, 68, 94, 100, *100*, 201; vice president of, 106, 111–112

Jackson, Robert, 269, 307, 343, 348

Jacksonian era, 61, 65–72; major presidential powers introduced, 94

Japan: World War II and, 33, 247–248, 342, 344, 388; World War II surrender, 346, 389, *389*

Japanese American internment (1941), 49, 68, 266, 303, 305, 345

Jay, John, 323

Jayalinthaa (Indian actress), 109

Jay Treaty (1794), 61, 217, 314, 324, 338

Jefferson, Thomas, *99*, 204, *401*; historical view of, 97; judicial review and, 287, 319; political party development and, 61, 62, 233–234, 239, 240, 242, 277; presidency of, 62–63,

Jefferson, Thomas (*continued*)
68; presidential power and, 63, 93, 99–100, 324–325; war powers and, 298, 299, 346
Jeffersonian Republicans. *See* Democratic-Republican Party
Jeffords, James, 232
Jews, 132, 136, 137, 247
Jim Crow, 134
Jindal, Bobby, 105, 116, 137
Johnson, Andrew, 81, 82, 205, 351, *403*; impeachment of (1868), 27, 36, 80, 83, 225, 242, 316, 347, 352
Johnson, Lyndon B., *405*; congressional relations, 200, 372; executive orders, 50, 268–269; Great Society programs, 90, 91, 193–194, 352, 372; imperial presidency, 90; judicial appointments, 282; liberals' break with, 353; malicious attacks on, 398, *398*; policymaking, 199; reelection campaign withdrawal, 104, 124–125, 131, 353, 372; succession to presidency, 104; television use, 249; as vice president, 10, 104, 112, 126; Vietnam War and, 91, 96, 115, 131, 352–353, 372, 374, 390, 393, 398, *398*
Johnson v. Eisentrager (1950), 304–305, 309
Joint Chiefs of Staff, 9, 162*b*, 169, 327, 331, 357, 358–359, 363; chairman's increased power, 375
judicial imperialism thesis, 293
judicial review, 280, 284, 286–289, 318, 319–322, 382; Supreme Court case establishing, 287, 319
Judicial Watch, 315
judiciary, 5, 280–322; appointments to, 3, 20, 41, 232, 241, 248, 280, 282–286, 289–290; Article III vs. Article I courts, 282; constitutional sources of power, 280–286; executive orders and, 50, 316–317; executive support policy, 289–292; federal districts, 70; FISA Court, 334, 335, 336, 337; function of, 2; impeachment of judges, 225, 282; lifetime appointment to, 282; nineteenth-century judges' legislative backgrounds, 290–291, 317; political milieu and, 283–284, 289–290; presidential enforcement of rulings, 284–289; Senate confirmation of appointments to, 206–207, 232; senatorial courtesy and, 84, 248, 282; separation of powers and,

2; signing statements and, 40–41. *See also* Supreme Court
Judiciary Act (1789), 319
Justice Department, 26, 170–171, 190, 382, 385; executive branch misconduct probes, 223; functions of, 163b, 170; signing statements and, 40, 270; war on terror and, 382
J. W. Hampton & Co. v. United States (1928), 312

Kagan, Elena, 262, 283, 284
Kansas, 74–75
Kansas-Nebraska Act (1854), 74–75, 351
Kasich, John, 116
Kemp, Jack, 109–110
Kennan, George, 356–357
Kennedy, Anthony, 283
Kennedy, John F., 186, 199, 285, 390, *405*; assassination of, 91, 104; Cuban invasion and, 393; executive order, 268; executive power expansion, 372; judicial appointments, 282; media events and, 249; national security affairs and, 363, 365; New Frontier program, 90–91; political family of, 112; popular approval of, 96, 242; press conferences, 244; *Profiles in Courage* Pulitzer Prize award, 96, 107; stepping stones to presidency, 107, 108, 112; televised campaign debate, 144; vice president of, 10, 103, 112, 126
Kennedy, Joseph P., 107, 112
Kennedy, Robert F., 112, 115, 186
Kennedy-Kassebaum Act (1996), 193
Kernell, Samuel, 247
Kerry, John, 124, 142, 143, 153, 329–330
Kerwin, Cornelius, 180
Key, V. O., 133, 234
King, Martin Luther, Jr., 134, 352–353
King, Preston, 351
King, Rufus, 38
kings. *See* monarchy
Kissinger, Henry, 258, 329, 363
Knight, Peter, 149
Korean War, 266, 269, 321, 326, 339, 355, *389*; allied troops, 371; financing of, 367, 371; president's emergency powers, 306, 386; president's inherent power and, 33, 34–35; president's military deployment, 34, 359, 370–371, 389; unpopularity of, 371; U.N. Security Council resolution and, 369, 370, 380, 389

Korematsu v. United States (1944), 305, 345

Kuwait, 378, 380, 383

Labor Department, 85, 263; functions of, 164*b*

labor policy, 49, 271, 272–274, 347

labor unions, 84, 132, 136, 150, 151; Democratic Party and, 237, 238; striking worker replacement and, 269, 272, 287, 317

Laden, Osama bin, 169, 325, 326–327

La Guardia, Fiorello, 137

Landrieu, Mary, 39–40

Landrum-Griffin Act (1959), 248

Laos, 365–366

Largent, Steve, 110

Lavtov, Sergei, 329

law enforcement, 46, 190, 285; federal agencies, 170–173

laws: congressional appropriations for, 48; congressional delegation of power, 311–312; congressional enactment refusal, 36; congressional oversight of (*see* legislative oversight); congressional presentment clause and, 22; executive orders and, 269; federal agencies and, 53; federal rules and regulations implementing, 175–185; judicial review of, 280, 284, 286–289; political campaigns and, 117–119, 147; president's faithful execution of, 28, 30, 33, 42–48, 77, 93, 101, 193, 195, 200–203, 284, 298, 300, 302, 303; president's leadership and, 94, 95, 200; president's power to veto (*see* veto power); president's signing statement as circumvention of (*see* signing statements); tripartite division of power and, 2

leadership PACs, 146

League of Nations, 86, 209, 245, 352

Lebanon: hostages in, 393; U.S. forces in, 371, 379–380

Legal Services Corporation, 161

Legal Tender Act (1872), 79

legislation. *See* laws

legislative districts, 117–118

legislative oversight, 203–205, 216–220

legislative veto, 313, 379

legislature, 5; function of, 2; judiciary and, 290–291, 293, 311. *See also* Congress; Parliament

Lend-Lease Act (1941), 343

Lever Espionage Act (1917), 341

Lever Food and Fuel Control Act (1917), 341

Lewinsky, Monica, 226, 230, 254

Lewis and Clark expedition (1804–1808), 63

Libby, Lewis ("Scooter"), 27

liberals, 352–353

Liberia, 362

Libertarian Party, 113

Libertarians, 123

liberty bonds. *See* war bonds

Libya: Benghazi embassy attack, 143, 188–189, *188*; U.S. air strikes, 35, 380

Lilly Ledbetter Fair Pay Act (2009), 196

Lincoln, Abraham, *100*, *403*; Cooper Union address, 76; executive orders, 49, 50, 77–78, 266, 300, 340; habeas corpus suspension, 21, 34, 52, 77, 78, 101, 287, 300, 301, 340; judicial review and, 287–288, 300–301; martial law declaration, 34, 78, 236, 301, 340; presidential greatness of, 96, 97; Republican Party and, 110–111, 113, 233, 235–237, 239, 240; war powers of, 33, 34, 72, 77–80, 100–101, 339, 340, 346, 386, 388, 399. *See also* Civil War

Lincoln, Blanche, 39–40

Lincoln-Douglas debates (1858), 76

line-item veto, 201, 206, 313–314

Little Rock (Ark.) school desegregation, 285

Little v. Barreme (1804), 281, 299, 320

Litvinov Assignment, 296

lobbyists, 137, 146, 149–151, 264–265; presidential staffers as, 200

Locke, John, 300, 303

Lockheed aviation, 360

Lodge, Henry Cabot, 352

Logan, John, 352

Louisiana Purchase (1803), 34, 49, 52, 233; frontier squatters and, 235; presidential power assertion and, 63, 99–100, 266; slavery extension and, 73–74, 75

Lowi, Theodore J., 252; *The Personal President*, 242

Lowry v. Reagan (1987), 308

loyalty program, 288, 347, 352, 366, 371, 385

Loyalty Review Board, 366

Luther v. Borden (1849), 292

MacArthur, Douglas, 108–109, 370

machine politics. *See* political machines

Madison, James, 5, 25, 36, 111, 227, 231, 319, *401*; Democratic-Republicans and, 62; "dogs of War" phrase of, 346, 354; foreign policy and, 338, 354; pocket veto introduced by, 64, 93; presidency of, 63, 64, 65–66; war powers and, 298, 346, 394

mail censorship, 100–101

Mansfield, Harvey, 8

manufacturing, 73

Marbury v. Madison (1803), 281, 287, 319

Margolies, Marjorie, 118

Marine Corps, 172, 189, 358, 359; troops in Lebanon, 371

marque and reprisal, letters of, 298

marriage, 139, 203, 287

Marshall, George C., 199, 356, 368

Marshall, John, 285, 289, 299, 312, *319*, 325; executive privilege and, 314; foreign relations speech (1800), 34; judicial review doctrine, 287, 319

Marshall Plan (1948), 368

martial law, 34, 78, 236, 303, 340; Supreme Court ruling, 301

Mashaw, Jerry L., 176, 331

Massachusetts, 6–7

May, Christopher N., 301

Mayer, Kenneth, 260

Mayhew, David, 150

McAdoo, William, 342

McCain, John, 28, *56*, 102, *102*, 124, 147–148; natural-born citizen issue, 56–57, 104; presidential campaign of, 126, 127, 151, 158–159, 196

McCain-Feingold Act (2002), 152, 193, 241

McCarran Internal Security Act (1950), 347

McCarthy, Eugene, 115, 124, 353

McCarthy, Joseph, 249, 347, 352

McConnell, Mitch, 368

McCubbins, Mathew, 53, 181, 219

McCutcheon v. Federal Election Commission (2014), 145, 152

McDougal, Susan, 27

McFarlane, Robert, 27

McGovern, George, 353

McGovern-Fraser Commission, 120, 241

McGrain v. Dauherty (1927), 217

McKinley, William, 83, 84, 156, 243, 295–296, *404*; assassination of, 85

McKitrick, Eric, 79, 236

McRaven, William, 169

Meat Inspection Act (1906), 85

media, 85–86, 219, 223, 226, 253–256; attacks on presidents by, 253–254; focus on president of, 227; investigative journalism and, 222, 229, 253; military combat-zone access for, 376–377; Nixon campaign against, 222; opposition research and, 254; partisan press and, 62, 68, 234, 243, 247; presidential campaign coverage, 124–125, 131–132, 241; presidential press conferences, 86, 244, 246–247, 248, 249, 254–255; presidential use of, 243, 246, 249–254, 279; social media campaigns, 116; Watergate investigation, 222, 229. *See also* press; radio; television

Media Fund, 148

Medicare and Medicaid, 91, 173, 213; funding for, 210

Meese, Edwin, 40, 41, 270

Merryman, John, 285

Merton, Robert, 248

metadata, 336–337

Mexican-American War (1846), 47, 70, 71, 74, 349, 386–387, *387*; postwar political alliances, 351

Mexico, 314, 325, 332

MGM (Metro-Goldwyn-Mayer), 247

Middle East, 170, 326, 371

Miers, Harriet, 207–209, 221

Military Academy, U.S., 63

military commissions: Civil War, 78, 236, 340; Cold War, 355; war on terror, 35, 273, 305, 309, 325, 382; World War II, 303, 304–305, 345

military forces, 359–371; advanced weaponry and, 375–376; as all-volunteer, 373–375, 385; Cold War doubling of, 359, 365; congressional powers and, 24, 29, 47, 216, 298, 323, 338–339, 362; defense contracts and, 331, 360–361, 385; Defense Department and, 161, 162*b*, 169, 189–190; desegregation order, 49, 50, 266, 268, 330; draft and (*see* conscription); European alliances and, 368–369, 371, 383; executive orders and, 77, 266, 279; funding of, 24, 47, 203, 298, 338–339, 366–371, 375–376; HIV-positive personnel, 41, 271; president as commander-in-chief

of (*see* (commander-in-chief); president's
control over, 357–363, 370, 371–372;
president's deployment of, 47, 326–327;
president's inherent powers and, 34, 100,
340, 384; private contractors and, 166–167,
168, 361–363, 365; professionalization of,
357; recruitment of, 245; reorganization
(1947) of, 357–360; spending levels on, 212,
213, 215, 232, 366–370; undeclared wars and,
339; unification of, 357, 358; war heroes as
presidential aspirants, 69–70, 71, 108–109,
154–155; wartime mobilization of, 348. *See
also* National Guard; *specific branches*
military-industrial complex, 361
Military Professional Resources, Inc. (MPRI),
361, 362
military tribunals. *See* military commissions
militias, 77, 236, 298, 300, 348–349, 357, 358.
See also National Guard
Milkis, Sidney, 246, 258
Mill, John Stuart, 217
Miller v. United States (1871), 301
Milligan case (1866). See *Ex parte Milligan*
minimum hours and wage, 240
minority hiring. *See* affirmative action; Equal
Employment Opportunity Commission
Missile Defense Agency, 330
Missouri Compromise (1820), 73, 74; invalida-
tion of, 75, 287, 351
Mistretta v. United States (1988), 316
Mitchell, Billy, 358
Modern Whig Party, 113
Moe, Terry, 39, 59, 276, 289
monarchy, 4, 8, 21, 300, 391, 397
Mondale, Walter, 112, 144, 195
monetary policy, 66, 79, 84, 371; components
of, 174, 213; exchange rates, 332; executive
control of, 93, 94; federal agencies and,
173–174
money supply, 79, 174, 213
money swapping, 150
Monroe, James, 63, 65–66, 74, 111, *401*
Montesquieu, Baron de, 2; *The Spirit of the
Laws,* 2
Montgomery, Robert, 248
Montgomery Ward & Co. v. United States (1945),
306
Moore, Michael, 142

moral issues, 4, 254; president's character and,
138–143, 399–400; slavery as, 73, 74, 76
Morrison v. Olson (1988), 316
Morse, Wayne, 353
mortgages, 165, 268
Moseley-Braun, Carol, 147
muckrakers, 243–244
Murphy, George, 109
Myers v. United States (1926), 27–28, 316

Nader v. Bork (1973), 316
NAFTA. *See* North American Free Trade
Agreement
Nannygate, 207
national bank. *See* Bank of the United States
national conventions, 113–114, 119, *278*, 350
National Defense Act (1915), 358
National Defense Act (1916), 340
National Defense Act (1917), 340, 344
National Defense Act (1947), 159
National Defense Council, 341
National Defense Establishment, 169
national emergencies. *See* emergency powers
National Emergencies Act (1976), 35, 373
National Enrollment Act (1863), 236
National Environmental Policy Act (1969), 184
National Federation of Independent Business,
322
National Gazette, 62, 234
National Geospatial Intelligence Agency, 169
National Guard, 140, 161, 358, 360, 374–375
National Highway Traffic Safety Administra-
tion, 264
National Industrial Recovery Act (1933), 215,
287, 312
National Institutes of Health (NIH), 173
National Intelligence Director, 327
National Labor Relations Act (1935), 238, 269, 272
National Labor Relations Board, 37, 288–289
National Military Establishment, 357. *See also*
Defense Department
national monuments, 274
National Oceanographic and Atmospheric
Administration, 46
National Passenger Railroad Corporation, 161
national security, 168–169, 209, 233, 327–385;
directives, 50, 51, 371–372, 397; executive
departments, 168–169, 233, 363–366, 370;

national security (*continued*)
executive privilege claims, 315; loyalty legislation, 288, 371, 385; National Emergencies
Act, 35, 373; presidential power statutes, 356;
as salutary campaign issue, 13. *See also* emergency powers; war on terror; war powers
National Security Act (1947), 90, 101–102, 189,
357; effects of, 260, 358–359, 360, 363, 365
National Security Agency (NSA), 162*b*, 327,
329, 330, 385; electronic surveillance program, 35, 167, 220, 325, 334–337, 397; functions of, 169, 333–337; improper practices
charges, 220; private contractor, 167, 220;
Snowden disclosures, 336
National Security Council (NSC), 9, 10, 169,
171, 199, 205, 337, 358, 360, 363, 365; creation of, 90, 95, 102, 258, 357; members of,
327; staff of, 364
national security directives (NSDs), 365
National Security Resources Board, 360
national sovereignty, 33, 36
National War Labor Board, 266, 305
National Youth Administration, 238
Native Americans, 60, 68, 150, 156, 299
NATO (North Atlantic Treaty Organization),
368, 381
natural-born citizen, 12, 20, 81; definition of,
55–58, 104
naval campaigns, 6, 281, 298, 299, 320, 339
Navy, 189, 298, 340, 343, 357, 358, 359
Navy Department, 51, 162*b*, 218, 357, 358; creation of, 160, 168–169
Navy Seals, 169
Neagle, David, 302
negative ads, 131, 143
Negotiated Rulemaking Act (1990), 182
Nelson, Ben, 39–40
Netanyahu, Benjamin, 325–326
Neustadt, Richard, 195, 205
Neutrality Act (1940), 342
neutrality proclamation (1793), 61, 62, 324
New Deal, 88–90, 310; factional opposition
to, 240; federal bureaucracy expansion, 31,
88–89, 101, 238, 239; "First" and "Second,"
88–89; increased presidential power, 53,
193–194, 198–199, 237–239; popular mobilization and, 242; Supreme Court invalidations of, 287, 312–313, 320–321

New England Confederation (proposed), 64, 386
New Frontier, 90–91
New Hampshire presidential primary, 104, 124
New Orleans, Battle of (1814–1815), 64, 68, 386
New Politics (1970s), 350, 352–353
New Republic (magazine), 250
newspapers. *See* press
New York City: draft riots (1863), 349; ethnic
politics, 136, 137
New York Times, 222, 253, 335
New York Times v. United States (1971), 307
NFIB v. Sibelius (2012), 322
Nicaraguan civil war, 202, 204–205, 223–224,
229, 339, 378, 379
9/11 Commission, 140–142, 171, 195
9/11 terror attacks, 35, 93, 163, 171, 190, 250;
intelligence agencies and, 333, 334; presidential responses to (*see* war on rerror)
Nitze, Paul, 357, 359
Nixon, Richard M., 56, 141, 153, 232, 249, *322,*
326, 352, *405;* all-volunteer military and,
373–374; character flaws of, 392, 398; chief
of staff, 10; core constituency, 139; domestic
security surveillance program, 307; executive orders use, 222, 269; executive privilege
claim, 61, 314–315, 321–322; Ford's presidential pardon of, 27; foreign policy adviser,
329; impeachment probability, 36–37, 92,
223, 224, 229, 288; impoundment of funds,
202, 204, 211, 222, 288; judicial appointments, 282, 283; judicial decisions enforcement, 285–286; judicial review and, 204,
288; malicious portrayals of, 398, *398;* media
and, 222, 253, 255; national security advisers,
363; New Politics coalition against, 353;
Philadelphia Plan, 268; "plumbers squad,"
92, 222; presidential power expansion, 90,
92, 221–222; regulatory review, 259–260;
resignation of, 11, 12, 17, 37, 92, 126, 223,
224, 229, 231, 255, 353, 372; resignation of
vice president of, 12; Southern strategy of,
285–286; stepping stones to presidency,
108; Supreme Court rulings and 288. 315*b;*
televised 1960 election debate, 144; as vice
president, 10, 112, 249; Vietnam War withdrawal, 372; White House taping system,
61, 218, 223, 229, 288. *See also* Watergate
affair

Nixon v. Administrator of General Services
    (1977), 315
No Budget, No Pay Act (2013), 216
No Child Left Behind Act (2001), 203
nominating caucus, 113, 114, 120, 121, 125
nominating convention, 70, 113–114, 154
nondelegation doctrine, 311
Noriega, Manuel, 380
Norquist, Grover, 150
North, Oliver, 224, 229, *229*
North American Aviation, 266, 303, 343
North American Free Trade Agreement
    (NAFTA), 111, 232, 332, 364
North Atlantic Treaty Organization (NATO),
    368, 381
North Korea, 167, 328, 332, 389
Northrup Aviation, 361
Northrup Services, 362
North Vietnam. *See* Vietnam War
"notice-and-comment rulemaking," 89–90, 182
NSA. *See* National Security Agency
NSC. *See* National Security Council
NSC-10/2, 365
NSC-68, 359, 365
NSDs (national security directives), 365
nuclear weapons: Cold War and, 12, 359; Iran
    and, 135, 325–326, 332
Nullification Crisis (1832), 67–68, 73

oath of office, presidential, 20, 21, 77, 94, 101
Obama, Barack, 153, *159*, 198, 225, 275, *278*,
    279, *406*; birth certificate, *57*; budget battles,
    48, 199, 215–216; congressional hostility
    toward, 37, 203, 208, 215, 232, 281; debt
    ceiling and, 168; domestic policy initiatives,
    194, 196; drone strikes and, 35, 325, 382, 384;
    electronic surveillance and, 337; evolving
    positions of, 393; executive agreements,
    297; executive orders, 49–50, 51, 93, 131,
    185, 232, 270, 274, 279, 303, 395; executive
    power and, 47, 203; executive privilege and,
    314; First Spouse, 17, *17*; foreign policy, 135,
    325, 326–327, 329–330, 332, 382; haters of,
    392, 400, *400*; health care proposal, 39–40
    (*see also* Affordable Care Act); immigration
    reform, 49–50, 51, 93, 125, 131, 232, 274,
    279, 303, 395; inherent presidential power,
    35; Iranian nuclear agreement (2015), 135,
    325–326, 332; Iraq War and, 194, 325, 354;
    judicial appointments, 41, 232, 241, 283,
    284; judicial review and, 280–281, 288–289,
    318; killing of Osama bin Laden and, 325;
    legislation and, 178, 180, 203; media use by,
    250–251; natural-born citizen issue, 55, 57,
    104; political consultant, 116; presidential
    campaigns, 110, 121, 123, 124, 126, 132, 135,
    144, 146, 151, 158–159, 391; public approval
    ratings, 252; recess appointments, 37; reg-
    ulatory review, 32–33, 187, 265; secretary of
    state, 17, 112; Senate blockage of nominees,
    208, 232; signing statements, 41–42, 272;
    stepping stones to presidency, 106–107, 108;
    surveillance practices and., 335, 337; torture
    and, 28–29; Twitter followers, 116, *278*, 279;
    unilateralism, 93, 270, 275, 303; veto use, 22,
    201; vice president of, 11, 126; war powers,
    383; White House "Czars," 9
Obama, Michelle, 17, *17*, *159*
Obamacare. *See* Affordable Care Act
Occupational Safety and Health Administra-
    tion (OSHA), 32, 177, 178, 184, 219; presi-
    dential "prompt letter" to, 264; regulatory
    review and, 261
O'Connor, John J., 240
O'Connor, Sandra Day, 291
Office for Emergency Management, 343
Office of Censorship, 266, 343
Office of Civilian Defense, 266, 343
Office of Customs and Border Protection, 168
Office of Economic Opportunity, 91
Office of Information and Regulatory Affairs
    (OIRA), 10, 180, 181–182, 184, 186, 259–262;
    creation of, 260; increased power of, 264,
    265; "prompt letters," 264
Office of Management and Budget. *See* White
    House Office of Management and Budget
Office of Personnel Management, 47
Office of Price Administration, 266, 304, 345
Office of Production Management, 343
Office of Strategic Services, 357
Office of the U.S. Trade Representative, 331–332
Office of War Mobilization, 266
Ohio, 129, 139
oil resources, 232, 273
OIRA. *See* Office of Information and Regula-
    tory Affairs

Olson, Theodore, 274
O'Malley, Martin, 115
O'Neill, Thomas P. ("Tip"), 251, 252
open primary, 120, 122; vs. closed, 121b
organized labor. *See* labor unions
OSHA. *See* Occupational Safety and Health Administration
Overman Act (1917), 341, 344

PACs. *See* political action committees
Padilla, José, 310
Padilla v. Kentucky (2010), 310
Pakistan, 170
Palin, Sarah, 126, 127
Panama, U.S. invasion of, 326, 376, 380
Panama Canal Treaty, 232
Panama Canal Zone, 56, 104, 297, 380
Panama Refining Co. v. Ryan (1935), 294, 312
Panic of 1837, 66
paper currency, 66, 79, 94
Paperwork Reduction Act (1979), 186, 260, 261
pardon power, 20, 22, 25–27, 224, 230, 395; petitions 2001–2012), 26t
parental paid leave, 263
parliamentary system, 3–4, 239, 252
partisan identification, 37, 88–90, 135–138; Congress and, 37, 200, 231–232; divided government and, 197; media and, 62, 66, 234, 253; voters and, 135–138. *See also* political parties; *specific parties*
Pataki, George, 116
Patriot Act (2001), 335, 382, 385
patriotism, 236, 251, 350
patronage, 67, 69, 94, 115, 130, 239; Jacksonian era and, 67, 94, 234–235, 239, 277–278; New Deal and, 237, 239; political machines and, 86–87, 136–138; Progressive era reform and, 87, 165–166
Paul, Joel R., 297
Paul, Rand, 116, 123
Paul, Ron, 123
PAYGO accounting rules, 212–213
Peace Corps, 49, 90, 91, 266
Pearl Harbor attack (1941), 33, 247–248, 342, 344, 386, 389
Pearson, Drew, 107
Pendleton Civil Service Act (1883), 87, 165–166
Penhallow v. Doane (1795), 293

Penn, Mark, 116
pension funds, 151
Pentagon. *See* Defense Department
Pentagon Force Protection Agency, 162b
Pentagon Papers, 222, 307
People's Party. *See* Populist Party
Perot, H. Ross, 111
Perry, Herman, 108
Perry, Rick, 116, 123–124, 131
Pershing, John J., 358
Persian Gulf War (1990–1991), 5, 33, 140, 232, 252, 369, 371, 374, 375, 376; background and conduct of, 380–381; coalition nations and, 378
personal liberties. *See* civil liberties
Pfizer, 151
pharmaceuticals, 173, 191, 192, 196
Philadelphia Committee of Privates (1776), 348
Philadelphia Plan (minority hiring), 268
Pierce, Franklin, 70, 71, 75, 351, 402
Pinckney, Charles, 8
piracy, 6, 46, 299, 339
Plato, 393–394
pocket veto, 22, 37; Madison first to use, 64, 93
police. *See* law enforcement
police power, 34
political action committees (PACs), 115, 116, 145, 148; definition of, 146
political clubs, 65
political coattails, 111–112
political consultants, 115–116, 133–134
political families, 112
political machines, 86–87, 136–138
political parties, 233–242; core constituencies of, 132–133; corruption and, 84, 86; early power of Congress and, 52–53; "era of good feelings" and, 64; forming of new, 110–111, 154–155; ideological factions and, 240; impeachment charges and, 225–226; Jacksonian era and, 65–72, 94, 153, 234–235, 242, 277–278; Jeffersonian origination of, 234, 242, 277; judicial appointments and, 283–284, 289–290; media outlook and, 253; minor parties and, 113; New Politics and, 350, 352–353; patronage and (*see* patronage); presidential history and, 59, 61–62, 233–242; as presidential power basis, 233–242, 274–275, 277–278; Progressive era reforms

and, 86–87; state organizations, 69, 154; third parties, 111, 113, 129–130, 156; volunteer workers, 116–117. *See also* partisan identification; *specific parties*

political philosophy, 2, 152, 217, 300, 303

Polk, James K., 60, 152, *402*; as "dark horse" candidate, 70–71; Mexican War and, 47, 70–72, 300, 349, 386–887; presidential accomplishments of, 71–72, 88, 94

polls. *See* public opinion polls

pollution. *See* emissions standards; water pollution

popular mobilization, 86, 233, 242–256, 274, 277, 278–279

popular sovereignty, 75

populism, 66, 274

Populist Party, 111, 156

Porteous, Thomas, 225

Postal Service, 160

Post Office Department, 160, 218

Powell, Adam Clayton, 292

Powell, Colin, 329, 376

Powell v. McCormack (1969), 292

power sharing. *See* checks and balances

preemptive war, 25

presentment clause, 22, 201

president, 391–400; administration components, 9–11; approval ratings, 252; biographer portrayals of, 96, 392; broader meaning of, 9–11; bully pulpit of, 86, 94, 214, 255; candidacy process, 105–113; career backgrounds of, 105–111; character flaws of, 139–143, 392; compensation of, 20; death, incapacity, resignation of, 11–14, 20, 70, 126; elected term of, 19, 61, 103; election mechanisms for (*see* presidential elections campaigns); eligibility requirements, 12, 20, 55–58, 104–105; executive branch management and, 185–187; fallacy of presidentialism and, 394–397; family dynasties and, 112; first African American as, 158; fixed four-year term of, 36, 49, 61, 103; former vice presidents elected as, 112; form of address for, 61, 391; function of, 2; greatness rankings, 95–98; as head of state, 21; historical view of (*see* presidential history); image building by, 66; independence of, 49–51; individual personalities, 152–153; as institution, 391–400;

judicial review and, 286–289, 318, 319–322; judiciary empowerment of, 292–316; legislative agenda of, 193–195, 200; legislative powers of, 310–314 (*see also* veto power); line of succession, 12–13, 13*b*; malicious campaigns against, 392, 398–400; media coverage of, 85–86, 227; military heroes as, 108–111, 154–155; nominating process, 70–71; oath of office of, 20, 21, 94, 101; personal conduct of, 139–143, 226, 230, 254, 318, 392; physical threats to, 392 (*see also* assassinations); political ambition of, 198–201, 392–393; portrait gallery, *401–406*; powers of (*see* presidential powers); precedents set by Washington for, 61; public appeals of (*see* popular mobilization); removal from office of (*see* impeachment); "rights, duties, and obligations" of (*see* inherent powers); spouse of (*see* First Spouses); State of the Union message, 21, 61, 195, 199; stepping stones to office of, 106–108; succession provisions, 11–14, 20, 229; supremacy development of, 384–385; temporary incapacitation of, 12; term of office of, 252–253; two-term limit for, 104, 157, 347; two-term tradition of, 61, 88; as unitary actor, 28–29, 30, 38–42, 49–50, 53; veneration of, 391, 392; vesting clause and, 21, 28. *See also* congressional-presidential relations

presidential campaigns. *See* presidential election campaigns

presidential decrees. *See* executive orders

presidential election (1800), 62, 127

presidential election (1824), 64–65, 127, 154, *155*

presidential election (1828), 65

presidential election (1836), 127, 155

presidential election (1840), 154–155, *155*, 235

presidential election (1844), 70

presidential election (1856), 75

presidential election (1860), 75–76, 83, 110, 113, *156*, 235; issues and significance, 155–156

presidential election (1864), 260, 349

presidential election (1868), 83

presidential election (1876), 293

presidential election (1880), 111

presidential election (1892), 111

presidential election (1896), 156, *157*

presidential election (1912), 111, 156–157, *157*

presidential election (1916), 157
presidential election (1932), 83, 157, *158*
presidential election (1936), 157, 238, 257
presidential election (1940), 157
presidential election (1944), 157
presidential election (1948), 88
presidential election (1956), 107, 114
presidential election (1960), 144
presidential election (1964), 56, 91, 104, 131
presidential election (1968), 56, 91–92, 112;
     Johnson withdrawal, 104, 124–125, 131, 353,
     372; third-party candidate, 111, 130
presidential election (1972), 92, 120, 350. *See
     also* Watergate affair
presidential election (1976), 129
presidential election (1984), 144
presidential election (1988), 131, 144
presidential election (1992), 111, 133–134, 233,
     252, 326
presidential election (1996), 110, 111
presidential election (2000): Florida vote
     recount, 118, 119, *158*; popular vs. elec-
     toral vote, 129, 157–158; primary, 124, 147;
     Supreme Court resolution of, 158, 284,
     292–293; televised debate, 144
presidential election (2004), 124, 139–143, 148
presidential election (2008), 41, 56–57,
     106–107, 112, 119, 126, 158–159, *159*, 196, 391;
     Democratic delegate selection, 121; financial
     crisis issue, 135; Internet strategy, 132; public
     campaign financing, 151; televised debate,
     123; vice presidential candidate, 126, 127
presidential election (2012), 110, 113, 131, 135,
     159, 175; Internet strategy, 132; televised
     debate, 123–124
presidential election (2016), 17, 105, 107, 110,
     112, 113, 135, 137; character issue, 143; Repub-
     lican and Democratic aspirants, 114–115;
     Super PACs, 147; televised debates, 123, 124,
     148
presidential election campaigns, 3, 103–159, 197;
     battleground states, 129, 130, 139; campaign
     methods, 130–133 (*see also* advertising;
     media); campaign organization, 115–119;
     career backgrounds of candidates, 105–111;
     challenges to incumbents, 115; character
     issues, 139–143, 144; coattail candidates,
     111–112; "dark horse" candidates, 70–71,

83, 87, 92, 116, 125; debates, 123–124, 131,
     142–143, 144, 175; disputed vote reso-
     lution, 62, 127–128, 292–293; electoral
     vote (*see* Electoral College); ethnically
     balanced ticket, 136; funding of, 114, 132,
     144–153; funding reform, 118, 151–152, 174,
     193, 241, 274, 283; funding restrictions
     lifted, 146–147, 152, 283; funding sources,
     148b; general election, 125–127; history
     of elections, 154–159; independence from
     congressional elections, 103–104; interest
     groups vs. voters, 147–152; issue categories,
     134–135; lawyers and, 117–118, 147; mecha-
     nisms for, 3, 8–9, 13–14, 19–20, 62; national
     conventions, 70–71, 87, 91, 113–114, 119, 125,
     278, 350; new technologies, 131–132, 241;
     nominating processes, 70–71, 83, 87, 91–92,
     105–108, 113–115, 120, 121, 125, 154, 199, 241;
     party platform, 125–126; party primaries
     (*see* primary elections); political coattails,
     111–112; popular vs. electoral vote, 129, 157,
     284; Supreme Court intervention, 284,
     292–293; themes and tactics, 133–134; third
     parties, 111, 113, 129–130, 156; vice presiden-
     tial choices, 126–127; volunteer workers,
     116–117; vote count accuracy, 118–119
presidential history, 59–102; six eras of, 60–65
presidentialism: elements of, 394–397. *See also*
     unilateral presidency
presidential powers, 18–54, 59–102, 231–279;
     acceleration of, 53–54, 87–88, 92–93, 226;
     administrative strategy, 256–265; budget
     consolidation and, 72; checks on, 2–3, 8,
     14, 36–38; Cold War and, 355–357; congres-
     sional curbs on, 48, 92, 353–354; congres-
     sional early power over, 60; contemporary
     routine application of, 394–395; continuing
     expansion from 1930s of, 88–102; dele-
     gated powers, 30–33, 36, 201, 208, 310–314;
     executive branch management tools,
     187–188; executive energy components,
     38–52; expressed, 22–27; foreign affairs
     and (*see* foreign policy); forms of decree,
     49–50; imperial presidency, 61, 90, 94–95,
     357, 370; implied powers, 27–30, 32–33,
     101–102; independence of office and, 49–51;
     "inherent" argument (*see* inherent presi-
     dential powers); instruments of, 277–279;

Jacksonian elevation of, 65–72; judicial enhancement of, 292–316; limited range of, 187, 265; Lincoln wartime precedents for, 79; modern supremacy of, 384–385; oath of office as source of, 20, 21, 77, 94, 101; pardons and, 20, 22, 25–27, 26t, 224, 230, 395; party-based organizations and, 233–242, 274–275, 277–278; policy tools, 231–279, 363–366, 394–395; popular mobilization tools, 242–256; Republican era of, 61, 83–88, 94; Roman model of, 4, 52, 265; six historical eras of, 93–98; Supreme Court's enhancement of, 314–317. *See also* Article II; commander-in-chief; unilateral presidency; war powers

presidential proclamation, 5078

presidential succession, 11–14, 20, 329

Presidential Succession Act (1947), 12–13

presidential unilateralism. *See* unilateral presidency

President's Committee on Administrative Management (Brownlow Committee), 257

President's Surveillance Program, 334–335

press, 243–247, 250, 253; partisan, 62, 66, 234

press conferences, 244, 246–247, 248, 249, 254–255

press secretary, 10, 247, 254

price controls, 269, 303, 304, 312, 341, 345, 346

primary elections, 52–53, 87, 88, 91–92, 104, 113, 114; binding vs. nonbinding, 121b; debates, 144, 148–149; delegate selection rules, 121–122b; open vs. closed, 120, 121b, 122; procedures, 119–125; public mobilization and, 242; state legislatures and, 117–118; superdelegates, 122, 122b; Super Tuesday, 124; winner-take-all, 120, 121b

prime minister, 3–4, 27

Pritzer, Penny, 108

Privacy Act (1974), 353

private contractors, 166–167, 169, 188, 268, 272, 273–274, 368; Defense Department, 330–331, 353; Iraq War, 166, 361–363

Prize Cases (1863), 78, 300, 309, 340

Progressive era, 291, 298, 395, 396; reforms of, 52–53, 85–88, 198, 241

Progressive Policy Institute, 133

property seizure, 303, 306

proportional representation, 120, 121b, 129

Protect America Act (2007), 335

protective tariff, 61, 67, 73, 234

public appeals. *See* popular mobilization

Public Company Accounting Reform and Investor Protection Act (2002). *See* Sarbanes-Oxley Act

public disclosure, 182–183

public employees. *See* government employees

public interest, 395–396

public land, 274

public opinion polls, 130, 241

public relations firms, 243, 244–245, 248, 249, 254

Pure Food and Drug Act (1906), 85

Putin, Vladimir, 329–330

Qatar, 383

Quasi War with France, 281, 299, 320, 324

Quayle, Dan, 144

Quirin case (1942). See *Ex parte Quirin*

Radical Republicans, 80–81, 82, 240, 351

radio, 246, 253

Railroad Administration, 342, 346

railroads: regulation of, 85, 243, 244, 278–279; transcontinental, 75; wartime takeover of, 342

RAND Corporation, 165, 331, 360–361

Randolph, A. Philip, 360

Randolph, Edmund, 8

Randolph, John, 140

Raso, Connor, 181

Rasul v. Bush (2004), 309–310

rationing, 341, 345

Ratner, Sidney, 367

Rayburn, Sam, 107, 112

Reagan, Ronald, 29, 138, 269, *405*; acting career of, 109, 251, 252, 399; agenda of, 199; "arms for hostages" statement, 393; assassination attempt on, 392; Boland Amendment violation, 202, 204–205, 339 (*see also* Iran-Contra affair); budget deficits, 212, 213; Christian right and, 116–117; Cold War and, 355; core constituency of, 139; federal bureaucracy and, 175, 186–187; image development, 251–252; impeachment potential, 224; judicial appointments, 284; legislative program, 232, 252; malicious portrayals of,

Reagan, Ronald (*continued*)
398–399, *399*; media coverage of, 253, 255; military buildup, 365; national security directives, 365; popular approval of, 96, 252; popular mobilization by, 242, 251–252; presidential election debate, 144; regulatory review, 47, 260–262, 265; Senate rejection of Supreme Court nominees, 207; signing statements, 40, 95, 270–271; stepping stones to presidency, 108; tax cuts, 212, 213, 232, 274; television use by, 251–252; temporary incapacitation of, 12; unilateralism, 92–93, 95, 270, 379–380; war powers violation, 308, 378–380, 381. *See also* Iran-Contra affair
recall, 156
recess appointments, 21, 22, 52; first (1795), 61, 93; partisan reasons for, 37; Supreme Court limitations, 22, 37, 288–289, 318
recession. *See* financial crisis
Reciprocal Trade Agreements Act (1934), 364
Reconstruction era (1866–1872), 80–83, 347, 351
Reconstruction Finance Corporation, 344
Red Cross, 348
Reed, Ralph, 149
referendum, 139, 156
Reform Party, 111
regulatory agencies, 174, 186, 259–262
Regulatory Flexibility Act (1980), 185
regulatory policy, 49, 85, 175–185, 203
regulatory power, 175–185, 217
regulatory review, 29, 32–33, 47, 53, 93, 95, 272, 273, 275, 394; unilateral president and, 102, 186–187, 259–265, 266
Rehnquist, William, 284, 297–298
Reid, Harry, 208
relief spending. *See* welfare
religious right, 117, 120, 123, 133, 138, 139, 148, 149–150
removal power, 27–28, 314, 316. *See also* impeachment
renditions, extraordinary, 35
Reorganization Act (1939), 257
reprieves, 20, 22
Republican era, major presidential powers introduced, 94
Republican Party: Affordable Care Act opposition, 47; African American voters switch from, 37; campaign issues, 135; Civil War

and, 72, 79, 235–237, 239; Clinton investigations by, 225–226, 230; Contract with America, 313; core constituency, 133, 136, 137, 138–139; district redrawing and, 117–118, 197, 396; entitlement curbs and, 48; federal bureaucracy critiques, 175; first presidential victory (1860) of, 110, 113, 235; formation of (1854), 75, 155–156, 349, 351; line-item veto and, 313; media and, 253; national convention, 125–126; Obama's executive orders and, 51; presidential era of, 61, 83–88, 94, 156; presidential primary system and, 91, 119–125, 148, 148–149; 121*b*; Progressive movement and, 86; Reconstruction and, 80–81, 82, 351; religious right and, 117; signing statement introduced by, 41, 49; social conservatives and, 138; as Southern majority party, 136, 285; Tea Party movement and, 215; veterans organizations, 350; volunteer workers, 116–117
Resource Conservation and Recovery Act (1976), 180
Reuther, Walter, 360
Revenue Act (1862), 78, 367
Revenue Act (1942), 367
Revolutionary War, 6, 7, 61, 348–349
Rice, Condoleezza, 141, 329
Rich, Marc, 27, 395
Richardson, Elliot, 223
Right-to-Know Act (2000), 179
RIP (revelation, investigation, and prosecution), 223–224, 228, 255
Roberts, John, 283, 284, 288, 322
Rockefeller, Jay, 220
Rockefeller, Nelson, 12
Rogers, William, 363
Roman executive power, 4, 52, 187, 265
Romney, George, 56, *56*
Romney, Mitt, 110, 123, 124, 131, 132, 135, 159
Roosevelt, Eleanor, 16, *16*
Roosevelt, Franklin D., 5, 88–90, *101*, 157, *158*, 211, 316, *404*; administrative strategies, 256–257, 356; antidiscrimination order, 268; assassination attempt on, 13; death in office of, 10, 88; Democratic Party and, 237–239, 240–241, 245; executive agreements, 90, 209, 296; executive branch extension under, 88–90, 94–95, 101; executive orders, 49,

89–90, 268, 270, 304, 305, 342, 343; federal bureaucracy and, 31, 170, 257–258; federal tax system and, 367; First Spouse, 16, *16*; foreign policy advisers, 356; inauguration of, 83; legislative initiative, 198–199; military and emergency orders, 53, 302–305; popular mobilization skills of, 242, 245–248; presidential greatness of, 96, 97; presidential power of, 53, 193–194, 384; Social Security and, 173; stepping stones to presidency of, 106, 108; Supreme Court "packing" plan of, 248, 256, 287, 312, 320–321; third and fourth terms of, 61, 88, 157; treaty ratification and, 363–364; Truman as successor to, 10, 88; vetoes and, 201, 205; war powers and, 302–303, 342–345, 388–389; wartime executive orders and, 49, 89–90, 266. *See also* New Deal; World War II

Roosevelt, Theodore: Bull Moose Party formation, 111, 156, *157*, *404*; direct popular appeals by, 242, 243–244, 278–279; executive power and, 85–86, 87, 94, 198; historical view of, 97

Rossiter, Clinton, 302

Rove, Karl, 116

Rubio, Marco, 105, 116, 137

Ruckelshaus, William, 223

Rudalevige, Andrew, 199

Rumsfeld, Donald, 111, 365, 376

Rusk, Dean, 369

Russia, 329–330, 332, 383. *See also* Soviet Union

Safe Drinking Water Amendments (1986), 270

St. Clair, Arthur, 217, 218

Sallie Mae, 165

salutary issues, definition of, 134–135

same-sex marriage, 139, 203, 287

Sanders, Bernie, 114–115

Sandinistas (Nicaragua), 205, 380

Santorum, Rick, 116, 123

Sarbanes-Oxley Act (2002), 32, 177–178

"Saturday Night Massacre" (Watergate), 223, 229, 316

Saudi Arabia, 378, 383

Scalia, Antonin, 283, 310

Schechter Brothers Poultry v. United States (1935), 294, 312

Schlesinger, Arthur, 90, 347, 356, 370

school desegregation, 285–286

Schwartz, Thomas, 53, 181, 219

Schwartzkopf, Norman, 376

Schwarzenegger, Arnold, 109

Schwerin, Dan, 107

Scowcroft, Brent, 327

secession: Federalist threat of, 64, 386; of Southern states, 76, 77, 82, 95, 156, 198, 235

Second Bank of the United States: functions of, 66; Jackson veto of, 52, 66, 68, 100, 201

Second War Powers Act (1942), 345

secrecy, 7, 8, 167

Secret Service, 163, 171, 173

Securities and Exchange Commission (SEC), 32, 89, 174, 177–178

Sedition Act (1918), 302

Seidman, Harold, 173, 290–291

Selective Service Act (1917), 341

Selective Service Act (1940), 344

Selective Service System, 360

Selma civil rights march (1965), 134, 249

Senate: advice and consent of, 20–21, 22, 36, 37, 42, 208–209, 280, 283, 316, 323; appointment by state legislature to, 69; appropriations subcommittees, 210; cabinet confirmation by, 9, 84; celebrity members, 110; censure of Jackson, 68–69, 201, 316; CIA operations and, 170, 220; direct popular election to, 3, 244; impeachment trial, 36, 224, 225, 226, 230; intelligence and surveillance hearings, 123; isolationist members, 209, 244, 247; judicial appointment confirmation, 282; League of Nations rejection, 86, 209, 245; McCarthy Communist investigations, 347; oversight committees, 217, 220; political pressure and, 244; post–Civil War power of, 83; presidents with prior service in, 109, 118; presidential appointments confirmation, 27, 36, 37, 41, 232, 248, 280, 282; presidential appointments denial, 206–207, 231; presidential candidates prior seat in, 11, 112, 114; presidential line of succession and, 13*b*; president pro tem of, 329; pro forma session, 37; Radical Republicans in, 80–81; recess appointments by president, 21, 22, 27; sixty-vote supermajority, 41; treaty ratification by, 36, 37, 86, 90, 195, 208–209, 295,

Senate (*continued*)
  323, 363–364; Versailles Treaty rejection by,
  90, 245, 347; vice president's roles in, 127,
  195; Watergate hearings, 222–223
Senate Commerce Committee, 220
Senate Foreign Relations Committee, 295, 353,
  369
Senate Government Affairs Committee, 219
Senate Intelligence Committee, 220
Senate Judiciary Committee, 232
senatorial courtesy, 84, 248, 282
senior citizens, 137–138
Sentencing Commission, U.S., 92, 316
Sentencing Reform Act (1984), 316
separation of powers, 2–3, 7–8, 25, 195, 231.
  See also checks and balances
September 11 attacks. *See* 9/11 terror attacks
sequestration, 48, 204, 215, 216
Sessions, William, 186
Seventeenth Amendment (1913), 3, 144
Seward, William, 77
Shays, Daniel/Shays's revolt (1786), 6–7
Shefter, Martin, 223, 228, 255, 303–304
Sheldon, Lou, 150
Shenkman, Richard, 153
Sherman, Roger, 8
Shinseki, Eric, 186
Shipping Act (1917), 341
Shipping Board, 346
Sierra Club, 315
signing statements, 28, 30, 40–42, 53, 93,
  95, 102, 201, 202, 266, 270–277, 279; as
  line-item veto replacement, 201; Reagan
  administration expansion of, 40, 95
Silverstein, Gordon, 307, 313
Simas, David, 221
Skocpol, Theda, 348
Skowronek, Stephen, 97, 194
slavery: emancipation, 49, 50, 78, 156, 266;
  extension to territories, 73–76, 155–156,
  349, 351; political division over, 75, 156, 351;
  Southern state sovereignty claim and, 69
Small Business Administration, 175, 182
Small Business Regulatory Enforcement Fair-
  ness Act (1996), 184, 219
Smith, Al, 106
Snowden, Edward, 167, 220, 336
social conservatives, 138–139

Socialist Party, 113
social media campaigns, 116
social networking, 132, 336
Social Security Administration, 48, 161, *192*,
  262; established funding for, 173, 192, 210
Sofaer, Abraham, 299
soft money (campaign), 241
Solow, Alan, 108
Somalia, 47
Sorensen, Theodore, 107
Sotomayor, Sonia, 283, 284
Souter, David, 283, 289
South: Black Codes, 80; black disenfranchisement, 80–81, 91; civil rights demonstrations
  in, 133; Civil War blockade of, 34, 77, 300,
  340; Fourteenth Amendment reaction, 81,
  82, 83; Jacksonian party and, 66; Jim Crow,
  134; Kansas-Nebraska bill and, 75; Lincoln's
  election and, 76, 156; nullification claim,
  67–68, 73, 235; political parties, 62, 136,
  285–286; school desegregation ruling and,
  285–286; secession of, 76, 77, 82, 95, 198,
  235; state party congressional coalitions, 69;
  state's rights advocacy, 235. *See also* Civil
  War; Confederate States of America;
  slavery
South Carolina, 65, 67–68, 76–77, 80, 124
South Korea, 371, 389
Soviet Union, 296, 346. *See also* Cold War
Spanish-American War (1898), 84, 358
Speaker of the House, 87, 127, 128, 198; presidential line of succession and, 13*b*, 329
Special Forces, 372
special interests. *See* interest groups
Special Operations Command, 169, 383
special prosecutor, 223, 224, 229, 316. *See also*
  independent counsel
Specie Circular, 66
speechmaking, 243, 244, 246, 248, 249,
  250–251, 255–256
speech writers, 10
spoils system. *See* patronage
Stafford Act (1988), 36
Stanton, Edwin M., 316, 351
Starbucks, 119
Star of the West (supply ship), 77
Starr, Kenneth, 226, 230
state and local elections, 151, 239

State Department, 166–167, 218, 327, 328–330; Communist infiltration charges, 347; creation of, 160, 328–329; diplomacy, 167, 328; Foreign Service merger, 356; functions of, 164*b*, 188–189; policy planning staff, 356–357, 359, 363, 364, 365; secretary of, 9, 11, 17, 112, 143, 329

state electoral votes, 128*t*

state governors, 109, 201, 236

state legislatures, 9, 38, 67, 82–83, 151, 244, 279; judiciary and, 289–291, 317; presidential elections and, 3, 12, 63, 64, 65, 117–118, 128, 238, 292; senatorial appointments by, 69, 76

state militias. *See* militias

state of emergency, 35–36

State of the Union message, 21, 61, 195, 199

state party organizations, 69, 70, 237

state redistricting. *See* gerrymandering

state's rights, 33, 67–68, 235

Statue of Liberty, 251–252

steel mills seizure (1952), 34–35, 50, 275, 287, 306–307, 321, 348

stem cell research, 49, 50, 273, 395, 396

Stevens, Christopher, 189

Stevens, Thaddeus, 80

Stevenson, Adlai, 116

Stimson, Henry, 360

Strategic Command, 169

striking worker replacement, 269, 272, 287, 317

Student Loan Marketing Association (Sallie Mae), 165

Subversive Activities Control Act (1950), 288

suffrage: district redrawing and, 117–118, 197, 296; expansion of, 65, 154, 239, 339, 348–349; property ownership requirement, 63, 349; Southern black disenfranchisement, 80–81, 83; voting age lowering, 349; Voting Rights Act, 91, 249, 284, 287; women's, rights 349

Sumner, Charles, 80–81

Sunstein, Cass, 265

super PACs, 116, 145, 145*b*, 146–147

Super Twiggy (cartoon character), 48

Supreme Court: appointment of justices to, 41, 207, 280; campaign finance rulings, 118, 145, 146–147, 151–152; *Chevron* standard, 312–313; Civil War rulings, 287–288, 300–301, 340; equal pay suit dismissal, 196;

executive privilege rulings, 61, 218, 223, 314–315; "intelligible principles" standard, 312; justices of, 282, 283–284, 289–290; line-item veto rejection, 201, 206, 313–314; New Deal program invalidations, 287, 312–313, 320–321; presidential election (2000) decision, 158, 284, 292–293; president's dominance in foreign policy rulings, 294, 296–298, 325; recess appointments ruling, 22, 37, 288–289, 318; F. D. Roosevelt "packing" plan, 248, 256, 287, 312, 320–321; steel mill seizure invalidation, 35, 269, 275, 287, 306–308, 316, 348. *See also* judicial review; *specific cases*

surveillance, 169, 220, 315, 353; emergency powers, 93, 95, 373; FISA Court and, 334, 335, 336; metadata and, 336–337; Nixon domestic program, 307; NSA secret program, 35, 167, 220, 325, 333–337, 397; Patriot Act provision for, 382; by private contractors, 361; Senate subcommittee hearings on, 123; Snowden disclosure of, 167, 220, 336; warrantless, 307, 334; warrants for, 385; wire taps, 307

Sutherland, George, 294, 296, 297, 298, 325

Swearingen v. United States (1896), 296

Swift Boat Veterans for Truth, 142

Symmes, William, 29–30

Taft, William Howard, 84, 86, 87, 156, *157*, 198, *404*

Taft-Hartley Act (1947), 306, 347

Taiwan, 167, 209, 297, 328

Taiwan Straits, 371

"take care clause," 21

Talbot v. Seeman (1801), 299

Taliban, 170, 250, 308, 309, 325, 381–382

Taney, Roger, 34, 285, 287, 289

Tariff Act (1890), 311

Tariff Act (1897), 295

tariffs, 61, 73, 75, 234, 332; Nullification Crisis and, 67–68, 73

Tax Court, U.S., 282

taxes, 86, 175, 213, 232, 234, 367; Affordable Care Act and, 288; Congress's power to levy, 37; federal system, 78, 367; government spending and, 173–174, 212; post-Revolution revolts against, 6–7; progressive

taxes (*continued*)
income tax, 367; Reagan cuts, 212, 213, 232, 274; war financing and, 371, 375–376. *See also* Internal Revenue Service
Taxpayer Relief Act (2012), 215
Taylor, Zachary, 60, 70, 71, 108, 109, *402*
Teamsters Union, 150
Tea Party movement, 215
telecommunications. *See* communications technology
telegraph, 85, 243, 341
telephone, 85, 341; user surveillance, 335, 336
television, 131, 147, 149, 241; presidential candidate debates, 123–124, 142–143, 144, 148; presidential use of, 248, 249–252, 253, 254, 255–256
Telman, Jeremy, 299
Tennessee, 77, 82
Tenure of Office Act (1867), 27–28, 225, 351; repeal (1887) of, 316
term limits, 104, 157
territorial expansion, 63, 71–72, 293; extension of slavery and, 73–76, 155–156, 349, 351; Free Soilers and, 75, 349, 351; frontier squatters and, 235; Mexican War and, 351, 387. *See also* Louisiana Purchase
terrorism. *See* war on terror
Texas, 71, 74, 76, 126; annexation of, 49, 266; district redrawing, 117
Texas Air National Guard, 140
think tanks, 133, 194, 199, 253
third parties, 111, 113, 129–130, 156
Thomas, Clarence, 207, 283, 284
Thompson, Fred Dalton, 109
Thoreau, Henry David, 74; *Civil Disobedience,* 74
Thornburgh, Richard, 46
Tippecanoe, Battle of (1811), 69–70, 156
"Tippecanoe and Tyler too" (1840 campaign slogan), 106, 156
Titan Corp., 363
tobacco products regulation, 263
Tocqueville, Alexis de, 187, 265
torture, 28–29, 102, 170, 250
Total Information Awareness program, 336–337
Townsend, Kathleen Kennedy, 112
Toxic Substance Control Act (1976), 184–185
trade policy, 331–332, 364–365; congressional regulation of, 323, 338; dumping and, 332;

early presidency and, 61, 62, 63; embargo and, 35, 332; executive agreements, 295, 297, 364; fast track procedure, 39, 364; free trade and, 62, 67, 72; International Agreement on Tariffs and Trade, 90; International Trade Organization, 364; NAFTA agreement, 232, 364; North-South division over, 72–73; as political campaign issue, 111; protectionism, 61, 67, 73, 234; reciprocal agreements, 364–365; sanctions, 332. *See also* tariffs
Trade Representative, U.S., 167, 332, 337, 364–365
Trading with the Enemy Act (1917), 269, 341
Traditional Values Coalition, 149–150
Train v. City of New York (1975), 204
Transportation Command, 169
Transportation Department, 382; functions of, 164*b*, 174
Transportation Security Administration (TSA), 163, 171, 190–191, *190*, 218, 382
treason, 46, 77, 340; as impeachment cause, 21, 224
Treasury Department, 10, 72, 79, 218, 263, 345, 371; bond issuance, 79, 188, 214, 236, 370; creation of, 160; debt ceiling and, 168; federal agencies, 167–168, 173–174; foreign policy and, 327, 331–332; functions of, 164*b*, 168, 173–174; secretary of, 9, 316. *See also* Bureau of the Budget; Internal Revenue Service
Treasury notes, 79
treaty power, 20, 293; congressional and presidential, 2, 294–295, 338, 368–369; executive agreements replacing, 90, 209, 295, 296, 297, 363; of president, 33, 100, 208–209, 232, 295, 323; ratification by Senate, 36, 37, 86, 90, 195, 208–209, 295, 323, 363–364. *See also key word for specific treaties*
Truman, Harry S., 96, 185, 208, 258, 354, *404*; congressional relations, 347, 352, 356; defense budget, 366–367, 380; domestic policy, 355–356; executive agreements, 364; executive orders, 50, 316, 366; executive power growth under, 90, 95, 199; Fair Deal program, 90, 355–356; foreign and security policy, 356–357, 360–361, 363, 364, 369, 380, 384; foreign policy adviser, 329, 363; foundation for presidential supremacy

and, 384; inherent power claim, 33, 34–35; loyalty measures, 288, 366; military control, 370; military desegregation order, 49, 50, 266, 268; National Security Act and, 356–357, 370; national security advisers, 363; overrides of vetoes of, 205, 347; Republican filibusters and, 208; signing statement use, 270; steel mills seizure, 34–35, 50, 269, 275, 287, 306–307, 316, 321, 348; as vice president, 10, 88, 112. *See also* Korean War

Trump, Donald, 110, 113, 116, 145, 148

TSA. *See* Transportation Security Administration

Tulis, Jeffrey, 243

Twelfth Amendment (1804), 62, 127

Twentieth Amendment (1933), 12–13, 128

Twenty-Fifth Amendment (1967), 11–12

Twenty-Second Amendment (1951), 61, 104, 157, 347

Twenty-Sixth Amendment (1971), 349

Twenty-Third Amendment (1961), 127

Twitter followers, 116, 132, 227, *278*, 279

Tydings, Millard, 240

Tyler, John, 60, 71, 156, 201, *402*; succession to presidency, 11, 70, 106

Tyson, Don, 108

Ukraine, 330, 332

undeclared wars, 339, 379–380, 386, 389

Unfunded Mandates Reform Act (1992), 185

unilateral presidency, 35, 38, 42, 47, 49–50, 52, 61, 63, 102, 205, 209, 233, 236, 261, 262, 265–270, 275, 276, 279, 303, 357; definition of, 49, 95; development of, 92–93; foreign policy and, 266, 268, 297, 324–325, 363, 370, 379–380; instruments of, 53; introduction of major presidential powers and, 95; national security and, 363; regulatory review and, 186–187, 259–265, 266; war on terror and, 93, 308–310. *See also* executive agreements; executive orders; regulatory review; signing statements

unitary executive theory, 8, 28–29, 30, 38–42, 95

United Arab Emirates, 378, 383

United Nations, 167, 188, 325, 355; Security Council war resolutions, 369, 370, 380–381, 383, 389

United States v. American Telephone & Telegraph Co. (1978), 315

United States v. Belmont (1937), 296, 298

United States v. Butler (1936), 320–321

United States v. Curtiss Wright Exporting Company (1936), 34, 294–295, 296, 297, 309, 325

United States v. District Court for the District of Columbia (2004), 315

United States v. House of Representatives (1983), 315

United States v. Mead Corporation (2001), 313

United States v. Nixon (1974), 61, 314–315, 321–322, 322

United States v. Pink (1942), 296, 297, 298

United States v. U.S. District Court (1972), 307

United We Stand America (third party), 111

Universal Training and Military Service Act (1951), 360

University of Alabama, desegregation of, 285

Unlawful Internet Gambling Enforcement Act (2006), 203

urban voters, 136, 237, 238

USA Patriot Act (2002), 335, 382, 385

U.S. attorneys, 170

U.S. bonds. *See* government bonds

U.S. budget. *See* budget, U.S.

U.S. Trade Representative, 167, 332, 337, 364–365

Utah, 71

Vallandigham, Clement, 78

Van Buren, Martin, 65, 70, 71, 106, *402*; stepping stones to presidency, 106, 111–112

Vance, Cyrus, 363

Ventura, Jesse, 110

Versailles, Treaty of (1919), 85, 90; Senate rejections of, 209, 245, 347

vesting clause, 21, 28, 95. *See also* unitary executive theory

veterans, 40, 350, 351–352

Veterans Affairs Department: functions of, 164*b*; hospitals, 186, 218; House investigation, 219

veto power, 2, 52, 66, 310, 313; bills vetoed, 1780– present, 23–24*t*; congressional override, 22, 36, 195, 201, 205–206, 206*t*, 347; Jackson's routine use of, 68, 94, 100; line-item veto and, 201, 206, 313–314; pocket veto and, 22, 37, 64, 93 vice president, 9; defeated presidential bids by, 112; elected term of, 18; election campaign debates, 144; election process for, 62, 127; executive privilege and, 315; factors in choosing, 126–127; impeachment of, 224; nomination of, 124, 126–127; powers of, 195; presidential relations with, 10–11; removal from office of, 21; separate electoral ballot for, 62; as step to presidency, 111–112; successions to presidency of, 11–12, 13, 20, 70, 85, 106, 126, 329; temporary rule of, 128; term limits, 104

victory bonds. *See* war bonds

Vietnam War, 92, 222, 326, 339, 355, 366, 369, *389*, 390; Congress and, 47, 372, 378; draft resistance, 26, 350, 353, 373; lessons learned from, 375–384; L. Johnson policies, 91, 96, 115, 131, 352–353, 372, 374, 390, 393, 398, *398*; media critics of, 253; military lessons learned from, 375–376; opponents of, 140, 350, 352–353, 374, 389, 398; political mobilization and, 352–354; as presidential election issue, 115, 140, 142–143; presidential pardons of draft resisters, 26; U.S. withdrawal from, 372, 373

Virginia Electronics, 362

Volunteer Act (1898), 358

voting rights. *See* suffrage

Voting Rights Act (1965), 91, 249; Supreme Court weakening of, 284, 287

Wade, Benjamin, 240

wage controls, 269, 305–306, 345, 346

Wagner Act (1935), 238, 269, 272

Walker, Scott, 116

Wallace, George, 111, 130, 285

Wallace, Mike, 107

Wal-Mart, 151

Walton, Reggie B., 337

war. *See* antiwar movements; war powers; military forces; *specific wars*

war bonds. *See* government bonds

War Department, 218, 316, 341, 357, 358; creation of, 160, 168. *See also* Defense Department

War Finance Corporation, 346

War Food Administration, 266

War Industries Board, 341, 346

War Labor Board, 343

War Labor Disputes Act (1943), 266, 303, 345

War Mobilization and Conversion Act (1942), 345

Warner Brothers (Jack and Harry Warner), 247

War of 1812, 63–64, 154, 299, 338, 349; burning of Washington, D.C., 64, 386, *387*; New England secession threat, 64, 386; war hawks, 52, 63, 386

War on Drugs, 362

War on Poverty, 91, 249, 310

war on terror, 11, 28–29, 49, 93, 95, 102, 140–142, 195, 233, 250, 252, 256, 385; CIA operations, 170, 171; congressional 2001 resolution, 171, 382–383; executive agencies, 31, 190–191; as government surveillance justification, 337 (*see also* surveillance); Guantanamo Bay prisoners, 42, 305, 309–310; intelligence agencies, 333; military commissions, 35, 273, 305, 309, 325, 382; preemptive actions, 326; presidential-congressional relations, 371–380; presidential emergency and war powers and, 308–310; presidential inherent powers and, 35; presidential unilateralism and, 93; as salutary campaign issue, 134, 308–310; signing statements and, 272. *See also* Homeland Security Department

war powers, 6, 24–25, 47, 131, 195, 298–308; antiwar movements and, 349–350; cessation of war and, 346–354; congressional, 6, 24–25, 29, 33, 47, 84, 216, 298–299, 302, 327, 338, 346, 381–382, 386; congressional vs. presidential, 301, 327, 370–371, 372, 394; costs of war and, 346; executive orders and, 49, 77–78, 89–90, 266; framers intent, 25, 298, 327, 394; judicial decisions and, 293, 298–306; lessons from Vietnam War, 375–384; politics separated from, 354; presidential extent of, 384–385; presidential inherent power claim and, 33–34, 77–78, 94, 100–101; presidential primacy in, 25, 94, 95, 339–345, 378–390; undeclared wars and, 339, 379–380, 386, 389; UN Security Council resolutions and, 369, 370, 380–381, 383, 389. *See also* commander-in-chief; declaration of war; emergency powers; military forces

War Powers Acts (1941! 1942), 344–345, 379

War Powers Resolution (1973), 33, 92, 93; presidential disregard of, 308, 378–380, 381, 386 warrantless searches and surveillance, 307, 334–337

Warren, Earl, 283, 289

War Trade Board, 346

Washington, D.C. *See* District of Columbia

Washington, George, 7, 60, 108, 109, 324, 338, *491*; executive privilege introduced by, 61, 93, 217–218, 314; myths about, 392; presidential greatness of, 95, 97; presidential precedents set by, 61, 62, 88, 93, 95, 217–218, 391; stepping stone to presidency, 108, 109; vetoes by, 68; war powers view, 299

Washington Post, 222, 229, 250, 253, 336, 337

Washington state, 72, 129; gubernatorial 2004 election vote recount, 119

Washington Times, 253

Watergate affair, 10, 11, 17, 141, 204, 207, 224, 225, *228*, 231, 366, 372; background of, 92, 222, 229; executive privilege claim, 61, 218, 314–315; firing of special prosecutor, 223, 229, 316; Ford pardon of Nixon, 27; prosecution of Nixon, 36–37, 92, 141, 353; Senate hearings, 221–223, 255; White House tapes, 61, 218, 223, 322

water pollution, 263

Watts, J. C., 275

Wayman v. Southard (1825), 312

weapons of mass destruction, 382, 393

weapons systems, 360, 361, 375, 376

Weaver, James B., 111

Webb, Jim, 115

Weber, Vin, 149

Weekly Standard, 253

Weems, Mason, 392

Weinberger, Caspar, 27

Weko, Thomas, 260

welfare: Clinton reform, 233; New Deal programs, 238, 239, 240, 248

West, William, 181, 183

West Publishing Company, 40

Whig Party, 69–70, 75, 106, 154–155, 235

Whiskey Rebellion (1781), 7

whistleblowers, 167, 219–220, 222, 229, 336

White, Edward Douglass, 342

White, Leonard, 60, 84–85

White House advisers, 9–10

White House Communications Office, 250, 255, 256

White House "Czars," 9

White House Office of Management and Budget (formerly Bureau of the Budget), 10, 90, 174, 179, 180–181, 182, 184, 186, 211, 219, 232, 257–260, 262, 264, 265; "quality of life" review and, 259–260

White House Office of Political Strategy and Outreach, 221

White House Staff, 194, 257; components of, 9–10, 60; executive privilege and, 315

Whitewater probe, 141, 225–226, 230, 253, 255

Whitman, Meg, 110

Widmer, Ted, 107

Wilkinson, James, 377

Wilmot, David, 351

Wilson, Edith, 16, *16*

Wilson, James (Constitutional Convention delegate), 7

Wilson, James Q. (political scientist), 172

Wilson, Woodrow, 83, 84, 87, 90, 106, *388*, *404*; direct popular appeals of, 242, 243, 244–245; executive orders, 341–342; First Spouse, 16, *16*; legislation enacted, 86, 198; postwar isolationist opponents, 209, 347, 352; presidency of, 156–157; stroke incapacitation of, 12, 245. *See also* World War I

wire news services, 85, 243, 244

Wisconsin, 129

Wolfowitz, Paul, 393

Women's Christian Temperance Union (WCTU), 348

women's rights, 15, 137, 226; equal pay act, 196; suffrage, 349

Wood, Kimba, 207

Woods v. Miller (1948), 345

Worcester, Samuel, 285

Works Progress Administration (WPA), 101, 238, 239

World Trade Center attack. *See* 9/11 terror attacks

World Trade Organization, 364

World War I, 86, 90, 157, 244–245, 334, 340–353, 358, *388*; civic and service organizations, 348; draft resistance, 349–350; government bonds, 79, 369, *388*; postwar congressional power, 347; postwar political alliances, 352; presidential powers, 302, 339, 340–342; Treaty of Versailles, 85, 90,

World War I (*continued*)
    209, 245, 247; Wilson's positions on, 388;
    women's suffrage and, 349
World War II, 209, 246, 247–248, 342–345,
    384, *388, 389*; civic and service organiza-
    tions, 348; Congress's declaration of, 386;
    defense contracting system, 360; domestic
    shortages, 345; emergency orders, 302–306;
    executive branch growth, 89, 343, 344;
    executive orders, 49, 89–90, 266, 303–305;
    generals as potential presidents, 108–109;
    German agents case, 304, 345; government
    bonds, 79, 345, 369; Japanese American
    internment, 49, 68, 266, 303, 305, 345;
    military commissions, 304–305, 345;
    postwar congressional power, 347; postwar
    European economic recovery program,
368; postwar political alliances, 352–353;
    postwar revocation of emergency powers,
    346, 347; presidential constitutional and
    extraconstitutional powers, 33, 53, 246,
    247–248, 266, 302–303, 304, 339, 341–345,
    388–389; taxation, 367; veterans organiza-
    tions, 350

Yakus v. United States (1944), 304, 345
Yalta Conference, 347
Yemen, 170, 382
Youngstown Sheet & Tube Co. v. Sawyer (1952),
    269, 306–307, 308, 309, 316, 321, 348
Yugoslavia (former), 362, 363, 381

Zahn, Paula, 377
Zangara, Giuseppe, 13